FORTUNE'S FOOL

FORTUNE'S FOOL

STAR-CROSS'D BOOK 3

David Blixt

Books by David Blixt

The Star-Cross'd Series
The Master Of Verona
Voice Of The Falconer
Fortune's Fool
The Prince's Doom
Varnished Faces: Star-Cross'd Short Stories

Will & Kit
Her Majesty's Will
Fire At Will - Coming Soon

The Colossus Series
Colossus: Stone & Steel
Colossus: The Four Emperors
Colossus: Wail of the Fallen – Coming Soon

Nellie Bly
What Girls Are Good For – A Novel of Nellie Bly

Eve of Ides - A Play

Non-Fiction
Shakespeare's Secrets: Romeo & Juliet
Shakespeare's Secrets: Macbeth (with Janice L Blixt)
Fighting Words (with Kirby, Leoni, & Gerard)

For Jan -

"Thou and I are too wise to woo peaceably."

Dramatis Personae

♦ a character recorded by history
◇ a character from Shakespeare

Della Scala Family of Verona

♦ FRANCESCO 'CANGRANDE' DELLA SCALA – Ruler of Verona, Imperial Vicar of the Trevisian Mark

♦ GIOVANNA DI SVEVIA – Cangrande's wife, great-granddaughter to Emperor Frederick II

♦ ALBERTO II DELLA SCALA – Cangrande's eldest nephew

♦/◇ MASTINO II DELLA SCALA – Cangrande's youngest nephew

♦ VERDE DELLA SCALA – Cangrande's eldest niece

♦ CATERINA DELLA SCALA – Cangrande's middle niece

♦ ALBUINA DELLA SCALA – Cangrande's youngest niece

♦/◇ FRANCESCO 'CESCO' DELLA SCALA – A bastard

◇ PARIDE DELLA SCALA – Cangrande's great-nephew, son of the late Cecchino della Scala

1

Nogarola Family of Vicenza

♦ ANTONIO NOGAROLA – Vicentine nobleman, elder brother to Bailardino

♦ BAILARDINO NOGAROLA – Lord of Vicenza, husband to Cangrande's sister, Katerina

♦ KATERINA DELLA SCALA – Sister to Cangrande, wife of Bailardino

♦ bAILARDETTO 'DETTO' NOGAROLA – eldest son of Bailardino and Katerina

♦/◊ VALENTINO NOGAROLA – youngest son of Bailardino and Katerina

Alaghieri Family of Florence

♦ PIETRO ALAGHIERI – Knight of Verona, son of the poet Dante

♦ JACOPO 'POCO' ALAGHIERI – Dante's youngest son

♦ ANTONIA ALAGHIERI – Dante's daughter, in holy orders as Suor Beatrice

Carrara Family of Padua

♦ MARSILIO DA CARRARA – Lord of Padua, cousin of Gianozza Montecchio

♦ NICCOLO DA CARRARA – cousin to Marsilio, brother to Ubertino

♦ UBERTINO DA CARRARA – cousin to Marsilio, brother to Niccolo

♦ CUNIZZA DA CARRARA – sister to Marsilio

♦ TADDEA DA CARRARA – daughter of the late Il Grande da Carrara, cousin to Marsilio

Montecchio Family of Verona

◊ ROMEO MARIOTTO 'MARI' MONTECCHIO – Lord of Montecchio, father to Romeo

◊ GIANOZZA DELLA BELLA – wife to Mariotto, cousin to Carrara, mother to Romeo

◊ ROMEO MONTECCHIO – son of Mari and Gianozza

AURELIA MONTECCHIO – sister to Mariotto, wife of Benvenito Lenoti, mother of Benvolio

BENVENITO LENOTI – Knight of Verona, husband to Aurelia, father to Benvolio

◊ BENVOLIO LENOTI – cousin to Romeo, son of Benvenito and Aurelia

Capulletto Family of Verona

◊ ANTONIO 'ANTONY' CAPULLETTO – Lord of the Capulletti family, born in Capua

◊ ARNALDO CAPULLETTO – uncle to Antony

◊ TESSA GUARINI – wife to Antony, mother to Giulietta

◊ THEOBALDO 'THIBAULT' CAPULLETTO – nephew to Antony

◊ GIULIETTA CAPULLETTO – daughter of Antony and Tessa

Supporting Characters

ABBESS VERDIANA – Benedictine abbess of Santa Maria in Organo in Verona

♦ ALBERTINO MUSSATO – Paduan historian-poet

ANDRIOLO DA VERONA – Capulletto's groom, husband to Angelica

ANGELICA DA VERONA – Tessa and Thibault's nurse, wife to Andriolo

AVENTINO FRACASTORO – personal physician to Cangrande

BAPTISTA MINOLA – Paduan noble, father of Katerina and Bianca

♦ BERNARDO ERVARI – Knight of Verona, member of the Anziani

♦ BERNARDO GUI – Dominican Cardinal, former head of the Inquisition

♦ BISHOP FRANCIS – Franciscan Bishop, leader of Verona's spiritual growth

◆ FRA BONAGRATIA DA BERGAMO – Franciscan friar, former lawyer

◇ FRA LORENZO – Franciscan friar with family in France

◆ FRANCESCO DANDOLO – Venetian nobleman

◆ FRANCESCO 'PETRARCH' PETRARCHA – Florentine exile, aspiring poet

◆ GHERARDO PETRARCHA – Florentine exile, younger brother to Petrarch

◆ GUGLIELMO CASTELBARCO – Veronese nobleman, Cangrande's Armourer

◆ GUGLIELMO II CASTELBARCO – Castelbarco's son

GUISEPPE MORSICATO – doctor, knight, living in Ravenna

◇ HORTENSIO & PETRUCHIO II BONAVENTURA – twin sons of Katerina and Petruchio

◇ JESSICA – Venetian Jew, daughter of Shalakh

◇ KATERINA BONAVENTURA – Paduan-born heiress, wifc to Pctruchio Bonaventura

◆ FRANCESCO 'PETRARCH' PETRARCHA – Florentine exile, aspiring poet

◆ MANOELLO GIUDEO – Cangrande's Master of Revels, a Jew

MASSIMILIANO DA VILLAFRANCA – Constable of Cangrande's palace

◆ NICCOLO DA LOZZO – Paduan knight, changed sides to join Cangrande

NIKLAS FUCHS – German-born friend to Mastino

◆ PASSERINO BONACCOLSI – Podestà of Mantua, ally to Cangrande

◇ PETRUCHIO BONAVENTURA – Veronese noble, husband to Katerina Minola

◇ SHALAKH – Jewish Venetian money-lender, father to Jessica

THARWAT AL-DHAAMIN – Moorish master astrologer, called the Arus

TULLIO D'ISOLA – aged steward, Grand Butler to Cangrande

◆ WILLIAM MONTAGU – English knight, distant relation to the Montecchi

◆ WILLIAM OF OCCAM – Englishman, Franciscan friar and scholar

◆ ZILIBERTO DELL'ANGELO – Cangrande's Master of the Hunt

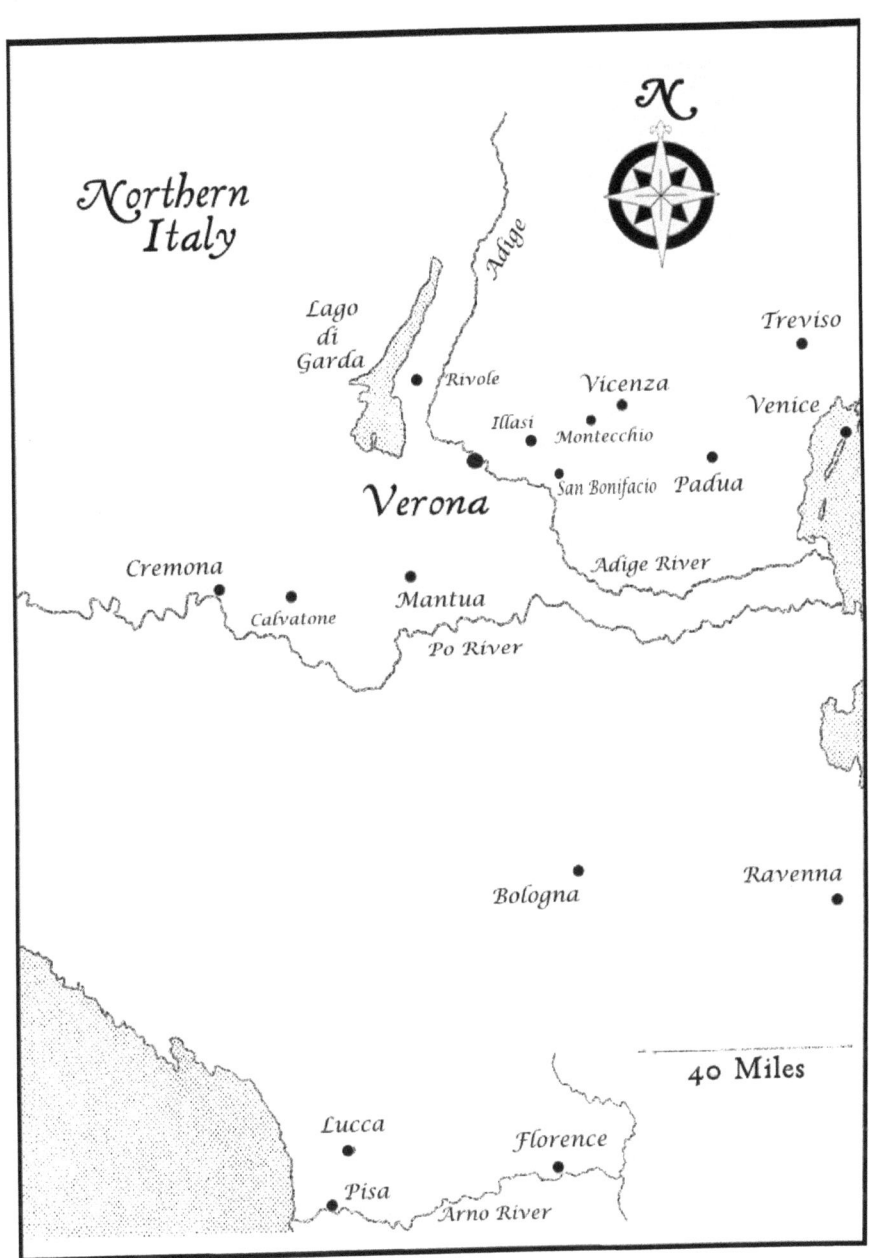

NORTHERN ITALY

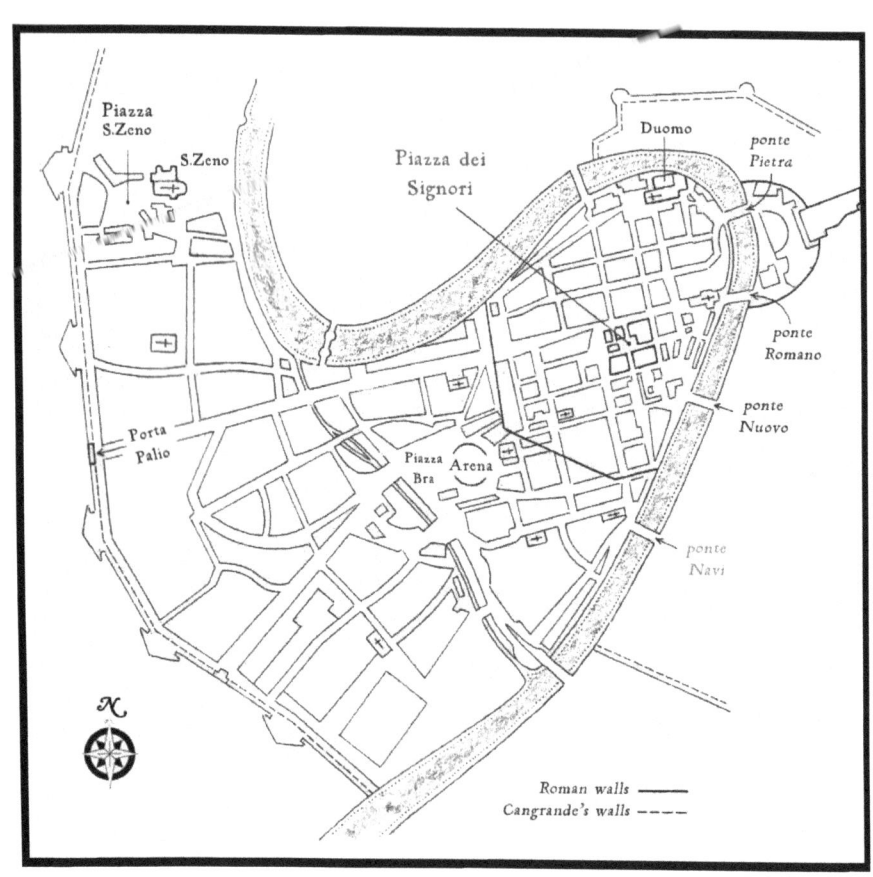

THE CITY OF VERONA

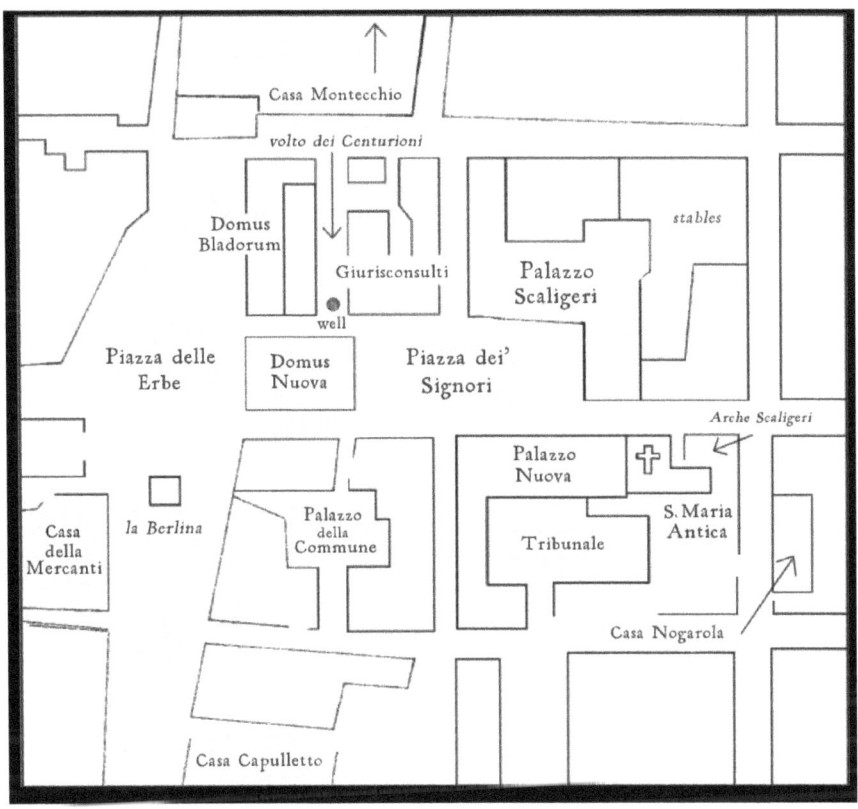

PIAZZA DEI SIGNORI

...Patris iam detegam falsi dolos
Infausta mater. Non diu tellas nefas
Latere patitur; durat ocultum nichil....

'...Now shall I reveal
The wiles of your deceitful sire, distraught
Mother that I am. The earth refuses
To hide for long a crime. Secrets will out...'

The Tragedy of Ecerinis
Albertino Mussato
Act One, Scene One, lines 4-6

Death is the mother of beauty; hence from her,
Alone, shall come fulfillment to our dreams
And our desires.

Sunday Morning
Wallace Stevens

Prologue

Lyons, France
1 October 1316

So red they might have been made of actual flame, the banners snaked out, unfurling with hearty cracks before whipping back under the fury of the mighty wind called the Mistral. Oarsmen swept and heaved in rhythm with the choir that sang holy songs in both Latin and French – but not Italian. The gentlest hint of things to come.

The banks of the Rhône were teeming with onlookers. It was almost a holiday, an impromptu festival along the river's edge. Some hapless souls plunged in, pushed by those eagerly seeking a better view. When again in their lifetimes could they lay eyes upon Saint Pierc's heir? Especially as there was so much pressure to return the papacy to Rome, making Clement's transplanting of the Holy See a temporary aberration, a Gallic hiccough in the history of the Church. So French citizens between Lyon and Avignon now flocked to the riverbank to watch the new pope pass, that when they prayed they could attach a face to their pleas.

Not that anyone could see his face. Aboard ship, the throned figure was practically swallowed by his hat and gown, despite their being tailored to him. A gnome of a man, delicate and diminutive. Even the throne itself, high on its pedestal, was cleverly designed to hide the fact that his feet couldn't reach the deck. A step pretended to be a footrest for the most mighty man in all of Christendom.

His might was more frightening because as yet no one knew how he planned to wield it. Pope for less than two months, as yet there was no sign of his nature. Would he be benevolent or tyrannical? Waiting for some sign, his fellow cardinals were growing uneasy. In the absence of a pope these last two long years, they'd grown used to life without an overlord. Added to that was the unimpressive stature of the new Holy Father, more suited to a foole than a prince.

Disappointed by the dwarf on the papal throne, several young ladies on the shore cast their eyes about the massive barge for a sight more pleasing to their eyes. Almost at once they found a most deserving figure tucked away on the lower level, far from His Holiness. The young man's naturally fair complexion was tanned but not burned, his fashionably long black hair whipping in the wind from beneath his square, feathered cap. Dressed to perfection in demi-cape, high boots, and hose cinched so tight it showed the muscles of his thigh, he was the very ideal of the modern knight. More, his slight air of suffering made him all the more attractive. And the cut of his doublet was so high as to be almost scandalous – just below the richly embroidered hem, girls could see the faintest curve of his firm buttock. How daring! How delightful! How *French!*

Had he known he passed for French, he would have been deeply gratified. Nineteen years old now, married for over a year and still yet a virgin (a status which many French maids had attempted to correct), Ser Mariotto Montecchio was the epitome of chivalry. And true chivalry, as everyone knew, began in France.

A youth stood near him, just twelve years old last July. He was rather plain, with drooping eyes and a face that was still sorting itself out. Dressed in a drab second-hand gonella and a floppy cap that was woefully out of style, the lad gazed at Mariotto as if he were a god.

Summoning his courage, the boy pointed to the girls on the shore. "They're staring at you."

Mari was pleasantly startled. The lad had an Italian accent! Was it Florentine? Too honest to pretend he had not noticed the girls, Mariotto chose to be generous. "Perhaps they're staring at you."

The boy looked ruefully at his poor clothes. "No. You're like the sun. I'm just a cloud blocking their view."

Mariotto felt a curious pity rising in him. "Very poetic. What's your name?"

"Francesco. Though I suppose it should be François. We live here, now."

"Me too," said Mari, hiding his sadness behind a smile. He had no inkling how long this noble exile would last.

Young François surprised Mari by nodding. "I heard the story." He pointed at the girls on the Rhône's bank opposite them. "If they heard it, they'd drown themselves like the Donna di Scalotta did for Lancelot du Lac."

Mariotto winced. The reference to Lancelot was apt. As Lancelot had betrayed Arthur with Guinevere, so Mariotto had betrayed his closest friend by stealing his betrothed.

Aloud he said, "That would be a shame, as I'm married." *Though not yet a husband*, he reminded himself.

The boy continued to nod wisely. "Some men say you did wrong. I don't think so."

"No?"

"No! If chivalry is all about the wishes of women, great deeds in their names, hardships for their sakes,

you did the right thing. You made her happy by marrying her."

To Mari that argument rang false. "Alas, François,
chivalry is about pining from afar, the idea of an
unattainable woman. Dante never wed his Beatrice."

"Dante is an idiot."

The youth pronounced the words with such certainty that Mariotto had to laugh. "Be careful! I'm a
friend to his son."

"And my father is friends with Dante himself." The
twelve-year-old shrugged. "I don't mean to smear his
poetry. Just his notion of love as an idea. Love is real,
and real love makes you act. That's why you married
your friend's betrothed."

Mari didn't want to answer that, so he argued
for love. "It's the relationship between Beatrice and
Dante that's legendary, a love that transcended the
physical. Ideally, love and marriage are not meant to
be joined. Marriage soils love's perfection."

"So why did you marry her then?" asked the
young man with direct simplicity.

Gazing out at the cheering folk on the shore, Mari
was silent. His unspoken answer was equally simple,
and eternally shaming. *I wanted her. I couldn't bear
to be a great lover, to love from afar. O, Gianozza...*

Yet Fortune had conspired to make theirs a great
tale of love after all. Fate, in the guise of the Lord

of Verona, had separated them, sending Mari here to the papal court on the very day of his wedding. His exile from his bride made him pine, and long, and dream. From her letters, Gianozza felt the same. Theirs was indeed destined to be a great love, like Dante and Beatrice, Antony and Cleopatra, Odysseus and Penelope.

"My son isn't troubling you, is he?" asked a grave man, dressed exactly as young François.

Mariotto recognized the exiled Florentine as a notary to one of the cardinals. "Not at all, Ser Petracco," said Mari with a winning smile. "We were debating the nature of chivalry and the love of poets."

The notary's chin lifted as if to remove from his nose a foul smell. At the same moment his son shot a reproachful glance to Mari. With apologies for troubling the Veronese knight, Ser Petracco took his son off, a firm grip on his shoulder. Not an admirer of poetry, mused Mariotto.

A burly cardinal approached, a smile bursting through his beard. "I know that look. Has little Francesco been reciting verses again?"

Mari bowed. "Cardinal Orsini. My fault, I'm afraid. We were discussing courtly love."

"Ah. l'amour." With that polite acknowledgement, Cardinal Orsini took up station beside Mariotto to stare out over the water slipping by.

Mari knew that most men on this ship thought him a damned romantic fool. During the past year, as he grew more and more worldly at the leaderless papal court, he'd been forced to rebuff – sometimes physically – the attentions of dozens of girls. This drew laughter from many prelates, and earned him a few equally unwelcome advances from his own sex.

The only man who had never mocked him was Cardinal Napoleone Orsini. In spirit both the lion and the bear his name indicated, he was a generous, gregarious, and bluntly gracious man. Upon arriving in the summer of 1315, Mariotto had attached himself to Orsini's party. Back then the cardinal had been rumoured as a favourite for the papacy, and as they spoke nearly the same language (Veronese Italian differed from Roman Italian, but only in dialect), it seemed a natural move. Mariotto had orders to lobby the new pope in Verona's favour, and if he had a friendship with that new pope before the office was granted, so much the better.

The election of Jacques d'Euse had come as quite a shock, and not only to Mari. After two years without a Holy Father, the latest French king had bullied and bribed all the cardinals together and forced them into a castle to do their duty and choose a pontiff. It gave new meaning to the term conclave – con clave, literally, 'with key'. While they held the key to God's heir on Earth, Philip V held the key to their freedom.

Mariotto remembered waiting with so many others outside the castle, watching for the telltale smoke that would signify Orsini's election. But when the white smoke had come and the doors had opened, it was instead a cordwainer's son who had mounted Saint Peter's throne. The little man had taken them all by surprise, doing the unthinkable and nominating himself. Trained in both law and medicine, his career in the clergy had been mostly spent presiding over the seaside See of Frejus, a pleasurable duty, and in Avignon, providing advice more legal than spiritual. How he had swung them around to vote for him, no one quite said. Certainly Orsini had been mute on the subject. But rather than look displeased, Orsini appeared quite content.

Now looking out over the water, Orsini softly murmured, "Illyria, I am coming."

"Pardon?" said Mariotto.

Abashed, the cardinal rubbed his whiskered chin with the back of his hand. "I have a cousin, prince of a city on the coast of Anatolia. It's called Dubrovnik, but he has renamed it Illyria."

"Illyria? After—?"

"—Ilium, yes, the fabled city of Helen and Paris." Orsini smiled smugly. "He's a fanciful fellow, for all that he's a good prince. In fact, he's rather like you! He pines. O, how he pines! He writes of a young maiden for whom he would eat every apple in the world. Her father is a great man of the city and her brother is one of the handsomest men in the land – by report, he would even rival you," added the cardinal with a cheerful wink. "Certain that with such men in her life already he would pale in comparison, my cousin has talked himself into loving the lady from afar."

Mariotto pulled a face. "That's falling off the horse before you get to the rail."

"I told you, fanciful. Come to think of it, he's not at all like you. You abandoned convention and seized your moment. That's the difference between true love and this airy popular nonsense. True love demands action. Only in false love can a man wallow, peak, and pine."

"You and young Petracco see eye to eye. But it's contrary to what the poets—"

"Pfah! Poets love words, not women. It's like the Church. There are men of the cloth who mouth the words of Christ, and those who live them. Love of Christ demands action. Misguided as many of the crusades have been, one cannot fault the passion with which the crusaders spurred off to fight. Christ himself was a man of action – his love of his Father made him perform miracles, and he beat the craven moneylenders. I tell you, if I have been tempted to any violence in my life, it has been to emulate him in that act. For I swear to you, Ser Montecchio, I detest even the smell of money!" The steel in Orsini's voice underscored his vehemence.

Mariotto paused, then returned to his original query. "So why do you say you are coming to Illyria?"

Again the cardinal looked abashed. "Your fault! I was thinking about courtly love – desire as the be all and end all. To me, my cousin's Illyria is all about desire. An ideal, a mythical state, a place where one pines for the thing one wants most in the world. And therefore that thing is most often denied." Orsini chucked Mari on the shoulder. "We all know what your Illyria is – your Gianozza."

Mariotto grinned. "And yours?"

"Rome," said the cardinal simply. "As Rome has been denied us these many years, Rome is my Illyria." Orsini released a huge, happy breath. "But at last we are returning."

Mariotto perked up at once. This was news! "His Eminence is returning the Holy See to Rome?"

Orsini nodded. "There is no harm I think in speaking of it, now the election is past and he is enthroned. Our new Holy Father has sworn an oath to me, upon the consecrated Host and before all the entire conclave, that he will never again mount a horse or mule except in the direction of Rome."

Mariotto lacked a lawyer's mind, but this seemed a convoluted oath to take. "Is that why—?"

"—we float instead of ride? Yes," answered the cardinal. "He is keeping his word. Rightly, he points out that Avignon is the current site of his authority, and he must attend to matters there before he makes such a drastic change."

"No disrespect, but he is very old, and quite frail," observed Mariotto. "What if, God forbid, he does not live to see his promise carried out?"

"Then we shall elect another who will. But that won't be necessary. Jacques d'Euse is famous for being a man of his word, else he would not have been elected."

They sailed on for hours, the cardinals and bishops and knights waving and smiling to the throngs along the Rhône. There was great cheer, particularly among the Italian clerics – they were at last to return to San Pietro's true throne. They were going home.

The sun was low in the autumnal sky when Avignon came into view. With great decorum the little pope lifted himself from his throne and crossed to the rail where Orsini and Montecchio, along with many others of their nation, had congregated.

"Mon frère!" cried the wizened pope to Orsini. "See how vibrant the heavens are above my beloved France."

"Indeed!" agreed the cardinal warmly. "I am certain it seems all the more lovely, as you contemplate leaving it behind. If death is indeed the mother of beauty, then exile is the father of patriotism."

"What you say is both profound and true," said the pontiff in his curious style of speech, both headlong and monotonous. "I find in me no inch that is not tilled with love for France. And it is for that reason I have decided that I must delay preparations for a return to Rome."

Orsini's generous spirit was devoid of the suspicion that Mariotto, listening intently, felt all too keenly. "For how long?"

"Indefinitely," said the little pope, his sorrowful expression not reaching his eyes.

For a suspended moment Cardinal Orsini wrestled with the meaning of this word. Then like a thunderclap the pontiff's purpose was made clear. Orsini looked as though his ribs had been levered open and his heart removed before the gaze of all the world. "You do not intend to return the Holy See to Rome?"

The little man in the grand hat and gown blinked several times. "You wish me to leave my own country for all eternity, to lock myself away in that ruined country you call Love? No. I fear Roma is not Amor for me."

"But – it has been the home of the papacy since the first pope, the blessed Peter himself. He chose Rome as the finest and grandest city in all the world!"

"But is that true today? The world has shifted away from Rome, *mon frère,* and we must follow the world's lead."

"Holy Father, you are charged to lead, not to follow."

"And so I am, by leading us away from blind adherence to tradition. But in one way you are mistaken. I must lead my flock, but I must follow God. God has led the papacy to Avignon. Where He leads, I must follow."

Orsini kept his voice level by sheer force of will. "My Lord, one of your titles is Bishop of Rome."

"I have so many titles, I can do without that one. My dear Orsini, the same Lord that gave the blessed apostle Peter the power to bind and loose – he is everywhere, is he not? Certainly he is as present in this lush and vibrant land as he is in the decayed maw of the seven hills. I am afraid this journey has quite determined me to stay in Avignon. No, I pray you, do not protest! Your Italy smiles to you, but for me it would only be a land of exile and despair."

Struggling, Orsini's obedience lost to his need to protest. "Your Grace, Rome is the capital of the Christian world."

"The Christian world needs no capital, mon frère. The Lord our God is everywhere, ever present. He will forgive the whims of an old man too tired to travel so very far."

"But your Holiness, your promise – you vowed upon the sacred Host—"

Jacques d'Euse held up a hand. "My dear friend, I promise you I will not be forsworn."

Mariotto spied a litter awaiting the pontiff on the quay. A litter that had already been arranged, did not have to be sent for. He had sworn never to ride again, unless it was towards Rome. And as Cardinal Orsini had said, Jacques D'Euse was a man of his word.

Jacques d'Euse, now Pope John XXII, possessor of immense – and irrevocable – power.

As Mariotto Montecchio joined the procession that followed the dwarfish Pontiff back onto French soil, the bear-like cardinal lingered behind, as bereft of words as of recourse. Like his cousin and name-sake in distant Illyria, all that remained in Orsini was his longing.

ACT I

Naught's Had,
All's Spent

One

Ten Years Later
Caprino, Italy
24 March 1326

"The Greyhound? Why the Devil is that devil coming here?"

"A fit enough cause for a devil. He's coming to inspect the forge."

From his seat behind his elaborately carved desk, Gaspardo Rienzi thumped his fleshy fist. "Rubbish! He never comes unless there's been trouble with production, and we've been exceeding even our own estimates this last six months and more!"

This was addressed to a teen that greatly resembled Rienzi, only taller and with tighter-fitting skin. "He's bringing his heir."

Mouth open for a further curse, Rienzi clamped it down in a sour grimace, looking very much as if he had bitten his tongue. "Of course he is."

The winter months around Verona had been quiet for once. The Greyhound's prodigious energies were nowhere to be seen – no games, no festivals, no grand hunts. The Palio had come and gone in a rather lackluster fashion, since the great man had taken himself off to the Lago di Garda with this fabulous heir everyone was praising. It was the first time in memory the Greyhound had missed seeing the Palio run.

More, there were murmurs of a family quarrel – the Greyhound's bitch sister had followed to the palace at Garda, only to be refused entry at the gates.

Now, two days after Easter, both hound and pup were coming to inspect the forge. God alone knew why. Behind the desk Rienzi girded himself. "Very well. I'll meet them myself."

"I can do it, father."

"No, Adamo. That family is the Devil's own. I don't want you to have any contact with them. Not you, and certainly not Lia. They're dogs, the lot of them." Eyes turning inwards, Rienzi gnawed his lower lip. "When is he coming?"

"Tomorrow, sometime after dawn."

"Probably worried about the Emperor coming across the Alps. Damn the Scaliger and his damnable ambitions. Still, we can use the day to demand more money and maybe a few more concessions. Inform the smiths to keep the fires going all night, just in case he tries to surprise us."

"Yes, father."

Rienzi averted his gaze, looking out the window and blinking rapidly. "Leave me."

Adamo bowed to his father and exited the chamber, pulling the heavy oak door shut behind him. As he started down the hallway he was not surprised to discover his sister waiting.

"You shouldn't have told him," scolded Lia.

"You shouldn't listen at keyholes."

"Don't try to joust with me."

Adamo grinned crookedly. "You don't even have a lance."

Lia persisted. "You shouldn't have told him."

"I had to, didn't I?"

"Well then, you shouldn't have agreed."

"To what?"

"To let father meet him! You know how much he loathes the Greyhound!"

"Oh yes, Lia, I know precisely how much. Just enough to bad-mouth him, not enough to refuse his money."

"That money is for you, you ungrateful—"

Adamo raised his fist and Lia stepped back. Tripping on her skirts, she fell hard on her rump and curled into a ball, expecting to be kicked.

But Adamo was a man now, fifteen years old, and deemed their childhood squabbling beneath him. Though the sneer was still present. "Lia, you truly are an idiot. We should sell you to an abbey to live with the other girls too stupid to be ornaments to their families."

"At least I'd be away from you."

"Is that any way to talk to your loving brother?"

"I'd rather be sister to a cur!" Struggling to her feet, she muttered curses at her voluminous layers. Despite nearing her fourteenth birthday, and despite flowering a year before, she was still unused to the layers and layers of formal feminine gear. But her father liked to have her dress as his pretty angel, and Lia strove to be obedient. "At least go with him!" she urged.

"No," he said. "I will obey father's wishes."

"Why start now?"

"It frees me to do other things." Chucking her under the chin, Adamo strode away.

Concerned, Lia knocked on her father's door, hoping to cheer him up. But the old man refused her entrance, demanded to be left alone. Shoulders sagging, Lia returned to her room to discard her many layers. She had gotten all bound up for nothing.

Damn the Greyhound, she thought. Him, and his heir.

25 March 1326

Snow stirred, performing effortless pirouettes just off the ground as the two horses halted before a spectacular view. The burgeoning sun to their right cast an almost blinding reflection off the river. Across the shimmering water, the ground climbed steeply, rising from nearby hills to become the monumental Alps. This was the northern boundary of the Feltro, the northernmost region of Italy.

It was cold, and to breathe was to be bitten in the throat. Yet Cangrande della Scala, master of Verona, ruler of the Feltro, took in a lungful of brisk winter air and expelled it with gusto. He flicked the reins in his fur-covered gloves, and the horse under him turned away from the sun's glare. In truth, the dappled charger was too well-bred for simple rides such as this, but the Scaliger had a yen for fancy beasts as well as fancy clothes. And fancy games.

The second horse was a young palfrey, not fancy but a little wild for its small stature. It had been chosen to match its rider. Francesco della Scala, master of himself, ruler of his wits, sat upright in his saddle and forced himself to take in the eternal greys and purples of the land before him. Looking out at the snow-covered trees, the ice-crusted river, and mountainous peaks, a poem suggested itself, but the lump of wet ashes that had replaced his brains couldn't form it. It was happening more and more, this lack of words – a dreadful prospect for one who loved language as much as life.

Say something! Cesco's mind cried out. At once his mouth obliged. "What, Alexander, not weeping?"

Cangrande had been enjoying the boy's silence, and his famous smile had an edge as he answered. "It is not the breadth of the domain, but its fertility that matters." Removing an apple from his saddlebag, he bit deliberately into it.

Cesco kept his eyes off the apple, but that didn't stop his stomach from roiling with lust. "Why must you always retreat into ribaldry?"

"You'll understand once your balls drop. Now be silent, I'm enjoying the view."

It was indeed magnificent, but Cesco's eyes clouded, his ears filled with each crunchy bite of apple. Closing his mind to sound, he employed numbers to distract him. 237 days, precisely. Grandfather Dante had always said to be specific. 237 days equals 34 weeks equals 8 months.

Eight months of stolen sleep. Thirty-four weeks of eating scraps. Two hundred thirty-seven days of humiliation. A seventeenth of his life spent for a mouthful of dust. Two thirds of a year without breaking.

For that was the game – breaking him. Last summer Cangrande had welcomed his heir back to Verona by taking him on as squire, claiming it was to better know the eleven-year-old after so many years apart. But the true reason was to break this willful, insolent, daredevil child. Cesco was being treated as one of the Scaliger's hawks – starved, tasked, deprived of sleep or comfort – all to bend him to his master's will. It was a miracle that Cesco had lasted so long.

Of course, I've been cheating. All unwilling, his thoughts drifted to the small wafers hidden in his boot. He couldn't help imagining the sensation of energy and confidence he would feel once one passed his lips. He couldn't swallow one now, not in front of his tasker. He would have to endure until the opportunity presented itself.

Cesco filled the time by trying to guess why they had come. Usually his days were spent learning some new fighting technique or bending under some grueling physical labour – riding, running, climbing, hunting, swimming. On rare occasions he was allowed the great pleasure of a book, and then only to recite it verbatim on the next ride for his master's amusement. Success in all these was met with indifference, whereas failure was greeted by severe punishment. *At least he doesn't blindfold me, or sew my eyelids shut. That was a common practice with birds. Best not mention it, though. It would give him ideas.*

Often Cangrande would farm out a day's training to one of his lords or retainers. But today their predawn exodus from the hunting retreat at Garda had been made without pages, guards, or friends. Just a knight and his squire. And the path hadn't been marked, meaning they'd come to a secret place. It was enough to cause Cesco a little paranoia, a perversely welcome sensation. Mystery made his blood flow faster. Tired as he was, any stimulant was to be treasured.

What is in that churning violence you call a mind, my lord? Where are you taking me? Somewhere along the river, certainly. Perhaps a swim? That would wake me up, at least. And while we're undressing I could sneak a wafer...

Cangrande cocked his head at Cesco, and the boy realized he'd missed the sound of horses. *Damn.* "My lord. Horses."

Cangrande tossed his half-eaten apple into the snow. "Don't be afraid. We are expected."

Once, Cesco would have bristled at the implied hint of cowardice. Now it rolled off his back as a battle not worth fighting. Realizing this meant he had indeed been altered by the hawking, he instantly set about being mulish. "Finally giving up? Selling me into slavery?"

"You'll be dead long before I give up. If I cannot tame you, no one else will be allowed to try."

"That's rather like burning down your city so the enemy cannot claim they seized it."

"It's exactly like that. Bear it in mind. Now hush."

Not a novel exchange, nor particularly clever on either part. But the fact that it had even taken place meant Cesco had won a victory. Not broken yet! Pleased, he trained his eyes on the small party approaching them.

Like Cangrande, all five riders were wrapped in furs and leathers, denoting their wealth. Whereas Cesco was dressed in itchy homespun, with only the leather he had cured himself to protect him. Looking like a patchwork vagabond, he felt like one too, and had to constantly refrain from scratching.

The leader was on the best horse, but his place in the group was obviously due to deference, not saddle skill. A pudgy old man, more fit for a coach or carriage. Cesco couldn't see much of his face, swaddled as it was, but something in the man's demeanor made Cesco's fingers itch.

The old man reined in just short of sword's reach. "Capitano. You look in health."

"Thank you, Gaspardo! It's true, I have never been so robust. A winter without wars, only good meals and better company. The exception is this dolt of a squire. But he has a family claim on me, so..." Cangrande shrugged to suggest his helplessness.

All eyes turned to Cesco, and for the millionth time he felt himself being measured. Despite Cangrande's light words, they all knew this was the bastard Heir of Verona, and they scrutinized his features for any similarity between him and his lord.

In height, there was none. Cangrande was a near giant, towering over other men both in the saddle and on foot. Whereas Cesco was lacking in stature even for one just shy of his twelfth birthday. Nor did they share a frame, Cangrande being large and just a little too well-fleshed, while Cesco was leaner than one of the great man's hounds.

But there were echoes in the lines of the face, the arc of the chin, and the wryness of the smile. Similar too were the curls of chestnut hair that in summer sunlight became fringed with blond. Both wore their hair shorter than was the fashion, and both were dressed in the same colours, which showed the sameness of their skin tones. Naturally, Cangrande's garments were superior.

The chief difference lay in the eyes. Cangrande's were of a rich blue that might have come from

Maestro Giotto's own palette, whereas Cesco's were changeable – or so he'd been told. Some days they were said to be a muddy blue-grey, but mostly they were green. Women loved to tell him how magnificent a green it was, with gold flecks and a pale ring around them, resembling nothing so much as a lush isle in the midst of a turbulent and stormy sea. Himself, he'd never seen them but by reflection, and even the finest mirrors failed to show him what other people saw. To him, they looked like the eyes of an animal trapped in the body of a boy. But that was a fancy born of circumstance.

Bruised, tired, and hungry, Cesco contrived to smile brightly. "I hope, masters, you find my company less irksome than does my lord Cangrande. If I have any virtue, it is a knowledge of all my faults. He has catalogued them for me."

"King among them is impudence," agreed Cangrande. "Gaspardo, allow me to introduce my heir, Francesco. Infant, this great man is Monsignor Gaspardo Rienzi, master of the river and all its fruits and labours."

"Neptune, Poseidon, and Rienzi – a god among us. I am in awe." Up close, Cesco could make out the broken veins of the sot and the pale yellowness that bespoke a dying liver. Doffing his cap to the old man, Cesco's numbed fingers almost dropped it, but he managed to make the mistake appear an extra touch of foppishness.

Rienzi was far from amused. In fact, the man looked downright venomous. *What did I ever do to you, Lord Rienzi? Did I steal your daughter? Burn your lands? Fish your pond? Or am I merely condemned by association?* But the old man found a polite reply. "You are fortunate in having a son so quick-witted, my lord."

"Wait until you know him. You'll see it's only his tongue that's quick. Still, it's true that I'm lucky in all my bastards. But there are so many, how could I not be? Now if we could, let's away. And please, not a word of our destination. It's a surprise."

Under his layers of furs and hoods, Rienzi made a noise Cesco couldn't decipher. Then the old man turned his horse's head back the way he had come. Cangrande and Cesco followed, surrounded by Rienzi's men.

There was no speech for the next half mile until, cresting a hill, Cesco spied a mass of stone spanning the water, marring the sun's reflection. A solid bridge led to a huge building perched above the river's center, with two brick chimneys belching forth black smoke. Attached to the building was the largest waterwheel Cesco had ever seen.

This had to be their destination, as Cangrande proved by watching his squire's reaction. "You know what it is?"

Cesco looked wide-eyed at the Scaliger. "You mean you don't?"

Cangrande clucked his tongue. "That's another meal you'll have to forego. Really, I'm surprised you haven't wasted away to nothing. Answer the question."

Cesco squinted at the structure. "It's your famous water-forge."

"O, that's a shame! I was hoping you hadn't heard about it."

"Is it supposed to be a secret?"

"Well, everyone knows it exists," said Cangrande easily. "But not its location."

Cesco was genuinely bemused. "You're joking! Everyone knows where the forge is."

"Ah, they only think they do. I had another waterwheel built several miles from here, and there's smoke rising from it, too. However, rather than stoke the fires, that wheel grinds wheat. This is the true forge."

"And it goes unnoticed?"

"Who goes looking for something when they already know where it is?" A typical piece of Scaligeri subterfuge – allow your foes to see what they expect, while the truth lies hidden close by.

Yet Cesco was intrigued. "Why secrecy at all? A water-forge is not novel, not in this day and age."

"I suppose not," said Cangrande tartly. "So tell me, O master of modernity, what is the purpose of a water-forge?"

"Making weapons out of water?"

"Amusing. Keep it up and I'll have you turning that wheel by hand."

Cesco bowed his head in mock subservience. "But my lord Capitano, it's technically true! The water turns the wheel, which powers the bellows, which stokes the fires, which allows the blacksmith to work with hotter flames than the average forge. And you can use the river to cool the metal. So the water makes the weapons stronger."

"That's only half its genius! Rienzi? Can you illuminate this young know-it-all as to the other advantage of our treasure?"

Despite his cold demeanor, Rienzi couldn't disguise his pride. "The wheel also powers trip-hammers to beat the metal. Raw ore can be shaped into wrought iron in less than half the time it takes a common smith."

"As an experiment," added the Scaliger, "it has paid for itself time and again, allowing me to equip men twice as fast as my enemies."

Hearing this, the famished Cesco forgot his stomach, hungering instead to enter the forge and explore. He made a show of yawning. "And why are we here? Am I to learn a trade?"

Cangrande clapped his gloved hands. "Now why didn't I think of that? It would be a good way to put some muscle on your frame."

"So would letting me eat."

The lord of Verona laughed. "True at that. However, if you can curb your appetite, we will enter and have a look around. Then we can leave poor Rienzi in peace."

Rienzi glanced up out of his swaddling. "You're not supping with us, lord?"

"Thank you, no. I wouldn't dream of imposing upon your household – not with this little monster in tow. His manner at table is worthy of a kennel. No, Cesco can snare us some game for supper. As he points out, he lacks employment."

Reaching the bridge, Cesco noticed an image painted on the wall of the forge. An amusing emblem, a beaver racing through flames. "Is that your crest, Lord Rienzi?"

"Yes," grunted Rienzi. "Granted us by the Capitano."

Cesco studied the flaming beaver. "There's a joke in there somewhere."

Reins in hand, Cangrande grinned. "No dammed jokes. It burns me up."

"O!" In mock pain, Cesco urged his horse forward.

Cangrande kept pace. "That's you, always forging ahead."

"I cry a foul! For there's nothing fouler than a pun."

Cangrande wagged a finger. "You know, I'd willingly let you share in the meat you catch so long as you laugh at my jokes."

"I'd rather starve," said Cesco bitterly.

The seven riders dismounted, hobbled their horses on the metal rings at the bridge's end, and entered the structure.

From the edge of the treeline, they were observed.

After more than an hour, the same party emerged, Rienzi in the lead, Cesco doggedly bringing up the rear. Both Cangrande and Cesco were blackened and begrimed, blisters on their fingers and palms. All the adults save Cangrande wore bemused expressions, as if uncertain what they had just witnessed.

They were followed by a massive fellow in a leather smock whose shoulders and biceps proclaimed his profession. Ruffling Cesco's short curls with his callused hand, the smith spotted his own teenaged apprentice lingering in the doorway. "Oi! Get back inside. This is no holy day!" As the apprentice scampered off, the smith confided in Cangrande. "Sorry, m'lord. He doesn't often see lads his own age."

"Understandable. I was told once that fools delight in other fools," replied the Scaliger. "Still, that was refreshing! Despite all our modern amenities, sometimes it's healthy to do some good, old-fashioned work! But duty calls. Cesco, see to the horses."

Bowing, Cesco did as he was bid without comment. As he plodded away, the smith said, "S'truth, my lord, he's a determined one, isn't he? Never seen a lad so young work so hard to impress a father."

Cangrande flexed his right arm. "Couldn't do it, though, could he?"

"He's just a mite! An' he did a more creditable job than any beginning apprentice I've ever had. Give me a month, I wager he'd be as good with the hammer and anvil as I am today."

Smiling his famous allegria, Cangrande clapped the smith on the shoulder. "If I could spare him for the month, I'd gladly take that wager!"

At the end of the bridge, Rienzi was already being lifted into his saddle by two of his retainers. Unhitching the dappled charger and the palfrey, Cesco heard Rienzi grudgingly say, "I was impressed by your questions, boy."

Cesco bowed gravely. "I'm here to learn."

In truth, he'd been fascinated. He'd seen forges before, of course, but nothing like the horrible, marvelous inferno within those walls. The troughs for good and bad ore, the firebox, the releases to dump the detritus into the river. Clearly it was a mechanism still in flux, with additions made every few months to improve on the theory. The smith had explained two such changes to them, and Cesco had instantly voiced his thoughts on how to improve the improvements.

Foolish. Open your mouth, you invite trouble. Cangrande had instantly taken up the hammer and tongs and begun working a piece of metal like a professional, stroke after hearty stroke. A casual barb stung Cesco into trying it himself. He knew he hadn't done a good job – his metal was weak and unshaped while Cangrande's was almost perfect. But he had neither faltered nor given up. That was something.

Even Rienzi seemed impressed, in spite of himself. "Your suggestion about the firebox had merit."

Cangrande approached them. "Yes, the lad does a decent job of emulating intelligence. A shame his mental muscles so far outstrip the ones on his arm. Gaspardo, I thank you. Truly, the forge could not be in better hands. My trust was not misplaced."

Rienzi bowed his head. "I am gratified you think so, my lord."

"Though you should try your hand at the anvil from time to time – bracing! It might dispel your bilious humour."

"Rude labour is not in my blood," replied Rienzi.

"While it's certainly in mine," laughed the Scaliger, picking up on the hinted insult. "I've often wondered where the ladder in my family crest gets its origin – were we carpenters? I find myself in divine company, then."

"Or perhaps just social climbers, like the Capulletti," observed Cesco.

For all Rienzi's obvious dislike of the Scaliger, something had softened his opinion of Cesco. "Are you certain you will not sup with us, lord? I could have some soup brought to your squire, who has laboured so hard this morning."

Cangrande waved the offer aside. "We won't impose any further on your hospitality. But please pass my respects on to your family. Your son must almost be of age, no?"

"Past," said Rienzi stiffly. "Fifteen last fall."

"Excellent. We must see him in the lists this summer. Perhaps he can be the warrior you never were." With this casual slight, Cangrande swung up into his saddle and clicked his tongue. "Come, Cesco. The smell of the forge keeps the game away. Let's go where you can catch me a nice meal."

Cesco clambered up and urged his mount to follow the Scaliger's trotting charger. He could feel the eyes of the gouty old man burning his master's neck, and made sure to twist around and wave cheerfully before pulling his palfrey alongside Cangrande's steed. "Is it clever to bait the man who makes your swords?"

"Cleverer than letting him think he has any importance in the grand scheme of things. For ten years he's kept the forge running, and been well recompensed for his services. But does he thank me? No. Instead, he carps and complains."

"It's certainly true he doesn't like you."

"He's not required to. But he must respect my authority." Cangrande pulled a face. "It's his own doing entirely. His discourteous nature means I have to belittle him just to remind him who the master is."

Cesco managed a dry chuckle. "So you treat him like me?"

"By no means," said Cangrande seriously. "You two are entirely unlike. You have ability. It's humility you lack. He has neither. It's something you'll find as you grow older. Men of lesser ability will resent you, no matter what you do. If you succeed, you are a cock on a fence. If you fail, they delight in ridiculing your faults. Because they all harbour a secret belief that, had they only been in your shoes, they could have done it all better. But that's a fallacy. If they were able, they would excel. Instead, all they can do is resent you for showing up their failings."

Cesco's fascination kept him awake. "Aut Caesar, aut nihil."

"Exactly."

"Isn't that hubris?"

"On my part, or theirs?"

"Both."

The Scaliger considered. "Hubris is false pride. So in regards to myself – and you, for that matter – it cannot be hubris, but rather an honest assessment of our abilities. Rienzi will never be more than he is, nor could he be. Rather than admit his limitations, he chooses to resent me for pointing them out to him."

It wasn't often that Cangrande spoke seriously. Most of their days were spent in sparring, both verbal and physical. But once in a fortnight the Scaliger would open up and speak frankly. These conversations were rare, and treasured. Cesco recognized these nonces of solace for what they were – a hint at the finishing line, of the life that awaited the conclusion of the hawking. A true training, not of body but of mind, a rapport between lord and heir that would benefit them both.

But Cangrande had also made it clear that the hawking would only end when Cesco capitulated, when his spirit was broken. Which meant, to Cesco, that it would never end if left in Cangrande's hands. It was up to Cesco to end it. On his own terms.

Leaving the forge, they'd ridden south. Cangrande now turned east, steering his mount towards the sun. Following, Cesco hoped the confidences would continue. "You make Rienzi sound dangerous."

"All men are dangerous, given the opportunity. Take our friend Passerino. He does have some meager ability to rule. But rather than be content with his post as lord of Mantua, he believes he deserves more. He deludes himself into imagining he could rule the whole Feltro. So he tries to have me killed, despite our years of friendship."

At last! Passerino was a topic Cesco had desired to broach for months. "You haven't confronted him."

"Yet," said Cangrande, eyes twinkling. "I allow him to live on in ignorance, convincing himself that I know nothing of his plots and schemes. I will let him have just enough rope to hang himself. Never fear. When the time comes, I'll be there to draw the noose tight."

"I'd like to be there, too," said Cesco seriously.

"What, still angry over that nurse's brat?"

"Yes." Because of the plot against Cangrande, an infant girl had been murdered before Cesco's very eyes. He'd named his hawk after her.

"Tch. There is a sentimental streak in you quite opposed to your nature. Must be Ser Alaghieri's doing. Still, anger can be useful, properly applied. Now tell me what you really think of my forge."

"I wouldn't want to fish in that water."

Cangrande laughed. "Nor I! That's why I had it built on this offshoot of the Adige, so as not to interfere with the true river. And I have a small dam further downstream to catch anything harmful." The Scaliger cocked an eyebrow. "But as you weren't planning on catching our supper from the river, that was an evasion. What are your thoughts on the forge?"

"I'm astonished so few men can keep such a beast running."

"It's an astonishing modern age we live in. The smith only has to make certain that fuel is regularly added – though I imagine that's what his apprentice is charged with. Still, not everyone could keep such an industry alive. The cost in coal and limestone is prohibitive. Fortunately, I can afford it. Hyah!" Speeding up, Cangrande leapt his horse over some bracken. Cesco did the same, only to find his master had not slowed, but continued on at a gallop. Cursing, Cesco kicked hard, following in an impromptu race that he was already sure to lose.

Still, if I'm going to lose anyway… He pretended to slip sideways in his saddle as if losing his balance. As he heard Cangrande's mocking laugh from ahead, his forefinger and thumb darted into the rolled cuff of his high boot and removed one of the sticky waferish chews. Pulling himself upright, he brushed his chin, sliding the confection between his lips. At once he felt relief and renewed energy. How much of that is my imagination, and how much the Moor's drug?

Despite his doctor's utter dismay, for the last several months Cesco had been consuming small quantities of a mixture of drugs, including both hashish and opium. He was careful not to over-indulge. He'd done that once, with disastrous results.

After twenty minutes of weaving in and out of trees and jumping short gullies, they reached a barren patch of snowy grass beside a clear stream. Cangrande had already dismounted and was brushing his horse's neck. "Bracing! But disappointing! I'm thinking of sponsoring a tourney, but not until I know my heir will not embarrass himself. Or his master."

"His what?" asked Cesco innocently.

"That's five races in a row you've lost. We really must get you a better horse."

"Seven, actually," said Cesco, his mind fixed on the idea of a tournament even as his mouth carried on. "But on different horses. The fault must be in the rider. Or maybe the saddle? Perhaps I could sit in your seat next time – you know, try it out for size."

Cangrande's eyes narrowed. "I wouldn't let you near my saddle looking like that – you're filthy!" He glanced down at his own hands and feigned shock. "Good lord! So am I! Come, we must cleanse ourselves before we dine!"

At once the great man was stripping off his clothes. Cesco did the same, determined to be the first into the water. He succeeded, barely, running across the snowy patches and throwing himself chest-first into the stream seconds before the Scaliger. The cold made them both gasp and laugh swearingly. Since the water was not deep enough for a proper swim, they couldn't race from bank to bank as they often did. Instead, Cangrande splashed at Cesco and began to advance on him.

Forcing himself not to shiver, Cesco took up a wrestling stance. The next few minutes could not be termed a pleasure for either man or boy, but both took satisfaction in humiliating the other. Cesco worked desperately to stay out of the big man's grip, while Cangrande fought to keep his feet under him as Cesco used every trick to upend him. At last, by mutual consent, they trudged back onto the bank and wrapped themselves in their horses' blankets. Together they built a fire. Normally Cesco's chore alone, the possibility of frostbite demanded a faster resolution. Cangrande's tasking was pragmatic.

Long minutes later their clothes were once more upon their backs and their teeth had ceased chattering. They allowed their unsaddled mounts to drink from the stream while Cangrande rubbed his chest with his hands and Cesco hunched over the fire, hands out as if in supplication.

All at once Cesco said, "It would be interesting, though."

"What's that?"

"Using water as a weapon."

Cangrande raised an eyebrow. "A water-sword, perhaps?"

"I was thinking more along the lines of a water-ram. Beat a wall with water instead of stones to weaken it. It would be a stunning attack for the people behind the walls."

Cangrande's eyes lost focus. "I like the concept. But the amount of water would be colossal, and the delivery system a problem. How would you go about it?"

For the next half hour they discussed possible uses for water in battle. They chased the most ridiculous notions, trying to find practical ways around creating enough pressure behind the water to make it effectual.

When the topic was exhausted, Cangrande said, "What time do you imagine it is?"

Cesco looked up at the sun. "Almost noon."

"Well, we have a good half of the day ahead of us. Yet already I'm exhausted. Age, I defy you! You're not tired, are you?"

"Not at all." Because of the wafer, it wasn't even a lie. "I'm invigorated!"

"Ah, to be young again. Of course, I was already a knight when I was half your age. You're going to have to go far to eclipse me."

Turning his face to the fire, Cesco said, with forced ease, "Who said I plan to eclipse you?"

"Does it require speaking aloud to be true? You speak it in your every move, in your every look. In every battle you begin and lose, just to be sure the battle was fought. You shout it in your refusal to be obedient. Do you think this is how I wish to spend my hours? Mucking about in the river, catching my death. Teaching you swordplay, axeplay, and every other kind of play that can bring glory. I have better things to do."

"I don't think that's true. Or else you'd be doing them."

"By God, but you're clever! And yet a fool. Have you ever stopped to think why I'm taking such trouble with you?"

"I assume it's so that, even if I excel, you can take the credit."

"How devious I am. You must feel the deepest despair, knowing that you will never be free of my shadow."

"I do not fear the shadows, my lord."

"Good for you. There is enough strife out where men can see it for us to go hunting danger in the dark, like a cat."

"Or a falcon." Cesco did not care for cats, a fact Cangrande found amusing.

"Speaking of which, my little red hawk, if it's noon, it's time to eat." Stretching himself out full length next to the fire, he propped his saddle under his head as a pillow and closed his eyes. "I'm in the mood for hare."

Cesco sat considering all the ways a man could die. Then he stood and, removing the hunting gear from his own saddlebags, stalked off into the forest. Behind him, out of sight, the Scaliger began to snore.

Le feu épure l'or, Cesco recited to himself. Le feu épure l'or. On this of all mornings, it was an apt analogy.

Within moments among the trees, Cesco was aware he was not alone. He was about to crouch low and reach for a weapon when a tall figure in dark traveling clothes stepped into view. He signaled Cesco to be silent, beckoning him further from the clearing.

Relief coursing through him, Cesco fell in beside the man and spoke softly in Arabic. "I wondered if thou wouldst find us."

"I cannot always keep pace, unseen," rumbled a deep and broken voice in the same tongue. "But I will always find thee, little dancer."

"My own Aldebaran. Which creates me as Pleiades. Together we form the bull's eye. I wonder, art thou truly a skilled tracker? Or dost thou cheat? Where is thy pendulum?"

"With my cards and charts, at the palace. If I am stopped, I need no hints at witchcraft about my person. My skin is damning enough."

"Charred black at birth by the fires of Hell," agreed Cesco lightly. "Sometimes I wish I owned some trait so fearsome. Then perhaps I could frighten men into respecting me."

"A pitiful lack," agreed the Moor gravely. "Thou must earn it instead."

"Now you sound like him," groused Cesco, switching back to Italian and throwing a thumb over his shoulder.

The Moor switched tongues as well. "How was the forge?"

Cesco's face lit from within. "It was fascinating. I've never seen how much work it takes to make a simple idea come to life. Have you been inside?"

The Moor shook his head. "I arrived in time to observe you come forth."

Cesco felt the unspoken half of the sentence hanging in the air. "And?"

"And I was not the only one watching."

"No?"

"There was a lad, taller than you–"

Cesco pulled a face. "Let's face it, who isn't?"

"He seemed intent on the Capitano."

"A gawker. Someone come to stare at the famous Lord of Verona."

"Perhaps," admitted the Moor.

"Well then," said Cesco, yawning.

"I see I am wasting your time."

"Not at all. It's just that I have a hare to hunt. Or, more hopefully, a brace, so I might get one of my own."

"You settle in here," said the Moor. "I'll find your hares."

Cesco sighed in perfect bliss. "May the blessings of the Prophet alight on thy shoulders, I was so hoping you would say that." Slipping into the nook of a tree, he tucked his gloved hands under his armpits and was asleep before he closed his eyes.

The Moor threw his cloak over the boy, watched over him for a time, then moved off silently in search of game.

Two

The ship rocked gently at anchor, under a closed cavern of a sky. Cesco's arms encircled his love as her legs twined about him, pulling him close. Nearby, through a haze of red, men worked to bring down the sails, remove the masts.

"My love," murmured Cesco, pulse rising.

"Aye, love," whispered the honey-tongue in his ear.

A trumpet blast shook the boat and the hard, low sky parted in a crimson gash. Through the rift drifted a man, naked but for his helmet, his body hairless like the god he was. Little wings beat madly at the air, sending up a wind from his ankles.

The god waved his staff over Cesco and his love, the two snakes pulsing up and down its length, hissing words that sounded like death. Cesco's heart hammered wildly as he looked into the divine eyes, clear and cold as his own.

The golden-hair beneath the helmet stirred in the vicious wind aroused by divine rage. "Son of the goddess, how can you sleep so soundly in such a crisis? Can't you see the dangers closing about you now? Madman! Can't you hear the Westwind ruffling to speed you on? That woman spawns her plots, mulling over some desperate outrage in her heart, lashing her surging rage, she's bent on death. Why not flee headlong?"

Turning away from the god, Cesco closed his eyes and nestled closer to his love's breast. "Go to Hell, giant-killer."

"Go to Hell," repeated the god, swimming off through the torn red sky.

Waking with a violent start, Cesco looked quickly around. The snowy ground was quite still, undisturbed. The sun overhead had hardly moved – he hadn't slept long. Had he cried out? Had Cangrande heard? He waited, willing his shuddering heart to still. There was an added discomfort lower down, embarrassing in the extreme. Unsure what to do about it, Cesco willed that, too, to relax.

Pressing his back against the treebark, he scrubbed his eyes clear. What the Devil was that? Unconsciously he touched the disc hanging by a thong at his throat – an ancient coin, forged in the time of Virgil. On one side was inscribed the word PAX over the image of a laurel wreath. On the obverse was a winged helmet, and the single name – MERCURIO. Cesco had worn it as long as he could remember.

Bad dreams were nothing new. From earliest childhood Cesco had been plagued by them. He never spoke of them, not to anyone. Not even to the poet who'd helped raise him, who would have delighted in them. For there was nothing Cesco feared quite so much as dreams.

At some early point in his life he had read L'Inferno. From that moment on his dreams had been peppered with images from the epic poem, his natural creativity fusing with the most grotesque verses to create a catalogue of demises horrible and fascinating.

Soon his mind began to create new ways to die – inventive deaths, even ingenious. Not simply hangings or stabbings, but death by crushing darkness, by water drops, by music. Death at the whim of friends. And always on the other side lurked the true inferno.

Thus Cesco's earliest lesson, taught to himself by himself – how to wake before he died in his dreams.

Once he'd actually dreamed that he was dead. The dream began with his death as established fact. Even as he was amazed by the strangeness of a dream that let a dead boy think, he was horrified to find that death was neither peace nor torture. No forest of wailing trees, no men carrying their heads like lanterns. Instead, Cesco's dreaming death was a constant rush of people and words and action and ideas.

In short, death was madness.

These were the wages of dreaming. If he was grateful to Cangrande for anything, it was for teaching him that a body could become too tired to dream.

The irony was that Cesco felt as much fascination as revulsion for his dreams. The moment he awoke, he always made a list of images, picking out their sources – reality, fiction, or pure imagination.

This dream, for example, was simplicity itself. Virgil's Aeneid, Book Four. Aeneas and Dido, with Cesco in the hero's place. The words spoken by Mercury were the very ones the ancient god uttered in the poem.

There were discrepancies, though – Dido hadn't been on shipboard when Mercury had delivered this second warning. Nor had the sailors been dismasting, but rather preparing for departure. Aeneas was planning to leave Dido, whereas in the dream Cesco seemed to be staying. Let Mercury threaten how he may, Cesco had turned his back on death-bringer. Interesting.

Feeling a pressing need, he loosed his points to make water. Only as he finished did he notice the hare hanging from a low branch, trussed and ready for skinning. The Moor was probably out attempting to deliver a brace, but one was enough to satisfy the Scaliger, with perhaps a little left for Cesco. Though

Cangrande was like enough to over-eat, just to make Cesco suck the marrow from the tiny bones.

Cleverly, the Moor had not bothered to skin the animal himself. By now the Scaliger knew the quirks of Cesco's knife and would recognize the difference. Hungry, Cesco decided not to wait. Let the Moor eat his next catch himself.

With his unearned trophy slung over his shoulder, Cesco left the Moor's cloak hanging and made his way back towards the bare ground where the Scaliger waited. It was a short journey, and he arrived at the clearing with an eager anticipation of waking his master and presenting the meal.

Cangrande was still there, sleeping. But he wasn't alone. There was movement in the snowy grass of the clearing. For a moment Cesco imagined it was a boar, dripping tusks and all. Then he blinked and saw the tusk was actually a glint of steel.

The figure hunched close to the ground was more a bundle of rags than a man. In the right hand was held a long misericordia, the thin dagger used to find a chink in an opponent's armour and violate the heart or lungs.

Cesco remained unmoving in the shade of the tree. For the briefest heartbeat he thought, How simple. How delightful.

And how callow to sit here and let it happen. Clearing his throat, Cesco called out, "O Jacob! Esau, the cunning hunter, is approaching your tents!"

Waking instantly, Cangrande leapt to his feet, his sword hissing from its scabbard. At the same moment the bundle of rags turned tail and ran for the far treeline. Small, hardly a man at all. A youth. Quick as a doe in flight, the figure stole into the covert of the wood.

Cangrande looked after his would-be murderer, then turned to Cesco. "What are you waiting for, squire?"

"An order, my lord," said Cesco.

"I expect more initiative," drawled Cangrande, resheathing his weapon as Cesco approached. "Especially when my life is threatened."

"But I would have had to drop this fine hare," replied Cesco.

"I would rather have you skin that fellow."

"He was hardly a threat. If he'd had a tail, it would have been between his legs. And after this morning, I am in no condition to chase another rabbit," added Cesco, settling himself by the fire. "Just how many people want you dead?"

"How many stars are in the heavens, how many grains of sand on a beach?" Cangrande sat down again, laying his sheathed sword near at hand. "At least I wake to find a meal."

Cesco knelt, holding the hare before him as if in majestic offering. "Even as Nimrod the mighty hunter before the Lord."

"A little thin, but serviceable."

"Him, or me?" Cesco set to work skinning the animal. "I'm surprised he got so close. Didn't you hear him?"

Cangrande looked rueful. "I thought it was you, creeping close to have another go at besting me."

"We are dressed alike. He could be my tatterdemalion twin! Though if you thought he was me, he's certainly lucky to be alive."

"You know better. I hate to kill my enemies."

"Well do I know it. Best to see them broken."

"Best to see them join your side! There is nothing in life so sweet as having a sworn enemy give you his absolute allegiance."

"Does that mean you'll give Passerino another chance at life?"

Cangrande made an enigmatic gesture. "Perhaps." He stood to examine the markings left by their uninvited visitor.

Finished with the quick work of skinning, Cesco reached into his saddlebag and removed a long pointed metal rod with a wooden handle. On this he placed their meal. With the ease of practice he fitted two more rods into the ground at either side of the fire and settled the skewer bearing the hare across them to roast.

Cangrande returned. "I have a mind to discover who that was."

"Shall we track him?"

"No," said Cangrande. "He was no expert. A professional would have used a bird-bow to bring me low. Which means he's a local bearing a grudge for some imagined slight."

"Probably bedded his wife. Or his mother, judging his size."

"More than likely. Though I think I'd remember taking lice from some wench."

"So, being local, he knows these parts."

"Which makes hunting him an exercise in futility. A practice in which you excel, I know, but instead let us provide him another opportunity. We'll camp here tonight, under the stars."

"We'll be missed at the palace."

Cangrande grinned. "One of the grand things about being the lord of all I survey is that I'm not tied to other men's schedules. No, you and I shall idle away the afternoon, then I'll lie here and present a most inviting target."

"I notice the singular case. Where shall I be?"

"Paying the price for your lack of initiative. You shall keep watch tonight. All night."

Cesco bit back his cutting reply. The smell of the roasted hare had his stomach rumbling again, and Cangrande was unwrapping a block of hard cheese. "Of course, lord."

They ate, then spent the rest of the afternoon in mock-duels. By now there were no new tricks, only slight innovations to familiar moves. Though Cesco was smaller and weaker than the Scaliger, he was able to keep his feet and was only smacked twice by the flat of Cangrande's blade.

They hunted together for their evening meal, catching another scraggy hare and two small birds with their bows. After supper, Cangrande again rested his head on his saddle, leaving Cesco in an uncomfortable perch against a spidery tree, the better to keep himself alert.

Cesco thought wistfully of where he'd been a bare year earlier. Sweet Ravenna. He had not appreciated the warm, safe, gentle comfort of that city. Nor had he truly appreciated the bed he'd had in the household of Ser Pietro Alaghieri. Shivering, he consoled himself with another sticky chew and the certainty that the Moor was out there, watchful as ever. The would-be murderer would stand no chance of slipping by them both.

◆ ◇ ◆

The low winter moon cast slanting shadows. The sun had set almost six hours past. The effect of the sticky chew made Cesco's body seem far-off, yet full of movement – his toes kept wiggling in his boots. He was trying to recall word for word the section of the Aeneid that had birthed his dream when suddenly he felt a knife at his throat.

"Don't make a sound." A youthful voice, artificially lowered, like a boy pretending at being a man.

In answer, Cesco's lips formed silent words.

"What?" hissed the youth.

"Oh, may I speak?" asked Cesco in a low whisper. "I thought that perhaps you could read lips."

"Don't be clever."

"Can't help it. Ask the Greyhound."

"It's him I want. I have no quarrel with you."

"I beg to differ," said Cesco, allowing his eyes to slide down towards the naked blade on his skin. "If you mean to kill him, you'd best murder me as well."

"That loyal?"

"That practical. Anything happens to him, I'll be blamed. I stand to inherit the most. Qui bono?"

"I benefit," hissed the youth. Perhaps realizing the betrayal of Latin schooling, the next words were rougher still. "I am his death. You can live and risk the blame, or you can die. The choice is yours. But if you call out I'll slit your throat."

"And if you cut his throat," rasped a deep voice from inches away, "you'll find your own slit before his blood touches the earth."

Cesco felt rather than saw the Moor's blade at the youth's neck. As always the aged man was nigh invisible, and quieter even than death.

The pressure of the knife at Cesco's throat did not slacken – he could feel the beating of his own pulse against the metal. "Tharwat, this is Death. Death, Tharwat al-Dhaamin. But then, you two ought to be close friends by now." Cesco switched to Arabic. "O Shadow, while I appreciate thy timely intervention, it would be best if the Scaliger were not made aware of thy presence."

"Shall I let him murder thee?" responded the Moor sourly.

"Stop that!" hissed the youth.

"No skill at barbarous tongues?" asked Cesco lightly in Latin. When there was no answer, he switched to the Lombard dialect. "I was simply telling my shadow not to murder you before you could tell us the reason you wish the illustrious master of Verona dead in his sleep."

"When one sees the Devil, one does not need a reason to strike. It is enough that he is the Devil."

"Well reasoned and well-spoken. Perchance, do those voluminous rags hide someone of better birth?"

"Better than yours."

"There we are agreed," said Cesco. "I am a bastard, and a bastard of a bastard as well."

"Enough," growled the Moor. "Child, release the blade and lie flat on the earth."

There was the slightest hesitation. The would-be murderer couldn't help a glance at the supine figure of Cangrande, golden head still resting on his saddle. Whoever this ragamuffin is, he doesn't lack for nerve. He's still determined to do it.

Then the knife was removed from Cesco's skin and dropped, point first. Instantly the Moor had hold of the scruff under the hood and was forcing the assassin to the snowy ground.

Cesco stood, casually brushing the side of his neck. Using their private tongue he said, "If we present this fellow to the Scaliger, he may let slip thy presence."

"Dost thou advocate death?"

"No," said Cesco uncertainly. "I was just observing—"

With serpent speed the youth rolled to face the sky. The feet kicked, the back arched, the hands braced, and suddenly the whole body was arcing upwards into a standing position. The Moor's lunging knife missed. The acrobatic ragamuffin had already broken into a run.

Not for freedom. For the Scaliger.

"Father!" cried Cesco.

That forbidden word conveyed the urgency. Cangrande roused in time to grasp the arm holding the plunging dagger. Still it met flesh, cutting Cangrande's cloak and breaking through the hard leather doublet beneath.

Even wounded, the Scaliger's years of training dictated the moves that followed – a step, a twist, a throw – and the ragamuffin went tumbling across the frozen earth.

Cesco's feet pounded the snow-covered ground, Tharwat running beside him. Knife embedded in his shoulder, Cangrande drew his sword even as the youth rolled and fled towards the water.

The Moor overturned the blade in his hand, gripping it by the point. He raised it to the level of his ear, prepping the throw.

"No!" Cesco nudged the Moor sideways, altering the dagger's course. Instead of a killing blow, the dagger entered one ragged sleeve, slicing the arm within. The cry came in the youth's genuine voice, high and trembling. But the ragamuffin kept running, disappearing into the bracken by the water's edge. There was a splash.

The trio reached the waterline. Already the figure was well downstream, swimming awkwardly with one arm, letting the current do most of the work.

Cesco started kicking off his boots. The Moor grasped his shoulders. "What dost thou do?"

"He'll drown!"

"Let him," replied Cangrande, also in Arabic. He grunted as he yanked the bloody dagger from his shoulder.

"He'll freeze," protested Cesco. "And we won't learn who he is, what he wants."

Kneeling, Cangrande began packing his wound with snow. "We cannot always receive the answers we seek, for they do not always exist."

"There are always answers," growled Cesco, rejecting the proverb by changing tongues. But he stopped struggling – the would-be killer was gone. "We could walk downstream, along the bank, until he surfaces."

"We could," mused the Scaliger. "However, I am more interested in the apparition before me. Tharwat, did you just happen by?" His words conveyed amusement. His tone did not. "At last I comprehend the boy's supernatural endurance. How long have you been shadowing us? How many of the tasks I set for him did you complete in his place?"

"It is no more than I did for you, when you were his age."

Eyebrows raised, Cesco looked with open interest between the Greyhound and the Moor. Cangrande's jaw set. "Perhaps my memory deceives me, but I don't recall you performing my chores for me."

The Moor was impassive. "You were not so tested."

"In body. My spirit, however, suffered far more."

"If you recall, I relieved that as well."

"The unkindest cut of all." When Tharwat did not answer, the Scaliger changed subjects. "Cesco, you spoke with our young friend. Who was he? Another bastard with delusions of grandeur?"

"A noble child, or at least educated and pretending not to be. And nimble! He did a walk-over and plucked his dagger from the ground before Tharwat could prevent him," added Cesco, impressed.

Cangrande regarded the Moor. "You must be aging. And this cold certainly could not be healthy for your old bones. We must see what we can do to remedy your ills." Fair words did not disguise the threat. "Come, let us three warm ourselves by the fire as we bind my wound and pity the poor frozen boy who has eluded and outsmarted us all."

As they returned to the clearing, Cangrande looked up from the reddening snow at his shoulder and cocked his head at his heir. "By the by, what was that you called me?"

Cesco had been expecting the rebuke. "A slip. I mistook you for the Lord our God, who died untimely at the hand of traitors. He was father to us all."

"So when you called out 'Father,' you weren't calling to me?"

"No," said Cesco with absolute finality. On their first meeting he had been forbidden to call the Scaliger by the name of 'father'.

"A pity," replied Cangrande. "If in a moment of distress you had called me father, I might have been moved enough to give you permission to use the term in company. But since it was an error, you will refrain from ever using it again."

Colour flooded Cesco's cheeks. Unwisely, he chose to respond. "As if I could call you father! The only man I have ever known to have earned that name at my lips is across the Alps, treating with the Pope on your behalf. If Pietro Alaghieri were here, I might have called him by that name."

Cangrande smiled. "Tender-heart that he is, he would have been struck dumb by such a show of devotion, only to be struck dead a moment later. No, we must be thankful Ser Alaghieri is far from such peril of being your father-figure. Else he would surely be dead."

Three

Avignon, France
11 April 1326

The cold body lay on the marble altar as none other than Cardinal Orsini performed the funerary rites.

"Requiem æternam dona eis, Domine; In memoria æterna erit justus, ab auditione mala non timebit."

The church was not as crowded as it might have been. But most of those present mourned honestly enough, appreciative of the august personage delivering the dead man's final mass. Unlike a peasant death peopled with the unwashed and unlettered, this funeral mass was attended by men who knew Latin as well as their own tongues, and the mental translation was instantaneous: 'Eternal rest grant unto him, O Lord. He shall be justified in everlasting memory, and shall not fear evil reports.'

That last was doubtful, for he'd lived a life of devoted, if single-minded, honesty. Such men were never without their detractors.

"Absolve, Domine…" continued the Latin drone. "Forgive, O Lord, the soul of your faithful departed servant, Pietro, from all the chains of his sins and may he deserve to avoid the judgment of revenge by your fostering grace, and enjoy the everlasting blessedness of light."

The literati, in honour of father and son alike, were here in force. Most were clerks and men in minor orders – Avignon was an industry town, and that industry was religion. Hardly a man of birth and ambition escaped its calling. Yet there were many who read things other than religious documents. Foremost among these was poetry. This was France.

"Day of wrath, a day that the world will dissolve in ashes, as foretold by David and the Sibyl..." The cardinal's voice became more animated, almost eager. The end of the world was, to him, a glorious prospect these days. He seemed to envy the corpse, so peaceful under his shroud.

Wind stirred, plucking at the gauze shroud that lay over the body on the altar. Father and son had looked much alike in life, and the corpse showed still the echoes of kinship – the nose, the lips, the high forehead. Comely, stately, grave. Well, that was fitting.

"Lord Jesus Christ, King of glory, free the souls of all the faithful departed from infernal punishment and the deep pit. Free them from the mouth of the lion; do not let Tartarus swallow them, nor let them fall into darkness; but may the sign-bearer, Saint

Michael, lead them into the holy light which you promised to Abraham and his seed…"

Listening from the steps outside, Pietro Alaghieri bent his head in prayer. Though barred from entering, he remained devout. Indeed, his excommunication had only proven how devout he was, and how obedient. He obeyed every injunction, suffered every slight, and still rose barefoot to pray in the middle of the night. He had not known how precious was his faith until it was denied him.

A light misting of rain fell. The wind that blew the drizzle sideways into his eyes was by now familiar. It was the Mistral, blowing off the Alp-fed Rhône and chilling everyone who dared to brave it. Pietro had heard that it never truly disappeared, not even in summer. He prayed he wouldn't be here long enough to find out.

Pietro tightened his cloak, a voluminous piece of clothing with a heavy hood to hide as well as protect his face. If apprehended here, it would damage his suit. Fortunately there was little danger. All around him men hid their faces, though not for concealment. The Mistral carried a foul smell, a miasma of feculent odor coming from the Palais des Papes down the road.

It was rumoured that the papal palace itself had the most modern of facilities, a whole tower whose lower two floors were made entirely of latrines. The stone seats emptied into a pit that was flushed into the river by a diverted underground stream. It had been designed so the palace was upwind of the pit.

Unfortunately the same could not be said for the city. It was horrible to think he'd been here long enough to get used to the smell. For four months Pietro had resided in the meanest hovel, the only place that would open its doors to him, while he petitioned the powerful Colonna family, papal gate-keepers, to grant him an audience. Despite having known the son of the great Stefano Colonna from law school in Bologna, Pietro found himself politely but firmly rebuffed. As yet he didn't know if it was for himself, his father, or the man he represented.

The funeral concluded, and the mourners began to rise. Pietro left his place by the church doors, walking swiftly across the street. There were a good number of papal guards emerging from the basilica. Or rather, mercenaries kept in the Pope's employ. They were obviously not here to honour the dead but to herd the living – two men were in their midst, looking around them as if they had not seen the open air in a great while. They were not restrained, but the implication was clear. These men were not free to go where they pleased.

Well-dressed elderly men emerged, mostly clergy. It made sense, as the deceased had been a papal clerk. Hearing the eulogy, Pietro had felt a little strange. The man bore his name, and this could easily have been his life. It was the vocation Pietro had been destined for, until God had claimed the life of his elder brother and thrust him into the uncomfortable role of heir to his poetical father. There had followed knighthood and the Law – and the wonderful, terrifying boy he'd fostered as his own. When Pietro prayed, it was mostly for Cesco.

Cardinal Orsini swept from the basilica with a brisk step, his practical manner bespeaking more important duties. Next came Cardinal Sciarrillo Colonna, with whom Pietro had been desperately trying to get an appointment. A more crass man might have seized this chance to plead his case. Pietro remained where he was.

In Colonna's wake came the chief mourners, the family of the deceased. First through the doors was the one Pietro knew least, the late man's daughter Lucia. She was a vision, all bedecked in ribbons and frills. The white of mourning couldn't disguise her voluptuous figure. Nor did she want it to.

She came on the arm of her younger brother, who was well fleshed and dressed in the latest French style. Pietro recalled his own flights of sartorial fancy at that age, a habit his father had deplored. Perhaps Gherardo would outgrow it as well. But it would take time – a long time, if his elder brother was any example.

And here he came, the son and heir. He had gone the distance in his attire. Instead of a rented or borrowed white robe, he sported a finely tailored white doublet of the most modern style, with matching hose and hat. Only his curled shoes were black, but to offset the effect on the eye his hat bore a black feather, and his outer cape was of the darkest black as well. It was as if he had stepped from a chessboard into society.

Indeed, Francesco Petrarca practically glowed as he left his father behind forever. It was as if the death of Ser Pietro Petracco had released a brake. Both sons now resembled a pair of runaway carts, associating with a racy crowd of thinkers, poets, and philosophers that their stern and serious father had always condemned. Theirs had been a tempestuous relationship, Petracco utterly unable to comprehend his eldest son, and vice versa. He'd even burned his son's books to discourage reading poetry.

Petracco, Petrarca, Petrarch. Names were malleable, as Pietro Alaghieri well knew. His own family name had suffered every variation under his father's pen, marching in step with each change of fortune. Even his father's Christian name of Durante had been shortened, and at the end of his life the poet's signature had read Dantes Alaghieri.

A few years ago Pietro had been obliged to sign Alighieri to a legal document while executing his father's will in Florence. But Alighieri was the Florentine spelling, and while ever Pietro lived in exile from that city he would follow his father's example and eschew their customs. Instead he used a much older version of the name, one that stemmed from their ancestor Alaghiero.

Petrarch had done something similar, though for the reverse reason. Rather than honour his late father, the twenty-one-year-old had wanted to distinguish himself as something other than a loyal son. As early as ten years before, the son had begun using a different name to distinguish himself from everything his father held dear.

Lost in thoughts of names and fathers, Pietro didn't realize he was staring until Petrarch met his gaze. Quickly Pietro ducked his head, but too late. The other man was already crossing the damp and slippery street, hand outstretched. "Hell-boy! Hell-boy, is that you? This is a delightful surprise!"

Pietro winced even as he laughed. "I wish you wouldn't call me that."

"But I simply cannot resist!" cried Petrarch, no evidence of mourning in his delighted mien as he clasped Pietro warmly by the arm. "Especially when it makes you turn red enough to justify the title! But perhaps I should try something more formal for the Knight of Hell. Ser Alaghieri, the ignoble Hellequin. Or should it be Rubicante, for the crimson cheeks?"

Petrarch was amusing himself by playing off a famous passage from the great epic written by Pietro's father. Pietro said, "I thought you hadn't read it."

"I'm resisting, it's true. But one can't escape the juicier bits. People feel the need to retell, recite, regurgitate it until one must clap hands over one's ears and sing la-la-la! And still some of it sinks in! In fact, there is a better title for you. Since you serve the Greyhound, shall I call you Cagnazzo, the low hound?"

Cagnazzo was the name of one of ten demons tricked by a mortal. Pietro's retort invoked another. "If you do, I'll call you Alichino in return."

He meant it as 'the allurer.' But Alichino also meant 'droop-winged,' and Pietro regretted the phrase the moment it passed the hedge of his teeth. Francesco Petrarca was a comely young man, handsome in every respect save two – his eyes, and his chin. Not that there was anything wrong with the orbs themselves. Neither milky nor crossed, they were a perfect if watery blue. But the skin under them bagged and sagged heavily, endowing him with a permanently imploring look, rather like those dogs that have too much skin for their faces. The problem with Petrarch's chin was simpler – he didn't have one. His mouth seemed to run straight down to his neck.

The reference to drooping anything brought Petrarch's mind straight around to his eyes, and at once he tensed his cheeks as if to tighten his skin. Pietro hurriedly added, "I came to pay my respects, as best as I can."

"I wish I'd known, I would have insisted you come in. O, the scandal!"

Ignoring this, Pietro said, "I'm very sorry for your loss."

"I'm not," replied Petrarch simply. He'd penned an ode to his mother when she had died six years before. Pietro remembered reading it and thinking it was very good. There was clearly not going to be a companion piece eulogizing his father.

Petrarch's face lit with a sudden idea. "Come home with us to Carpentras! William and Bonagratia have been given leave to join our midday meal while they prepare the vault for the final interment. They'll be glad of the company – as will I!"

"Francesco…" began Pietro in a half-hearted protest.

"Petrarch," corrected his friend. "You have enough Francescos in your life."

I know which I would be rid of. Yet Pietro was grateful for the invitation. Four months of almost absolute solitude had worn on him more than he would have dreamed. So he allowed himself to be guided over to the men under the papal guard.

Ignoring the mercenaries, Petrarch presented Pietro to his guests. "Ser Alaghieri, allow me to introduce William of Occam and Bonagratia of Bergamo. Gentlemen, this is Pietro Alaghieri, knight of Verona, student of law, and woeful excommunicant."

Occam cocked his head. "Really? You must tell us how you have fared."

"Yes," agreed Bonagratia wryly. "Since we are surely soon to join you outside of God's grace."

Pietro had heard of them, of course. It would be difficult to find two more famous friars. Both were members of the Frati Minori, known as the Franciscans for their adherence to San Francesco's beliefs. Thrown together by circumstance, both had been papal 'guests' in Avignon for nearly two years, awaiting trials for very different offences – trials that seemed destined to never occur. Too dangerous to condemn, too dangerous to release, permanent detention was the Pope's solution, stifling the dangerous challenge these monks posed without making martyrs of them.

Petrarch's introductions reached his family. "You remember my sister Lucia. And this, of course, is my brother Gherardo."

"Well met!" said Gherardo, clasping Pietro's hand. They had known each other at university. "Come, shall we go? Dinner is waiting."

"Ser Alaghieri," said Lucia, sidling up against him, "will you give me your arm? The streets are so treacherous." She tucked her arm in his, pulling his bicep close to her ribs.

Feeling the bodice holding her bosom in place, Pietro tried not to flush. "Of course. An honour." He caught a dark look in Petrarch's eye, but the glower was not aimed at him.

Fighting the wind through the streets, Petrarch ranged himself at Pietro's right side. "You've come from Verona, yes? Have you seen Mariotto? Is he still besotted?"

Their mutual friend Mariotto Montecchio had spent two years in Avignon attending the Pope to curry favour for the Scaliger, and during that time young Petrarch had befriended him. In answer to the question, Pietro nodded. "They have a son called Romeo."

"And the rivalry?"

"Simmering, but not boiling. They don't like each other, but there's not much call for them to meet outside of the city council."

"Good. Mari often bemoaned that whole business – though he didn't regret it."

Gherardo shook his head. "Fancy stealing your best mate's girl. Why lose a friend for une femme? Where's the sense in it?"

"It sounds romantic to me," observed Lucia, pulling so tightly on Pietro's arm he almost stumbled. Fortunately they were walking very slowly. Though Pietro owned an old wound just above his right knee that occasionally hindered him, it was not Pietro but Petrarch who held them back with a ginger gait. At first Pietro thought his friend was limping, then realized that the long curling shoes were impeding Petrarch's progress.

Apparently Occam had noticed as well. "Why not buy proper shoes?"

"I am a living example of form over substance," replied Petrarch lightly. "It is better to look good than to feel good."

"Impractical, idiotic, and impertinent," said Occam with a shake of his head.

"You should be a Bishop," laughed Bonagratia.

"That would make his father proud," said Occam.

"Meaning I utterly refuse," said Petrarch, mincing along.

The six of them had to squeeze into the carriage, with the mercenary guards mounting horses to ride alongside. For most of the ride out of the city Lucia prattled on and on, dominating Pietro's attention. She asked questions that she never allowed him to answer, flitting from one topic to the next like a butterfly newly emerged from its cocoon. Twice she touched on the subject of Pietro's wealth, remarking that, as the heir to the most famous poet in the world and also a knight with a fine stipend from his lord, he must be quite rich.

Pietro demurred. Money was an uncomfortable topic. He was indeed becoming rather affluent – bankers were the only men who never seemed to notice his excommunicant status. And lately he'd been spending lavishly, with fresh bedding each day and plenty of light around him at all time. After a month in a dark, dank Venetian cell, he was fond of the comforts of life. But he never forgot the impoverished days of his youth, nor how swiftly his father's fortune had been confiscated after the exile from Florence. Thankfully, Lucia wasn't quite gauche enough to ask him his worth outright.

Casting about for something to discuss, Pietro decided to harass Petrarch. "Tell me again, why won't you read the *Commedia*?"

"For fear of its influence. I intend to be the greatest writer of my age, as your father was for his. But I want to do something new! Find something that has never been done before!"

"Good luck in that," said Occam, seated opposite them. "The Lord God created all there is in the first week of creation. Therefore, logically, there is nothing new under the sun."

"Or what is new is the work of the Devil," added Bonagratia.

Occam shook his head. "There is no creation without God. Lucifer is out of God's view, no longer connected to the divine. Ergo, the Devil cannot create. He can only twist what exists to his purposes."

Nearly an hour later they reached the hamlet of Carpentras and the small but well-appointed house that had belonged to Petrarch's father. Their mercenary escort took up a post beside the doors as the guests were ushered in by a single servant.

Entering the house, Bonagratia turned to one of his guards. "Wouldn't you rather be within doors? It would be more comfortable." The man declined, but the friar persisted. "Shall I have them send some food out?"

"Thank you kindly," said the soldier, trying to check his grin. Clearly the mercenaries thought well of their two prisoners.

Following the troupe up the stairs to the living spaces higher in the house, Pietro was unavoidably reminded of his childhood home – the austere, cramped tower, his mother's fierce domination of the servants, his father's absence. So long ago.

Lucia tugged on Pietro's arm. "A real knight! You must sit with me. Such a pleasure. Avignon is stuffed with clerks and clerics. You're not married, are you, Ser Alaghieri?"

"Ahh – no, no I'm not."

"Pity," said Lucia with the ghost of a wink. "I hear married men make the best—"

"Lucia!" Petrarch's voice was the crack of a whip. "Why not go check the kitchen, make sure supper will be ready."

Rebellion simmered in Lucia's eyes, but she left the room, moving with an uncanny gait that brought attention to her hips.

The five men sat down to table, Petrarch at the head, Pietro on his right, with Gherardo on Pietro's other side. Both Occam and Bonagratia threw back their cowls, showing carefully tended tonsures, though in Occam's case there wasn't much tending needed.

Bonagratia was the taller of the pair, and since most of that height was in his torso he towered over his neighbour at table. Probably closer to fifty than forty in years, his genial eyes were those of a youth.

The dominating presence was Occam. It wasn't for looks – his hooked nose was too wide for his face, while his chin tapered to an almost comical point and his ears jutted at the lobes. Taken together, his whole face seemed to point down. His mouth was incongruously small, and when he spoke it hardly opened at all, creating the illusion of a masque with intelligent and fiery eyes peering out from beneath.

Prayers said, Pietro settled in at the table with ease and pleasure, once again in the company of brilliant men. Evidently Bonagratia felt a similar relief. "O, this is pleasant. Despite the sad occasion, it is a treat to be eating different food, seeing different faces."

"So what news in the world, Ser Alaghieri?" Before Pietro could respond, Petrarch turned to the two friars. "Pietro is the most well-informed man I've ever met. Always up to the moment on the happenings of foreign courts and sub rosa dealings. It made him the treasure of Bologna."

Bonagratia tore a hunk of bread. "Is that how you know each other? From university?"

"We go back much further than that. Ser Alaghieri the heretic and I lead parallel lives. Both sons of Florentine exiles, both students of law. Both have lost our fathers. But mine is a far happier lot. Pietro is my shadow-self."

Pietro's answer was a little more helpful. "Our fathers knew each other. Both were members of Florence's Bianchi faction, and were exiled for it. When the Bianchi were gathering troops to raid the city, my father advocated diplomacy instead of violence. Ser Petracco joined him. They were ignored, and when the battle turned into a disastrous rout, they were blamed."

Occam's eyes narrowed. "What was the rationale for such a claim?"

Gherardo answered, sounding rightfully bitter. "They were accused of sabotaging the enterprise. Of dulling the spirits of the men before the battle, of not supporting the soldiers."

"I imagine the souls of the soldiers look more kindly on them than upon the men who sent them to their deaths," observed Bonagratia.

"Well they're all united now, and I wish them joy of each other's company." Petrarch's tone was a little too jovial for Pietro's taste. He did not consider the loss of his own father a boon. But he refrained from saying so, allowing Petrarch to continue the narrative. "Unlike Dante, my father was offered the chance to return. He could either pay a fine the size of his whole fortune, or cut off his right hand. He chose exile."

Pietro chuckled. "Ah, Florence. My father was offered amnesty, if he paid a fine and walked naked on his knees through the city carrying a candle."

Petrarch laughed. "Can't imagine why he refused. So both our fathers were stripped of status and wealth. Dante went first to – where?"

"Verona," said Pietro. "Then Bologna for a time. Then Paris, Lucca, back to Verona, and finally Ravenna."

"Meanwhile my father went to Arezzo, then Pisa, then finally in 1310 he came to Avignon and set up as a holy scribe." Petrarch shivered. "He meant the same fate for me and Gherardo. Ecclesiastic lawyers. Brr!"

"What would you rather be?" asked Occam. "A poet?"

"Actually, yes. Father loathed the idea. No matter how I pointed to Maestro Dante as an example, Father insisted it was no life for a son of his."

There was real venom in the memory. Before his old friend could out and out slander the deceased, Pietro said, "Whereas my father would have liked nothing more than for me or Jacopo to follow in his footsteps. But I have no skill with verse – believe me,

I've tried. So it's law for me. I actually enjoy it," he added defensively.

"And that's where we really got to know Pietro," said Gherardo, bolting down his food to finish his brother's tale. "Pietro, did you hear? Mundinus is dead."

"No!" Mondino de' Luzzi, more simply known as Mundinus, was reputed to be the greatest doctor of the age. Certainly he was the most scandalous. Pietro had been present for the public human dissection that had so shocked the city of Bologna ten years before.

That brought Petrarch out of his angry reverie. "Yes, and we've been debating – do you think they'll actually dissect him?"

Pietro drew back a little in revulsion. "Why would they?"

"It was in his will!" explained Petrarch with relish. "He insisted on his corpse being used for his students to… you know. He said he owed them one final lesson."

"Ghoulish." Bonagratia crossed himself. "May God have mercy on his soul."

Occam didn't look as though he thought it ghoulish, but he let the subject pass. "Ser Alaghieri, didn't you accompany your father to Paris?"

"I joined him there just before he left to follow Heinrich back to Rome." He fell silent at the memory of the failed Holy Roman Emperor, whom his father had adored. Pietro often wondered if Dante would have loved Cangrande so completely had Heinrich lived.

"I was in Paris before my 'invitation' here." They spoke for a time of Paris, and Occam explained that he had come to lecture at the university there much the same way Pietro's father had fifteen years before. "While I was at Oxford the doctors debated if they should issue Dante an invitation to lecture for us instead. It was a lively back and forth, but eventually the offer was made. As I recall, he declined."

Pietro laughed. "I'm surprised he went as far as Paris! He only accepted because he was interested in finishing both Dei Vulgari Eloquenta and Il Convivio."

"Why not just sit and write them out?"

Unlike Petrarch, Pietro enjoyed talking about his father. He explained that both works had been started as lectures at the University of Bologna. Impoverished by his exile, the great poet had needed to earn some kind of living. "He required an audience. He liked to think on his feet."

"It's still talked about," added Petrarch. "He was apparently quite the entertainer."

"When he chose be," admitted Pietro. "As he got older he preferred to cultivate an air of refinement and – what's the phrase I'm looking for? Placid disdain."

"I wish I'd come when you invited me, I might have met him. How titanic that would have been! Ah, the next course. Everyone, please enjoy. At least we may agree this soup belongs to us," added Petrarch lightly.

Bonagratia rolled his eyes. His papal imprisonment stemmed from his Order's claim that Christ had owned no property, had shared everything in common with the apostles. But not all Franciscans agreed on this point, and many brothers had left the Order while chanting, My soup is mine!

Occam ignored this sally. "Ser Alaghieri, our friend says you keep an ear to the ground. We hear woefully little news of the world. Tell me, is it true that the Duke of Austria has finally been released?"

"So I'm told," said Pietro.

"More than released," said Gherardo, still sopping his bread and devouring it. "Made co-ruler of Germany!"

This was the piece of news that had all of Europe chattering. Until recently there had been two claimants to the imperial throne – Ludwig the Bavarian and Frederick III of Austria. For nine years both had struggled for supremacy, a duel that ended with Frederick's imprisonment. But news had come that Frederick had renounced his claim in return for his freedom and a high position in Ludwig's court. It was a small enough concession, as it left the Bavarian as the undisputed head of the Holy Roman Empire.

"A Christian act on the part of Ludwig," observed Bonagratia. "Having beaten Frederick for the throne, he could have kept his rival in prison forever. Instead he is a ruler once more, though his curtailed authority is limited to Austria alone."

"Your master must be living in anguish," observed Petrarch to Pietro. "He backed the wrong horse."

It was true that Cangrande had supported Frederick, though Pietro suspected it was only a ploy to extend the confusion over the succession. A strong emperor was not in Verona's best interests. "I'm not certain he even cares. There are more pressing matters for him closer to home."

"His heir, perhaps?" Like everyone else, Petrarch had recently learned that the child raised in Pietro's house as his orphaned nephew was in actuality the bastard heir to the great Greyhound of Verona.

Pietro was reluctant to discuss Cesco. "That, too. But things are not going well for the Ghibellines. After the two significant victories at the end of last year, the Florentines bolstered their armies by submitting themselves to Carlo di Calabria, son of Roberto di Napoli."

"The appointment of a strong cardinal in Lombardy won't be a help, either," said Petrarch. "In fact, I hear the Guelphs are feeling feisty enough to send envoys to Verona in the hope of detaching the Scaliger from the Emperor. What will he do?"

"He'll listen – and be seen to listen."

Bonagratia wiped up the last of his soup with a hunk of charred bread. "Speaking of Lombard politics, what's happening in Padua? The little we hear is very confused."

This was a tender spot for Pietro. Though no one knew it, he had been a part of last year's uprising. Disguised in borrowed armour, Pietro had fought to unseat his old foe Marsilio da Carrara from the leadership of Padua. The attack had failed, thanks to another of Cangrande's devious games, and now Pietro's life was in jeopardy. It was one of the levers the Scaliger used to make Pietro do his bidding. If Cangrande let it slip that Pietro had been there, the young knight would find himself under a death sentence from three distinct nations – Florence, Venice, and Padua. But whereas the former two were content to deny Pietro access to their lands, Pietro had no illusions about Carrara's revenge.

Being an excommunicant, Pietro had no recourse, could seek no sanctuary. Any man was free to offer Pietro insult or violence without peril to his soul. There were many men who would welcome a ransom from Padua and approval from the church for killing a heretic. One more reason he had to succeed in his mission here.

Petrarch knew none of this, of course. He was merely referring to the most recent upheaval. This past February, just months after the failed uprising of Paolo Dente, Paduan exiles again tried to retake their city. They failed as well, mainly due to the lack of support they received from the lord of Verona, who turned a mysteriously deaf ear to their pleas. Some rebel leaders were captured, few of whom lived to see their trials.

Pietro said only that he had heard the same as everyone else – Padua was in a state of chaos, with no firm hand on the reins. After that, the conversation wandered to another land in chaos, England, and the fears of many that the French would make an attempt at claiming the throne.

"Rubbish," said Occam stoutly. "Even if the Queen is French, the king has an heir."

"Who is in Paris," said Petrarch slyly, tweaking the Englishman's nose.

Occam seemed to have perfected the habit of ignoring his host. "Speaking of Paris - Ser Alaghieri, while you were there, did you ever hear a lecturer by the name of Eckhart?"

"The Dominican philosopher? I heard of him. Why?"

"He seems likely to join us. The Archbishop of Cologne has recently charged Brother Eckhart with heresy."

Patting his stomach, Bonagratia nodded. "We're in excellent company."

"Has your confinement been difficult?" asked Pietro. "Are you often allowed into the city?"

Occam shrugged. "Ours is a rather loose house-arrest. We are allowed visitors at the monastery, and on such occasions as this we are permitted to venture into society. The guards are more to prevent us passing papers to our adherents than to keep us from escaping. They confiscate our letters, read our correspondence."

"Mine too," said Pietro. "Though they're more subtle about it. But the seals show clear signs of tampering."

Occam laid down his bread and spoon, his bowl still quite full. The rich fare of Petrarch's table was too much for his Franciscan belly. "You know you weren't condemned for yourself." His Latin held more than a tinge of French, and a guttural sound underneath. Could that be English? "Rather, you are the victim of their unreasonable ire at your famous father."

"I know." The injustice of it kept Pietro's answer short.

Occam swept on. "A victim of circumstance, of poor timing. They could not attack the great Dante Alighieri while he was alive, because they rightly feared his pen. Florence, one of the greatest cities in the world, will never erase the blot he put on their name. And Boniface, Clement, Philip the Fair – they will be remembered through your father's eyes. Pope John is not such a fool to call down the wrath of poets on his head. And to defame such an illustrious man after his death looks what it is, spiteful and cowardly. In you, they have the perfect vessel for their revenge."

"Can that be the only reason?" demanded Bonagratia. "What was it you did? What was the pretext?"

"I failed to collect an unfair tithe levied on the people of Ravenna."

"But that's absurd!" cried Bonagratia. "There are dozens of men who have refunded the tithes from their parishes without punishment. Oh, they are called onto the carpet, to be sure. But excommunication! Ridiculous!"

"Is that the only cause?" asked Occam.

"As far as I know," said Pietro. "They didn't cite any other reason in the proclamation."

Occam's eyes narrowed shrewdly. "Nothing about your master?"

"No. I had my knighthood from him, true, but at that time it was generally thought we were estranged, the better to protect his heir. Though now we are lumped together as one." Which was no accident, of course. Cangrande had forced Pietro to represent them both here in Avignon.

"Disgusting!" cried Bonagratia. "Sacrilegious! I tell you, money will be the end of the Church!"

Occam chuckled. "Heretic."

Bonagratia shook his head. "His Holiness must see reason!"

"That's demanding a miracle. Ser Alaghieri, what do you mean to do? Why have you come?"

Though prisoners, these were famous holy men. Could they help? Pietro laid out his case. "I'm here with a double petition. To intercede on behalf of the Scaliger, and to have my own excommunication removed. I would appreciate any advice you can give me to achieve both ends."

"Of course," said Bonagratia feelingly. "My first advice is prepare to be patient. Nothing in Avignon moves with speed."

Occam shook his head. "That's God's own truth. Moreover, it won't help your case to be seen with us. I am heretical for my interpretation of Scripture favouring a separation of powers, temporal and spiritual. That puts your master on my side. Brother Bonagratia here is feared because of his vocal support of ecclesiastic poverty – the very thing you seem to be condemned for. In each of us, you have both your causes defined. And we are in prison. It does not bode well for your chances." He paused, considering. "Have you thought that you might achieve one of your aims at the cost of the other. You could gain your own reinstatement, but fail your master. Or worse, the reverse. Your mission seems at cross-purposes with itself."

Pietro had indeed considered that. His face must have proclaimed as much, for Petrarch suddenly began to laugh and clap his hands. "I have it, I have it! I'll be your advocate!"

"What?" said Pietro, startled.

"Yes! With the aid of these great minds," said Petrarch, waving his hand at his two clerical guests, "I shall present your case, leaving you free to argue for your master. O, what a sensation it will cause! And in the meantime, you shall live here!"

"No," said Pietro firmly. "I cannot blight your—"

"My good standing will aid you much more than your odiousness will stain me. The Colonna family has a high opinion of me. I dress the same way they do, and I can recite a verse as quick as you please. And the Colonna are the key-bearers to the Pope! No – I insist! I shall represent you, be your advocate, while you ply your trade for your master!"

"Excellent!" cried Bonagratia.

"A sound plan," said Occam.

Reluctantly, Pietro consented. Even as he did, it was on the tip of Pietro's tongue to say, Cangrande is not my master.

Late that afternoon, while the bereaved family attended Petracco's interment at the grave dug in Carpentras, Pietro returned to his inadequate quarters to pack. Giving orders for his belongings to be transferred, he discovered a letter had been delivered. The seal showed obvious signs of tampering, and Pietro suspected that by now a copy of the contents were being pored over. He smiled, certain that the papal cryptographers would have no success. Everyone from bankers to papal legates wrote in code, and no doubt John had many skilled cypher clerks in his employ. But the day they were able to break this code was the day Pietro learned to breathe water.

There was a sound reason for Petrarch's praise of Pietro's knowledge of current events. Pietro's home in Ravenna had been the clearinghouse of all intelligence and gossip that could possibly be of use to Verona. Though his present circumstances kept him from continuing in such employment, he still received dispatches from Tharwat and other, unknown correspondents who kept him abreast of the latest world events.

Breaking the seal, Pietro saw this was not an intelligence letter. Heart beating faster, Pietro recognized the cramped hand of Cesco. His last note had relayed all that had happened in Caprino, and the wound Cangrande had received. This note was brief, but still breathed the boy's unique style, picking up as though their conversation had been interrupted:

> For the last month my training has, of necessity, been farmed out to other men – Castelbarco, Nogarola, Bonaventura, Montecchio, Capulletto, da Lozzo, dell'Angelo. Cangrande's wound is healing very slowly, but he's been diligent in arranging a system that would keep me walking the knife's edge. Charming, no?
>
> Meanwhile, our Moorish friend has been unusually busy making charts for each

member of the Anziani. I'm sure you can guess who created that commission. Dottore Morsicato tried to take his place, leaving poor Esta's side long enough to follow me on one of my hawkings. But the Scaliger is wise to our tricks now, and the doctor has discovered the consequences of slipping me food. I disappeared for five days, first up in the Alps with Alberto Nogarola, then three days and nights toiling in his 'secret' forge on the river.

(It's an amazing piece of engineering. I learned a great deal, despite the burns. The blacksmith and his boy were grateful for the help, and told me all they could of metalwork.)

By the time my sojourn ended, my limbs had turned to liquid and I'd lost more weight. I was willing to accept another offering, but Morsicato took one look at me and refused. I think I saw tears in his eyes. So the Scaliger has won that turn.

By the bye, the Scaliger was not with me during my second trip to Caprino, so there was no further attempt by the youthful hunter. A shame, as I thought we had a good rapport.

Antonia is well, and Jacopo seems in good spirits. As ever, he is in the throes of some illicit affair with some lesser-born female. It seems your brother has received your share of the famous Alaghieri libido – didn't your father have an affair when he was first in Verona? That is the rumour. It's amusing to think that you, too, have little bastard siblings running about. Though I doubt Grand-father Dante's libido could ever have matched Cangrande's.

Speaking of your brother, the other night I heard him declare his intent to return to Florence – he's found some-one willing to pay his fine, and they're waiving the other stipulations. They seem very eager to have someone called Alighieri back within their walls. 'Godi, Fiorenza, poi che se' sì grande..!'

But why, you ask, is he returning to the pestilent paradise that birthed him? He's talking of following Antonia's foot-steps and taking at least minor orders.

Can you imagine? Though he is determined to remain in Verona until the tourney at the start of July.

I'm sure there is more news, but I cannot think of it. I am bone weary – I suppose 'dog tired' would be more appropriate. But without him hounding me, my hawking is a little relented. I will survive, no matter what you may hear. Enjoy your stay in Avignon, by all means. Do not come back. We do not need you.

That last was a stab in Pietro's heart, for he could hear Cesco's voice, the irony, the plea, the resistance to admitting he was alone and helpless. If he'd demanded Pietro's return, Pietro would have left in a moment, despite the risk. The indictment without the plea cut far deeper.

Pietro took a moment to fret for the doctor and his wife – Esta had been unwell ever since their return from Ravenna, preventing the doctor from reestablishing his practice. Pietro thought of how Morsicato had quizzed him about Mundinus and his dissections. Notes for a long anticipated treatise on anatomy were said to exist, but Pietro doubted anything would come of it. Too gruesome a field of study. Yet he decided to write to his Bolognese friends and have copies of the notes sent to Morsicato. It might serve to distract him from his ailing wife…

Even with Morsicato's most-understandable pre-occupation, Cesco still had both Tharwat and Pietro's sister, Antonia, to rely upon in extremity. Whatever roadblock the Scaliger threw in their path, Pietro was certain those two would allow no harm to come to their charge. As long as that was true, Pietro felt secure enough to stay and make the Pope aware of the Scaliger's demands.

As well as one of his own devising.

Four

Verona, Italy
2 May 1326

"O sweet sweet irony," cried Cesco, laughing uproariously as his horse cantered into the long enclosure. "I wish we had a poet or a bard with us to record this momentous, epic, most historic day!"

The tiltyards were of the design common to all Europe, with armoured men of wood and straw set upright on each of the dividing rails. Half-men, actually, their upper bodies supported upon a pole that could be rotated, raised, or lowered to suit the trainee.

Though there were three separate tracks for riders to use, the guests had the tiltyards to themselves today. The grizzled veterans who ran the yard were present only to serve the two men and the boy who had just arrived.

"Ooo, what do those do?" asked Cesco, pointing to the dummies in a parody of ignorance. "Tell me, cos! I long to learn!"

His insolent delight arose from the choice of men ordered to teach him jousting: Mastino della Scala and his close companion, Niklas Fuchs.

Mastino was eighteen years old and, until last summer, the presumed heir to his uncle Cangrande. Then Cesco had appeared as if raised from the earth to torment all Christian souls. Since then Mastino's life had been a misery. Worse than being the butt of Cesco's jokes was the fact that he was now overlooked, forgotten by the very people who had cheered him barely a year before.

Fuchs was a shade older, perhaps twenty. Where precisely Mastino had found Fuchs was something of a mystery. That Fuchs hailed from the far side of the Alps was certain, based on his accent and colouring, fairer even than the fairest Veronese. His hair was actually lighter than his skin. But if he had come to Verona on his own and found Mastino, or if Mastino had met him at some tourney or spectacle, no one knew.

Technically both were still squires, though it was only a matter of time – Cangrande would knight them just as soon as Mastino fought in the field. He should have been part of the great battle against Bologna last fall, but Cangrande had inexplicably withdrawn Verona's troops before the hostilities opened, forcing Mastino to wait for another good war. Until then, he could only earn honour in the lists.

Typical of the Scaliger to craft a moment so fraught with meaning. On their third public encounter, Cesco had outridden both Mastino and Fuchs, leaving them both with their faces literally in the mud. So today Cangrande had naturally set the duo the task of testing Cesco's skill on horseback. Everyone had something to prove, scores to settle.

Mastino turned to the yard-master. "Fetch us some helms and lances. And armour for the hyena," he added sourly.

"Jackal, please," retorted Cesco. "Because I'll be feasting on your hide by midday." He had swallowed a sticky chew before departing the palace, and already the elation was flooding him. A day without Cangrande, a day of sport! Even with two avowed enemies as his teachers, he felt more joy than anxiety. Something new! If only he weren't so tired...

Snap out of it! Keep talking – talking is always the answer. "I've missed you, cousin! Where have you been all this long, cold winter?"

"If you only knew," replied Mastino tauntingly.

"Oh cousin, that's cruel. Mayn't I be allowed to live vicariously through my beloved relation, who can wander off free of the cares of being anyone's heir?"

Mastino's jaw worked silently, but before he could discover his voice, Fuchs said, "We went north, to Augsburg and Vienne. There were winter sports."

"You'll have to tell me all about it," said Cesco, eagerness only partially feigned. "Is that why the Capitano commanded you to try me in the lists?"

"I suppose," said Mastino, temper under rein. "Fuchs is a famous tilter."

Cesco eyed Fuchs up and down. "He does seem a little off kilter. So when do I get my spurs?"

"When I am sure you're not going to rowel them over the back of my neck."

"As if the *filzlaus* could reach your neck," said Fuchs.

"He's right," said Cesco with the cheerfulness that drove his cousin to distraction. "I'm so small I'd have to stand on my hands. Fortunately..." He flipped himself into a handstand on his saddle and flailed his feet menacingly. "I la!"

Mastino looked tempted to knock him over, but Fuchs simply ignored Cesco, dismounting instead. The Mastiff was prone to anger, whereas Niklas Fuchs was methodical and cold. *Which is why*, thought Cesco, *you are the more dangerous of the pair.*

Mastino followed Fuchs' example, taking up practice armour from the trunks the servants brought forward. Both owned suits of armour for parade and war, but there was little sense in scoring them in practice with a child.

Disliking being ignored, Cesco flipped down from his horse and strode over. "Do I get to dress for the ball?"

"You certainly do." Mastino chose the heaviest armour that fit across Cesco's front and back.

"I'm entitled to a shield with my arms on it, and a helmet."

"You're also entitled to a beating. Care to guess which you'll get first?" As the servants buckled them in, Mastino kept talking. "I know you think you were born in the saddle. But there's a difference between the trick-riding you do and real jousting. And the major difference is *this*." He slapped his hand down hard on Cesco's metal backplate.

Cesco almost fell over. It was far heavier than he'd guessed. Or he was weaker than he suspected. Even offered breakfast, he hadn't been able to eat more than a few bites. His stomach was too used to going hungry. He was already paying for the folly of the handstand. It was all he could do to keep his knees from trembling.

"My lord," said one of the yard-hands, a man with many scars across his arms and hands. "Mostly we don't put on full armour when we teaches. Just the chest and head, so that—"

Mastino gave the old man a withering look. "He's being brought along quickly. He doesn't mind, do you, boy?" He slapped Cesco's helmet.

"Eh?" asked Cesco. "Sorry, there must be an echo in here."

Mastino ran his tongue across his teeth. "Once he's in the full complement, let's find him a good charger. No palfrey, you hear. Something hot!"

The veteran bowed. "Very good, my lord."

They finished strapping Fuchs in first. As he pulled on his gauntlets he pointed. "What is the monstrosity on the center rail?"

Unlike the two outer rails, the straw dummy along the center course had been replaced by a metal vat on a pivot, with steel rods for arms. One arm was crooked and holding a sword. The left arm bore a shield.

"It's a new kind of quintana," replied the veteran, looking skeptically at the contraption. "The Capitano's own invention. Had us install it last night. Haven't tried it out yet."

"Should we keep to the outer rails?" asked Mastino.

"Obviously not," replied Cesco. "He had them install it for us. I'm sure we have orders to stick to the central rail, no?"

"I'm afraid so," said the servant, with a pitiable look to Mastino.

"What is that mechanism under it?" asked Fuchs, squinting.

"Forgive me, I'm afraid I'm forbidden to answer. I'll go find that horse." The man scampered off

Mastino groaned. "Trust my uncle to saddle us with something no one's ever used before."

"We do have a perfect Judas Goat," observed Fuchs.

"Baa-a-ah," said Cesco, the bleat multiplying from the echoing helmet.

The horse arrived, a massive-boned creature that could have been a destrier for sheer height. Yet it had been fed not for bulk but for speed, taut and sinewy and slightly wild-eyed. Cesco looked him up and down. "I'm supposed to ride that monster? He won't even notice I'm on his back!" But he crossed awkwardly to the stirrups and gripped the saddle. "A little help, please."

Once Cesco was in place, Mastino mounted his own horse. Spurs jangling, he trotted close and pointed. "Do you know what that is, infant?"

"What the French call a quintain, from the Latin *quintana*, a street between the fifth and sixth maniples of a Roman camp where the legionaries practiced their martial exercises. Today it means the target for swords and lances. I think the first modern one was actually a tree trunk, about the height of a tall man's head—"

Mastino broke in. "Yes, parrot, fine, fine. Since you know so much, why don't you show us how it's done. Fuchs?"

Fuchs snatched the lead away from the servant and led Cesco's horse over to the starting place along the center rail. "Baa-ah!" repeated Cesco. "Like a lamb to the slaughter, yes?"

His delight died as the lance was settled in his grip. Like the armour, it was heavier than he'd expected. He had to torque his wrist and stiffen his shoulder almost to breaking just to keep the blasted tip off the ground.

A shield was fitted onto his left arm, one with the L-shaped gap in it for the lance to angle through. Taken together the weight threatened to drag him straight through the horse down to the ground. Leaning forward even an inch would be disastrous.

Mastino cantered up alongside Cesco. "Let's see what the old dog has crafted to torment us. Ready?"

Without waiting he stabbed a spur into the flank of Cesco's horse.

The beast leapt forward and Cesco lurched back in the saddle, shield and lance dipping towards the ground as he tried to hold his seat. Mastino and Fuchs jeered, their laughter audible even over the thundering hoofbeats.

Bouncing this way and that, Cesco dragged up both shield and lance. He'd seen tilting at festivals and tournaments around Ravenna, and once in Venice during an escapade of which Ser Alaghieri was blissfully ignorant. So he knew where the target was supposed to be hit, and how. But it was a far more difficult feat than he would have guessed. The horse moved with such speed that the quintain hurtled at him like the ground at a falling man. The long lance was tip-heavy, the shield awkward, and the line of sight through the helmet was close to non-existent. Cesco tried to imagine what it would be like if his target wasn't stationary, and he was astonished that anyone survived the *giostra* at all.

His wandering thoughts caused his lance tip to sag. It made contact with the quintana low and to the right, striking at about the level of a man's belly.

Instantly there was a metallic groan and whine, and Cesco gasped as a chill ran over him, water pouring into his helmet and over his shoulders. As he opened his mouth to cry out, he was struck a blow in the back so sharp it sent him sprawling over his horse's neck, lance and shield toppling from his hands.

He could hear the hoots and applause from behind him. "O, how I wish we *had* brought a poet! He's right, Fuchs, we should be immortalizing this moment!"

As the charger slowed – it was well-trained and didn't require guidance, thank Heaven – Cesco used his right hand to pry his slippery helmet from his head and turn. The quintana was rocking gently on its pivot, still turning. Water sloshed from the open top with each motion, and the blunt sword in the crooked metal hand kept turning.

"Water weapons," murmured Cesco. Dripping, he joined Mastino and Fuchs to examine the device.

The *quintana* was open-topped, with a great quantity of water within – though less than there had been a moment ago. The bottom of the vat was on a strong pivot supported by several ribbons of metal so thin they bent. The pivot was rigged to move not only right and left, but up and down as well. If hit dead center of the chest the vat would rock backwards, spilling water on the far side of the rail. A mishit would do one of three things – a low hit would spill water on the attacker; a glancing hit to the left would bring the sword around, an actual danger; a hit to the right would bring the shield into the horse's face, or possibly strike the attacker and spin him sideways in the saddle.

Cesco reconstructed his charge in his mind. *Two mistakes.* By hitting low, he'd been doused. By hitting to his right, he'd brought the sword swinging around to smack his back. There was a palpable irony – the armour Mastino had insisted he wear was responsible for saving Cesco's life. Cesco said as much, causing Mastino to scowl.

The device was Cangrande all over: ingenious, inventive, and invidious. Trust the Capitano to find a way to cause torment even in his absence.

The morning did not improve for Cesco. Over and over they made him charge, and over and over he was doused, smacked, and rocked. They only paused each fourth or fifth run for the servants to replenish the water. While this was done, both Mastino and Fuchs would come over to mock Cesco's latest attempts, with very little in the way of helpful criticism. "I thought you knew how to ride!"

"He only knows idiot saddle-tricks."

"Drop that tip again and we'll make you carry a longer one."

"Fool! You let the horse bounce you off target."

"Pathetic! Not a single solid hit all morning."

Cesco had replies for each insult, but he also recognized the truth of what they were saying. He was failing, something he was unused to. But this was not like juggling or swordplay or poetry, all of which he could master on his own time, in the privacy of his bed chamber. Nor was it quite like the horse tricks he'd mastered in Ravenna. This was not a skill he could gain solo. For this exercise he required equipment and the aid of several men. Which made him all the more determined to improve.

Novice that he was, he saw the advantage of Cangrande's new *quintana*. A cruel but effective instructor, at once brutal and completely fair. A better teacher by far than Mastino.

Close to noon, after dozens of runs and almost as many blows, another upside to Cangrande's invention revealed itself – both Mastino and Fuchs were eager to try their hands at mastering it. Satisfied that Cesco was spent and hurting, they curtly commanded him to climb down and clean the soaking armour so it wouldn't rust.

"I think *I'm* in danger of rusting," he said, allowing the servants to unbuckle the straps.

"Impossible," retorted Fuchs. "You've shown no steel at all."

"Then I shall steal some from you." Wordplay was a reflex.

"See that he scrubs and oils every inch," Mastino told the servants. "And don't help him, or we'll use you for a quintana instead." He turned to Fuchs. "Shall we show him how it's done?"

"With pleasure."

They set about it, Mastino first. He rode well, and with a practiced blow he rocked the quintana backwards, barely causing it to twist at all. Fuchs was even more precise, sloshing a vast quantity of water on the far side of the rail. The metal arms didn't rotate an inch.

Cesco learned more watching the pair take turns at the quintain than he had in the saddle. Mastino was highly skilled, and was only doused once. He did tend to draw his lance to the right, just inside the target's shield, which meant he was forced to protect himself on each run from the swinging sword. But it may very well have been deliberate, Mastino trying to build a necessary skill.

Fuchs, on the other hand, remained perfectly dry and entirely unscathed. Every blow rocked the metal vat backwards without the slightest rotation, and Cesco could imagine a man being hit with such accuracy. In jousting, of course, most lances were built to splinter. Dangerous, but rarely fatal. But on the field of war or in a formal duel, the lances were like these – solid cores of ash-treated wood. Woe unto anyone who felt the impact, for it would likely be his last sensation. At least it was a death to please the divine Caesar – swift.

After an hour they broke for their meal. Cesco sat with them, gnawing on his own hunk of bread and nibbling at the edges of some cheese. "I see why I was entrusted to you. You both are phenomenally skilled."

Mastino's eyes narrowed as he tried to discern the insult under the praise. Finding none, he nodded once. "Yes, we are."

"Is it natural ability, or practice?"

Again failing to find malice in the query, Mastino answered. "Both. It was hard for me at first – though I didn't do near as badly as you on my first try. Still, I'm here most of the year, practicing. Fuchs is the natural."

"There is not much to choose between us," said Fuchs, complimenting his master. "And I started even younger than you."

"I'm fortunate to have you both to teach me," said Cesco. Then he added, "If only you were willing to teach."

Hearing criticism at last, Mastino snarled. "How can we teach a child unable to even lift his lance?"

"The Capitano has a method where I'm concerned," said Cesco lightly. "He teaches me everything he can, and is seen to do so. Therefore when I fail, it's my own inability. But when I succeed, he takes the credit. By placing me under your tutelage, he is offering you the same chance. Everyone will know that I learned to joust at your hands. If I succeed, it will be all to your credit. But since the Scaliger has successfully taught me so much, any failure in this arena will be seen as a failure of my teachers." Cesco shrugged. "So truly, it's in your best interests that I do well. We both know about the tourney this summer, and we both know I won't be allowed to just sit and watch. He'll put me in the thick of it, to test both me – and you."

Mastino was silent. Finally Fuchs said, grudgingly, "You try too hard to maintain your lance with your arm-strength alone. Use your back, leverage your shoulders."

"Thank you. What else?"

Mastino echoed Fuchs' brusqueness. "Concentrate on the target. Forget the incoming lance, forget the horse, forget safety. Just keep your eyes on the place you're aiming for."

"Shouldn't I be worried about defense?"

Fuchs shook his head. "If you think of your shield, you have already conceded."

"Explain, please."

"You have decided your own blow won't matter, and his will. Thinking defensively will get you killed."

"That's a rather contrary piece of direction. I like it. May I try?"

Re-armoured, Cesco spent another hour tilting at the metal dummy, with Fuchs and Mastino calling out scraps of instruction after each go – still heavy with insult, but more helpful than before.

Finally he made a nearly perfect run. Like Mastino, he still hit more to the right than center, but this time he stayed dry. Both his tutors were silent, praise in itself. Exhausted but delighted, Cesco cantered his horse closer to them and pulled off his helmet. "I've got the hang of it now. If we were careful, could we try it without the quintana?"

"What, us against you?"

"Yes. Slower, perhaps, and with the thinnest straw lances—"

"Not a chance," replied Mastino.

"Why not?"

"First off, the horses are well-trained, they won't run slower. This is a sport that must be learned at speed, or not at all."

"At speed then."

"Secondly, you're cursed, and I want nothing to do with someone who is doomed to die. It might be said that I caused your death, then I would be as damned as you."

As Cesco's smile widened his eyes creased. "Cursed? Damned? Did you go to some old hag and give her some of my hair, or an old boot?"

Mastino shook his head. "This was all of your own doing. You murdered Federigo. You spilled the family blood."

Federigo della Scala had been Cangrande's cousin, until he had conspired with Passerino Bonaccolsi, the lord of Mantua and Cangrande's bosom friend, to murder Cangrande and rule in his place.

"Federigo died by his own hand," said Cesco. "An accident."

"A curious accident. Tied in a chair, his neck broken. Deny it however you like, you spilled family blood. I know you weren't raised here, but there's a curse on our family, and you've invited it down on your head. I just hope I'm there to see it. Though not too close," Mastino added.

Cesco felt a frisson of joy as he realized that Mastino's hatred for him was fringed with just a little fear. "My dear snarling mastiff," he said delightedly, "I had no idea you were so superstitious! I'm going to bring you a rabbit's foot the next chance I get."

"Keep it. You're the unlucky one."

"You're the only one who thinks so. But cousin, you haven't thought this through."

"No?"

"No. If indeed I am guilty of what you think, it's not because I'm cursed that I'm dangerous. I'm dangerous because I'm willing to do what you're not."

"Child," said Mastino with a dark glint in his eye, "you have no idea the lengths I'm willing to go to ruin you."

"And you have no idea what I'll do if you try. Why not be friends, then? Set aside our poor meeting and declare a truce."

Before Mastino could answer, Fuchs said, "I will ride against the *trottel.*"

Cesco's teeth flashed winningly. "The perfect solution! Unless the *trottel* is somehow related to our darling Niklas as well?"

Mastino shrugged at Fuchs. "Don't kill him."

"He's smarter than that," said Cesco, eyes bright. "No, from Fuchs it will be a knife in the back or not at all."

Fuchs scowled. "I won't kill him. Just make sure he lacks the breath to insult us further."

"That might mean killing me," warned Cesco lightly.

"*Halts mau,*" snapped Fuchs.

The quintana was removed and Fuchs took his place on the opposite end of the yard. They faced each other, the long rail to each rider's left dividing them so that their horses could not collide.

For this they used practice lances. Different from lances of war, these were not a single piece of hardened wood but several thinner slats around a hollow center. At the tip was a ball of hard wood. It packed a terrific punch, but the moment it encountered any resistance the slats supporting it would bend outwards and shatter. Designed for sport, it would hurt a man without severely damaging him.

Or so went the theory. Cesco had heard of several men mishit with a sporting lance who were killed by broken slats piercing their throat or eye. He reached up to be sure his helmet was entirely in place, then tried to match Fuchs' careless pose.

The veteran in charge of the tiltyards had a flag. He walked to the center of the rail where the ground had been turned to mud by the quintain. He called out for the riders to prepare themselves and offered the common instructions to a *giostra*.

As the flag went down, both horses bolted forward almost of their own accord. As instructed, Cesco forgot about his shield, trusting instinct to guard him. He focused his whole being on the center of Fuchs' breastplate. Which was hurtling towards him with an impossible speed! What would happen if he was hit? For an instant he took his eyes off his target to watch the ball of the sporting lance. In that moment time seemed to contract and instinct screamed at him to turn, to twist away, evade. Obediently his body tried, but under the weight of the armour he hardly shifted. Like the sun to the earth, his whole world seemed to revolve around that tiny wooden ball.

Time expanded and Cesco felt the impact of the ball right in his chest. The cracking sound in his ears could have been the supports splintering, or his ribs. The world went bright and dark all at once as he was lifted clear from his saddle. He landed on his left side in the mud, his unbroken lance beside him. He'd missed Fuchs entirely.

Mastino was laughing uproariously. Fuchs rode back along the rail, holding the remains of his shattered lance. "Who is eating the muck now?"

"I am." Chest and side throbbing, Cesco hacked and spat. "Mmm. Yum." Rising in a series of metallic staggers, Cesco straightened his helmet. "Best of three?"

"Why not? If you are determined to be beaten to a pulp, I am your man."

They resumed their places, Fuchs with a fresh lance. Again they were given the signal, again they raced together. But this time Cesco understood the injunction against defense and concentrated all his attention on his target. He still took the worst of the exchange, but his lance came away broken and he remained in his saddle.

It was difficult to tell under the helmet, but Cesco thought Fuchs was bemused. He wasn't hurt – Cesco's ball had caught him in the right shoulder, breaking only half of the thin slats of wood. Still, it was great progress from first to second try. Mastino was silent. Again, compliment enough.

Cesco examined his oddly deformed lance. The ball was still attached to half a dozen strands of wood, its weight making the weapon droop. He tossed it away and took another, returning to his post at the end of the rail.

Fuchs had done the same. There was an eager lean to the German's body, like a hound straining its leash. Cesco felt his own body echoing the sentiment.

The veteran servant took up his stance for the third and final run. As he raised his arm, the flag in hand, he paused. His head turned towards the gate, and in practiced caution he threw up his free hand to grasp the flag tight, the universal signal to hold.

Even through the helmet Cesco could hear it. A commotion outside the walls, the hue and cry of panic. Automatically both Fuchs and Cesco turned their horses towards the gates. Mastino was already there, pulling the doors wide and grasping the nearest frightened citizen. "What is it? What's happened?"

"Bursa! It's fallen – fallen to the Infidel!"

"It's panic like I've never seen. The end of the world. As if they've ever heard of Bursa before now."

Cesco's audience was Suor Beatrice, novice in the Benedictine Order and, more importantly, daughter of Dante. Born Antonia Alaghieri, she was Pietro's sister, and Cesco had been raised to think of her as his aunt. It was his habit to sneak away from the palace in his few spare moments for the comfort of her arms.

She was defying her Order by allowing these secret midnight visits, but it was the only time she saw him, and she treasured these moments even more than he. At twenty-six years old, Antonia's guiding principle was to be useful, and when Cesco was with her he could unload his cares and for a brief time be the child he truly was. Leaving her beloved convent in Ravenna to bring Cesco back to Verona, Antonia had sworn an oath to stay with him until the state of his soul was certain.

Now she sat in the darkness, stroking his hair. The Scaliger made him keep it short, cutting away all those beautiful curls. "I don't even know where Bursa is."

"In Anatolia, a hundred miles south of Constantinople, not far from Nicea." He spoke with absolute authority – he, who'd never been farther east than Venice.

"And who has conquered it?"

"The Infidel."

"Any particular one?" asked Suor Beatrice wryly.

Eyes closed, Cesco said, "You've heard the name Osman Gazi?"

"I think I have. A leader of some new band of Turk. Was it he?"

"It would be the Devil's own work if it were," said Cesco. "Or some very disturbing miracle. He's dead. Natural causes, called to Paradise by Allah, peace unto the Prophet."

"Francesco della Scala," scolded Suor Beatrice in uncompromising tones. "This is a house of the Lord."

"Forgive me, Suora. I thought it fitting to hope he was called to his own benevolent Creator, rather than damned to burn by ours."

Suor Beatrice took her hand from off Cesco's head to cross herself. "There is only one...! Ooh, you've been talking too much with Tharwat!"

"I imagine that will soon be remedied," said Cesco cryptically. But before she could force him to explain, he returned to his tale. "It seems that upon Osman's death, his youngest son appointed a caretaker for their lands and marched an army to the long-besieged Bursa."

"Long-besieged?"

"No one's been paying attention, but it seems that Bursa has held out against the Turk for nine long years, with push and pull from the Greek Emperor in Constantinople. Is it strange that there are two emperors, East and West? Like the Sun and the Moon, divided only by the *mare nostrum*." He caught himself rambling. "Anyway, upon this new warlord's arrival the mighty walls of Bursa crumbled like paper, to the shame of the Greek Emperor Andronikos, currently engaged in an uncivil civil war with his grandson."

"Was there horrible slaughter?"

"Surprisingly, no. The invaders showed remarkable clemency towards those of other faiths. No forced conversions, no executions. It might be said that this new Turk showed more Christian charity than the Christians would. Not that I think there will be much praise for him. He has declared Bursa the new capital of something called the Kayi Clan."

This time she didn't bother to challenge Cesco's heretical streak. "Do you know his name?"

Mid-yawn, Cesco shifted to a more comfortable position, laying his head in her lap. "Didn't I say? I must be tired. His name is Orhan, son of Osman. They're calling him the new Saladin."

"Is it enough to cause a crusade?"

Cesco shrugged. "I doubt it. After the perversion of the Fourth Crusade, no one believes in them. We can yearn and tear our hair all we like, but I believe the Holy Land is lost to us. We're more interested in fighting in our own backyard than in being away for decades, and far more interested in tourneys than holy war. I know I am," he added laconically. "Though I would like to stroll around Golgotha, pluck some olives from Gethsemane, climb Sinai. See what all the fuss is about."

Antonia changed topics. "When will the tournament take place?"

Cesco squirmed in anticipation. "The first two days of July. He's in the midst of planning it – you know our Capitano, he likes the details. I suppose that's why he's fobbed me off on Mastino for the moment. But if it means I get to participate, I'm game."

"And Mastino and Fuchs are teaching you to tilt?"

"Yes."

"That must be – interesting."

"It is, actually. Though they're loath to do it, they have much to offer. I'm hardly able to move at present, but I learned a great deal in just this one day."

"They didn't have to teach you to ride, at least. Didn't Pietro buy you a pony back in Ravenna?"

"He did. And later I borrowed some horses to practice on."

"Stole, you mean."

"I liberated them from captivity, but always returned them, none the worse for the outing. In fact, I did many a Ravennese horseman a favour by exercising his horses for him."

"Remind me, how did they repay you for this incredibly selfless behavior?"

"Threatened to have me stocked," Cesco admitted. "If I'd been older, they would have demanded I lose a hand or an eye. I confess I exploited my tender years for all they're worth."

"Meaning those years are behind you?"

Cesco chuckled sleepily. "I would hardly call this past year tender."

"You've grown some."

"Hardly at all, but you're kind to say so.

"I miss your hair."

"Next time I'm sheared I'll save a lock for you."

"How is Susanna?"

Antonia could almost hear the smile. "She's a fantastic footer, and she can pitch so high! Lord Bonaventura says he's never seen a bird hang quite as she does. I'm sure he's shining me on, but it's pretty to believe him. And while I'm in the city I can care for her."

"Where is she when you're away?"

"Detto looks after her for me." Bailardetto Nogarola was more a brother to Cesco than a cousin. Entirely unlike each other, they'd bonded as children and the link had only strengthened over time. "In fact, we're the only two she'll mind. Not even Bonaventura can handle her without getting nipped." Petruchio Bonaventura was a Veronese noble, wild in his youth and now married to a woman as beautiful as she was outspoken.

"Do you get to fly her often?"

"Once a week, at least. It's the only time the Capitano really gives me my head. I think it amuses him to have me play out our little drama with my own hawk. I have to treat her almost as badly as he treats me, just to train her. If I coddle her, she'll be spoiled and no use to anyone." Antonia felt him shake his head. "The man works on many levels, one being rather heavy-handed metaphor."

Listening, Antonia's mind turned to one fact about his little falcon that he never mentioned – her name.

Unusual for a bird, chosen as a kind of penance for a perceived failure. Even in this activity he loved so much, he flogged himself for past mistakes.

Antonia hugged him closer and he made a loud strangling sound. "Shhh," she said, glancing at the shut door. These visits had to be kept secret for both their sakes. Antonia knew she was suspected of having a lover. It was why the Abbess hadn't allowed her in the general dormitory, keeping her in this guest chamber. Suor Beatrice was from a different convent, and so many holy houses doubled as brothels that an abbess could never be certain what kind of nun she was receiving.

Celibacy was something of a joke among the laity, mostly referring to the friars. There were a hundred amusing tales that began, 'There was once a brother who lived with ten women...' Which made it all the more important to maintain a firm stance. No abbey could risk an unknown girl from another house that might have more liberal ideas.

But Suor Beatrice brought with her a peculiar skill that made it impossible for the Abbess to eject her from either the building or the Order. Cesco invoked it, asking, "How goes the copying?"

Antonia sighed. "Slowly. They have no trouble scraping the vellum with the pumice, but for some reason they're stingy about the chalk to soften it. So the ink doesn't set properly into the pages."

"Frustrating."

"Quite. And there's quite a bit of chatter about women creating books. But the Bible for Lord Castelbarco is nearly complete, and we've had a second commission – another Bible, of course. The price is enough to feed the abbey for six months at least. I believe the Abbess is beginning to warm to me." She and Cesco shared a chuckle.

"Who was the new commission from?" asked Cesco shrewdly.

"Lord Montecchio."

"Meaning your friend Gianozza, the causer of conflict, founder of feuds, votaress of vengeance, wanton of warfare—"

"She might have said something to her husband," said Antonia drily. "Otherwise my days are full. I find time to visit Fra Lorenzo and his gardens at San Francesco al Corso."

"Ah, the good friar. Have you divined the cause of his inexplicable hatred for your knightly brother?"

Antonia had indeed learned the reason Fra Lorenzo detested Pietro. In return for Lorenzo's aid, Pietro had refrained from exposing some heretical deed in the friar's youth. But the friar hadn't enjoyed the threat of blackmail, and was proving quite capable of holding a grudge.

Antonia couldn't decide if she liked or disliked Fra Lorenzo. Certainly he was a man of many parts, frank but never inappropriate. Happily, his anger at her brother hadn't extended to her. In fact, he was perversely pleased, because for the first time he had someone in Verona in whom he could confide the tale of his youth. It was disturbingly salacious. While she applauded his survival of the affair, she recognized in him a strong streak of self-preservation that clashed with his high-sounding morality.

But that was not for Cesco's ears, so she changed the subject, speaking instead of her other frequent port of call – the Chapter Library of Verona's Duomo. Until recently the books within had been the Scaliger's private collection, bought sight unseen and in such numbers that most of them remained unread still. In her role as overseer of a newborn book-making enterprise, she could plead to the Abbess that the research was necessary. With her status as both a sister in Christ and the daughter of a great poet, she was granted an unusual measure of freedom. Her lifelong love of reading was understandable, if not quite respectable in a woman, and the brother in charge of the books left her mainly to her own devices.

"Though their system is hopelessly shoddy," she said, repeating a frequent complaint. "There are so many scrolls the brothers haven't even catalogued. I've offered to help."

"And were refused, naturally."

"Naturally. Fools. Pardon me." As she crossed herself he yawned again, and she pulled a blanket snug up under his chin. "Sleep. If you mean to participate in the tourney, you must survive the training. Which means rest."

"I'll go at Matins," he said drowsily. "There's a feast tomorrow at midday. Don't know why. I'll try to have you invited." Almost mumbling now, he turned onto his side. At once his breathing became regular. It was the one blessing of this horrible ordeal Cangrande was putting him through, he no longer had trouble falling asleep. She had spent so much of his youth at his bedside, talking with him in just this manner until he could resist Morpheus no longer. And yet he would awaken in less than an hour, wild-eyed and staring. He never told them what dreams haunted him so, and eventually they stopped asking. Now he slept, if only from fatigue. Suor Beatrice thanked God for small blessings.

At the bell for Matins, four hours before dawn, she woke him and they both rose from her pallet. The boy kissed her cheek in the dark and she departed, knowing he would steal away once all the sisters were in the chapel. It was their routine by now, one that filled her with contentment. She was his escape, his solace. As Cesco was the sole reason for her prolonged sojourn in Verona, she felt she was fulfilling her purpose. Her father would be proud.

Suor Beatrice's guest suite was on the north side of the building. The enforced privacy rankled, but she knew the Abbess was guarding her institution from charges of unchastity. Being on her own made it possible for Cesco to visit her, which compensated her for her loneliness.

When the prayers were finished she returned to her room. Closing the door, she dropped her over-robe and was moving towards the bed before she sensed a presence in the room. "Did you change your mind and decide to raid the kitchens instead?"

A hand grasped her clumsily by the arm, then with more confidence about the throat. "Don't scream," whispered a voice. A man's voice.

She was thrown roughly onto the floor, the breath knocked out of her. Confused, dazed, Antonia tried to rise. But she couldn't. As if it was happening to someone else, her mind registered the weight on her, the businesslike lifting of her shift. An instant later it was intensely personal – a hand groping between her legs, right to her most private self. She felt the need to scream, but fear and horror closed her throat. She could barely breathe.

The weight shifted as he used his knees to force her legs apart. Gasping, she clawed at the stone floor with her hands, breaking her nails, trying to escape, but he clutched her hair in his hands and his weight was too much for her to dislodge.

Then it happened. He removed one hand from restraining her just long enough to reach down and find her vagina, guiding himself into her. It was clumsy, dry, and rough at first as he positioned himself. Then he thrust hard and she felt something in her tear, rip away, like the seal on her soul.

Now he thrust, using her blood to move fast and faster. Again and again she tried to scramble away, but with his hands above her shoulders and his hips grinding down on her, all she could do was whimper, eyes wide in shock and horror and disbelief.

It seemed to last an eternity. Finally he held still, grunting as he spasmed in her. Tears came as her intellect recognized the moment.

The pressure eased as her attacker withdrew himself. He yanked her up to her knees by her hair, squeezing her breast in one hand and giving her neck a quick bite before pressing his lips to her ear. "No quarter."

He shoved her back to the floor wet with her tears and her blood. Still cloaked in darkness, he stood. There were sounds of cloth being adjusted. She felt him absently use his toe to push her legs back together. She tried to rise but a booted heel shoved her back to the stone floor. The door opened and shut. He had gone.

When Abbess Verdiana came by the door a few minutes later and heard the hitched breath of Suor Beatrice's weeping, she didn't pause but passed the door by. She'd heard two voices earlier and now congratulated herself on not allowing the visiting novice to contaminate her other nuns. The girl was proving valuable to the house, but if she was foolish enough to tryst, she had to accept the consequences.

Five

Tessa Capulletto sat focusing on the yarn in her fingers, endeavoring to ignore her rising gorge. She couldn't decide if her illness was due to this latest child growing inside her, or her company.

She was at the Scaligeri palace, seated on a comfortable chair with a back to ease her condition. The other women sat on cushioned boxes, backs erect, enjoying a breeze that fluttered the drapes of the grand loggia.

Their husbands were all below in the hall, no doubt drinking – wherever the Scaliger was, wine was never out of reach. Tessa wondered if he was quite recovered from his wound. It was information she would have to wheedle out of her husband. Antony Capulletto did not naturally confide in his wife, considering her a necessary evil, and a child.

I am no child. I have a child of my own. I am a woman now.

As proof, she was here, invited for the first time to join the other wives, though the next youngest was almost twice her age. It was a strange gathering. Apart from servants, there were only six women present. Too few to fill the long arcade of the enclosed palace balcony. Their hostess had cleverly dealt with that by having screens erected, partitioning off their little corner of the loggia to create an intimate space.

Tessa felt under-dressed, despite her embroidered and brocaded panel dress being among the most expensive in the room. It was not the clothes but how she wore them. She was still short, and her breasts hadn't filled out properly, not even after giving birth. Angelica said it was because she wasn't using them, but Tessa could think of nothing worse than letting the little leech bite down on her with those teeth just coming in. Let Angelica coddle and nurse the brat – it would help make up for the loss of her own child. And soon Tessa would have another hungry mouth to pass off to the nurse. A boy, all the wisewomen said. She prayed they were wrong.

As if in answer her stomach roiled, and she distracted herself from it by considering the other women. The one she knew best was seated closest. Tessa could not help liking Kate Bonaventura, in spite of her rather unwomanly conversation. Red-haired, full-chested and full-hipped, the Paduan-born lady was known for being slightly mad – a reputation earned more in her past than in her present. Kate and her husband Petruchio were the guests of honour each year at the revels Tessa's husband threw for San Bonaventura's feast. Last year the event had been memorable for several reasons. Retiring from her first attempt at playing hostess, Tessa had given birth to her daughter. At the same moment, the bastard Cesco had interrupted the feast by stealing a horse, and then the Scaliger's sister had re-entered society after her stroke.

That lady was here, too. Katerina della Scala. The rancor between the two siblings was famous. They behaved more like husband and wife than brother and sister. At Christmas, Cangrande had refused his sister entry to his palace. Arriving today in the company of her husband and elder son, she could not be turned off, so Cangrande had exiled her to the society of women.

Sitting with her gloved hands folded, Donna Katerina was the sole woman without occupation. Though recovered from her stroke, her left hand was sheathed to cover an old wound, a dreadful burn. Thus disfigured, Katerina had taken to wearing gloves to put others at ease. It meant, however, that she lacked the fine touch for weaving. Another form of exile. In a less formidable woman it might have been pitiable.

Seated beside her was Donna Elena, wife of Lord Castelbarco. Tessa had met her only once before, but she was a pleasant elderly woman of fifty or so, hardly younger than her husband. No threat there.

On Elena's far side was Giovanna da Svevia, the Scaliger's wife and today's hostess. Much older than her spouse, she was somewhere between Katerina and Elena in age. Rumours hinted that, like her husband, Giovanna despised her sister-in-law. But so far they were exceedingly polite to each other, even sweet. Surprising, as Giovanna was the great-granddaughter of Frederick II, last of the Hohen-staufen Emperors and famous for fits of temper. Tessa had come expecting to witness a better show than this.

Yet if there was to be a drama, the likeliest source was from the woman seated across from her. Clos-est in age to Tessa, she was the person Tessa most wished to ignore. Actually, she wished the puttanna would drop dead at her feet so Tessa could grind her heel into that creamy face. Slender, with hair like raven-feathers and eyes like sapphires, Gianozza Montecchio fit her expensive French clothes per-fectly. Just the right hint of cleavage – of course motherhood had endowed her with perfect tits! – and bare shoulders, all wrapped and warped into an hourglass of brocade and jewels that screamed, 'Look at me! I'm perfect!'

Tessa had never met Donna Montecchio before to-day, but she'd seen that face often enough. It was painted on the walls of her house, adorning fres-cos whose religious pretext couldn't hide their true meaning. This bitch Gianozza had been betrothed to Tessa's husband, just as Tessa herself had been be-trothed to someone else. But unlike Tessa, the bal-dracca had deliberately broken her bond and mar-ried her betrothed's best friend instead. Leaving Antony Capulletto in need of a wife.

Tessa hated Donna Montecchio on two counts. First, because Antony made no effort to disguise the fact that Gianozza was his one true love. He still re-ferred to her by that stupid pet name, calling her 'my Giulia'. Some kind of reference to the women of Cae-sar's family, and their ability to make men happy. Ridiculous, and obviously false. Who had ever been made happy by this simpering harpy? Not that this plain truth had stopped Tessa's husband from nam-ing their daughter – Tessa's child, born of her loins! – after her. Giulietta. The Little Giulia.

Tessa's second cause for hate was that if only the bagascia had married where she had promised, then Tessa would still be a maiden looking forward to her wedding night with Theobaldo Capulletto. Her beloved Thibault. Now her nephew by marriage. Though she vaguely understood these two causes were contradictory, to her they were both perfectly valid reasons to hate.

Thus, before they'd even met, Tessa saw Gianozza Montecchio as her personal tormentor. Now Tessa was astonished to find a woman so plainly stupid! All this fuss over her? Pretty, yes, it was undeniable. But that breathless little pant she emitted every few minutes, as if always on the brink of tears! And the soulful look she had perfected, like a sad dog pleading for a treat. Tessa's opinion of her husband plummeted even further.

Upon arrival today, Donna Montecchio had tried to embrace Tessa like a sister, which had only caused Tessa to stiffen and protest her delicate condition. Exchanging the formal kiss of greeting, Tessa could smell the orange blossoms in Gianozza's hair and on the puttanna's breath. For the rest of her long life, Tessa hated oranges.

The sporca madonna wasn't busy with a needle or a hand-loom. No, she'd been invited to read aloud to them. Love poetry, of course. It was all Tessa could do to block out the vapid, vapourish voice.

Tessa, Giovanna, Katerina, Elena, Kate, and Gianozza. Six women. Yet there were seven seats. Who was missing? Tessa filled her mind with women absent. Verde della Scala, Cangrande's niece. Nico da Lozzo's wife, whose name Tessa couldn't recall. A homely girl, much taller than her husband. Who else?

When the doors to the loggia opened and a woman in a dun-coloured habit entered, Tessa recognized her at once. The girl who was becoming a nun, Ser Alaghieri's sister—

"Antonia!" Dropping her book, Gianozza flew from her cushioned box to throw her arms around the newcomer. But her fashionable skirts were not made for such a move, and her loss of balance made her embrace less a hug and more a desperate clutching. Tessa deliberately let the laugh escape her lips, even as she pretended to smother it. Stupid strega.

But Gianozza was laughing too, giggling in a fashion more suited to the maiden she had once been rather than the matron she now was. "Forgive me, darling, I'm just so happy to see you! O but Antonia, you look dreadful! What's the matter, love? Are you ill?"

"I do have a – a cold," replied Suor Beatrice, who the bitch insisted on calling Antonia.

She's lying, thought Tessa. She's been crying. Can't the flighty donnaccia see it?

Apparently not. "I'm so glad you're here," said the Montecchio bitch in what she mistook for a confidential whisper. "You must shield me!" She then turned around to beam at the rest of them. "You all remember Suor Beatrice?"

"How could we forget her?" said Giovanna da Svevia. Their hostess rose to politely kiss Suor Beatrice on either cheek. "As her very interesting name indicates, she is the bringer of blessings."

There was something very cool in that embrace, and Tessa wondered what lay between them other than age. Suor Beatrice said, "Forgive me, lady, for coming so late. I had to speak to Fra Lorenzo on my way."

"Holy business must of course come first," said Donna Giovanna. "You know everyone here, of course?"

Suor Beatrice said she did, and worked her way around the arc of seats, duly greeting them each in turn. Though she did not know the novice well, Tessa thought that she behaved quite unlike her usual brisk self.

Tessa's feelings about Suor Beatrice were mostly positive. She'd been one of a very few women who had come throughout the winter to see how Tessa was faring after the awful events of November. But she was also sister to one of Antony's dearest friends, and linked to the boy Cesco. That wild little imp, nearly Tessa's own age, had not only almost cost the life of her daughter, but also wounded Thibault's pride. Tessa's dislike for the Greyhound's bastard went deep.

Katerina della Scala rose to kiss Antonia warmly. "A pleasure, as always. I hope you have news of your brother to share."

"Nothing, I'm afraid – unless you mean Jacopo."

Katerina smiled. "No, your younger brother is below with the men. I imagine they are raising cups to his imminent departure. I was referring to Ser Pietro."

"I'm sure he's well," said Suor Beatrice, moving on to embrace Kate.

The red-haired woman kissed her smackingly. "Another youthful face! Thank heavens! We women under forty are now in the majority. Though you'll be the envy of every one of us, young or old. A body unravaged by children. I can hardly recall what life was like before my little monsters. Don't you dare sit beside me, I'll die of jealousy."

Suor Beatrice looked curiously stricken at this, but rallied and said something pleasant. Tessa hardly noticed it, for Gianozza was hovering over the nun's shoulder as if to guide her away from Tessa.

Quickly Tessa rose, and there was nothing the Montecchio bitch could do but watch their embrace. As they parted, Suor Beatrice looked down at Tessa's belly, eyes widening. Tessa said simply, "Yes, I'm increasing again."

"So soon?"

Resuming her seat and her hand-loom, Tessa shrugged her tiny shoulders. "Our girl is healthy, and our nurse has laid absolute claim to her. My lord says he wants a boy, then the business will be over and done with." Seeing the look of distaste on Antonia's features, Tessa said, "I'm better able to be a wife now I am older. And as soon as this one is born, I will be able to do as I please."

"When you get older, it's the business that pleases," said Kate with a secret smile.

Suor Beatrice shuddered. Their hostess found the comment in poor taste as well. "Donna Bonaventura, there are no men present to impress, and therefore no earthly need for your earthy wit."

"Where are the men?" asked Suor Beatrice, glancing around in a much more mousey way than usual. "I would like to see Cesco."

"The men are below, doubtless plotting great feats for the tourney. While we wait, I have asked Donna Montecchio to entertain us with reading. Suor Beatrice, will you sit by me? I know you have no man to weave for – your pursuits are far more lofty. But will you mind holding this?" Cangrande's wife held out the massive ball of yarn that she was using on her own hand-loom.

Almost Donna Montecchio protested – obviously she wanted her friend at her side. But the vapid idiot resumed her seat opposite Tessa and took up her book. Blessedly, before she could resume reading, Cangrande's sister spoke.

"Perhaps, now she is here, Suor Beatrice should read to us," said Katerina. "I say nothing against your reading, Madonna Montecchio. But Suor Beatrice is the daughter of a poet, and is herself the maker of books. It might be more suitable employment for her than holding yarn."

Tessa blinked. Was that a rebuke? It seemed so, judging by the way Cangrande's wife and sister were gazing at each other. There might be sparks yet.

However, before open hostility could break out, Suor Beatrice said, "I'm afraid my cold would make it difficult. I'm happy to hold the yarn and listen."

Katerina tilted her head in acknowledgement. Meanwhile, the bitch was fluttering in her seat. "O, if only my Romeo were here. You all must hear him. Five years old and already he can recite a hundred cantos, word for word."

Donna Elena was bemused. "Is that what you're teaching him?"

"Yes! Only love poetry," exclaimed Gianozza. "No offense, Antonia, but your father's *Commedia* is far too violent for one so young. He's a very sensitive soul."

Instantly Tessa decided to have Thibault read L'Inferno aloud to Giulietta each night at bedtime.

The stupid witch flaunted the book in her perfect white fingers. "You know this one, of course!"

Suor Beatrice looked at the volume blankly for a moment. "Filippo."

"Yes!" Gianozza turned and spoke to Tessa as if to a child. "Rustico di Filippo, a Florentine of two generations past. He is better known for his satiric verses, but this book contains his love poetry." She looked to the hostess. "Shall I?"

"Please."

Tessa turned her face down to stare at the yarn she was working, trying to block out the breathless whispering voice reciting verses that the faithless idiot probably didn't even understand. What tripe!

But despite her iron determination, eventually the words crept in. The general sentiment was that Love is impossible inside the bonds of marriage, for marriage stifles the spirit, denies free will.

Well, that's certainly true. But if she believes it, why did she rush off to marry the first man that caught her fancy? Stupid fica!

The more I humble myself to love,
The more he shows me fierce power –
And the more my desire increases,
And the more night and day make me suffer.

O, how I suffer! What will I do,
If you don't aid me, my lady?
If you deny me, beautiful, in my heart,
Life won't be able to last, but will leave.

Everyone looks me in the face and wonders,
Seeing my changed expression:
For I hide my suffering with words—

The donnaccia's faux-dulcet tones were interrupted by Donna Katerina. "Suor Beatrice, are you quite well?"

The Alaghieri girl's shoulders were shaking, and the odd tear escaped her eyes to trail down her nose and fall onto the ball of yarn in her lap. Tessa had always thought of Suor Beatrice as pragmatic, levelheaded. It was a disappointment to find the nun more like Gianozza than herself. The idea of being emotional about poetry!

Predictably, Gianozza dropped her precious book to the floor so she could rush over and lay hands upon Antonia's shoulders. "Oh my dear! I am so sorry! Of course you are moved! As am I!" The hussy began crying as well. "He suffers so, in silence. It is true love!"

Tessa was delighted to see Kate roll her eyes. "Actually, I think he was remarking on his inability to be silent. It's a common fault," she added pointedly.

Tessa found herself saying, "Shall we have music instead? I have always thought that it was unladylike for a woman to read."

Stung, Gianozza turned her too-beautiful face towards Tessa. The bitch even cried prettily – though Tessa noticed how quickly the tears went away as she began to speak. "Antonia reads. There is no woman more devoted to words than my Antonia."

"That is only natural," said Elena. "Suor Beatrice has lived with books all her life."

Having had her discourtesy of using Antonia's birth name pointed out, Gianozza obviously felt rebuked from all corners. She responded in character. "Even holy orders cannot overcome her true self! And Antonia Alaghieri is her father's daughter."

"Rubbish," replied Katerina della Scala. "Suor Beatrice is herself. She needs no qualifier."

"Really?" Giovanna da Svevia smiled warmly at her sister-in-law. "How else is she to be defined?"

"How else but through her actions, her very being."

"A radical notion," replied Cangrande's wife. "What are we if not daughters, sisters, and mothers?"

"I don't know about you, dear sister," said Katerina smoothly. "But I am myself first."

Giovanna clapped her hands lightly. "Admirable. But does that make you a good woman, I wonder? What is the first duty of a woman?"

This was a lesson that Tessa's father had literally beaten into her. Almost mechanically she answered, "To love our husbands."

"To be loved by them," corrected Gianozza Montecchio.

"To partner them," said Kate Bonaventura.

"To advance the causes of our men," said Elena Castelbarco.

"Yes," said their hostess, agreeing with this last statement. "Be they fathers, husbands, sons, what have you. We are here for their sakes, not our own."

Katerina blinked rapidly. "I'm surprised to hear you say so. Do not we have souls? Do not we yearn, desire, have opinions?"

Giovanna da Svevia shook her head. "The Bible says we come from Man. First Adam, then Eve. We are derivative, and sinful."

"I hope so," said Kate with a secret smile.

Ignoring this, Katerina pressed her sister-in-law. "Perhaps it is because I am indeed a woman and do not understand, but why would the Lord create a thing without a meaning? Why put Evil into the world to no purpose?"

"The purpose is to test us."

"Not us," corrected Elena Castelbarco. "Men."

Katerina seemed to grow taller in her seat. "Is it fair, then, that we suffer judgment? Do not women go to Heaven, to Hell?"

"We do," answered Giovanna, equally erect. "But we are judged for our relations to men, not for ourselves. Notice in Dante's trip to Hell, sinful women are in the ranks of the adulterers, not among the heretics or the betrayers. We do not suffer the worst torments, because we are incapable of great things without the men we tie ourselves to. We are either anchors around our husbands' necks, or else wings strapped to their feet. There is no higher cause than the advancement of our men."

"I am stunned to hear you think so poorly of our sex," answered Katerina. "Myself, I know a good number of women who deserve to suffer in those lowest rings. Women may betray more than simple fidelity. We are none of us so shallow that we cannot burn."

Giovanna's lips were thin. "Nor so deep that we might escape it."

The tension was thick. Cangrande's wife and sister were locked in stares, strained smiles etched deep into their features. Elena deliberately continued her yarnwork while a grinning Kate waited for the first blow to be thrown. That stupid little bint Gianozza looked confused, the debate far above her ability to understand.

There was a slight sniffle from Suor Beatrice. "I am sorry to have caused a disagreement. I am fine, only – I did not sleep, and I am a little unwell."

"Poor dear!" sighed Gianozza feelingly. "You should drink something."

"A little food and wine would do us all well." At their hostess' signal, low tables were produced laden with breads and fruits and finely-presented roast fowls. Apparently the women were to eat here on the loggia. Again, unusual. The Scaliger eschewed the separation of the sexes at table, preferring a more celebratory air – though certainly he did not temper his conversation to suit female ears. Tessa wondered how deep the siblings' hatred went, that all the women were to be excluded to keep Cangrande from his sister.

Whatever the answer, his wife was complicit in his exercise in exclusion. Which meant it fitted in to her own agenda. Even Tessa knew that when Giovanna spoke of working for the advancement of the man in her life, she was not referring to her husband. Her focus was her great-nephew, Paride, younger even than the Scaliger's bastard.

Tessa was fascinated by the politics of the nobility, moreso since she had married into it. Her family was in trade. There was even a rumour, spread no doubt by her husband, that the Scaliger's heir was to marry her little Giulietta. Which meant that Tessa might be grandmother to some future prince of Verona. A heady thought.

Donna Katerina did not allow the introduction of food to dim the discussion of the role of women. "How far is a woman allowed to go to uphold the men in her life? May she break customs? Laws? Commandments? There are women who, after the loss of their husbands, have dressed in armour and led soldiers in the field to protect her son's lands. Is that a sin?"

"I hear the voice of experience," said Giovanna. "Haven't you yourself adopted male dress?"

"Old stories are often exaggerated."

"That is hardly a denial."

One result of her stroke was that Katerina's smile was crooked. "Neither is it a confession. I have no desire to be burned at the stake for flouting God's design. All I will say is that I have ever worked to advance the interests of the men in my life. Again I ask, is that sinful?"

"It is, if you desire to behave so. I believe a woman may act from necessity, but not for personal glory. That was Eve's fault."

Donna Katerina made a face. "Why is it that when we speak of women, we invariably return to one of two examples? Eve and the Madonna."

"Exactly," agreed the red-headed Kate beside her. "A woman who acted, however wrongly, and a woman around whom things happened."

"Blasphemy," muttered Elena Castelbarco.

Giovanna da Svevia shifted her gaze. "Suor Beatrice, your father called Eve praesumptuosissima, did he not? The most presumptuous."

It was the stupid whore that answered. "Dante even insisted the Bible was mistaken, that it was Adam who spoke first, not Eve. He felt that such a defining act must have been performed first by a man. And I agree!"

Oh stop talking, porca puttana! It doesn't matter how much literature you memorize if you don't understand it!

"Eve was among the first that Christ lifted from Hell at the harrowing," said Kate. "Meaning he thought her worthy of redemption – free from sin."

Elena shook her head. "There is only one woman without sin. The Madonna was created by the immaculate conception – a birth without sin. Only a sinless woman was fit to receive the Holy Spirit. Eve sinned, and was forgiven. The difference is enormous."

"I wonder," said Donna Katerina. "Is Eve damned for biting the apple? Or for convincing Adam to do so? If she alone had eaten of the tree, would she be as reviled as she is? Or was it that she caused her husband's fall from grace that blackened her so thoroughly? If that is so, she is as defined by her husband as the rest of us."

"Of course she is defined by him," said the idiot. "She was born from his rib."

"If we are defined by our husbands," demanded Kate, "what does that say for Suor Beatrice? She has forsaken men. Is she thus useless?"

Elena was utterly scandalized. "Suor Beatrice has undertaken to serve the greatest husband of all. She is a bride to Christ, and works to advance His interests through the holy Church."

Kate turned. "Suor Beatrice, whose side do you take? Eve's, or the Madonna's?"

Suor Beatrice looked more ill than ever. "I take no side. We are all at the – the mercy of men. So they will always define us. But Eve defined Adam as well. And Christ could not have existed without Maria." She seemed to be struggling with something, a thought she couldn't quite articulate. "It is better to sacrifice your all for a man you love than to watch him fail. Love is the key. God is love. Christ died to prove his love of us. We must not sacrifice our selves for anything less. But if we love... if we love, how can we not sacrifice?"

Kate was nodding. "Exactly! What I said before, a partnership. A woman's power comes from the man in her life – the lord bestows the keys upon his wife, creating her as chatelaine. Yet the man cannot exist without the woman. Setting aside the basic act of birth, what great man did not have a woman to guide him?"

"Excellent points, both," said Donna Katerina. "Tessa, you've been silent so far. Do you have a contribution?"

Tessa felt herself flush. Katerina was talking down to her, when in reality they were the ones being childish. She told them so. "This is inappropriate."

Katerina raised her eyebrows as Giovanna said, "What is, dear?"

Tessa's mouth turned down, creating a mulish expression. "All of this – talk. This is a debate fit only for men. It is unwomanly. Forgive me, but I am sure that

Suor Beatrice does not endure such – such prideful talk in the convent."

Katerina's smile was infuriating. "Perhaps we should return to reading. It was less contentious."

"So long as we have a man come in to read to us," added Kate, clearly baiting Tessa further.

Steeling herself, Tessa turned to address their hostess. That shows them! "Lady, please let me thank you again for the summer bonnet you sent my daughter. It is adorable."

Giovanna looked amused, but the conversation was clearly behind them. "And how is little Giulietta?"

Precocious. Demanding. Willful. Aloud she said, "Well, thank you. She doesn't cry as much as I expected, which is pleasant. And she is walking."

"Already?" Genuine surprise showed on every face.

"Yes, too early, it seems. She keeps walking into doors and walls. She hasn't learned yet not to—"

She was interrupted by a shout outside, quickly followed by another, then the unmistakable crack of a blow. As one, the ladies rushed to open the curtains to look down into the Piazza dei Signori.

In the center of the public square a massive elderly black man was wielding a curved sword, threatening a dozen men who advanced on him with clubs and staves. Suor Beatrice muttered a foreign-sounding name. Squinting, Tessa could tell that it was indeed the Moor who had invaded her home last fall, the day Susanna had died. The astrologer, a dabbler in heathen magics and dark arts. She feared for the men he was attacking.

Fortunately, they had him at bay. He hadn't yet unsheathed his great curved sword, nor was he doing more with the scabbarded weapon than to fend off jabs and thrusts from the men surrounding him. After a moment even Tessa could tell he was not the aggressor in this fight, more the pity.

"Damned Moor!" cried the leader of the mob, swinging an arm-length hunk of timber.

"For Bursa!" cried another, and together with three others rushed at the Moor. More men followed until there was such a crush of bodies that Tessa was certain that the Moor could not survive.

"Why don't they do something?" demanded Suor Beatrice, pointing to the soldiers dressed in Scaligeri livery. Though they recognized the Moor, the palace guards were just standing and watching. Good for them, thought Tessa. Let the heathen sorcerer die!

The doors beneath their loggia opened and men came spilling out of the palace – Cangrande, his arm still in a sling. Katerina's bear-like husband, Bailardino Nogarola. Kate's long-haired wild-man, Petruchio Bonaventura. Elena's husband, Lord Castelbarco. And, side-by-side, Tessa's husband and his nemesis, Lord Montecchio.

From above, she identified them mostly by hair and build. Not that she would recognize Lord Montecchio – she only knew him from the fresco vilifying him on the wall of their house, and the painting was obviously an injustice. Everyone said he was handsome, but Antony was quite careful that his wife never had congress with the 'bride-thief', lest she too might fall for his charms. Tessa knew he had hair as dark as his wife's, whereas Antony's was ugly, the colour of sand. But Antony was quite the bigger of the two, strong and muscular, whereas Montecchio was lean, though by no means weak. The difference between a destrier and a courser.

At their backs came squires and lesser knights. Mastino and his brother Alberto. The handsome German, Fuchs. Jacopo Alaghieri, brother of Suor Beatrice. Cangrande's second cousin, young Paride…

And there was the Greyhound's heir, little Cesco. She'd heard of his magnificent head of curls, but they'd been shorn away before she had ever laid eyes on him. What little hair he was allowed was chestnut coloured.

At his side was Bailardetto, Katerina's elder son. Like his friend, he had chosen to be called by a diminutive – Detto. The black-haired Detto was Bailardino's son, Bonaventura's squire, and Cesco's close friend. That last meant that Tessa didn't care for him, either.

The men paused for only a heartbeat upon the threshold of the square, taking in the action before them. They shouted orders, but the guards played deaf – though, in fairness, the enclosed piazza was now filled with noise.

Typically, the Greyhound's bastard didn't wait for anyone else to act. Running forward, he kicked the nearest brawler in the knees. The man fell forward and Cesco stepped onto his back and launched himself flying at a descending club.

"Cesco!" For the first time today, Suor Beatrice seemed wholly present. Tessa was forced to admit the boy had courage – close to her age and hardly bigger than she, yet he threw himself into the thick of the scrum. Mid-leap, he grasped the arm holding the club at both elbow and wrist. What happened next Tessa was later able to reconstruct with Thibault, leafing through his collection of fightbooks. Using his right forearm, Cesco pushed down on the brawler's elbow while his left hand pushed up on the wrist holding the club. The bent elbow brought the club up to meet the man's nose, which shattered in a spray of blood. Twisting around like a spinning top, Cesco came away with the club, which he immediately applied to another man's knee.

The heathen Moor called out something. Though the words were foreign, the intent was clear: Leave me. But Cangrande's bastard only laughed and continued to lay about him with his stolen club.

Tessa felt a pressure at her arm and noted the presence of Katerina della Scala beside her. She expected the woman to shout out as Suor Beatrice had. Instead, Katerina merely watched as Cesco used his club in a series of sweeping arcs that reached up and over his head to ward off any blows, ending in low blows at knees and hips.

Tessa felt a new source of jealousy, again for her beloved Thibault's sake. Though Thibault was of an age to become someone's squire, her husband refused to let him train. Whereas the Scaliger was flouting convention and training his own boy. Everyone had heard tales of the hard, grueling fall and winter the boy had endured, ending in the Scaliger's wound.

Now the effects of that training could be seen. The young bastard was a whirlwind of motion, striking down men twice his size and three times his age. One man lifted a stave and sent a pair of strikes at the boy's shoulder and knee. Cangrande's heir dodged the stave's tip by leaning out of the way, then caught the blow to his knee with the back of his club. Slight as he was, he somehow muscled the butt end of the stave up and around to strike another brawler on the ear. The man holding the stave now had his back to Cesco, but couldn't turn because of the crush. The boy pitched the club at the back of the man's head. The brawler crumpled.

Grasping the falling man's stave, Cesco started jabbing, pushing, and swinging it until he cleared a little room behind him, taking up a stance at the Moor's back. He shouted something in a heathen tongue. This time the bruised and bloodied Moor said nothing, but together the two began to wheel, each one stepping to his right. The image that presented itself to Tessa's mind was of the innards of one of her father's windmills – three separate sets of circles in constant motion. The first set of circles was the Moor's blade, still in its scabbard, making the shape of an 8 in the air before him. The second was the stave in Cesco's hands, describing two halves of the same arc. The third was made by the pair of them walking in step, warding off the attackers as they edged towards the noblemen on the periphery of the square.

The Scaliger's bastard was calling out taunts and jeers, and Tessa almost laughed as he paid for his temerity when one brawler struck him on the ear.

Suor Beatrice cried out, and below so did young Detto, until now restrained by his father's grip. With a howl, Detto broke free and hurled himself into the fray. Only eleven years old, he was far more solid than Cesco, and in his fury he needed no weapons to knock adults aside to reach his friend.

Young Paride started forward to aid Detto. "Paride!" shouted Donna Giovanna, his great-aunt, from the loggia window. He stopped and twisted around to look up at her, eyes wide. "Don't you dare risk your life for that creature! Stand off!" Amusingly, Paride obeyed, hastening to stand with his back to the palace wall.

Detto's fury kept him from fighting rationally, and he was elbowed in the face. That brought a cry from the boy's mother and father both. His son having been struck, Lord Nogarola bodily lifted the three men who separated him from Detto off their feet, pitching them into their fellows. Petruchio was by his side, feeling quite as strongly about men beating his squire.

Suddenly all the nobles were wading into the mob, dispatching them with ridiculous ease. For the first time Tessa witnessed her own husband in a fight, and she was struck by how fearsome he looked, and how brave. This was something he was not too coarse for, neither too boorish nor too bold. Here in the thick of fighting, he looked manly and even handsome. He was enjoying himself! There was a smile on his face as he looked up and waved—

Not to Tessa. Antony's wave was for Gianozza Montecchio, who stood biting her knuckle and emitting squeals of fear and excitement.

Seeing the wave, Lord Montecchio threw one hapless citizen directly into Antony's back, toppling him. Tessa laughed aloud at the comical face her husband made as he went down.

Angry citizens turned to find famous faces behind the fists pummeling them. Dismayed, and fearing retribution at law, the crowd dispersed, running pell-mell for the four exits to the open-air piazza.

The whole fray had lasted only three minutes, perhaps less. Cangrande's bastard was bleeding but still on his feet, Detto beside him, holding a hand over his own eye and laughing. Sagging, the Moor grasped Castelbarco's arm as he was led indoors. The guards, roused to their work at last, cleared the square and made their limp excuses to the Scaliger.

He alone had not participated in the fight. Perhaps it was due to his arm. Perhaps it was that he didn't wish to tarnish his reputation by saving a heathen from a richly deserved beating. Or perhaps he wanted to observe how his heir handled himself.

Their hostess turned away from the balcony rail. "We should see to their injuries. And hear their tales, so as not to injure their pride."

The women all turned to go, Gianozza breathlessly in the lead. Tessa had absolutely no desire to take part in the coming scene. Gianozza would fuss over Lord Montecchio, while Tessa's husband would play the fool to attract her attention. Tessa herself would be forgotten. Better to retrieve her weaving and wait to be summoned. He would be angry, but better that than subjecting herself to playing a role in the farce that awaited below.

Stepping behind the screen to where they had been sitting, Tessa was surprised to hear someone returning to the loggia. Two someones, from their voices.

The first was Suor Beatrice, who was saying, "...should be seeing to Cesco."

The second voice belonged to Donna Katerina. "He's fine, and won't thank us for fussing over him as we would a child. However hard this 'hawking' has been, its effect showed most clearly."

"He was always skilled," answered Suor Beatrice. "His hawking has made him weaker."

"For the short-term. In time it will be his strength. But that is not the reason I wished to speak to you."

Suor Beatrice sounded apprehensive. "Yes?"

"You may have heard that I've been trying to see our Cesco. But my brother has prevented my being alone with the boy. He suspects me of some treacherous design. In our ongoing war, Cesco is less a pawn than the Queen, to be guarded at all times. To possess Cesco is to be the victor, so we spare each other no quarter."

"No quarter," echoed Suor Beatrice. There was a brief silence. "Why do you want to see Cesco? What do you wish to tell him?"

"I wish to give him a weapon. One that will strengthen his resolve, help him endure his trials. I offered once before, and he refused. But I would like to renew the offer. Will you tell him that? That I wish to arm him against his tormentor?"

Suor Beatrice was reluctant. "It may lose something in the telling."

"I will write you a letter, then, which you may pass to him the next time you see him. He does sneak off to visit you, no?"

"Does – how many…is it common knowledge?"

"Certainly not," said Katerina. "But my brother suspects, as do a few others. The boy has few bolt-holes in the city. You are an obvious source of comfort to him."

"Obvious," repeated Suor Beatrice dully.

"Are you well?" Katerina seemed genuinely concerned.

Suor Beatrice's answer was brisk. "Perfectly. Write your letter and I will give it to him. This once. I do not intend to be a courier between you."

"I understand, and I thank you. You shall have it by this evening. Now, shall we visit our triumphant boys and revel in their glory?"

Tessa remained still for a time after they had gone, absently closing the ends on the little loom in her hands. Then she emerged from behind the screen and drifted closer to the window, gazing out at the afternoon sky.

Interesting. Katerina wanted access to Cesco. Access Cangrande was loath to grant. A weapon? Tessa wished she could ask her husband about it, but he wouldn't know. Or if he did, he wouldn't tell her. She would have to discuss it with Thibault.

Six

For several days after the brawl in the street, Antonia's routine was exactly as it had been, but her distraction kept her from understanding when others spoke to her. Mistakes were made in the copying, and she avoided the solitude of the monastery library entirely Every male voice seemed to resonate with the calm, businesslike violence of her rapist.

She felt outside herself, and there was a dark part of her that wanted to scoff at her own reactions. Her first thought after he'd left was that she did not have the energy to be a victim. She knew for a certainty she had done nothing wrong. This had been a calculated assault on Cesco. She was only a side issue. Somehow that was more insulting. Whoever he had been, it hadn't been about the sex but the violence.

As smart as she was, she tried talking herself out of everything she was feeling, and grew disgusted with herself when she could not put those wretched feelings aside.

On the sixth night after the event (that was how she counted time now, how many days since she had been attacked, how many hours since her virtue had been torn from her), Cesco reappeared. Exhausted as ever, his inquiry after her health seemed perfunctory. She made a fuss over him, passed along Katerina's note, and let him sleep again in her arms.

By the mid-night bells he was gone. She walked shakily to join the other sisters in prayer, but when the chanting was over she did not return to her bed. She remained on her knees in the chapel all through the night, right up to Prime, every noise jolting her from fervent prayer. When the sun rose, she felt victorious.

The next night she locked her door and wedged a chair against it. She was awakened by a weight on top of her, a filthy cloth shoved into her mouth. This time there was real violence to the attack. She tried to fend him off with the knife she'd carried for seven days, but he took it from her with contemptuous ease and held it against her throat. This night he stayed to assault her twice more, in different ways. She wept and fought and screamed futilely into the rag. He said nothing, which somehow made it all the more horrible. His occasional grunts and the violence of his body spoke for him.

She was rescued by the bells, when he lifted her to her feet and shoved her bleeding and fouled into the hall. When she finally had nerve to return to her cell, he was gone. Yet their mingled scents lingered in the air, making her retch.

That day she almost asked Abbess Verdiana to move her into the common cells with the other sisters. Yet she refrained. It would remove her from danger, yes. But so too would it remove any possibility of Cesco finding her alone. She sat in her cell all day, turning the matter over and over in her mind until she felt faint.

No quarter. It was a message. Not for her, she wasn't important enough. For Cesco. He was to be allowed no respite, no relief.

Could she tell anyone? Tharwat or Morsicato would protect her, surely. The stealthy Moor might even be able to trap her rapist and murder him as he slipped out. But if this was done by Cangrande's orders – something she couldn't rule out – the repercussions would be endless. The murder would give the Scaliger a pretext to remove the Moor, thus stripping away another layer of Cesco's protection. And who was to say it would end with the man's death? She couldn't even be certain it was the same man between the first and second nights.

Worst of all, Cesco might learn of it. This was something her brilliant boy did not need on his conscience. Despite his nature, she harboured no doubt of his love for her. She feared that this might achieve what the hawking had not – break his spirit.

No quarter.

Could she tell Abbess Verdiana? No. Perhaps her own abbess, whose bark was far worse than her bite. But this old woman, as suspicious as she was concerned with reputation, would certainly repudiate her and throw her out, not only from the nunnery but from the Order entirely.

She knew Pietro would come to her aid in an instant. But if her brother returned to Verona, he'd find a price on his head within the month. Poco was preparing for his new training, in Florence of all places, and would depart at the start of July, after the tourney. Though he would surely stay if asked, she could not imagine telling him.

She pondered telling Fra Lorenzo, but after some thought ruled it out, too. What could he do, an herbalist friar? Unless it was to give her a draught of some potion to ease her nights between. That, at least, she could ask for. She had already called upon him for the means of ridding herself of any pregnancy, claiming it was for someone else. Her character was such that he did not doubt her.

At noon she roused herself for prayers, working hard on her grooming before emerging from her cell. Her attacker had been careful – her bruises were all in places that did not show. Only her haggard, sleepless, fearful eyes betrayed her.

At Vespers that night she joined the other sisters in singing a theody, the second psalm of the hour, the hundred and twenty-third of the bible. Mechanically, she sang:

Nisi quia Dominus erat in nobis, dicat nunc Israel:
nisi quia Dominus erat in nobis.

But the next lines shook her from her thoughts, and a trembling purpose filled her as she sang.

When men rose up against us:
perhaps they had swallowed us alive.
When their fury was angry against us:
perhaps water had swallowed us.
Our soul hath passed through a brook:
perhaps our soul had passed
through an intolerable water.
Blessed be our Lord:
which hath not given us for a prey to their teeth.
Our soul as a sparrow is delivered
from the snare of the fowlers.
The snare is broken: and we are delivered.

Tears on her cheek, she found her voice. She would not be done in by this. She would rescue Cangrande's falcon from the snare. If solace was denied Cesco in every other quarter, she would continue providing it.

No matter the cost.

A balmy midnight, the thirtieth day of June. Being the eve of the tourney, the Scaliger hosted a feast for the visiting knights, and there were preliminary jousts, premieres commençailles, to whet the crowd's appetite.

Thus Cangrande was too busy to keep a strict eye on his heir. Longing to watch the events, Cesco used this time to slip away to a deserted cellar chamber of the palace, just off the old Roman baths. Concealed in a corner with his tallow candle, he huddled down to write a long letter to Uncle Pietro in Avignon.

Typically, he began with a bit of news utterly divorced from his immediate self:

> From Egypt has come a crushing blow to the scholars of antiquity. The Lighthouse of Alexandria, fabled in poem, song, and story, is no more. Wholly functional for over a thousand years, the marble edifice was leveled in an earthquake. Those Veronese familiar with the authors of ancient Rome are pulling their imaginary togas over their heads to mourn.
>
> But their dour spirits can do nothing to dim the excitement surrounding this

tourney. The Scaliger is not participating, due to his eternal injury. He's certainly playing a minor wound for all it's worth. I believe he'd let it fester if he didn't fear losing the whole arm. Perhaps he plans to mimic his sister and experience a miraculous recovery when least expected. Though after rising from the dead last year, he's set the bar rather high.

Speaking of Detto's mother, I believe I already mentioned the invitation I received through our beloved Suor Beatrice, promising me a weapon to use in my hawking to ward off my tormentor. A greater lure was never known and I confess I was curious. But I put off answering for almost a fortnight so I could parse the underlying intent. You haven't yet told me why you harbour such deep suspicions of her, but I imagine she must be very like her brother, since it was she who raised him. You say she raised me as well in my first few years, a time I barely remember. But I find myself mirroring you – I don't trust her.

Divining her invitation had a motive other than my welfare, I determined to lay a trap for them both. I called on Donna Katerina yesterday, during the night. I did not tell her I was coming, I just climbed in through the second floor window – as her house was the scene of my convalescence last summer, I remember it well. I found her alone, reading, though I suspect she had been waiting for me every night this last month. She greeted me and we bantered as you might expect. It was a type of dueling I've learned well, but she has mastered it. Yet I learned a great deal even before we reached the topic of the weapon.

She broached the subject obliquely, asking what I knew of astrology. I informed her that I was raised in close proximity to one of the foremost astrologers in all the world, and dull as I am I had picked up a few tricks. She then asked me if I knew my birthdate. I said I knew the month, but not the day. Oh, did I not tell you, Nuncle? Yes, I know I was born under the sign of Gemini. So much for your efforts to keep it a secret. But she offered to tell me the day, and produced several scrolls.

I can see you stiffening as you read this. Why? Do you know what is in those scrolls? I think you do. I think they are the reason you've kept me in the dark as to the date of my emergence into the world. Well, Nuncle, you may relax. I never saw what was charted in them, for at that precise moment we were interrupted by the Capitano.

This was my trap, you see. I thought I might learn more in witnessing a failed attempt at secrecy, so I allowed myself to be trailed to her door. I was alone with her for all of five minutes before Cangrande himself was demanding entrance.

Not that he was anything less than his suave self. And we were not there long. He clouted me on the ear for neglecting my duties, then chided his sister for 'seducing the boy as you seduced his keeper.' Does that refer to you? Now that's a story I long to hear! I hope it is salacious, but somehow I doubt it.

Rather, I imagine Donna Katerina was the woman you loved from afar who had feet of clay. You've hinted as much.

It might seem that my snare was a failure, but not so. I learned more from the Capitano's face than I could from a hundred scrolls. When he saw those rolls of parchment, the air seemed to drain from the room. So my star-charts frighten and enrage him. Interesting. It is indeed a weapon – though one I must be careful about using. As long as he believes I have not read them, he will treat me carefully. If I do read them, as Katerina desires, I may gain a weapon only to lose the war. A threat is far superior to a blow. Ask Damocles.

Thus you may rest assured, the secret is still a secret. For the moment. If the Scaliger hawks me too hard, I may resort to perusing those scrolls. I suppose it lies in my stars.

Cesco laid his quill aside and flexed his fingers. The cypher came so easily to him he barely had to think of the encoding. Instead his mind was engaged with the matter of his birthday, which Katerina had in fact let slip. June 15th. Passed unremarked just two weeks earlier, it meant he was now twelve years old. Infuriatingly, the extra year had added very little to his height.

It was thanks to Mastino that he could fix the month of his birth. A year ago, just a fortnight after he'd arrived in Verona, he'd been introduced to a lady with an odd lilting accent. Donna Maria. Taking her for one of Katerina's attendants, Cesco had ignored her words until Mastino informed him that this Maria was in fact his mother. Since then he'd reconstructed the conversation until he had it sound for sound, gesture for gesture.

You must have been born under it to have such a strong attraction.

Mercurio. He suits you, my boy.

Mercury, the ruling planet of the Gemini sign. Cesco reached into his shirt and withdrew a collection of rough astrological charts. They'd been sketched in darkness during snatches of stolen time. Each bore the mark of Gemini. Most were now useless – and damning. If Cangrande found them, he would assume Cesco had indeed seen Katerina's charts. Reluctantly, Cesco put his hard work to the candle's flame and set them alight.

Picking up his quill, he continued to write:

It does make me wonder, why more than one chart? Surely I was only born once! Or was I put back in the oven like an unfinished loaf of bread? One would think my mother would have objected. I must ask Morsicato if he has heard of such a thing – if I ever see him. He's in Vicenza still, doting on his wife. She doesn't improve, doesn't decline. She exists in a state of discomfort. In that way—

He almost finished the line with 'she is like Suor Beatrice.' But he instead made a reference to himself and his hawking, still debating making mention of his growing concern for his Auntie Antonia. Over the last couple weeks Suor Beatrice had turned sour. Oh, not towards him! If anything she was over-enthusiastic for his presence, coddling him, covering him with unaccustomed kisses and hugs.

But there was a new furtiveness to her behavior, an unwelcome timidity in her eyes. I wonder if Fra Lorenzo knows what the matter is. Sadly, he and the good friar were not on the best of terms at present. Encountering him that morning, they had passed bland words, until suddenly the Franciscan had grabbed Cesco's face in his hands, pulling at his eyelids. Cesco had recoiled, hands beating the friar away. But the holy man had seen everything he needed. "I know that look in the eyes. You're a lotus-eater."

"Names are unkind, Frater. All things in balance. It is part of a discipline I learned at the foot of one of my many keepers. I applaud you for your perspicacity."

"Does your doctor know?"

"Yes. He, too, disapproves. But how else can I endure my hawking? Herakles couldn't have done it, and he was half a god. Have no fear, I know the risks."

"I doubt it." Lorenzo's voice had been grave. "If you continue, you will abuse it, and it will consume you."

"Too late." Flushed with anger, Cesco had stormed off. He needed no reminding of his failures. They lived in him, he carried them everywhere.

Deeply concentrated on recalling that scene, Cesco almost missed the sound of steps approaching. He stashed the sheet he was writing upon. Since there was no swift way to dispose of inks and quills, he had another sheet prepared. Like the one he'd been labouring upon, it was written in code. But this code was of his own devising. Early on he had simply written gibberish, but as time passed he decided that should he ever be discovered penning secret messages, they should at least be entertaining. So the fake coded letter was addressed to the Emperor Komenos of Trebizond, and related to a matter of gardening that, read properly, had a delicious double meaning.

The footsteps stopped and there was a knock on the door. Meaning it was not Cangrande, who would never ask permission. "Come." Tharwat entered and Cesco pulled a face. "You allowed me to hear you."

"You deserve as much privacy as you can earn." The Moor did not ask to whom Cesco wrote. He probably already knew.

"Let me put a seal on this." Cesco produced the genuine letter, rolled it neatly, then poured wax from the tallow candle to form a rough seal. Leaning forward, he used the coin at his neck to impress the wax. There was no other like it that he knew of. Pietro would know the letter was genuine.

Sitting back, Cesco handed the roll of paper to the Moor. "There. You can take it to Ser Alaghieri yourself."

Tharwat frowned. "I will see it sent."

"No, you will hand it to him."

The Moor shook his head. "I am not leaving."

"Three attacks in as many weeks. The last time the mob handed Cangrande an official petition for your head."

"He declined."

"This time. But he wants you gone, far away from me. I would be surprised if the petition wasn't his idea."

"All the more reason to stay. Besides, the tourney begins tomorrow."

"Exactly. The city teems with men, all of them good Christians, all of them with a taste for blood – they're here for a tourney after all."

"You are scheduled to joust. You ask me to leave you in peril."

"No, I'm telling you to leave because you're in peril. If you stay, you will certainly be attacked. By men who won't be content to come after you with clubs and staves."

"It is nothing I have not endured in the past."

"You're wrong. Bursa has changed everything. It may die down, in time. Ludwig will start a war with the Pope, or France will invade England. But at the moment everyone is mourning the loss of yet another Christian city. Even if you were not a Moslem, your skin marks you as heathen. You needs must leave."

"I will not."

"Of course you don't think so. But if you stay you'll be killed."

Tharwat was ever obstinate. "I will not leave you."

"You will if I ask you to. Don't fret for me. I have Suor Beatrice for occasional respite, and the doctor in extremis. Now go, and Allah guide you." Cesco made the Islamic salute from heart, head, and spirit. Then he held out the scroll.

Tharwat al-Dhaamin stood entirely still for a full minute, his eyes unfocused. Or perhaps they were focused on something Cesco could not see. At last he stretched out a hand and took the scroll. "Very well. I will see the doctor. You must have a continued supply of hashish."

"He won't like that."

"All must endure the vicissitudes of fate. His burden will not tax him beyond his endurance." Moving to leave, the Moor paused. In his painful rasp he spoke in Arabic. "Thou once asked a question."

The boy matched the switch of tongues. "Once only? How very incurious I am."

"Almost a year past, I offered thee an answer to any question thou couldst devise."

"And I posed to thee what question I would be wisest to ask. My memory has not suffered the trials my stomach has."

"I have thy answer."

Cesco leaned back and folded his arms behind his head. "Oh?"

"Truly if I wore thy skin, I wouldst ask what occurred to make Cangrande send you to Ravenna with Ser Alaghieri."

Cesco's lips formed a kind of half-frown. Unconsciously he switched back to Italian. "A man kidnapped me, and Pietro was the one who... No. Clearly not. Your face speaks volumes." Fatigue forgotten, the boy rose and began to pace. "But then why would – no, there's more. Why that question, if it doesn't lead to where I should go?"

"I cannot tell you more than I have."

"Sworn to secrecy?"

"Yes," said the Moor. "I am."

Cesco's smile grew. "Thank you again. Quite a bargain – two clues at the cost of one."

Seven

Verona
1 July 1326

Trumpets blared a volley to shake the skies, nine hundred ninety-nine singers raised their voices, and a cheer echoed off the stone walls of the fabled Arena of Verona. The tourney had begun!

'Tourney' was the name popularly given to competitions of chivalry, mock fights staged for sport. The name itself was born two hundred years before, thanks to the accidental death of Count Henri III of Brabant during a sportful meeting between his knights and those of the castellan of the city of Tournai. The monks at the nearby church of St. Martin recorded the event, and forever after the name of the town was associated with daring military sport.

Verona's tourney was planned as a two-day spectacle of martial prowess. After the initial entertainments – a play, a mime, etc – the first day would consist wholly of jousting, while the second day would be split into two separate parts. In the morning there would be a series of wrestling matches, open to all comers. Unlike the jousts, solely available to the nobility who could afford the gear, the wrestling matches were open to every citizen of Verona, be he base or proud. A fine tradition, mirroring Verona's famous Palio, the twin races held during Lent. The horse race was exclusive, the footrace was not. Cangrande had decided this was an excellent precedent to follow.

Yet it was the second afternoon that held the greatest attraction, the one everyone came to see: the mêlée, a general engagement of two 'armies' battling for each other's standard. Blades would be bated, their edges dulled, and the horses muzzled so they did not bite the flower of nobility as they engaged in the most exciting and deadly of sports.

That loomed on the morrow. Today was the time for individual knights and squires to distinguish themselves.

In most tourneys, including the frequent jousts in France, the main events would be held outside the city walls, where stands could be erected for spectators. Verona needed no such arrangements. It held the Arena. Built by the Romans of antiquity, the massive marble edifice was Dante's inspiration for the design of Hell – not the insult it seemed. Neatly perfect concentric circles created order out of the chaos of thousands of bodies crammed into one place. Like everything Roman, the Arena was perfectly engineered to hold the entire population of the city, a full twenty thousand souls, and still have room on the steps for a few thousand more.

Naturally it occurred to the Capitano that this would be an opportune occasion for foes to launch a sneak attack. With so many foreign knights inside the city walls, it might prove too great a temptation for his many enemies. Especially as they could rid themselves of all opprobrium by claiming they were helping to overthrow a heathen excommunicant. Not that he suffered deprivations for his unholy status. The Bishop of Verona knew upon which side his cheese was toasted.

Still, it behooved the Scaliger to take precautions, such as manned barricades down major streets, or deadlines disguised as garlands. Deadlines were barbed ropes or chains hung at the level of a mounted man's neck, well clear of the thronged citizens below. A knight riding at full tilt had been known to lose his head due to a deadline.

The east side of the Arena was reserved for foreigners, the west for native Veronese. This meant that the natives would be squinting into the sun during the play, but would have a better view of the jousts. Citizenship should have privileges.

North and south above the entrances were kept for the nobility. Cangrande had ordered massive awnings to shield the more august members of the crowd from the merciless summer sun.

Ser Giuseppe Morsicato, knight, doctor, and man of many parts, sat under one such awning feeling grateful for the innovation, as his bald head fried like an egg if left out too long. Dressed in his formal robes of crimson, his matching doctor's cap was not designed to be practical, hanging long and limp, sliding off his head the moment he began to sweat.

He'd aged this last winter and he knew it. There were bold streaks of silver in his new beard. He still mourned the loss of his old one, the product of years of careful grooming, and despaired of ever again achieving so fine a fork.

It was because of the damned Moor that he had shaved his face, and it was due to the same man that Morsicato was not now by his wife's side, where he belonged. Al-Dhaamin had appeared at his gate in the small hours of the morning, steam rising from his clothes and horse. The animal was about to collapse, meaning Tharwat had ridden it past hope of recovery. Tharwat, who'd raised the creature from a foal in Ravenna.

The sight of the blighted horse impressed the doctor with the urgency of the Moor's errand. "What's the matter? Poison again?"

"In private." Tharwat pushed past the doctor and waited until the servants were dismissed before saying another word. "He has dismissed me."

"Cangrande?"

"Cesco. Out of concern for my safety, he has sent me to Ser Alaghieri in Avignon."

Morsicato's jaw dropped. "Avignon? Isn't that exchanging stocks for a noose? The fervor there must be even greater!"

"Avignon is close to Spain. A man of my skin will pass more easily, at least as a slave. But the timing is unfortunate. Tomorrow he jousts for the first time. He needs one of us there, in case of a crisis."

"Do you know of any danger? I mean, besides a twelve-year-old jousting."

"I have read the stars. He will not die, but there is injury in his near future. He will need your services."

"Fracastoro is there," said Morsicato, referring to Cangrande's personal physician. "He can manage. I cannot leave my wife."

"Is she worsening?"

"It changes day to day. Some are better than others. Nothing I do seems to matter."

"Whereas what you can do for the boy may matter very much." The doctor frowned at the harshness, a frown that only deepened as Tharwat added, "He also will need a new supply of hashish. You are the only man I trust to—"

"I won't!" cried Morsicato, much louder than he'd intended. Wincing, he listened for his wife, but there was only the familiar sound of her cough from above. Fixing the Moor with a steely eye, he continued in a lower tone. Lower, but not softer. "You can't ask me, a doctor, to feed the boy's addiction."

"He is not an addict," the Moor replied. "The fright last fall has made him cautious, and he actually receives a very small amount, mixed with other herbs. Hashish itself is not addictive."

"Mixed with poppies it is!"

"Can be. Which is why I require your skill. I will leave exact instructions. I tell you now, so you will not be shocked, in addition to the opiate there are a number of known poisons in the mixture. I have spent the winter building his immunity. There will never be a repeat of last July."

Morsicato was less shocked than another man might have been. Indeed, had he been in Verona he might have instituted a similar practice. But not one involving the regular consumption of this special concoction of hashish. "I won't assist you in making him a lotus eater."

"If you do not, he is certain to become one, for he will procure his own. What he finds will be far purer than the mixture I make for him, which is a recipe handed down through generations of men who studied the herb for its beneficial properties."

"Hashashins!" hissed Morsicato. "A band of killers! Using the stuff to induce a frenzy—!"

The Moor stood with his hands folded before him, immovable as a rock, determined to make his case. "Do not believe wild tales. These were professional men. It was not frenzy, but clarity, aim, and energy. All traits the boy has needed this last year."

It took time, but eventually Morsicato saw the sense in Tharwat's arguments about regulating the hashish, and once he studied the mixture he was much less vexed – it was an ingenious combination. And the doctor also saw the chance to wean the boy off the stuff for good.

Which is how Morsicato came to be sitting under an awning in the Arena, watching a religious play concerning David and Goliath. It would have taken literal torture for him to confess his secret relief to be once again in the society of men. For all their squabbling, he loved his wife very much, but he could honestly say there was nothing more he could do for her. And the Moor had made a persuasive argument. Though Morsicato was not a man to believe in the stars.

Coming late, he'd resigned himself to baking slowly in the sun. But fortune favoured him in the form of Lord Castelbarco, who found him in the crush and issued an invitation to sit under the awning just behind the Capitano's balcony. Morsicato eagerly accepted, and now they both sat on cushions in the middle tier of Veronese nobility, ignoring the play and scanning the crowd instead.

"I see a great many French colours," observed Morsicato.

"Can you blame them? Fifty years jousting has been banned in France. Most of them have to travel to England to show off their skill, and who wants to do that?"

"Is your son participating?"

"He's been in the tiltyards all month. Even persuaded me to spar with him. I'm still sore." The elder Castelbarco shook his head. "I'm too old for jousts."

"Aren't we all?" Morsicato continued to scan the crowd for banners. "No one from Padua that I can see. A shame Carrara hasn't come. I'd love to see him unhorsed."

"Too many memories here, I imagine. Besides, he has his hands quite full." They chuckled together at Padua's continuing misfortunes.

A latecomer jostled the ranks of watchers to join them. It was Jacopo Alaghieri, younger brother to

Pietro, known colloquially as Poco. A wastrel, a reveler, a failed and disgraced soldier, and eternally famous for finding the last cantos of his father's great epic. Leaving at the end of the week for his native Florence, he was tolerated for the sake of his family, and for his almost unquenchable good spirit. "Ah, la lonc sejor! I love tournament season!"

"Why aren't you with Alblivious?" demanded Castelbarco, referring to Cangrande's eldest nephew, who was Poco's fast friend.

"He's riding today. Has to, doesn't he? Does anyone have something to drink? I'm parched!"

Morsicato gestured to the servants walking the stairs with jugs and cups. "There's water in the jugs."

"I said a drink, not something to wash in." Poco settled in uninvited to join Castelbarco's party.

"I'm surprised Alberto is riding," said Castelbarco. "I can't recall him ever being in the lists before."

"He's tired of Mastino getting all the praise. He wants to be more warlike, and since there's no good war on at the moment, he'll ride today. There's as much honour to be gained in the lists as there is on the field – more, since women are watching."

"He's willing to break his skull to impress a few ladies?"

Poco laughed. "Is there any other cause worth a few knocks?"

"So why aren't you down there?" asked Castel-barco lightly.

"I don't need to impress women," said Poco with a complacent smile.

"Alberto isn't worried about his lack of—" Morsi-cato almost said skill, "—practice?"

"Nullo interveniente odio, pro solo exercitio, atque ostentatione virium," said Poco, proving he'd absorbed at least some of his father's Latin. "Not in hostility, but solely for exercise and the display of prowess. They're all perfectly safe, no?"

Castelbarco frowned. "You're a fool if you believe that. Who is he scheduled to ride against?"

"Fuchs."

"God help him."

The initial matches were all arranged well before-hand, and Cesco was listed for the later afternoon. Naturally he would not be facing off against a full-grown knight. No, his opponent was to be his friend Detto. And unlike the adults, the boys wouldn't be using the solid oak lances. Until they reached their majority – fifteen years of age or a knighthood, whichever came first – they would have to satisfy themselves with practice lances that broke apart like straws.

As the plays ended and the stages were disman-tled, Morsicato saw Cesco and Detto running together at the edges of the Arena floor, excitedly watching the events. There was something about Detto that brought out the child in Cesco, a phenomenon Morsicato was thankful for.

Having not clapped eyes on the boy in over two months, the doctor's breath hissed through his teeth. A wiry boy by nature, he now appeared to be muscle stretched over bone. But he didn't look like a victim of starvation – Morsicato had seen more than enough of those. The image that came first to the doctor's mind might have been driven by fancy. The boy looked like a greyhound, fleet and taut and light as the air.

A rail was set, the posts sunk deep into pre-dug holes at north and south. At the same time, barricades were erected, just in case a lance or horseshoe went flying. The view from the lowest seats was thus obstructed, making the poorer spectators decry their own protection. But this was standard practice for the Palio, the annual race for which the Arena was both start and finish line.

After prayers, trumpets, hymns, speeches, and cheers, the tourney began. Due to his injury, Cangrande had yielded the place of eminence to his nephew Mastino, who was to inaugurate the event in a joust with the leader of nearby Mantua, Passerino Bonaccolsi.

Morsicato was one of the few present in the Arena who knew that Bonaccolsi had twice tried to murder Cangrande and usurp his power. Cangrande's own cousin had been in league with the Mantuan leader, but Federigo's death had removed all evidence. Publicly a staunch ally of Verona, Bonaccolsi himself had no idea that Cangrande suspected his treachery. Morsicato wondered what Mastino's instructions were.

It was swiftly clear that Mastino had been told to win, but not to humiliate their chief guest. Both men scored, both kept their seats. After three passes Bonaccolsi's armour showed the worse damage and Mastino was judged the victor, meaning he would ride again later in the day against another winner.

Bonaccolsi took his defeat graciously, as he still had another joust scheduled. Out of curiosity, Morsicato asked who Bonaccolsi would face next, and was disappointed to learn it was some foreign knight from England. Then Morsicato heard the name and frowned. "Montagu? Is he—?"

"Some relation to our Montecchio, yes," confirmed Castelbarco. "Despite the troubles of his nation, he's come to meet his distant cousin and honour us with a show of English bravery. Perhaps if he wins, he can repay the loan Cangrande gave him years ago to claim his title."

"I hear the English are all drunks," said Poco dismissively, quaffing a skin of wine. Morsicato stifled a laugh. Castelbarco studied the sky. Heaven help the priests of Florence charged with his training.

The next hour was joyful, and Morsicato forgot his cares as he cheered himself hoarse with the rest of the spectators. Depending on the skill level of the combatants, the varying guisti were run with lances, swords, or axes. One man was killed, another blinded in one eye. Morsicato considered offering his services, but there were plenty of medical men in the Arena tunnels already. His duty was to watch over Cesco. Besides, he was enjoying himself for the first time all year.

Typical to a Scaligeri event, after every five or six contests the field was over-run by dancers or mummers or acrobats to relieve the tension. After a particularly skillful set of jugglers had collected their knives and torches, the heralds announced the next race, crying out the names of Alberto della Scala and Niklas Fuchs.

Alblivious lined up beneath Cangrande's balcony, while Fuchs took his place at the Arena's south end. Poco hooted and whistled, drawing a great deal of attention. Alblivious heard the whistles and turned to wave. He was so busy laughing at Poco's antics he had to be reminded to close the visor of his helmet.

The flag dropped and they were off, their horses kicking up clods of dirt. Fuchs' lance caught Alblivious in the center of his chest and lifted him clean out of the saddle. The crowd gasped as Cangrande's nephew landed in a heap, the metal on his body clanging loudly on the Arena floor.

Poco stood, ashen-faced, watching as squires and servants rushed from behind the barricades to see if this hapless member of the ruling family was still breathing. Cangrande himself leaned forward in concern.

Alblivious raised a wrist limply into the air and waved. The crowd cheered as he was carried off on a board. Poco took a moment to loudly abuse Fuchs before departing to join his friend in the catacombs below the Arena.

Poco was not the only person to abuse Fuchs. Known far and wide as a master tilter, the German was deemed unsportsmanlike to have so devastated a less-skilled opponent on the first try. Especially one so beloved as Alblivious, as much a favoured city pet as kinsman to the prince. In spite of his prodigious skill, Fuchs was hissed the rest of the day. He didn't seem to care.

More bouts, mostly among foreigners. Italian, German, English, Scottish, French, Spanish, Greek, and Polish knights and squires were in evidence, all vying for fame and glory. One knight from Brindisi found eternal glory, dying in a bad fall when he was unhorsed. Far from casting a pall on the event, the crowd's enthusiasm only heightened.

Castelbarco's son won his first series against a French squire, with honour for both. Petruchio Bonaventura, now in his middle thirties, proved he was a better hunter than tilter, losing his first bout against a Scotsman in only two tries. His unorthodox wife was vocal in her abuse of the winner, and finally her husband had to climb into the tiers above and silence her with a passionate kiss, at which the crowd cheered and cheered.

Then two names were called out that made Morsicato groan. "No! They're not—!"

"They certainly are." Castelbarco grimaced in kindred dismay. "Montecchio and Capulletto. Arranged through a proxy, as they refused to speak to each other. I imagine their go-between was Montecchio's brother-in-law, Benvenito Lenoti. He's over there."

Tracing Castelbarco's gesture, Morsicato saw Lenoti, a decent-looking fellow, seated beside his wife and son, little Benvolio. Beside Benvolio was Montecchio's five-year-old son Romeo, whose dark hair kept getting into his eyes. He looked excited, not frightened. But his mother kept trying to cover his eyes. The cause of the whole ridiculous feud, Gianozza Montecchio looked stricken, but in a theatrical way, as if that was how she was supposed to look, not how she truly felt.

That's uncharitable, the doctor told himself. Who am I to judge her? She may be truly conflicted, and she probably is genuinely upset.

Castelbarco continued to speak. "I confess I'm surprised – they've made a point of not competing against each other outside of the Palio."

"I'm surprised the Capitano is allowing it," said Morsicato as he watched Mariotto Montecchio and Antonio Capulletto take their places. "Isn't this very like dueling?"

"This is legal, he can't argue it. To be sure, he gave them a stern lecture. And he forbade anything but lances, in case they were tempted. But I think the Capitano hopes it will purge their ill humours, like a good bleeding. Or else he's just given up," added Castelbarco.

Morsicato looked around. Gianozza was now clutching her raven-haired boy tightly in her arms. The child's eyes were wide and his mouth hung a little open in anticipation, but he didn't wriggle away from his mother's grip, as Cesco would have done. Recalling what Cesco had been like at that age, the doctor wondered if it was fair to judge any other boy by that standard.

Morsicato missed the lowering of the flag, but the thunder of hoofbeats brought him around in time to witness the first pass. Both men caught the onrushing lances on their shields, to polite applause from all. Skill was only appreciated by those few who knew how. Most people came for the horrendous injuries, and were disappointed if someone was not unseated or at least bloodied.

The second and third passes were the same as the first, all skillfully deflected. No solid hits, so it was up to the men officiating to determine which knight was the victor. Based on an examination of the shields, they chose Montecchio. Capulletto stalked off in a huff while the crowd gave Montecchio a half-hearted cheer, having expected better from two men so famous for their enmity. Good show, well done, may we have some blood now please?

Morsicato glanced sideways again. Little Romeo was standing on a bench applauding wildly, while Gianozza made a show of weeping her relief. Foolish woman.

Nico da Lozzo won two of three runs against a massive Pole, and Passerino Bonaccolsi was mildly (and embarrassingly) wounded when the English Montagu's lance caught him low in the saddle. Bonaccolsi was eliminated from the competition, while others like Mastino, Fuchs, Montecchio, and da Lozzo moved on. Recalling what Castelbarco had said about Montagu owing the Scaliger money, Morsicato wondered if he might not have just witnessed that debt's repayment.

Another break in the action was called, and from out of the two opposing tunnels came a dozen unsaddled horses with acrobats on their backs. The two lines of hot-blooded steeds passed each other as the riders leapt from back to back to the awe and amazement of the crowd. The performers had olive-dark skin and were dressed in the most outlandish fashion, more like a collection of scarves than proper clothes.

All at once a figure raced out from one of the tunnels. *Dear Christ, what is the little monster doing now?* Morsicato watched as Cesco held up a hand to a passing acrobat. The performer made the mistake of ignoring him. *Humiliating for anyone, let alone the Scaliger's heir. Though they likely don't know who he is.*

They were about to learn. Morsicato watched with mingled dread and pride as Cesco grabbed the bound tail of a passing horse and kicked up his heels, swinging first to one side of the horse's rump, then the other. He had to push off hard each time to avoid being clipped by the powerful legs and their metal shoes.

On the third swing he was able to cast his pronated legs up and over the unsaddled back, laying himself sidelong across the galloping horse. He twisted around into a handstand then flipped neatly down to his feet. He was only there a scant second, though, because the acrobat whose horse this was did not appreciate being outshone by a child. He took a swipe at Cesco, who ducked and launched himself in a hands-free cartwheel onto another horse's back.

Sending sport, the other acrobats began to incorporate the intruder into their act. Picking up their rhythm, Cesco was soon flipping and diving with the rest of them. When they brought the horses into a trotting line and made a human pyramid across their backs, Cesco was put on the shoulders of the man who was the apex.

The crowd was beside itself. Most of them had heard stories of the boy's skill, but to have lived to see it…!

Morsicato's applause was less enthusiastic. He knew the cost this performance would demand, and he could almost see the opiate ring in the boy's eye. Damn Tharwat, damn Cangrande, and while you're at it, God, damn the boy as well. It was unnecessary, it was theatrical, it was foolish. In short, it was Cesco to the hilt.

The next event was affectionately known as the Children's Run, a chance for young squires to show their skill. Cesco and Detto were scheduled to be the first to run, but after that display the organizers decided to move them back a few places, giving Cesco opportunity to catch his breath.

This sent the twin sons of Petruchio Bonaventura into the lists. Both Hortensio and Petruchio the Younger resembled their father, but showed better skill than he did. In three runs, the matter was so close that it took an examination of their lances and armour to decide which of the ten-year-olds came off the better. Hortensio was adjudged the victor, and his brother congratulated him by punching him in the nose. Brawling good-naturedly, with the mocking voices of their sisters hooting them, the pair had to be carried from the Arena floor before the next run could be set up.

Castelbarco wiped tears of laughter from the crinkled corners of his eyes. "A shame! That was a contest worth wagering on. I hope they'll be allowed to take part in the wrestling tomorrow."

"After that performance, I doubt their mother will allow it," observed Morsicato, belly aching from an excess of guffaws.

Paride della Scala came trotting onto the field next. By all accounts the lad was the nicest of fellows. Great-nephew to both Cangrande and his wife, he'd perhaps had the best claim on the title of heir before Cesco had arrived. Indeed, as he was legitimate, his claim might have been better. Certainly it was stronger than Mastino's or Alberto's – they did not have the blood of Frederick the Great in their veins. The only stumbling block was his age. He'd been born in 1315, a scant eleven years before, making him a year younger than Cesco and the same age as Detto.

None of which had stopped Cangrande's wife from trying to promote his interests. With no son of her own, Paride was the only blood relative Giovanna da Svevia had left, and she was determined to put him on Verona's throne. It made Morsicato furious that such an obviously decent boy would be the object of devious schemes.

Facing Paride at the opposite end of the rail was a fellow his own age and size, with a shock of hair so blonde it was almost white. Morsicato thought he looked familiar, but couldn't attach a name to the face until the heralds cried out the names. "Paride della Scala and Theobaldo da Verona!"

Something itched Morsicato's memory. The name, the name was wrong. Not Theobaldo, but close, more Germanic...

"Thibault!" cried the doctor aloud. "That's Thibault Capulletto!"

"Antony's nephew?" asked Castelbarco, craning his neck. "I don't know that I've ever seen him. Why the devil isn't he using his proper name?"

"Probably because his uncle won't approve of him jousting. He won't let the boy be a squire, plans for him to be a religious."

"And he's here anyway?" said Castelbarco, impressed. "Good for him. But if he hasn't been practicing, he's going to lose."

"He probably knows it. It's enough for him to be here, flouting his uncle's wishes."

The riders were in place, the flag raised, when a sudden shout the volume of a thunderclap reverberated around the Arena. Antony Capulletto, still half in armour, stalked from the tunnels in a towering rage. Thibault looked desperately at the man holding the starter's flag, but it was not lowering, and Paride had turned his horse's head. There would be no charge.

Thibault remained rebelliously in the saddle, forcing Antony to physically haul him down, pull off his helmet, and twist his ears. Thus ended Thibault's first giostra, with him being marched from the Arena, howling in rage while the crowd howled with laughter.

"O, this alone is worth my aching posterior!" cheered Castelbarco, enjoying the scene.

"Yours isn't the only one that will be aching tonight," observed Morsicato. "Poor Antony – he's not having a very good day of it."

Paride was declared the victor by default, and it was finally time for Cesco's run against Detto. Morsicato leaned forward – this was, after all, the reason he was here. But everything looked well, nothing out of place. The herald called their names as they took their places. Fittingly, Cesco was on the north side, just below the Capitano's balcony. He looked splendid in armour that was fitted perfectly to his size – apparently the Scaliger hadn't indulged in the extra humiliation of dressing his heir in mean armour. Probably thought it would reflect poorly on the family. Besides, nothing could be quite as humiliating as the scene they'd all just witnessed.

Cesco scored on the first pass, his practice lance splintering marvelously. For all that they were less dangerous, there was something more dramatic in the breaking lances than in the sturdy oak ones. Morsicato wondered if it was simply the joy of visual destruction.

Detto's lance hadn't splintered, though he had connected. Not a straight hit, but a glancing one, causing the lance to break on one side and hang wobbling down. He reached the squires and servants below the Scaliger's balcony and exchanged it for a fresh one, while at the far end Cesco was doing the same. Detto twisted in the saddle to wave to his mother, but she missed the wave, busy staring at Cesco.

Both lances splintered on the second run. Because more of Detto's lance had broken, he was determined the victor. One win each, and a final run would decide who would face bloody-nosed Hortensio Bonaventura.

Again below the Scaliger's balcony, Cesco removed his helmet to speak a few words to the Capitano, and the pair of them bantered as Cesco's new lance was handed up. Morsicato couldn't hear the words, but based on the roaring laughter of those seated around the Scaliger, both were exercising their fabled wit. If wit was a weapon, those two have murdered each other a thousand times.

While replacing his helmet, Cesco's lance slipped from his grip. It fell to the earthen floor with a resounding thud. Quickly it was handed back up to him and he took his place long the rail.

Something about the lance bothered Morsicato. It was painted in the crimson and gold colours of the Scaligeri, just like the others Cesco had used. Since Cesco was resting it on his hip, the point was high in the air and the doctor could see the ball at its end. All seemed well, yet something had the doctor's palms itching.

The official raised the starting flag and Cesco and Detto lowered their lances into position. But Cesco had to fight to keep his from dipping too low. Clearly he was struggling to maintain its level.

Now the hair was standing up along Morsicato's neck and forearms. Something was very wrong, he knew it in his bones. He just didn't know what it was. He opened his mouth to shout, but just then the starter's flag came down and the crowd's cheers swallowed his warning.

As Cesco raced down the length of the Arena, his lance kept drooping lower. It was almost as if the thing was too heavy for him. But practice lances were hollow. Which meant—

"Those are real lances!"

"What?" asked Castelbarco.

"They're real! They're—" He turned back to watch the collision. Cesco must have recognized the danger, for he allowed his lance to drop off-line. He was deliberately going to miss.

But had Detto realized it? He seemed not to have. Strong for his age, Detto's lance was perfectly level, aiming directly for the armour above Cesco's heart.

Morsicato tried to calm himself. Even if Detto's lance was real, surely the blow wouldn't be fatal.

One knight has already died today, he reminded himself. And Cesco is too small to take such a blow. Morsicato glanced down at the back of the Scaliger's head. Cangrande was sitting a little straighter – he, too, had noticed something was wrong. So why wasn't he stopping them?

It was too late, the moment of impact was upon them. Cesco's lance missed entirely, and Detto's splintered upon impact, just the way it was supposed to. Morsicato felt a wave of relief. A simple mistake, giving Cesco the wrong lance...

Suddenly Cesco fell from his saddle onto the ground. Wheeling his horse about, Detto cried out in terror, and Morsicato saw a flash of metal in the stub of Detto's broken lance.

As one the crowd surged to its feet. Morsicato scrambled, shoving bodies out of his way. Reaching the bottom tier, he crashed through the space between the barricades and raced towards Cesco's limp form. Dismounted, Detto was shedding his armour as he ducked under the rail.

Leaping from the balcony, Cangrande was the first to reach Cesco's side. Morsicato arrived moments later to hear Cesco say faintly, "A scratch, just a scratch..." There was blood running down his right arm.

Together Cangrande and Morsicato got the boy's armour off of him and the doctor began to wipe away the blood, looking for the source. Detto kept murmuring, "I'm sorry, I'm sorry, I'll never joust again, dear Lord, just let him not be hurt—"

"Detto, I'm fine," said Cesco a little more heartily. "Wait – Morsicato? Whatever are you doing here?"

"Enjoying the day," replied the doctor distractedly. "Or trying to." He found the wound, a nasty cut at the base of the armpit, tapering to a slight cut on the shoulder. "Can you move the arm?"

"You're growing your beard back," observed Cesco brightly, smiling into the doctor's face.

Morsicato couldn't help an eye roll before repeating his question. Flexing, Cesco winced, but the arm moved well. "The tendons are intact. If we clean the wound, you'll keep the arm."

"Burn it clean, just in case." Cangrande was examining the scoring on Cesco's petta. The gouge on the breast-plate began just to the left of Cesco's heart and reached up to the shoulder.

"It isn't actually very deep," said Cesco. "Help me up. They have to see I'm not dead."

A crowd had formed as more nobles and professionals gathered to offer assistance. Detto and Morsicato aided Cesco to his feet. Leaning against the doctor, the boy used his good arm to wave. The crowd cheered.

"Someone's always trying to do you in," muttered Morsicato in Cesco's ear.

The boy's mouth curled. "Must be a flaw in their characters. It certainly isn't me."

"Of course not," replied Cangrande. He pointed to the remains of Detto's lance, some ten yards away. "Let me see that."

Obediently, Detto ran to fetch it, and when he returned his eyes were on the thing in his hands, blood drained from his face.

The exterior of the lance broken apart, revealing a spearhead on a truncated shaft about half the length of the lance. The hidden spearhead was cross-hatched, designed to puncture armour. It was pure luck that the blow from the ball at the lance's tip had twisted Cesco in his seat. Otherwise it would have punched a hole in Cesco's armour and straight through his chest.

Morsicato looked down at the X-shaped point and shook his head. Damn you, Tharwat. You and your stars. Must you always be right?

Eight

"They examined the rest of the lances, which took some time. Mine and Detto's were the only ones tampered with. So they finished the rest of the scheduled jousts." Cesco sat in the dark, listing off the day's events to Suor Beatrice as he lay curled at the foot of her pallet, his injured shoulder away from her gentle caresses. "Fuchs ended up taking the prize, meaning he'll be the leader of one army in tomorrow's mêlée."

Antonia was aghast. "But how was the switch made?"

Cesco laughed wryly. "The Scaliger blames me, naturally. Says the distraction of my antics with the acrobats created an opportunity to switch out the lances. It was clever, to give me a solid one with a ball on the end. Whoever it was knew I wouldn't let Detto be hurt. Thus I was sure to take the hit."

"Why not give you both real lances?"

"If they'd given Detto a real lance like mine, he would noticed and likewise missed. Instead they supplied him with a doctored practice lance." He shifted a little, lifting his chin away from the shoulder in its sling. After a quick scorching, Morsicato had slathered the injury with poultices that made Cesco wrinkle his nose.

"Is it bad?" asked Suor Beatrice in a hoarse whisper.

Cesco pulled the arm out of the sling and patted her knee. "Not nearly as bad as it might have been. I think the burning did more damage than the weapon. They're worried about poison, I think. Which is clearly ridiculous – I've already proven I have the intestinal fortitude of a hundred men."

Antonia blew out an exasperated sigh. "Cesco! Someone tried to murder you! What if they try again?"

"O, I doubt that will happen, not with everyone watching for it. And besides, it was so very public an attempt, with much that could go amiss. If my death was the goal, there are easier ways. This was more likely a message of some kind."

"A message? Saying what?"

"I'm not sure. Jousting is dangerous? Ow!" cried Cesco as Antonia nudged him.

"I thought it didn't hurt," she chided. "Any idea who it was?"

"I'd hate to speculate."

"You don't seem particularly worried."

"On the contrary, I am," said Cesco, sitting up. "About you. Won't you tell me what the matter is?"

Even in darkness he could tell that she was looking away from him. "Nothing is the matter. I'm only worried for you." She hugged him, careful of his shoulder. Her hugs had grown fiercer over the last few weeks, even as the haunted look in her eyes had increased. She was like a ghost determined to be corporeal.

When she'd entered the cell and seen him waiting, he'd seen the wince before the smile. And there was an unsheathed dagger resting in the frame of her bed, something he had discovered entirely by accident as he'd sat down to await her. Yes, something was very wrong. Tonight he was going to find the cause.

But first he would behave normally – which meant abusing the Scaliger and lamenting his state. With genuine anger, he said, "I'm too young! I can't match him for strength or endurance. Eventually he will wear me down." He took a breath. "This is a battle I can't win."

"Surely you've been learning—"

"Oh, I've learned! No squire has ever received such an education."

"You're playing with double meanings. But ignore the sarcastic one for a moment and think! Does anything he's taught you this past year apply to your present condition?"

He wanted to be glib, but he recognized her good intent and obediently ran through the thousands of lessons he'd had. After a moment, one particular instance came to mind. "He said something once. He was riding hard, forcing me to keep pace while he listed a general's thoughts on generaling. 'If the war is unwinnable,' he said, 'change the rules, alter the stakes, do something wild and nonsensical, do whatever you must to throw your foe off-balance and gain the initiative.'"

"So the challenge isn't surviving your hawking. It's changing the stakes. Which first means you must define them."

Interested, Cesco considered. "He means to break me apart so he can build me again in his image. The obvious responses are to resist or feign the breaking. The first isn't cutting it and the latter has no appeal."

"There must be a third option. One that will allow you the space you need to become a match for him."

"I'm too tired," sighed Cesco at last. "But there's good sense in what you suggest. Thank you. In the meantime, I think I need a break." He paused, then began to laugh. "Oh yes! A break is exactly what I need!"

Antonia smiled in the dark. "You've come up with a scheme."

"Not for the long war. But I have a battle tomorrow that I can win. Ha! Will you wake me at Matins?"

"Are you sure you cannot stay until dawn?" There was strain in her voice, but he honestly couldn't decide if it meant he should stay or go. He decided to try her defenses once more. "Why should I, Imperia, when you don't really want me here?"

Normally she would have snapped at him for the use of a hated nickname. Instead she hugged him tighter. "Of course I want you here. I'm here for you, always. You know that. No matter what."

"Beatrice. Antonia. Dear, dear auntie – tell me what's troubling you, please! I can help. I'm ever so clever."

Antonia shook her head. "I have trouble sleeping, is all. But don't let that stop you. I'll wake you at Matins."

As he fell asleep in her arms, he felt a tear drop onto his cheek.

Waked at Matins, he slipped out of the abbey and started back for the palace, as usual. But after a few streets he doubled back and climbed a roof to hide himself in the shadow of a bread-maker's chimney across the grassy sward enclosing the nunnery. Hidden from the moon's light, he crouched against the brick chimney, stealing its warmth, and waited.

After some time a man emerged from a door at the side of the nunnery. Alone, no sign of a porter. He must have entered while Cesco had been making his circular maneuvers, for no one had entered since.

The waning moon was just a sliver in the sky. Cesco crawled forward to the edge of the roof to stare at the man. Tallish, but stooped to disguise his height. The voluminous cloak outlined broad shoulders. That was all Cesco could see until the hooded face glanced up at the moon.

It was Lucifer. A long grotesque nose that hooked over an eerily wide smile. The eyes were not eyes at all, but holes. And the colour of the face was blacker than the darkest night.

Cesco's breath caught. For a terrible and wonder-filled moment, the world of L'Inferno was real. Magic existed, for if demons walked the Earth then so too did dragons and gryphons and centaurs and gods, the old gods, Jupiter, Venus, Mars, and Mercury. In that moment Cesco felt more alive than ever before. As horrible as the creature was, if it existed, then anything was possible.

It took Cesco only a second to realize this was one of those carnevale masques that he'd once seen in Venice, like the one he himself had worn a year before to the Capulletto ball. They'd become fashionable in all of Lombardy, and no one thought much of a man in a masque walking down the street anymore. A welcome form of anonymity in a world grown too familiar. A masque was license to do as one pleased, without fear of consequences. A masque was liberty.

But liberty to do what? Was he meeting with Aunt Antonia? Was she betraying Cesco? Was that the cause of her furtiveness, her excess of care? Was it guilt that made her flinch when she saw him?

Under the heavy cloak it was difficult to tell if this was someone known to him. But as the demon strode along the path away from the convent, he did something that filled Cesco with horror. He adjusted his belt and points, then his codpiece. There was something utterly, practically sensual in the gesture, conveying a whole world of meaning.

Though only twelve years old, Cesco reached the inevitable conclusion. No. Oh no...

Before he was even aware what he was doing he'd pried up a clay tile from the roof and stood. Nocking it in his bent elbow like an ancient Olympic discus, he hurled it with all his might at the demon's head.

The projectile shattered with a crack just above the hooded figure. The demon ducked instinctively, hands moving for his dagger. The dagger Cesco had found in Antonia's room. She'd tried to defend herself, only to have the weapon taken away. She might even be dead...

Cesco was already flinging a second tile and reaching for a third. The second was better aimed than the first, and the demon had raise a hand to protect himself from shards. He was running before the third could strike, bolting into the shadows of the next street.

Cesco cursed himself. Stupid! Foolish! He'd simply reacted. He should have followed the man home, learned his identity, then murdered his body, piece by piece.

It isn't too late! Leaping into space, Cesco landed atop an awning, wincing as he rolled down to the ground – he'd forgotten his injured shoulder. But already his feet were propelling him in pursuit of the demon. Like every male in Verona, Cesco never traveled anywhere without a good knife at his belt. As his feet pounded the marble paving slabs, he drew it and gripped it tightly in his fist.

Whoever he was, the demon was fit, and his longer legs were putting distance between himself and Cesco. He slowed only to overturn water-barrels or boxes that might trip up his pursuer. For he knew he was being pursued – Cesco removed all doubt by shouting to imaginary friends, calling for them to cut him off.

The demon didn't swallow that hook. Save for the occasional drunk, the streets on this side of the river were deserted. The foreign knights were being housed outside the city, and the town militia were all manning the walls, not wandering the streets.

Just as well. When I catch him, I'll have him all to myself.

So far the demon had not spoken, only grunted. Focused on gaining ground, Cesco couldn't pause to note any clues to the demon's identity beyond one clear fact – the man knew Verona well. Looping away from the river towards shops and homes, in this chase side streets were used, blocked alleys avoided.

Of one more thing was Cesco certain. This was not Cangrande. Though strong and agile, Cesco's prey had less ingenuity. Cangrande would certainly have lost Cesco by now.

Unless I'm meant to draw that conclusion. He's just wily enough to pretend to be less than he is. But no. After a year of close quarters, he would certainly recognize the Scaliger. Wouldn't he? What does it say about us that I could even imagine him harming Antonia that way?

Antonia. Feeling another surge of boiling blood, Cesco flipped his dagger, holding it by the tip in the manner he'd seen Tharwat use, and threw.

He'd practiced a little since that night near Caprino, but not enough. The tip of the blade missed its mark. It was the dagger's pommel that struck the fleeing demon on the shoulder blade, bouncing off and causing no more harm than a stone.

Cesco couldn't recover his weapon – the demon was far too fleet. Instead he pressed on, silent now as he focused on drawing breath. His usual torrent of gibes was absent. Nothing existed but revenge.

They were approaching one of the tall barricades erected for the tourney. It blocked the street from any horses, with a wooden door for people to use. The door was open, and unguarded. This bastard could slip through, then bar the gate from the other side. Cesco had to stop the demon here! He was now within twenty paces of his prey – not close enough! In desperation he scanned the street for a possible projectile, anything...

There! A hook on a long wooden rod, used to open high shop windows. Cesco plucked it up as he passed. But what could he do, hurl the rod? That would have even less effect than the dagger.

The demon entered the intersection, only seconds away from the door and freedom. Cesco had to act! The deadline was on him—

Deadline! Cesco looked up. Just overhead, running at an angle across the intersection, was one of Cangrande's deadlines, a flower-bedecked rope of spikes. Beginning at the near corner, it ended at the barricade.

Without thought, without measure, Cesco took a running step onto a windowsill and swung the hook into the air. Falling as it caught, he pulled with all his might.

Tension was crucial to a proper deadline. This one was as taut as a bard's lute-string. The sharp hook snapped the rope with a crack. As the rope parted just above Cesco, the remaining length lashed across the intersection like the arc of a whip.

Halfway to the barricade door, the demon's back was raked from shoulder to hip by the deadline. It was almost comical, as flowers covering the deadline made it appear that the demon was being lashed by a bower.

The masqued figure howled and twisted. For a moment it seemed that one of the deadly little spikes had actually severed the spine, for the demon collapsed to the stone street.

Cesco landed, sprawling. Face flat on the ground, he watched, heart beating with triumph.

But the demon was stirring. Pushing up lithely onto the balls of his feet, Cesco launched himself forward, pole in hand, ready to crack the man's skull.

Lifting the slack deadline that had just injured him, the demon turned and swung it whip-like at Cesco's head. Cesco ducked and the deadline caught the pole, tearing it free from Cesco's hands.

The demon swung again, and Cesco had to roll to avoid the garland of spikes that scraped the marble slabs. Flowers scattered free with every swing of the rope. Cesco clambered to his feet and tried to rush forward, only to dodge aside again.

The demon's gloved hands showed expertise as he swung and coiled the rope, dancing it back and forth through the air. It snaked at Cesco's ankles and he leapt over it, like in a child's game.

Cesco took a step closer, but the spiked rope came flicking back, this time at waist level. Cesco leapt up and clutched one of the massive signs hanging out over the street. He flipped himself over the sign and scrambled back onto this roof's tiles just as the rope uncoiled itself towards his chin. It lacked the length to reach him, and Cesco crowed in victory.

Giving Cesco the fig, the silent demon dropped the deadline and turned for the barricade door.

"No!" screamed Cesco, his fleeting triumph forgotten. Victory belonged to the demon, too far away now to stop. Cesco yanked up the nearest clay tile, but the man in the demon masque was already through the doorway. It swung shut and Cesco heard the bar sliding into place. The demon could go off in half a dozen directions before Cesco found a way around.

The tile in his hands fell limply to the roof, sliding past the edge and shattering on the cobblestones below.

All his training, all his cleverness, and when it actually mattered he still failed. Just like with Susanna. When that infant girl had died, he'd blamed the hashish. Tonight proved he needed no assistance to fail. If he'd chosen a sign on the other side of the street, if he had braved a blow of the rope, if he had been smarter, quicker, better – then the demon would be dead and Antonia avenged.

Antonia! Cesco squeezed his eyes shut. How long? Two months? Three? Or, dear Lord, could it have started after his first visit back in August?

His eyes misted and for the first time since Dante's death, Cesco della Scala abandoned himself to tears. He stood on the rooftop howling and baying at the stars. His fists shook, his nails drew blood, his knees buckled back and forth. He bent down and pounded his fists against the tiles, turning them to shards and powder.

Then, as suddenly as the storm had come, it was over. He slumped limply down to the roof. When he wiped away the fluids from his nose and eyes, he was surprised to notice his hands were bleeding. His injured shoulder throbbed fiercely, threatening to open afresh.

"I am a sad and sorry ass." He made a sound that might have been a laugh, but was not. In Ravenna, with Donati, he'd made light of rapine. Now he felt sick at his own sense of humour – sicker, as he was certain to do it again someday. His tongue was always quicker than his conscience.

When at last he had his breathing under control, Cesco dropped to the ground and began walking towards the Ponte Pietra and the palace. He could inquire of all the bridge guards as to the identity of every man crossing this hour. But which bridge? Would the bastard even cross tonight? He could join the rest of the knights entering tomorrow morning and never be missed.

Cesco's thoughts turned back to Antonia. What could he say to her? How could he ease her suffering? Knowing her, to confront her would do even more harm. And trying to catch the demon in the act was too much a risk – she'd suffered too much already. There had to be another way.

And of course, there was.

"It's too much," he whispered, trying out the words. "Every time I see you, he gets worse. I'm actually getting less sleep now than before. I need to stop coming. I love you, but he'll break me if I don't."

He tried the lie a few times more, refining it, rehearsing the scene to perfection. The next time he saw her – definitely not at night! – it would play out. He would say his lines, witness her grief, and try not to see her relief.

Goodbye, Suor Beatrice. Aunt Antonia. Mother.

Two weeks shy of the anniversary of his arrival in Verona, Cesco was finally stripped of every refuge, every aid, every protection. Ser Alaghieri was in Avignon, the Moor was on his way to join him there, and the doctor's presence was clearly temporary. Now Antonia was lost to him.

From this night forward, Cesco belonged solely to the mercies of the Greyhound.

No quarter.

Nine

The second day of Verona's tourney was centered around the *mêlée*, a general armed engagement where knights were divided into two 'armies' and charged at each other. The ultimate goal was to unseat all the enemy riders, or else gain the enemy standard.

But before the *mêlée* came the wrestling matches. Being open to all comers, it was not unheard of for a smith or even a baker to win over a full knight. Verona owned an odd egalitarian streak and, as in the old Roman Saturnalia, once or twice a year the city's rich and poor were deemed equals.

As wrestling was not a danger to the crowd, the sheltering walls were removed for the morning, allowing a clear view for all. After the opening prayers and some light-hearted theatre, the contestants came running out into the already sweltering heat. Three separate squares were marked and the first matches began.

Among the knights and squires were butchers, smiths, tinkers, even one tailor. There was always a great cheer when some ignoble bully pinned a nobleman to the dirt. Some fought in half-dress, some in the nude. The only ladies in the crowd today were the relatives of the nobility, presumably above hooting or recoiling in shock.

"Look look!" cried Detto to Cesco from their shared vantage point on the balcony. "That one's plucked all his hair! And shaved his head!"

"And probably coated himself with pig grease," replied Cesco. "Anything for an advantage. After all, the monetary prize is astronomical." Despite being dog-tired, he cheered with the rest when they heard the crack of a broken bone. But it was a hollow shout, as his mind was racing. There was a great deal to accomplish today. Which meant indulging the sticky-chews again. With the Moor gone, he had to preserve his stores. But if he succeeded today, he might not need them again for some time.

Somehow he had to force the Scaliger to admit him to the *mêlée*. All his plans hinged on that. There was a way, but only if he acted soon. And there was the additional imperative of eliminating possible faces behind the demon masque.

Running over possibilities, Cesco noted that neither Mastino nor Fuchs were down among the wrestlers. Too far beneath them, rubbing shoulders with common citizens. They would wait for the *mêlée*.

Cangrande interrupted his train of thought by turning in his seat. "Boy! Do you see who is taking the center ring?"

Squinting, it took Cesco only a moment to place the man's massive frame and cheerful face. Last Cesco had seen him, both had been begrimed past hope. "The smithy!" he cried, applauding.

It was indeed Rienzi's smith, who had instructed Cesco in the workings of the water-forge a few months before. Which meant that...

Twisting around, Cesco scanned the banners behind them under the awning. And there it was! The flaming beaver banner stood proudly among the lesser nobles and invited guests. The Rienzi family was sitting off to one side, about halfway up the Arena seats. Rienzi himself was sweating heavily under heavy layers of formal attire. *Fur in July?* He was surrounded by servants, but there was no evidence of a wife, though it appeared he'd brought his children, a boy and a girl. They were like the sun and moon, the boy a fitter version of the father, probably in his middle teens, whereas the girl must've taken after her mother – the hair that showed under her hair-ribbon was a deep brown, her colouring fairer than her brother's.

"You're missing it!" said Detto, elbowing him. Wincing, Cesco shifted his arm in its sling and shot his cousin a nasty look, but Detto was far too excited to be contrite.

Rienzi's smith was holding the center ring, refusing to leave it after his first victory and demanding to be tested again. He felled his second opponent, and a third, still looking as hearty as when he'd begun.

The crowd suddenly had a favourite and Cesco joined Detto and the rest in cheering him on. When at last he was taken down, he had thrown or pinned eleven men.

"His bed won't be empty tonight," observed Nico da Lozzo.

"It's a strong bed that can take anyone in addition to him," replied Petruchio Bonaventura. "Good Lord, what a brute!"

"I'd like to know his diet," murmured Morsicato, who'd been hovering just behind Cesco all morning.

Cesco called down the row to Cangrande. "Surely he's won?"

"I think he has," agreed the Scaliger. "If we give the prize to anyone else, the crowd will swallow us whole."

Cesco stood. "I'll tell him."

Cangrande shrugged. "If you like. Tell Rienzi first – as his patron, he's entitled to a share of the winnings."

"And you wouldn't want to insult the old goat," said Cesco winningly.

Cangrande waved him off with a very public laugh. "Never!"

Though he could have pushed through the crowd, it was easier to duck into the tunnel behind the balcony and cross underneath to an entrance closer to Rienzi. Detto in his wake, Cesco skipped down the steps into the tunnels that ringed the underside of the Arena.

Wary Scaligeri guards kept the passage behind the balcony clear, so the two boys had no trouble navigating to the next opening. Here and there were the square pock-marks of holes bored into the stone, where once the timber struts had been placed to create housing, in the dark times after the fall of the Caesars. On the path between the invading Germans and their prey, Verona had suffered mightily, and the city's poor had erected housing within the Arena itself when their houses had burned. The Arena had been an object of awe for the invaders, and they'd kept well away from an edifice surely built by the gods.

For hundreds of years thereafter the Arena had served as shelter for Verona's poorest, until Charlemagne had come and swept the place clean. He'd loved Verona, as had his son Pepin, each exerting great pressure to restore Verona to her former glory. It was said that they had even resurrected the tradition of the Palio.

Those dark years had left scars, and an earthquake a hundred-odd years before had removed most of the outer wall encircling the great stadium. But still it stood, second in size only to the Colosseum in Rome and the largest one still in use, the site of great barbarity and even greater glory.

Turning left at another passage, Cesco and Detto ascended the stairs back into the light, dimmed only by the canopy overhead. But the sun-screen did nothing to deaden the noise, which swelled for another set of wrestlers.

Rienzi was seated a few steps up and in the middle of a row, resting upon many large cushions. His son and daughter flanked him, with four others, two minor nobles and two Rienzi servants. Recognizing Cesco, the ignoble-nobles stood and bowed, as did several people from nearby rows. Cesco waved in acknowledgement, then gestured to Rienzi. The old man huffed but rose from his comfortable cushions and edged past the people in his way. His son and daughter followed.

"I've come to tell you informally that your man's won," said Cesco, beaming. "Certainly no one is going to outshine him!"

"My thanks, Master Francesco," said Rienzi formally. "May I present my son Adamo and his sister, Rosalia."

"Charmed, my lady Rienzi," said Cesco, nodding absently at the girl. His eyes were on Adamo. "Signore, I'm not sure – have we met? I seem to feel a tickle on my throat…"

Adamo frowned, as if trying to discern the insult he was sure the comment contained. "I don't believe we have, my lord." It was clearly galling for him to call a bastard 'lord'.

"My mistake. I'm surprised you are not in the lists yourself. You look fit, trim. Even acrobatic. How do you keep such a fine figure – do you swim?"

Both father and son gazed at Cesco as if he were mad. Unsure if he was being baited, Adamo shrugged. Old Rienzi said, "My son is a great hunter, and of course living so close to the Adige, he swims well enough."

"Ah!" said Cesco, as if this were the answer he was seeking. He raised his chin to study the flapping Rienzi banner. "Monsignore, I've been meaning to ask, why a beaver? It's not a dam you run. Or is there a jest about a burning beaver being damned? Are there beavers in Hell, do you think?"

"You shouldn't blaspheme," said Rienzi's daughter. "The Lord hears all."

"I do it so He'll pay attention."

"A pity, as He is more impressed with deeds than words," she answered tartly.

A wide smile blossomed across Cesco's face. "But I tire of performing blasphemous deeds, so my words must suffice."

"Your words are not worth the air you spend to utter them."

"On the contrary, they cost me nothing."

"And are therefore worth nothing," she replied.

Nonplussed, Cesco studied her for the first time. A year or two older than he was, Rosalia was taller, though about as thin. Emerging from her awkward years, there were a few scattered blemishes, but no marring scars. She was one of those girls who could go either way – unremarkably plain, or breath-takingly gorgeous. Only time would tell.

More interesting was the directness of her gaze. There was nothing coy, nothing shy. She held his eyes with hers, daring him to look away first. But he couldn't. Behind her eyes there was something coiled, something bright, something alive. Was it anguish? Or amusement? Cesco couldn't tell, but he felt a twisting, gnawing desire in his belly, and a huge weight landed on his chest. Her eyes were arresting, a pure green, lush as a grassy sward.

It was as if a lever had been thrown in his liver. *O grandfather Dante, is this what you spoke of? It cannot be. I refuse to be so foolish…*

Clearly something in his face had changed, for Adamo Rienzi stepped between Cesco and his sister. "Don't speak to her!"

"Adamo…" said old Rienzi warningly, focused on the rows of nobility and merchants intently watching this scene, closer and more entertaining than the wrestling.

"That's right, Adamo." Their gaze broken, Cesco smiled charmingly as he looked Rienzi's son up and down. "It's not wise to antagonize your patron's heir – at least, not publicly. Wait for moonrise."

Adamo reached out to grasp Cesco's uninjured arm, but Rienzi seized his son and whispered very softly, "It's death to molest the Scaliger's heir. You understand? Death."

Cesco was unperturbed. "If you would like, Adamo, I would be happy to join you down in the Arena for a quick throw or two. But perhaps you should ask your smith for a few lessons before you try. Myself, I was trained at the Capitano's own merciful hands."

Before her brother could accept, Rosalia said, "Then why not go challenge *him*."

Cesco cocked his head to stare at her, his grin widening with wicked delight. "O, excellent suggestion! My darling Rosalia, I am ever in your debt." Bowing deeply to her, he skipped down the stairs so quickly that Detto had only followed three steps before Cesco was vaulting the low barrier to the Arena floor.

The nearest wrestling square was unoccupied at the moment. Cesco strode into the middle of it and turned to face the balcony. "Maestro! Is it time for my next lesson?"

"No," said Cangrande in a bored tone that nonetheless carried all around the Arena. "I tire of teaching one so rude. Let them continue! I'll thrash you tomorrow."

Ostentatiously, Cesco removed his sling. "But now I match you, wound for wound. Won't you come and give me another lesson?"

Cesco's mention of their perfectly matching wounds harped on a subject that many had debated all the previous evening. Rumour blamed the boy for the Capitano's injury. Could Cangrande have switched out the lances to balance the scales? Was the boy even now accusing him of just that?

None of this was part of Cesco's plan – it was *extempore*. But this opportunity might not come again. And he could achieve two kills with a single stroke.

If he pulled this off and then survived the *mêlée*, he would be free. And would know for an absolute certainty that Cangrande was not last night's disguised demon.

That's right, he told himself. *It has nothing at all to do with impressing the girl.*

A larger fellow would have already stripped his doublet and shirt off. But Cesco knew that his cord-thin frame would only create pity in the crowd, an emotion that the Scaliger could exploit by refusing to take on so pitiful a creature. So instead Cesco did a backwards flip from a standing position, then reached down to rub dirt on his palms. "Come, if not for my training, then for a wager! If I win, I may ride in the *mêlée* as full member of the nobility, armed with lances and swords. If I lose, I must carry the flag of Verona and preserve it in the rear ranks. Thus if Verona loses, the shame will be entirely mine!"

This was known in the streets of Ravenna as the Trickster's Force. It set the stakes in such a way that, regardless of victory, the real goal was achieved. And Cesco's goal was to ride in the *mêlée*.

Nobody's fool, Cangrande knew it for what it was. But the wager having been offered, he could only accept or reject, not alter it. Now it became a matter of shaming the Scaliger into accepting.

Cangrande did not seem so inclined. "I do not fight children! Not even ones of my own blood."

"Then let me lie about my age. I'm just half your height, so I must be half your age! How old are you again, Lord Capitano?"

Young enough to be baited, it seemed. "Too old to think there's honour wrestling children." Though Cangrande's response was typically glib and mild, Cesco saw the glint in the Capitano's eye, a look he knew all too well. *Good. All he needs now is an excuse.*

"If I am half the man you are, then reason says that two of me should equal one of you. I have a brother-in-years, also blood of your blood. Perhaps together we woodpeckers can topple the mighty oak!"

Without further prompting Detto came running out to stand side by side with Cesco. Two against one. It was irresistible. No matter the outcome, Cangrande would walk away with honour. Not that there was much chance of his losing.

The Scaliger provoked a great cheer by removing his sling. "Very well. On your own head be it!"

Cesco was busy whispering instructions. "You, high or right, as opportunity permits. I'll be low and left."

"Sinister suits you," replied Detto, earning a surprised laugh from Cesco. "What? I know things."

"You must teach me sometime. Ah, here he comes."

Cangrande dropped gracefully from the balcony and stripped himself to the waist. As he turned to show off his body to the applauding masses, Cesco could see his back. It bore no scars. The Scaliger was definitively acquitted of last night's dark crime. That in itself was a kind of victory.

An evil voice, one that never left Cesco for very long, whispered to him. *It means It was not he in the masque. It does not mean he is innocent.*

Cesco shook off the thought as he stripped down and focused on the trial at hand. That he'd already won his aim was some comfort through the following ten minutes of ceaseless, remorseless effort. Twisting, gripping, choking, rolling, evading, swiping, gasping effort.

That Cangrande emerged victorious was more a testimony to his guile than his strength. He employed every underhanded trick that would escape the crowd's notice, and Cesco's flesh was red with pinches and tweaks. Detto escaped that kind of treatment, though he took some hard falls. Cesco ended pinned between Cangrande's legs while Detto lay immobile in a hug that pressed his arms against his sides.

The crowd went wild. Doubtless there were some foreigners who would have delighted in the Scaliger's overthrow by two children. But the vast majority of those present, even his enemies, considered Cangrande the ideal man. In war, in art, in conquests (both territorial and feminine), in wealth, in manner, in speech – in every way, Cangrande was the prime specimen of perfection in this, the 14th century since Christ.

Under cover of the cheering, Cangrande remarked, "You lost your wager."

"And I'll pay the price."

"You know, I once made Alaghieri a banneret. As I recall it didn't meet his expectations." The Scaliger laughed, and Cesco made a face at his receding back.

Having taken his public share of pity and ridicule (he'd seen both Mastino and Fuchs laughing uproariously), Cesco retired with Detto to the bowels of the Arena, where they were washed and scraped clean by the medicos. At one point Detto's newly-pinked face swiveled towards Cesco. "Tell me it was to get into the *mêlée*."

"That, and for the fun of it."

"Good," grunted Detto, well satisfied. "I was afraid it was for the girl."

Plunging his head into the tub of water before him, Cesco pretended he hadn't heard.

Though clearly recovered from his wound, Cangrande declared that he would not take part in the *mêlée*, as it might be prejudicial. So the main event went ahead as planned, with some luckless banneret replaced by Cesco.

The event officially began with a parade around the edges of the Arena floor, each rider calling out his war shout, the chivalric 'cry of the heart.' Though the barricades were back up, most riders could see over these to address the crowd. Some made gallant shows to the ladies while others made rude gestures to their detractors.

Cesco himself cantered atop a great destrier. Wearing full armour for the first time, he was absurdly pleased with himself despite the extra padding he'd had to secret here and there to make the thing fit – forged with his age in mind, it had gaps for sudden growth that sadly hadn't happened yet.

In his gloved hands he held a pole from which fluttered the Scaligeri colours, a ladder with the two-headed imperial eagle perched at the top, a snarling greyhound just below the bottom rung.

That same device was repeated on the gold and red *caparison* draped over his horse's back under the saddle, fully visible across the hindquarters. The rest of the horse was hidden by armour. Along its face was the metal and leather *testiera*, with a pair of goring spikes that made the beast resemble the Devil's own steed. Below this was the *collo*, buckled to the underside of the neck, which in turn connected to the *pettiera*, chest armour that neatly made way for the legs to run. A curved plate called the *fiancali* was strapped across the beast's belly.

In front and back of Cesco's leather saddle were the two *arciones*, hard wooden barriers protecting his groin and lower back. Behind the saddle, across the horse's rump, hung the many scaled layers of the *groppa*. And extending out of the *groppa* was the *guardacorda*, the small, ornamental device meant to protect the horse's tail. In the case of Cesco's horse, the *guardacorda* was shaped like a snarling greyhound from whose mouth the horse's tail flowed.

The caparison lay under the saddle but over the *groppa* so the device was clear to view. Cesco was the target for the opposing army, and had to be marked as such.

As the parade finished its circuit of the Arena, Cesco tried to resist looking directly to where the Rienzi family had sat this morning. Failing, he saw all three there now, the father fanning himself, Adamo glaring daggers at Cesco, and the girl ignoring him entirely, instead looking at the balcony where Cangrande was making speeches to the jubilant throng. Cesco had his helmet in place and so couldn't distinguish the Capitano's words. Just as well. He'd heard quite enough of the Scaliger's voice this last year.

If I can pull this off, I can be free of it – and him. So forget the girl and the fact that she's not watching you. Focus!

Cesco joined the other Veronese as they massed beneath the Scaliger's balcony. The most famous faces of Verona were behind these helmets – Bonaventura, Nico da Lozzo, young Castelbarco. Montecchio and Capulletto competed for a spot in the front ranks. Bailardino Nogarola was present, representing Vicenza. So too were the Mantuans, represented in the person of their podestá, Passerino Bonaccolsi, recovered from his mishap the day before. Cesco wondered if Cangrande had any other surprises in store for this false-friend, but doubted it. When Bonaccolsi's time came, Cangrande would want to drop the hammer himself.

As the tunnels were only wide enough for three or four horses abreast, Cangrande had forbidden a proposed charge from beneath the Arena. Instead the two 'armies' would line up as on a formal field of battle. When the signal was given, they would charge at each other, lances leveled. Whoever kept their seats would wheel about, unsheathe swords, and engage in combat.

The main draw for these events – indeed, the reason they were so very popular – was not honour but ransom. If a man yielded in single combat, his captor was allowed to demand payment for his freedom, just as on a real battlefield. And the captor of the enemy colours could demand a sum from every knight who had gathered beneath it. A great motivator for both sides.

Where this *mêlée* would differ from all others held in the world was the scope. Most often a *mêlée* was held in a vast open field, providing many avenues of escape. *Mêlées* were sometimes known to last over a day, so desperate were the vanquished not to be caught.

But there was no escaping the Arena. In this relatively tight space, it would be a fight to the finish for everyone involved. Despite the blunted weapons, some were sure to die. More importantly, some were sure to become quite rich.

One of the most likely beneficiaries was Fuchs, who had already amassed several fortunes in the lists. He sat calmly bestride his saddle, fully-barded, with the signal honour of a scarlet general's cloak hanging from his shoulders. As the victor of the *giostri*, he was to lead the charge from the front ranks of Verona's knights and squires.

In even finer armour, Mastino sat nearby him. Cesco noticed that the Mastiff was moving a trifle gingerly. But that could be from the hard knocks from yesterday's jousts. There was not a single member of the nobility who was moving with ease today. No, that was not enough to accuse him...

Pay attention! Cesco stopped studying his usual foes, who were today to be his allies. Instead he scanned the foreigners.

Though there was no room for individual banners, the caparisons on the other horses declared their nationality and family titles. The more recognizable devices were Paduan, Venetian, Cremonese, Trevisian, Bolognese. But scattered here and there were French lilies, English lions, Spanish crosses, Polish and German eagles, each worked into some other design denoting regional or familial ties. Perhaps fifty foreigners in all, against just under forty Veronese, Vicenzans, and Mantuans.

Being a kinsman to Mariotto Montecchio, the Englishman William Montagu was given the signal honour of bearing the opposing side's banner, the target of all Veronese eyes.

Cesco's wondered how, of all the knights present, these men were chosen. *Were they limited by the size*

*of the Arena floor? Did the Scaliger make them draw
lots? Or are these the only men willing to risk their
necks and fortunes?*

Both sides took their places. There were too many
bodies for a single line, so instead walls of horses
ranked three deep would crash together. Those in
the front ranks ran the greater danger, as they had
to pass more fresh lances. Thus they were accorded
the most glory.

Cesco was in the middle ranks. He'd expected to
be placed at the rear, but Fuchs had instead done
the sensible thing and given Cesco a more defensible
position. At the rear, he would have been protected
from the initial charge, only to be horribly exposed
when both sides wheeled for swordplay. Centered,
he was surrounded by shields.

In a wider space, each combatant would normally
be allowed three lances. In the Arena they could use
only the one they carried, which altered the general
strategy somewhat. Breaking an enemy lance was
now of paramount importance.

Cesco had no lance at all. As banneret, he was
more target than combatant. But if he could manage to carry the banner one-handed, he could draw
his sword. He was determined to at least try. For this
was it – the first chance to show that he was worth

all the trouble, that the Scaliger hadn't broken him, that he was the future of Verona.

Men spoke, but he had trouble distinguishing words with the roar of the spectators reverberating around his helmet. Uncle Pietro had once described armoured battle as 'fighting in a bucket.' It wasn't an exaggeration. When the trumpets blared Cesco understood why that instrument was used to command armies – he heard every note.

Here we go. Spurring with the rest, Cesco pulled the banner in tight, right hand high, left at his hip. Lances would be aimed primarily at him, and he could draw his sword after the turn.

With breathtaking speed the first crash came, lances cracking upon armour and men tumbling half or wholly from their saddles. Those whose lances broke were quickly targeted, fending wildly with their shields. Many of these were felled in Cesco's path.

Then the first lances were upon him, a forest of boar teeth aimed for his unshielded breast. Bonaventura and young Castelbarco, assigned to guard the defenseless banneret, folded him in their protection, riding just ahead, tight to his horse's neck. Castelbarco received a punishing blow to his shield, due entirely to his refusal to deflect it in Cesco's direction. Bonaventura managed to trap two lances angling for

Cesco between his front *arcione* and his shield, allowing the motion of his horse to snap them both.

The next row was more dangerous still, for these were men who had not suffered in the front lines. But their rush was not quite as frantic, having been checked in their charge. They too aimed their lances for the little heir. Cesco dodged one lance entirely and allowed another to scrape his armour. He used the shaft of the banner to tap the hands holding a lance, forcing the enemy to drop it to the dirt.

Grasping fingers plucked at the banner. *Why didn't I think to tie it to my wrist? A falcon's jess would be the perfect tool. Too late now!*

Then he was through, the staff still safely in his grip. He followed his protectors as they turned about. *Turn, turny, tourney!* The *mêlée* was now truly begun, a free-for-all of skill and honour.

The next ten minutes were among the most exciting of Cesco's young life. Against his initial intentions, his sword remained scabbarded. He had no time to draw it, requiring each second to evade anew. His war-horse, bred from the famous Montecchi stock, was marvelously responsive. Riding it was like being astride a battering-ram, and he barreled through knots of dueling men, upsetting friend and foe alike, the Scaligeri banner streaming behind his head.

As more and more men were unhorsed, pages and lackeys ran out to claim riderless mounts and guide them out the tunnels beneath the Arena. Few knights were so fortunate, but the removal of horses gave the contesting forces welcome room to maneuver.

Cesco owed Mastino and Fuchs a debt – their training had been ruthless, but effective. He used the slowly-widening space to good advantage, always in motion, twisting this way then that in an unpredictable circuit.

Nevertheless he encountered real danger. The flag he carried meant wealth and glory for whoever attained it. Yet whenever he was threatened, some Veronese knight would come to his aid, abandoning personal fortune for communal victory. Surprisingly, Mastino was one of these – he left off chasing a rich Pole to lance away two Spaniards descending upon Cesco.

"*Grazie*, cos!" cried Cesco.

"Have to keep the pretty infant safe!" The Mastiff pointed at the banner. "Try not to drop it!" Cesco had a biting reply ready, but Mastino was already off chasing Montagu for the opposing flag.

The Englishman was skilled, guiding his horse without the reins as he clutched his banner close. Time and again he would simply ride clear of trouble,

plunging himself into a knot of his fellow foreigners for protection. Because few of the foreigners had
the same tongue, they all spoke French as best they
could.

As the object of every foreign eye, Cesco hadn't
much time to watch. But it struck him that Montagu
was playing an excellent defensive game – which
was all well and good, but lacked spice. The Englishman was not making as much use of his banner as
he might. *Methinks he requires a demonstration.*

Though it was a little lack-honour, Cesco swung
the staff in his hands so that the banner wrapped
around itself, leaving nothing trailing. Then he stood
in the stirrups (not nearly as impressive as when
Cangrande did it) and rode directly for a cluster of
enemy knights facing the wrong way. He gave his
mount its head, and as the beast bashed into a gap
half its size, Cesco used the banner's pole as a quarterstaff, aiming for heads and shoulders. *Crack crack
crack!* Three knights were struck, two with the butt
end, one with the wrapped banner itself. As his horse
muscled through, Cesco let the banner unfurl, and
the crowd encircling him cheered his daring assault.

There was a penalty, of course. More enraged than
injured, the three knights were in prime position
for pursuit. He could almost feel their spurs as they

launched after him, and he willed his mount on-
wards.

Instantly Capulletto was beside him. A moment
later Montecchio was on his other flank. Together
the pair dropped a step, forming a barrier between
Cesco and his pursuers. Cesco found it amusing. *The
stories are true! As much as they hate each other, they
never fail to find one another in battle.*

Free again, Cesco repeated the tactic on another
group. If only the armour didn't impede his move-
ments so! He knew he owed it his life several times
over, but he resented not being able to slide in and
out of his saddle, to flip and trick as he was wont.
This was clearly not the place for such flamboyance,
but he hated being reduced to common riding. If it
was common, Cesco wanted no part of it.

Verona's forces were gaining the advantage. The
numbers were even now, meaning the natives had
removed more foreigners than they had themselves
lost.

With less of a crush, Cesco finally had time to
cinch his banner under his left arm and reach down
to draw his sword from the saddle's scabbard. His
first time drawing a man's blade in contest. Even if
the blade was bated so as not to cut, it was worth
savouring.

His momentary relish nearly cost him, for seconds later there was a surge after him. He now held the banner one-handed, and enemy knights anxiously chased. Cesco's first cut had him matching blades with a Frenchman whose colours held the royal lily in prominence, denoting a royal relative.

"Give me the staff and I'll take you back to meet *le Roi!*" promised the Frenchman.

"Let me crown you instead, *monsieur!*" Cesco cracked the Frenchman's helmet with the staff, then spurred away hard.

Clear for a moment, he allowed his sword to sag as he stretched his arm. His injured shoulder was ablaze with pain, action and weight combining to aggravate it to white hot intensity.

Which meant the hashish was burning away in his blood. *Soon, or never.*

Cesco spied a crush of men in which Fuchs was matching swords with Montagu. Like Cesco, the Englishmen had cinched his banner tightly under his left arm, wrapping his forearm around it to lock it in place. Fuchs had long ago abandoned or lost both lance and shield, and was now wielding a bastard-length blade. Montagu's sword was shorter, but he'd taken Cesco's example and was using the haft of the banner's pole to strike Fuchs' unprotected sides.

Earlier, when entering the Arena, Cesco had had an idea. An awful idea. A terrible, wonderful, awful idea. Reason told him he had to stick to his plan, yet the idea refused to leave him.

Seeing Fuchs face Montagu, he saw a way to make both plan and idea coincide. *O Fuchs, you lovely villain – thank you! This is just what I need!*

Cesco brought his horse hard into the fray, slinging his steel, parrying with wild abandon. Never a careful fighter, he let his instincts lead him on. So long as he held the banner, everything was well.

Any moment now!

Fighting grew fierce around the two bannerets as both armies smelled the finish fast approaching. Fingers grasped and Cesco was forced to abandon his sword to keep the banner, which he again employed as a quarterstaff.

There were two styles to using a staff. Short-form was for closer, more defensive fighting. Eschewing short form, Cesco gripped the staff at one end – a longer reach meant a better attack. In long-form, he laid about him, swinging wildly and jabbing for chinks in armour, each swing and thrust bringing him closer to where Montagu and Fuchs battled.

Suddenly the two opposing bannerets were side by side, fending off very different attackers. Mid-parry, Cesco said in French, "Is it this warm in England?"

He heard Montagu laugh through his helmet. "Not often!" Unable to resist, Montagu swung his own banner at Cesco's head. Cesco blocked it with his own, knocking it aside and feinting for Montagu's midriff. Reversing the pole, he scooped his flapping banner around to strike the Englishman a wicked blow across the shoulders.

Fuchs wedged his mount between Cesco and Montagu. "Get out of it, *trottel!*"

"He means me!" explained Cesco to Montagu, who laughed again.

"*Verpiss dich!*" demanded Fuchs, his sword meeting Montagu's staff. "You risk losing all!"

Ignoring Fuchs, Cesco swung again for Montagu. Fuchs blocked the blow, knocking the tip of Cesco's banner down into the ground. He was instantly reviled by the crowd, watching breathlessly and hoping for their young banneret to strike down Montagu and win the day. Whereas Fuchs wanted the victory – and the prize – to be his alone.

The repulsed banner's pole came to rest beneath Fuchs' horse. Cesco glanced at Montagu. *Now now now!*

Still gripping the staff in long-form, Cesco struck upwards, hitting Fuchs' horse underneath the hindquarters. Thoroughly gelded, the great beast was trained for all kind of blows. That one elicited an especial, and quite natural, response – it reared.

Cesco kicked hard with his right spur and sawed on his reins. In answer, his horse turned sideways to Fuchs, placing its rump against Montagu's saddle. As the rearing horse came down, the flailing spiked hooves struck to either side of Cesco's saddle, one leg before Cesco's eyes, the other behind his back. He leaned desperately away from the muzzled teeth that snapped and bit. *This might have been a bad idea—*

As the forelegs raked the metal *fiancali* and *groppa*, Cesco's horse tried to flee. Fuchs' mount slipped free and descended to the earth, bringing the massive weight of the beast squarely down. The solid front of Cesco's saddle, the *arcione*, met the metal chest protection of Fuchs' *pettiera*, trapping Cesco's leg.

"*Scheisse!*" Fuchs pulled back on the reins and his horse obediently tried to turn. There was a great cracking sound and Cesco shouted in dreadful pain just as Fuchs got himself free. The banner in Cesco's hand drooped again.

Seeing an opportunity, Montagu lunged, reaching for the butt-end of Cesco's staff.

Though in agony, Cesco managed to bring his staff around to catch Montagu hard in the neck. Trying not to move below the waist, Cesco struck again with the banner-end. This time his target was the Englishman's forearm. He connected, and involuntarily Montagu's fingers relaxed. It was only a moment, but long enough. Cesco grasped.

But it was another of Verona's knights who seized the enemy banner and pulled it free. As the bugles called an end to the fighting, Cesco looked at the man riding victoriously around the Arena, displaying the silver and blue banner for all to see.

Passerino Bonaccolsi. The lord of Mantua, opportunist to the core, was the victor.

Seated in his saddle with the tattered Scaligeri banner still in his grip, Cesco panted like a bellows that had lost its wind. His left leg was hanging limply in the stirrup. He glanced up to the crowded balcony. Cangrande was watching him closely. So too Katerina. Morsicato was on his feet, pushing bodies aside to gain a better view.

But strangely it was not these faces Cesco sought. He scanned until he saw the Rienzi girl. She too was staring at him, and he wondered if she'd cheered him even once. *I bet you didn't, you little harpy. Which is fine, because I don't like you either.*

Suddenly she vanished, and Cesco wondered what had caused the sun to go dark...

Custom dictated that the day following a tournament there be held a banquet, during which the patron offered prizes to the victors. As this was to be thrown by Cangrande, naturally it had to be more lavish than any before seen. From food to entertainment, he spared no expense. No man would go to bed sober, or alone.

This was also the farewell feast for Jacopo Alaghieri, who found himself the butt of a drinking game, wherein any time someone mentioned a foreign place, he had to drink. A cruel game, as the whole feast was rife with the latest rumours from France – the English Queen and her lover had quarreled in public, ending in her threatening to return to her husband. Roger Mortimer, once the English king's stoutest supporter, had reportedly replied, "I'll cut you with my own knife if you try." Being French-born, Queen Isabella was said to have soothed him to tranquility between the sheets.

This report made it likely that the looming storm of civil war would pass England by, having done no more than ruffle court feathers and sent the bankers scurrying. Being English and acquainted with the foolish, over-fond king, William Montagu was plied with both questions and alcohol, in the hopes that the latter would aid in answers to the former. He passed out beside Poco, and both had to be taken back to their rooms in a cart.

Of course, the other talk that day was of Verona's heir. When asked, Cangrande maintained that the boy was recovering well at the hands of the best physicians in the land. He gave no hint of the conference that had occurred the night before in the old palace across the square, outfitted with a warm room in the basement for relaxing. The palace had been built upon a Roman foundation, and Cangrande's builders had brilliantly resurrected the ancient baths here. Meant for the Scaliger's own use, the warm healing waters were now turned over entirely for Cesco's care.

The conference had begun baldly enough. Morsicato and Fracastoro, Cangrande's personal doctor, were binding Cesco's leg. Detto was making idle chatter to Cesco, whose replies were a trifle dizzy but not incoherent.

Suddenly Cangrande entered. "Ser Dottore, Lord Physician – will he walk?"

"Undoubtedly," said Fracastoro. "It is a clean break."

"Good. I want him up on horseback in a fortnight."

"Not less than two months," replied Morsicato.

Cangrande scowled as Fracastoro backed up his colleague's opinion. "At the very least. If it heals crooked, he'll be lame for life. No, my colleague is correct, two months. Better three."

When the splinting was completed, Cangrande dismissed the doctors, then politely asked Detto to fetch some wine.

Alone, the two stared at each other for a time. Becoming bored, Cesco paddled a hand in the bathwaters beside him. "A wonderful feat, recreating the baths."

Cangrande nodded. "It never fails to astonish me, the knowledge we've lost over the last thousand years. Why can we no longer make devices the Romans saw as commonplace?"

"Like so much else, it is trial and error," said Cesco. "In time everything old will be new again."

"Just like your leg. Do not look upon this as a reprieve."

"*Au contraire*," said Cesco. "I'm sure it isn't."

Arms folded, Cangrande leaned against the stone wall, gazing at Cesco in the light of the glowing brazier that cast a red glow over the room. "Many are saying someone is trying to murder you. Again."

"We have another commonality." Shifting, Cesco knew better than to wince. Pity would not be forthcoming.

"Indeed. But it does make me wonder – who switched your lances yesterday? I thought I put you in charge of the practice lances." When Cesco said nothing, the Scaliger continued. "I might forgive one doctored lance slipping by you, but two? Shoddy, very shoddy."

"If I could bend, I would grovel for forgiveness."

"Still," continued Cangrande, "it was quite a feat, your not being skewered."

"A compliment? I'm gratified. Astonished, but—"

"Quite a feat," repeated the Scaliger. "Almost as if you knew it was coming."

"It's due entirely to your training," said Cesco lightly. "I'm always expecting the sharp end of the stick."

The Capitano barked out a single laugh. "Ha! Yes, well. Taken as a whole, it certainly appears that someone is attempting to murder you. After today those suspicions are alighting on one set of shoulders. Poor Fuchs is bearing all kinds of dark glances, and Mastino by association."

"That is a grave injustice," said Cesco.

"It is, since they are guiltless."

"Innocent of this," answered Cesco sharply. "Not guiltless."

Cangrande looked amused. "Have they been abusing you so much in the practice yard? It can't have been so terrible, they taught you well enough." He paused theatrically. "It's quite remarkable, isn't it?

You are wounded – not once, but twice! – before the eyes of the whole city. Neither injury proves fatal, yet combined they are quite enough to win you the sympathy of every feeble-minded fool on the Anziani. It is a unifier, gathering you quite a bit of political clout. If someone wants you dead, you must be a force to be reckoned with."

"The same could be said for you," replied Cesco. "You are impervious to attack, so your foes will destroy you through your heir."

Cangrande nodded absently. "If they were not suspicious of me for causing it all."

Cesco threw up his hands in mock horror. "You? *Ma, no!*"

Again Cangrande nodded, this time in satisfaction. "Just as I suspected. Well done. I've been wondering when you would fight back. It's well past time."

Cesco's face betrayed nothing. "I have no idea what you—"

"*You* planted the lances. *You* caused the accident." Cangrande gazed at Cesco with a menacing grin. "I'm impressed, actually. I was wondering how you would escape. Short of self-slaughter, this is perhaps the best way. A broken leg, an injured shoulder. Public, heroic, with a whiff of suspicion alighting upon your foes. Just what I've been waiting to see you do."

Suddenly pleased to be seated, Cesco felt his blood drain as a hundred contradictory thoughts ricocheted around his skull. Cesco wasn't changing the rules after all. He was dancing exactly to the tune the Scaliger played. *Fut.*

Unless— "You're making that up. You didn't think I would break free, just break. Now I'm free you can make it sound as if you plotted this all along."

"I have no objection to your nonce of freedom. Because at the end of the tunnel you'll see me waiting for you. You know what is coming this time. And I promise you, boy – short of death, you will not escape me again. When our contest resumes, I *will* break you. Not your leg. You." Cangrande appeared suddenly thoughtful. "Meanwhile, if you cannot train, you can at least be put to work. When I 'died' last year, Mastino made free use of my personal effects. Most of them were easily recovered, but one treasure trove was lost to me. My library. Hundreds of books and scrolls, innumerable scraps of parchment from Roman times and earlier. All given to the brothers at the Chapter Library."

"You want me to make copies," said Cesco hopelessly, imagining cramped fingers and squinting eyes.

"I think not. I've seen your handwriting. No, the works are available to me if I desire them. The trouble is, neither the brothers nor myself ever had the opportunity to properly organize and catalogue the contents."

Cesco's voice was wooden. "You want a list of everything in the library."

"Oh, nothing so basic! I want a proper codex, with cross-references to each work. You must read every one of them, noting the names of each person referenced, the page, the volume, et cetera. Obviously you will be living with the holy brothers while you perform this feat. You will not leave their walls for any reason."

Cesco sat upright. "The feast of San Bonaventura is in a week! Capulletto's ball—"

"—is much too risky for a body in your condition. No, no more feasts for you, boy. We must get you well! Besides, even were you in peak form, you'd be hard pressed to surpass last year's escapade. No, you'll spend that and every other night within the monastery walls, reading Latin and Greek – so fortunate that you are skilled in languages." Cangrande stepped away from the wall, looming over his heir with palpable delight. "What say you?"

What else was there but to agree? It was the cleverest of all punishments. Cesco had anticipated being an invalid in the palace, with access to other people. Whereas inside the monastery he would be effectively imprisoned. He would hear the general news, but no more.

It also cut Cesco off from the continuing intrigues of Detto's mother and her veiled hints at some weapon to be used against the Scaliger. For the first time he was tempted to accept her offer.

But no. This battle was his to win or lose. Cesco refused to be a pawn in their ongoing duel, whatever that was about.

Besides, for a child raised in the household of the poet Dante, being locked up with a few hundred books was hardly a cruel fate. Cesco was certain he would emerge out the other side whole and ready for the next step in his plan. Once he figured out what that step would be.

"I agree," he said, bowing to the Scaliger's will.

Thus it was that the revelers at the celebratory feast were ignorant of all save that Cesco was convalescing. Passerino Bonaccolsi was awarded the victor's prize, and the Veronese 'army' shared in the spoils. Montagu's ransom was paid by the Scaliger himself in homage to the English knight's bravery. Crowns were awarded, and torques, and swords, and horses. No one would leave Verona without experiencing the extravagance of the Scaliger's court.

In the midst of the revels there was a resounding knock on the doors to the great hall. Repeated four more times, each blow reverberated tremendously around the chamber. Mid-quaff, Cangrande gestured for the doors to be opened.

In strode nine men in immaculate dress, richly jeweled and exuding authority. Nine men – a heavenly number. This deliberate calculation was not lost on Cangrande as he set down his wine and stood. Instantly he understood the meaning of this invasion.

Though he had not yet achieved an audience with his Holiness, Ser Pietro Alaghieri had succeeded thus far at least: the Pope had sent his own emissaries to learn the condition of the Greyhound's soul.

ACT II

Rock of the Lord

Ten

Cangrande waited a whole week after the festival's end before granting the papal envoys a public audience, but backroom conversations informed everyone of what was happening.

Though they had lost two major battles, the Guelphs of Lombardy felt they were winning the on-going war. Florence's fractured factions had been unified under Carlo di Calabria, and Lombardy had a new papal legate: the pragmatically pious and energetic Cardinal Bertrando del Poggetto. Born Bertrand de Poyet, he was nephew to Pope John, and somewhat resembled that dwarfish prince with his rounded shoulders, protuberant lips, and over-large eyes.

It was this man himself who had arrived with fanfare at Verona's gates demanding to see the Scaliger. His mission? Publicly, he was here to discuss tithes. Privately, it was quickly learned, the Pope wished nothing less than to detach Cangrande from the Ghibelline cause.

The actual interview was fraught with tension. The new cardinal was near to bursting with suppressed hope, his arguments well in order and his purse at the ready. The Anziani were equally fidgety. They knew their Capitano well enough to recognize they had no idea which way he would jump. The new emperor had been no help in the recent wars, and since his victory over his rival his demand for taxes had only grown. Perhaps Cangrande would see profit in changing his coat and, in effect, ending all strife in Italy by bringing his lands into the papal embrace. His forces combined with those of Florence, Padua, and Treviso would conquer all, and he would be honoured forever.

But then he would be just one among many. Something the Scaliger had ever balked at being.

Of all the people gathered in the Domus Nuova, only Cangrande presented a careless demeanor. The Anziani were all aflutter, with low whispers behind hands and narrowed eyes beneath furrowed brows.

Seated behind the Scaliger, splinted leg sticking out awkwardly, Cesco watched the back of the great man's head, trying to read the mind within. His monastic exile had been lifted for a single hour, and not to gratify his curiosity. The arrival of nine ecclesiastics gave Cangrande an all-too-convenient patsy for the question of 'Who tried to murder the Heir?'

Here to drive home the connection, Cesco was under strict instructions, publicly given, not to speak. This once, he intended to obey. *Unless an opportunity arises...*

The entire business was civilly borne, and took only ninety minutes. The Capitano welcomed the cardinal in lavish terms, congratulated him on his elevation, then invited him to speak. The cardinal was equally eloquent in his praise of his host before launching into a history of the Guelph-Ghibelline strife. It took him an hour to reach the present situation, whereupon he laid out all the advantages of the Guelph cause and all the acclaim that would heap itself in Heaven and on this mortal plane if only Cangrande would set aside this pernicious emperor and declare the Pope as God's ultimate authority on Earth.

It was, perhaps, simplistic to claim that the strife was about papal or imperial authority. That was certainly how it had all started, but Italian regional and familial rivalries had fed the struggle. The ancient feud between the original Cappelletti and Montecchi, for example, had divided down Guelph and Ghibelline lines, but become far more personal over time.

However, by giving Cangrande the noble-sounding option of ending the struggle in the name of Christ, the cardinal was opening a grand door that promised riches, fame, and glory everlasting.

As the cardinal drew his address to a close, the lounging Cangrande made a show of considering for a goodly length of time. Then he straightened, smiled, and stood. "Your Grace, you have made a compelling argument, one that I know resonates with every man here. This struggle has gone on far too long, with much blood shed and wrongs performed on both sides.

"I approach, as a poet once said, the midpoint in the journey of my life, and I find the glory of battle dimming in the memory of friends lost, and the glory of diplomacy growing, as it keeps the blood of my still-living friends from being shed."

He's going to do it, everyone thought. *Verona is about to change allegiance, and the whole world will change because of it. The Emperor will lose all hope of Italy and be reduced to mere King of the Germans. All on the Scaliger's whim.*

Cangrande faced the cardinal. "The fact does not change, though, that I have sworn an oath. Several oaths, to several men, some living, some dead. An oath is a sacred bond, made before God and witnessed by his representatives. It charges not the body but the soul with a duty. Who is the keeper of oaths, your Grace?"

The cardinal answered at once. "God is, through his son Jesus Christ."

"I must respectfully split hairs with you. I am the keeper of my oaths. The great Lord in Heaven gave us free will. And, as a wise friend of mine once told me, a man is responsible for his actions, if not his stars. God will hold me responsible for my choice, but the choice is mine if I am to keep it or no. Should I join your cause, I would be damned. Unless," he added, "your pope would grant me absolution."

"He is your pope as well, you have only forgotten." Yet the cardinal beamed. "I have no qualms about assuring you he will grant that absolution."

Cangrande pretended to stagger back a step. "In truth? If he will let a man foreswear himself so easily, then he is no fit keeper of God's flame on Earth!" With visible effort, a reasonable facsimile of genuine decision, the lord of Verona composed himself. "You have made up my mind, your Grace. I thank you for your time and for your considered, and considerable, volley of words. I do agree there must be an ultimate power in this temporal world. But I believe that such power belongs not to the Pope, but to the Emperor."

The cardinal bowed, his original suspicions confirmed. It had been a valiant try. Now he could work to destroy this cur with a clear conscience.

There were polite formalities, though strained. Farewells were taken, gifts bestowed. But the moment the papal delegation had passed through the doors Cangrande addressed his nobles. "My lords, six days ago I sent messages to all the Ghibelline leaders in the Feltro, asking them to gather in the city of Mozzo tomorrow evening. If the Guelphs believe they are strong enough to sway us with mere words, then we must prove to them that we are unswayable. I leave tomorrow morning to meet with our allies and propose we summon Ludwig from Germany to receive his much delayed coronation in Rome."

First amazement, then cheering, and cheering, and cheering. Cesco cursed inwardly. A great adventure, and he was stuck in the monastery. Ill-luck – or ill-favoured stars. Whatever the cause, the mistiming of it made him throw a mental curse in Pietro Alaghieri's direction. *Truly, Nuncle, couldn't you have been just a little less persuasive?*

Carpentras, France
3 August 1326

Petrarch roared with laughter as he set the letter aside. "Your master certainly isn't going out of his way to make your job easier!"

"Indeed." Because of the vagaries of messenger services, the tale of Verona's tourney had arrived scant hours before the report of Cangrande's meeting with the papal embassy, both nearly a month past.

Pietro's more immediate concerns were the letters from Morsicato and Antonia. Thus he had to drag his attention back to the official letter from the Anziani, written by Bernardo Ervari with a laconic coda from the Scaliger himself.

Petrarch was still tittering. "Forgive me, it's just – all your hard work, gone in an instant! I suppose it's something that he didn't actually fling manure at them, but still..." He chortled himself to silence.

"It is beyond insulting," admitted Pietro. His frustration was palpable. Cangrande's refusal ensured that Pietro would not be granted a papal audience this year. *Not unless something changes...* But it was not in Pietro to actively wish for Cangrande's death. At least, not until Cesco was of age.

Cesco, who it seemed was once again the subject of murderous designs. *I should be there!*

Seeing Pietro was not inclined to laugh at this latest reversal, Petrarch composed himself. "Come! I know what will cheer your spirits!" He called for horses and cloaks. Despite the summer heat, there was always a strong wind blowing through the region, and it was a foolish man who did not dress against it.

They mounted and rode the seventeen miles into Avignon. Stabling their horses, they emerged into the street and Pietro had to turn to avoid several passers-by who made no concession for him. He was, after all, a known heretic. It was something he was slowly growing accustomed to. *How awful is it that I am becoming inured to insult?*

Not for the first time, Pietro asked, "Where are we going?"

This time Petrarch answered. "To meet with cooler heads."

As Pietro realized their destination, he almost protested. Bonagratia and Occam had been quite correct in their assessments. In the four months since their introduction, Pietro had followed the advice of the imprisoned ecclesiastics and avoided their company. Not only because associating with them would stain his endeavors. He also avoided their society because the reverse was true – being seen in the company of an excommunicant would do them no good whatsoever.

Apparently Petrarch thought that Cangrande's rebuff of the papal overture had altered matters significantly enough that Pietro now had nothing to lose.

"Besides, they've declared Occam guilty of heresy. There's nothing more either of us can do to ruin him."

Being a favoured up-and-comer with the Colonna family, Petrarch had no difficulty gaining access to the monastery. Indeed, the men at the gate knew him well, indicating he was a frequent visitor. "Yes, I come here two or three times a week. No one even thinks to question my intents – I am seen as harmless." He laughed and flapped his gargantuan slashed velvet sleeves. "There are advantages to seeming feckless!"

Informed of their visitors' arrival, the two friars emerged into the common yard and gave the Florentines a warm welcome.

"You both seem to be wearing your imprisonment well," said Pietro.

"Too well," said Bonagratia, patting his stomach. "We're being Frenchified. We've traded the Sirocco for the Mistral, the Tiber for the Rhône, the Tarpeian Rock for the Rock of the Lord. I hear even the papal wine has changed, from *vernaccia* to *beaune*. It's insidious. My French robes are a little too comfortable. I'm not one who believes in mortifying the flesh, but too much comfort makes a man soft, weakens his mind."

"That is the blight of the Church in general," added Occam as they strolled the sunny edges of the yard.

"An expectation of comfort, of ease. Our Lord did not indulge in ease when there was work to be done."

"You're beginning to sound like Fra Bonagratia here," observed Petrarch with amusement.

"Ha!" It seemed odd to find a sense of humour in so learned a thinker. "I am political not by nature, but by necessity. Their mistake has been to closet the two of us together for so long. Our heresies are completely separate, but we're growing to see them as stemming from the same corrupted root. So we've been honing our arguments, sharpening our wits on each other." The English friar was visibly pleased, a wrinkly grin etched across his masque-like face.

"Meanwhile, we are being treated to the best Avignon has to offer," said Bonagratia. "Airy rooms, fine food – better by far than our usual fare. They are killing us with kindness."

"In the hope that comfort will persuade us where illogical arguments won't," added Occam.

"We touched on your so-called heresies back in April," said Pietro, "and of course I've heard bits and pieces. But I'd like to hear your causes from your own lips."

Both friars were pleased to have a fresh audience. Occam gestured for Bonagratia. "Let you begin. Your cause is the grander, while mine is a mere quibble."

"Being a lawyer," objected Bonagratia genially, "Ser Alaghieri must enjoy quibbles. But as you wish."

As they took their exercise around the walled garden, Pietro listened to two separate but complementary ecclesiastic causes. Bonagratia's was rooted in a very simple collision of ideal and venal interpretations of Scripture. The friar was not confined for his own ideas, but rather for the ideals of the Order he represented: the Frati Minori, also known as the Franciscans.

The debate had begun between the Dominican and Franciscan orders, who wrangled over whether it was heretical to assert that Christ and His Apostles possessed property, a contest rooted in the Bible. In Matthew 19, Jesus says to a man, 'If you wish to be perfect, go, sell all you have, give your money to the poor, and come, and follow me.' San Francesco of Assisi had taken this passage literally, and his followers naturally took this as a tenet of their Order. An earlier Pope had given his sanction to their refusal to own property, even the clothes on their backs, by claiming papal ownership of all things Franciscan. He then allowed them use of the clothes, food, and lands that were now, technically, his. Thus the Franciscan Order owned nothing.

To prove their point, the Franciscans had called a general chapter of the order in Perugia four years earlier. There the Franciscan leader, Michael of Cesena, together with Bonagratia and others, had published two letters affirming their belief that Christ owned no property.

But ecclesiastic poverty was not a popular topic in Avignon's new and ever-expanding Palais des Papes. Displeased, Pope John XXII renounced ownership of the Franciscan goods and published a papal Bull asserting that ownership of a thing could not be separated from its actual use. If Christ wore shoes, they were his shoes. Therefore Christ had owned property and it was just and good that the Church should do the same.

Ill at the time, Michael of Cesena had deputed Bonagratia to speak for the Franciscans at Avignon. "That was three years ago. There was a public debate in the presence of his Holiness and several cardinals. I showed perhaps more passion than discretion, and was justly humbled for my pride. John republished his Bull with even greater ideas of Church property, and I was cast into this silken prison."

As Pietro's own supposed heresy was similar, he knew these details fairly well. Yet it was enlightening to hear the tale from Bonagratia, himself so passionate about a cause that Pietro had unwittingly joined. "Michael of Cesena is your leader?"

"Indeed. With Ubertino da Casale. The Pope wants Michael here to answer for our order. And he wants Ubertino dead."

Having once been destined for the Church, Pietro knew these men by name at least. "I thought they were friends!"

"No more. Last fall Ubertino fled Avignon, hurling insults as he went. He referred to the Pope as the anti-Christ."

It was unusual for something so momentous to have escaped Pietro's notice. But then, fall had been a distracting time – especially the month he'd spent sitting in a Venetian prison.

He turned now to the other disgraced ecclesiastical, more famous by far. Occam had never finished his degree at Oxford, earning him the title of *Venerabilis Inceptor* – 'Worthy Beginner.' In the years since leaving school, he'd earned a second nickname – *Doctor Invincibilis*. The heresies of the Unconquerable Teacher were more convoluted than his friend's, and far more numerous. Taken separately they did not match the grand nature of Bonagratia's cause, but together they were a landslide of logical contradictions and impossibilities in Church doctrine.

Bonagratia chimed in. "In many ways, Brother Occam's persecution is due to ill timing, or an ill-choice of orders. Had he worn the robes of a Dominican, he would have been able to espouse all the same views in peace. But as a brilliant Franciscan in a time when the Pope was fighting that order, he is seen as dangerous."

"How?" asked Pietro, fascinated.

"I am an unwitting advocate for the imperial cause," said Occam ruefully. "For my reason tells me that while Holy Church has complete authority over matters of the spirit, matters of the temporal world are outside the scope of the Holy See."

"How so?"

"This is good," said Bonagratia with relish.

"The chain follows thus," said Occam. "God, in His infinite wisdom, gave Adam the power to name the beasts, thereby signifying that Man has authority over the creatures on this temporal plane. For the word *nomen* derives from *nomos*, the Latin word for 'law.' Thus did the Lord grant Man the power to make laws on Earth. And by Man, I do not mean a single man, for any single man may be a fool, or addled, or dim-witted, or mendacious, or mean-spirited. I mean Man as a collective whole, rather like the Athenians of old, or the noble Roman senate. For one man might make a bad law, not to the general good. This is not true of a collection of the best and brightest, combined together to create laws governing Man's actions on Earth. And please note, I do not suggest that Man has any influence over God's Law, which is separate and inscrutable. Are we thus far in accord?"

"Absolutely," agreed Pietro. It was an argument that would have pleased his father.

"Very well. Having thus established that the governance of earthly matters is separate from divine and spiritual rule, which is God's province, it then follows as sure as night follows day that the Church has no authority over temporal matters. To say it does is to diminish the Church."

"What do you mean?"

"This is the best part," whispered Bonagratia, nudging Pietro's arm.

Occam took no note, caught up in forging the links in his chain. "God has gifted Man with reason, and with the rule of Law over earthly things. But, in His infinite goodness, he did not gift this only to those who have seen the divine wisdom of Christ and been blessed to follow Him. All men have this ability, for did not the Romans do this? Was Caesar not capable of reason and good governance, despite being denied the example of Christ? What of the heathens in other lands? Do they not have the ability to rule themselves wisely, but for their staggering omission of denying Christ? They may be damned, but the great God of hosts, God of Israel, Father of Christ, has bestowed upon them the same capacity for earthly law that he gave to Adam. All Mankind is so gifted, for if it was not, then His greatest gift would mean nothing. What is God's greatest gift to Man?"

Pietro puzzled for a moment. "Breath. Life."

"Dogs breathe. Mice breathe. Even fish must breathe, I imagine. What is it they lack?"

"The capacity to reason."

"Just so. And Reason leads to Choice. Choice is indicative of Free Will. Therefore God's greatest gift to Man is Free Will. But if all men are not gifted with reason and the power to make earthly law, then his gift is a Trojan one, which is unthinkable in the Almighty, God of Heaven."

Pietro was feeling a little breathless. "Everything you say makes perfect sense. But why do you say that claiming power over temporal matters diminishes the Church?"

Occam looked grave. "Pietro, can I fly?"

"Excuse me?"

"Am I possessed of the ability, like the birds in the sky, to open my arms and take flight?"

Pietro glanced at the grinning Bonagratia, wondering if this were some sort of trick question. "I – I doubt it."

"You are right to do so. And if I were to make claim to such an awesome power, you would be correct to call me both liar and fool. To claim a power I do not have opens me to ridicule. Now follow me in this. If the Church claims to have authority, by virtue of its seat as the Voice of the Lord on Earth, over affairs of Man, then it must mean all Mankind. But you will agree that other nations, heathen nations, Mohammedan nations, pagan nations – you must agree that they do not respect Mother Church's authority over them. And just as I would be a fool to claim I have the power of flight, the Church would be a fool to claim a power it does not possess, that of dictating mortal law here on Earth. Tell me, does the great Khan obey the will of the Pope?"

"Of course not."

"Does the savage cannibal of Africa? Does the Oriental of Captain Polo's tales?"

"No."

"So if the Pope insists he has authority over all Mankind laws, he looks as foolish as the parent who says he has absolute command over a disobedient child. Impotence is laughable, and every time the Church insists it has authority over all men in creation, it shows its impotence. But this is impossible, is it not? God's representative on Earth cannot be impotent, for God in His holy wisdom would never allow such a thing. So it is clearly God's will that the Church should not have sway over this mortal coil.

In fact, Christ himself says that they are separate. 'Render unto Caesar the things which are Caesar's, and unto God the things that are God's.' What could be a clearer statement that there is a separation between Divine Law and mortal law?"

"What about Mosaic Law?" pressed Pietro, fascinated to hear the answer. "The laws brought down by Moses from Mount Sinai? Are those not for all Mankind?"

"Not at all. Those are for the followers of the true faith, which we are blessed to be, thanks be to God. 'I am the Lord thy God. Thou shalt have no other gods before me.' There is an implicit acknowledgement of other gods, those belonging to heathens and unenlightened souls who have not found the blessing of Christ. While those are, yes, Divine Laws, they apply to our spiritual selves, setting up the scales by which we will be judged in the hereafter. They are not Man's law, though often they overlap. But who has ever been dunned at law for coveting? Coveting is of the soul. It is the *taking* of another Man's property that troubles man's law, while the sin of *coveting* troubles God."

Bonagratia was annoyed by a seeming digression. "Brother, please finish your thought on the foolishness of the Church reaching past its own arm."

Occam held up a hand in submission. "Forgive me – quibbles! We will certainly all agree that the authority of the Pope stems from blessed Saint Peter, the first pope, the rock upon which our Lord and Savior Jesus Christ built our beloved Church. And as Peter's power is derived from Christ, so Christ's power derives from the goodness of His Holy Father, God in Heaven. If it were the will of God that the Church should have power over the affairs of mortal man, then It would be Divine Law, not mortal law, and be enforced with all the power of the heavenly host. But God gave all Mankind the ability to make the laws, and the free will to choose to follow them, without temporal punishment for Man's acts. God's divine punishment will be meted out after death, but God's representatives have no power to enforce His divine will on Earth. Ergo, they are not meant to. If God wished them to have such authority, He would have granted them commensurate power. And if Mother Church claims to hold sway over Man's law without God's sanction to enforce it, then they make themselves fools."

Occam spread his hands. "Thus I come to the inescapable conclusion that our beloved Holy Church should not meddle in the affairs of mortal laws, states, or princes. We must be above those cares, though not above those laws, for we are mortal too, and must therefore be subject to the laws of Man."

Bonagratia laughed. "Unconquerable indeed! You see now, Ser Pietro, why he terrifies so many of our esteemed brothers. In the space of ten minutes he has concluded that not only should the Church not influence statecraft, but should even subject itself to the laws of kings and princes!"

Shrugging, Occam rubbed his bald pate. "To flout the laws of a prince diminishes the prince's power. God gave Man sovereignty on Earth, and to question Man's law is to call into question the wisdom of the Lord. I, for one, find that sinful."

Pietro was laughing even as he felt a door open in his mind. It was the same way he'd often felt talking to his father, or to Cangrande. "Is that why you are here?"

Occam pulled a face. "Indirectly! It's envy has pinioned me here in this – place." If the word he was clearly longing to say was Hell-hole, he couldn't bring himself to speak so of the Holy See. "My accuser is one Brother John Lutterell. He came to Avignon after being expelled as chancellor at Oxford, to complain to the Pope of losing his post—"

"Thanks in large part to you," interjected Bonagratia.

"Not at all! He was a poor thinker, and a poorer guide in studies. If we clashed, it was no fault of mine. Besides, I had already departed when the faculty voted him out. Truly, his actions threatened to create a schism in the whole English church. Alas, I am afraid brother Lutterell has a very poor grasp of reason. But that is not always the sign of a deficient mind. I'm sure he would have been a most excellent mender of soles, if not souls." This was, of course, a most impolitic statement, as the Pope was himself the son of a shoemaker.

To Pietro, Occam continued. "As proof of my heresy, Lutterell produced my commentaries on the Sentences of Peter Abelard – we all write them, it's a common teaching tool. But Lutterell was able to convince several prominent inquisitors that my commentaries contained fifty-six heresies. Many were decided to be in theological error – the fools – but none were deemed heretical. So, rather than release me, they started a second inquiry into ten new charges, of which they've found me guilty. But other than seizing my writings, they've done nothing to me. Whenever they call me before them to pass their sentence upon me, I show them their errors in such a way that they are forced to convene a new commission."

"Which is why they've stopped trying to pass sentence." Bonagratia was darkly amused. "They can't out-argue you, so they keep you in this temporal Limbo."

"Far easier than challenging their own thinking," grumbled Occam.

Upon being urged, he went on to list more of his heresies, clearly enjoying his audience. The most contentious one was Occam's challenge to the Sacrament of the Altar, when the wafer and wine transformed into the body and blood of Christ. After tracing the logical fallacies of transubstantiation for Pietro, he concluded by saying, "It does not diminish the miracle of the Resurrection to say that the sacrament of the altar is symbolism. Otherwise it is cannibalism, a paganistic return to ideas of magic incompatible with the modern world."

"It all sounds like good theology to me," said Pietro. "Aristotle would be proud."

His attempted agreement brought groans from Bonagratia and caused Occam to shake his head vehemently. "I defy theology! God is not logical! Faith and reason are separate entities – as the Trinity alone proves."

That surprised Pietro. Most educated holy men embraced theology, the Logic of God. "How so?"

"The Trinity defies logic. In simple terms, the Trinity states that God is the Father, yes?"

"Yes."

"It also says that Christ is God, no?"

"No – I mean, yes, it does say that."

"Well, logic tells us that if God is the Father and Christ is God, then Christ is the Father. Is Christ the Father?"

"No, Christ is the son."

"A logical fallacy," concluded Occam. "Proving that logic cannot be applied to God as we apply it in philosophy. The laws of men are logical, reasonable. But Man is a fool if he thinks he can unravel the mysteries of God Above. Anyone who says they know the Will of God is a liar, a sinner, or selling something."

The lawyer in Pietro wanted to pursue this conversation, but Petrarch had long ago grown restless. "To divert you from your imprisonment, we've come for your advice," he told them, and laid out the recent events in Verona.

Like the aspiring poet, both friars found more to laugh at than lament in the tale. Less amused, Pietro said, "He has made my mission impossible."

"Nonsense!" cried Bonagratia. "There is a simple way out of your predicaments, both personal and official. One not open to us."

"There is?"

"The trouble is that you're a philosophical lawyer! You think in terms of arguments, moral force, law, justice. Those things mean absolutely nothing in Avignon."

"As we continue to learn, to our cost," added Occam.

"Then what carries weight?" asked Pietro.

Bonagratia's sunny countenance clouded over. "Money. Money would quieten the waters your lord of Verona has disturbed. No matter how insulting he is."

Occam nodded, biting his lips to keep himself from commenting.

To their surprise, Pietro was actually smiling. For once Cangrande would pay for his deeds. Literally.

"For your case, though, there is an additional obstacle."

Pietro blinked. "Why is mine different?"

Bonagratia folded his hands before him, as if in prayer. "At Petrarch's request I have been making discreet enquires. There is a good deal of sympathy for your plight among some of the lower and mid-level clerics. The fact that you have not lobbied for yourself has been noted with approval, and the fact that you are known to pray each night while not forcing yourself unwelcomed into a church is admirably martyr-like."

Pietro shot a look to Petrarch, who shrugged. "The light is often lit, and the servants have remarked your devotion. I believe they wish me to emulate you." He laughed, causing the two holy men to frown. Petrarch was being groomed for minor orders, and despite their current ill-odour, both men were devout enough to wish Petrarch might not laugh so at the idea of midnight prayer.

Bonagratia continued. "Petrarch and his brother have spread the word of your devotion, and your humility. It is said that your error was born of compassion for those in your care, rather than some form of deliberate heresy."

"Then what's the obstacle?" asked Pietro.

"There appears to be someone who is entirely opposed to your regaining your rightful place in God's view. This person is whispering into the Pope's ear, and thus holds all talk of an audience at bay. It seems quite personal."

"Who?" demanded Pietro.

"We do not know," said Bonagratia apologetically. "We are shut out from any real intelligence. We can only work through the rumours that reach us here in our confinement."

"Is there any one man that you have offended grievously?" pressed Occam. "Or even slighted?"

Pietro thought hard, running down a list of enemies. There were several, but none had much sway with the Church, not even Carrara or Dandolo. He shook his head.

"What about your father's enemies?" suggested Petrarch.

That was a possibility. "If so, I might not know it. He placed so many holy men in Hell… And in life he wrote to so many people, especially in the cause of returning the papacy to Rome."

"It is very likely that," said Occam with satisfaction. "The obvious solution."

"And easily remedied," said Bonagratia. "The son should not be held to account for the transgressions of the father. Discover this man's identity and reconcile him to you. His is the lone voice that drowns the choir singing your praises. Gain his approval, then open your master's purse and all shall be well for both you and the Scaliger."

"Thank you. Both." The knowledge that someone was actively working against him was disturbing, but also lighted an avenue to explore.

"I can play the bloodhound for you, Pietro," said Petrarch cheerily. "Stefano Colonna will certainly know who it is that's so objectionable. But the matter of how much money still remains."

Occam and Bonagratia exchanged a look. "We may be able to assist you," said Occam slowly.

Both Pietro and Petrarch stared. "In fixing the price of a *bribe*?"

"A moment, please." Bonagratia took Occam by the arm and the two men stepped aside to converse in low tones. Their conference ended with Occam departing into the cloisters while Bonagratia returned to their guests. "We have come into possession of an item that will be of use to you. But no one may know that it reached you through us. Indeed, it would be best if you were careful to never reveal its existence. It would be fatally embarrassing for his Holiness, and would damage the cause of any man possessing it."

"What is it?" asked Petrarch excitedly.

"A weapon of sorts." Bonagratia clearly had misgivings. "At least, that was the intent of the misguided soul who bequeathed it to my care. He meant me to publish it, I think. But that would not serve any purpose other than complete the alienation of the Pope. We have been arguing how best to rid ourselves of it. In fact, after reading it, I wish I could scrub clean the balls of my eyes."

"What is it?" repeated Petrarch, breathlessly.

"You shall see."

A few minutes later Occam returned, carrying a copy of Aristotle's Polemics. At least, that was what the cover proclaimed. Yet when Occam placed it in Pietro's hands, he brushed his fingers and palms on his robes as if to cleanse himself. Hardly the way a man devoted to reason would treat the great philosopher.

"What is it?" asked Petrarch a third time, cracking the cover a fraction.

"The official ledger for papal indulgences," said Occam softly.

"What's so remarkable in that?" Indulgences were monetary prayers, amounts of gold paid to the Church in exchange for forgiveness of sins. It was common practice, a well-established part of Church doctrine.

"You will understand when you read it. Now hide it about your person. If it were known that we ever possessed such a ledger we would surely be put to death. Use it carefully. If asked, we will deny all knowledge of its existence."

Pietro did as he was bidden. Better he carry it than Petrarch, having far less to lose. As he placed it in his satchel he caught an odor rising from the book, something familiar yet disturbing. "What is that smell?"

"That," said Bonagratia in disgust, "is the smell of money."

Though anxious to rush back to Petrarch's house and open the ledger, Pietro resumed this pleasant stroll around the cloister garden. Bonagratia and Occam were not often allowed guests, and it would be sinful to deprive them of company after all their good advice.

They discussed news of the world, starting with the ongoing contest raging across the Channel. Because three of the conversants were Italian, the discussion focused on the repercussions on their homeland. Banking families in all the major communes watched with rising dread the waning power of the English king, to whom they had loaned vast sums of money. The war with Scotland had drained the coffers of the island nation, and word was the Scots were about to hold their own Parliament, while the Irish were revolting again. Last year the new French king had snaffled up all English possessions on the mainland. Edward II had sent his wife to negotiate, only to have her refuse to return. At present Edward II was demanding the return of his son and the death of the queen's lover, Roger Mortimer. Edward couldn't even control his wife, let alone his country.

"Roger Mortimer is said to be a level head, but he's playing the fool." Petrarch winked at Pietro. "Another Mariotto – a fool for love."

Occam shook his head. "Take it from a fellow Englishman. Mortimer is no fool."

From there the talk turned to Charles IV, the fourth French king in ten years. Pietro recalled the curse of the last Templar knight, damning the French royal line to the thirteenth issue. So far the curse was proving quite potent.

Talk shifted to Germany. "Bonagratia and I hear that Ludwig has consented to the invitation issued by the Lombards."

"Where did you learn that?" demanded Petrarch.

"Even imprisoned we have our sources," said Occam cryptically. "He plans to travel to both Milan and Rome to receive the imperial crown. With or without papal blessing."

"Another excommunicant," said Bonagratia sadly. "It is a weapon His Holiness wields too lightly."

Petrarch asked the unaskable. "Are you in communication with the Emperor?"

"Of course not," replied Occam at once. "All my correspondence is read before it comes to my hand. It would not aid my circumstances to be thought in league with imperial forces."

"Nor mine," agreed Bonagratia. "To ally ourselves with him would put us at war with the Pope. Still, we hear things..." His voice trailed off.

"Well, your sources move more swiftly than ours," said Pietro. "We've only just heard the Lombards were issuing the invitation."

"With Pietro's unrepentant heretic master leading the call," added Petrarch.

Pietro couldn't restrain himself. "He's not my master."

"So you keep saying. Yet you serve him."

"I am willing, in this instance, to carry out his wishes. For the good of Verona."

"For the good of Verona's heir, you mean," said Occam shrewdly.

"One and the same," answered Pietro.

When they returned to Carpentras, Lucia was lying in wait. "Ser Alaghieri, I'm afraid I must trouble you to explain another passage to me."

Lucia was a problem whose solution Pietro could not see. She flirted with him mercilessly, especially when her brothers were not present. He had taken to locking himself up in his rooms, or else absenting himself from the house as often as possible.

His only solace was when she left the house to go visiting – another source of shame for the family. Girls of good families did not wander off alone. Indeed, they didn't venture out of doors without a family member and a troop of attendants and guards. Petrarch had tried to tie her to the hearth after their father's death but, as it had with her siblings, the death of Petracco had released some kind of brake in Lucia. She liked to elude her keepers, and would often return from God knew where bearing armfuls of new clothes or trinkets. Since her purse was not so deep, these must have been gifts. From whom, and in exchange for what, was unclear.

Petrarch was beyond distracted at his sister's behavior. Pietro recalled the stories of his own sister marching around Florence doing their father's business at the age of twelve. Knowing Antonia, Pietro had been able to excuse much – she was not a girl given to flights of silliness. Yet, viewed dispassionately, it was almost scandalous. Lucia's similar behavior made him acutely aware of how damning Antonia's actions must have been in the eyes of his countrymen. A girl's virginity was her only value. Pietro knew his sister had always aspired to a cloistered life, but most probably assumed Antonia's holy vows were only taken to free her from the taint of her earlier life.

Somehow Pietro doubted that Lucia was destined for a similar fate. He couldn't imagine her in a convent. At least, not voluntarily.

Her latest tactic was a good one. Petrarch's refusal to read the *Commedia* made Pietro the only man in the household who could assist her in parsing the poetry. Fortunately today Pietro was able to beg off, citing business with her brother.

Closeted in Petrarch's office with doors locked and windows shuttered, Pietro and Petrarch hurriedly opened the ledger. After several pages of instructions to cardinals not to allow this tome to fall into 'less enllghtened' hands, they came to a list of indulgences.

For the first few pages these seemed innocent enough – the price for missing Church services, the price of a late baptism, forgiveness for ill thoughts or similar sins. Then all at once the list grew more complex, and Pietro felt his skin begin to crawl:

> If an ecclesiastic commits the sin of the flesh, be it with nuns, his cousins, his nieces or his goddaughters, or with any other woman, the guilty one shall be absolved for the sum of 67 pounds, 12 sous.

> If, outside the sins of fornication, he asks absolution of the sin against nature or of bestiality, he shall pay 219 pounds, 15 sous; however, if he has committed this

sin only with young boys or with animals and not with women, the fine shall be reduced to 131 pounds, 15 sous.

A nun who has given herself up to several men, either one at a time or on successive occasions, in her convent or outside it, and who would wish to obtain the rank of abbess, shall pay 131 pounds, 15 sous.

"This is appalling! They've taken every clerical sin imaginable and fixed an exact price for forgiveness, down to the smallest coin! What kind of mind does that?"

"A lawyer's mind," answered Petrarch sourly. It was not a jab at their shared occupation, but rather an acknowledgement that John XXII had studied law in his youth. Which implied that his was the guiding light behind this book of simony.

For that was what this was. Legend told of Simon Magus of Samaria, also called Simon the Sorcerer, who offered money to San Pietro in exchange for the gift of the Holy Ghost. Forever after the commerce of spiritual things for material gains was known as simony, and strictly forbidden.

Until now, it seemed. They read on:

> Priests who would obtain authorization to live in concubinage with their female relatives shall pay 76 pounds, 1 sou.
>
> For every sin of lust committed by a layman, the absolution shall cost 27 pounds, 1 sou; for incest one shall in conscience add 4 pounds.
>
> The adulterous wife who asks absolution to be sheltered from all proceed ings and to have wide license to continue sinful relations, shall pay the Pope 87 pounds, 5 sous. In a similar case, the husband shall submit the same tax; if they have committed incest with their children, they shall in conscience add 6 pounds.

"Dear Lord. Is incest truly that common?"

Petrarch affected a jaded air. "Where have you been living?"

"Among civilized peoples, I guess."

"O come! Just because it isn't known doesn't mean it isn't happening."

Stifling a disgusted shiver, Pietro returned to the ugly siren song of the ledger:

> A husband who has struck his wife roughly shall pay into the treasury of

the Chancellery 3 pounds, 4 sous; if he has killed her, he shall pay 17 pounds, 15 sous. If he has committed this crime to marry another, he shall pay an additional 52 pounds, 9 sous. Those who have assisted the husband in the murder shall be absolved at 2 pounds per person.

The wife who shall destroy the child in her womb, and the father who shall have aided in accomplishing this crime, shall each pay 17 pounds, 15 sous. The person who shall procure the abortion of a child of which he is not the father shall give a pound less.

Whoever has killed a Bishop or a high Church official shall pay 131 pounds, 14 sous, 6 deniers.

Whoever would wish to buy in advance absolution for any accidental murders that he might commit in the future shall pay 178 pounds, 15 sous.

Petrarch laughed hard at that. "There's a handy clause! A free murder, absolved in advance?"

"Be fair," chided Pietro, so horrified he was laughing. "It does say 'accidental' murder."

"True."

A heretic who is converted shall pay for his absolution 269 pounds. The son of a heretic burned or killed by any other torture shall be rehabilitated only by paying 218 pounds, 16 sous, 9 deniers.

An ecclesiastic who is not able to pay his debts and would like to escape prosecution by his creditors shall give the Pope 17 pounds, 8 sous, 6 deniers, and his credit shall be re-established.

The permission to set up merchandise shops and to sell different commodities under the portico of a church shall be granted at a price of 45 pounds, 19 sous, 3 deniers.

For the making of contraband and for defrauding the Prince of his rights, one shall pay 87 pounds, 3 deniers.

"What does that mean?" asked Petrarch.

"Smuggling," answered Pietro distractedly, still reading.

A virtuous monk desiring to pass his life in a hermitage shall pay to the treasury of the Pope 45 pounds, 19 sous.

A wandering apostate desiring to re-enter the fold shall pay the same sum to be absolved.

Monks and priests desiring to travel in lay clothing shall have the same tax imposed on them.

The illegitimate child of a priest desiring to serve in his father's parish shall pay 27 pounds, 1 sou.

An illegitimate child desiring to enter Holy Orders and possess benefices shall pay 15 pounds, 18 sous, 6 deniers.

Laymen who are crippled or deformed and who desire to enter Holy Orders and possess benefices shall pay to the Chancellery 38 pounds, 2 sous.

Whoever may wish to break his oath and still be guaranteed against all prosecution and all ignominy shall pay to the Pope 131 pounds, 15 sous.

And on, and on. Crimes of every size and every nature, with a price at the end of each. Crimes against God, Nature, the Church, or all three together. Crimes that should require a lifetime to repent, forgiven for a sum of gold.

Closing the cover on the final page, Pietro walked to the window and opened the shutters, breathing in the late summer air. "Dear Lord."

"In one way," said Petrarch, "you have to admire it."

Pietro understood what he meant. "It is certainly thorough. And I suppose it's the natural outcome of the concept of indulgences. If one can pay to remove a sin, then logically all sins have a price."

"Still," said Petrarch warily, "our friends were right. This isn't something the Church would ever like to see published."

Pietro's mind went instantly from the word 'publish' to his father. What would his father have thought of such a document? Certainly there would be one more pope burning in Hell – but where? The Eighth Circle mostly likely. The third chasm? The fifth, the sixth? Where did such a soul belong?

Pietro was startled to hear Petrarch say, "Still, this is excellent for us."

"What do you mean by that?"

"Isn't it obvious? What we must do is determine which of these apply to both you and the Scaliger, then gather the appropriate sum. Unlike your master, your excommunication is only about money. There's a reason for the local saying: 'If you can pay, you may pray.' This tome only proves it's true." Petrarch grinned. "Welcome to New Babylon."

Eleven

Caprino
17 October 1326

Gathered in the pre-dawn light, over a hundred men thundered across the countryside near the Lago di Garda in pursuit of a pair of hinds. Petruchio Bonaventura galloped in the front rank, with both Guglielmo Castelbarco the younger and elder vying for second place. Young Castelbarco was a man of fifteen years, thin and grave as his father.

Nico da Lozzo rode hard after them, looking young as ever despite pushing middle-age. At his side rode his squire, young Paride della Scala, eleven years old and dogged in his pursuit of honour. They were flanked by Montecchio and Capulletto, doing their damnedest to ignore each other.

The whole hunting party was raucous. Bishop Francis shouted for joy – the holy man was an avid hunter. Ziliberto dell'Angelo, the Scaliger's Master of the Hunt, was equally excited. He never tired of the thrill of the chase. Mastino and Fuchs both rode hard among the leaders. Alblivious and Poco were further back, whooping and hollering with the rest while not interested in actually competing. Otto the Burgundian, captain of a mercenary force and a current favourite of the Scaliger's, wore no expression whatsoever as he pressed his horse, his excitement showing only in the tension of his posture and the crack of his flail. Even the ancient Massimiliano da Villafranca, Cangrande's Constable, had been coaxed out of Verona for a holiday.

Before Cesco's advent, this had been the Scaliger's favourite pastime. His followers, most of them lords in their own right, would gather outside his palace at Caprino to carouse or doze in their saddles until the great man himself joined them. Then the hunt was on and it was up to each man to keep pace.

Bailardino Nogarola and Petruchio Bonaventura were longtime revelers, for whom hunting was as natural as breathing. Today they were instructing the boy they had in common - Bonaventura's squire, Nogarola's son.

Detto was thrilled to be present, and not just for the hunting. It was his first chance to see Cesco since his friend's leg had healed, and while he knew his uncle would be showing Cesco off to the world, he hoped they'd find time to ride and raise Cain as they had back in Ravenna, in the good old days.

Among the throng too was Morsicato, who'd received a laconic note from Cesco announcing his release from 'fraternal hell' and a return to 'the dead-liest game.' Construing that last phrase in its dark-est way, Morsicato had come to observe matters for himself.

Over the last three months Morsicato had made weekly visits to check on Cesco's mending limb. The leg was well, and its owner was even better – at least physically. Confined among the holy brothers, the boy knew better than to become a sloth, but there was definitely more meat to him. He looked rested, though all the reading had given him sore shoulders and bad posture. Best of all, his eyes showed no sign of barbiturate.

But Cesco's restless spirit chafed at his imprison-ment, especially as Verona's summer had been full of lively delights. Cangrande held one joyful event after another – feasts and races, jousts and goose-pulls, poetry salons and bear-baitings. And hunts, hunts, hunts. All of which Cesco heard through the walls of the monastery as he choked on the dust from scroll after scroll, his hand cramped from writing and his eyes blurred with Latin, Italian, German, and French words.

During his visits, Morsicato had asked Cesco what he was learning. "A great deal, all of it useless. What does it matter if someone at Caesar's court was in-triguing to fiddle with the grain dole? Or if Charlemagne paid his barber his weight in silver? I'm no historian. All I learn is that Fortune's wheel is ever turning, and that nothing ever truly changes. There is nothing new under the sun, only the illusion of novelty. A truly devastating thought," he'd added in disappointment.

Two weeks ago the boy had been pronounced fit by both doctors. At once the general invitation to hunt went forth, bringing everyone here, to the end of the Earth. Or so it felt. Caprino lay at the base of the Brenner Pass and had some of the most variable landscape in Lombardy. Flats and forests, lakes and slopes, it made for intriguing game and dangerous sport.

It was also the scene of Cangrande's wounding. Morsicato knew from Tharwat that Cesco was innocent of any misdeed. But that was not what was generally believed, hence the number of attending guests. Everyone wanted to see what would happen next in the battle between the Scaliger and his heir.

Uninvited, the doctor hadn't expected a ringing welcome from Cangrande. But upon emerging from the crowd of servants, pages, and retainers of the palace, the lord of Verona had come directly to him and kissed him in welcoming condolence. "I hope Esta's improving?"

"She is, lord," lied the doctor.

"I'm glad."

Appearing beside the Scaliger, Cesco also kissed Morsicato in greeting. His hair was razored close again, the first sign of the renewed struggle. "Here, give her this," he'd added, handing across a poem he'd scribbled on a scrap of paper. "An invention of my poor brain."

Intercepting the poem, Cangrande had scanned it. "Oh Cesco, this would only serve to hasten her ill-ness back again." He tore the paper in quarters and let the pieces drift away on the air.

Cesco had bent low into a bow. "I submit to your superior judgment. After all, I was only raised in a poet's house, suckled at the teat of the finest word-smith in living memory. I have not your rarified tastes."

"Was it *his* teat you suckled at? It must have been rather dry."

"Dry as your wit, lord."

"Quite." The Scaliger had turned to the assembly. "Well come on, let's loose the hounds! Remember, we eat only what we catch! Cesco will starve unless his little hawk catches something."

Everyone had leapt to their saddles, and now they were in full-throated chase, vying with each other and the elements on this drizzly autumn morn-ing. Wine had been flowing long before dawn and most riders showed the effects of bibbery, some even falling from their saddles to the laughter of their neighbours.

Knowing what damage such falls could cause, Morsicato hadn't touched a drop. Nor, of course, had Detto, who kept to his saddle with ease. He never used spurs or a switch to urge his horse on. The beast under him just seemed to know what the boy wanted, be it a canter or a full charge. It was said that Detto had animal magic, and he'd been known to call birds down from the trees to eat from his palm. But his rapport with animals did not dim his enthusiasm for the hunt – he was very much his father's son.

Unlike many lords, Cangrande did not like easy game. Not for him the hares or deer released seconds before the chase. The hinds they were after had been tracked through the night by dell'Angelo but were nowhere in sight when they started. It was up to the hounds to find them. There were twenty such hunters, of a variety of breeds, though naturally greyhounds were the most prevalent.

Cesco was at the front, driving his horse hard with spurs and flail. Though he never passed Cangrande for the lead, several times they were neck and neck. Watching, Morsicato saw their hostility had become something else entirely. Expert horsemen both, they bantered and even sang as they rode across the countryside.

There was very little similarity between them in size and shape. Yet no one doubted they were related – so similar in act, in voice, in daring. And in the eyes. Despite the difference in colour – one set blue, one green – they laughed at the world in just the same way.

Cangrande's servant followed with the merlin the Scaliger favoured, but Cesco carried his own hawk with him. It rode on the bar in front of his saddle, a small falcon, hooded and tethered so it couldn't take wing. It bore the movement of the horse well, rocking with the rhythm of each separate hoofbeat.

After a while some older men fell out. Though sore and breathless, Morsicato wasn't yet so aged that he couldn't end a hunt. And there were pauses when the hounds lost the scent, during which men could catch their breath and chat about trifles. Then the dogs would pick up the trail again and they were off.

The first hunt of the day ended after two hours of chasing, with the hounds baying the hinds at the edge of a stream at the foot of Monte Baldo. Cesco managed an amazing shot from full tilt that took the larger hind in the throat. He missed the sight of his arrow going home, though. The moment the shot was loosed, Cangrande's horse had bumped into his, forcing Cesco to struggle to keep both horse and bird upright. The Scaliger hurtled on and took the smaller hind with an equally expert shot.

The party came to a rest, panting and laughing. Rights of the next kills were divvied up, two for each hunt. In honour of his return to health, Cesco was allowed to air his hawk first.

Hawking was not one of Morsicato's pastimes, but he knew the mechanics well enough. First came the transition from the saddle-bar to Cesco's left arm, which was gloved in hard leather from knuckle to elbow, protection from the razor-sharp pounces. Cesco was using only one jess, which made for a quicker release. Nor did the boy use a brail to secure her wings, a bell to announce her, or a leash to haul her in. He seemed to like her unfettered.

Nearby, Petruchio clucked his tongue in disapproval. Last year, at Cangrande's insistence, Bonaventura had taken Cesco through all the steps of taming – the darkened room, the slow feeding, the blindfold, the gentle clicks of the tongue and the soft caresses and repeated praises. The midnight ventures into the city to acclimate the bird to people, yet not frighten it. The perpetual state of flack, of half-liberty that kept a bird uncertain, dependent upon its master.

Now Cesco was using his own style, a private level of communication with his trained bird. Susanna felt his touch and spread her wings, bating slightly, craving free flight. Then with a twist and a push the blindfold was off and the bird beating high into the air.

Morsicato joined the applause, and Cangrande was just calling for his merlin when a pair of breathless riders approached from the south. He was handed a slip of parchment, which he read at a glance. "To the palace, everyone! There's work to be done!"

Nico da Lozzo sawed his reins. "Is it the Paduans? Is the truce over?"

Cangrande shook his head. "Sadly, no."

"Passerino?" asked Cesco, *sotto voce.*

"Nothing quite so nice," said Cangrande in an amused whisper. "No, rather some unwelcome news." Raising his voice, he flourished the communication in his hand for all to behold. "It appears that there is civil war in England. On the twenty-fourth of last month, Queen Isabella returned to her kingdom to wage war on her husband. She has the might of France behind her and a powerful warrior in Mortimer to lead her armies. Technically she is asserting the rights of her son Prince Edward, to take his father's throne."

Bailardino scoffed. "What does that matter to us? Let's finish the hunt!" Many voices chimed in raucous agreement.

"Lord Nogarola, think for a moment," said the elder Castelbarco. "If this news is indeed only twenty-three days old, the bankers and traders will just be hearing it. There will be a panic."

"So I think," agreed Cangrande. "We must erect levies of common sense before waves of panic wash over us. It won't matter as much in the countryside, but cities will be awash in fear. Bail, ride for Vicenza immediately. All of you, go to your city dwellings, not your castles! We must show our support for commerce. Montecchio, I need you especially – you must tell me everything you learned from your cousin regarding English dispositions."

Pleased to be singled out, Mariotto Montecchio cantered forward, nudging Capulletto out of his way as he passed. Everyone else sullenly turned their horses back towards Caprino, from there to ride to their respective city homes to help calm the lenders and creditors.

"If you please, my lord," said Cesco, reining in beside Cangrande. "I would like to remain until my falcon has finished her hunt."

"I may need you," said Cangrande.

"If I go, I lose the bird."

"Let someone else fetch it."

"Very well. Whom should I leave behind?"

Whom indeed? No one could come near the bird, not without fear of losing a finger or an eye. Not Ziliberto, the Master of the Hunt. Not Cangrande, not Petruchio, skilled hunters both. Not even Detto with his animal magic. For reasons only known to God and Cesco, Susanna responded to no one but her master. For transport she had to be hooded, her beak tied shut, her wings pinioned, her pounces corked. But on Cesco's arm she was all gentleness. Cesco had broken her, the way Cangrande meant to break him.

Hunting animals were precious. If the Scaliger was considering ordering the boy to leave the bird, he well knew it would look poorly before all these nobles. It was no part of the Scaliger's design to turn the boy into a martyr. "Very well. You may stay until she's done airing. Then return to the palace with all speed. There is a great deal to do, and since you have a mind for puzzles, perhaps you can watch as we resolve this one." He was speaking for all to hear. "If the English king loses this war, his debts will be lost to us. The bankers will be frenzied. They need our assurances." He lowered his voice, speaking softly just to Cesco. "Enjoy your brief flight."

"When will my hawking recommence?"

"Tomorrow."

"Tomorrow *and* tomorrow – always with you it is tomorrow."

Cangrande arched an imperious brow. "Be afraid when it is today."

"Thank you, lord," said Cesco, bowing his head in formal obedience.

"Hup!" Cangrande's horse galloped away surrounded by hounds. The rest of the nobles followed suit.

Petruchio Bonaventura didn't need to see the look in his squire's eyes. He simply waved his hand. "Yes yes, stay, Detto, by all means. But tomorrow you'll be polishing every scrap of armour I own. Twice."

"Yes, lord! Thank you, lord!" cried the delighted Detto.

"Coming, doctor?" asked Bailardino, his horse bucking back and forth eagerly.

"I think I'll stay," replied Morsicato. "Make sure the bird doesn't turn on them."

"Figs," said Cesco. "She'll build a nest in your beard. Oh wait – it isn't big enough yet, is it?"

Bailardino laughed, punched his son on the arm, and headed off with the rest.

There followed an uncomfortable silence. Uncomfortable for Morsicato at least, as he watched Cesco watch his bird. Finally the doctor said, "So how are you?"

Cesco held up a hand. "Quiet, please. She doesn't know you, and this is a tender moment." He cantered north across the open field, heading for the treeline. Detto followed, with the doctor bringing up the rear.

Balked, Morsicato whiled the time by examining Detto, communing with his horse. Serving as Petruchio's squire suited him. He was well-muscled for one so young. "What are you now, ten years old?"

"Almost twelve!" said Detto resentfully, puffing out his chest.

"My mistake. How is Bonaventura treating you?"

"He's magnificent. His wife gives me harder chores than he does." Detto jerked a thumb at Cesco. "I'm treated better than he is. You saw Uncle Francesco veer into him?"

"I saw them come together and Cesco's horse lose balance."

"Uncle Francesco likes the first kill of the day to be his."

"He killed a whole skin of wine before we started," said Cesco over his shoulder. "I thought that would have sated his need. Now seriously, be quiet, the pair of you. A little reverence is appropriate."

Above them the dark-eyed falcon ringed, gliding on the faint wind from off the river.

"Be careful," said Morsicato.

"O God – thank you! If you hadn't warned me…"

Detto snickered. The sound was familiar from their time in Ravenna, and elicited a familiar rise from the doctor. "Shouldn't you be using two jesses?"

Cesco looked right, then left, then under his horse. "I don't see Lord Bonaventura. Do you? Then we won't tell him."

"The bird may, if she decides to take off your nose."

"Perhaps it's your nose you're worried about. Is my sin so rank? Do I offend?"

Morsicato wagged an admonishing finger. "You'll be sorry."

"Pull in that finger or you're the one who'll be sorry. Susanna's beak is free, and those long fingers are a trifle wormy."

"I'm here to look after you, boy. Even if you don't need me, pretend."

Cesco studied the doctor for a flicker of time. "You didn't wed me when I wasn't looking, did you? No? Then save your husbandly instinct for Esta. Shouldn't you be by her side, instead of acting the thorn in mine?" With that he turned back to watch his falcon rise higher and higher in the sky.

Morsicato's teeth gnashed. "Very well. I'm going back to the palace to see what's happening. Let me know if you need anything."

"If my arm needs a bleeding, my belly a leeching, or my nails a paring, you are my first port of call." The boy didn't take his eyes off the bird.

"Well done. You've turned into *him*." Furious, Morsicato yanked on his reins and trotted away, leaving the two boys on their own. *I hope the bird rips his guts out! A bleeding might do him good.*

Watching the doctor go, Detto edged his horse nearer to Cesco's. "You were pretty rough. Esta *is* ill."

"Then he should be with her, not chasing after my skirts. Besides, it's been forever since you and I had an adventure." They grinned at each other, and Detto's heart swelled – he was still at an age where friendship was everything in the world.

But Cesco had another reason for sending the *dottore* away. He still did not know the identity of the demon who'd hurt Antonia, and he was determined that none of his protectors ever be imperiled for him again. He worried about even having Detto along, but he couldn't deny himself the pleasure of his friend's company.

A cry from above made Cesco glance up and smile. "Here she comes."

The falcon had enjoyed her freedom. But now the thrill wore thin and she circled back, nearer her master. She watched for movement in the tall grass of the field and at the edge of the trees that marked the rise of the mountain.

"She's got a high pitch," observed Detto. They watched the bird pull away in a wider and wider circle. Just as Detto thought she might be raking out, Susanna dropped like a stone to the ground. At the last moment she spread her wings and rose away, an animal in her pounces as she sailed just above the tall grass.

Even though he'd seen the Moor out hawking, Cesco kept to Petruchio's western style of catching, keeping the bird on the sinister arm. Eastern rules had the bird on the right, but as Bonaventura had pointed out, that tied up one's sword arm unnecessarily. "Cangrande sometimes uses birds in battle," Petruchio had said. "It's good to think in flexible terms."

Just before she reached his arm, Susanna dropped her prey at the boy's feet. It was a large cat, wild and feral.

Taking her weight, Cesco stroked the bird's cere the way she liked. She pressed her head into his hand. "Have you brought me a Thibault? Or is this some other pussy?"

Detto dropped down to collect the dead animal. "He's an idiot."

"Thibault the cat? I think I pity him, actually. Or I would, if he were just a hair less arrogant."

"That's what he accuses you of."

Cesco shrugged. "Doesn't mean I'm wrong." The cat was bagged and Susanna was treated with a bit of older meat. "Want to put her up again?" When Detto didn't answer, he added, "I know he said to return right away, but it's been months since Susanna has had a good airing. Me too, for that matter. The brothers were kind, but I've lost a good yard of eyesight from all that reading. And I think I've got piles. At least, my backside itches in the worst—"

Detto was frowning at the treeline. "I think I saw something. Someone. Watching us."

"Oh?" Cesco continued feeding Susanna while edging his eyes sideways towards the rising woodline. "I don't see anyone. Could be nothing."

"Or it could be the person who tried to kill you in the tourney," suggested Detto.

As that person was actually seated in Cesco's saddle, it seemed unlikely. But Cesco saw an opportunity for a little sport. "Let's act like we're still hunting, send her up, but towards the mountain this time. We might see something. Or better, she might rake whoever's spying on us."

"It could be the doctor," warned Detto. "Watching out for us."

Cesco scoffed. "Then he can practice his craft on someone other than me for once."

Thrown aloft a second time, Susanna took wing, gliding up over the trees. This time she was quick to dive. But before she could reach her target, something shot up from out of the trees and crossed her path. The hawk screamed and spun away, frightened.

"Susanna! Susanna!" called Cesco, but she was winging hard up and away. In moments she had disappeared into the sky. "Gone." Tears in his eyes, Cesco's voice quavered. "My bird is flown."

"What was that, a bat?"

"An arrow," snarled Cesco. "One that some stupid Cupid is going to regret loosing." Leaping from his mount, he ran for the treeline.

Detto dropped to the ground and scrambled up the slope of the mountain after him. Entering the wood, they fought their way through the lower brambles and growth until the trees grew tall enough not to impede them.

Reaching the spot the arrow had come from, Cesco halted. Catching up, Detto looked around. There was no sign of an archer.

Cesco knelt, examining the ground minutely. Suddenly he whirled, his arm flicking out. The knife from Cesco's boot whisked past Detto's nose and up into the branches behind him. There was a cry from the leaves and a series of branches rustled.

A long silence ensued.

"I take it I missed," said Cesco loudly.

There was no answer.

"I have another knife here somewhere."

"And I have you at the end of an arrow." It was a young voice, trying to sound older.

"Ah-ha! I know that tremulous tenor! Detto, allow me to present the invisible Death. Death, Detto."

"You aren't very original," said Death from the trees. "You said the same thing last winter."

"And you're still a poor marksman. You missed my bird."

"Your fault! He would have taken a piece of me."

"*She* would have scared you, nothing more. She knows not to attack men – or whatever you may be. A bird that gets a taste for human flesh is no use to anyone. Such a skillful hunter must know this." Cesco's voice bled sarcasm.

"Skillful enough to put an arrow in your throat!" raged Death.

"A loss the world would mourn for an age of ages."

There was a snort from above. Detto started to edge sideways towards the nearest tree. An arrow came hurtling from the leaves and planted itself in the dirt between his feet. "Not another step!"

"You're improving," acknowledged Cesco. "But I feel obliged to warn you, frightening my bird is one thing. If you shoot my blood-brother you will not leave this wood alive."

"What if I just wound him?"

"Like you did Cangrande? You might indeed escape the wood – only to die in your home within the week. I'm something of a hunter myself."

Death scoffed. "You couldn't track me last winter."

"Couldn't and didn't are two separate concepts. You were too small to fish for, we'd only have thrown you back."

"Look who's talking!"

"Though small in stature, I am a giant in spirit."

Death actually laughed. "Who are you, Ser Modesty incarnate?"

"I'm Castor, he's Pollux."

Stringing together this lighting-fast dialogue, Detto realized this archer was the same person who had stabbed Cangrande last winter. "Why are you after Cangrande?"

"Yes," echoed Cesco. "We're all over excitement to learn your motives. But we seem to have started this dance on the wrong foot. If my friend and I lower ourselves to the ground and sit on our hands, may we then trade pleasantries?"

There was a pause. "I'm waiting."

Cesco seated himself with his back to a tree, Detto beside the grounded arrow. "We're down. Perhaps we might be treated to a face."

A branch shivered, then another. From between the leaves appeared a hooded figure, still mostly hidden. Ragged clothes hung loosely on the thin frame. The only visible feature under the hood were cold eyes of green ringed with grey.

"Better." Cesco's gaze narrowed as he studied the archer. Then he smiled and cocked his head to one side. "Detto, have you ever read Ovid? No? Pity." Cesco returned his attention to the figure in the branches. "*You dare to crown your long hair with a turban! White poplar leaves are more fitting for Hercules.*"

The answer was immediate. "*By as much as you are the less, greatest of men, so much the greater her victory over you, than yours over those you conquered.*"

Cesco blinked, then grinned playfully. "In hindsight I'm grateful I didn't name my bird Icarus. You would have felt the need to shoot her down out of poetic justice alone."

"Hindsight is the prayer of the unimaginative."

"True. Yet if only we could choose our names at the end of our lives, every man's title would become him. I've often wondered what name I'd give myself, were I not already bespoke. The old folk say names have power, and that our true names uttered aloud give others power over us. The spirits do not take such transgressions lightly, they say, and—"

"Do you *ever* stop talking?"

"You've deduced my cardinal sin! Is that what you do, go from place to place observing the sins and just deeds of men, as gods do? Did the Scaliger fail your judgment? Is that why he has to die?" The stranger's green eyes gazed evenly out at him from under the hood. When the archer refused to answer, Cesco continued. "I was disappointed, you know. Here I was, back in Caprino in May, but without the Capitano I was clearly unworthy of your attentions. O Death, you are cruel!"

"Kind enough not to kill your bird."

"Hear that, Detto? Susanna has been judged worthy of life. Tell me, Death, what sins do you find here, in us?"

"An abuse of poetry."

Cesco threw back his head and roared with laughter.

"And the sin of posing," added the archer.

Cesco's mirth didn't stop at his mouth, it reached all the way to his eyes. "Then I'm not alone. We're both creatures of art. You're not quite the poor vagabond you seem."

"It is true. I am not what I seem."

Detto broke into the conversation. "You're hunting on the Scaliger's lands without permission. Someone knows who you are."

"I'm permitted."

Cesco brightened. "Even better. We'll have your name by nightfall."

"Not if you're pinned to that tree by your ears." The threatening arrowhead was visible between the leaves.

"Naughty varlet. Don't you know that bows are forbidden against men. Mother Church would be very angry."

The archer was beginning to sense the danger of remaining. "Leave me be, or I'll murder you both."

"Figs." Cesco held up a hand. "If you think you can get us both with one bolt, please do. It would be an honour to witness such a shot. Otherwise give us a name, just to satisfy my friend. For myself, I don't much care. It doesn't have to be real – any name will do."

The archer considered. "Hercules."

Cesco shook his head. "Cangrande is hardly the Lion."

"No, he's the stable. Fine. If you're Castor, I suppose Death is as good a name as any."

Cesco made a show of scratching his back against the tree. "Melodrama. How nice. I suppose, being immortal, I must throw myself in front of my egg-friend here to save him from you."

The archer snorted. "You could come towards this tree and test that theory."

"I thought you'd never ask." Cesco's hands came up from the earth quick as a striking snake. The rock missed its mark, but still caused the archer to lose aim. Loosed, the arrow buried itself in the bark just over Cesco's head.

"I've got him!" Detto was already up and racing for the archer's tree. Cesco scrambled just as fast but in an arc around the tree to prevent escape.

They hadn't reckoned with their quarry's familiarity with the wood. Leaping from one branch to the next, the archer was two trees away in a heartbeat, every step moving higher and into deeper growth.

Detto met Cesco at the base of the second tree, scanning upwards. Branches were shaking all around. "Where is he?"

"Light as a sparrow, already gone." An arrow lighted in the tree a foot above his head. Cesco blinked at it. "Or not."

Detto grabbed Cesco and threw him to the earth, stepping in front of him and blocking his friend with his own body. "Coward! Come out and fight like a man!"

"That's asking too much," said Cesco from the ground. "We're hardly men ourselves. Don't worry. Our mystery hunter is gone. That was the final gesture of defiance."

But Cesco was mistaken. When they returned to the treeline at the base of the mountain, they discovered their steeds missing. Ten miles from the palace, they faced a decent walk over some very hilly terrain.

Detto cursed once, gazing around the lush landscape. Cesco wagged a finger angrily. "I was willing to let this go. Anger at the Scaliger is inevitable, and self-defence is admirable. But this – *this* is a declaration of war."

"I didn't get a good look at him. Did you?"

"No better than you," said Cesco.

"Do you think dell'Angelo would have a clue?"

"We're not asking dell'Angelo. Look, if you start out now—"

"No," said Detto, shaking his head.

"—you could make it back to—"

"No."

"—the palace and bring back some—"

Detto put his fingers in his ears. "La la la. Not going."

Cesco made a rude gesture. "Figs. Fine, then. Come. But you'll be horribly in the way."

"You won't say that if an arrow comes out of nowhere."

"I'm too small to hit. You're the perfect size target."

"At least I'm good for something," said Detto. "What's your excuse for living?"

"If you ever find out, please let me know. No one's ever told me. Now come on." Together they started off on the trail of the stolen mounts.

After a while Detto said, "I don't know 'egg-friend'."

"You're just admitting it now?"

Detto hung his head. "I'm so ashamed."

"Shame on Shame, for shaming you." As they traced the hoof-prints Cesco told the story of Castor and Pollux. "They came from twin eggs, along with a pair of women, famous in their own right. The boy and girl from one egg were immortal, the others weren't. Castor and Pollux looked alike, so they stayed together, never out of each other's sight, so Death couldn't tell them apart."

"What happened?"

"They lived forever."

"Good story!"

"I think so," said Cesco, grinning.

"Which one am I again?" asked Detto.

"Pollux."

"And he's…"

"The mortal one."

Detto rolled his eyes. "Low man again!"

Cesco made an emphatic appeal to the heavens. "Look, if we come across Death I'll wave my arms and leap around while you run for it." He made a cartwheel and began spinning, arms thrown wide. "Here I am! Take me now! Dammit, Detto, run for it! Don't just sit there laughing! I'm trying to die for you! The least you could do is not laugh at a dying man!"

Detto gave Cesco the fig. "So much for sneaking up on Death."

"We'll just have to outfox the old fox, then, and live forever. I'm game. How about you?"

Four long hours later they found their mounts, back almost where they'd started. Resting on the saddle bar was Susanna, her head tucked into her wing as she slept off her tiring flight.

Detto was amazed. "She came back!"

Cesco shook his head. "Look at her leg."

Detto did, and saw the bird's single jess was tied to the saddle bar, ensuring Susanna would not fly off while she awaited her master's return.

"Your friend Death really is a good hunter," said Detto appreciatively. "I wonder how he managed to coax her down."

"I have no idea. But this is the second time Death has given me the slip. I'm beginning to feel unwanted."

"By Death? We should all be so lucky. What's that?"

Detto was pointing at a note attached to the jess, scrawled in a childish hand. Cesco plucked it up and read:

One bird has come to roost, the other has flown. Let it go.

"O no, my deadly Cupid! We'll meet again."

Twelve

Though aware from Cesco's letters that Tharwat was coming to France, it was late October before Pietro actually set eyes upon the Moor. Dressed in homely Western garb, Tharwat appeared one morning seated opposite Petrarch's house, working the kinks out of a bit of rope.

Spying him from a window, Pietro raised a hand and opened his mouth. He quelled the impulse at once. There was always a purpose to the Moor's pretenses. And there were compelling reasons for Tharwat not to be seen in Ser Alaghieri's company. Lobbying for papal forgiveness, it would do Pietro no end of damage to be seen consorting with a Moor. As ever, Tharwat was playing the protector.

Strange, in a former Hashashin. As a youth, Tharwat had been made to endure their training. He had only spoken of it once, and then only to explain his similar training of Cesco. It was something Pietro was still uncomfortable with, but he recognized the value of having an Assassin in their ranks.

Over the next five weeks Pietro would occasionally glimpse the Moor out of the corner of his eye. He was careful not to betray himself by sending secret signals. He did wish the Moor would make contact, if only to explain what long game he was playing. But the lack of contact told Pietro there was, as yet, no news.

This only added to his frustration. Petrarch had so far been entirely unable to attach a name to the unknown cleric who so opposed Pietro's reinstatement. In the meantime they pored over the ledger and calculated the sum it would take to buy Cangrande a papal forgiveness – a vast figure indeed. Pietro's own price was far less, but then his own purse was not as deep. Petrarch suggested bundling together the holy bribes (for in essence that's what indulgences amounted to), and let Cangrande pay for Pietro's pardon. Tempting as it was, Pietro knew that his excommunication had nothing to do with Cangrande, and could not therefore excuse such chicanery. It was not the way a knight behaved. Besides, he was loath to be in the Scaliger's debt.

November was lightened by the visit of another acquaintance from Bologna, Guido Sette, whom Petrarch counted as his closest friend in the world. For the three weeks of his stay, Lucia forgot Pietro's existence, which was such a blessing that Pietro was tempted to offer Sette money to stay on longer.

One late November day, Tharwat brushed hard against Pietro in the street. Tharwat immediately ducked his head and made a groveling bow. Pietro barely nodded in return before resuming his walk.

The moment he achieved his room he removed the note slipped into the laces of his sleeve. Uncoding Tharwat's messages was harder than any except Cesco's, who delighted in altering the code a little each time to test and torment the recipient. Or maybe the boy only did it to Pietro.

Tharwat's note was brief and concise:

> Boy is mended.
>
> Beware of your shadow.
>
> Could riddle be backwards? DXV, not VXD?

Three parts. First, because Tharwat knew how Pietro's mind worked, the reassuring fact that Cesco was healed. Pietro wondered how the Moor had that bit of news before he did, but let that pass.

The second was a personal warning, and the reason for the sudden communication. Beware of my shadow? It could only mean that there was someone in it. Pietro was being followed.

344

It was not as worrying an idea as it might have been. Pietro had assumed that His Holiness would have set someone to watch Pietro from the moment he arrived, almost a year ago.

Pietro then realized that if Tharwat was issuing the warning now, after lurking about for almost a month, that it was new. Which meant Petrarch's enquiries were beginning to ruffle someone's feathers. Excellent.

The third part referenced a continuing puzzle – a communication from Cesco's vanished mother, a series of letters that shaped the letter *M*. Tharwat was sharing his latest attempts to parse her message, a message they'd not yet shared with Cesco. The boy had enough concerns.

Cesco had met his mother only once, and briefly, and hadn't been told her true identity. Pietro himself was hardly better informed, knowing her only as Donna Maria. She'd vanished just after meeting her son, and the Moor had traced her to an abandoned building in the country. There, covered in her blood, was the message she had carved into the wooden walls with her fingernails. Pietro and the Moor had burned down the whole building, agreeing that no eyes but theirs should see the message before they could decypher it. The woman herself had disappeared, likely spirited off by Cangrande's enemies. Which made her message all the more urgent.

Hanging from string at his neck, Pietro carried a tiny scroll-tube in which he kept his copy of the message. He removed it now to try the Moor's key. Unfurled, the message read:

M	R	C		T	S	M
A		A		T		A
B		V	X	D		B

To Pietro's mind, MAB was the vital portion of the message. Why else repeat it start and finish? And the shape of the whole message bore a meaning – but what meaning? *M* – for Maria, the sender? Or was it the initial Cesco was meant to beware. For that was the only part that Pietro was sure of, it was a warning. CAV. Cave. Latin for 'Beware'.

The center trio of letters, VXD, was just as incomprehensible as the rest. For some time Pietro had tried to substitute proper names for the first and last letters, using *X* as 'ex', meaning from. The best he could devise was VERONA EX DIO. Verona out of God? Nonsensical.

Following Tharwat's suggestion, the reversed letters became DXV. That was a sequence that bore meaning for Pietro and Cesco both. In the last canticle of his father's *Commedia*, there was a prophecy to a future hero who would bear the DXV. It was more cryptic than Dante usually liked to be. In fact, Pietro was fairly certain that his father had not penned it. It was much more like something Cesco would have invented.

But what did it mean? Was it the numbers 500, 10, 5? Or some bastardized version of DVX, meaning Duke.

Beware the Duke. Which in common parlance could mean 'Prince'.

Cangrande was the Prince of Verona. Beware Cangrande. Was that the message? Had the Scaliger himself kidnapped Cesco's mother, removing her as a threat to his plans for their child? It tallied with as much information as they had.

But Pietro had learned that not every evil deed could be laid at the Scaliger's doorstep. Personal likes and dislikes had to be taken out of account, leaving matters to be judged impartially. He had to follow his training, not his heart. In this, most definitcly, he had to be a lawyer.

The rest of November passed with Pietro mentally combating three separate wars – Maria's message, Cangrande's reinstatement, and his own unknown foe. Added to that were the unwelcome advances of Petrarch's sister. Amazing his hair hadn't turned white with the strain.

This day, the fifth of December, passed in the usual manner. Pietro kept mostly to the house, though by now Petrarch's neighbours had grown weary of abusing him for his unholy status. He read, he wrote a little poetry (all of it poor), he watched out the window for a sign of his shadower, he wrote several letters of no real import, and he talked with Petrarch upon the latter's return from the papal enclosure. Still there was no answer to who was pouring poison in the Pope's ear.

After supper, Pietro retired to his rooms and was astonished to find them already occupied. Tharwat al-Dhaamin was seated in a corner, away from the tower window and out of sight of the door. Pietro shut both then crossed to embrace the older man. "Your disguise is quite a step down from your usual attire."

"Yes," rumbled the Moor. "I have resurrected the guise of the Arūs, now an animal-trainer to princes and kings. His Holiness enjoys spectacle, and the occasional execution by lion or bear satisfies his need."

An unpleasing prospect to an accused heretic, Pietro passed it by. "You've actually seen the Pope? You've had better luck than I."

"So I understand. You will not be successful, as matters stand. In either of your tasks."

The breath hissed from between Pietro's teeth. "Is that divination or intelligence?"

"The latter." Tharwat handed over a bundle of clothes. "Dress. There is something you must see."

At once Pietro stripped off his workaday doublet and put on the borrowed garb. Examining himself, he asked, "What am I?"

"My master, ruler of the papal menagerie. I hired a man who resembles you, just for this purpose. And he has been diligent in his limp." It was Tharwat's habit to employ men to pretend mastery over him. He subscribed to the same philosophy as the Scaliger, that the finest disguise was to let men see what they expected. In this case, an Italian with a scarred Moorish slave. Pietro had seen this method at work over the years with great success.

Dressing, Pietro felt his heartbeat accelerate. "You can't just tell me?"

"If I could, I would. This you must confirm with your own eyes. Come."

Stealing from the house the way Tharwat had come, across a balcony and down a rope, they evaded any spying eyes. It was cold. The winters these last ten years had been the hardest in memory, each one progressively more bitter. Pietro remembered his father debating some clergyman about the underlying meaning. The holy man had asserted that cold brought perfection, as Heaven was the opposite of Hell, and Hell was fire. But Dante had countered that all warmth in the universe came from God above, and for that reason he had depicted the lowest point in Hell as a frozen lake, as far from God as one could get.

Feeling the stab of the Mistral wind, Pietro was inclined to his father's point of view. This cold was ungodly. Ironic, then, that the Holy See should be located here, where such frigid winds cut a man to the bone all year round.

Braced against the chill, they rode into foul-smelling Avignon and walked bold as brass through the streets. "Your name is Anselmo of Battavia," said Tharwat softly from his servile place at Pietro's right shoulder. "You speak neither Latin nor French, so your slave must translate for you. You find this humiliating, and therefore avoid conversation. Turn right at the corner."

Obeying, Pietro committed the tale to memory. "Where is the real Anselm?"

"Closeted with a companion he could never afford himself. He will not emerge before dawn."

Pietro hated himself for blushing. He'd just turned thirty, and yet had never been with a woman, despite many veiled offers (not to mention Lucia's unveiled ones). Morsicato had teased him once, early in his excommunication, saying that as long as Pietro was damned he might as well enjoy it.

But Pietro's fleshly longings were still subject to his strict sense of honour. In this, he was unlike the other males of his line. Despite both his marriage and his romantic devotion to his beloved Beatrice, Dante had engaged in several renowned affairs during his exile. While it was not in Pietro to condemn such behavior in his sire, he could not imagine imitating that example. He left that to his little brother. Poco had enough libidinousness for them both.

God had decreed the marriage bed the place for such things. Besides, a knight was meant to honour women, not dishonour them. Having survived this long without indulging in the pleasures of the flesh, he was determined to remain true to himself and his honour.

Lost in thoughts of a sin he'd never yet committed, Pietro came to an alley between a butcher's shop and a massive stone wall. "Turn here." At the end of the alley was an arch bored in the stone, and in it a well-guarded gate. He knew from his walks around the city that the papal palace faced west, which put them now on the east end, the very rear. This was clearly the back entrance to the Palais des Papes, where men on less-than-savoury business could exit without drawing too much attention.

Tharwat said something to the guards and they were admitted without fuss. Pietro walked boldly past them as if familiar with the place, and thus entered the papal enclosure for the first time. I hope leaving will be as easy.

They emerged into a wide garden at the rear of the palace, planted with pleasing trees and well-tended shrubberies. Opposite them, the castle – it was more castle than palace, fortified against all threats – was magnificent, and constant construction promised to make it grander still.

Tharwat led him to a small but solid building opposite the palace, nestled into the crook of the garden wall. It scented more like a stable than a residence. The massive doors were bolted on the exterior, and within Pietro heard a low grumble of several creatures greeting their keeper's scent. Tharwat removed a key and worked the lock. The well-oiled door made no sound as it swung wide. Pietro entered, Tharwat behind him.

"Stay by the door," instructed the Moor, brushing past him.

Pietro was more than willing to obey. Outside of horses, hawks, and hounds he had very little care for animals.

Though he'd known this was one of Tharwat's many skills, he was astonished at how well the animals minded the Moor as he moved from cage to pen. There weren't many – two female lions and one male, in separate pens. A pair of shaggy wolves with the whitest fur Pietro had ever seen. And a single pard, sleek and black.

The sight of the pard made Pietro recollect the very night he and the Moor had met. A leopard had been enraged by a devil named Gregorio Pathino in a failed attempt to kidnap Cesco, then just a babe in arms. Pietro still bore faint scars across his forehead from the creature's claws.

Tharwat had stepped in to wrestle the beast and come away unharmed. Pietro now understood why – like Detto, the Moor had animal magic. The caged pard prowled forward and actually nuzzled Tharwat's outstretched hand. It sent a growl Pietro's way, then settled in to gnaw the cured meat Tharwat gave it.

After feeding each of the animals and speaking to them in an unintelligible tongue, Tharwat returned, a collection of leather bits and pieces in one hand, and bladder of wine in the other. "There is no window, so we must watch from without. We have made it our habit, my 'master' and I, to sit out upon an evening, taking the air. No one complains. My master drinks while I mend the whips and leads."

Tharwat brought forth a chair and placed it in the snow outside the menagerie door. He settled down beside it, and Pietro took the indicated seat. Clearly they were waiting for something. Tharwat busied himself with small tasks while Pietro pretended to drink the wine. He actually drank more than he intended, as it aided him to hold off the chill night air.

There was little to see. The high wall before them was dotted with glassed windows, some bearing light, some dark. Wanting to ask what lay within, Pietro refrained. He doubted the Moor had been allowed to wander the papal palace, and even if he knew the floor-plan, this was not the time to speak of it.

Occasionally clergymen in rich robes entered or exited the palace. Some took the air, some wandered off to corners to pray or converse with their fellows in low tones. Many strode to the arched doorway and exited behind the butcher's shop, off about some secretive errand.

It was an hour after the last light of dusk had faded and night was setting in when Tharwat gave a small grunt. It seemed due to some trouble he was having with relashing a whip he had untied, but as a cue it was obvious enough. Keeping his chin low over his wine, Pietro lifted his eyes to scan the yard.

There were scattered men in the hooded robes of friars – far more Dominicans than Franciscans or Benedictines, Pietro noted – and one in a cardinal's red galero surrounded by a cluster of clerks and no-

354

taries. But they had been in the yard some time, therefore not what Tharwat was hinting at.

Turning his hooded eyes towards the rear gate, Pietro saw a man just entering the snowy yard. Dressed in Dominican robes, the man's hood was slung heavily over his face. He was exceedingly tall and painfully gaunt, making his voluminous robes hang upon him as if on a post.

Already Pietro felt a pricking sense of familiarity, but as yet he couldn't put a name to his fear. It wasn't until the door was shut behind him that the new arrival felt free to lower his cowl, revealing his face.

It was the Scaliger's visage gone wrong. The cheeks, the chin, the perfect teeth. But this face had never smiled, and bore none of the meat that Cangrande had added these last years. It was a face deliberately starved of life, hiding an equally starved soul – starved of compassion, of mercy, of justice.

Gregorio Pathino. Bastard son of Alberto della Scala and half-brother to Cangrande himself.

The spaventapasseri.

The Scarecrow.

Thirteen

Inhibitions loosened by the cheap French wine, Pietro couldn't help his gasp. Immediately he lifted the bladder to his lips and was careful not to look up again until the unholy friar had passed him by. "Did he see me?"

"I do not believe so," replied the Moor casually, still working on his knots. "Certainly he did not pause."

Feeling a panicked roiling in his bowels, Pietro wanted to berate the Moor for not issuing some kind of warning. He'd almost betrayed them both!

The larger part of his mind was grappling with the concept of Pathino's presence. Ten years before, Pathino had been in league with the Count of San Bonifacio and Cangrande's wife, Giovanna. Though their motives differed, their combined aim was to remove Cesco from the field of play. Pathino believed himself to be Il Veltro, the mythical Greyhound, a title Pietro and Tharwat knew belonged to Cesco – the boy had a destiny, a great role to play in a new age of man. It was a fact carefully hidden from all, including the boy himself. It was the weapon that Cangrande's sister kept hinting at, a vital piece of information in her private war with her brother. Pietro understood that if Cesco ever came in possession of this knowledge, Cangrande would spare no effort to reduce the boy even further. Only in ignorance was Cesco secure.

Had Pathino learned of Cesco's destiny? Or did he still believe, as most the world did, that Cangrande was his competition for the title? Did he still have hopes to step into that great role? And if so, why was he here?

Unable to sit still, Pietro rose and went within doors. At once the Moor scooped up his busy-work and followed, barring the door behind them.

Within the safety of the menagerie's solid, windowless walls, Pietro sank shaking to the straw-covered earth. For him, Pathino had been the thing of nightmares. "How in the name of all that's holy could Pathino be here?"

"So it is Pathino," murmured the Moor.

"You didn't know?" A moment later he answered his own question. "Of course not. You never saw him for more than a moment, in a crowd." It also explained Tharwat not warning Pietro. He didn't want to plant an idea in Pietro's head and thus taint the recognition.

"Yet I thought it must be he," rumbled the Moor softly. "Your description was apt. And he has something of the Scaliger about him, even now."

"The resemblance is greater than it ever was. Or perhaps, knowing their kinship, I just recognize it better."

"Kinship in form, or in spirit?" asked Tharwat, shrewdly guessing Pietro's double meaning.

As that did not require an answer, Pietro returned to the immediate question. "Who is he pretending to be? Why is he here?"

"He is called Brother Gregor, and his abode is the Dominican monastery two streets over."

"For how long?"

"I first saw him three weeks ago," answered Tharwat. "He's been in residence for some years. He is well known, and his devout practice of mortification is much admired by some. But it keeps him from advancement, as it makes others uncomfortable."

"I've been in Avignon for months," said Pietro. "How is it that I had no idea he was even here?"

"He keeps within the Dominican walls, leaving them only for this weekly visit to someone in the palace. His name is altered. As long as you are excluded from the papal presence, there is no danger of discovery."

"Years," said Pietro, repeating the Moor's earlier statement. It explained so much. His excommunication – both his and Cangrande's, in fact – was the long machination of this one man. For years, it seemed, Pathino had been waging an unseen war against the Scaliger and Pietro both. Content to wait in silence and watch as his victims were picked apart from afar. How very Scaligeri.

Pietro asked more questions, but Tharwat had already shared all he knew, save for one ominous fact. "He is closely linked to several prominent inquisitors, including one Bernardo Gui."

That was a name to conjure with. Ironically, Pietro had once used that same name to threaten Fra Lorenzo with exposure. For, besides being a noted historian, Gui was the literal author of the manual of Inquisition, and skilled in dozens of ways of co-ercitio – torture. The idea of Pathino being intimate with such a man was frightening in the extreme.

Tharwat continued. "Now that I am sure of his identity, I will make further inquiries. But first, I must ask – do you want him dead?"

Pietro blinked in astonishment. "You mean murdered?"

"It would not be difficult. It was the task you and I undertook, so many years ago, with poor Ignazzio. Find him, question him, and remove him as a threat. The difficulty always was finding him. We have him now. Would it not be wise to simply slay him?"

Two images of Pathino came to Pietro's mind at once: him throwing the infant Cesco to the leopard, and him holding a knife to the three-year-old Cesco's eye. Several more followed, imaginary images of crimes Pietro had not witnessed – the stabbing of Pietro's treacherous groom Fazio, Montecchio's noble father stabbed with Capulletto's dagger, the astrologer Ignazzio slit from groin to sternum. All these and more could be laid at Pathino's doorstep. If ever a man deserved death...

The temptation was great. Yet Pietro had trod just such a winding path last year, skirting the edges of his conscience. It was a path paved with slick stones, and led only to Hell. He was petitioning to be restored to God's sight. Did he want to tempt the Lord's wrath by committing murder, even a deserved one? For though a man with Tharwat's training would no doubt find the task simple, the blood would be on Pietro's hands.

I am a knight, and a lawyer. I am not a judge. Nor am I a prince. Most importantly, I am no Scaligeri. "No. That is not who we are."

Tharwat bowed his head. "As you say. I will learn all I can."

They laid plans for a time, there in the company of lions, wolves, and a leopard. It was not lost on Pietro that these were the very beasts that faced his father in the opening canto of L'Inferno – the same canto that related the prophecy of the Greyhound. If there was meaning in their society, Pietro couldn't fathom it.

When they were finished, Pietro felt inexplicably better. Now he knew his enemy. Knowing, he could retaliate. Perhaps not murder, but he could see justice done. It was his duty, as both knight and lawyer. And in fighting an imposter in Dominican robes, he would be doing God's own work. He would wage a holy war on Pathino. Pietro's personal crusade.

As there was no going home that night, Pietro settled in. He was too wary to remove his boots – he might have to run for his life at a moment's notice. But he loosened them and stretched, while Tharwat organized some papers on a nearby table. The Moor smiled over one, a smile Pietro had only ever seen Tharwat give for one reason. "What did Cesco say?"

Looking up, the Moor tapped the page in his hand. "Cesco? No. This is a letter from an old friend. He invites me on a journey of exploration."

"Another adventurer?" asked Pietro wryly. After the fabulous and wholly unbelievable travels of Marco Polo two decades earlier, many youths dreamed of seeing the world. Since his death two years ago, many more were the traders who hoped a new traveler would rise to firmly establish this new route to the East. "Polo's tales were ridiculous. A pack of lies, surely."

Tharwat eyed him. "There are many who would say that your life story to date is impossible. Yet here you are."

Pietro blinked. "A hit. You're tempted?"

"I would be a liar to say I was not. But I am too old. And I have seen many of these places already. Though not China. I will be impressed if Battuta goes so far."

"Battuta?"

"Abū ʿAbd Allah Muḥammad ibn ʿAbd Allāh al-Lawātī al-Ṭanjī ibn Baṭūṭah," said Tharwat, giving the young explorer his full name as he laid the letter aside. "He is on his way to Mecca, and plans afterwards to make his name and his backers' fortunes by exploring. A blessing upon his endeavors. But I have no time for such things. And, as I say, I am no longer young. Exploration is for the soft bones and hard muscles of youth. I have seen enough of the world to know humanity is the same everywhere. The rest is mere gilding." With that, Tharwat blew out the lamp.

Pietro laid his roiling head to rest on the game-keeper's pallet. In darkness, Tharwat checked the animals, then he too retired.

Lying awake in the dark, Pietro thought again of Tharwat's earlier offer. It was only the second time he had ever referred to his skills at murder. Twice, in a dozen years. For all that they were friends, the Moor kept himself very close, hiding his secrets like the stars hid their designs.

But then, Pietro had never asked. Not about the scars on his neck, nor about his youth. Nor even how he had come to serve Cangrande. I cannot resent him his secrets if I've never asked to share them. And he could hardly blame Tharwat for not volunteering information. The one time he had done so, Pietro had shunned him. It was only the Moor's loyalty and generosity of spirit that had kept their friendship alive. Shame on me.

"Tharwat. Tell me about your youth. What happened to you?"

There was a long silence from the next pallet. Beginning to regret the question, Pietro was about to apologize for prying when, in a soft voice, the Moor began to tell his tale.

"Tharwat is not a Moorish name. It is Persian. Though born in Spain, I was raised among Persians, given into their care by my parents in repayment of a debt. Normally no Persian would have soiled his hands with a Moor, but these were men in dire need of strong backs, and even at five years I was strong.

"As for their need – I do not suppose you know much of the history of the fortress of Alamut? It was built sometime before the year 900 by a Daylami king. Alamut means 'eagle's teaching,' for when the king saw a bird perch upon the rock high above him he saw the strategic value of such a position.

"But it wasn't until two hundred years had passed that Alamut became home to the hashishiyya – the Order of Hashashins, what you call Assassins. The founder of the Order, the great and wise Hasan-i-Sabah, took the fortress by guile in the year of your lord 1090 and remained there for the next thirty-five years, until his death.

"As a Nizari Muslim, Hasan was considered an apostate by the Seljuk Turks who surrounded Alamut. But he was devoted to his faith. He exiled all musicians from his city and had his own son executed for consuming alcohol. A cultured man of great knowledge and learning, Hasan was well versed in mathematics, astronomy, magic, and alchemy.

"He was also a master of the revolution. Though not a military man in the sense of a leader of armies, his fidai – the faithful – were more feared than any conventional force. They used only the hand-held dagger, and never fled their deeds. In the time of Hasan it is said that over fifty men died at the point of a fidai blade, and several cities came to be controlled by Hasan without an army ever lifting a sword.

"Though Christians the world over tremble at the tales of the Assassins, I know of no use of the fidai against a Christian leader. The structure of the Knights Templar and the Knights Hospitaller, Islam's foes, rendered assassination useless. Murder one Christian knight, another would step into his place, just as skilled and probably more zealous than his predecessor.

"No, it was against the Seljuks and the Mongols that the fidai had their great successes. But the wrath of these foes, long in coming, was dreadful. It was the Mongol lord Hulegu's army that came some seventy years ago to Alamut. My heart breaks to think of that time, as it does when I imagine the barbarians sacking Rome. In Alamut, water ran through channels of solid rock to be stored in great wells carved from the mountainside. Trees planted by Hasan's own hand produced food to feed each mouth. And the library – where else had the learning of two worlds, east and west, been stored? Paradise.

"All destroyed. All gone. When years later I laid eyes on Alamut I could only imagine its former glory. The Mongol could not bring down the mountain, but he did what he could. Nothing was let live or stand, save the castle. Nearly two hundred years of Nizari history erased from Persia.

"But not from the world. Some Nizari survived, fleeing across Egypt, where they were persecuted, and to Spain, where they were tolerated. And here the few fidai remaining made their plans to regain the fortress of Alamut.

"I was born some sixty-four years ago near the mountain of Alhambra in Granada. Having too many children and too little wealth, my parents passed me to the Nizari in return for some service. I was perhaps five years old. At once my training began. Though the fidai were determined to regain Alamut, they knew they could raise no army to rival the Mongols. So they decided to rise the way Hasan had risen – through fear.

"It was at seven years that I first tasted the hashish which, mixed with herbs and a mere trace of opium, gives the user a sense of euphoria. I know now that the fidai used it to create a passion in me for their cause – I believed I had seen the face of God.

"But though much of my training was in stealth and murder, they remained faithful to Hasan's other teachings. When I was given my first lesson in astronomy I showed an aptitude. In only a few weeks I knew all the names and, along with methods of murder, it was decided to initiate me into the more mystical practice of astrology.

"My studies were interrupted in the year 1274 when we began the slow journey to Persia. There my mentors joined other escaped Nizari and formed an army. The next year we attacked by stealth and took Alamut back from the Mongols. I was twelve, and covered in glory.

"Our victory was short-lived. The following year our forces fell to the Mongol army. But during that sole, bliss-filled year I pursued almost nothing but astrology. There was a Persian whom I hadn't known in Spain, an old man who had been let live by the Mongols as harmless. He took me into his home and taught me all he knew of trines, sextiles, and oppositions. It was ancient knowledge culled from Greek, Roman, and Arab sources, all flowing together in this single man. And through him, in me. It was under his guidance that I drew my first star-chart, and with him that I saw the course my life would take.

"That idyllic year ended with the Mongol's return. They laid siege to the castle and we fell almost at once – we were killers, not soldiers. Most of my brothers died in the battle, or else threw themselves from the rocky slope to their deaths. But I was young and frightened. I hid.

"I was found, of course. They tortured me for days, but asked no questions beyond my name. I was a child, I knew nothing of value. They were merely amusing themselves. I was their plaything.

"Worse than their torture of me was their cruelty to my master. They had heard he had embraced the Nizari's return and so they plucked his eyes from him, took his fingers, his teeth, his manhood. I gave him what comfort I could, but could do nothing to ease his soul. He died in my arms without knowing me.

"I believe they grew tired of me – by submitting to their cruelties without protest, I gave them little pleasure. The day after my master's death they took me out onto the cliff before the castle. There a forge had been built. From the forge they removed a thin collar of metal. They said that since I was so devoted to that place, I should have a wedding band. They called me the Arūs. The bridegroom.

"They held my arms and forced me to my knees. I do not remember much of what followed. I remember weeping, and perhaps I prayed. I am quite certain I did not plead. I would not grant them that satisfaction. Once the burning collar was locked about my neck they released my hands so that they could watch my struggles. But I denied them their pleasure. In unknowable pain, I ran forward and threw myself from the rock of Alamut, hoping to end my suffering by dashing my brains out on the rocks below.

"As I hurtled through the air, I remember quite clearly cursing, not my tormentors, but the old man who had helped me make the chart for my life. The chart had shown a long life, with a purpose. I knew when I leapt that my life was over. I was certain that the stars lied. But of course, they did not.

"I have no memory of how I survived. Somehow the fall had broken the burning collar, sparing me. I awoke in a house, taken in by a goat-herd whose wife nursed me to health. They asked no questions of me, but had they I could have given them no answers. My voice was almost entirely gone. It was years before I could speak in any meaningful way.

"I lived in their house and gave them loyal service until together we deemed the debt repaid. Then I left them to return to the castle. Using all the knowledge the fidai had given me, I settled my debt there as well. Not only mine, but that of my fallen brothers. And my poor master. I used the name they had given me. The Arūs. I'm told it is still a name to frighten men in that part of the world.

"That done, I left Persia, traveling west for the land I once called home. But in the stews of Alexandria I was taken by slavers and sold into bondage. I toiled on a pirate's ship for a year, rowing, and here my knowledge of the stars became useful. The ship's master often consulted me with his charts. I guided them so well that I was eventually given my liberty.

"I journeyed with them for a time more, relishing the freedom of the sea. It was with these pirates that I first came to Venice, where I made some charts for the Doge's family. That was when I first met young Katerina and her father, the great Alberto della Scala. This was before the birth of her youngest brother. They asked for their charts, and I obliged them, the ship's navigator posing as my master. I left Italy, not knowing what seeds I had sown in Katerina's mind.

"Upon leaving Venice I finally returned to the land of my birth. When at last I saw Granada again, my family did not know me. Nor I them. I was a man now, and they feared my size combined with my up-bringing. So I left again, hiring Ignazio to pose as the astrologer, and taking ship for wherever the winds blew us.

"I returned to Verona in time to witness the birth of Alberto's third son by his wife. He was christened Francesco della Scala, and already there were signs of greatness in him. Through Ignazio, I was asked to make this child's chart, and did so, not knowing the trouble that would bring us all so many years later.

"That child was Cangrande. The rest you know."

As Tharwat finished his tale, Pietro sat in silent awe. He sensed this story had never before been told. At the same time knew there were pieces missing. But just this much was stunning, and he wrestled with this new insight into his old friend. "These faithful…"

"The fidai."

"Yes – they did this to you. They used drugs to win you to their cause."

"Yes."

"How could you – how could you use the same methods on Cesco?"

"It was only a part of the training. A system devised over nearly two hundred years. Without any one part of the training, it falls to ruin. I am certain that my training has helped him survive this last year, just as I am certain he is no addict. He knows the proper dosage to create energy, stamina, euphoria. He also knows the dangers of over-indulgence. You know him – he will walk a razor's edge, but never cut himself."

"Unless he's pushed," answered Pietro.

Fourteen

Trento, Italy
6 January 1327

Reports from England kept all of Europe grimly entertained. Queen Isabella and her lover-champion Roger Mortimer had forced King Edward to flee to London, effectively penning him in his own city. Already the queen had gotten her son Prince Edward appointed Keeper of the Realm, and arranged a marriage between the lad and the Countess of Hainault, sister to the emperor's new wife. A month later Isabella's forces captured her husband and placed him in Kenilworth Castle. Tales of the king's degradation at the hands of his wife were surprisingly inventive. In his letters to his new friends in Verona, William Montagu confirmed that at least three of them were true.

With the whole of Europe caught up in the scandalous coup, several statesmen missed what was happening in India. It was not, however, lost on the banks and trade guilds. Like the Byzantine Empire, India was suffering the Turk. Sixteen years after their initial attack, Muslim armies re-invaded Halebid, the wealthy capital of the Hoysalas, turning the city into a shambles. The Hoysaleswara Temple, dedicated to Shiva, was left unfinished for a second time, after a total of eighty-six years of work. The walls of the temple, covered with an endless span of gods, goddesses, animals, birds, and dancing girls, were guarded by a Nandi Bull. But this Bull, it was said, had turned his back when the invaders came.

Already concerned over the financial upheaval in England, this attack filled the money-men of Europe with a real fear of a loss of trade with the East, the major investment plan of many since Marco Polo's return. Bankers from Bruges to Constantinople curtailed their speculation in Eastern markets. Yet the major local resource prized by the Turk was something no European had ever bothered with – the berries known as qahwa which, steeped in water, provided a soothing and energizing drink. Goats had been said to dance on their hind legs when given the plant from which the beans grew.

Of nearer interest to Verona was the ongoing unrest in Padua. After the unsuccessful coup d'état under Paolo Dente last year, Marsilio da Carrara had recalled his cousin Ubertino and banished all of Dente's followers. There had followed a veritable reign of terror. Armed to the teeth, Ubertino's men swaggered through the streets of Padua while honest citizens hid in their houses or fled. Not bothering to even disguise themselves, brigands daily committed every kind of injury to the populace – assault, violence, robbery, kidnapping, rape, and murder. As a man walked along a street he'd find a sack thrown over his head, himself carried off to a Cararresi stronghold and held for ransom from his family or guild. Every morning at least one corpse was found lying in the gutters or in the center of the piazzas. No one was ever brought to trial for their deaths.

To anyone perceived to have wronged Ubertino or Niccolo da Carrara, retribution was swift. The judges who'd ordered Ubertino's exile were gruesomely executed, their records burned. The convent of Santa Agata was sacked, the nuns savagely violated. It was commonly known that Niccolo de Carrara had led the pillage, but only his less important followers were even charged, and none were convicted.

During all this the Capitano of Padua, Marsilio da Carrara, kept himself aloof within his palace, looking after his own interests. The people pleaded with any authority for aid. Heinrich of Carinthia, to whom the Paduans had always run for help against Cangrande, sent a representative to stabilize the city. But Heinrich's only interest seemed to be how much money could be wrung out of Padua before it swallowed itself in flame. Noble Paduans like Petruchio's father-in-law, Baptista Minola, became expatriates in Venice or Ferrara, leaving the poor city to the Carrarese and Heinrich's German soldiers.

Meanwhile things were calm in Verona. Cangrande's heir was seen everywhere and heard nowhere. Gone were the escapades of the past year. He appeared only in the company of Cangrande or one of a handful of great men of the city. Still considered a prodigy, there were now reports of humiliating failures – he'd missed an easy target at the butts; he'd slipped off his horse on a long ride; he'd fallen into a river during a hard crossing. These were so out of character that Pietro whisked off a worried letter to his sister.

Antonia's reply was bitter in its brevity. What did Pietro want of her? She saw very little of Cesco. What little she did see worried her. She wrote of the return of his skeletal thinness, of his first spots, of the wasted circles under his eyes. Morsicato was doing what he could, but he was barely keeping his wife alive and had little of his art to spare.

Cesco wrote snatches of greetings here and there. Typically, he did not mention his own health. He pointed out failings in their new code and provided bits of information the network had somehow overlooked – somehow in the midst of his hawking the boy was cultivating his own sources of intelligence.

Of his relationship with Cangrande he said not a word.

Thus did the year 1326 come to an end – at least in Verona where January, not Easter, was considered the start of the New Year.

However the year was counted, that Twelfth Night was momentous. That was the day the Emperor Ludwig IV arrived in Innsbruck on his way to Trent.

This was the first time an emperor had visited Italy since the unfortunate Heinrich had died besieging Rome in the company of the poet Dante. Hearing of Ludwig's arrival, Ghibelline generals and nobles flocked to Trent from all over Lombardy to greet their lord and master.

Last and greatest among their number, Can Francesco della Scala, son of Alberto I, Capitano del Popolo and Podestà of Merchants, Imperial Vicar of Vicenza and Verona, arrived on the Ides of January. The impoverished Emperor had fewer than a hundred knights in attendance at the great Trent city hall. Cangrande brought many more, all expensively decked out in matching capes and spurs.

That the Emperor was irked was evident from the first seconds of their audience. He sat upon his great throne on the dais in utter stillness, watching Verona's lord approach in opulent procession.

Friend and foe alike agreed that Ludwig der Bayer was well-featured. Full-sized yet trim, clean shaven with a rosy complexion. His hair was curly, a remarkable reddish-blonde. If his chin was a little too small, his strong neck and shoulders compensated that lack. Between his Hapsburg nose and the strong line of his brow, his oversize eyes were piercing.

It was on his personality that reports differed. Friends spoke of the smile that was ever on his lips, while Guelphs spoke at length of his querulousness. Ghibellines swore he liked a good jest, while papal envoys reported his restlessness and impulsive nature. Yet all could attest to his boldness, and to the charisma that radiated like heat from a hearth-fire.

Cangrande reached the dais and knelt, but Ludwig did not immediately bid him rise. "Ah, *François du l'Échelle.*" The Emperor spoke in French, stroking the gilded bear-teeth hanging about his throat. It was said that those teeth were plucked by his own hand. "*Bienvenue à notre présence.*"

Cangrande replied in the same language. "I was baptized Francesco, lord, so well you may call me François. But I hope my lord will know me by my more familiar name – Cangrande."

"Yes. Der Hund. The mythical Greyhound. It is a shame we have not met before now."

"I regret it extremely, lord, but my actions in the field protecting your interests have held my attention."

"Our interests? Our interests are clearly yours, since you do so well by them. Perhaps you could lend us a doublet for our coronation. We are sure we own nothing so fine."

Still on his knees, Cangrande shifted his cape to one shoulder, revealing the gilt doublet in its entirety. "Your Grace is too modest. But of course, what is mine is yours."

"Ours? To do with as we please? So said so done is well. But what if we found that Verona was mismanaged? Could we then replace the Capitano?"

Cangrande shrugged. "The office is an elected one, as my lord is well aware. Voted by the people of the city through their representatives."

"Yes, Capitano is elected. Imperial Vicar is not. It is bestowed." Ludwig looked to the banner at Cangrande's back, held high by a wiry boy still shy of manhood. Atop the embroidered ladder sat the two-headed imperial eagle. "You are free with the title."

Cangrande stood without bidding, causing a stir among the assembled nobles. "The title was bestowed upon me by the great Heinrich, your noble predecessor. It has been my honour to carry it these many years. Yet in many ways it is a hollow title, my lord."

The Emperor gazed at the lord of Verona for a long time, lips and brow set in a withering frown. "How, hollow?"

"The Imperial Vicar of the Trevisian Mark is meant to be overlord of Verona, Vicenza, Mantua, Padua and Treviso. Yet regrettably there is no force in the imperial decree. Verona, I was already lord of when the noble Heinrich invested me. I have had to fight for the rest. Vicenza I gained right away, and Mantua too is under my dominion." This raised several eyebrows, as Passerino Bonaccolsi was the titular head of Mantua. "But Padua and Treviso hold out to this day. They deny imperial authority, deny they are a part of the Mark, of the Feltro, of your domain."

Ludwig was grave. "Fifteen years of war and still you have not swayed them. Tell us, do they deny our authority, or yours?"

"Ours combined, my lord. It was my hope that you might grant a specific order commanding Padua and Treviso to bow to my authority, that I might rule them for you, in your name."

"And if we deem it wise to invest another of our subjects?"

Cangrande flashed his perfect teeth for all to behold. "Who else knows the players and the game so well? It takes an Odysseus to blind the Cyclops in his den."

As if summoned by magic, a whip-like man with one eye sewed shut appeared at the Emperor's side. This was Berthold von Neifen, Count of Marstetten and Ludwig's right hand. When years earlier the Emperor had needed a general to lift a papal siege on Milano, he'd sent Berthold. At court, the Count of Marstetten was the Emperor's chosen champion. Thus the Scaliger's cyclops reference was a carefully calculated insult.

The lean Count with the sewn eye was a head smaller than the Capitano of Verona, and the Scaliger had more knights in the great hall, if not more men. The Emperor waved a restraining hand at Berthold. "If you know the game so well, why have you not won?"

"Like poor opponents, the Paduans do not know when it is better to lay aside their queen and capitulate. They need to actually be placed in check. One way to do so would be to change the feather in my cap and become a Guelph. I've had offers, your Majesty, many offers. From Florence and its allies. For my aid in their cause, they would grant me Padua and Treviso. The Pope offers even more."

Stirs among the Emperor's many retainers, but no change of expression from Ludwig himself as Cangrande continued. "I would rather have such an honour from your hand. In return for which, I am pleased to part with these trifles."

He waved a hand and four chests were brought forth and upturned, spilling their contents on the slate floor. Gold discs piled higher and higher, some showing the side that bore a lily, symbol of Florence, some displaying the obverse bearing that city's patron saint.

As the last gold florin clattered to the floor, Cangrande said, "Two hundred thousand. A fair display, I think, of my loyalty. Think of it not as payment but as a minor donation to your Majesty's cause, one that I will better once Padua is mine." It was a blunt gesture, but perhaps better so, had not the Scaliger added a coda. "Then perhaps you could afford such a doublet as mine."

The Emperor shot out of his throne as if launched by a catapult. "You dare!"

"I dare much."

"Majesty!" cried Berthold in outrage as several men stepped forward to lay hands upon the Scaliger. Verona's knights moved to block them. As yet no weapons were drawn, but it was only moments away.

There was a sudden ripping sound, a great rending of fabric. Cangrande cried out in surprise and dismay. Two more quick cuts of the knife and the fabulous doublet was off the Scaliger's body and tossed to crumple in a heap atop the pile of coins at the Emperor's feet. The offending knife followed it closely.

"There, your Majesty." The new voice spoke in fluent German, notably in the Emperor's own dialect. "Another gift from Verona. My master looks far superior without it, as the court women no doubt agree."

"Who speaks?" demanded the Emperor in his own tongue.

Stepping out from behind Cangrande, Cesco knelt. The empty sheath at his hip told of the knife that had performed three swift cuts – one up the back, one under each arm – loosening the ostensible object of contention.

The Emperor peered at the boy. "Step forward, you!"

Cangrande spoke in a different Germanic dialect. "He is a mere page, my lord," he said, laying a hand upon Cesco's shoulder.

"Then he should be swift to obey his overlord," said Ludwig.

Cangrande's jaw set, but he released his grip. The boy stepped over the ruined doublet to prostrate himself before the Emperor in a pose of complete submission.

"Your name, boy."

Cesco's head remained completely bowed, talking to the stone floor, but his words were clear. "My name, your imperial Majesty, is not my own. I fear to bring disgrace upon my master should I utter it."

"How can such a quick-thinking and comely child disgrace anyone? If anything, it is your master disgraces you. We asked your name."

"I am told I was baptized Francesco, your highness."

"Like your illustrious Capitano. But you have doubts?"

Cangrande broke in. "My page is precocious, lord. He—"

The Emperor sniffed. "Learned from his master, I'm sure."

"Your highness—" began Cangrande.

"Lord della Scala, perhaps in your court men have leave to speak at will. But this is the Imperial Court of the Holy Roman Empire, and we do not address you at present." The Emperor returned his gaze to Cesco. "Tell us, young Fran-chess-ko, how you come to speak in our native tongue."

"I have heard it spoken in camp here, my lord."

The Emperor raised his brows. "And you learned to speak it so flawlessly? Look at us. Yes," said Ludwig slowly, glancing back and forth between Cangrande and Cesco. "We have heard tell of an heir to der Hund. Is it possible that you are related to this arrogant, insolent man?"

"I am as proud to claim him as my father as he is to claim me his son."

Seeing consternation raging across Cangrande's face, the Emperor smiled. "Fran-chess-ko. François, in French. That is the same as our Franz, no? Tell us, Franz der Hund, what you think of your father's demands."

Cesco blinked in surprise. "The humble Capitano of Verona would never make demands of your illustrious lordship! He speaks out of his passion to champion your cause. If I may, your Grace, setting aside all familial loyalty, I must tell you that the Capitano is the most able leader of men in Lombardy." Cesco's brow furrowed artfully. "Perhaps he lacks the false-modesty that causes men to hide their lights under a bushel, and thus is not as equipped for such an august gathering as this. He is a plain man, a soldier, more comfortable in the saddle than the salon."

The Emperor cast an eye over the Scaliger. "Plain is not the word we would have chosen. Arrogant. Posturing. Peacock, perhaps."

"I assure you, great one, this Apollo is no pavone. If his valet chose extravagant attire for today, the Capitano barely noticed it, so great was his desire to meet with you. It was, after all, his idea to call this gathering and attain at last your right of coronation."

If the rest was art, this last was true enough. But the Emperor was still angry. "Perhaps he issued the invitation to supplant us before our own followers."

An uncomfortable ripple passed through the crowd. The Emperor had spoken aloud what everyone had already deduced. Truth be told, there were many in the assembly who wondered if it might not be for the best. But it having been said, Cangrande's death was almost a certainty.

Cesco just laughed. "Giant he may be, but he is no Ephialtes, to test his spirit against mighty Jove's. There is no need to have him bound, great one."

The Emperor frowned. "Is that a reference of some kind?" A man stepped forward and whispered in Ludwig's ear. This was the favoured imperial poet, Hugo von Trimberg. Upon hearing the poet's explanation, the Emperor's face lit with delight. "L'Inferno! Oh-ho! Is this the child fostered with the great poet Dante? Tell us, boy, can you recite?"

Cesco bowed deeply. "If your highness pleases, I can even put his Comedy to music."

The Emperor took in a great breath, eyes darting between the Scaliger and his heir. "It would please us greatly. Do you require an instrument?"

Cesco's answer was to open his mouth and begin singing. The notes were high, clear and strong. But the words were not what Dante had written. Cesco was translating the opening Canto of L'Inferno to the Emperor's own style of German.

Ludwig coloured with pleasure. The court, seeing his evident delight, smiled and cooed. The Emperor had a new favourite.

Fuming, Cangrande listened closely. His own German was pure, bearing little relation to the Bavarian style favoured by the Emperor. Hence he'd followed only the gist of the rapid exchange between Ludwig and Cesco. But he understood that the boy was pleading Verona's case – something Cangrande was loath to hear. For Ludwig was quite correct, Cangrande's intention had been to march in and establish his dominance over the Emperor from the first moment. Everything had been calculated, down to the offensively rich doublet.

Everything except the boy's intercession. At first Cangrande thought his heir was aiming for simple humiliation. He now perceived that Cesco's planning had been as careful as his own. The perfect imitation of the Emperor's tongue. The literal laying bare of Cangrande. The loyal defense of a master he was clearly at odds with. The casual reference to Dante's poem, drawing out a new line of conversation. Now the song, showing off the boy's invention and musicality at once.

Out-flanked, the Scaliger immediately forged new tactics. The first was to wipe the scowl off his face and display instead an amused tolerance.

Ironically, the first Canto of L'Inferno carried Dante's version of the Greyhound prophecy. Even showing Cangrande up, the boy was literally singing his master's praises – or so everyone believed, including Cesco himself.

Cesco concluded the first Canto and the Emperor burst into applause. The whole court followed suit, remarking what a clever boy the Scaliger had. Even Cangrande slow-clapped while Cesco lowered his head with a modest smile.

"So inventive, so vibrant." The Emperor turned his head. "Berthold, have you ever heard the like?"

The man with the sewn eye shook his head. "Never, my lord."

"You, Hugo?"

"Nor I, my lord," said the Emperor's pet poet.

Ludwig crossed to lay a bejeweled hand on Cesco's shoulder. "Boy, will you bestow your time with us?"

Cesco appeared flattered but uncertain. "If my master the Capitano can spare me."

"We think he can be persuaded to." Ludwig turned to Cangrande. "Thank this boy, Hund. He is why you leave here unhindered. Leave the gold as well, for his upkeep and ours. And perhaps when next we meet you will have taken a lesson from your heir on how to petition an Emperor. You may go."

It was an order Cangrande could not courteously refuse. "I beg a word with young Francesco before I depart."

The word 'beg' being appreciated, the wish was granted. Cangrande leaned forward to kiss Cesco on either cheek. Ruffling the boy's hair a little more roughly than appeared to the watchers, he said softly, "I was a fool not to factor you into this interview."

Cesco grinned up at him. "A mistake I trust you won't make twice."

"Count on it. I expect detailed reports."

"If you can figure out the cypher."

Turning away, Cangrande bowed low to the Emperor and backed out of the hall at the head of his retinue. The moment he was outside he chuckled, gave a meaningful look to his friends, and sauntered away as if he hadn't a care in the world. As if this had been his plan all along. As if he had contrived all this to plant his spy in the Emperor's camp. They admired him all the more.

Tonight he would begin lessons in the Emperor's dialect.

Fifteen

Avignon, France
18 March 1327

"Is he hostage, or refugee?" asked Petrarch's brother Gherardo with a discerning smile.

"Both, I think." Pietro had heard the news with visceral pleasure. Cesco had freed himself from his hawking in a way that heaped praise upon him while blackening Cangrande's eye.

The letters had flown from Trent like startled birds. In Italy, Germany, Austria, Spain, and France, all were soon reading accounts of the encounter between the Emperor and the Greyhound, and the aftermath. Cangrande's heir was kept as hostage to the Scaliger's good behavior, but rather than being locked up in someone's castle for the duration, Cesco had been given a prestigious post at the imperial court – personal page to Ludwig himself. The Emperor made further provisions against his safety, namely signing a treaty of alliance with Heinrich of Carinthia, a longtime foe of Cangrande, in which the Veronese lord was passingly named, employing the dismissive and contemptuous version of his title, Der Hund. The Hound.

"So your boy has escaped?" asked Gherardo.

"For the moment." In his year as a guest in Petrarch's house, Pietro had made no effort to conceal the war between the Capitano and his heir. It was common knowledge already, and like everyone else not directly involved, the brothers Petracco found it greatly entertaining.

Entertainment wasn't the only fee Pietro paid for living in this house. Not wanting to be a burden, he had hired a servant to clean up after him and to help cook his meals. He'd also hired, at Cangrande's expense, a clerk to assist Petrarch in preparing his case. He insisted on paying for candles, inks, paper, quills, and a fair portion of the household food. Naturally, this flow of largesse freed Petrarch to indulge himself in the finest clothes and wines France had to offer.

Today Pietro and Gherardo were sitting in Petrarch's office, sipping water instead of wine. The change was likely due to Petrarch's absence. Gherardo didn't seem to have his brother's natural flair for flamboyant living. It seemed more an aspiration, a goal to be worked at. Pietro hoped that the fellow would find his own level, become his own man. But it was not the kind of observation a casual friend and guest could make.

"So the Emperor is being crowned?" asked Gherardo.

"After Easter, they say." Pietro's left leg was bouncing slightly, full of pent-up energy.

"Will your master attend, after this?"

"He's not my master."

"I wager he's smarting that he didn't take the Pope's offer when he had the chance."

"It's a wager you'd lose," said Pietro.

They paused as they heard heavy steps on the stair. The door was flung open and Petrarch entered in a rush. He'd shed his snow-covered cloak downstairs along with his boots, but his hose and fur-lined farsetto still showed traces of the weather.

"I have a name," he announced, oddly unexultant as he poured himself a heaping goblet of spiced wine. After months of scrabbling for this information, he should have been more triumphant. The lack spoke volumes.

"At last!" Gherardo was privy to everything except the book of indulgences. Petrarch wanted to shield his brother from any possible consequences of having that dangerous tome in the house.

Petrarch downed the goblet's contents in a single quaff. Setting it on his desk, he sank into his chair and sighed. "Cardinal Bernardo Gui."

Forewarned was forearmed. Thanks to Tharwat, Pietro had known the name before it left his friend's lips. This was the confirmation he had been awaiting.

Petrarch took Pietro's blank face for shock. "It seems the inquisitor has taken a very personal interest in the question of your reinstatement. And, as I'm sure you know, Gui has the ear of the Pope."

"Is there a reason? I mean, for singling me out."

Petrarch's drooping eyes seemed heavier today. "He cites your father's work, and your own intimate ties with another heretic. Hardly proof, but enough to damn you by association."

Pietro knew the true prime mover, but couldn't share it without betraying Tharwat. Absently he said, "My sister is a novice, and my brother is in Florence taking minor orders."

"That means nothing to Gui."

"Should I prepare to be arrested?"

"No! No, not at all. There is no proof of true heresy."

"I refused to tax the people of Ravenna," said Pietro.

"A mere pretext for your excommunication, and one that sits very ill with several cardinals. Many men have done far worse and received only a reprimand. To arrest you on such a charge would set a worrying precedent." Petrarch refilled his goblet. "I have requested an interview with Cardinal Gui."

"Is that wise? Meeting him may do me more harm than—"

"You won't be there. I'll dine with the Colonna family, and Gui will join us. I'll test the waters, see if there is any hope. I think the best way to proceed is to gain his favour. If he ceases to oppose your reinstatement, you can then petition the Pope on behalf of the Scaliger—"

There was a bump just outside the heavy office door, and the sound of quick steps in retreat, as if someone had stumbled while listening at the keyhole.

Gherardo was the first to the door. Opening it wide, he stepped into the hall, Pietro and Petrarch joining him seconds later.

Lucia was sauntering towards them. "Did you see anyone here?" asked Gherardo.

"No," she replied, passing them by.

Warily eyeing his sister's receding form, Petrarch shook his head. "Busybody."

Indeed, of late Lucia had shown a keen interest in Pietro's religious status, and when it might be mended. She had continued to plague him, blocking his path in the hallways and brushing her bosoms against him. Twice she had outright suggested marriage, wondering aloud if her brothers had welcomed him to the house so he might seduce her and so take her off their hands. "Not that I would object," she'd purred, batting her eyelashes.

"I am not a suitable man," Pietro had sternly replied. "An excommunicant, suspected of heresy. Your brothers would wish you to marry better."

"You don't understand women at all, do you? Being bad only makes you more desirable." She had kissed him quickly on the neck, then scampered off.

Now Gherardo closed the door and they resumed their conversation in closer tones. "No, Pietro, confronting a man of Gui's power is unwise," observed Petrarch sagely. "Best to work through intermediaries like myself."

When they descended to supper. Lucia joined them, dressed in a very alluring, and very expensive, dress. Petrarch scowled. "With what coin did you purchase that? The household funds?"

"I have money," she replied haughtily. "And many friends."

"Too many friends."

"Oh, brother!" she turned to share a conspiratorial whisper with Pietro. "For someone so busy being *à la mode*, he's shockingly conventional!"

The meal progressed, with a polite discussion of Latin poetry that neatly excluded Lucia from the discourse. When she excused herself, the young men remained to quaff off the last of the wine and talk of other things.

"Pietro, are you well? You seem distracted."

Pietro ceased his fidgeting. "Sorry. Just thinking."

Petrarch placed a comforting hand on his friend's shoulder. "This is not insurmountable."

Gherardo made reference to the setting sun, and Petrarch set down his cup. "Oop! Thank you, Gherardo! Pietro, I must leave you. I have a most pressing matter, one that cannot be delayed on any given evening!"

The twinkling in Petrarch's eye invited Pietro to inquire. Pietro obliged. "And that is?"

"Mirror time!" There were ways in which Petrarch was very like his sister.

Declining Gherardo's invitation to play chess, Pietro climbed the stairs to his room as he considered the facts. Pathino influences Gui, Gui influences the Pope. Discredit Pathino and with luck the case against me crumbles. But how to bring Pathino into disgrace? He hoped the answer was waiting for him.

396

Pietro unlocked the door to his room and closed it behind him before lighting a candle. Tharwat was there, asleep in a chair by the shuttered window.

They'd risked only two meetings since December, having worked out signals to be left in plain view if either of them required counsel. In February Pietro had summoned Tharwat to share news from Verona, doing so by leaving a full wineglass in an open window.

Then just a week ago Tharwat had marked the wall opposite Petrarch's house with a chalk drawing of a lion, ostensibly to advertise the next papal entertainment. Pietro told Petrarch's servants to leave his room in peace that night, because he had papers he needed to organize.

As appointed, the Moor had appeared just after dark. "Through my master, I have arranged for us to display our animals at the Dominican monastery. I have learned which cell Pathino occupies. During the display a wolf will break loose and race into the dormitory. My master will order me to retrieve it."

"Affording you the opportunity to search Pathino's things." Pietro's face had shown his concern. "I don't know. There's a lot that can miscarry."

"Which is why I warn you. If I am taken, they may assume I am a thief and I will be beaten. But being

397

a Moor, they will probably accuse me of witchcraft. If that is the case, I will attempt not to survive my initial interrogations. However, it might be wise, if I am taken, to vacate the city for a time."

"Good Lord." Pietro had gripped Tharwat's arm. "Don't do it!"

"The opportunity will not present itself again. There is nothing in my stars to say I die in France, or at this time."

"Not dying doesn't mean living well," Pietro had replied.

"True. But I deem this worth defying the odds. Pathino must be dealt with. He is a threat to both you and the boy. If I am caught, I will attempt to murder him. Do not argue. This is my choice."

Pietro had clamped his mouth shut, then waited this whole week for word. In due course he heard of the escape of the wolf and of the beating the Moorish slave had taken for letting it loose. Thankfully, that was the end to the gossip. Tharwat's deception had worked. Now it was a matter of waiting for him to return and reveal what, if anything, he had gleaned.

This morning the chalked figure of a wolf was scrawled opposite Pietro's window. He'd been fidgety all afternoon, anxiously awaiting this interview.

The Moor was deeply asleep, difficult to wake. Pietro had to shake him. "I grow old," said Tharwat simply, lifting himself from the only seat in the room. "I take rest where I may."

"Sit, please." Pietro lit a candle and perched on the edge of his bed. "You were beaten?"

"It was necessary to the ruse." Indeed, his face showed a split lip and much bruising. "I think my 'master' enjoyed the farce. His blows carried more weight than strictly necessary."

Instantly there was a new concern. "Will he betray you?"

"No. He has family, and I have made it clear that if I should come to real harm, so will they. It is false, but he believes." In the light of the candle Tharwat noted some papers in Pietro's handwriting. The Moor smiled slightly. "Poetry?"

Pietro shook his head. "No. I lack the skill. But since I'm doomed to this eternal stay with nothing to occupy myself, I've begun a commentary on father's *Commedia.*"

"Well done," replied the Moor. "You knew him best, and can explain his more obscure intentions."

"Honestly, it would be better if it were Antonia writing it. But as that's not a proper undertaking for a holy sister, it falls to me. Poco once said he fancied doing it." The Moor snorted and Pietro grinned. "Yes, I'd like to see that too." The grin faded. "So what did you learn?"

"Pathino, or Brother Gregor if you please, keeps no personal items in his cell other than instruments of self-inflicted penance. His hair shirt, his cilice, and the like. There are no papers at all. Or at least none easily discoverable."

"Damn." Pietro stared at the wall, thinking hard. "He must have documents. He keeps it secret, but proof of his heritage must exist. Some evidence that he is Cangrande's elder brother, the natural son of Alberto della Scala. If he ever plans to shed this holy disguise and return to his 'rightful' place in Verona, he must have some kind of testimony of his lineage."

It was what they had concluded in December when speculating on Pathino's aims. Discredit Cangrande, remove him from power, then return as the last living son of Cangrande's father to take up the reins. Only then could Pathino steal his destiny.

"What if Pathino's conversion is genuine? I remember how he used the Lord's name to justify much of what he did."

Tharwat's brow compressed. "If so, why bother continuing his revenges upon you and his half-brother?"

"Becoming holy wouldn't diminish his need for revenge. If anything, that madman would think he was the instrument for the Lord's justice."

"If it is justice he seeks, he will surely want to prove his claim."

"Which brings us back to the question of proof. He must have it hidden somewhere, somewhere safe. But that could be anywhere."

Tharwat considered. "Would he leave it to be found? He's not a trusting soul. Obsessive. Controlling. Would he not be more like to keep it upon his person—"

"The cross!" Pietro turned bright eyes upon the Moor. "You remember, Cesco once pulled a medallion with a cross from Pathino's neck..."

The Moor was nodding. "I carried that medallion for over a year as we tried to trace him. Rude, but rich. Missing two pearls. It had no writing upon it, but many knots and swirling designs, as though the pearls were stars in a swirling night sky. It cost Ignazio his life."

"We wondered at the time why it was so important. Why he was willing to chase half across the world and murder for it."

"We assumed it was valuable to him, beyond its intrinsic value. Then I learned it was a gift to Cangrande's father from a Scotsman in return for a service rendered."

"Pathino told me the same thing in the cave. Alberto had given it to Pathino's mother during their tryst." As often as they'd discussed Pathino over the years in Ravenna, somehow the medallion had not come up – at least, not in more than passing reference. "I never asked, who identified it for you?"

"Manoello Giudeo, the court fool. He was jester in Alberto's time as well. After Ignazzio's death, I drew a copy of it for the Scaliger. Manuel happened to see it, and remarked upon it. What is in your mind?"

It seemed a fairly thin hope. Yet Pathino had killed to regain the medallion. Clearly it had some importance. Was it merely sentimental? Or could it be more..? "Tharwat – what if the medallion is the proof?"

Tharwat frowned in thought. "Without writing, how can it be proof?"

"A seal ring is proof. A banner is proof. So long as he possesses it, he can prove his claim."

"Not unless there is someone who can verify its true nature, and testify that Pathino received it from Alberto. If we're even correct."

"If that," agreed Pietro. "Can you draw it again, do you think?"

"Give me paper."

As Tharwat recreated the medallion in ink, Pietro shared the news from Trent. The Moor paused in his drawing to gaze out at the snowmelt in the starlight. "Whose idea do you think it was, to elude his hawker?"

"His, I'm sure. A perfect solution, since he has lost all of us." Pietro pressed his lips together and stroked his bad thigh – it always ached in cold weather. "I need to get back to him."

"We serve him best by removing this threat. If he has shown anything, it's that he can survive."

"I know. I only fear what surviving costs him. Better he had friends to shoulder some of that burden. He's only a boy."

Tharwat handed the finished drawing to Pietro. Swinging one leg over the windowsill, he smiled. "Though perhaps young in years, he's never been only a boy."

Asleep that night, Pietro resisted yet another dream of Cangrande's sister. Katerina came to him not as she was, but as she'd been when he first saw her – beautiful, tyrannical, mocking, gentle, knowing. The knowledge that she was a monster, or had monstrous intents, lay yet in the future. Old enough to be his mother, yet ageless, tempting. He'd never quite recovered from the shock of finding her less than she seemed. Or was it that she was more?

Now she was toying with him, making his loins ache with teasingly light touches. "No. I hate you. I can't – we can't…"

"Oh, but we can." The lips brushed his ear, just before the teeth bit down.

Pietro's eyes sprang open and he bolted away from the warm body partially covering him. The candle he kept by his bed was out, and all was darkness. His hand scrabbled for the dagger on the bedpost, but in reaching for it he fell off the bed, barking his elbow on the tiled floor.

"Shhh!" hissed the figure in the bed. "My brothers will hear you!"

"Lucia?" Dumbfounded, Pietro looked to the door. Even in the dark he could see that it was shut. "How did you get in here?"

"Silly. We all have keys." She reached down for him and he slithered quickly away. "What's the matter? Don't you like girls?"

"What are you doing here?"

"Anything you like." Her voice was husky as she dropped off the bed onto the floor to crawl after him. Naked but for his shirt and his slippered feet, Pietro retreated until the wall was at his back. Her hands found his thigh, then his groin. "Are you a ship, to have a mast so tall?"

For a moment he was tempted – how he was tempted! Who could blame him, honestly?

Petrarch, for one, you fool. And Gherardo. And everybody in the world. He pushed her hands away, cursing his body and the girl and the dream that had put him in a state fit to combust. "Lucia, no. No. This isn't right."

"It isn't wrong, either," she murmured, biting his leg.

"Ahh! Lucia, don't make me call for your brothers!"

"And what will you say? How did I get into your locked room? Why am I naked?"

In the darkness he hadn't known that. His resolve wavered. "Get your clothes on. Please, this isn't the way—"

"No? Is this the way, then?" She lifted herself on top of him and he had to shift his desperate hips to keep from entering her, which he knew was doom – the moment he began, he would not stop. "Lucia!"

Stroking his hair, she pressed her pelvis against his chest, and through the thin shirt Pietro could feel her coarse hairs against him. There was a dampness, too. He was going to have to hit her.

Her hands dropped from his hair to lay along his neck, and her fingers found the bag that hung about his neck. "What's this? Some token from another lover?"

That brought him back to the world with a cold rush. Shoving her aside, he stood and crossed the room, throwing wide the window to let air and light in. "Find your clothes and get out."

She was on her knees by the door, making a pouty moue with her mouth, her shoulders forward to make her breasts fuller in the moonlight. "Who is she?"

"Lucia. Go."

She froze a moment, uncertain. Then a look of absolute loathing crossed her face. "What's the matter with you? Not man enough to take a willing woman? Or am I not man enough for you?"

"Just go."

Standing, Lucia grabbed up her gown from the chair, threw open the door, and stomped back to her room without bothering to dress.

Pietro was just closing the door when a flickering light approached from further down the hall. Damn. He stepped into the hallway to brave whatever unpleasant scene lay in store.

Lucia was nowhere in sight, but her elder brother stood there in his nightshirt. Petrarch's drooping eyes were shadowed from the candlelight, and Pietro couldn't tell what they held.

They stood staring at each other for a long time. The anxiety of the moment was murderous. Pietro didn't know what to say. Any excuse insulted his friend's sister. He was wholly innocent – perhaps too innocent. A part of him said if he were going to be blamed, he might as well have tasted of the apple.

At last Petrarch said, "We'll get you a better lock for that door."

"Thank you," gasped Pietro, sure he was about to be sick.

Petrarch opened his mouth, then seemed to think better of whatever he was about to say. He turned and entered his own chamber, closing the door behind him, casting Pietro into darkness.

Pietro could not sleep after that scene. Instead he lit a candle to write and seal an uncoded letter destined for Verona, Tharwat's drawing carefully rolled inside it. Then he pulled the parchment out of the pouch Lucia had found. Until dawn he distracted himself with the puzzle of MAB, for once feeling relief instead of fear reading it.

Maybe that's why Cesco is so enamored of puzzles. They keep you from thinking about life.

Sixteen

Milano, Italy

Cangrande's behavior during their meeting having left a foul taste in Ludwig's mouth, the Emperor avoided the obvious route to Milano, bypassing the Alps and skirting Verona by some miles in favour of Bergamo.

But such a rift could not be long entertained. Cangrande was the greatest Ghibelline power in the Trevisian Mark, his wealth phenomenal, his mercenary armies legion. Not even the Visconti of Milan could match him. After letting the great man cool his heels in Verona, the Emperor sent none other than the one-eyed Berthold von Neifen as his peacemaker. Their interview was private, but the result was Cangrande's journey to Milano in time for the coronation.

Arriving, Cangrande presented a subdued version of himself at the imperial court. His clothes were still fine, but muted in colour and pattern. The dark shades of his farsetto were costly but not flashy. Noting this with satisfaction, the Emperor invited Cangrande to dine with him – after the coronation.

The following day Ludwig personally made peace between a reluctant Heinrich of Carinthia and a grudging Cangrande. The pair had been vying for control of Padua for nearly seventeen years now, and the war was too profitable for either man to give it up easily. But as allies in the Ghibelline cause, they had no choice but to embrace and share the kiss of peace.

After that, the Scaliger walked a dangerous line. He'd brought over twelve-hundred knights to attend him, almost ten times the number of Ludwig's men. He held open court every day, something even the Visconti couldn't do. He spent money as though he could pluck it from the night skies. The day after Easter Sunday he attempted to buy up all the game in the area – every hen, hare, deer, boar, and cow he could find. Fortunately for the Emperor even Cangrande lacked the ready cash for that, and the imperial court was able to dine, if meanly.

On a glorious Friday the 29th of May, Emperor Ludwig took to the streets of Milano (or, as he called it, 'Mailand') to celebrate the Feast of San Massimo – an irony, to be celebrating the feast day of a sainted bishop of Verona. But it was a chance to parade his imperial majesty two days before he received the first of the crowns that would end all controversy over his claim to the throne. It was also a chance to make both the Visconti family and the thrice-damned Cangrande della Scala ride obediently behind him. That the Greyhound had to follow his own heir in the parade was particularly pleasing to the Emperor.

Among the multitudes cheering Ludwig's procession, a cluster of Veronese stood on a prominent step before a minor church. One young fellow waved a checkered flag that could not help but catch the eye. From horseback the Emperor asked his steward who they were, but it was his page walking beside the imperial mount who supplied the names. "The one with the forked beard is Ser Dottore Giuseppe Morsicato, knighted by your illustrious predecessor Heinrich. The man beside him is Lord Petruchio da Bonaventura, also a Knight of the Mastiff. And the young man with the flag is Bailardetto da Nogarola, squire to Lord Bonaventura. Also my cousin and close friend."

Ludwig reared back in mock shock. "I don't think I've heard you name anyone as a friend, boy!"

Cesco bowed his head. "Only your majesty do I hold in greater esteem."

"I do relish courtly lies, Franz, especially when framed so smoothly. I suppose you wish to be released from your duties this evening so you may spend time with your only friend in all the world."

"I had not even considered begging such a gracious boon of your majesty. Though," added Cesco thoughtfully, "I imagine it would irk the lord of Verona if he were present at your table while I was excused."

"An excellent reason, then! At the parade's end, go find your friend. And tomorrow he and his master may attend me in person."

Grinning, Cesco ran over and passed a few quick words with Detto and Petruchio, relaying the Emperor's invitation and learning the name of the inn they were at – as Petruchio hadn't intended to come to Milano for the coronation, he wasn't part of Cangrande's official retinue.

Just as Cesco scampered off, Detto spied his father approaching and waved. Bailardino's face split into a huge grin as he waved back. Petruchio bowed deeply to Cangrande, who waved carelessly. When they were past, Morsicato turned to Petruchio. "The rest of the parade will take an hour. Shall we catch up with your wife and children?"

"Oh hell," replied Petruchio, looking up at the balcony where his family had an excellent view of the procession. "I suppose I'll have to bring them to the audience as well. After all, it was Kate's idea to come."

This was only true in part. Kate had suggested this trip to her husband. But it was an idea Morsicato had in turn planted in her.

Days earlier, on his way to Milano, the doctor had stopped at Petruchio's estates. Lord Bonaventura had been out riding with his sons and squire, so Morsicato had sat down with Kate and her two daughters. "Your sons are well?"

"They are. Ferocious squabblers. I have to seat them miles apart at table. I'm occasionally tempted to tie them in a sack and drop it in the river to force them to work together. But I fear they would drown arguing over the order of precedence in leaving the bag. Thank Heaven they go to Vicenza this fall." Young Petruchio and Hortensio were destined to be squires to Detto's father, as Detto was to theirs.

After more pleasantries, Morsicato had casually let drop his destination. Katerina Bonaventura had looked mildly intrigued, saying, "I've never seen an emperor. Are they very different from other men?"

"Heinrich exuded majesty."

"Like the Greyhound," said Kate.

Morsicato always had to remind himself that most of the world believed Cangrande was the Greyhound. "Just like him, only fatter."

Laughing, Kate turned to her daughters, who had laid their sewing aside to listen. "What do you think, girls? Shall we shame your father into displaying us to the Emperor Ludwig?"

Her daughters were ecstatic at the idea. The elder, Vittoria, talked only of what she would wear. She was dark of hair and complexion, like her father, but had a delicate air. The oldest of the Bonaventura children, she would be twelve this fall. The twins had come between the girls, and would be eleven this August.

The youngest child, who next month would be ten, was redheaded like her mother. She'd sniffed scornfully at the doctor. "Why are you going?"

"To watch the coronation."

"You're not telling me the truth. You want to see Cangrande's son."

"Evelina," her mother had chided, "it's impolite to call people liars, even if they are. Of course he wants to see the boy he helped raise. It was a foolish question."

Eyes blazing, the girl had turned mulish. "What's more important, being polite or being honest?"

Rolling her eyes, Kate had sent both her girls to fetch something from her room. Once they were out of earshot she'd turned to the doctor with a frank smile. "My younger daughter doesn't know what questions matter. Now tell me, why do you want Detto to go?"

Laughing, Morsicato had stroked his forked beard, nearly its old self. "I hate being transparent. She's right, I want to see Cesco. But he might not want to see me."

"Whereas he can't say no to Detto. I see. And why do you wish to see him?"

"To make sure he's well, that's all. There's no danger."

In truth, Morsicato was worried about the hashish. Cesco's diluted supply must have run out long ago. Had he gotten more on his own?

"I am always least assured when being assured. I suppose we'd best start packing. Don't worry about my husband. I can manage him."

And so she had, bringing her whole clan – husband, sons, daughters, servants, and squire to Milano just in time for the great parade that opened the coronation festivities.

Two hours after the parade they were back in their cramped room at the top of an inn. They were fortunate to have even this. Everything had been booked long in advance, but Petruchio had made a wager with the room's inhabitant, a trial of skill at blowing snot across the yard. Being particularly skilled, Petruchio had won the wager and the room, much to his wife's disgust.

"You're only angry I didn't let you have a try. But I hate being outshone."

"I'm angry because our sons are going to practice day and night, and likely our daughters too!"

"Not me!" cried Vittoria in utter disgust.

"You'd get a nosebleed anyway," teased Evelina. "You're so delicate."

"Then she'll like the air here," said a voice from the door. "Here is where rare birds thrive, for the air is delicate." Cesco was instantly swept into a choking embrace. "Detto! You'll miss me when I'm you've strangled the life out of me!"

Laughing, Detto released his grip. It was too cramped for everyone to rise for a proper welcome. Young Petruchio and Hortensio came forward to thump Cesco on the back. Thirteen next month, he was their elder by nearly two years, yet they were taller than he, which clearly rankled.

Lord Petruchio Bonaventura remained sprawled in a chair by the window. "How's Susanna, boy?"

Cesco grinned. "She's a better gamer than any bird in the Emperor's keep, lord. I give you full credit."

"Excellent! Cesco, you remember my odious, odiferous groom Grumio."

"How could I forget? How are you, old man?"

Dozing by the window, the groom cracked an eyelid. "Eh? Sorry, are you speaking to me? I'm too old to hear young voices. Buzz buzz buzz."

Petruchio kicked the chair Grumio was sleeping in, jolting his servant. "And you remember my ravishing wife, though the Lord alone knows why she married me."

"I was drunk." Kate sat with a deck of cards before her. "No, wait – that was you."

"So it was! And these are my daughters, Vittoria and – Evelina! Pull your dress down and stand up straight! Lord! Kate, do something with that one!"

"What would you suggest? Shall I starve her, or keep her blindfolded in a dark room?"

"You could sew her eyelids shut, like they do for rebellious falcons!" suggested Vittoria nastily.

"Shut your face," said Evelina with an elbow for her big sister.

The last person in the room had so far refrained from greeting Cesco, so Cesco sought him out instead. "Dottore! Bearded once more! I'm so glad – Susanna needs a new nest."

"She's welcome to try." Embracing the boy, Morsicato looked deeply into his eyes and saw no trace of barbiturate. Thank God, he's not been indulging.

The face itself was in the process of growing – the lips were fuller, the nose larger, and there was more than a trace of hair along his chin, though it had been razored. "Your complexion has cleared. You look well rested. And well-fleshed, for you."

Cesco pulled his face away. "I always feel as if you're sizing me up for a meal. I take it you're responsible for this menagerie?"

"Menagerie!" cried Petruchio.

"Fair word, and that's the truth," muttered Grumio for all to hear.

"I thought you couldn't hear young voices," mused Petruchio.

The groom shrugged. "They so rarely say anything of merit."

Kate smiled. "I feel the same about men."

Ignoring the squabbles of this queer family, Morsicato answered Cesco. "I thought you might enjoy the company of boys your own age."

"Alas, there's no shortage here. The Emperor's son Ludwig is never far from his father, and little Stefan tries to keep up. There are a dozen other pages, including several Visconti boys. They're my bitter rivals – how these family feuds do breed! In our mock-duels they always try to uncinch my saddle girth or butter my boots. Amateurs! I've endured infinitely worse tricks before now – as they've learned to their sorrow."

"What's the Emperor like?" asked Hortensio.

Cesco pulled a thoughtful face, stroking his chin as Dante used to do. "In folly, wise. In difference, attentive. In adversity, successful. In despondency, strong-willed. He is a man of contradictions, but bears them lightly. Money is like water through his fingers. He's surrounded himself with philosophers, but he's not one himself. His greatest joy is hearing the hunting horn in the mountains. That and his entertainments." He grinned. "I had the honour of planning the imperial court's Easter pageant."

Petruchio nodded. "We heard about that. A string of pantomimes and a very convincing crucifixion scene, they say."

"Germans do like their blood. But the whole court wept at the resurrection mime, with the Madonna and Mary Magdalene beating their fake bosoms and tearing their wigs out in joy. Are you laughing, Detto? Here, let me show you how it went!"

There was a great deal of horseplay, with the four boys and little Evelina racing around the cramped room, crashing into walls and shaking clouds of dust from the rafters. Vittoria cringed and scowled at them all. Kate, Morsicato, Petruchio, and Grumio offered choice remarks while protecting the wine decanter.

Evelina especially tried to bait Cesco, much to the amusement of Petruchio. "Remind you of anyone, Kate?"

Eighteen months older, Vittoria was much smoother, and when the wrestling was finished she emerged to stroke Cesco's hair. He didn't seem to mind, but Evelina did – she pulled her sister's hair, prompting Kate to take her outside for a stern chat. Evelina came back holding her swatted bottom and with such an hilariously charming scowl upon her face that everyone had to laugh.

Cesco announced he had to depart. Hortensio groaned, Grumio thanked God, young Petruchio tried to start another wrestling match, but his father intervened. "We all have a big few days ahead of us. Tomorrow we are invited to court. Lad, when is the actual coronation?"

"Sunday, in the morning. Then we retire to the pitch to watch the jousts. The Emperor will face off against a ceremonial army, which will tremble and quake before him. Berthold the Cyclops will challenge all comers and win, until he faces Ludwig and suddenly loses all skill. Then I will paint my face and become the whore of the horse once more. They seem to love acrobatics. Maybe I'll let the black knight catch me just to put an end to these idiot shows."

Detto said, "Can I be the black knight?"

"Even if the Emperor said yes, I don't think Lord Nogarola would approve."

Morsicato seized on the reference to Detto's father. "Where are they staying?"

"Since their arrival, Verona's best and brightest have taken over the Basilica di Sant'Ambrogio, and right now Bailardino is overseeing their getaway route in case the Scaliger's little conspiracy requires a hasty retreat." Cesco saw their surprised looks. "Haven't you heard? Conspiring is all the rage. The Capitano di Verona is said to be filling the Emperor's depleted coffers in return for the title to one more city."

"Padua?" asked Morsicato.

"Pisa," guessed Petruchio.

"Milano," said Kate.

Cesco tapped a finger to the side of his nose. "The prize to the lady. Yes, rumour says they're coming to an understanding. The only people who have displeased Ludwig more than the Greyhound are the Visconti."

"Cangrande owning Milano," mused Petruchio. "That would be something. But is it true?"

Cesco smiled mischievously. "It's the rumour."

"One you've had nothing to do with," said Morsicato with a scowl. "Boredom?"

Cesco clutched his chest. "Dottore, are you accusing me of intrigue? Me? You cut me to the quick!"

"Don't tempt me. My scalpel is itching."

Petruchio said, "What's this about an escape route?"

"Well, because of this ugly and baseless rumour of Veronese ambition, there have been threats against the Scaliger's life. Nothing open, you understand. Just whispers. But enough to make the lord of Verona desire a link to his forces. Sant'Ambrogio is big, but not big enough to house over a thousand knights and their retinues. Our forces are camped nearby with numbers rivaling the holy host. But they are separated by all of Milano, whose citizens are loyal to the Visconti family. The Emperor has shown his concern for Cangrande's safety by graciously opening an old postern gate in case the Greyhound needs to flee with his tail between his legs."

"The point, boy," said Morsicato shortly. "I swear, you grow more tedious each year."

"As long as something about me is growing. But in brief, Cangrande's engineers are building a bridge over the city's moat. It was begun four days ago, so I imagine it's almost finished."

"We're Veronese," said Vittoria a little vapourishly. "Are we safe staying in the city?"

"Safe as houses," Cesco assured her. "Nothing's going to happen. Now really, I must go. No doubt this lovely inn has a feast prepared for San Massimo. Lord Bonaventura, could you possibly excuse your squire? I can guide him to his father's lodgings."

"By all means." Petruchio then had to quell his own children, who wanted to go along with Cesco and Detto.

The two lads departed, and as the rest of the menagerie descended for their holy day meal, Kate said, "It appears your fears were unjustified, doctor. Life with the Emperor hasn't changed him. He seems very much himself."

"Yes," said the doctor distractedly. "Now I'm just concerned what mischief those two will get into tonight."

Kate laughed. "It was your idea to bring them back together. Now endure the consequences!"

Seventeen

As the sun lowered and glowered in the west, the Basilica of Sant'Ambrogio was a beehive of activity. Poor petitioners lined the street leading to the door in hope of alms. Holding them back were a hundred or so of Cangrande's men, chosen for comeliness as well as bulk.

Inside the huge holy building, Cangrande and his knights were feasting. But it had become his habit each evening to emerge and toss out alms to the needy of Milano, another extravagant display of wealth that no one could challenge. It was said that the Scaliger was more generous than the Emperor – and had a far handsomer smile.

At the back of the throng stood Detto, his head low so he wouldn't be recognized by his father's colleagues. On the quick walk here, Cesco had made it clear that they were not in fact going to present themselves to their sires. But he was typically mysterious as to their true goal.

Arriving, Cesco had slipped away, telling Detto to wait. Now a tap on his shoulder made him turn, but no one was there. When he turned back he was looking at Cesco. "Funny. What's the plan?"

"Here, put this on." Cesco was now wearing a hooded peasant cowl, and he handed across one just like it. "We're hunters, and should reflect it in our dress."

"Hunters of what?"

"Not what, whom. I saw someone here the other day. An old friend of ours. I thought you might want to help me play hound to our hare."

"Who?"

"Death."

It took Detto a moment. "The archer that scared off your bird? How did you recognize him?"

"Same hood, same doublet, same hose. The tatterdemalion terror, no mistake."

"Really? He must be really poor, if that's his best outfit. Is he here for alms?"

"I don't think so. Our quarry was looking furtive and eager to reach the front. I spied the hare from across the piazza and tried to follow but got caught in the crowd. I think I was spotted, because Death vanished like a thief in the night."

"What were you doing here?"

Cesco made a balancing gesture with the back of his hand. "This and that. Little chores for the Emperor. Now come on and keep an eye out." Cowled, they plunged together through the masses of people.

"Where did you see him?"

"There, at the corner." Cesco pointed to a side-street that was slightly less crowded. "It's the way to the Scaliger's bridge. The Milanese can't use it."

"If it's Uncle Francesco's bridge, then Death must belong to someone in Verona."

"Astute. Let's wait here." They achieved an unobtrusive perch on some steps near the alley. Cesco's gaze seemed fixed on the door to the grand church where resided Verona's greatest lords. Detto's father was absent, but Nico da Lozzo was there, cheerful as ever. Bernardo Ervari was present to assist Castelbarco and his son in holding court in the Scaliger's stead, receiving petitions and offering the occasional largesse.

Bored, Detto tried to emulate his friend's nonchalance. But every now and then he couldn't help throwing a furtive glance over his shoulder.

The fourth time he did so his eyes widened. "Cesco," hissed Detto. "He's here!"

Cesco didn't turn. "Behind us?"

"Yes!" Detto started to point but Cesco stepped on his foot.

"Don't. The prey's nose will catch the scent of danger."

"What do we do? Grab him?"

Knowing Death was over his shoulder, Cesco pointed at the church door across the square as if he saw someone famous. "Fun as that sounds, we'd get pinched by the guards before we got any satisfaction. No, I thought we'd trail Death back to Hell – or Limbo, Tartarus, wherever Death calls home. Let's wait here for Goodman Death to pass us by, then slip back to the alley. The alley leads to the bridge, the bridge to the camp, the camp to our prey's nest."

Detto nodded. "You think he's here to kill Cangrande?"

"What else does Death want? After two tries, I would be surprised if it was something else. Three *is* a lucky number. I imagine if the Capitano di Verona were to show his head, he would receive the gift of everlasting peace. But Death is thwarted again, for tonight the Scaliger dines with the Emperor. So we may watch without fear, then trail our quarry home. Now act like eager peasants." Cesco waved and pointed again.

Detto followed suit, but couldn't help shooting one last glance back over his shoulder...

In the thick of the crowd a pair of green eyes were fixed on him. He met those eyes for a split second. Just long enough. "Oh no! Cesco, I —"

Cesco whirled around even as their prey spun about to walk briskly back towards the alley. "*Merda, merde*, shit, and *schiesse*. Come on!"

Leaping from their perch, they started dodging and weaving their way through the throng. Cesco was quicker, small and lithe, while Detto barked the adults with shoulders and elbows. Grown-ups cursed and swatted at them both, slowing them down.

Reaching the mouth of the alley, they broke through the crowd in time to see the roguish ragamuffin just turning the corner, legs pumping in a full out run.

Cesco sprinted in pursuit. "And we're off! Za!"

Detto dashed after him up the side street. Though Detto's legs were longer, by the time they reached the corner he found himself three full strides behind. "Come on, Detto! Don't spare! We're two hounds and a hare!"

A few Veronese in Cangrande's livery lounged along the cobbled route to the bridge. Guarding the Scaliger's path of retreat, they didn't much care about a footrace between children. A few even called out encouragement, while one threw a bale of hay across their path. Cesco vaulted it, Detto dodged it, bringing wry cheers at their backs.

They were catching up. Ahead, something fell from their prey's grip, clattering woodenly on the cobblestones. To Detto's eyes it looked like a flute. When Cesco reached it moments later he plucked it up and tucked it into his belt without breaking stride.

Their quarry reached the small postern gate the Emperor had opened for Cangrande. It was filled with more guards, lounging and guzzling drink with the bridge engineers. Death dove between a pair of legs and rolled into an upright run. Cesco whistled appreciatively even as he leap-frogged the same guard who had turned to discover what had passed him. Detto had to barrel the fellow over and evade the grasping hands of the others, just now realizing someone had got past them.

Through the stone gate they emerged onto the newly constructed bridge, the kind called 'flying,' a quickly-made wooden structure used to span a short gap or a moat. Fifty meters long, it was just three meters wide, supported by a double row of oak piles.

At the far end there were a dozen oxen roped to the end piles at all times, six for the right, six for the left. If attacked, Cangrande would retreat to his army, then start the oxen pulling, toppling the nearest oak piles and collapsing the bridge into the water. Owing to the depth and softness of the riverbed clays, the relatively narrow part of the river couldn't be forded by man or beast. Thus Cangrande would be safe with his army, ready for whatever came next.

The sprinting ragamuffin was already almost across. Cesco called out, "You can run but you can't hide!"

Bemused oxen drivers cursed at the running children, but the oxen themselves were unmoved. Detto imagined what would happen if their prey had started the oxen moving – he and Cesco would be running across a falling bridge, not a flying one. An exhilarating, terrifying thought.

A dirt path led up a hill to the hundreds of tents where Cangrande's army had disposed itself. Dashing up the road, their quarry turned right, disappearing among row upon row of milling men and boys.

Reaching the same spot, Cesco and Detto skidded to a halt, gazing around. "Gone," panted Detto.

"Fut," gasped Cesco. "Come on. You're the squire of the best hunter in Verona. Tell me you've learned something."

Detto looked at the earth and saw the imprint of a dozen boots and more hooves. Back-tracking up the dirt road they had come down, he found the toe imprint of badly soled boots. "Someone running doesn't leave heel marks, just toes," he explained, pointing. "This is him, here."

Rather than be impressed, Cesco made an exasperated noise. "Well, tracker – track!"

From sprinting they now began a slow crawl, Detto's nose almost to the ground as he attempted to trace the footprints in the trampled dirt. It was slow going, but Detto had indeed been trained by the best. Four times he was thrown off by false leads and twice they had to hide from knights who knew their faces. The second time they had to duck behind a hay bale as Massimiliano da Villafranca himself stalked down the path towards them.

While they were hiding behind the hay, Detto said, "What was that he dropped?"

Cesco produced the object, holding it up. "Look, but don't touch."

"Why not? It's just a flute," said Detto.

"Not one you'd want to hear played. Look again."

It wasn't a flute at all. There were no finger holes, nor a lip-shaped curve. It was equally open on both sides, like a tube, but with a small object wedged at one end. "A blow dart!"

"Just so. It seems Death was out hunting today, too."

"Someone in Uncle Francesco's camp wants him killed?"

"More than one, I would hazard," said Cesco laconically. "But only our friend is actively trying to achieve such a worthy goal."

"You're the heir. Won't he try to kill you too?"

Cesco shrugged. "Death had a chance in the woods and didn't take it. Don't look so worried. No boy with a blowpipe is going to get the better of me,

I promise." He poked his head around the hay. "Villafranca's gone. Let's press on."

It took another ten minutes to trace the marks to a large tent. "That's the one," said Detto.

Just like all the others in the row, it bore no telltale marks of a would-be murderer plotting within its hide walls. Cesco pulled Detto into the shade of another tent. "There's probably a guard just inside that flap just waiting for two idiot boys. Hm!" he added.

"What?"

Cesco pointed to the flag outside the tent. "Recognize it?"

Detto waited for the wind to pluck the cloth up, stretching out the design. It was a curious device, a beaver in what looked like a river of fire. "At the tourney last year…"

"Yes. Rienzi. Ha! I *thought* so."

"His son didn't like you very much."

"And I'm so personable."

"Should we confront him?"

"We'd be giving away the game. So to speak."

"But what if he's not in there? Maybe he used it as another false trail. You know, passed through and snuck out the back?"

"Good point. Let's go have a look."

They strolled back to the end of the row of tents, counting them off as they did, then circled around the rear to the next parallel 'street' of tents. Each tent stood back to back with another. Ducking under the criss-crossing guy ropes, they counted until they arrived at the back of flaming beaver's tent. Detto scanned the earth carefully for signs of anyone having exited. "No, he didn't leave."

"Excellent." Smiling, Cesco produced a short knife from his boot. Gathering a fistful of tent in his hand, he pushed and pressed until it slit the hide wall. He paused, listening, then worked it with care until he had rent a slit big enough for him to pass through. "Keep that flap open, and don't let anyone see you."

"I want to go in, too."

"I know, but let's take a page from the Capitano's book and leave an escape route open."

"Fine, idiot. Don't get killed."

"*Cianfa dove fia rimaso.*" Making a cheerful fist at the setting sun and giving God the fig, Cesco stepped through the rift into the cool dimness of the beaver's tent.

Seconds later Detto heard a shrill scream and a series of shouts. Cesco bolted out, face red with laughter and panic. "Run! For the love of God, run!" His legs were already pumping full tilt, leaping over the guy ropes and out into the dirt road.

Detto thudded behind him, tripping over those same ropes but somehow keeping enough footing to dodge a passerby's grasping hand. Voices all around were raised in alarum. "What happened?!"

Darting behind a moving cart, Cesco turned off the beaten path to run straight for the bridge. "There was this girl...!"

"A girl? Was it the sister?"

"It wasn't Aphrodite at her bath – though she was certainly surprised!" Cesco's laughter made him hard to understand. "Now shut up and run!"

Behind them the camp was in chaos. Someone must have cried rape or murder or ambush, because the whole of Cangrande's army was rousing itself. Any moment now an arrow might find their backs. Detto chugged harder, grinning in spite of himself. "Stupid way to die!"

"Then don't die!" They were racing down the hill towards the flying bridge. Ahead, soldiers moved to block their path. There weren't many yet, but the bridge was only three meters wide. "Cesco—!"

"I see them! Keep running!" Cesco himself was slowing down, fumbling something from out of his doublet – the blowpipe.

"What are you—?"

"Get onto the bridge!" Breaking stride, Cesco clapped the evil weapon to his lips. But he was laughing too hard, and had to force air into his lungs before he could blow.

Detto saw what Cesco was aiming for. "No! You're not—!"

The little dart was a blur, ripping soundlessly through the hazy summer air. The lead ox was far less soundless as the dart buried itself in its hindquarters. The creature startled its keepers with a sudden bellow of rage, then began straining forward. Chained to the first, the next ox followed its lead, and the next, and in seconds a half dozen oxen were pulling and straining against their harness while their hapless keepers tried to calm them. Fortunately the oxen on the other side of the path were still, calmly resting and unmoved.

Detto was running so hard he was sure his body would fly apart like a coach pulled by runaway horses. "You're insane!"

"Now you tell me – whoops! Look out, there!" His last laugh was at the soldiers who had taken up a position on the bridge. As the six oxen on the right side pulled, the closest pylon began to shift. The soldiers threw out their arms comically, dropping their pikes and spears as they fought for balance. Cesco and Detto raced past them onto the bridge.

Oh God oh God oh God! As his feet hit the wooden slats, Detto could already feel the bridge start to creak. He heard a sharp crack as a rope came undone, snapping and whipping at the struts beneath them. Legs pumping furiously, Detto pulled level with Cesco just as the planks in front of them parted. Wide-eyed, deaf to anything but the blood pounding in his ears, Detto leapt.

Cesco landed first, light as a ferret. Detto landed fully on both feet, but the force of his landing completed the parting of the loose planks, and suddenly Detto was disappearing among the clattering, tumbling bits of the dismantled bridge.

Cesco threw out a hand. Detto grabbed it, pulling his friend downward with him into nothingness.

Summoned from his supper with the Emperor, Cangrande stood the top of the ravine and looked down at the wreckage of his bridge. As only half the posts had been yanked free, the bridge was still half-standing, with slats and ropes twisted into fanciful shapes. "Children, you say?"

"Yes, lord." The captain of the guard was trying not to let his lord smell the drink on his breath.

Looking over Cangrande's shoulder, Bailardino said, "Maybe midgets."

The Scaliger's lips twisted wryly. "Midget saboteurs?"

Bailardino chuckled. "They never do anything by half."

Cangrande nodded. "They make short shrift of their enemies."

"They dwarf their competition."

"I think they were youths," said the captain, so stolidly that Cangrande had to smother another laugh. "Boys."

"Don't worry, I believe you," said Cangrande. "In fact, I even know which boys."

"Our boys, you think?" asked Bailardino.

"I have no doubt. Just as I have no proof."

"Well, whoever they were," said the captain, "they're goners."

Bailardino's levity vanished. "What? Why?"

"They didn't make it. They fell along with the bridge."

Bailardino leaned urgently forward to stare down into the chasm. "Francesco, we must—!"

"—go back to the palace and have a drink. That's what we must do."

"But they—"

"They'll show up later tonight with a lead-lined story as to where they've been all day. I'm serious, Bail. They're fine. Trust me." He turned to the captain. "I want this bridge reconstructed by morning. If it isn't, you'll have a choice of how I turn you into a midget – at the shoulders, or at the knees. If you succeed, I'll personally pour your next flagon of wine from my own store." The Scaliger turned on his heel and stalked away. Bailardino followed, still looking nervously over his shoulders for his son.

The captain wasted a moment wiping the sweat from his brow and rearranging his damp hose, then started bawling out orders. At once the engineers began the tedious task of rebuilding the bridge they had just finished the day before.

Twenty feet below, enveloped in the shadow of a still-upright stretch of bridge, Cesco and Detto listened and tried not to giggle. Right up against the moat wall, they were perched together on a tall pillar that somehow hadn't managed to fall. Yet.

"You're a monkey," whispered Detto.

"Says the monkey-boy. *You* grabbed the rope. I was planning on an early death."

"Sorry I interfered." Detto felt a ripple of pride, but immediately pushed it away. He knew Cesco – if he chased after praise for saving them, it would vanish like the morning dew.

Cesco pressed his back against the rough ravine wall. "Still miss me?"

Detto made a rude sound. "A girl."

"What?"

"A girl, you said."

"Ah, yes. The girl in the tent."

"Was she pretty?"

"Oh yes! I stopped to draw you a picture."

"Shh! They'll hear you."

"How would I know if she was pretty? I saw her for all of two seconds."

"Was it the sister?"

"I think so. Who else would it be?"

Detto shifted. The timber they were hiding under leaned against the rough earthen wall of the moat. The detritus of the wrecked bridge was littered below and around them, some boards wedged into the crumbling dirt. Detto eased himself into a more secure position. "How old?"

"Fourteen, fifteen maybe? I have little to compare to. I never had a sister."

"Death's sister. Does that make her Life?"

"Twins."

"Egg friends."

"Exactly."

Detto elbowed Cesco in the ribs. "So what did you see? Out with it!"

"The world still has some secrets, I'm afraid."

"That's not an answer. What did you see?"

"I saw the moon, and the stars in her eyes."

Detto tittered. "You saw her arse!"

"Shh!"

"What did it look like?"

"Like a dog's nose."

"What?"

"What do you think it looked like? It looked like an arse. In fact," said Cesco, considering, "it looked a lot like yours..."

Detto grabbed Cesco and the two wrestled until a stray board fell away from their perch. Watching it fall and splash into the water, Detto said, "We've got to get out of here."

"Agreed."

Detto stared at Cesco expectantly. "Well?"

"Well, what?"

"How are we getting out of here?"

"I thought you knew. You got us here."

"I didn't tear down the bridge!"

"Me either. The oxen–"

"Stop talking and tell me how." Cesco opened his mouth to point out the obvious contradiction, but Detto cut across him. "How!"

Cesco rubbed his nose. "Well, we have two options. Up or down."

"If we go down, we'll have to go up again."

"If we go up, we'll be seen and arrested."

"So that's no good."

"No." Cesco looked at the earthen wall behind them. "Hmm."

"What?"

Lifting one arm and pretending to hold a sword, Cesco touched Detto's shoulders, one at a time. "I dub thee knight." He waited, his expression impatient. "Well? I can't knight myself!" Pulling a face, Detto reciprocated Cesco's pantomime knighting. "Good. Now that we're knights, we can move like knights."

"I don't see any horses," said Detto drily.

"If we fall, you'll see horses."

It took Detto a moment, then he groaned. "Sea horses. What did your grandfather say about puns?"

"He loathed them. But he wasn't my grandfather."

"I'm waiting to hear how we're getting out of here."

"I told you – like knights. One forward, two to the side."

Detto squinted for a moment, puzzling. Then he smiled.

"Exactly," said Cesco. "Only on this chessboard, forward is up. Follow me."

Faces pressed against the crumbling dirt, they began edging to their left along the moat wall. They moved swiftly, not looking up at the flurry of activity above them. Miraculously, they reached a bend in the ravine wall without being seen. Sheltered from view, they began the more dangerous process of ascent. But they shared the invulnerability of youth. It was just a matter of finding handhold rocks that were so deeply embedded in the earth they wouldn't come away the moment pressure was applied. Lighter weight, Cesco led the way.

Near the top, Detto paused to flex his fingers. "Do we tell Uncle Francesco about the blowpipe?"

Cesco twisted to look down at him. "Only if we want a good tanning. If we tell him about tracing the would-be killer to his army, he'll have proof it was us who tore down his precious path to safety. Now I'm only guessing, but I think he's angry about that."

"He suspects you anyway," said Detto.

"Us, darling. He suspects us."

"Don't call me darling." Detto began the climb again, forcing Cesco, who was above him, to do the same.

"I just wanted to express my love before we plummet to our deaths." Cesco tested a stone and it tore free at once. It hit Detto on the head, and he swore. "Sorry. Here's one that's better. Anyway, you heard him. Suspicions are not proof. All we have to do is come up with the lead-lined alibi he thinks we already have."

Detto looked down at his filthy front. "What excuse can we give? If we go back to the inn, our appearance will tell all."

Cesco paused and shook his head, admonishing himself. "No. I have it."

"Yes?"

"Oh, I think we should confess our sins and beg divine intervention."

"Confess? You don't really mean that? Or are you saying we should go to church?"

"I'm very serious." Reaching the top, Cesco pulled himself over, then flipped around to reach down for Detto's hand. "We shall appeal to the highest power in the land. I think the Emperor will be just amused enough to help us lie to the great lord of Verona."

"Ha!" Clasping Cesco's hand, he climbed the last few feet and hauled himself up on the turf just outside the city wall.

They both lay in the early evening light, staring up at the sky. After some little time Detto said, "So what do we do about Death and his sister?"

Cesco hitched himself up to gaze over the moat at the tents, just visible in the distance. "I think – I think that I need a little time to decide what to do about our friends, the burning beavers. Surely we've scared Death away for the moment. Let it rest until I'm back in Verona."

"And when will that be?"

Cesco shrugged. "I serve at the whim of Fortune."

On the eve of the ceremony a stir was created by yet another papal decree. Pope John XXII had long troubled this emperor, and now, in the midst of his installation as the head of the temporal arm of God on Earth, Ludwig was suddenly removed from the Lord's sight altogether. Like Ser Alaghieri, like the Capitano di Verona, like so many others, Ludwig IV had been excommunicated.

Which didn't stop the festivities. The Crown of Italy was duly placed on Ludwig's head, the act being performed by two deposed prelates – the archbishop of Milano had chosen Avignon over Germany and flatly refused to perform the ceremony for the ex-communicated Emperor. With Cangrande in attendance among the rest of the Emperor's adherents, it was jokingly said that the number of excommunicants was greater than those still in the flock.

The crown was carried to the dais by Ludwig's eleven-year-old son (also Ludwig), the scepter by his eight-year-old son Stefan. His surviving daughters by his first marriage were present, as were the two little ones by his new wife, Margaret of Hainaut.

Many had vied for the honour of carrying the king's new sword, the Sword of Italy. But the champion was never in doubt. Young Franz der Hund, the Emperor's own page, walked among all the nobility of Germany, Austria, and Italy, bearing the fine blade in its jewel-encrusted scabbard and knelt to offer it to the newly crowned king.

Watching his bastard heir from an honoured place in the gallery, Cangrande made a show of smiling. Cesco had indeed owned an iron-clad alibi for the destruction of the bridge – he and Detto had been playing chess with the Emperor's pet poet. As was his wont when faced with ill-fortune, Cangrande laughed in public and laid plans in private.

The ceremony itself went off without a hitch, and the great feast that followed would be memorialized in several songs – not the least for a death that caused a great stir. But under cover of the reveling and mourning, much work was accomplished. When at last the days of celebrations were over, Cangrande returned to Verona well pleased.

Arriving at his palace, the Scaliger's mood was impervious even to the news that his sister was waiting for him in his study. Reading by the light of the sun that slanted in the tall palace windows, Katerina closed her book as he closed the door. "Welcome back. You come alone?"

"I am never alone. Even in private, I have you haunting my thoughts. Where's Giovanna?"

"Your lovely wife decided to travel to Rome for the month. She said she will wait for you to join her at the coronation."

"Ah. Well then, she'll be waiting some time." He began to unlace the calves of his tall boots. "The coronation in Rome is delayed. I regret to say there has been an attempt on the Emperor's life."

"Surely not! I hope he is well?"

"The poison never reached his lips. Like any wise man of power in a foreign land, he employs his lords as his tasters – myself among them. I am fortunate that the poisoned goblet did not come to me, or I would be as dead as his poor page."

The effect was wonderful. Katerina's languidly composed air vanished as she said, "Not Cesco!"

"Did I say page? I meant retainer. No, our boy is perfectly well. As are all of the imperial heirs, I'm happy to report. Alas, it was one of his host's family, Stefano Visconti. Oddly, it seems that the bolt hit close to home. Stefano's brother is being blamed. Galeazzo is something of a wild stallion, though his son may amount to something. But in my generation, there's only one Visconti worth a damn – Luchino. Perhaps I like him because he reminds me of myself. Eminently capable. Or because he dotes upon the only issue of his two marriages, a girl named Sylvia. Or perhaps because he, too, is an excommunicant. So many of us godless men running about these days. Hell will be overflowing. Certainly with Visconti. Stefano is an excellent start."

Katerina's calm was restored. "I'm pleased to hear you were not suspected."

"O, I'm sure I was. But my near-demise weighed in my favour – the wine almost came to me." Cangrande saw her gaze and laughed. "Truly, sister, I am entirely innocent! Poison is not my weapon of choice."

"Yet Cesco does not return with you."

"Sadly, no. The apple of the Emperor's eye won't be pried from the imperial presence until at least after the coronation in Rome. Whenever that may be. A continual hostage, encouraging me to be my best self."

"You seem well pleased."

"Why should I not? You behold the undisputed Imperial Vicar of Verona, Vicenza, Feltre, Belluno, Monselice, Bassano, and Conegliano."

"Not Padua? Not Treviso? Poor dear."

Cangrande chuckled. "All in good time. As the Emperor will be in Italy some months yet, there is time to move him to my cause. Meanwhile my old friend Passerino Bonaccolsi is confirmed in all his Mantuan possessions, and the Estensi family are Vicars of Ferrara."

"What of his hosts, the Visconti?"

"Ludwig is suspicious, but they are quick to condemn the black sheep of their flock. If they bring

Galeazzo to heel they should fare well. More's the pity." Boots removed, Cangrande wiggled his toes and wrinkled his nose. "I have a bath warming. To what do I owe the honour of this visit? Do you miss having someone under your thumb? Surely your second son is still at home. Or does he not provide enough stimulation? After your stroke, I would have thought you lacked the energy to ride herd over more than one at a time."

"Quite finished?" asked Katerina politely. "As you note, I grow weary more easily, and nothing tires me more than your whining. As for Valentino, he is well, working hard at home and hating every minute of it. Now that I am recovered, he seems eager to get out of the house and off to martial pursuits like his brother – though I doubt he'll ever be the natural soldier Bailardetto is. Still, his enthusiasm makes me proud. My boys are such good fellows, nice to the core."

"And loyal! You should see Detto spending his every spare hour with our boy."

" 'Our boy' is the reason I am here. I came in the hope that Cesco had returned with you. This month he turns thirteen. In two more years he will be a man. I thought it time to discuss his future."

"A heartbreak, then, that you must wait so long."

"Indeed. Almost as heartbreaking as it must be for you, seeing someone else play with your toy."

"How empathetic! Truthfully, Kat, I take a rather lopsided pride in our boy's escape. First the business with the tourney, then thwarting me before the whole world. If he reaches his majority, he'll be formidable."

"He takes after his father." There was a pause, then Katerina said, "Aren't you afraid that if you don't break him soon, he will be wild forever?"

"His need to escape says the breaking is close. All it will take is a single event. A crisis of sorts, where his high-flying spirit is blighted. Then he will cleave to me as his bird does to him."

"You speak as if from experience. What crisis broke you? Ponte Corbo? Or something far earlier?"

Ponte Corbo had been Cangrande's lone great defeat, where he had run from a battlefield like a whipped cur. Yet now his smile did not look at all forced. "You assume I am broken."

"I'm delighted to hear you are not. Perhaps now you will stop accusing me of being the one who broke you. Though in that case I wonder how you learned so well what it takes to tame your red hawk."

"You mistake the lesson. I learned how to avoid taming."

448

"Ah, that explains it. Certainly Cesco has profited from his tutelage at your hands, learning enough to elude his master."

Cangrande crossed to the door. "For the moment."

ACT III

Doom'd to Walk the Night

Eighteen

Carpentras, France
6 April 1327
Good Friday

...gi circa premissum secundum mem-
brum principale loqui ut non prenuntiet
hoc, scilicet de tali veltro...

Pausing to uncramp his ink-stained fingers, Pietro wondered, How did father do this?

Frustrations threatened to engulf him from all sides. This was the latest. Trapped in the pitch darkness of that dank Venetian cell two years before, Pietro had thought he had so much to say about his father's great work. But for months he'd tried to reconstruct the brilliant insights he'd had while holding madness at bay along with the rats. To no avail. All he was able to do was regurgitate uninteresting pabulum that was obvious to anyone with half a brain.

But until Petrarch met Bernardo Gui or arranged for a papal hearing, there was nothing else to do. Sighing, he picked up his quill, dipped it in ink, and continued to write Latin words in his neat script. At least my penmanship is better than my father's, if not my words.

Pietro had hoped in writing he would find solace. His unease didn't come from the lack of reply to his letter to Verona – it was far too soon to expect one. No, his discomfiture was far more personal. This was the third year he could not participate in the Easter celebrations. Christmas was difficult, to be sure. But for a devout Christian, Easter was the true holy day. Today's anniversary of Christ's death was a time to be with others, sharing in the communal mourning before the joy of Sunday's services honouring the Resurrection, proof of Christ's divinity and God's love for all mankind. It wounded Pietro's heart not to have set out with the rest of the household before dawn for services.

All I can do now is hope that next year I'll be back in God's view. For what is Easter, if not hope?

Almost angrily, he returned to his writing:

> ...ex se sed ut prenuntiata ab alio hic illa sequatur, ut puta prenuntiata a beato Methodio Episcopo qui, ut...

A hammering on the door made his quill stutter. Cursing, he reached for his sword, kept close to hand since he learned of Pathino's reappearance. Who was in the house on this day? Had they sent men to arrest him? Today, of all days?

With a ginger move, he rose and slipped the latch on the back of the wooden door. "Come!"

Petrarch came barreling through, breathless and crimson-cheeked. "Oh Pietro! Pietro!"

"What's the matter? Has something gone wrong?"

"Wrong? Wrong? What could be wrong? Oh Pietro – I am in love!"

Releasing his sword's hilt, Pietro eyes narrowed, his crooked smile rising into place. "In love?"

"I know! Me? It's absurd, ridiculous. O, but Pietro, I burn, I pine, I perish! She is a wonder! A beauty! A vision!" Petrarch fell to his knees, hands outstretched. "Forgive me, for your father's sake. I've often mocked your father's love for Beatrice. How, I asked, could a man fall deeply in love at first sight of a woman. Love is of the spirit, and how can eyes see a spirit trapped in mere mortal flesh. But now the scales have fallen from my eyes, and I see the world anew!"

Pietro sat, wry smile now firmly in place. "Where did this miracle occur?"

"In church. The church of Sainte-Claire. How fitting that here in the belly of Babylon an angel descends to give purpose to my life."

"Did you speak to her?"

"Speak? What could I say? What words could fall from my lips that would do justice to such a monumental moment? I wish I were a mason, to build a tower, a castle, a pyramid to her, that I might show her the sky-reaching height of the passion she's awakened in me. But I am a poet, so I must build her a monument of words! I've found my Muse! O, Laura! Laura!"

Pietro's smile twisted down as he laughed. "Laura? Really, Petrarch? Laura?"

That dripping skepticism checked Petrarch. "What? What's wrong with—?"

"Laura. As in, the Laurel." For a hundred years and more, the best poets were awarded a laurel wreath in the style of Caesar to acknowledge their greatness. Pietro's father had worn several, and his portraits carried them. "Really?"

Relieved, Petrarch laughed. "No no, I swear, Pietro, she's as real as you or I. More real! Come! Come come come, let me show you!"

Pietro pulled away from Petrarch's grasping hand. "I cannot enter a church."

"Ah. Quite." His friend was momentarily flustered. Then Petrarch lit up. "The demonstration! This afternoon there's to be some kind of show of magic or alchemy or something in the central square. The whole city is talking of it. She might be there! Come, dress, and we'll go see what all the fuss is about."

Pietro was reluctant, but it was impossible to deny a passionate Petrarch. Would he could show such enthusiasm for my cause, mused Pietro crossly. Still, he dressed and dined with the family, then rode out into the biting Mistral wind just as the bells were tolling the demise of the Lord.

They passed Lucia as they exited the house, but she gave them hardly a glance. This last month had been a relief. The night in Pietro's room had been a watershed, for she no longer made eyes at Pietro, or even seemed to notice his existence. She was coldly polite to him at meals, and was often absent, out with her friends or praying at church. Pietro hoped that some good had come of that embarrassing scene, that the girl had found God again, and would henceforth devote her passions towards a more proper avenue.

The ride to Avignon was familiar by now, and soon they were again walking in the bad air. Their horses hitched, they followed the crowd, Petrarch drawing many amused glances. He was dressed even more outrageously than usual, with a silken doublet so slashed and festooned with ribbons that one could hardly see the rich fabric itself, though it did entirely reveal his embroidered cream-coloured shirt beneath. His hose was maroon velvet, also ribboned up the seams, and it clashed with his scarlet cape. His broad hat was so floppy that it kept obscuring his vision, and his curled shoes made walking a real effort.

Whereas Pietro was wearing his habitual boots, half-trousers, tunic, doublet, and riding cape, with a featherless cap on his head. His doublet had been in the best style when he'd bought it two years before. But in Avignon he looked like a country bumpkin. Here, where men rode snow-white horses decked in gold (sometimes shod in gold as well), excess was everything. The original citizenry had been augmented by the Holy See, and not only with ecclesiastics, but with merchants, artisans, mercenaries, astrologers and fortune-tellers, thieves, prostitutes, and no fewer than forty-three branches of Italian banking houses. It was said that Avignon dined on gold, and on souls. Pietro could easily believe both.

The demonstration they were attending must have had the blessing of the Church, for it was being held in the square outside the Penitentiary, in the Place des Corps Sant on the Rue Sant-Michel. The Penitentiary was a looming structure, newly built like so many in Avignon – since the Church now seemed permanently mislocated here in France, there was a constant drum to build new basilicas and palaces to recreate the feel of the Vatican.

But unlike other buildings being raised to the glory of God, the grim-visaged Penitentiary sought to live up to its name and make those seeing it repent. Surely no one wanted to be within those forbidding walls, not ever.

Yet it was within those walls that Pietro's future would be decided. This was the abode of the Grand Penitentiary, whose office it was to judge excommunicants, issue indulgences, and deal with any sacramental impediments that might arise for the Holy See. The office had been vacant these last four years, since the death of Cardinal-Bishop Fredoli in 1323. It was this vacancy that had vexed Pietro and Petrarch so thoroughly. Had there been a Grand Penitentiary in place, he would have been forced to hear both Pietro's and Cangrande's suit. But the new building stood empty, with only minor priests dealing out indulgences according to their secret price-book of sins.

The open plaza before the ugly grey-stone building was cramped, full of people yet with a lane cleared as if for an archery tournament. In fact, Pietro saw a large metal target placed upon a bale of hay about the height of a man. "What is this? I thought someone was turning lead to gold."

"No one knows," replied Petrarch, distractedly scanning the crowd for his newfound love.

It was up to Gherardo to explain further. "Some are saying it's alchemy, but the Church would never allow a demonstration of that. This is supposed to be something altogether different. They showed it to the Pope, and he was evidently delighted. Says it will change the world, and drive out the heathen from Jerusalem once and for all."

There was such noise in the plaza that Pietro had trouble hearing his companions, let alone the man declaiming in the open center of the crowd. Snippets reached him. "…Far East…Marco Polo…from the heathen, a weapon of frightful force…"

Interested in spite of himself, Pietro watched as men in the garb of tinkers fiddled with an oddly-shaped covered metal pot. It looked like a head with an elongated mouth. There was a small hole at the top with a string hanging out, so that the head had a single strand of hair. Priests were praying over it as the leather-smocked tinkers poured cup after cup of shiny grey dust down the mouth. The dust was evidently quite precious, as they were careful not to let any spill or blow away in the Mistral's fierce pull. Pietro noted that several of the tinkers were missing fingers.

One priest fitted a stone arrowhead into the mouth of the pot, making the sign of the cross as he did. Then the bulbous metal pot was strapped down onto a heavy stand and aimed at the target. The crowd grew less noisesome as curiosity overwhelmed them. They watched as the priests and tinkers retreated – all save one, who held a closed lantern. A hush fell over the expectant crowd as he opened one of the lantern's doors and held up the string to the flame within.

The string must have been oiled, for the fire raced along it. The tinker ran back as if his life depended upon it. Gherardo laughed. "What, will it leap up and eat—?"

There was an inhuman roar, the sound Lucifer must have made when he'd struck the ice after being cast from Heaven. There were screams and shrieks of terror as half the crowd turned to run, while the other half fell to their knees to pray.

Spine shuddering, Pietro stumbled backwards, the hair on his arms standing upright. His ears were ringing, and a terrible smell assaulted his nose, fire and sulphur and an acrid scent of burnt air, as if lightning had struck – not from the sky, but from inside the pot.

In the center of the square, the pot had vanished in smoke. When the cloud at last cleared, the coughing tinkers went searching for the arrowhead. The metal shield at the center of the target was pierced clear through, near the top – even weighted, the fearsome weapon had rocked back the blocks holding it. The stone arrowhead itself was lodged deep in the wall of the Penitentiary.

"Dear Lord." The ringing in his ears made Pietro's voice echo in his head as if he were under water. Everyone was muttering, either prayers or curses. Petrarch was casting desperately about, looking for his Laura, praying for her safety.

Then the priests, having been forewarned, showed the audience how to react. They began to applaud. Slowly the remaining crowd followed suit. Even Pietro, flesh crawling, had to clap his hands.

Suddenly his eyes were arrested by the sight of Tharwat. The Moor was standing far to the back of the crowd, hidden until they had all knelt. Meeting Pietro's eyes, he jerked his chin at a balcony of the Penitentiary. Tracing the Moor's gaze, Pietro noticed a man in Bishop's robes. He was medium sized, perhaps fifty years old, with a trim little beard that was as much white as black.

Nudging Petrarch, Pietro pointed up to the balcony. "Who is that?"

His friend squinted up. "That – ah, that's the Bishop of Albano. Gauscelin de Jean. I meant to tell you – rumour says his cousin the Pope has appointed him Grand Penitentiary."

For several moments Pietro just stared. "What?"

"John just made him the new—"

"There's a new Grand Penitentiary? Good God, why didn't you—"

"It just happened! I heard about it this morning – right before I saw my Muse. And before this infernal…Good God, what was that?"

"Look," said Gherardo, pointing, "they're doing it again!"

"Francesco—!" Pietro was furious over his friend's omission, as ready to explode as that horrible pot of fire. But he was interrupted as the second demonstration got underway. Again the pot was filled with the glittering black dust, though Pietro noted they washed it out first, dousing the inside and out with water. A second arrowhead was slipped into place, a new string was lit, and again the square erupted in fire and noise.

Better prepared this time, Pietro watched in fascination as the arrowhead hurtled along, propelled as if shot from God's bow. The metal shield was pierced again, and again the projectile was wedged into the wall. Priests were emerging now to complain to their brothers in the demonstrating party of the damage being done to the Penitentiary.

While they wrangled, the tinkers began again to wash out the pot and prepare it for a third trial. Pietro noted they were quicker about scrubbing out the inside, and wondered what that meant. Clearly the black powder, dug up from some gateway to Hell, caused this horrible fire. They said this dust came from the East. Fitting, he thought, watching as they scooped another cup from a barrel and poured it into the pot's mouth. If there is a Hell on Earth, it must be—

This time the roar came without warning, without prayers, without the arrowhead fitted into place. A gout of flame ripped out of the metal pot to consume one tinker and two of the arguing priests. All three were still alive, though if God were merciful they wouldn't be for long. Each was screaming through charred lips as they clawed the air with blackened hands.

Now the entire crowd fled in earnest, vomiting and weeping as they poured out into the streets towards the nearest churches to pray.

Without a church to go to, Pietro found himself racing not away but towards the scene of destruction. His first thought was of the suffering trio, plus the dozen others who had suffered minor burns. He had lived with Morsicato long enough to know basic medicinal aid…

His eyes fell on the barrel containing the powder. The lid was still open, surrounded by charred bits floating in the air. He didn't know what the dust was, or where it had actually come from. But the evidence of his eyes told him the combination of dust and fire was disastrous. "Cover that! Cover that barrel!"

No one heard him. In the cacophony of agonized screams, prayers, oaths, and moans, his was just another voice. He ran harder, praying he would be there in time, yet certain he wouldn't. He pictured himself consumed in flame, his flesh flayed from his bones in hellfire – which some would call a fitting end. If I die now, I'm doomed to Hell. No Purgatory, no Heaven. I am out of God's sight.

Yet Pietro forced his pace on, shoving bodies from his path. Already his old wound was slowing him. Cesco had once described watching him run as seeing a chariot with a wheel on one side and a bouncing stick on the other. Once more cursing Marsilio da Carrara and his crossbow, Pietro gritted his teeth. Tears were in his eyes, though from exertion or the acrid sting in the air he didn't know.

He was just yards away when he noticed one flaming ember, larger than the rest, floating on the air just above the barrel. He stretched out his hand, as if he could close the distance by sheer force of will.

There's no way! O God, please hear me, save these people, save me, God save us...!

A figure hurtled from the side of the crowd and threw his chest across the barrel's mouth, covering the powder with his own body. There were more screams of terror as men saw a Moor in close proximity to the devilish powder. Doubtless they expected another burst of flame. Swords were drawn, but the wary men kept their distance.

Pietro reached the barrel, the smell of charred flesh assaulting his nose. "Tharwat!"

The Moor's head turned. "Run!"

Pietro reached out for the barrel. "Let me help!"

Tharwat clutched the barrel closer to him. "Run, you fool!"

Pietro understood the Moor's order – being seen together could damn one or both. But he refused to leave his friend in such danger. If the men with drawn swords decided Tharwat had caused the accident, he would surely die here and now. But if a Christian helped to remove the dangerous object, they might retain their senses. Throwing his riding cape over Tharwat for an added level of protection, Pietro bent down and took hold of the bottom of the barrel. "Let's shift it."

Lips tight, Tharwat rose, the mouth of the small barrel pressed against his chest. Pietro kept the bottom level with the Moor's rise so that none of this deadly powder escaped. "Where?"

"A corner of the yard. They mustn't think we're stealing it."

Together the pair of them crab-walked to the side of the yard, depositing the barrel safely away from any stray ember in the air.

"Is this Greek fire?" asked Pietro.

Tharwat shook his head. "Men describe that as liquid. This is something else."

Soldiers and citizens were now flooding the courtyard to help, and all eyes were on the duo by the barrel. Pietro called over to the men standing by the exploded weapon and the corpses. "You there! Bring the lid for this barrel!"

"Why?" demanded a priest. "What are you doing?"

"We're trying to keep this damned stuff from catching fire and killing us all! Didn't you see? If the fire kisses the powder, we'll all be consumed! Or do you want this brave fellow here to keep pressing his chest against the barrel and hope for the best?"

After several tense seconds of mutters and wary conversations, one brave man approached, the barrel lid in one hand, his sword in the other, as if the blade could ward off this terrible substance. Tharwat stepped quickly back and Pietro fitted the lid into place. Not knowing what else to do, he sat on it.

The helper retreated, and the crowd watched in suspicion as Pietro and Tharwat remained beside the barrel of hellfire. Pietro half wanted to draw his sword, and he wished the Moor was wearing his falchion. It seemed as though they were about to be brought up on charges and hanged. If they weren't rushed and torn to pieces by the mob first.

Then someone began applauding. A second pair of hands started up at once, but it was several seconds more before the rest of the crowd decided that Pietro and Tharwat were not fiends but heroes.

Pietro sagged in relief, and out of the corner of his eye he saw Tharwat release his tension, his hand moving away from the knife on his belt. The Moor made a deep bow to Pietro, as if to a stranger, then sidled away, leaving Pietro alone to receive all the accolades.

Once the heathen was removed from the picture, the applause grew. Reason began to quell fear, and they all slowly understood that Pietro had saved the lives of everyone in the square.

Authorities arrived, and the barrel was carefully taken away. Freed from his perch, Pietro found himself surrounded by well-wishers. First among them was Petrarch, eagerly introducing Pietro to every prominent layman and cleric in the crowd. The smell of burnt flesh still hung on their air as Pietro shook hands and exchanged bows with men who until this moment would have shunned him as a heretic. He received invitations to dine, to attend poetry readings, to speak of his father's great works and his own experiences in Verona and Ravenna.

As they returned to their horses, Petrarch was praising the Lord. "Thank God Laura was not there. I don't think I could have borne it had she seen that, much less been hurt."

Uninterested in this phantom love, Pietro said, "You began the applause."

Petrarch grinned. "Crowds are like sheep, they need to be herded. They were waiting for someone to tell them how to react, how to behave. I merely showed them the way."

"It had the added justice of being true," added Gherardo. "You are a hero. What you did – I was running the other way."

"As was I." Petrarch clapped Pietro on the shoulder. "Today changes everything."

Recalling that grainy black powder, Pietro couldn't help thinking that Petrarch was more right than he knew.

Nineteen

In the weeks that followed the incident with the pot-au-feu, as the locals were calling it (a sick joke, as the words 'pot of fire' in French also referred to a beef stew, and quite a bit of meat had been turned to bloody stew that Good Friday), Pietro Alaghieri, Knight of the Mastiff, became the most sought-after guest in Avignon. He dined with princes and prelates, counts and courtiers. He ate off silver and gold plate, partaking of the finest dishes France had to offer, with sauces and spices devised for the most discriminating palates.

The conversation of Dante's son, it was soon discovered, was learned and reasoned. Destined for the cloister before his brother's death had elevated him to the role of heir, he spoke of Hell, both poetic and theological, with insight, scripture never far from his fingers. While he spoke highly of his father, he downplayed his own achievements. His humility was tested as he was lauded for his bravery, but his natural reticence kept him from ever singing his own praises – a rare thing.

In Avignon, what was rare was valuable. Pietro di Dante became even more sought after. So long as no one was crass enough to mention his religious ill-favour, it was winked at.

This sudden social prominence had the unwelcome effect of renewing Lucia's interest in Pietro. She was no longer physically affectionate, thank Heaven, but she now insisted on bringing Pietro along to meet her coterie of friends. Pietro was shocked to see how many of these were males, and of the men how many were priests. But then at least half the males in Avignon were under some sort of holy orders – it was joked that the butchers had taken vows, if only to keep their livestock pure. Petrarch himself had told that jape, and Pietro had forced himself to laugh. His host's strong impious streak reminded Pietro of a different Francesco.

Cesco. Pietro was beginning to have trouble recalling his boy's face. A face that had surely changed in eighteen months. He wondered if the Emperor had let the boy grow his hair long again, as he preferred. He wondered if the boy was still monkeying over buildings, or if he had grown out of such antics. He wondered if the boy – young man! – was still risking life on a daily basis. He'd heard of the adventures in Trent, of course. After that, each new post from Italy had Pietro holding his breath for news of some terrible accident. Then a letter would arrive in the boy's own hand, carelessly relating irrelevant news and asking obscure poetic questions that Pietro could barely make out, much less answer. The last letter had seemed like gibberish, until Pietro realized that the boy had encoded it from German, not Italian. Little bastard...

The word bastard led him once more to Pathino and the medallion. Still no answer. And no sign of Tharwat since the business with the pot-au-feu. A clear precaution on the Moor's part – they'd been seen working together in the most public way, and therefore could not be seen together again. Pietro had in fact been asked about the Moor on several occasions, and could only reply that the helpful dark-skinned heathen had not been there with him. Which was strictly true. Pietro was working very hard not to lie, not to anyone – it was hardly fitting to be trying to return to God's sight by telling falsehoods. Even in a society filled with them.

Then came the important day. Finally – finally! – Petrarch had convinced his patrons, the powerful Colonna family, to host a reading of Dante's epic poem. "You have a powerful advocate – I mean, beside myself! Young Giacomo has been hounding his uncle on your behalf lo these many months. He remembers you fondly from Bologna and your newfound glory has given him the opportunity he lacked! Now all that remains is to choose what passage you will read."

"You have one in mind," observed Pietro.

"Indeed. The tale of Francesca da Rimini."

Pietro groaned. Doubtless Petrarch hoped his Laura would be present and swoon for the tale of thwarted love. "I thought you hadn't read L'Inferno."

"I haven't. But one would have to be living in Plato's cave not to have heard that particular passage. It's perfect!"

Perfect for Petrarch, perhaps. But Pietro regretfully declined the request. He had uncomfortable associations with that canto – Mariotto and Gianozza had used it to justify their breaking of faith with Antony. What no one ever seemed to realize was that God had put the cheating Francesca in Hell. Her deed was not romantic, but damnable.

Pietro settled instead upon one of his favourite passages, a diatribe his father had penned the night of Pietro's duel in the Arena, all about the internal strife tearing Italy apart. Another reminder of the split between Antony and Mari, it was also the one moment in all his life that Pietro had inspired his father's words, creating his own little corner of the canticle. Religiously unobjectionable, it was sure to

471

please the French guests and make the Italians nod ruefully.

As his taste for fancy hats had died long ago, Pietro declined to borrow clothes from Petrarch. Instead he dressed in a lawyer's gonella, as was his right, being Verona's legal representative in Avignon. The gown was not as comfortable or fashionable as a farsetto, and Pietro recalled his own disdain for his father's fuddy-duddy taste in clothes as he donned it. I must be getting old. He was thirty this year.

Together with Petrarch and Gherardo, mincing in their fantastical and torturously ill-fitting boots, Pietro made his way through Avignon towards the Palais des Papes. Their destination was situated just across from that impressive, ever-growing edifice. A three-story fortress of brick crowned with a tower rising a further four stories, the palace of Cardinal Giovanni 'Sciarrillo' Colonna was the center of intellectual life in Avignon.

It was also well fortified. The Colonna family knew something about reversals. The previous generation had been men of high standing with Pope Clement, but after his imprisonment by Pope Boniface, they had been not only defrocked but excommunicated, their property seized and their castles attacked. They had responded by making war on Boniface, attempting to abduct him and take him to France. His death

472

had ended the feud, and the Colonna were once again on the rise within the Church. But the outfitting of their new palace bespoke a commendable caution. One never knew what the future might bring.

It was a mark of Pietro's past life that as he studied the façade he scanned for handholds, wondering if Cesco could climb to the oddly angled roof at the top. Probably. Smiling to himself, he entered and climbed the stairs to the salon.

Seeing the stunningly august assembly facing him, Pietro was instantly transported back in time thirteen years to his first encounter with Cangrande's court. Just as then, here were knots of men seated or standing, arguing politics, religion, literature. His father was not present, nor Cangrande, nor Mari and Antony. But the feel was the same. The only major difference was that nearly everyone wore the robes of an ecclesiastic.

Just as Mariotto had been his guide long ago, today he had Petrarch tugging him by the elbow. "Over here. Pietro, may I present our hosts, Stefano and Sciarrillo Colonna. My lords Colonna, Ser Pietro Alaghieri."

"The hero of the hour!" Sciarrillo was the more notorious of the two, famous for his temper and his daring. A quarter of a century ago he'd slapped a pope right in the face. He was of medium height, with angry eyes, hollow cheeks, and a marvelous moustache that was so full that it seemed a thing unto itself, swooping across his lip like an artist's fancy. "Well met, ser, well met. I admire your patron. We Ghibellines must stand together." An odd statement coming from a cardinal, considering that the original Guelph-Ghibelline strife arose from the struggle between pope and emperor. But over the years it came down more to the politics of Italian cities. Besides, Sciarrillo was a man who knew well the occasional need to oppose the Holy See.

Sciarrillo's elder brother bowed his head. "An honour." Count of Romagna, several times the Senator of Rome and Imperial Vicar of Italy, Stefano Colonna was sixty-two years old, the same age Pietro's father would have been. Recently arrived from Rome, he was reputed to be a throwback to the ancient days of that city, a true patrician gentleman. Indeed, he and his brother claimed to be able to trace their lineage all the way back to the Julio-Claudian emperors of ancient Rome.

Clearly he was a gracious host who put a high price on civility, and also upon honesty, as his next words proved. "We regret not welcoming you before now. Rest assured, your many petitions have not gone unnoticed, nor your patience. My brother and

I have the utmost sympathy for your situation. Our father felt his excommunication keenly, and we have not forgotten."

Startled by this frank statement, Pietro found himself bowing even more deeply, his right leg extended, his left bent, hands wide. "Alas my lord, my father was the one with the skill for words. Your kindness in accepting me at all is a gift, an honour, and a privilege. I treasure your invitation, and am moved by it."

Stefano nodded, pleased. "Though I am a mere guest here, just as you are, I am certain my brother would henceforth welcome you at any time. I do beg your forgiveness if any soul here is less understanding of your presence. We have many guests, and not all of them are as civilized as one might wish."

Duly warned, Pietro allowed himself to make the rounds of introductions. The first was a familiar face – young Giacomo Colonna, son of Stefano, whom Pietro had met in passing in Bologna. As grave as his father, but somewhat less intelligent, he was a good friend to Petrarch and was able to pass several words with Pietro about their common acquaintances at University. There was another son, Stefano's heir, but he was still in Italy.

"What brings your father to Avignon?" asked Pietro.

It was a casual question, but Giacomo became instantly guarded. "Family matters. Nothing important."

"Ah." There was something in that, but it was none of Pietro's affair.

The next guest Petrarch introduced was the gregarious Cardinal Napoleone Orsini. His family were longtime foes of the Colonna, but evidently Stefano's nobility had been able to reconcile this sixty-four year old cardinal to French society. As bear-like as his second name, with a grizzled mane of his first, Pietro knew of Orsini from letters written a decade earlier when Mariotto had been exiled to Avignon and taken service with this holy man. Once a serious contender for the Papacy, Orsini had been a cardinal for thirty-nine years and voted in conclaves for five different pontiffs. He himself had placed the tiara upon this latest pope who'd proved such a lawyer in his oaths.

The intervening years had not been particularly kind to Cardinal Orsini. Blighted by the Holy Father's refusal to restore the papacy to Rome, he'd spent the last few with his head basically in the sand, penning a few biographies of saints.

Yet he was cheerful as Pietro mentioned Mariotto's name, recalling as everyone did the lovesick young man denied his wedding night with his stolen bride. "He was the perfect lover, always in a state of agony. Thank Heaven he did not choose the holy order. Such passion, transferred to Almighty God above, would have outshone us poor old men as the sun does a candle!"

Another man who caught Pietro's attention was Cardinal Luca Fieschi. Not only was he an Italian, he was related to both Pope Adrian V and the infamous Pope Innocent IV, who a hundred years before had declared the whole world under papal dominion and hounded Emperor Frederick II to his grave. In many ways Innocent was to blame for all the modern strife – and for Pietro's troubles, having reaffirmed the concept of excommunication.

But Pietro found Cardinal Fieschi a charming man – perhaps too charming, and certainly full of his own pedigree. Not content with just his famous papal ancestors, he also let slip that he was related to the kings of England through Edward I's mother. He seemed quite determined to awe Pietro with his importance and august lineage. Pietro made a show of being impressed, then quickly moved on.

He was slowly introduced around the whole room, and spent an hour in pleasant conversation with many different men. Despite Lord Stefano's warning, no one was the least bit rude. Praise was heaped upon him for his Christian bravery, for his piety, his dignity, his father, and his devotion to duty. As Sciarrillo put it, "Imagine accepting public disfavour in order to raise your master's heir in secret! You must be a poet's son! It's so – Romantic!"

More men were arriving, and Pietro quickly lost track of the names in a sea of introductions. There were women, too, wives and daughters of the laymen, as well as sisters, cousins, and nieces (or natural daughters called nieces) of the ecclesiastics. But as Stefano was a stickler for propriety, the men and women did not mingle, with the Eves removed to a different salon from the Adams.

Petrarch crept close, interrupting Pietro's conversation with a pair of prelates with a fidgety whisper. "She's here."

"Who?"

"Laura! I must go to her." He slipped away, leaving a flummoxed Pietro to wade through the sea of crimson with only Gherardo as his guide.

Pietro pulled a face. "Is she really here? Or is this an excuse to pose before the women?"

Gherardo could only shrug. He hadn't seen her either, and his brother was absolutely refusing to share her full name.

It was close to the hour appointed for Pietro to read when he felt a chill enter the room. It was indeed as if a physical frost had crept in, for that's how cool the whole assemblage became, as if an icy wind had blown into the chamber to take the bloom from the entertainment.

A new arrival was bowing to the hosts in a perfect display of guestly homage. Dressed in cardinal's robes, he was at least seventy years old, thin but unbowed by age. He spoke to Stefano, and the noble Colonna seemed non-plussed by the man's appearance. He sent a wary glance in Pietro's direction. With the air of a man resigned, he led the newcomer directly to where Pietro stood sipping hazelnut water and eating cruste rolle.

Seen up close, the newcomer owned the most chilling grey eyes Pietro had ever seen. His face had once been ravaged by pock-marks, which had left his cheeks scarred. He now radiated a polite hostility as he waited for Stefano to speak his name, though by this time Pietro knew who had to be.

"Ser Alaghieri, allow me to introduce his Excellency, Cardinal Bernardo Guidoni."

"An honour and a privilege." That slow chill which had quelled the room now crept shudderingly up Pietro's spine as he bowed before the cardinal's fixed smile. This was no longer a friendly gathering. Perhaps the Colonna brothers had intended it as such, but the advent of Bernardo Gui made this an informal hearing, an event far more dangerous than any courtroom. Here he could not call upon a lawyer to defend him, and any chance remark could be used in some future event to damn him.

Not that his lawyer was here. Trust Petrarch to abandon him in his moment of greatest need! Out of the corner of his eye, Pietro saw Gherardo scamper off to drag his brother away from his inane lovesick mooning.

There was nothing for it but to put on a brave face and pray not to end the day in a papal prison. Pietro was sure his would be far less comfortable than the one Occam and Bonagratia enjoyed.

Cardinal Gui was smiling, though the smile did not reach his eyes. "Our host has been requesting my presence for supper for weeks, and I understood it was to meet his protégé, young François. Who, as I hear, has taken up the role of advocate for the son of the infernal poet. When I heard of this gathering, I decided it was the perfect opportunity to accept."

"You honour me far more than I deserve," said Pietro, desperately glad he had eschewed wine today. "I have long wanted to meet you."

"Have you? Then this day is a blessing for us both. I understand that you are reading today. I must confess, I've longed to hear your father's words spoken by one so intimately associated with them. May I be so bold as to request a canto?"

Surprised to hear Gui knew his father's works well enough to request a passage, Pietro feared a trap. But there was no way but forward. "Of course, your Excellency."

"I would like to hear the fifth canto of your father's work called Paradiso."

The chill turned to sweat on Pietro's neck. The fifth canto. The Moon and Mercury. Damn. "I'm afraid I don't have a copy with me."

"I do." Gui produced one from his robes. "I've marked the page."

"Thank you." Pietro received the book as if it were poisoned. "I would be honoured to oblige – if our hosts have no objection?" Please object! Please!

Beneath his patrician reserve, Stefano Colonna was fuming. His brother looked just as angry. Gui had placed them in the position of being ungracious hosts. But they did not, could not, know the dangers that lay in that canto, and therefore had no grounds to prevent the request. "I am sure that any lines from your father's masterpiece will be a welcome diversion—"

"And educational," said Gui.

"— but I'd actually hoped for a little personal satisfaction. I was going to request canto twenty-seven from L'Inferno."

Pietro could have kicked himself. He had entirely forgotten the damnation of Guido da Montefeltro, suffering all the torments of Hell for his advice to betray the Colonna family! It was the obvious choice. "I had planned, actually, on a canto from Purgatorio."

"Why not all three, then?" asked Bernardo Gui with complaisance. "Hell, Purgatory, and Heaven. A trinity. Three is perfect in all things – even poetry."

A copy of L'Inferno was found. The lack of open hostilities had caused the room to relax, if infinitesimally. With the pervading silence around him and the leather-bound books in hand, there was no way to delay. Pietro took his place before the gathering, opening L'Inferno to the twenty-seventh canto as his hosts made the introduction. No one dared applaud until Gui began lightly patting his hands together.

Stomach in knots, Pietro made a few remarks, setting the stage for the canto he was about to read. His father had traveled deep into the bowels of Hell, reaching the eighth bolgia, where men suffer all in flame, looking like walking candles. "As Virgil tells my father, 'These spirits stand within the flames. Each one is wrapped in that in which he burns.'" Pietro quickly related his father's encounter with Ulysses and Diomedes, burning together in a single fire for their stratagem with the Trojan Horse, and for tricking Achilles into joining that war. Then Pietro began to read.

The passage began with Ulysses and Diomedes moving off, and another walking flame coming close and speaking Dante's native accent of Lombardy. This was a recent arrival in Hell, and though the poem did not name him outright, every reader knew by the description of his deeds that this was Guido of Montefeltro.

> *Mentre ch'io forma fui d'ossa e di polpe*
> *che la madre me diè, l'opere mie*
> *non furon leonine, ma di volpe.*

> *Li accorgimenti e le coperte vie*
> *io seppi tutte, e sì menai lor arte,*
> *ch'al fine de la terra il suono uscie.*

––––––––––

> *"While I still kept the form flesh and bones*
> *my mother gave me, my deeds were not*
> *a lion's but the actions of a fox.*

> *"Cunning stratagems and covert schemes,*
> *I knew them all, and was so skilled in them*
> *my fame rang out to the far confines of the Earth."*

Defeated, Guido had taken the monastic life until he was called from retirement by Pope Boniface, who was then besieging his enemies. The poem did not mention those enemies by name, but everyone present knew they were the Colonna – Stefano, Sciarrillo, and their father and uncle. The Colonna family had been much attached to the previous pope, whom Boniface had forced to abdicate under dark circumstances.

Calling Pope Boniface the 'Prince of the latter-day Pharisees,' Guido related how that evil Pope had asked his advice on how to take the Colonna stronghold, Praeneste. Absolved in advance of all his sins, Guido gave simple advice: 'Promising much with scant observance will seal your triumph to the lofty throne.'

Pietro heard his audience hiss as he read those lines. This indeed had been Montefeltro's advice, and Boniface had dutifully promised the Colonna family a pardon if they surrendered. Believing his lies, they'd agreed, only to have their stronghold demolished, their lives threatened, and their very souls placed in peril. This had led to their attempt to kidnap the Pope himself, when Sciarrillo had slapped the pontifex maximus in the face. That night had eventually led to the pope's death, which in turn led to the removal of the papacy to Avignon. So much strife due to one piece of fraudulent advice.

As Dante had written it, the dead Guido had started his ascent to Heaven when a devil arrived to claim him:

> *... li disse: 'Non portar; non mi far torto.*
>
> *Venir se ne dee giù tra 'miei meschini*
> *perché diede 'l consiglio frodolente,*
> *dal quale in qua stato li sono a' crini;*
>
> *ch'assolver non si può chi non si pente,*
> *né pentere e volere insieme puossi*
> *per la contradizion che nol consente.'*

> *... "No, wrong me not by bearing that one off.*
>
> *"He must come down to serve among my minions*
> *because he gave that fraudulent advice.*
> *From them till now I've dogged his footsteps.*
>
> *"One may not be absolved without repentance,*
> *nor repent and wish to sin concurrently –*
> *a simple contradiction not allowed."*

The fiendish cherub then gleefully added, 'Perhaps you didn't reckon I'd be versed in logic!' The weeping flame departed, and Dante moved on to the next level of Hell as Pietro finished the canto.

Now the applause was not strained or reserved, though Pietro suspected it was more for the damnation of the hosts' enemy than for his skill at reading. Pietro noticed Petrarch sidling into the room. He didn't know why, but he was relieved. Perhaps he just needed a friendly face.

Then Pietro's heart leapt up into his throat as Cardinal Gui spoke. " 'One may not be absolved without repentance, nor repent and wish to sin concurrently.' An excellent observation. I must make a note of it."

Again the room released a silently held breath, and conversation began to flow. Pietro answered a few poetic questions, saying that yes, his father had once praised Guido of Montefeltro, but that was before his false advice had become publicly known. Then the two Colonna brothers began relating the siege, and Pietro stepped back to sip his hazelnut water, hoping their story would last until nightfall.

But the tale was finished in just ten minutes, and Gui had another question ready the moment it was done. "Is it true, Ser Alaghieri, that your father based the plan for Hell upon Verona?"

Stepping back to the podium, Pietro forced a weak smile. "Upon the Roman Arena there, yes. He imagined the ancient days of gladiators and lions chasing good Christians, and saw in the blood-stained earth a river of blood. As the seats form rings around the center, his plan grew from there."

"Ah! Clearly Verona is a Hellish place. Are there nine rings?"

"No. He chose nine rings of Hell to mirror the nine heavens, nine being three threes. And three books for the *Commedia*, with thirty-three cantos each, creating a trinity of his own redemption."

Gui was not to be diverted. "Are there still lions in the Arena?"

"Lions on occasion, but no Christian sacrifices."

"I'm gratified to hear it. I feared your master, being out the sight of God, might make free of the ways of old Verona."

"On the contrary, your Excellency, Cangrande's father burned Paterene heretics in the Arena."

"The son is not the father. If the sins of the father do not damn the son, then neither can the good deeds of the father absolve the son. But back to this magnificent and most just poem – there was a reference I must confess I did not recognize. The simile about the Sicilian bull..?"

The answer that leapt to Pietro's lips was nothing dangerous. "It comes from the histories of Orosius and Valerius Maximus, as well as Ovid. An ancient tyrant had an artisan craft him a brass bull in which he could roast his enemies alive. The moment it was finished, the tyrant ordered that the craftsman be the first victim, to test his creation. My father called that justice, as did Ovid. 'There is no law more just than that the craftsman of death should die by his own handicraft.' "

Even as he said it, Pietro feared he had gone too far. Could he be perceived as challenging the Grand Inquisitor who had sent so many heretics to death?

Gui's frown was strong as he spoke. "If there is any objection to be raised to this fine work, and indeed all of modern secular literature, it is that – far too much reliance and reference to the works of the ancients. If I had my way, all pagan writing done before the birth of our Lord and Savior Jesus Christ would be burned and erased from history."

Pietro chose not to rise to that extraordinary bait. It was Petrarch who objected. "Cardinal Gui, surely you don't claim that there were no good men before Christ. Was it their fault that they had not yet received the gift of grace? Must we erase them only because they lived in a time before our Lord had come to save them?"

"You mistake me, young man. I do not object to the ancients because they are pagan. As you say, they could hardly help their sorry state. No, I worry because their words are too beautiful, too uplifting, too stirring to the heart."

"How is that a flaw?" Petrarch was not the only one curious as to Gui's reasoning.

The cardinal opened his hands in utter helplessness. "It makes us love this life too much. They had no notion of Heaven, as we have, so they quite naturally focused on their present, their temporal selves, their animal needs. We know better. If a man spends his days thinking of life here on Earth, then by process of exclusion he is not thinking of his salvation in the life to come."

Suddenly Pietro wanted nothing more than to hear a theological debate between William of Occam and Cardinal Gui. Though he rather imagined that Gui would use his position of inquisitor to back up his arguments if he found himself out-reasoned.

Amused by his imagination, Pietro almost missed Gui's next lance. "Now we come to the heart of the question. Ser Alaghieri – what is fraudulent advice, precisely? Does your father mean advice to commit fraud? Or advice falsely given? What is it the damnable Guido is damned for?"

Pietro's best answer was the truth. "I'm afraid I cannot say. I never asked my father to explain that passage. My apologies."

"Alas!" cried Gui. "But I confess I was merely curious. Both are worthy of damnation. I applaud your father's perspicacity. Though not his choice of tongues. Writing in the vulgare! Tell me, did your father ever advocate a translation of Holy Scripture into the vulgar tongue?"

"He believed it should be translated into every tongue, the better to reach those who have not yet heard the miracle of Christ."

Expecting a rebuke or a debate, Gui merely nodded. "A most noble sentiment. Shall we move on?"

Obediently Pietro opened his own book and read aloud canto six of Purgatorio, which was not overtly contentious, as it excoriated Italy for internal feuds. But there was one verse that made Pietro wince inwardly as he read it:

> *Ahi gente che dovresti esser devota,*
> *e lasciar seder Cesare in la sella*
> *se bene intendi ciò che Dio ti note,*
>
> *guarda come esta fiera è fatta fella*
> *per non esser corretta da li sproni,*
> *poi che ponesti mano a la predella.*

———————————

> *Ah, you who should be firm in your devotion*
> *and let Caesar occupy the saddle,*
> *if you but heeded what God writes for you.*

490

see how vicious is the beast not goaded
and corrected by the spurs,
ever since you took the bridle in your hands.

This could have been dangerous, as Dante was telling the clergy to stop meddling and let Caesar run things in Italy, meaning the Emperor. But when the canto was finished and other men were talking of this family faction or that, Gui let this pass by without comment.

Perhaps he's just waiting for riper fruit. Well, time to offer it up.

Pietro reached for Paradiso, and his own damnation.

Twenty

Trying to keep his hands from shaking, Pietro opened the copy of Paradiso Gui had given him. The passage was marked with a long duck feather, and Pietro was shocked to discover the volume was one of the originals, copied in Ravenna after Dante's death. How had Cardinal Gui come to possess it? Was it possible Gui was an admirer of Dante? Or was this some kind of statement? And why did the duck feather raise Pietro's hackles?

As before, Pietro began by offering a brief introduction. At this point in the narrative, Dante had been lifted by his beloved Beatrice to the sphere of the moon. Insubstantial, they were not on the moon, but within it. Bringing the beatific vision her name implied, Beatrice began to shine so brightly that Dante had to avert his eyes.

Canto V began with her explanation of this:

> *"S'io ti fiammeggio nel caldo d'amore*
> *di là dal modo che 'n terra si vede,*
> *sì che dal viso tuo vinco il valore,*

non ti maravigliar, ché ciò procede
da perfecto veder, che, come apprende,
così nel bene appreso move il piede..."

———————

"If I flame at you with a heat of love
beyond all measure known on Earth
so that I overcome your power of sight,

do not wonder, for this is the result
of perfect vision, which, even as it apprehends,
moves its foot toward the apprehended good..."

These lines and those that followed were perfectly fine. The problem was yet to come, as Beatrice repeated Dante's question:

"Tu vuo' saper se con altro servigio,
Per manco voto, si può render tanto
Che l'anima sicuri di letigio."

———————

"You want to know if a vow unfulfilled
may be redeemed by some exchange
that then secures the soul from challenge."

Beatrice then went on to make the speech promised by Virgil in Purgatorio, a discourse on free will. Oddly echoing Occam, the fictional Beatrice

493

proclaimed that the greatest gift God gave to creation was 'the freedom of the will,' saying that only men and angels were so endowed:

> *... ché, nel fermar tra Dio e l'omo il patto,*
> *vittima fassi di questo Tesoro,*
> *tal quale io dico; e fassi col suo atto.*
>
> *Dunque che render puossi per ristoro?*
> *Se credi bene usar quell c'hai offerto,*
> *di maltolletto vuo' far buon lavoro.*
> *To se' omai del maggior punto certo;*
> *ma perché Santa Chiesa in ciò dispensa,*
> *che par contra lo ver ch'I' t'ho scoverto...*

> "*... For when man makes a pact with God,*
> *this treasure, as I have suggested, then becomes*
> *the sacrificial pledge, an action freely chosen.*
>
> "*What, then, may you render in its place?*
> *If you think of doing good with what you've offered,*
> *you would do good works with gains ill-gotten.*
>
> "*Now you may be certain of the major point.*
> *Since Holy Church gives dispensations in this matter –*
> *which seems to contradict the truth I have*
> *declared..."*

Now they were in it! His father's dripping sarcasm about dispensations in place of real penance was unmistakable. Pietro thought of the book given to him by Bonagratia and Occam, the list of indulgences. Was it possible Gui knew Pietro had such a book? Had he requested this canto to force Pietro into confessing such knowledge? Or was the passage damning enough in itself?

Pietro's tongue stumbled a bit, and he refocused on his reading as Beatrice went on to explain the two elements of a vow – the oath itself, and the thing to be sacrificed. Using examples from both holy scripture and heathen times, Dante's muse laid out rules for those rare cases when a thing to be sacrificed had to be replaced.

Mopping sweat from his brow, Pietro came to the end of the troubling passage and read of his father's swift transport from the Moon to Mercury, where he met and addressed a glowing personage who would turn out to be the Emperor Justinian. The canto ended with Dante preparing to listen to what Justinian had to say. *Perhaps I should keep reading until I collapse, just to forestall the questions I know are coming.*

But Pietro bravely closed the book, using the feather to again mark the place. There was a smattering of applause, but this time Gui did not put his hands together. Instead he held up a hand for silence. "Fascinating! Tell me, Ser Alaghieri, why does Divine Radiance come in the person of your father's great earthly love, this mortal woman for whom he peaked and pined in life?"

"Beatrice in the poem is a figurative person, one that my father as poet uses to guide him, much the way his poetic inspiration, Virgil, guided him through Hell and Purgatory. The love he bears her, and she him, is a pure love, unsullied by mortal lust or entanglements. It is, in fact, the chivalric ideal of love – love of spirit, never consummated in flesh."

Cardinal Fieschi unexpectedly joined the debate. "But Ser Alaghieri, love outside the bounds of holy matrimony is not a love sanctioned by the Lord. Surely it's sinful to suggest it is."

What did I ever do to you? "This is no romantic love, your Eminence. Beatrice is here to be the figure of God's love, a bringer of holy light."

"As Lucifer was once the Lord's light-bearer," interjected Gui, clearly annoyed at Fieschi – he needed no help. "Interesting. But what does this blinding radiance signify?"

"That is up to the reader, of course. Literature cannot exist as the author intends, but is a process of shared experience. Just as the Law cannot exist without men to interpret it, so too art cannot survive on its own. It must have an audience. It is my experience that the artist can never fully control what others take away from his work."

"An interesting position. You say there is no one truth, only flawed interpretations. Does that apply to God's work as well as Man's?"

The answer was so obvious, Pietro was wary. "God's word is Truth. But I am sure your Excellency would agree that men often misinterpret it. Which is why we have the Holy Church to guide us," added Pietro before his adversary could.

Cardinal Gui smiled. "A point well argued. Though by making this case, you put your father in the place of God."

Pietro bowed his head. "Certainly that was not my intent."

Lord Stefano Colonna came to Pietro's aid. "Even the humblest artist is the god of his own creations. As we were created in God's image, it is only fitting that we emulate Him. For when we create something, anything, from the tailor his gown to the joiner his stool, are we not imitating the great Creator Himself?"

"Very well," said Gui. "We will agree that God's Truth is truth, and those who misinterpret His Will are heretics, and must be corrected in their misapprehension by Mother Church. If this is so, then are we not in danger of becoming heretics ourselves?"

Now it was Stefano's brother the cardinal who answered. "What does my learned brother mean?"

"I mean a heresy of poetics! If we interpret this fantastical piece of the great Dante's own brain, we may err. We are fortunate to have with us our own version of the church of Dante – his pope, as it were, the *pontifex maximus* of the *Commedia*, Ser Alaghieri, save us from ourselves! Enlighten us as to the meaning of this divine light your father bestows on this heavenly woman!"

It was a cunning trap, artfully sprung, setting Pietro up as a metaphorical pope, and therefore by definition a heretic. The best move would be to defer, to claim he was unworthy to speak before such a learned audience.

But his temper was rising. Taking a sip of water to calm himself, Pietro nodded. "Very well. In my father's Paradiso, the laws of nature give way to the laws of the spirit. The light you ask about is in fact the divine gift of Intelligence, which separates us from the beasts. But as we are above the animals of the field, so is God above us, and His light blinds. Figures in Heaven are almost unseeable to mortal eyes, so filled are they with illumination – there is a reason we say 'illuminate me' when we wish to understand."

Petrarch refused to let Pietro risk himself alone. "It is a sidelong reference to another of those pagan works you abhor, your Excellency. A work by Plato—"

"Yes, Francesco." Unwilling to endanger his friend, Pietro cut across him. "Just as men living in a cave perceive the creatures outside by their shadow alone, so too are mortal men incapable of perceiving the Divine Intelligence of the Lord. That was my father's point."

"Ah! Marvelous!" Cardinal Gui was leaning forward in his seat, hands clasped tight, pleasure etched across his face. "And you, Ser Alaghieri – do you agree?"

"Forgive me, I have not my father's wit. Though it seems true to me that God is greater than Man can understand." That perfectly safe statement was inarguable. But seeing the challenge in Gui's cold grey eye, Pietro was incapable of staying his tongue. "In fact, it's always seemed to me the height of arrogance for men to say they know the Will of God."

The room was silent as Gui said, "I quite agree. Which is why men must seek the guidance of the Church."

It was on the tip of Pietro's tongue to point out that the Church was run by men. He was only saved from that utterly damning statement by Lord Colonna, who broke in with a question. "Ser

Alaghieri, as I listened I was most interested in the matter of vows. Specifically, why such a learned and excellent debate occurs in the first verse devoted to Mercury. Is not Beatrice's argument that vows are not changeable at all? Then why does this discourse happen between those two fickle orbs, the moon and Mercury? The moon changes constantly, and Mercury was the bringer of death."

It was Petrarch who answered. "Forgive me, my lord Colonna, but there is a nuance there. Mercurius was not the bringer of death, but the bearer of it. Meaning he transported those who died to the Underworld. The caduceus, his staff with the twin entwined snakes, was his entry, being the symbol of a herald. In Ovid he is charged with bearing the nymph Larunda there."

"And seduces her along the way," observed Gherardo just loudly enough to draw disapproving chuckles. He wanted to prove he knew just as much about poetry as his brother.

Squaring his unimpressive jaw, Petrarch pressed on. "In classical times, my lord, Mercurius was not only the messenger of the pagan gods, he also held dominion over trade, and therefore contracts. So his planet has great sway over legal proceedings. Which is why I imagine Pietro's noble father placed the great Roman Emperor Justinian there."

Pietro nodded, thinking of the caduceus. He'd once found an old Roman coin with Mercury on it. For years it had been about the neck of his dog. When that dog died saving Cesco's life, Cesco had taken it for his own neck, where it hung to this day.

Cesco – what am I doing here? I should be there, keeping you safe, not risking my life in a game of words with cardinals and bishops and popes.

Then Pietro recalled who it was that little Cesco had needed saving from – Gregorio Pathino, who was here, pouring poison in Gui's ear. This was as important to Cesco as it was to Pietro.

Meeting eyes with the inquisitor, he gave a small smile. Come, your Excellency. You wanted me to read this for a reason. Ask your real question. Let's have done.

Gui obliged. "All this talk of pagan gods is well enough for a salon on the classics. But I am more interested in another part of Lord Colonna's question. Ser Alaghieri, if this is any example, I take it your father had very strong opinions about vows."

"He did, your Grace. It was my father's belief that a vow undertaken of a man's free will could not be amended or altered, and a broken vow of that kind, large or small, was damning."

"That seems just and wise. At first glance, at least. But are not all vows undertaken freely?"

"Some vows are enforced. A child being baptized has no concept of the vows undertaken in his name. Which is why a grown man must reaffirm those vows of his own free will."

"Free will, yes. Your father spends a great deal of time on that topic here."

"He believed that it was God's greatest gift," said Pietro simply.

"Greater than life?" asked Gui.

Pietro found himself using Occam's argument. "Beasts have life, your Excellency. Man has free will. Ecclesiastes 15 says, 'In the beginning, God made Man and left him in the power of his own counsel.' By which we can infer, his own free will. The Glossa of that passage says that free will was given only to Man, of all creatures. Animals have senses and appetites, not volition and reason, and so they lack free will. Men alone have it. Or rather, men and angels."

Gui did not pounce, but rather eased closer to the point. "So Man is not alone in having free will and reason? Does that not make a mockery of Genesis, where Man is made in God's image?"

"In God's image, not with His abilities," countered Pietro. "We are in His shape. What gifts He bestows must be outside that. And if God in His divine wisdom bestowed reason upon us, might He not have done so on the creations of Heaven?"

502

Before Gui could answer, Cardinal Orsini came to Pietro's defense. "Come, Bernardo! Admit the poor boy's point. Clearly angels have free will – they must, for Lucifer chose to rebel against the Lord, along with one-tenth of His angels. If the heavenly host did not have free will, then it was God's will that His favourite rebelled, which is cruel. For if the angels have no choice between Heaven and damnation, then what chance do we have? And if life is all predestined, then why does a man's behavior matter? What would the Church have to regulate and absolve if Mankind had no choice? Men could sin freely, knowing the outcome to be predetermined."

"Forgive me, Cardinal Orsini," said Gui. "I hope I do not give the impression of finding fault. Unlike the theologians, I am not overly interested in predestination, nor in the rationality of angels. I am merely intrigued by the Alaghieri version of free will, and how it applies to oaths and vows. Ser Alaghieri, I will happily stipulate that man has free will, and I think – with the reason endowed unto me by God! – that a vow is indeed a sacred thing, a pact made before God."

Though dangerous, Pietro interrupted Gui to correct him. "Forgive me, your Excellency, but according to my father it is even more than that. A vow is a sacrifice of will, freely made. And having been entered into freely, it cannot be broken."

Gui was clearly unused to being corrected. But to contradict Pietro outright would place him in the position of saying a vow was breakable. Instead he steepled his fingers. "Yet your learned father seems to also state that some vows ought not be kept. How can this be reconciled?"

Pietro recalled countless nights debating this point in Ravenna. "There are indeed some vows that are on their face invalid. A foolish vow, or an illegal one – meaning one against the Lord's laws – those are invalid from the start. As we saw in the passage from L'Inferno, one cannot make a vow to undertake something forbidden, like murder. Nor may one undertake vows against reason. As the blessed Saint Augustine says, 'When a man misuses free will, he destroys himself as well.' A good example of this is the one my father uses, of Jephthah. Having foolishly vowed to sacrifice the first thing he saw when he got home if God granted him victory, he was forced to sacrifice his own daughter. Was that vow pleasing to the Lord? Yes it was fulfilled, but it should never have been made."

The watching crowd was both frightened and fascinated, wondering if this was in fact an ecclesiastical courtroom in the guise of a salon. Yet Gui was serene as a knife on the table – dangerous, but not immediately threatening. "So you think Jephthah should have renounced the vow, breaking his pact with God?"

It was not lost on Pietro that Cardinal Gui kept trying to make this about Pietro's views instead of Dante's. "My father would argue that Jephthah should never have entered into such a pact."

"Yet it was a vow made of his own free will, the very thing your father prizes so highly. And if men were allowed to leave off fulfilling foolish vows, there are many who would stray from their marriage beds – more than they already do, I mean," added Gui, to general amusement. "Does your father mean that such a vow is invalid, just because it is foolish?"

Pietro chose his words carefully. "Not at all, your Excellency. A vow has two parts. The oath itself, and the thing promised. The oath is sacred, and cannot be annulled. But the promised thing, the sacrifice, is open to change."

"Ah! Just as Abraham was allowed to substitute a ram for Isaac," observed Gui happily.

"Yes. And as Leviticus tells us, once something has been consecrated to God it must go to God, unless it is by the will of God."

"So substitutions are permitted?"

Pietro was glad of his dark lawyer's gonella, which hid the fact that he was sweating through his tunic. This was where the danger lay. "Not by Man's choice."

"How, then?" asked Gui sweetly.

"Only with the twin keys Beatrice mentions, the gold and the silver."

"Which represent what, precisely?"

"Authority and Reason. By which my father means, God's authority and the reason He gave us."

"And who holds God's power on Earth?"

"The blessed Pope, of course. And through him, his cardinals and bishops." Pietro bowed to the assembly of holy men, and took a moment to wipe perspiration from his brow. The quick staccato of their last exchange had been as dangerous and frightening as the cut and thrust of sword-play.

"All this is plain good sense, artfully expressed," said Gui, evidently at his ease as he enjoyed Pietro's discomfort. "So why does it seem that your father does not approve of alterations of this kind?"

Pietro cocked his head as if confused. "I'm sorry, your Excellency?"

Gui held out a hand, and Pietro crossed to give him back his copy of Paradiso. Removing the duck feather, Gui went straight to the thirty-fourth line of the verse.

Tu se' omai del maggior punto certo;
ma perché Santa Chiesa in ciò dispensa,
che par contra lo ver ch'I' t'ho scoverto,

convienti ancor sedere un poco a mensa,
però che 'l cibo rigido c'hai preso,
richiede ancora aiuto a tua dispensa.

"Now you may be certain of the major point.
Since Holy Church gives dispensations for this
which seems to contradict the truth I have declared,

"you'll have to linger longer over dinner,
for the tough food that you have swallowed
still requires some aid for your digesting."

"Tell us, Ser Alaghieri, why is it such a tough meal to swallow, this idea that the Church has power to grant dispensations and indulgences?"

Damn you, father. It was not a heartfelt oath, only one of the moment. Taking a deep breath, Pietro said, "It is the toughness of reason, a seeming contradiction that is in fact clearly explained as the canto goes on, that only the authority of the Church, married to its good sense, can grant dispensations." There! That sounded very well.

"Why all this talk of good sense? Cannot the Church do what it pleases?"

"If so, it abuses God's gift of reason. And surely you will agree there are some vows that should not be excused. Your own earlier example is apt – a married man, sworn to fidelity to his wife, cannot come to the Church and ask permission to forswear that vow. I am certain you agree."

"I do. Though when men stray, they must do penance."

"So they must," said Pietro earnestly. "And for penance to be accepted, they must repent."

"You argue most persuasively. What of a man who has vowed to go out upon a crusade, to travel ultramarino to the Holy Land and fight the infidel? Surely that is a vow of fidelity. Can not the Church excuse such a man in exchange for some other service?"

"It can," said Pietro. "Though it should not."

"Ah! The fervor of youth. I recall that you have yourself fought in the field to great renown. Is that your opinion, or your father's?"

"Both," admitted Pietro.

"There are times, my young friend, when money is more useful than a sword. What does your father say to that?"

"That the thing substituted must be of greater value than the thing originally promised."

"Was Abraham's ram of greater value than his son?"

"To God, it clearly was. And I believe the point was that Abraham was willing to sacrifice his son. The vow was fulfilled, and the substitution made by the grace and mercy of a benevolent God."

"Indeed, God above is magnificent, both for His justice and His mercy. Let us make another example, less extreme. What if a man undertakes, of his own free will, some holy office – a benefice, say – and then chooses not to administer it? Is not that a vow broken? A substitution of his judgment for God's?"

Here it was, at long last, a direct attack upon Pietro. He chose to answer like the lawyer he was. "If such a man indeed failed to carry out the duties of his office, and neglected the welfare of those placed under his care, then it would certainly be a vow broken."

"Would such a man deserve punishment?"

"If he had broken faith with his charges, and with God, then yes." It was a careful point, placing Pietro in the right by making him the champion of those in his benefice. By refusing to over-tax them, he could argue that he had not betrayed their interests. The opposite, in fact.

Gui saw this, and struck. "You mention the people, and God. You leave out the intermediary between the two. Does not this man owe a debt to the Holy Church as well?"

"A debt?" asked Pietro pointedly. "Certainly he owes the Church obedience in all just commandments."

"Who decides what is just for the Church?"

"God, of course."

"Not the man?"

Pietro was being backed into a theological corner, and knew it. "According to my father, no."

"Do you agree with your father's position?"

"The third commandment says I must honour my father."

"And the eighth says you shall not bear false witness. It is no sin to disagree with your father, unless the disagreement itself is a sin."

Pietro took a sip of water. "Forgive me, your Excellency – what was the question?"

Gui smiled, as if he was being kind to repeat the damning query. "Do you, Ser Alaghieri, agree with your learned father that a man does not have the right to alter a vow of his own initiative, but only with the blessing of Holy Church?"

It was an elegant trap. There was only one answer. "I do. A man may not alter an oath made freely."

There was a murmur throughout the room as the men wondered if Pietro had just condemned himself. The triumphant smile on Gui's countenance made Pietro's blood boil. He quickly pressed on. "I also agree that a vow to do something illegal or unjust in the eyes of God is no vow at all, and should not be honoured."

The smile vanished from Gui's face as if he'd been slapped. "Is it not legal and just to collect tithes and donatives in the name of the Church?"

"Tithes are every Christian's duty," answered Pietro, heart hammering in his breast. "For the rest, render unto Caesar what is Caesar's, and unto God what is God's."

The moment it passed his lips Pietro saw the blood drain from Petrarch's face, and someone in the crowd actually gasped. He had just committed a terrible crime. Speaking not for Dante nor anyone but himself, Pietro had used Christ's own words to call into question the right of the Church to collect money beyond the ten percent due to God. And by invoking Caesar, he had made reference to the Pope's current battle with the Holy Roman Emperor. With one sentence, he had tied himself to the causes of both Bonagratia and Occam.

Gui seemed to swell in his seat, growing larger and more upright. No longer placid, his cold eyes smoldered. Not with anger, but with hunger. He clearly wanted to tear Pietro's words apart. But they were the words of Christ. He had to consider how to challenge this without contradicting the gospels.

Standing nearby, Lord Colonna was mortified his brother's home had turned into the arena where this unseemly battle was being fought in the guise of a social event. "I think we have strayed from the poem we are discussing. Let us proceed – Ser Alaghieri, when your father ascends to the next planet, Mercury, he meets Justinian and a second man. Who is that?"

Tearing his gaze from the aged inquisitor, Pietro's forced smile was shaky. "Romieu of Villeneuve, the namesake of a friend of mine."

"And of mine," added Cardinal Orsini, meaning he too was a friend of Mari's, whose full name was Romeo Mariotto Montecchio. It was a small thing, but one that heartened Pietro. The bearish cardinal could easily have distanced himself from any association with Pietro.

Pietro went on to describe Romieu's story, who'd been a lord's loyal counselor until his rivals spread lies about him that cost him his position. Impoverished, he had to beg for bread, but never said an ill word against his former lord.

"I would have killed the man, myself," said Sciarrillo Colonna.

Frowning, his noble brother pressed on. "Certainly such a devout steward deserves a place in Heaven. But why Mercury?"

"He is only visiting in Mercury," explained Pietro, still on edge. "All spirits in Heaven are free to go where they wish. But I think my father placed him there to be a counterpoint to Justinian, who was the source of so many excellent laws. He's there as a reminder that ingratitude is often the reward for faithful service." It took all Pietro's will not to look at Cardinal Gui as he spoke.

There followed a slightly strained discussion of Dante's arrangement of the planets of Heaven. Just as the atmosphere was growing more comfortable, Gui silenced everyone by speaking again. "I wonder that you are so versed in astrology, Ser Alaghieri. Wherever did you gain such knowledge?"

A fresh chill ran through Pietro. "My lord della Scala once employed an astrologer called Ignazzio. Sadly he was murdered while visiting Aragon." *By your friend Pathino.*

"And he taught you?"

"His apprentice. And of course my father made an extensive study as he prepared this final volume."

"I see. A noble study, the motion of the heavens. Though I often wonder if it is not paganism at its core. The planets themselves are named for pagan deities, and so many infidel cultures make it their study." Gui threw up his hands. "But this is not to the purpose! Please, continue your discussion. I did not mean to distract you."

Then why did you mention astrology?

It was already growing dark, and the salon was soon ended. There was applause for Pietro, though mostly polite – no one wanted to be seen as enthusiastic for a man who may have just doomed himself. Everyone listened as Cardinal Gui came over to shake Pietro by the hand.

"An illuminating and enjoyable afternoon. Ser Alaghieri, I look forward to seeing you again. Soon, I hope."

"I'm humbled, your Excellency. It cannot be soon enough."

Gui moved off, carrying the volume of Paradiso with the duck feather sticking out the end.

Watching him go, Pietro let out a long breath. Once upon a time he had fought a duel with Marsilio da Carrara in Verona's Arena. As he walked out of the Colonna salon, Pietro felt as weak and empty as he had at the end of that contest. It was an apt comparison. He'd emerged from that contest in the same manner – alive, but the loser.

Petrarch, however, seemed joyful. As they strolled down the stairs and out to the carriage, he pinched Pietro's elbow. "You did well!"

"Did I?" The breeze outside made his damp clothes cling to his body.

"You were humble, learned, and firm. You gained more friends than you lost."

"But Gui—"

"Gui was never going to be your friend. You stood up to him. That's almost unheard of. I swear, Pietro—" Petrarch seemed at a loss. "I wouldn't have. Couldn't have. I lack the courage. I see now why you deserve your knighthood. Being your friend is an honour. Truly! And I will do everything in my power to free you from this mess."

Pietro found there were tears at the corners of his eyes. "I didn't make it easier for you."

Petrarch laughed. "You certainly didn't! But now that battle has been declared, we will win." As Gherardo climbed into the carriage, Petrarch pulled the door shut and rapped the roof. Before the driver could crack the whip Petrarch lurched forward and pointed out the window. "There! Pietro, there she is! My Laura! Isn't she a vision?"

Pietro turned, but the carriage pulled away before he could see the woman in question. He laughed. "I tell you, you're making her up!"

"Would that I were. I'd get so much more accomplished. I tell you, my soul is on fire!"

"Dampen it, please. Or else it will be me in the flames."

It wasn't until he was in his bed, replaying all the words exchanged that day, did Pietro have the revelation that shook him to the core. He was turning over that last exchange with Gui, the part about Pietro's astrological training and how it was an art studied by infidels.

That could have been simple talk, Pietro kept telling himself. It needn't be a reference to Tharwat...

All at once he realized the significance of Gui's book mark. For Tharwat had long made a practice of fletching his arrows with duck feathers.

Twenty-One

11 July 1327

Pietro became even more fascinating to the people of Avignon after his now infamous encounter with Cardinal Gui. Yet the flood of invitations gave him pause. Were they eager to meet him just for his company, or because he was surely going to die?

He accepted fewer of them than before, and made certain there would be no more readings, no more opportunities to be hanged by his father's verse. He did accept a lovely private dinner at the Colonna palace, their unspoken apology for the unseemly confrontation he'd endured under their roof. Petrarch said it was an excellent sign, as Cardinal Sciarrillo was the papal gate-keeper, and was now kindly disposed towards Pietro.

That dinner provided Pietro with his only opportunity to ask after Tharwat, if obliquely. He mentioned that he'd heard the papal palace kept a menagerie, and he'd like to see it. The Colonna admitted they knew of the existence of the private zoo, but didn't know anything about the keeper or his assistant. Pietro tried to reassure himself that if anything dramatic had occurred, these two were close enough to the papacy that they would have heard something.

He also learned that they were both to travel back to Italy at the end of August. "We have duties there. Just because His Holiness has decided to root himself here in France, it does not mean the Church has abandoned its true home. Rome was Peter's rock, and Vatican Hill is still where the world looks for guidance."

And you're leaving here just as Emperor Ludwig is heading to Rome to crown himself. Meaning you plan to have a foot in both camps. But Pietro kept his scurrilous insights to himself.

More worrying was the idea of losing an ally who had the Pope's ear. Uninterested in currying favour, Sciarrillo was a man who spoke his mind, was never mild in company. If he felt Pietro was being abused, he would speak up. Pietro hoped his trial – for that was what it was sure to be – happened soon.

They spoke of Cangrande, of course. Stefano had met the Scaliger on several occasions. "I always found him to be a gentleman, if a bit cocksure. Likes to own whatever room he's in. There is nothing humble in him." Laughing, Pietro agreed, and told a few innocuous, if mildly embarrassing, tales.

There followed some very pointed questions about recent events, and Pietro confessed that relations between Cangrande and the Emperor had not improved. Hearing this, Stefano said, "For this he burned his bridges with the Church? I hope your master knows what he is about."

He usually does, Pietro did not say.

Talk turned to news from Florence (where Pietro was an exile), Venice (where Pietro was under a death sentence), and finally Padua (where Pietro's damning part of the Dente revolt was still a secret). Privy to much information about each of these places, thanks to Cangrande's network of intelligence, Pietro knew the most about Padua, only some of which did he share that night. The rest was secret, as were his sources.

His best font of information was Petruchio's father-in-law, Baptista Minola, struggling mightily to maintain his grip on his minor holdings in the city and country. From him Pietro had learned that his old foe Marsilio da Carrara was a worried man. Carrara's cousin Niccolo had formed his own following and was beginning to grow larger than his frame. Baptista suspected that soon Cousin Niccolo would usurp the leadership of Padua, nominal though it was. He was courting the Ghibellines of Padua, entertaining them with lavish parties and holding secret meetings in his home. Straddling the fence of having two Ghibelline sons-in-law while living in a

Guelph city, Baptista had elected to avoid such gath-
erings, protesting his frail health much the same way
he had when eager suitors had called years ago for
his younger daughter.

Baptista wasn't the only one to hear the rumours.
In a pre-emptive strike, Marsilio had recently banished Niccolo's major followers. Upon Cangrande's
return from Milano, Niccolo's best friend was seen
with the Scaliger, thick with intrigue. The moment
that news reached Marsilio, Cousin Niccolo had fled
Padua, rounded up all the other Paduan exiles (even
those who had fought his brother) and brought them
to Cangrande to plead for aid. The Scaliger agreed
to support their efforts, but denied them troops – he
refused to break the current truce.

Nevertheless, Cousin Niccolo did get troops out
of Verona. He found a sympathetic ear in Mastino
della Scala, who was itching to prove himself in the
field. The Mastiff had Fuchs recruit and arm a private army of German mercenaries from across the
Alps, soldiers disaffected with the Emperor and longing for spoil. Mastino promised them wealth greater
than Pluto's mine, and they pledged their loyalty,
not to Verona, not to the Scaliger, but directly to
Mastino.

The implication was obvious. If at some future
date there was any question of succession, Mastino

meant to have an army at his back that would not defect to Cesco.

There was also news from Verona that was strictly personal, related in a letter from Antony Capulletto. Leaving for Florence, Pietro's little brother Poco had left behind a wench who'd apparently given birth to a son. Being a relation to one of Antony's servants, she'd come to him for help. Capulletto wrote that he'd taken the child in, for the sake of Pietro's family. As a mark of respect, Antony even had the boy christened Piero.

Thus Pietro gained his first namesake, a bastard nephew who would be brought up in a house containing a fresco of Pietro as a saint. Reading all this in Antony's letter, Pietro had no idea if he should laugh or hire a swordsman to have his brother killed. Maybe Tharwat remembers his Hashashin training...

Of course, that would require knowing where Tharwat was.

At the end of June, while Petrarch was busy at the Colonna palace, Pietro did something foolish – he called on Bonagratia and Occam. Having tied himself, however philosophically, to their causes, it was more dangerous than ever to be seen with them. Yet receiving their invitation, he'd felt obliged to accept.

"Young fool," chided Occam as they again took the air of the cloistered yard. "Crossing swords with the High Inquisitor? That was utter stupidity."

"Brave, though," observed Bonagratia with a smile.

"Certainly. And other fools will cheer our young knight even as he's burned at the stake."

"I had no choice," said Pietro.

"Rubbish. You could easily have said many things that would have balmed that wound. Instead you gave that detestable man exactly what he wanted – a challenge. He has an unparalleled record as an Inquisitor. During his fifteen years in Toulouse he convicted and condemned over nine hundred souls. Breaking you will be his pleasure. Here." Occam reached into the heavy pouch at his belt and produced two books. "Since you are committed to this folly, these may assist you."

"More terrible tomes?" asked Pietro. "I'm still reeling from your last one."

Bonagratia smiled. "This might be more practical."

"Yes. Since Gui armed himself with your father's words at your last meeting, you may repay him by arming yourself with Gui's words for your next. You may just survive."

Accepting the books, Pietro glanced at the titles. Practica Inquisitionis Heretice Pravitatis and *Le Catalogue des Évêques de Limoges*. "Gui wrote these?"

"He did. The Latin one is his guide for inquisitors, giving examples of how to cross-examine a heretic and make even an innocent soul look guilty. He employs several logical fallacies that you should gird yourself against. The other is his own history of the Bishops of Limoges. He's written several such, and it's rumoured he plans to unite them into a tome of general knowledge."

"Interesting that he wrote them in French," observed Pietro.

"He thinks in French," said Occam dismissively.

"As does the Pope," observed Bonagratia pointedly.

"And Pietro, be warned. He believes in this notion of coercitio, that truth can be found through physical coercion."

"Meaning torture," explained Bonagratia.

Occam nodded emphatically. "There is a foolish idea that a man will speak the truth if put under enough pain. Whereas it is far more logical that a man will actually say anything, true or not, to make the pain stop. There is a reason we've condemned so few heretics in England. Say what you will about Edward II, but he upheld his father's decree against torture. The Inquisitors say we are not diligent enough to root out the heretics, whereas we maintain we are not forcing innocent men to proclaim their guilt. Truth comes from reason, and a man on the rack or being flayed is beyond reason."

Pietro could not help a twitching of his fingers at the thought of the skin being flensed from them. Quickly he changed the subject. "Is there any advancement of your own cases? Surely with a new Grand Penitentiary they cannot delay any longer."

"Surely they can! They'll fill the schedule with less contentious cases, such as, forgive me, yours. The Church is not eager to display the divisions within its holy ranks."

"But there is progress," said Bonagratia eagerly. "There are rumours of a congregation in some God-forsaken abbey in the north of Italy. There will meet the brothers of our fractured orders, including my beloved Michael of Cesena. They are planning it for November, and we all pray that being gathered in one room will mend the rifts and, with the guidance of God above, discover a means of going forward that will be the satisfaction of all. I hope to attend," said Bonagratia.

"I do not," stated Occam. "Any overt show on either of our parts would be fatal to both our causes. Though I confess it hurts my heart. I hear Guglielmo da Baskerville is going. I would enjoy seeing him again." Shaking off a fond smile, Occam returned to his original point. "Regardless, we hope that these books will give you shafts for your bow by offering you a chance to observe how Gui thinks."

Thankful, Pietro took the books back to Carpentras, fully intending to start poring over them that night. But he was waylaid at the front door by Petrarch's sister. Lucia was just preparing to leave, which caused both her brothers to frown in consternation. "At this hour? Without a chaperone?"

Lucia rolled her eyes. "I'm staying in town with the Fieschi family – I'm sure I told you. Cardinal Fieschi has a niece visiting. Isabella, daughter of the Count of Savignone. I've been asked to be her companion and guide to Avignon. I'm certain it is entirely proper!" she huffed.

Pietro recalled the pompous and charming Cardinal Luca Fieschi who'd joined Gui in attacking Pietro. He felt uncomfortable at the idea of a woman he'd spurned and who had access to so many of his secrets being closeted in a household aligned against him. But there was nothing to be said.

In his room, Pietro settled down to read the writings of Cardinal Bernardo Gui. To his dismay, he found the history excellent, and the cross-examination of heretics uncomfortably familiar.

Just eight days later a richly appointed prelate arrived at Carpentras with the sealed summons for Ser Pietro Alaghieri to appear before the Bishop of Albano, the new Grand Penitentiary, for an examination of his soul, and his master's. In honoured attendance would be the Cardinal Orsini, Cardinal Colonna, Cardinal Fieschi, and Cardinal Guidoni – all of whom had been present at the reading.

There were two more names Pietro knew only by reputation. One was Cardinal Bertrand del Poggetto, nephew to the pope, avowed detester of literature, and the man who had been rejected by Cangrande the year before. The other was Cardinal Jean de Baune, a Dominican Inquisitor who had once held office in Narbonne.

Studying the list again, Pietro summed it up neatly. "Not a particularly friendly assembly."

"Better many than one or two. They are like to wrangle – it's their sport. All you have to do is divide them, or at least not give them cause to unite against your master. You shall argue for the Scaliger, and I for you," said Petrarch, taking the parchment to read it over again.

"When?"

"Monday, the second of September. Hmm. The feast of Saint Agricola."

"The farmer? Or the Roman general?"

"A local saint, the Bishop of Avignon five hundred years ago. The current pope created the college of Saint Agricola just six years back. It's a very important day for locals – feasts and celebrations and what-not."

Pietro didn't have to search far for a reason. "They don't want public attention focused on my trial. Which means they plan to condemn me. Not Cangrande, the crowds wouldn't care about that. Me. I'm to be arrested, and they want everyone too busy reveling to make a fuss."

"Possibly," admitted Petrarch. "Or it could be they're just preparing in case you are condemned. It doesn't mean they've decided in advance."

"September second. That date is ringing bells in my head. And not for Saint Agricola."

"Let's see. It was the death-date for Emperor Constantius III."

"No, something earlier. Isn't that the date for the Battle of Actium, when Mark Antony lost his war against Augustus?"

Petrarch snapped his fingers. "Mark Antony! Yes, of course. That's also the date in 44 that Cicero made the first of his Philippics, condemning Antony for being a tyrant. 'Illud magis vereor ne ignorans verum iter gloriae gloriosum putes plus te unum posse quam omnis et metui a civibus tuis quam diligi malis. Quod si ita putas, totam ignoras viam gloriae.' " Petrarch laughed. "But I doubt they know enough of the classics to choose a date of such import deliberately. Never fear, my friend. As Cicero himself said, 'Verum enim amicum qui intuetur, tamquam exemplar aliquod intuetur sui.' And I am your friend, through and through."

'A friend is like a second self.' Pietro recalled the last part of that quote. 'And in his friend's life he enjoys a second life after his own is finished.'

I hope if things go badly, my friends do not suffer as I will.

His mind returned to the thing he'd been fretting over since March. Now that the date was set, time was a real factor.

If only I had an answer to my letter! Antonia – I need you!

Two months earlier, his letter had found itself safely delivered into the hands of the person he least suspected of suffering, his sister Antonia. She received it eagerly, then steeled herself. She had promised – no secrets. So she marched directly to the door of Abbess Verdiana and knocked.

"Suor Beatrice. Come in, my child. Close the door. Now, what is it?"

"A letter. From my brother."

"He is a long time at Avignon. I trust his petition goes well."

"I do not know, Mother. I have not read it."

The Abbess looked pleased. "Then let us read it together."

It was difficult, as it was in code. But Antonia dutifully translated everything, reading the contents aloud. "He is worried for a friend, the Moor I told you of."

"Ser Alaghieri keeps strange company."

"They met through the Capitano. Tharwat saved my brother's life."

"Well then, that debt must be paid. And it's not for me to say what friends the Capitano di Verona should have. Though we must note that he, too, has been excluded from the sight of the Almighty."

Antonia read on. She had not shared the code itself with the Abbess, but she had sworn to reveal the contents of all messages that came to her within these walls. It was the price. The price for safety.

She had tried, a year ago. Tried herself to defend her honour. But again the man had laughed at her feeble attempt with the knife, then beaten her savagely where it wouldn't show.

529

The next day Cesco had broken his leg. She'd rushed to visit him, every step an agony, only to hear him declare his intention to stop his secret midnight visits. "It's too hard. This wouldn't have happened if I'd just stayed at home. His punishments are worse than not sleeping."

She'd pleaded with him to keep the option open, use her for a refuge when the world was too harsh, as he had as a small child. But the twelve-year-old had been firm, and she had cried real tears of grief. Horribly, the relief was greater. If Cesco never came again, she would not be subject to further attacks.

But though the attacks ended, Antonia's condition did not improve. Indeed, her nerves became worse. She found herself shrinking from shadows, fearing her own room – she'd never learned how the man had come and gone without a trace. She dedicated herself more than ever to work and prayer, so long as there were other women present. She began to loathe the society of men. She stopped going to the monastery with the tremendous library, despite the fact that Cesco was there, doing his catalogue. Even Fra Lorenzo, whom she had come to think of as a friend, was an unwelcome sight. She found herself stealing candles from the workshop where the books were made, just to leave them burning in her room at night.

Worst, in her weakest moments she found herself thinking ill of Cesco, despising his posing, his antics, his determination to be special. If he had only submitted to Cangrande, bent to his will, then none of them would have their present woes. Pietro could come home, Tharwat too, and Antonia could return to her beloved convent in Ravenna.

She loathed herself for harbouring these thoughts. In her rational mind she knew them unjust, unfair – Cesco didn't even know of her plight!

Yet she could not banish them. Weeks and months of these constant terrors, of losing the confident young woman she'd once been into this mouse that she detested, of restless sleep and feverish work-filled days, of waiting and waiting to see if Cesco needed her.

Then all at once he'd gone to serve the Emperor. Without even a word of farewell. Leaving Antonia without a thought.

The moment she heard the news of this defection, she had steeled herself and gone to the Abbess. "Mother, I would like to join the other nuns in the main sleeping hall."

The Abbess looked sternly up at her. "Why? Have you and your lover had a quarrel?"

Stunned and shocked, Antonia had blinked, then all at once found herself on the floor, bawling, shaking, howling. The story came tumbling out: her mothering of Cesco, the rapes, even the moon tea she had asked of Fra Lorenzo. She confessed everything that was in her, every sin, real and imagined.

Antonia had been astonished when the Abbess had knelt and held her tight, rocking her as one would a child. When she was quite recovered, the Abbess invited her to share her own rooms that night. Antonia was so relieved she almost cried again. That night, for the first time in months, she'd slept soundly. The Abbess had allowed her to sleep through the night hours of observance, and even through Compline.

Then they had sat together for an interview.

"Suor Beatrice, you have been subject to wicked deeds. I see now that I misjudged the situation, and I beg you to forgive me." Her normally stern visage grew even harder. "But I trust you see your wickedness, too. This is the fruit of poisoned trees that you harvested. You came to this house filled with secrets and deceptions. You may have thought you were doing good. Surely your intentions regarding this poor child are excellent. But your misfortunes came about from being too sub rosa. Secrets are like your attacker – they require darkness to survive. Sunshine is their enemy. The sun is God's own light. Darkness is the Devil's realm. So secrets, good or ill, lead to deviltry.

"Today we start anew, you and I. You have been a tremendous asset to this house. The money your Bibles fetch has allowed us to repair the dormitory roof, not to mention feeding many poor wretches who cannot feed themselves. But you have held yourself apart from us, to preserve a piece of your secular self. You must choose, girl – are you Antonia Alaghieri, of plots and secrets and lies? Or are you Suor Beatrice, a Benedictine nun, a bride of Christ, devoted to truth, chastity, and light? If the former, you must leave, whatever financial loss this house may suffer. For no good comes of a relationship based on lies. There will be no repercussions, no ill wishes or rumours. We will part as friends."

The Abbess had seen Antonia's stricken expression. "If you choose to remain, my girl, there must be no more secrets. I will keep you here, as my personal aide. You have certainly earned such a post, no one will question it. You will help me run this house. But I must know I have your absolute devotion and trust. Which means no more secrets. Of any kind."

Desperate to accept, Antonia had forced herself to speak the sole objection weighing upon her. "Some secrets are not mine to share."

Frowning, Abbess Verdiana was very still for a long time. "Very well. You may leave."

"No! Mother, please, no! I swear I will keep no secrets of my own from you. Nor will I act in secrecy to hide the deeds of others. But I cannot break a solemn vow to God, which I would be doing were I to reveal other people's secrets."

The tiny woman with the slight hump of age under her mantle had gazed at Antonia for a seeming eternity. At last, pressing her lips together, she sighed through her nose. "Needs must. Certainly I cannot tell you to break a vow to God above. One member of your family has been condemned for that already. But we are agreed – no more secrets from me?" Antonia nodded submissively. "Then you may stay."

There had been one more condition for Suor Beatrice to remain in the convent. An Abbess was, of course, not empowered by the Church to hear confession and grant absolution. Antonia was commanded to go to a priest and confess her sins, cleanse her soul before she took up her newly dedicated role. She'd fretted over the choice of priest, but at last had chosen the one she knew best. Though shocked, Fra Lorenzo had comforted her marvelously. She found afterwards that she was not so frightened as she had been. She did not even feel uncomfortable in his presence. But then, he was a holy man. More her brother now than even Pietro or Poco.

That had been January. In the months since, Antonia felt somewhat more like herself. Abbess Verdiana was a crotchety bird, but Antonia came to know her moods and see the sense behind her commands. Having experienced the tenderness buried deep within the old woman, it coloured every order with more compassion than Suor Beatrice had perceived before.

Until this latest letter, the burden of secrets had not been too heavy. There had been a few notes from Cesco, rambling and full of boyish news. Letters from Morsicato focused mostly on his wife's ill-health. Poco wrote occasionally from Florence, and spoke mostly nonsense. Only in Pietro's letters were there matters that had to be spoken of indirectly. So far she had managed not to betray his confidences without breaking her vow to the Abbess.

That changed with this letter. She'd finished reading aloud the passage about facing Bernardo Gui over their father's work (she was unable to conceal her anger at Gui, nor her pride in her brother) and was in the midst of translating the next section when all at once she stopped.

"What is it?" asked the Abbess.

"Pietro found the answer," said Suor Beatrice, shocked. "Well, not an answer, a clue…"

"What's this? Another of his secrets"

"Forgive me. This will take a moment." She read carefully over the request that would cross a metaphorical line. Were she to obey, it would cease to be *his* secret, and become hers as well. She had to either refuse her brother, or…

"Mother, he writes to ask my help."

The Abbess waited, then said, "I think you must explain."

Suor Beatrice did, telling the whole tale of Pathino, the murders, the kidnappings. She shared the drawing of the medallion.

They had to pause to attend the prayers of Sext, then returned to the Abbess' office to resume the story. At the conclusion, the Abbess' nostrils were flaring in anger. "And this detestable man, who murdered Lord Montecchio's father and tried to murder the Greyhound's heir while he was a babe in arms, this man is now wearing holy orders, and speaking poison into Cardinal Gui's ear?"

"So it seems."

"And what is it that your brother wishes you to do?"

"He has some questions regarding the history of the medallion, and how it came into Pathino's possession. He wishes me to ask among those who knew the Scaliger's father, and to journey to Montecchio, on whose lands this evil man's mother was in service. He wants enough information to take into court." Antonia went on quickly. "Mother, I know this is secular work. But the Church is involved, and this speaks directly to the interest of Verona. Pathino is a definite threat. I have no doubt that he has had a hand in the excommunications of both the Scaliger and my brother. Surely it is the Church's duty—"

Abbess Verdiana held up a hand. "Enough, girl. This certainly is no surprise to me. I knew this day would come, when you would beg to meddle in the affairs of the world again. It is in your nature. Indeed, it is a sign that your nature is at least somewhat restored, that you wish to again partake in statecraft."

Dropping her head, Antonia forced herself to remain silent, reminding herself that she was no longer the foolish girl who took command of her father's printing business and marched through the streets of Florence, Verona, and Ravenna as boldly as a knight in arms. She'd vowed herself to humility, then failed to show it, and so had it thrust upon her. "I will write to Pietro and tell him I cannot help him."

"Nonsense," said Abbess Verdiana. "You will write to him with all the answers he requires. For you are quite right about the duty of the Church. And it will garner our house the good will of the Scaliger."

Antonia's head snapped up. "You mean – I should venture out and find the information he needs?"

"I mean, my daughter," said the Abbess with a downturned smile, "that I have lived in Verona a very long time, and have all the answers you require."

Twenty-Two

2 September 1327

After twenty months of kicking his heels in Avignon, Pietro Alaghieri entered the massive stone structure of the Penitentiary for the hearing that would determine the fate, not only of his body, but of his soul.

Having bid perhaps his last farewell to Carpentras, (though not to Lucia, who was ill that morning), Pietro had joined Petrarch in a carriage and ridden through darkness to arrive in plenty of time for the hearing.

The heat of August had not abated, and the stench of Avignon was heavy in the air. But inside the new stone palace it was significantly cooler, and the incense burning at each window filled the nose with spices, not shit. At least the interview wouldn't be physically unpleasant. Unless they decide to resort to coercitio.

They climbed the stairs behind the priest who served as steward for the Grand Penitentiary. The session was to be held in the grand salon on the second floor. There were rushes on the ground floor, but two flights up the slabs of marble were bare, and their boots echoed resoundingly.

Passing through a pair of imposing doors, they entered a high-ceilinged room paneled with carved wood. At its center stood a small table with two chairs behind it – at least they would be allowed to sit.

Ten feet past the table was a long, raised platform upon which stood seven high-backed chairs, fashioned from wood so dark it was almost black. Just behind this dais stood a statue of Christ crucified. Recently finished, it still gleamed with polish. The savior's left hand was nailed to the cross, as were his feet. But his right hand was free, touching a small purse at his hip. This addition was all the rage in Avignon art, a direct slap at those who believed in the poverty of Christ. Pietro couldn't help wondering why, even if the savior *did* own property, the Romans let him keep his money on the cross?

The holy judges were all in place, with lower orders of priests and prelates acting as clerks and scribes. At the center of the seven sat Gauscelin de Jean, Bishop of Albano, the new Grand Penitentiary. To his right sat Cardinal Colonna, Cardinal Orsini, with Cardinal Fieschi on the end. On Bishop Gauscelin's sinister side sat grave-faced Bernardo

Gui, with two men who must have been Cardinal Poggetto and Cardinal de Baune.

There were no warm welcomes, no private good mornings or well-wishing. The penitent and his lawyer were escorted to their places. There was a pitcher of water on the table, which Pietro suspected was an invitation to display weakness. Ignoring it, he took the place on the right of Petrarch, putting him almost directly opposite Cardinal Gui. They made eye contact, and Gui inclined his head as if in respect.

With the judges already seated, it seemed as if Petrarch and Pietro were late. Nor did they have an opportunity to organize their papers. The moment they took their places beside their chairs, Bishop Gauscelin nodded and a priest banged a heavy gavel three times. "This gathering of the Grand Penitentiary Court is in session. Let us pray." He went through a long, stentorian invocation of God Almighty to aid them in bringing truth to darkness, falsehoods to light, and showing the faithful the way to everlasting salvation. Pietro's prayer for all those things was heartfelt.

There was a brief period of introductions, where Pietro was formally presented as Cangrande's representative, and Petrarch as Pietro's. All the cardinals were named in turn, and while Fieschi looked bored, both Orsini and Colonna smiled thin encouragement. Pietro found himself wishing it were Stefano Colonna and not his brother the pope-slapper present here today.

Seated on the other side of Gui, Poggetto was a squinch-faced man with wispy stray facial hair, as if he only shaved a portion of his face each day. He had a long nose, slack skin, and droopy eyes that were almost a match for Petrarch's. But Petrarch was far more handsome than this forty-seven year old cleric.

Cardinal de Baune had a Gallic strength of face and nose that rendered him a painter's dream – no lines, but round planes perfect for swooping brush-strokes. He was in no way fat, simply rounded and ruddy, with a drooping moustache that made him more suited to joining Vercingetorix than to wearing a pontifex's crimson robe. Pietro had to remind himself that this jolly-faced Frenchman was a notorious Inquisitor, with a fearful reputation second only to Gui.

The Grand Penitentiary himself looked rather more like Poggetto – which made sense, as both were relations to the Pope. He too bore the sagging eyes and heavy flesh, though the Bishop of Albano was far more kempt and groomed. His two chins were nicely shaven, and the hair sprouting from his ears was trimmed into perfect tufts.

"You may be seated," he said gravely to the two young men before him. Pietro and Petrarch took their seats. "We are here for a dual – purpose." The pause made it sound as though he'd said 'duel.' Pietro saw Gui's mouth twitch in amusement. "The first is to examine the charge against Ser Alaghieri, that he willfully failed his duty to the Holy See by refusing to collect tithes in his benefice. The second is to look into the matter of the present lord of Verona and his transgressions against God and men."

He held out a hand, and it was instantly filled by a priest standing behind the platform. "I have here a statement from our own Cardinal Bertrando del Poggetto, papal emissary to Lombardy, describing in great detail the words and deeds of that Veronese scoundrel, Cangrande della Scala, who has been excommunicated for supporting the infamous and impious Ludwig of Bavaria, who styles himself a Roman Emperor. These are the two matters before us. After hearing the evidence in both cases, we will vote to restore their souls, or no."

"Pardon me," said Cardinal Poggetto, author of the letter. He looked down at Pietro. "While no man's soul is a trifle, and no crime against God Almighty is excusable, it seems that the violations of an Italian tyrant are far more urgent than the transgressions of a knight of a minor order. Must we hear both cases today?" Having been insulted by Cangrande, he was eager to dispense justice.

"We can hardly allow an excommunicant to argue before us on behalf of someone else," countered Cardinal Colonna. "We must first sort out Ser Alaghieri's status, then move on to the Scaliger's."

"If Ser Alaghieri is acquitted," added Cardinal Fieschi dubiously.

Cardinal de Baune's brow furrowed comically. "Is this a trick of some kind? Linking the two cases in this way?"

Cardinal Orsini rolled his eyes at the younger man. "Alaghieri was made a knight by the Scaliger. He fostered the Greyhound's son. He was sent here to argue on the Scaliger's behalf by the Scaliger himself. They are linked."

Petrarch rose. "Thank you, your Eminence. To that point, I have here a letter from the Capitano di Verona stating that he instructed my client to forego the extra tithes over the citizens of Ravenna—"

"I have the same letter," replied the Grand Penitentiary, holding out his hand and receiving it. "It seems of little import. The lord of Verona has no claim over Ravenna. That city is under the stewardship of Lord Guido Novello da Polenta, and it is through him, not the Scaliger, that Ser Alaghieri had the benefice in question. Monsieur Petrarca, did Lord Novello command your client to fail in his duty to collect the Church's portion?"

"No, your Eminence, he did not. But as my client was in Ravenna for the sole purpose of raising the Scaliger's heir, and that with the blessing of Lord Novello, it can be argued that Ser Alaghieri never stepped out of the sphere of Veronese influence."

Cardinal de Baune's face showed bewilderment. "Was his acceptance of the benefice then a pretext? Did he never intend to fulfill his duties? Or did he make a vow to serve two masters, and find himself in a position of choosing the secular lord over God in Heaven?"

"Your Eminence, my client is a man of immense honour for one so young, and was entrusted with a sacred duty by his liege-lord. His vows as a knight are made before God, and are as sacred—"

"It seems foolish," said Bernardo Gui, speaking for the first time, "to be listening to a lawyer when the man is present here, in his own person, to answer these questions."

Petrarch bowed. "Your Excellency, Ser Alaghieri is here to answer questions regarding his lord, the master of Verona, not about himself."

"But seeing his presence here in this very room, surely it would be remiss of us not to avail ourselves of his person. A lack of reason, as it were." Gui smiled.

"He is no plebian farmer, no mendicant or half-wit, incapable of arguing for himself. He is a knight and judge of Verona, a student of law at Bologna. And, if I may say so, an excellent debater. I had the honour earlier this summer to have a pleasant exchange in regards to poetry, and found his wit the equal of mine. If not greater!"

It had been the risk from the start. Both Pietro and Petrarch had known that having Pietro in the room, the judges would almost certainly demand to question him directly. Pietro could refuse, of course, but then it would appear that he had something to hide, that he feared examination in the open court. So they had rehearsed the formal statement from Petrarch refusing outright to breach his client's rights, and Pietro's quick interruption, offering himself up. Performing it now, Pietro seemed honest and eager, held back only by his zealous and devoted lawyer.

Having volunteered to answer questions himself, Pietro took Petrarch's place, standing before the seven men on the raised platform. Holding no notes, he clasped his hands behind him and lifted his chin to receive questions.

Oddly, the first question was not aimed at him. It came from Cardinal de Baune, and was directed at none other than Cardinal Gui. "Forgive me, my friend, but I must pause to question your personal stake in this. You say you met with this young man once before. You even seem to admire him. Can you be quite objective in this interview? Should you not, perhaps, recuse yourself?"

For a junior cardinal to ask his senior to recuse himself was a rather large insult. But as the question had been arranged in advance, Gui took no offense. "I shall try to keep my personal feelings at bay. Indeed, I will strive to overcome them. Perhaps my learned and wise colleague the Bishop of Albano would allow me to ask the initial questions? Then those more impartial spirits might judge from on high, like God Himself, who sees all and knows all."

Though it was artifice, it was artfully done. In moments Gui was also upon his feet, coming down from his place at the high table to stand barely in the periphery of Pietro's sight, seeming to hover behind Pietro's left shoulder. The symbolism was clear. To the audience facing them, Gui was on the right, while Pietro occupied the sinister position. Well, he's done this many times before.

"Pietro Alaghieri, son of the poet and exile Dante Alaghieri, you are accused of disobedience to Mother Church, and are therefore suspected of being a heretic, of believing otherwise than Holy Church believes. And of disseminating such beliefs in the form of 'poetry' written by your late father."

If Gui had intended to surprise him with the charge of heresy, he was to be disappointed. "I never held any faith other than that of true Christianity."

"You call yourself a true Christian. Do you consider our faith false and heretical? Have you ever believed as true a faith other than that which the Roman Church holds to be true?"

Pietro knew enough not to turn to face Gui, but offered his answers to the six men seated before him. "I believe the true faith which the Roman Church believes."

"Perhaps you belong to some sect that calls itself the Roman Church."

"I have only ever belonged to one church, and that is the Holy Roman Church, whose head is Pope John, and before whose elders I stand today."

That solid declaration was not the answer Gui had wanted. "Say simply, do you believe in one God the Father, and the Son, and the Holy Ghost?"

"I so believe." So far, this was precisely from the book given him by Occam and Bonagratia. Gui had a pattern he liked.

"Do you believe in Christ born of the Virgin, suffered, risen, and ascended to heaven?"

"I so believe." Come on! Ask a real question!

"And do you, like your father, believe that the Church lacks the power to make dispensations for sin?"

Finally! "Neither I nor my father believed what you say. In fact, he states quite plainly in his writing that the Holy Church has exactly that power, to make substitutions for an oath or a sin."

"As you yourself once noted, writing is open to interpretation."

"But not all interpretations are what the author intended. In your own writing, you place the blessed Saint Dominic in the church before the battle of Muret, praying for the victory of the crusaders. Yet others have interpreted that to mean that the blessed saint was in the midst of the battle himself – which is not what you wrote. Is that what you intended?"

Out of the periphery of his vision, Pietro saw Gui stiffen. Unused to being countered, the Inquisitor was obviously taken aback at having his own words thrown in his face. In truth, he had been the first historian to insert the blessed Saint Dominic into the battle proceedings at all. Before Gui, it had been unnamed monks and priests praying for victory, while Dominic was credited with a prophecy concerning the crusade as a whole. To support the idea that the founder of his order had supported lay violence against heretics, Gui had placed Dominic at the battle itself, and in the dozen years since he first published this account there had grown stories of Dominic walking around the battlefield with a giant cross, warding off arrows.

"We are not here to question me, young man. We are after the truth about you, and your father."

Petrarch stood. "His father? Lord Penitentiary, we are not here to try a dead man. Is it the intent of this court to hold a man accountable for the sins of his father?"

Cardinal de Baune answered rather snappishly, quoting Exodus. " 'Yet He will by no means leave the guilty unpunished, visiting the iniquity of fathers on the children and on the grandchildren to the third and fourth generations.' "

Cardinal Colonna countered with Deuteronomy. " 'Fathers shall not be put to death for their sons, nor shall sons be put to death for their fathers. Everyone shall be put to death for their own sin.' And as yet I have heard no sin."

At the far end, Cardinal Fieschi leaned forward. "The sin, as I take it, is the disobedience of not collecting an added tithe levied upon those under his benefice. Thus Alaghieri broke his vow, and disobeyed the Church."

"And for this he was excommunicated?" demanded Cardinal Orsini incredulously. "Why was he not simply removed from his post and ordered to do penance? Excommunication seems unfathomably extreme."

"For once Cardinal Orsini and I are in agreement," said Colonna. "Who presented the order for His Grace the Pope to sign?"

"I have it here," said the Grand Penitentiary, producing the document.

Desperately trying not to look eager, Pietro listened intently. This was the paper that had removed him from God's sight, the document he and Petrarch had petitioned to examine without success. Now Cardinal Colonna received it and read it over. "Why, this petition came from Cardinal Gui." His head snapped up. "What's this nonsense about you being too partial in this lad's favour, if you're the one who wrote the order for his excommunication in the first place?"

Gui spoke in level tones. "I did it with a heavy heart. And I did not then know the young knight as I do now. I have encountered his mind, and know it to be formidable. He has his father's way with words. Indeed, had I known then all that I do now, I would proceed along entirely different lines."

"Are you saying that you would not request his excommunication?"

"No, that is not what I am saying, Cardinal Colonna. I am saying I would have written the order for crimes far more grievous than merely refusing an order to collect money."

Pietro turned to stare directly at Gui, but wisely remained silent, allowing Petrarch to ask, "To what crimes do you refer?"

"If I may continue with my questions, that shall become clear. First let us finish with this business of the refusal to collect the Church's due. Ser Alaghieri, when we met this summer you said that the Holy Roman Church does not have authority to levy money beyond the tithe of one-tenth a man's wealth."

"I did not say that," replied Pietro, returning his gaze to the men on the platform. "I said that tithes were the duty of every Christian, and that for the rest, render unto Caesar that which is Caesar's, and unto God that which is God's. If you took a meaning from those statements, it was inferred by you, not implied by me."

"Does the Church have the right to collect money?"

"Of course."

"Did Christ collect money?"

"I do not know. I am certain he was not one of the publicani, collecting taxes for the Romans."

"But surely you feel his reaction to the money-lenders in the Temple speaks of a certain dislike of money in Church dealings."

"Again, those are your words, not mine."

"So you were not attempting to emulate Christ when you refused to collect an extra tithe from your beneficiaries?"

"I would not presume to believe I was in any way emulating the Lord Christ." Pietro fixed his eyes upon the Grand Penitentiary. "I did not mean disobedience to the Pope, or to the Church. My decision not to collect the extra tithe was a refusal to over-burden peasants who had little enough to live on. They had paid the one-tenth that was their duty. I felt it wrong to demand more from them before a winter that promised to be harsh."

Gui had a question ready, but Cardinal Poggetto got in first. "Then this sworn statement from your lord, Cangrande della Scala, is false. He swears he ordered you not to collect the tithe. Or is it you who is lying, to protect your lord?"

Hearing Petrarch clear his throat, Pietro ignored his friend's obvious advice to let Cangrande take the blame. "I am a knight and a Christian, and though I am no longer within the sight of the Lord, my vows as both keep me from ever bearing false witness. Perhaps my lord della Scala wrote that to shield me from harm, claim my sin as his own, as a good lord must." No, he did it to bind my cause to his. So much for false witness. "I am sorry he tried it, as it puts him in more peril for swearing falsely. But upon my honour, the decision not to overcharge those in my care was solely mine. I wrote at the time to explain my action, and offered to pay the sum myself in time. What I received in return was an announcement of my excommunication." He was longing to question Gui, to demand why he'd asked for the order. But it wasn't time yet. He couldn't let his shaft fly until Gui had loosed all his own bolts. Pietro had just one arrow in his quiver. He had to make it count.

"It does seem excessive," opined Cardinal Orsini, "and hasty. We have men here in Avignon who are accused of far greater sins, and are as yet untouched by something so drastic as excommunication." He was obviously referring to Occam and Bonagratia. "If Ser Alaghieri offered to pay the fee as a fine, surely that was more than enough for the Church. Especially the Church in Avignon," he added sourly.

"I agree," said none other than Gui's fellow inquisitor, Cardinal de Baune. "It is a minor offense, hardly meriting mention. Therefore I feel Cardinal Gui must enlighten us as to these other crimes he has uncovered, as they may explain the Holy Father's thinking in signing this order. For I am certain our illustrious pope has never condemned a man out of hand, or without the cause of Heavenly Justice on his side."

Gui bowed to his fellow Dominican. "Cardinal de Baune speaks most wisely. If perhaps I acted in haste to write out so a strong an order over so small a matter – though I think Ser Alaghieri would agree that all broken vows carry the same weight with the Lord – again, if I was indeed hasty, then I must have been guided by God Almighty, who led me to condemn blackest sin where none was seen. Which grieves me, as I know this young man believes himself to be a man of honour, a devout man, a man of the Church. But he believes erroneously! As I shall now demonstrate." Gui stepped closer, directly into Pietro's line of sight, forcing Pietro to address him and not the court. "Pietro Alaghieri, what do you know of astrology?"

Though expecting it, Pietro felt a shudder. Behind him, Petrarch rose. "Astrology? My lords of the Church, nowhere in any of these complaints is there a single mention of astrology as a crime against God. Nor is astrology itself a crime!"

"And he shall not be accused of practicing astrology. I simply ask what he knows of it."

The Grand Penitentiary nodded. "Alaghieri will answer."

Alaghieri. No Ser. That was a bad sign. "I know the basics of the planets, your Excellency. Their rotation around the Earth, and the angles they make between them. I can read star charts, though I have never tried making one."

"Impressive!" cried Gui. "I am sure you know more about such things than any other man here. You may recall I asked you this summer where you gained such detailed knowledge. I remember you answering that your father had done an intensive study for his work entitled Paradiso."

"Yes." Get on with it.

"And you mentioned another source. The Greyhound's personal astrologer. What was his name again?"

"Ignazzio." And he had an apprentice…

"Yes, Ignazzio. He died, you said, and you continued your tutoring with his apprentice."

I didn't say tutoring, you bastard, but why quibble? "Yes."

"And where is this apprentice now?"

You tell me. Aloud Pietro said, "I honestly don't know."

"Honestly? Meaning up until now you have not been honest?"

"I mean precisely what I say. I do not know the whereabouts of Ignazzio's apprentice."

"Then allow me to enlighten you." Smiling thinly, Gui snapped his fingers. Pietro braced himself. He had already spied the box behind Gui's chair just large enough for a head. Was that what the servants would now bring forward? Was he about to look upon his friend's severed head? Had Gui finished what heathens had started decades ago with a flaming collar?

But the servants did not bring forward the box. They opened the doors, and Pietro breathed a momentary sigh of relief. He's alive! Thank heaven, at least he's not...

Then Pietro saw Tharwat, and wished with all his heart that his friend had died instead.

Twenty-Three

Tharwat al-Dhaamin's arms were chained to a long metal rod that ran across his shoulders and behind his head, like a milkmaid with her pails. But here the pails were weights, bowing the Moor forward. If he had been able to walk, this weight would have been a burden. But his bloodied feet dragged, leaving a smeared trail on the marble. Pietro saw the two spikes still sticking out from Tharwat's ankles, a chain trailing between them. Two strong acolytes had to carry the rod, supporting Tharwat between them.

Orsini looked sick, and Fieschi physically recoiled. Poggetto was grinning, and de Baune was fanning himself and looking skyward, as if bored. Colonna scowled, not in horror but distaste. Even the Grand Penitentiary looked squeamish as he said, "Cardinal Guidoni! What is this?"

"This, brother, is the astrologer's apprentice we were speaking of."

The acolytes had set Tharwat down to Pietro's right, forcing him to kneel under the bar's heavy weights. His head was down, lolling to one side. But at the sound of Gui's voice the Moor lifted his face.

Pietro's almost cried out. One eye was shut – or so he first thought, looking at it. It was crusted over with blood, and Pietro wondered for a horrible moment if it had been removed. But then he saw the orb move and realized this was something far worse. Tharwat's left eyelid had been cut away, leaving the Moor unable to blink. The excruciating pain of this was hardly imaginable.

"Pietro Alaghieri," said Gui lightly, "do you know this man?"

Tearing his gaze from his friend, Pietro answered through clenched teeth. "I do."

"And will you tell the court his name?"

"I'm not certain I know his birth name. When I first met him, he was called Theodoro of Cadiz. He has sometimes been called the Arūs. But the name by which I've known him best is Tharwat al-Dhaamin."

That lengthy answer surprised Gui, but only for a moment. "Is this the man who posed as a servant in your household for all the years you lived in Ravenna?"

"He never posed as anything. He was a guest – first my father's, then, after his death, mine. I am also honoured to name him my friend."

That shocking pronouncement was almost enough to damn Pietro then and there. A Christian man, friends with a blackamoor astrologer? Pietro did not have to glance at Tharwat to know what his good eye was trying to communicate: Shut your mouth and save yourself.

Cardinal Gui was beside himself with delight. "I see. And did you know he was in Avignon?"

Thou shalt not commit false witness. "I knew he came to Avignon. I have seen him, I think, a total of six times, though it might be seven." Pietro cleared his throat. "I must state for the court that my host had and has no idea who Tharwat is, and never laid eyes upon him until the day of the accident with the pot of fire. Monsieur Petrarca had no reason to know Tharwat, and Tharwat was never invited into his home." That was treading a thin line, but Tharwat had always broken in, never entered as a guest. A lawyer's quibble, but Pietro was a lawyer as well as a knight.

The Grand Penitentiary leaned forward, hissing through his teeth. "This creature, your so-called friend, had a hand in that dreadful business in the square?"

"If by 'had a hand in' you mean that Tharwat helped me save the people in the square that day, risking his life to save mine and many others, then yes, he did. I have not heard from him since."

Gui answered that. "The reason you have not heard from him, Ser Alaghieri, is that he was being detained for lies and heresy."

"Has he confessed to heresy?" demanded Petrarch, rising to his feet.

God in Heaven bless you, my friend! thought Pietro, swelling with pride. You could have washed your hands of me here and now, and I'd never have blamed you. Pietro had long anguished over telling Petrarch all this, but the desire to shield his host had overwhelmed his personal need.

Yet here was Petrarch continuing his role of lawyer. He still had at least one ally among the Christians in this room.

In answer to Petrarch's question, Gui shrugged. "He has said nothing in any tongue that I or my fellow inquisitors comprehend – which in itself speaks volumes. For a man who speaks the Devil's tongue must himself be a devil, in league with Lucifer himself. And when he talks, his very voice is choked upon human noise."

"That's because he was tortured as a child – by Mohammedans, I might add. Those scars about his neck are from a burning collar they tried to kill him with. It is why he left heathen lands and began living among the Christians, whom he deemed more charitable," added Pietro scornfully. He turned to address the Moor. "Tharwat, if you can, what language were you speaking?"

Tharwat paused, then swallowed. His broken voice was harsher and more rasping than Pietro had ever heard it. "Hejazi."

"And where did you learn it?"

It was a risk, but the answer paid for itself. "Mount Sinai. Saint Catherine's monastery."

"I hardly think they speak Arabic at a Christian monastery," replied Gui demurely. "Even a Greek Orthodox one."

Tharwat blinked the one eye he could, keeping his gaze on Pietro. "They speak it to trade with the locals. I learned it to help them barter for better oil in winter."

Pietro nodded. "And what were you doing there?"

"Studying the stars," Tharwat answered thickly through his swollen lips. Pietro noticed that three of his teeth were either missing or broken. "They possess a copy of the astronomical tables of Al-Kuwarizmi, translated by Abelard of Bath."

Gui seemed to sense the danger of Pietro's line of questioning. By making the beaten heathen into an interesting man, one that the other judges would grow curious about, Pietro was transforming Tharwat from monster to curiosity, and possibly from there to learned man. So Gui put a stop to it. "And was that what you were doing in Avignon? Or were you here on some far more diabolic mission? I must tell you, my brothers in Christ, that this creature has been hiding himself in our very bosom for nigh on a year now! Living in the Pope's own palace, if you please! This thing that Ser Alaghieri sees fit to name as friend was hiding under a false name and profession. You might have seen him with the menagerie at the back of the palace yard, grooming the lions and whispering to the tigers. Yes, fittingly he hid himself among the beasts! I would not be surprised if we discovered the mark of the Beast upon him. Tell me, heathen, whatever you're calling yourself today, if you are feeling so loquacious, perhaps you will answer the question I put to you a hundred times these last weeks. Who was it sent you to Avignon?"

Tharwat breathed in once, twice. Then he smiled. Despite the missing teeth, the smile was pure and proud. "The Greyhound of Verona."

Pietro had to work to hide his own smile. The perfect answer! Everyone present would assume Tharwat had been sent by Cangrande. Only Pietro and Tharwat knew the title belonged to Cangrande's heir, the bastard of Verona.

Gui was delighted. "Ah! We come full circle, it seems. And you, Ser Alaghieri. You say you knew he was in Avignon. Did you know that he was posing as an apprentice lion-tamer to gain access to the papal palace and spy upon the Holy Church?"

"No," said Pietro.

"You didn't know? I find that difficult—"

"No, he was not here to spy upon the Church." Pietro paused, creating the breach he hoped Gui would charge into.

Gui obliged. "Then what was he here for?"

Despite his two decades interrogating heretics, the Cardinal was a student of Church Law, not worldly Law. As such, Gui was about to learn the first rule of a true lawyer: Never ask a question to which you don't already know the answer.

Squaring his shoulders, Pietro spoke in a soft, clear voice. "He was here hunting a murderer."

That simple statement might have been another pot of fire for all the uproar it caused. The cardinals and bishop upon the platform had no idea what had happened to their simple hearing, but clearly they were all agog over it. If not for the presence of the bloodied moor, they would have been grinning in delight over this exciting day's proceedings.

Gui himself looked bemused. He had expected denials, protestations, even oaths that Pietro had never heard of Tharwat, had nothing to do with him or his schemes. Doubtless the cardinal had heaps of documents and testimonials as to the relationship between Pietro and the prisoner. That was why the hearing had been delayed for the whole summer – they'd had to send to Verona, to Ravenna and Bologna, anywhere that Pietro might have been seen with Tharwat.

All that effort, wasted. More than admitting the relationship, Pietro had embraced it. Worse, he had flung out so much that was delightfully scandalous, so deliciously titillating, that it would be the talk of Avignon for weeks. Nay, months! The minor priests and acolytes in the chamber were all aflutter, and Gui's fellow judges were no better.

The man who had literally written the book on the Inquisition had no choice but to plunge blindly ahead. "Murderer? What murders do you mean?"

"I know of three people murdered by this man's own hand. The first was Tharwat's master, the astrologer Ignazzio. The second was my groom, a boy named Fazio. And the third was the father of my friend Mariotto Montecchio. I'm sure Cardinal Orsini recalls the details."

Alert and bewildered, Orsini explained matters to his fellows on the platform. "Mariotto Montecchio was the Scaliger's ambassador to Avignon ten years gone, and during that time I got to know him well. Cardinal Colonna, you may remember him, and I'm certain His Grace, the Holy Father, would recall the handsome young Italian who liked French fashion almost as much as young Petrarch there. This lad's father was murdered just a week after he returned home, and for a long time my young friend Montecchio blamed his former friend, Capulletto. But as I understand it, Montecchio's father was ambushed by a man who had kidnapped the Scaliger's heir. The child was rescued by Ser Alaghieri here, and the man escaped by murdering Montecchio's father and stealing his horse."

Pietro was quietly crowing. He couldn't have hoped for a better summary, nor had he expected Orsini to be so voluble in such a dangerous setting. *Perhaps I have two allies remaining.* "Just so, your Excellency. It was because of that kidnapping that Cangrande's heir was sent to live with me in secret. If not for unforeseen events in Verona two summers past, we would be there still, hiding from the threat of this murderous kidnapper until my charge reached his majority."

Gui was frowning. He may have begun to suspect where this was heading. Pietro had to get there first, not allow the cardinal to minimize the damage. He pressed on. "Tharwat revealed his presence in Avignon to me once he had found this man. This murderer has been posing as a Dominican canon. We knew him as Gregorio Pathino, and he kept part of that name when he hid himself behind a cowl. He calls himself Brother Gregor, and he has been pouring poison in the noble and honourable ears within the Church these last three years or more."

Gui was ashen-faced, for though Pietro had not said so, all men present knew Brother Gregor. Moreover, they knew whose creature he was. "This is outrageous! To accuse a member of my Order of murder and falseness! This is a mere masque, a diversion to distract us from Alaghieri's own sin!"

"I can prove what I say," replied Pietro simply.

"Send for Brother Gregor." The snap in the Grand Penitentiary's voice was sharp as he sent the acolytes scurrying. This was no longer exciting. One of his own was being accused, and the Bishop of Albano was not well pleased.

Nor was Cardinal Colonna, who looked sharply at Petrarch. "Francesco, did you know any of this?"

"No, your Excellency." Petrarch sounded breathless. And angry. "I confess I knew none of this – or rather, nothing of this Brother Gregor. I admit my own friendship with Montecchio, and that the details related by the learned Cardinal Orsini are the same that I know. I have heard the name Pathino in that context, but never anything about his being here in Avignon, or having taken orders."

"That is because this was part of the defense I was to mount for the lord of Verona," announced Pietro, "and to be spoken to none but your Graces."

The Grand Penitentiary's jaw was set. "Ser Alaghieri, you realize the gravity of your charges, and the punishment if they are false."

Alea iacta est. "I do, your Eminence. They are not false."

The doors opened and Pietro turned to behold two acolytes beckoning a man just out of sight. A moment later the reluctant *spaventapasseri* appeared. Tall as ever, emaciated and bloodless, he walked with a slight limp. Probably from wearing the cilice Tharwat had mentioned, that small metal chain with spiky prongs that dug into the flesh. Having been actually wounded in the thigh, Pietro was disgusted to think anyone would wear such a thing willingly.

Doubtless the Scarecrow had been close at hand, the better to relish Pietro's final defeat. Yet he could not be in the room without revealing himself. He'd probably planned to make himself known to Pietro only after the final sentence was pronounced, to relish his victory.

Unexpectedly summoned to the chamber, Pathino appeared as wild-eyed and uncertain as he had in that cave long ago. He met Pietro's triumphant glance for just a moment, and there passed between them the charged air of a decade of hate and loathing. Pietro wondered if the others could feel it. Himself, he would not have been surprised if lightning burst between them, so thick was the atmosphere. The Scarecrow had given Pietro his worst day on Earth. If God was as just as He was merciful, justice would be had this day.

Tearing his gaze from Pietro, Pathino broke into a quickened stride and did something wonderful. He knelt before Cardinal Gui. "You called for me, your Eminence?"

Gui looked ill, as well he might. Pathino had just linked them in the eyes of the other judges. "I did not, brother. It was his Excellency the Bishop of Albano, who wishes you to answer unfounded allegations made by the accused here today."

Turning, Pathino pretended to notice Pietro for the first time. "And do the accusations of a man outside the sight of God have such weight to call a brother from his holy work?"

"The search for truth is often unsettling," observed the Grand Penitentiary. "Ser Alaghieri has claimed that you are here falsely. I summoned you to hear his accusations in person and to refute them as best you may. Ser Alaghieri, produce your proof."

Pietro bowed deeply, leaning back on his right foot. "To begin, I testify that I've met this man twice.

Once during an attempt to kidnap the Scaliger's heir when the boy was just an infant. In his haste to get away, he threw the child to be mauled by a leopard. The helpless infant was rescued by myself and Tharwat al-Dhaamin, who put himself between the leopard and the boy. It was that night we met." He gestured to the tortured Moor, still suffering under the weight of the bar. Soon, my friend. Either I'll have you free, or I'll join you.

Pietro continued. "Pathino escaped, but tried again two years later, this time succeeding in spiriting away the child. I traced him to a cave once used by horse-thieves and there I confronted him. This man confessed not only his crimes, but the fact that he aspired to take over Verona and all the Feltro."

"And how would he achieve this?" asked the Grand Penitentiary.

"By telling the world the name of his father. He claims to be the bastard son of Alberto della Scala, half-brother to my lord Cangrande della Scala."

Another buzz of murmurs and exclamations. As the accusations grew more outrageous, Pietro's case became less believable. In proof of this, Gui scoffed. "Brother Gregor has never made such a claim to my ears."

"Nor would he. But if any of you had ever seen the Scaliger, you would see the resemblance plainly. And there is proof."

"Then produce it. So far I hear nothing but your own testimony, backed up by this heathen creature on the floor. Hardly unimpeachable witnesses."

"Very well. Though the proof must come from Pathino himself." Pietro turned and carefully produced a document from his bag. "Here is a drawing of a medallion. You can see by its strange swirls and knots that it is unique. It was torn off the kidnapper in the first attempt to snatch the child. A year later, in the kingdom of Aragon, it was then stolen from the corpse of Ignazzio, the murdered astrologer. I myself saw it about Pathino's neck during the second kidnapping, the night Pathino murdered my groom and Montecchio's father." As the drawing of the medallion was passed from his hand up to the dais, Pietro saw Pathino stiffen and Gui's eyes narrow. "Recently I realized that this medallion, so important to the murderer, might be significant in other ways. And I was correct." Pietro produced a second document from his bag. "This is a letter from Manoello Giudeo, Master of Revels at the court of Verona. He is very old, older even than the Scaliger's steward. And he writes that he can identify this medallion."

"What is it, then?" asked Cardinal Poggetto, practically drooling in excitement.

"Yes, lad," droned Cardinal de Baune, fanning himself in perpetual boredom. "Out with it."

Pietro obliged. "This medallion was a gift to Alberto della Scala from Sir William Wallace, a Scottish knight, as recompense for the aid of a few Veronese soldiers at the battle of Stirling Bridge in the year of our Lord 1297."

A greater stir than any before it. William Wallace was a name well-known in this land, so close to England. Thirty years earlier he had thwarted the English king Edward I, and done much to pave the way for Robert the Bruce to expand his realm and demand Scottish liberty.

Gui turned a pleading face to the Bishop of Albano. "Brother, this tale grows wilder by the minute. Are we to take the word of a jester, and evidently a Hebrew one at that? This story can only be a fiction!"

Pietro pulled out a second letter. Bless you, little sister! "Your graces, I have here corroboration from the Abbess of the convent of Santa Maria in Organo, in Verona. She too remembers the medallion, and especially the circumstances surrounding it coming to Verona. It seems that not only did Verona lend soldiers to Sir William, but that many died, among them Alberto della Scala's own nephew. The

572

medallion was sent by Wallace to honour the dead Scaliger's bravery. It was then given by Alberto della Scala as a love token to Pathino's mother, a serving wench on the Montecchio lands."

Pietro turned to gaze at Pathino. "Her name was Speranza Pathossa, whose name meant the Hopeful Pity. She befriended Alberto della Scala in his early years, and when she discovered her pregnancy he gave her the medallion as proof of her son's heritage. He then bestowed her in a convent in Verona where she was delivered of her burden, whom she named Gregorio." Pietro held Pathino's glare, trying to make each word cut like a knife. "She lived there until 1298, when for some reason she departed with her son in tow for parts unknown. It is still remembered by some of the elder nuns that the boy was called Pathino in a play on his mother's name. 'The little pity.'"

Rage rippled through Pathino as his mother's sin was laid bare for all to hear. Pietro braced to defend himself physically, should it come to that. But Pathino looked as bewildered as he was enraged, his eyes darting about the room from cardinal to cardinal. Gui was gazing at Pietro with grave interest, as if he were impressed with a clever child he'd thought to be a dolt.

"All this, your Graces, comes from the written testimony of Abbess Verdiana, who was a young novice when Speranza Pathossa entered the convent of Santa Maria in Organo. She recalls Alberto della Scala visiting the abbey on the eve of Speranza's departure. It is likely that the medallion was bestowed upon young Gregorio at that time."

Gui was about to object, but Cardinal Fieschi did it for him. "Very well, very well. Even if we accept that this medallion is what you say, and that this sadly common story is true, what does it have to do with Brother Gregor? You say you saw him wearing it, but that's hardly proof. How do we know this man is the pathetic child you speak of? What connects Brother Gregor to this medallion?"

Pietro pointed. "He's wearing it now."

It was a huge risk. Tharwat had searched Pathino's rooms and come away empty. It was possible their foe had hidden it somewhere safe until Cangrande and Cesco were out of the way. But having killed for it, Pietro could not believe that Pathino would let it out of his sight again. Tharwat's life, Pietro's own life, his very soul, all hung in the balance on this single guess.

Everyone was staring at Brother Gregor, waiting for him to refute this claim. When he made no move of any kind, Pietro knew he'd been right. Lowering his accusing finger, he returned the glare of hatred that the false friar turned towards him.

"Brother Gregor," said the Grand Penitentiary softly, "please show us what hangs about your neck."

Pietro expected him to resist, to run. But instead Pathino reached down his tunic's front and withdrew the chain bearing the medallion. It was still missing the pearls, but otherwise shone as brightly as a polished sword. A sword of justice.

"Your Graces," said Pietro loudly. "Twice failing to unseat his legitimate brother and gain control of Verona, this man came here to trick the Church into doing his work for him. His plan was to put Cangrande into conflict with the Holy See and have both the Scaliger and his heir removed from power. Then, with this medallion as proof, he meant to return to Verona, claim his rights as the last son of Alberto della Scala, and get himself elected Capitano."

"And you, Ser Alaghieri?" asked Cardinal Colonna. "Where do you fall in this?"

"Your Excellency, through luck and the grace of God above, I thwarted Pathino's two attempts to kidnap the Scaliger's heir. Because of this, I became a personal vendetta for him. Pathino used his position to sully my good name, and that of both my father and the lord of Verona, creating conflict with the Church where there was none. I daresay Pathino's lies drove the Scaliger into the arms of Emperor Ludwig."

As Pietro spoke, an examination was made of the drawing, the letters, and the medallion itself. When all the judges had read and seen for themselves, the Bishop of Albano turned to Pathino. "Do you have anything to say, brother?"

"I do. Much, in fact. But not here, and not to you."

"Do you deny the accusations?"

"Of what am I accused?"

"Of kidnapping, murder, treachery. Most grievous of all, of deceiving the Holy Roman Church by taking false orders to gain a temporal victory."

"Your Excellency," said Pathino, his eyes near feverish, "I take no charge more seriously than following the will of God. And I tell you now, God Himself has ordained my path. I am destined to greatness, and I am now as ever His willing instrument. I have broken no oath that God did not tell me to break, nor done aught but in His name. Holy execution is not murder, nor is it wrong to remove unholy creatures from God's light and presence. I have done nothing wrong."

This extraordinary speech sealed Pathino's fate. He might have been able to talk himself out of his plight. But to say before a collection of Inquisitors that he alone knew God's will was tantamount to putting his body on the rack and turning the wheel himself.

Hearing these words, Gui stepped away from Brother Gregor and swiftly crossed back to his seat on the platform. This retreat was a physical and metaphorical distancing of himself from this terrible mess in which he'd found himself bemired.

Pietro took that moment to launch his summary. "My lords, your most gracious Graces, I hope it is now plain to this court that the accusations against both myself and Cangrande della Scala are false, a direct result of a coordinated campaign, devised and carried out over several years, to discredit us before just such a court as this. We have lost our position in the view of God Almighty, not because of our sins, but because of this envious, scheming, devious, murderous person who has used Holy Mother Church to his own ends, playing upon innocent priests and noble prelates as a musician does his lute. He has spread lies. He has poisoned the holy well against us.

"Neither the Scaliger nor I lay claim to perfection. Far from it. But our sins are not unique. They are the common sins of Man. Both he and I hope for salvation, as do all men. We strive to know Christ and follow His teaching. All we ask is the chance to again walk in His light, and try as other men do to find the path to the Lord." He pointed at Tharwat. "Nor has this good man, heathen-born though he may have been, committed any crime against the Church. He undertook his actions in the employ of Verona, but for the good of all, in the cause of justice—"

The Grand Penitentiary waved Pietro to silence. "Ser Alaghieri, enough. This matter demands consideration. In light of the numerous shocking revelations of this afternoon, there is much to mull over. We must send to Verona, and Scotland, and Ravenna, and Aragon, to determine if all that has been claimed is indeed true. And I must warn you, Ser Alaghieri, if you have trifled with this court, if you have played us false, I will see you damned to the lowest pit of your father's Hell."

The Grand Penitentiary paused. After a moment, he shook his head. "Yet it seems to me that you may indeed have been abused. If this is so, we shall do what we can to make amends. For this time, take both the Moor and Brother Gregor away. Guards, release the Moor from his bonds and tend to his wounds. Though I cannot condone what he has done, clearly we are in his debt for exposing a viper in our midst. But neither may I free him without making certain of all these facts." He turned to Cardinal Gui. "Brother Bernardo, if all this is true, you have yourself been grievously wronged by one in whom you placed your trust. What say you?"

Quivering in rage, Gui bowed his head. "I say you are most wise, brother. We must take the time to find the truth to all this. For myself, I find these reports difficult to believe."

"For myself," said Cardinal Colonna imperiously, "I think the good Cardinal should recuse himself. Whatever the truth of the matter, he has clearly been a part of the drama, and cannot be an impartial judge of it."

It was an enormous insult, monumental. But what was that to a man who'd once slapped a pope? Seeing an opportunity, Pietro put on a grave expression. "If I may speak to that, your Excellency? I would prefer the learned Cardinal Gui to remain upon the council. For all that Pathino played him false, he is as intelligent and reasonable a man as I've ever met. I trust his judgment implicitly."

As Gui purpled, Pietro schooled his face to remain placidly sincere. To force the great Inquisitor to stand there and be defended by an accused heretic was a divine balancing of scales that would warm the cockles of Pietro's heart for years to come. *If I live that long.*

Pietro's smug self-satisfaction vanished as Tharwat was carried out, no longer attached to that horrible bar, but still in agony. *His eye! How can you repair his eye?*

579

The judges departed, full of conversation. O, the stories they would tell! Pietro felt sure he was about to be subjected to a new round of dinner invitations.

As the guards came for Pathino, the spaventa-passeri finally roused. Shaking them off, he took two quick steps towards Pietro. He was grasped at once, but his face strained forward, his teeth bared in a twisted version of Cangrande's famous allegria. "The Count of San Bonifacio isn't done with you, boy." Pathino was hauled away, straining towards Pietro, grinning like a maniac.

The Count of San Bonifacio? He'd once been Pathino's partner, along with Cangrande's wife, to remove the Scaliger's heir. But he'd paid for his crimes and expired the same night Pietro had saved Cesco. What could he have to do with any of this?

Confused, Pietro was wrenched back to the present by the expression on Petrarch's face. It was such a look of betrayed fury that he wondered if he'd lost yet another friend in his quest to retain his honour.

Then Petrarch burst out laughing and joyfully threw his arms around Pietro. "Pietro, you scoundrel! Wait until I tell my Laura!"

Twenty-Four

For several days thereafter the whole of Avignon was buzzing about the extraordinary happenings at the Penitentiary. A Moorish spy from Verona! A murderer hidden in a friar's robes! Bernardo Gui humiliated! And at the center of it all the handsome, brave, and devout son of a poet, who for three years had suffered under an unjust papal interdiction, only to prove himself a perfect son of Christ. It was the stuff of song, and there were many who tried their hands at composing it.

But they lacked for details. Thus Petrarch found himself besieged by callers and letters. Gherardo was invited to dine everywhere. Oddly, Lucia stayed at home, her ongoing stomach sickness a frustrating prevention to this amazing social opportunity. Pietro felt a shameful relief that she was not out there spreading gossip, though doubtless she was writing of it to everyone she knew.

Pietro himself made no calls. It would be poor form, he thought, to be seen reveling in his victory. If indeed a victory it had been. He remained guilty of the original crime, and understood all too well that the Church might condemn him just to save face. So he did nothing that could be interpreted by the holy fathers as arrogant or presumptuous. He celebrated his thirtieth birthday in relative silence, quietly accepting goblets lifted in his honour by Petrarch and Gherardo.

There was one invitation, however, he could not refuse. Four days after the hearing he called upon Bonagratia and Occam. They were beside themselves with praise, both for his daring and his ability to keep such remarkable secrets for so long.

"Petrarch, you truly knew nothing of any of this?" demanded Occam.

"Neither jot nor tittle," confirmed Petrarch ruefully. "Ser Alaghieri wanted to shield me from his plans, lest they swallow us whole."

"As they might have done!" exclaimed Bonagratia. "Pietro, you have no idea what a cat you've put among the cardinals! Gui is in seclusion, refusing to speak to anyone at present. In fact, I hear he's planning on traveling abroad."

Pietro tried not to appear relieved. "Oh?"

"You may recall I mentioned there was to be a gathering at a remote monastery in Italy. There my Franciscan brothers will confer with the Dominican emissaries of Pope John and thrash out the matter of the poverty of Christ. Gui is now going. As am I! I may well find myself traveling with him. I hope I can resist gloating over his recent misfortunes." Bonagratia's smile belied his stated hope.

"And you, William? Are you going?"

"I am not invited. Though I have grown quite sympathetic, it is not my cause. And I do not think Gui would welcome a logical refutation of his position by an Englishman – not so soon after he was out-foxed by a young Italian pup. I fear, my friend, you have made the lives of whoever he next fixes upon much more difficult. I pity his future victims."

"Speaking of victims," said Bonagratia, "have you heard anything of your Moorish friend?"

"Only that his injuries have been tended to. I hope he will find himself included in a blanket pardon. In this case he was acting for Verona, not for me."

"You must tell us all," said Bonagratia.

Having received so much help from these two ecclesiastics, Pietro could hardly deny them. He allowed Petrarch to tell the tale of the trial itself, then laid out the chain of events from the day of his knighting all the way through the final words of Pathino to the court.

When the tale was through, Occam stroked his chin. "I wonder that Cardinal Guidoni has not applied his many inquisitive skills to Brother Gregor. If any man was deserving of such attentions…"

Pietro had to agree.

On the way back to Carpentras, Petrarch was mulling some idea, a smile shifting across his face. "Pietro, so far I've not made any splash in this case. All my glory is reflected. Would you object to me making a point?"

"As long as the point doesn't turn into an edge to cleave my head from my shoulders."

"The point I have in mind is one they cannot object to without opening themselves to scorn." He explained his idea. "The Church will be furious, but they'll have no choice save consent."

Pietro didn't like Petrarch's scheme, thinking it too clever by half. Still, after keeping Petrarch in the dark for so long, he owed his host. "I'll consider it."

They arrived at Carpentras to find the household staff oddly furtive and subdued. It was up to Gherardo to explain. Leading them into Petrarch's study and shutting the doors, he looked both angry and sick.

"What is it?" asked Pietro. "Have we heard from the Penitentiary?"

"No. Nothing like that." Gherardo looked back and forth between them, then blurted it out. "Lucia isn't ill. She's pregnant. And she says – she says it's yours."

Under the reproachful glare of both brothers, Pietro hardly seemed able to breathe.

"I suppose marriage is out of the question," said Gherardo. "At least until you can go into a church. She can't marry an excommunicant."

"It wasn't me!" protested Pietro for the hundredth time. "I swear, Gherardo, I swear, I have never in any way taken advantage of your sister!"

"You didn't have to take advantage," answered Gherardo heavily. "We've all seen the way she's thrown herself at your head. I doubt any man could have resisted. But I thought you, of all men—"

"I'm not the father!"

A new day had cooled tempers, though it had been a loud and restless night. Petrarch had gone to confront Lucia, and she'd declared in no uncertain terms that the child was Ser Alaghieri's. "You yourself saw him throw me out of his room after having his way with me!" she'd screamed for all the house to hear.

Pietro had himself demanded an interview, and been flatly refused. "You've done enough damage," Petrarch told him shortly. "And damaged your cause as well. This will be about Avignon by tomorrow. Suddenly the noble and pious victim is a lecher and ungrateful guest."

Pietro wanted to weep. He offered to swear upon a Bible, upon his sword, upon his own life that he'd never had congress with Lucia. But Petrarch had simply stormed off in a towering rage. Having weathered the betrayal of the trial, it seemed his sister's lost virtue was a bridge too far.

After a restless night, Pietro had come downstairs to whatever fresh Hell awaited him. He found Gherardo alone. The young man looked sad and disappointed, but clearly attempting to be a voice of reason. He just as clearly did not believe Pietro's repeated protests.

"I understand why you wouldn't admit it," said Gherardo patiently. "It doesn't look well for you, I confess. But living in this house for two years, there's only so much pressure a man can take before he succumbs to his needs. I understand that. If the stories are true, your father and brother certainly knew it too."

Pietro clapped his hands to his forehead. Yes, his father had fathered a few bastards, and Poco was notorious for it. *And they think I'm just another randy Alaghieri dog who chases after a bitch in heat. Bitch! Just the word! I cannot believe Lucia is doing this! Why me? What did I ever do?*

You refused her, you fool. This is an exquisite revenge for that monumental insult.

Gherardo was still attempting to convince Pietro to admit his fault when Petrarch walked in. He looked better rested than Pietro had expected, and when he spoke his voice was subdued, but reasonable. "Leave him be, brother. I believe his innocence in this."

Pietro sagged in relief while Gherardo stared. "Did she confess it was someone else?"

"No," said Petrarch, taking an apple from a tray and biting into it. "But I know my sister. And by now we should certainly know Pietro. I ask you, Gherardo, as much as it pains me to – whom do you believe? Whose word is better? The knight, or the whore?" Pietro and Gherardo both flinched, but Petrarch carried on. "Do you think our flighty, flirty sister is telling the truth? Or should we believe the man who may keep secrets, but never lies about them."

Gherardo sank into a chair. "Pietro, of course. Damn. Sorry, Pietro." He slammed his hands together. "Damn!"

Squinching his face, Petrarch threw his sour apple aside. "I know."

Pietro needed to say something. "I thank you. You didn't have to believe me. Not after what you saw."

"I know what I saw. I saw you putting a woman out of your room. I know that, had she been there at your request, you would never have treated her so roughly. No," said Petrarch wearily, "this is my sister's attempt to save face. She's dishonoured herself and our house. She's probably hoping I'll force you to marry her and rescue her from disgrace. But that I cannot ask. Especially now, after she's played you so false."

The effort to speak these words was clearly costing him. But Pietro was grateful beyond reason. He could imagine little worse than being married to Lucia. "I'm so sorry, my friend."

"It's for us to be sorry. She has dragged your good name into this, at just the moment when you should be shining brightest. Alas, what Gherardo was saying holds true. It will reflect badly upon you. Because – I'm sorry, I can't publicly accuse her of lying."

"I understand." Pietro sighed heavily. "I should leave, take a room in Avignon."

"Don't be foolish." Petrarch's protest was half-hearted.

"If I stay and don't marry her, it will hurt you, too. Everyone will assume you approve, that you're my pander."

"Or that I know there's not a lick of truth in it. You cannot go."

"I must. Here, I'm a focus for scandal. And Lucia can make a scene every day. I don't think I could endure that. Besides, one way or another, I'm leaving soon. You have to live here after I've gone. You need to cut me dead."

Recognizing the truth of Pietro's words, Petrarch sighed. "I could murder her."

Pietro gave a wry laugh. "At least we know what forgiveness for that would cost."

Petrarch flashed a weak smile. "I will continue to serve as your lawyer. *That* I insist upon. And if we can root out the real father, we can make him take responsibility."

"I'll look into that," said Gherardo, a dark gleam in his eye.

Pietro nodded. "Very well. And there's one more thing I can do for you both in return." He took a breath. "I won't deny it. In public, I'll say nothing. Nothing at all. If the real father doesn't come forward, let them think it was me. As Gherardo says, my father and brother are famous for philandering. Cangrande, too. It's certainly not unheard of."

Petrarch had tears in his eyes. "Are you sure?"

"No," admitted Pietro ruefully, his lopsided smile flashing briefly. "But I owe you more than I can ever repay for the last year and a half in your house."

"You've paid—"

"I don't mean money. I couldn't have done any of this without you. If it helps you to share a little of this disgrace, I'll shoulder some. I should have done even more to discourage her."

"Short of castrating yourself, I don't think there's any more you could have done. Thank you." Petrarch held out his arm. Pietro clasped it, then Gherardo's, then went upstairs to pack his things.

The scandal was a pleasant autumn diversion for the people of Avignon. Pietro leaving the house made his guilt obvious to all, and his refusal to speak of it sealed his sin in everyone's eyes. "Feet of clay," they all said. "These knights are all a randy lot. And to treat his friend's sister so! Tch tch."

Days turned into weeks. Men smiled at him in the street, while women turned up their noses at the sight of him – though some of the younger ones tittered behind their hands. Living again in the fetid reek of Avignon put Pietro off his food, and worry kept him from sleeping. Not worry over the rumours – there was nothing he could do about those. No, he fretted for his friend. It took every ounce of Pietro's restraint to keep from marching up to the Penitentiary and demanding to see Tharwat. His dreams were filled with knives laid to his eyes, and he could not imagine how the Moor's sight in that eye might be saved. The eye would surely dry out. Beside the unthinkable pain that would cause, was Tharwat now blind in that eye?

Frustrated, Pietro busied himself with his lackluster commentary on the *Commedia*, and with writing letters to Verona's many informants. If, as he hoped, he was soon to return, he had to know what was going on.

There were always tales of Cesco. Some were worrying – risks taken, contests, challenges, games with mortal stakes. But Pietro had to admit that none of them were particularly unusual. There were no attempts on his life, no plots, no surprises.

The same could not be said of the Emperor, who was still looking askance at his Italian lords, wondering which of them had known about the poison that had so nearly claimed him.

The imperial court had not yet arrived in Rome – after the poisoning attempt, Ludwig was suddenly very cautious of his Italian allies. It was October and the court had gotten only as far as Cortona. Founded by a son of Noah after the great flood, the ancient city of Cortona had jubilantly welcomed Emperor Heinrich VII fifteen years earlier, and Frederick II sixty years before that. But the city had just recently been bought by a papal bull restoring its diocese within the communal bounds, so Ludwig's welcome was tepid at best.

Over in Padua, Marsilio da Carrara would have been wise to have men tasting his food as well. The same day that Pietro had stepped before the Grand Penitentiary's court, Carrara's cousin Niccolo had launched a campaign into Paduan lands, using soldiers paid for by Mastino della Scala. Not only paid for, but led – in person. While Cangrande was dealing with the Emperor, Mastino had breached the truce and launched an offensive against Padua, upon the pretext that he'd been invited in as liberator.

He and Fuchs rode at the front of the army of Italian, French, and German mercenaries. At first they tried to stay on the good side of the locals, paying for food and drink as they went. But when the natives of the Padovano remained hostile, Mastino let his troops off the leash. Crying 'havoc,' they pillaged and burned, destroying what crops and livestock they didn't eat.

Mastino versus Marsilio, thought Pietro as he read. *May they bring about a mutual destruction.*

The letters described two attempts to surprise the city of Padua itself, but both times Mastino's forces were betrayed. In retaliation, Marsilio da Carrara arrested his cousin's sons and sacked his house, burning it to the ground.

Finally Mastino and Niccolo withdrew to Este, under Veronese control since the last war. There they wintered and waited for the campaigning season to begin anew.

There was a piece of good news out of Verona, by way of Vicenza. Morsicato's wife was recovering. The doctor still had no idea what had caused her long decline, but she was on her feet again, and he'd been able to dispense with the hired nurse. Pietro was relieved for them both – unable to cure his own wife, Morsicato's medical practice had withered on the vine. Luckily he had his knight's pension to live on, as well as a steady income from the Nogarola household. But Morsicato was not a man to sit idle, and Pietro knew his lack of work would have driven him half-insane.

All at once came some shocking news from England. A letter from Cesco's friendly rival at the tourney, Sir William Montagu, was forwarded to Pietro from Cesco, but by then the story had permeated the whole of the Avignon court, quite quelling any remaining interest in the sordid dalliance of an Italian knight. This was a scandal that was far more delicious!

When Edward II's iron constitution seemed likely to last unto eternity, his wife devised a final trial for him to endure. It was well known at Court why the queen despised her husband so deeply, and her evil inspiration stemmed from that same root. According to Montagu, the queen had her husband trussed pinioned by a table, his legs spread-eagled under him and his arms pulled forward, exposing his backside. A drenching horn, such as was used to medicine sick animals, was then inserted in the king's anus, through which a burning, barbed poker was rammed up Edward's rectum, where it was slowly turned, each turn bringing a little more pressure, until he was dead.

The horrified Montagu penned an ironic coda:

> On the eve of the King's burial, it was given out to the common people that he'd died a natural death.

Never one to let another have the last word, Cesco had scrawled his own *bon mot*. Cicero seemed to be a recent favourite, and this quote was from the defense of Publius Sestius on a charge of violence:

> Cum dignitate otium.

Which, in this context, translated as, *"With retirement comes dignity."*

Laughing in spite of himself, Pietro reflected once more on his ward's dubious sense of humour.

Twenty-Five

Rumours continued to swirl around Pietro, with many remarking upon the myriad of letters flying between his rented rooms and Carpentras. Most asserted that it was Petrarch demanding Pietro do the right thing and marry the girl. But there were several who knew the girl in question, and had their doubts as to who the father might be. Whichever, everyone was certain there was a rift between Alaghieri and Petrarch.

Yet, when the papal summons came at the end of October, Petrarch joined Pietro once again at the door to the Penitentiary, and they were seen to smile together, and even embrace. As they entered, gossips went flying with this fragment of news, to be trumpeted around the streets with more import than a papal bull. This was life at Avignon.

"How are things?" Pietro asked, allowing Petrarch to choose how to answer.

The would-be poet cut right to the heart. "Lucia has at last admitted to me that you are not, and could not be, the father. But she will not say so publicly. Nor will she tell me who the father is. However, we cannot allow my sister's disgrace to keep you from dining with us tonight. The house is sad and lonely without your presence."

"If I'm free to come, I will. Of course if I do pay a call on your household, it will look as though I am admitting paternity."

"Or sharing a celebratory feast."

"Let's not count our chickens yet. There are many ways yet for them to damn me. Gui will be looking for revenge, I'm sure."

Petrarch looked startled. "Gui? Haven't you heard? He won't be present. He's left Avignon already. He and Bonagratia both departed for that conference on Christ's poverty in some Godforsaken monastery in Italy. You won that battle. That's one less vote we need worry about."

Despite his manifest relief, this raised a new concern. "Then who will be the deciding vote? We have two right now, I think – Orsini and Colonna. And I think the Grand Penitentiary may be on our side. But there's no way Fieschi, Poggetto, or de Baune will vote in my favour. Which means the scales are evenly balanced. Who makes the decision in the case of a tie vote?"

Petrarch shrugged. "All we can do is present the facts. Unless you have any other surprises for me?"

Pietro shook his head. "I used them all last time."

"Alas!" Petrarch grinned. "I was looking forward to another spectacle. Guess I'll have to create one myself." A remark that worried Pietro no end.

They were ushered up the stairs and into the same salon as before. There were still seven chairs, although this time the central one was grander than before – the Grand Penitentiary was likely asserting his authority.

This time the judges were not here before them, and the duo had an opportunity to lay out their papers. The two that mattered most sat at the center of the table, enclosed by sheets of leather. Before leaving Carpentras, Pietro had agreed to Petrarch's daring plan to poke the Holy See in the eye. Now he worried that they were brandishing a club where a smile might be better. But Petrarch was determined to impress his Laura, whoever she was.

The doors opened and six judges filed in. For a moment Pietro wondered if Gui's chair was to be kept vacant. But, instead of sitting on the central throne, the Grand Penitentiary took Gui's seat for himself. *What does that—?*

The doors behind them opened and a voice rang out, "His Holiness Pope Johannes the Twenty-Second, Most Holy Father, Pontifex Maximus, the Bishop of Rome and Avignon. Praise be unto him and his glory, the vicar of Christ on Earth, ruler of nations and of men!"

In contrast to the magnificent titles, the figure that shuffled in was tiny, delicate and diminutive, practically swallowed by his hat and gown, despite their being tailored to him. Even the red shoes, modeled after the boots worn by Roman Emperors, bore high heels to give him added height.

Goggling, Pietro quickly straightened. The Pope? The final vote was to be cast by his Holiness himself? Why had they not, then, convened at the papal palace?

Because they meant to surprise us. Or else not draw attention to this proceeding until it is decided...

The Pope coughed as he climbed the platform steps, and Pietro recalled that John was a consumptive. Avignon's foul air must have been murderous to him. Little wonder his palace was so perfectly constructed.

The short figure crossed to the central throne, and Pietro saw that the throne itself, set on the pedestal, had a cleverly designed footrest to disguise the fact that the Pope's feet couldn't reach the floor.

In his late seventies, the cobbler's son looked like a bearded gnome. But there was a great mind in there. He had studied law at Montpellier and medicine in

Paris. And rumour said that he'd been the chief architect of the destruction of the Templars, bringing about the dark Friday 13th, marking that day as unlucky forever more. All that before maneuvering himself into being elected pope, offering oaths and promises like the lawyer he was. True to his word, he had never ridden a horse from the day of his election to this. This man was nobody's fool.

In his appointed place, the Pope nodded to his cousin, the Grand Penitentiary, to proceed. The other judges took their seat as the Bishop of Albano began a long speech. A much more formal affair than before, the history of the charges was given great weight. After all, it had been Pope John himself who had signed the order to excommunicate Pietro. This time there were no voices raised questioning the cause.

Then the Grand Penitentiary reached the events of the previous hearing. "Under close interrogation, this villain Pathino, who was known to us as Brother Gregor, has confessed all his crimes. He has also had the audacity to proclaim himself the heir apparent to the Scaligeri titles and lands, as the eldest remaining son of Alberto della Scala. Though we have sent to Scotland to look into the history of this medallion, and sent to Verona and other cities to probe further into all the matters testified to before this court, the confession of Pathino makes matters simpler, at least so far as he is concerned.

"But we must confess that we are troubled by any number of matters. The placing of a spy within the Holy Palace itself, for whatever cause, cannot be winked at. Nor can your master be excused his hubristic embrace of the renegade Ludwig, who styles himself Holy Roman Emperor. Especially when said embrace involves throwing a gracious and Christian offer of forgiveness in Cardinal Poggetto's teeth. What is the Holy See to do when the kindness of Mother Church is cast aside with careless negligence? How are we to reconcile the Scaliger's stated desire to rejoin the fold with his public disdain of our benevolence?"

This was Petrarch's moment, and he seized it. "Your Holiness, your Graces, I believe I have a solution. Ser Alaghieri is guilty of one crime only, that of refusing to collect an additional tithe from his benefice. On the other hand, the Scaliger's list of sins is long and varied. So long, indeed, I had to write the sins down individually to keep track of them. If you'll allow me, Your Holiness, I have here listed out each offense, and placed upon it a monetary value we feel would be fair."

Pietro was hardly breathing as copies of the list were passed around. His nerves were high because the numbers were calculated directly from the list of indulgences given them by Occam and Bonagratia. They had counted Cangrande's various sins down to the last sou.

The meaning was plain. So too the threat. We have the list of indulgences. If you do not yield, then we will make the list public, and in the outcry that follows you will lose your battle with the Franciscans over the poverty of Christ. In short, Petrarch was telling the holy fathers to restore Pietro and Cangrande, or else be exposed to an even greater scandal than Pathino.

The Grand Penitentiary looked taken aback, Colonna dismayed, Orsini and Fieschi disgusted. Poggetto was doing divisions with chalk on a slate tablet, while de Baune's eyes burned into Petrarch's head. Only the Pope seemed to take the menu of sins calmly. He even smiled a fraction. He opened his mouth, and Pictro was startled to hear such a strong, clear voice bellow up from inside so small a figure. "You came to these figures yourself, I trust."

Petrarch bowed his head. "Your Holiness, how else?"

"How else indeed." There was a long pause. "Double them."

Cardinal Colonna hissed through his teeth. Orsini balled up the paper in his fist. The others did not react in any way. The Pope had just made clear what all knew, but was never spoken – that salvation was for sale. It was just a matter of haggling over the price.

If that was the case, then Pietro had hope. "Your Holiness, forgive me. I think that price is still too low for what we desire." The Pope raised his eyebrows and gestured for Pietro to go on. "First, the Church is precious to me. Having been cut off from it these last three years has been a terrible burden, and there is no price I would not pay to be again admitted into the ranks of the faithful." There, that didn't sound so bad. And he hadn't accused the Pope of being wrong in evicting him from the faith. "Secondly, there is the matter of Tharwat al-Dhaamin. As the Bishop of Albano has rightly stated, it is a grave crime to enter into the employ of the papal palace under a dual purpose. That he fulfilled the one, looking after the animals, does not excuse his second, nor does the fact that the information he discovered has rescued the Church from harbouring a fugitive and villain.

"But the fact is that this crime is not his own. As the good bishop said in his opening statement, this deed must be laid at the feet of the Capitano di Verona. It was under Cangrande's orders that Tharwat al-Dhaamin came here. I ask that Tharwat be excused this – he has already suffered enough punishment – and that this charge be added to Cangrande's list of offences."

"You do not seem to love your master," observed Cardinal Poggetto as he rubbed his nose, accidentally smearing it with chalk.

"I hope I love him as much as he deserves. But I am here begging for reinstatement before God, and it does me nothing but ill to deal doubly with this court. I speak only as an honest man. To that end, your Holiness, I will be entirely frank. Though I am here to restore both myself and the lord of Verona to God's sight, and beg the freedom of the elderly Moorish slave who has never been a threat to the Holy See, there is a cause even nearer to my heart. As you all know, I was entrusted with the care of the Scaliger's heir. As you are also aware, he is illegitimate. While I am here, unworthy as I am, before the Holy Father, I would be remiss to my sworn duty as the boy's foster father, as one of four men present at his Christening, if I did not beg for his status to be legitimized. I have met his mother, and she is a good Christian lady, despite producing a child on the wrong side of the sheets."

Cardinal Fieschi shifted uncomfortably as Cardinal de Baune leaned forward. "Who is she? Where is she from?"

Where was she from, you mean, thought Pietro. He felt in his bones that she was dead. "Her name is Donna Maria. I know no other. She gave up her son to protect him, surely the act of a Christian lady. There had already been an attempt on his life."

The Pope spoke again, his loud tone erupting from his tiny frame. "So many plots! I doubt he will live to his majority. But what proof do we have that he is on the side of the angels? Does he not now reside with the imposter Emperor, who even at this moment Is trekking to Rome to gild his brow with another false crown?"

"All this is true, your Holiness," said Pietro, bowing his head. "But he is not there by choice. Francesco is a hostage to his father's good behavior. As you may have heard, after the Lord of Verona rashly refused the offer sent to him by your Holiness – a refusal born, I believe, from Pathino's villainy in setting Cangrande against the Holy See – after this, Cangrande and Ludwig met. It did not go well. Cangrande did not allow for Ludwig's pride, and the German responded by taking Cangrande's heir hostage."

"I see," said the Pope, stroking his chin. "Would we not be strengthening his hand, legitimizing Cangrande's son while he is in the Bavarian's hand?"

"Possibly," admitted Pietro. "But it would also show Lord della Scala that he has options open to him other than the Emperor. That, combined with his own reinstatement, might be enough to make Ludwig worry. Already he has enough to be fearful of, with attempts on his life. It would make Ludwig need Cangrande more, and Cangrande need Ludwig less."

"Are you saying we could pry the Scaligeri family from their Ghibelline ways? That seems doubtful."

"Your Holiness, Cangrande della Scala is a man who looks always for Verona's best interests. For the last decade and more he has been a loyal Ghibelline – but that was when the imperial throne was in dispute. With Ludwig and Heinrich quarrelling over the German title, Cangrande was left alone to run the Feltro as he saw best. With Ludwig's ascension, things have fundamentally changed. He will not want imperial forces meddling in Verona. He is a man accustomed to rule, not being ruled."

"Then why should we ever take him in? For he must submit to the Church if we are to claim him back."

"Your Holiness, if the Holy See were still in Rome, there might be cause for concern. But I believe distance will make the Scaliger an excellent friend. He will obey papal bulls, tithe and convert, root out heresy as his father did before him. Yet the daily running of his lands will be entirely in his hands. He is an autocrat, and a pragmatic one. But also a man who holds oaths inviolable. He will obey them to the letter."

"A lawyer, eh? Well, an oath is a contract with God, and all contracts must be negotiated. Though I am confused. I was told you did not believe the Church should be involved with money. Render unto Caesar, you said."

Startled, Pietro found sudden inspiration in one of the pope's many names, barked out a few minutes earlier. "Money may belong to Caesar. But one of Caesar's titles was pontifex maximus, a title held today by Your Holiness. When Constantine combined the empire and the church, he made the Caesars the heads of Christianity. So, by extraction, the Holy See is Caesar's heir."

"Well argued! I see why our Cardinal Gui was so impressed by you." Pope John nodded to the Grand Penitentiary, effectively ending the interview.

The Bishop of Albano stood. "Ser Alaghieri, you have presented your case. If you will leave us to deliberate, we shall discuss your petition, and the penance you have offered."

"When shall we know?" asked Petrarch.

The Pope chuckled. "You'll have an accounting in God's own time."

Twenty-Six

Petrarch was smiling as they reached the outer doors. "Double wasn't enough? That's going to cost you, my friend."

Pietro grinned back. "It's Cangrande's money, not mine."

"Someone's going to make his master unhappy."

"He deserves some unhappiness. When do you think they'll vote?"

"This minute, I imagine."

"And how do you like our chances?"

Petrarch's saggy eyes squinnied tight. "I don't know. Colonna will support you. Orsini didn't like the offer of money – he wants the case decided upon merit alone. Fieschi seems to hate you, regardless. Poggetto will vote for you if the money is enough. I have no idea about de Baune."

"And His Holiness?"

"There's no way of knowing. He was friendly, but I hear he's friendliest with his enemies. If he thinks you're insulting him, he'll vote against you, and I'm afraid the Grand Penitentiary will vote with him. There's really no…"

Petrarch trailed off as he looked back over Pietro's shoulder. Turning, Pietro saw the unlikely pair of Cardinal Orsini and Cardinal Colonna descending the steps surrounded by their attendants. Orsini gave Pietro a half-smile. Then he shot a look of true revulsion at Petrarch and stormed off.

Sciarrillo Colonna was grinning as he strolled over to the young men. "We must forgive him. Old-fashioned. But money is the heart of Avignon, as it was the heart of Rome before. Without money, the Church cannot do its many great deeds. It is the grease for the axles of our holy carriage – it befouls the hands, but lets us run. Say, that's rather good! I'll have to remember it."

Both Pietro and Petrarch were close to leaping upon the elderly man. "Pardon me, your Excellency, but was there a vote?"

"A vote? Don't be foolish, lad. I'm here speaking with you, aren't I? I would hardly be doing so if you both were in disfavour. Ser Alaghieri, as we speak the Holy Father is signing a decree to restore both you and your master to the sight of God, and to legitimize the Greyhound's heir. You were persuasive, and where your silver tongue did not move heart, your golden purse did."

Petrarch whooped, kissing Pietro on both cheeks. Pietro himself was breathing easier than he had these last three years. But he noted the one omission in their victory. "And Tharwat?"

"Ah. The Moor. We don't quite know what to do with him. We execute heretics, not heathens. But this Mohammaden snuck into the papal palace and lived there for months, spying on the friars."

"He did the Church a service," said Pietro carefully.

"Which is why he continues to draw breath. And to be sure, he's paid for his offense. But no one feels he can be released as easily as that. Certainly not publicly. Then there's the matter of Pathino." The cardinal breathed in, coughed, and gagged. "O, what a stench!" Pulling a small bottle of perfume from his belt, he wagged it under his nose. "I must get away from this sewer. Ser Alaghieri, I presume you're heading back to Verona soon? Give this to your master." He handed across the Scottish medallion that had saved Pietro's life. "And call on me before you go!"

"I will," promised Pietro, slipping the chain around his neck. "And thank you."

"A pleasure! Especially entertaining. They'll be talking about it for months. Farewell, Ser Pietro Alaghieri. I feel we shall meet again very soon." With that cryptic statement, Sciarrillo turned to leave, but Petrarch called out to him. "Your Excellency! What was the count of the votes? Which way did the Holy Father go?"

Cardinal Colonna shrugged. "We'll never know how he would have voted. It wasn't necessary. Ser Alaghieri had four votes out of six in his favour. The pope did not have to commit himself at all."

"Four?" asked Pietro.

"Indeed! Mine, of course. Poor Orsini. The Grand Penitentiary. And Cardinal Fieschi. That was a surprise, I'll tell you. Euech – this air! Farewell!"

As the cardinal trotted off through the crowd, attended by his priestly servants, Pietro turned to Petrarch. "Fieschi?"

At first Petrarch looked confused. Then his face slowly hardened. "Pietro, come to dine. There is much to discuss, and not in the street."

Reaching Carpentras, Petrarch summoned his sister to his study. She was beginning to swell already, meaning she was several months gone. She was one of those women who positively glowed with the new life within her, in spite of its bastard status.

Seeing Pietro, she did a very slight curtsy, a smile curling her lips. "Ser Alaghieri."

Petrarch scowled. "Do you have an apology for him?"

Lucia's expression was sweetly blank. "Does he need one? I'd have thought his vindication was enough for one day."

Petrarch pointed a finger. "So you knew."

Pietro frowned. "Knew what?"

"That we'd win, that you'd be acquitted of any crime and restored. You knew, didn't you, sister?"

Lucia smiled. "I hoped. Prayed. Talked to my friends."

"Is one of those friends Cardinal Luca Fieschi?" demanded Petrarch.

Suddenly Pietro understood. Lucia had not been visiting with Fieschi's female relations. They had been brought to Avignon to hide her affair with the cardinal. She couldn't accuse him, or even hint that he might be the father. The wrath of the Church would come down and ruin her whole family, dependent as they were upon the Church for their living. So she had gone the obvious route, blaming someone as far outside the Church as could be, yet noble enough to excuse her. And Pietro's family was Florentine, as was hers.

In answer to her brother's question, Lucia didn't even blush. "He is a close friend."

"And in return for Pietro allowing men to think he was the father, Fieschi was willing to vote his way." Petrarch's appreciation was tempered by his disgust.

"I'd planned to ask Pietro to bear the shame, for my sake and his. But as it turned out, I didn't have to. He kept silent all on his own. Such a good man. I wish we had married. You'd make an excellent husband."

"And you, a horrible wife," retorted Petrarch.

Pietro shook his head, then said the right thing. "I suppose I owe you my thanks."

Lucia laughed. "I didn't do it for you! I did it for my brother, so he could win his case. He'll be famous now, and find a good post – either here, or in Verona. You can arrange that, I'm sure. You owe him, now. And me. At least as far as the public is concerned." She smirked at him. "Don't you wish now that you'd enjoyed me?"

The next few days were a blur. On Sunday Pietro attended mass for the first time in almost three years, and he could not help weeping silently at being admitted. Indeed, he was greeted with many congratulations after the service, along with winks and knowing looks. He now possessed quite a reputation.

Petrarch had chosen the church, his new favourite, Sainte-Claire d'Avignon. A pleasant place, and today the homily seemed aimed directly at Pietro – the story of the Prodigal Son. While he didn't quite agree with all of the bishop's conclusions, Pietro was so pleased to be back that he felt like he might shatter into shards of light.

Standing upon the Church steps on this brisk October morning, Petrarch was reveling in his own success while shielding Pietro from too many salacious stares. "If they think me a pander, so be it. We have nothing to be ashamed of. God knows it, and so do we. Let them gossip as they – there! Pietro, there!"

Pietro whirled about, expecting to behold soldiers or murderers or Pathino escaped and out for blood. Instead he beheld a breathtaking young woman emerging from the church. About seventeen years old, she was fair, with reddish-blonde hair under a richly jeweled mantle. She had not only the beauty of youth, but an undeniable refinement. A small mouth over a tiny, round chin, all below hooded eyes with thinly arched brows a painter would have envied. She bore herself with modest dignity, though she seemed to have a touch of resignation when she saw Petrarch staring at her.

Plucking Pietro by the arm, Petrarch guided him to where the young lady stood. "Pietro Alaghieri, allow me to name Mademoiselle Laura de Noves. Laura, this is Ser Alaghieri."

"Laura de Sade," corrected the lady gently, allowing Pietro to take her hand and kiss it. "I must congratulate you, ser. Our church was blessed this day with your presence. It is not often we see one brought back into the fold so dramatically."

"Thank you, mademoiselle. You are all too kind. I am equally honoured and blessed to be allowed to return."

"In truth, it was a most magnificent case," said Petrarch, literally shoving Pietro back a step. He was grinning like an idiot, and Pietro longed to slap sense into him. This was going to be a scene. "And so dramatic. Would you like to hear the details, mademoiselle?"

"Countess," she corrected again, also gently. "Ah, here comes my husband. Perhaps he would like to hear the details himself. Then he can relay them to me, if he thinks it fitting. Hugues, you remember Monsieur Petrarch, I'm sure. And this is Ser Alaghieri, of whom we hear so much that is excellent. Ser Alaghieri, this is my husband, the Comte de Sade."

Pietro hid his surprise in a deep bow. "I'm honoured—"

The Count had eyes only for Petrarch. "Again? My patience grows thin, boy. If you keep at her, I'll dun you at law the way you dun her in the street. Ser Alaghieri, I understand your friend here has saved you. I suggest you save him in turn, and keep him from the point of my sword."

"Hugues!" Laura's expression was one of consternation. "We are fortunate, with so many people eager to meet Ser Alaghieri, that we are able to have this introduction. And we can hardly blame them for attending church, can we? Come now, my love. Forgive us, Ser Alaghieri, Monsieur Petrarca. We must be going." Taking the Count by the arm, she led him away.

Having completely ignored the Count's warning, Petrarch was practically transported, staring after the lady as she held her husband's arm into their carriage. "Now Pietro, admit defeat. Not only is she real, my Laura is a beauty. Do you not agree?"

"A beauty," echoed Pietro.

In that moment, had his life depended upon it, Pietro would not have given voice to his actual opinion. Yes, Petrarch's Laura was a beauty. And resembled no one so much as Petrarch's own sister, the fallen Lucia.

Pietro called once more on Occam. After accepting the Englishman's heartfelt congratulations, Pietro offered to return the dangerous ledger. Occam declined, saying it was too perilous for him to hold. "Besides, you might need such a weapon someday. But I do have a request. Your ward is a page to the

Emperor, yes? Do you think he could give him a letter? Unofficially, of course."

"Of course." Accepting the sealed letter and tucking it away, Pietro waved off Occam's thanks. "No, thank you. For everything. It has been an honour to know you. And please say farewell to Bonagratia for me when he returns."

"I hope he does return. I have horrid dreams of Cardinal Gui's carriage overturning and killing all those within. Fortunately, I have never believed in the prophetic nature of dreams."

Pietro remembered a dream, long ago – fire, and a river of blood. "No. Better that dreams not come true. Not those kind, anyway. But my dream of being restored to the faithful has come to pass, and I thank God for it."

"As well you should! God gave you the tools to win a just victory in His name. Now be sure you honour Him by living a life worthy of His grace. And do that by continuing to use His greatest gift – reason."

Pietro laughed. "You sound like my father."

There were just two pieces of unfinished Avignon business left before Pietro could depart: Pathino, and Tharwat. Of the two, he cared far less for the spaventapasseri's fate than for his friend's freedom.

To that end, he used the feast thrown in his honour at the Colonna palace to corner Fieschi. The cardinal was uncomfortable, especially when Pietro hinted he knew who had fathered Lucia's bastard. After making clear he was willing to go on allowing men to think he was the father, Pietro issued his conditions. "My trouble is the longer I stay, the harder it is to remain silent. I grow tired of knowing looks and ribald remarks."

"Then you should return to Verona with all speed," observed Fieschi, sweating.

"I would love to. My dearest wish, really. But I cannot leave until I have my friend Tharwat safely with me, and Pathino either imprisoned for life or executed."

"You don't want to take Pathino back to Verona?"

Pietro had thought of that. But he knew the curse on the Scaligeri family. Sanguis meus. 'Blood of my blood,' old Alberto had said, decreeing that no member of his family should murder another. Cangrande would balk at ordering even Pathino's death. "No. Better he should pay for his crimes against God."

Fieschi shrugged. "I'll see what I can do. Please, excuse me." And the holy man had scurried away.

The potential scandal must have frightened Fieschi badly, for the very next day Pietro was invited back to the Penitentiary. He felt wary, fearful that his return to God's sight might be reversed. But he braved it, and was escorted down to the lowest cellar, where the cells had bars upon them. In one of them sat Pathino.

Pietro had expected to find him suffering the ills that Tharwat had experienced – weights, spiked ankles, burns, thumbscrews, and the like. Instead, he seemed remarkably whole. Thin and unshaved, but unbruised. In fact, he looked more like a scarecrow than ever before, as they had left him his hair shirt – if he wanted to punish himself, he was more than welcome. But after confessing to his sins so freely, there was apparently no need to apply coercitio. That felt infuriatingly backwards.

Seeing Pietro, Pathino stood. He said nothing as the attendant priest unlocked the door, nothing as he was guided up a flight of stairs and out a door at the back of the building, and nothing as he was made to kneel before a chopping block under the open sky. Finally, when the executioner reached for his axe, he spoke. Jerking his chin at Pietro, Pathino said, "Let him do it. My last request."

The executioner turned his hooded head to ask the silent question. It was rare, though not unheard of.

Pietro nodded. "I'll do it."

Executioners received special dispensation for taking a life. For himself, Pietro had only killed men in the heat of battle, never like this. Stepping forward, he took up the axe. But feeling its awkward weight, he shook his head and handed it back. He had not worn a sword to this holy building, but there was one on the executioner's hip. Receiving it, Pietro took up a position to the right of the chopping block and waited.

Snow fell lightly, wafting on the air and melting as soon as it touched the earth. Pathino was praying with the attending priest – there were no bishops or cardinals here today, though some were probably watching from the windows above. This inner yard was walled off so passers-by could not see in – this execution was not intended for the public. Pathino might say something embarrassing to the Church. The clergy were nearly as eager he should die as Pietro.

Listening to Pathino pray for salvation, Pietro felt his anger building. If I'd died any time these last three years, I'd have been damned without hope of salvation. Yet Pathino, a monster who has murdered and lied, wrecked countless lives, is absolved. A prayer before death, with the absolution of a priest, guaranteed Heaven. That very notion made Pietro's sword-hand twitch.

Finished, Pathino grasped the chopping block with both hands. "Very well, Alaghieri, knight of the Mastiff. Take the Greyhound's head."

Pietro did not want to speak, did not want to engage this fiend. Yet he could not help himself. "You are not the Greyhound."

Again the feral version of Cangrande's famed allegria. "Am I not?" Closing his eyes, Pathino began to recite:

To Italy there will come The Greyhound.
The Leopard and the Lion, who feast on our Fear,
He will vanquish with cunning and strength.
The She-Wolf, who triumphs in our Fragility,
He will chase through all the great Cities
And slay Her in Her Lair, and thus to Hell.
He will unite the land with Wit, Wisdom, and
Courage,
And bring to Italy, the home of men,
A Power unknown since before the Fall of Man.
He will evanesce at the zenith of his glory.
By the setting of three suns after his Greatest Deed,
Death shall claim him.
Fame eternal shall be his, not for his Life, but his
Death.

Pathino reopened his eyes, gazing not at Pietro, but to the heavens. "The Greyhound will usher in a new age of man, but will not be there to see it. I have set matters in motion that will ensure I am remembered. I go to my death willingly, as God has ordained. My destiny will be complete, with or without my life."

That sounded ominous. But Pathino had always been madly grandiose. "Do you have any message for your brother? For the nephew you tried to kill?"

Turning his head, Pathino thought for a moment. "No. From me, there is no last communication. I let the future speak for me. But there is a message. From the Count of San Bonifacio. Until there is a new Count, the old one's curse will lie heavily upon Verona and all those who caused his downfall. That includes you, Ser Alaghieri."

This was the second time Pathino had hinted the long-dead Count was still a fearful presence. Could it be true? Or was the Scarecrow mad, hearing voices from beyond the grave?

No matter. The time for his evil was at an end. Pietro lifted the sword.

The executioner held up a restraining hand. "You must ask him for forgiveness."

Pietro almost laughed at the sick humour of the moment. "Do you forgive me, Gregorio?"

Pathino's jaw clenched. He had to. It was the Christian thing, to forgive the man chosen to execute you. It was even more imperative, as Pathino had chosen Pietro himself. But he couldn't bring himself to say the words. He simply shook his head.

"Then damn you to Hell." Pietro swung with all his might.

It had been nearly two years since he had wielded a sword. Despite his racing blood, his first stroke did not quite sever Pathino's head from his body. Amid the spurting blood, Pietro wrenched his sword free and finished the job with a second blow.

Pathino's head landed in the small woven basket while the long, spindly body twitched and pumped blood for several more useless heartbeats.

The priest who had prayed with Pathino now prayed with Pietro, absolving him of sin, since Pathino had not. Pietro handed the sword back to the hooded executioner, letting the professional clean his own blade. He almost apologized for not doing the job better, then left the yard wondering if God would forgive him for the deep satisfaction he felt.

Guided upstairs, he entered a room more comfortable than Pathino's cell. There was open air, and a basin to wash in. There was even a prayer mat. *It's amazing, what we choose to care about. They hate him, were willing to torture him, but will not be uncivil to him.*

Tharwat was seated in a window overlooking the rear yard. Pietro said, "You saw?"

The Moor did not move. "Yes."

Pietro knelt beside his friend. There was a patch over Tharwat's eye, and his hands were wound in linen as the fingernails regrew. His ankles, too, were bandaged. To ask how he was would be foolish. "Tharwat – I'm so very, very sorry, my friend."

The rasping voice was a little less clear than it had been. The missing teeth made diction difficult. "It is done?"

"All of it. Cesco is legitimate. Cangrande and I are reinstated. Pathino's dead. And you're free."

Tharwat showed nothing. He stared, his remaining eye turning inward as he wrestled with the notion that he was not going to die. When Pietro saw a tear in Tharwat's eye, he stood. "I'll leave. I have to fetch a litter to bring you back to my lodgings—"

Tharwat lifted a bandaged hand. "Stay. For a time. If you would."

Sitting again, Pietro remained there until the sun began to set.

The silence was heavy. But it was shared.

The following day Pietro met Petrarch and Gherardo for a final farewell. It was a sober affair, thanks to Lucia's disgrace and Pietro's concern for the Moor. But they had succeeded in all they'd set out to do, and he owed these brothers more than he could say. They spent the whole time discussing poetry, fashion, and love – in short, the things Petrarch held most dear.

At dawn on Thursday, the Fifth of November, 1327, Pietro helped Tharwat into the hired carriage, then took a seat beside him. The driver rattled the reins, and together they left Avignon, the New Babylon, heading towards Italy to discover how the world had changed in their absence.

Twenty-Seven

Rome

For the first time in decades, Rome was alive again. People thronged the streets, traders came from Florence, Napoli, Brindisi, Venice, even as far as Vienna to hawk their wares. The locals cheered and cheered as Emperor Ludwig IV took up residence in the city where he would claim his third crown.

The loss of the papacy had devastated both the population and industry of the City of the Seven Hills. Built on a swamp, Rome was not a fertile land for crops or cloth or steel or wine. For the past thousand years, Rome had really produced only one thing – religion. With that industry removed to Avignon, there was nothing left for the people to do, leaving the inhabitants of the Eternal City staring into eternity.

Even before the vacating of the Vatican, the holy city had been a hollow shell of itself. Since the fall of the old Roman Empire centuries before, the population had dwindled to barely a tenth of its former size. But without the papacy to make the city a destination, there only remained the few local lords like Ste-

625

fano Colonna, the occasional pilgrim, and the peasants who housed their livestock in buildings once used by the Caesars.

All this changed with the arrival of Ludwig. Indeed, much of the delay in his coming was due to the need to restore Rome to some semblance of its former glory. Streets were now clean, banners flew from rooftops, and markets were alive with men and women thronging to witness the arrival of the Holy Roman Emperor, come to claim the final imperial crown.

Upon Sunday the 17th of January, 1328, Ludwig the Bavarian of the house of Wittelsbach was anointed the head of the Holy Roman Empire. Lacking a pope, the ceremony was performed by a cardinal – none other than Sciarrillo Colonna, with his elder brother watching gravely nearby. The old scoundrel had decided his pope-slapping days were not over, though this time the insult was only metaphorical. But the message would not be lost, nor the insult any less stinging. The Colonna family was one of Rome's oldest, and their allegiance was as much to Rome itself as to the Holy Roman Church. To them, the Church of Rome belonged in Rome. If the Emperor was willing to make that happen, he had the support of the Colonna clan.

Clearly this was what Sciarrillo had meant when he'd hinted that he would see Pietro soon. But Pietro was not there to witness the crowning. Though he could easily have reached Rome in time to attend, he received an order from the Scaliger to remain in Verona. Furious, he had to admit the Scaliger's reasons were excellent, as laid out in Cangrande's letter:

> The Emperor plans to install a new pope in Rome and declare John the Anti-Pope. At the moment papal fury will be reserved for the Colonna. If you arrive with the official decree of my reinstatement by Avignon, two things will happen. First, the new pope will excommunicate me for seeking the blessing of the old one, and second, John will excommunicate me all over again for partaking in the appointment of his rival. I refuse to allow your excellent work to be undone. So you must keep the official decree with you until my return.
>
> I know you're eager to see your former ward. As am I. I fear what a year in the imperial court has done to his manners, already shamefully lax from his soft life in Ravenna. Certainly there's been no

shortage of escapades, both in Milan and in Rome. But on the whole he has pleased Ludwig, which is something.

I must confess to being just as pleased with you. I never doubted for a moment that you would do anything but succeed in your tasks. But to have removed the threat of Pathino – there are no words to describe my relief. Though you are now so much a part of our family that I fear my father's curse may well touch upon your burdened shoulders, too. You realize, of course, that was his intent. With you as my agent, the curse was to fall upon my shoulders. But since we both know you are truly Cesco's, does that transfer the curse to him? Or are you still your own man, making the curse irrelevant?

You have practiced patience for so long, a little longer will harm nothing. And keep a low profile. Though your excommunication has been lifted, Florence yet has a death-sentence upon you, as would Padua were it discovered you'd had a part in the Dente uprising. So take my advice, stay in Verona, and ease yourself back into Veronese life. Call upon my sister.

That last made Pietro grimace wryly. A visit with Katerina was hardly easing himself into Veronese life. It was more a plunge from a high cliff.

But he would have to call upon her, as he'd decided to disobey the Scaliger, at least in part. He would remain, not in Verona, but in Vicenza. Morsicato was there, rebuilding his practice now that Esta was recovering from her mysterious illness. If any man could help Tharwat mend properly, it was Morsicato.

This was demonstrated the instant their carriage arrived in early December. Pietro had sent ahead, so the moment they arrived Morsicato was out of his door and chivvying the servants to carry Tharwat indoors. He didn't cluck over the Moor's condition, merely tugged his forked beard and said, "What have you gone and done to yourself now?"

Tharwat almost smiled. "Had I done this, I would have finished the job."

"Leaving me with nothing to do? You wouldn't be that cruel. Once you're fed, let's bathe you and see the damage."

Through the whole journey, Pietro had refrained from asking after the eye. Sometimes Tharwat would reach for it, then restrain himself. Often he would pour water over his head, or place a handful of snow beneath his eye-patch.

Morsicato explained why. "He's in agony. The eye is dead, but somehow he's kept it wet enough to move. Hideous to look at, and murderously painful, I'm sure."

Pietro shuddered. "What can you do?"

"I can't regrow his damn eyelid for him, or give him a new eye, can I? I'll do what I can. I'll try pulling the skin enough to sew it shut. If I can't manage that, then the eye will have to go. Bastards! Pathino is really dead? A pity. He deserved far worse. Gui as well."

"When will you operate?"

"Tomorrow, when there's enough light. I don't know how he's lasted this long without going mad. Stoic doesn't begin to describe him. Cato of Utica would be proud. You should have seen a doctor there."

"He said no. He trusts you. Now more than ever, there are very few of whom that might be said."

The surgery to close the socket was successful, though only because the eye itself had withered so badly. That done, Morsicato moved on to mending Tharwat's ankles, which had been pierced. "He won't say, but judging by the way the flesh is stretched, they had him upside-down, hanging from those spikes. The fact that he's walking is a miracle."

Pietro shook his head. "He told me his stars did not having him dying in France. I remembering glibly remarking it didn't mean he'd live well. Damn it, I should have done something!"

Morsicato grunted. "What could you have done? Stormed the Penitentiary and removed him by force? You had an army, did you?"

Pietro recalled his own imprisonment in Venice. "Cesco would have found a way. Cangrande too."

"They weren't there. And judging yourself by them is like Nestor comparing the heroes of the Trojan war – useless."

Pietro didn't like holding the Scaligeri up against the icons of antiquity, but he was intrigued by something else. "That's the latest in a series of very literary references. Have you been to university while I was gone?"

Morsicato pulled a face. "No. While you were off doing great deeds for Verona and posterity, I was fulfilling my duties as husband and doctor both. I had to fill the hours sitting by Esta's bed somehow, and reading was the easiest. After I went through all those dissection notes – thank you again for those –

I went back through the classics, hoping I'd understand your father's work better."

"And?"

The doctor shrugged. "I get the references now. But I still think half the point is lost on me. Why can't poets write plainly, like ordinary folk?"

This made Pietro laugh for the first time in what felt like years. It was good to be home.

For all that he was a renowned hero there, Pietro had never lived in Vicenza. His longest stay had been while he recuperated in the palace after his first battle, fourteen years earlier. Fourteen! *I was so young.* This year would see Pietro turn thirty-one. *Four more years, and I'll be at the middle of my life. And what do I have? No property except a burned-down house in Ravenna. A law degree I'm not using. A knighthood that causes me more grief than ease. And now a reputation for philandering and deflowering my friend's sister.*

He'd told Morsicato the truth of that, if only to avoid the doctor's constant ribbing. But when it came time to call upon Katerina della Scala, he kept up the pretense. He'd long since learned that any information in her hands was a weapon. If she ever found it desirable to drive a wedge between her brother and the Holy See, a bit of extortion would be of use. So he made sure not to tell her.

Otherwise he talked freely about Avignon and what he'd experienced there. In return, he learned from her a great deal that had escaped his notice while traveling.

"The new young king of England has by now taken a wife. The younger daughter of the Count of Hainault, whose eldest is now in Rome watching her imperial husband accept his latest coronet. The happy couple had already been married by proxy, a ridiculous practice to my mind. But the match strengthens Edward's position in Flanders and his children's claim on the French throne – both he and his wife had French royal blood in their veins. And they are nearly the same age. Which is also Cesco's age. Perhaps we should be looking for a bride for him?"

"Perhaps we should." Smiling, Pietro tried to imagine Cesco marrying.

Katerina carried on, showing no trace of slurred speech. "Of course, first we must find you a wife! I was hoping some French beauty would catch your eye. But all told, this is better. Now you're restored to spiritual health, with victories behind you and a great future before you. I'm sure that one day you will be in Castelbarco's place, or Bail's – the right hand of the Capitano. In fact, Bail feels much about my brother as you do about our Cesco. The first thing we must do is settle you down. Buy a house in Verona, and another here in Vicenza. Or an estate in the country between. Somewhere near your friend Montecchio. I will compile a list of respectable, presentable girls for you to wed."

The very last thing Pietro wanted was for Katerina della Scala to choose his wife. "You're too kind. But you were talking news. England is a long way off. Is there anything happening closer by?"

"In Padua, say?" Having read his thoughts, the lady looked sly. "Well perhaps you've already heard that the current podestà, a Venetian called Morosini, has fled Padua and is staying here as our guest. He makes the most shocking claim – that Ubertino de Carrara was plotting to murder him. Can you imagine?"

"Yes," admitted Pietro unhesitatingly.

"How uncharitable! But then, we share that trait, because I can imagine it as well. However, it appears that at present Ubertino is cowed by cousin Marsilio. With the support of the greedy German vicars Heinrich of Carinthia sent him, I'm afraid your old nemesis now rules Padua unchallenged. Didn't he once shoot at you with a crossbow?"

"Not at me. He actually shot me."

"That's right! How very rude. You'll be heartened to hear that his situation is entirely untenable. His citizens complain of high taxes and decry the unruly German garrison. Either Ubertino will find his spine again or another faction in the city will rise up."

Pietro was grim. "I wish I could be there to see it."

"You could always join Mastino and his German friend as they create havoc in the Paduan countryside. My lackwit nephew seems determined to reignite the war. His need to prove himself is ruining our best chance to gain Padua. Nothing unites Paduans more than fighting Verona. Fortunately, Carrara has accepted Cangrande's word that these attacks are unsanctioned, and that if the malefactors are caught Padua may do as it pleases. My brother didn't outright admit Mastino is the leader, just made clear he was playing Pontius Pilate."

Pietro couldn't help thinking that if anything could be better than Carrara's end, it was the ruin of Mastino. If both were removed, all Cesco's enemies would be laid to rest in a single year.

Katerina clucked her tongue. "But enough of war! We have our hands full figuring out a way to retrieve Cesco from the besotted Emperor. Oh, I don't mean to say Ludwig is inclined that way. Rather, he rightly thinks our boy is a wonder. So too does his wife, the sister-in-law to the new English king. The Emperor has already suggested a desire to take Cesco with him to Germany when the time comes."

Pietro had not heard that. "What does your brother say?"

"Francesco says mum. In a truly astounding act of self-negation, he's keeping his mouth resolutely shut. He will remain in Rome through the coronation and then return – hopefully with your ward. If not, we must lay our heads together and devise a means to bring him back to us."

The use of we, us, and ours was not lost on Pietro. Katerina desperately wanted to regain some measure of control over Cesco's life, of the kind she had possessed when he was a babe-in-arms. Pietro had no wish to engage the great lady in her plots to ensnare Cesco again. Seeing this, the lady smiled and politely asked after Tharwat's health.

Visiting Verona in mid-December, Pietro's first call was to Santa Maria in Organo to greet his sister. It was a surprisingly strained interview. Antonia was glad to see him, and clearly relieved at his restored status. But she also seemed somehow subdued. This was not the headstrong girl he remembered. Perhaps it's cloistered life.

Or perhaps she resents me being gone so long. I know I resent it.

The Abbess insisted upon being present, so he couldn't speak as openly as he might have liked. But he related all the events of the trial, thanking Abbess Verdiana for her sworn testimony – especially the part about Pathino's mother, which had been the bridge to connect the medallion's origin to its final recipient.

Relating the execution of Pathino, Pietro saw Antonia's genuine relief and pleasure. Her one tentative step toward romantic love, Petruchio's cousin, had died while out hunting Pathino. God's Justice had at last caught up with him. One more score settled.

Promising to return to the convent, Pietro made his next calls. He had to visit Montecchio and Capulletto separately, the idiots. He chose Mari first in order to pass along Cardinal Orsini's greetings. He then told the whole story of the trial to a satisfied Mari and a breathless Gianozza.

Mari's sister Aurelia was there as well, wanting to hear the final fate of the man who had murdered her father. With her she brought her son Benvolio to play with his cousin Romeo.

Little Romeo was as handsome as ever. But with parents as ravenly gorgeous as Mari and Gianozza, how could he help it? And he continued to be the main object of Gianozza's affection. She coddled and clucked at him, constantly referencing Lancelot and Paris, Abelard and Pyramus – the lovers of literature. Pietro thought the six-year-old was a bit precious, but when Mari gave him a stick he went through his sword paces like a man, far better than Pietro had at that age. Pietro was surprised that Gianozza approved until she pointed out that all great lovers were great fighters as well.

As Pietro was leaving, Mari plucked his sleeve. Struggling to say something, finally he got it out. "Pass on my condolences to Capulletto."

"Why?"

"You haven't heard? He's lost his son. Crib-death. I wouldn't wish that on anyone."

"You should tell him yourself," said Pietro sternly. But Mari only shook his head and went indoors.

Traversing a half dozen city blocks, Pietro indeed found the Capulletti household in mourning. Dressed all in white, Antony was beside himself with grief. He barely heard the details of Pietro's tale. He only perked up when little Giulietta tottered in. "My little ray of sunshine," he said, scooping up his daughter. "How now, how now? Look at her, Pietro! Scraped knees, dirty fingernails. Where have you been gadding, little imp?"

The two-year-old grinned up at him, her blonde hair falling across her eyes. "When I am five, I will kill a wolf."

Melancholy forgotten, Antony roared with laughter. "I imagine you will!"

Smiling dutifully, Pietro recalled the night of her birth. Cesco had been such a fool, starting a fire and chasing through the streets. So much had happened that night – Mastino sucking mud, Katerina's return, Cangrande introducing Cesco as his heir, Mari coming to Antony's house for the first time. It was as if the stars had aligned, the threads of their lives merging for a moment for a perfect tapestry. Such moments were rare.

Little Giulietta spied her cousin Thibault through the window. He was down in the yard practicing with a sword. She leapt off her father's lap and ran to join him, only to be scooped up by her nurse Angelica and carried away. The last time Pietro had seen Angelica, her daughter had just been murdered. Now another of her nurslings had been taken untimely. Yet her irrepressible spirit was clearly rallying as she mercilessly teased her lone remaining babe. Little Giulietta wriggled and laughed and let herself be diverted.

Watching them go, Pietro said, "Where is your wife?"

"Gone to Florence with her relations. Likes to visit the dress-makers there. Needed a holiday. Can't blame her. My poor little man!" Eyes welling, Antony apologized. "I'm sorry! I don't mean to—"

"I can't imagine what you're going through." Pietro paused. "Are things better with her, now she's older?"

"With Tessa? I suppose so. She's old enough now to be her own person. Nearly fifteen. She's hard sometimes. Harder than I am. Bitter, I think. But how else would she be, married to an old man."

"You're not old!" laughed Pietro. "Because if you are then I am."

"I feel old," said Antony.

Pietro hadn't known if he would say it, but now seemed the time. "Mari sends his condolences."

"Does he?" Pietro had expected to find suspicion in Antony's eyes. But he was wrong. It was hope. "Does he really?"

"He said so. He seemed very sincere."

"Good of him. Decent. So much stupidity." Antony frowned. "Did she say anything?"

Pietro didn't have to ask who 'she' was. "Not to me. Mari and I talked of you in private."

Nodding, Antony stared into the middle distance. Damn, thought Pietro. Every time the door is cracked open, there's Gianozza to shut it again. This feud won't end until one of them dies.

Before he left, Antony had his steward produce a toddling boy with straight brown hair and a slightly hooked nose. "Pietro, this is Piero. Piero, be a good lad and make a leg to this nice man."

The boy wiped his nose on his sleeve. "H'lo."

"A pleasure to meet you, Piero." Looking at his brother's bastard, his own nephew, Pietro didn't know how he felt. The lad was the spitting image of Poco, right down to the slightly sly look in his eyes.

Little Piero was being raised as Antony's page. Is that a good enough life for an Alaghieri? Should I take him in myself? Raise him to be my page instead?

A horrible answer came into his head. They'll think he's mine. After Lucia, they'll think he's mine. Damn. Do I really care what people think? I know it's not true. Does a knight do what is Just, or not?

But what do I have to offer him? An itinerant life of danger and intrigue. No stability, no security. He's better where he is. At least with Antony he has a chance at living, at not being used as a hostage or weapon against me. Or is that just an excuse? Do I balk at raising my brother's bastard? Is that what kind of man I am?

Wrestling with all of this, Pietro took his leave of Antony. Heading for the tunnel the led to the street, he paused to look up at the fresco that bore his face. It had been repaired since the fire three years earlier. Designed by Giotto himself, it depicted the story of King David, Bathsheba, and Uriah the Hittite. Everyone had a role in the painted drama. Mari stole the girl, Antony died nobly, and Pietro appeared as the voice of God's justice. Flattering, yes, but also embarrassing in the extreme.

"You look better in the painting," said Capulletto's nephew as he swung his sword in the cobbled yard.

"Most people do." Pietro had never really spoken to Thibault. He'd always felt rather sorry for the thirteen-year-old – not allowed to joust or practice war, he was destined for the cloister, a life for which he was clearly unsuited. But Pietro also remembered how the boy had once wished aloud for Cesco's death. All he could think now was to offer a bit of sword advice. "Reach. There's more power in extension than tension."

Rubbing his sore bicep, Thibault's expression was challenging. "That's not what the book says." He nodded to a fightbook open on the cobblestones. The drawings looked like monks fighting with swords and small round shields called bucklers.

"Because those books are written for men who already know the basics. Extend your arm and it won't get so tired." Thibault's expression was dubious, but the departing Pietro didn't care. He'd given the boy good advice. Perhaps it would save his life someday.

Before leaving Verona the next day, Pietro called at the monastery of San Francesco al Corso. It was early morning, and Pietro knew that despite the snow his man would be out among his plants.

Seeing Pietro approaching, Fra Lorenzo stood, clapping snow from his gloves. "Ser Alaghieri. I heard that you'd returned. Congratulations on being restored to God's light."

"Thank you. And thank you for your kindness to Antonia – Suor Beatrice. She wrote warmly of you."

"Is that why you've come? If so, there was no need."

The friar's expression puzzled Pietro. He'd become guarded at the mention of Antonia. But perhaps that was just Lorenzo's dislike of Pietro coming though. God knew he had cause.

It was for that reason Pietro had come. He cut right to the heart of the matter. "No. You may have heard I had two encounters with Cardinal Gui."

Fra Lorenzo's handsome face went grey. "Yes?"

"Your name never came up."

The friar pressed his eyes shut and sighed in sagging relief. After a moment his eyes flicked open again. "Then why call on me?"

"Because I owe it to you, after my behavior, to say so to your face. You have nothing to fear from me."

The friar stared for a time before finally nodding. "I see now what our sister Beatrice says is true. You are an honest man. Thank you. And again, my congratulations." With that he returned to his garden. Which was about as much forgiveness as Pietro could expect.

Departing via the bridge named for the saint that shared his name, Pietro returned to Vicenza. There he spent Christmas, reveling in each church service. Eschewing the larger houses of worship, he chose instead to bestow his time at the Basilica dei Santi Felice e Fortunato, Vicenza's oldest standing church. Each day he prayed to the remains of both the sainted brothers, whose very names meant happy and lucky. Despite all he'd gone through, or perhaps because of it, Pietro had cause to feel he was both those things.

Having been readmitted to the faith, he was seen to spend a great deal of time in public prayer. Some scorned him, saying it was too much showy piety. Others claimed such excesses were unhealthy. But most saw in his quiet, unostentatious hours in Vicenza's oldest church a truly humble and devout man celebrating his renewed relationship with God.

He accepted an invitation to celebrate the New Year with the Nogarola family – Bailardino was away, but his one-armed brother was here, as was Katerina. It was a quiet affair, livened only by the loud proclamations of Katerina's second son. Eleven now, young Valentino was itching to emulate his brother and go off to squire for someone famous.

In January Pietro heard the latest news coming up from Rome: of the coronation, of Sciarrillo's betrayal of the pope, of the ensuing hubbub and strife. Fortunately there was no word of Cesco beyond the extraordinary right bestowed upon him to again bear one of the crowns for the ceremony.

At the start of February came the papal retaliation, as Pope John XXII declared a crusade against the upstart Emperor. The people of Rome let their feelings for the French pope show by burning him in effigy, and Ludwig announced his intention to promote his friend, a defrocked priest called Pietro Rainalducci of Corbario, to the office of pope. Soon there would be two popes governing the spiritual world on Earth.

A crusade against a fellow Christian was not the only news coming from France. It seemed Pietro and Tharwat had left just in time. A rash of epidemics had broken out, the second such outbreak in ten years. This time the population was even quicker to point a finger. Lepers were accused of well-poisoning, and were burned. Their rumoured masters, the Jews and the Muslim king of Granada, were likewise stoned in person or burned in effigy. Jews were easy to distinguish, since Pope Innocent III had long ago decreed the Jews must wear badges of yellow felt, usually in the shape of a coin. That there were hardly any Jews left in France made the beatings all the more vicious.

A disease of another sort was rising across the Channel. Montagu's letters told of a weakening England, rife with ire and ripe for mutiny. First came a truce between England and France, signed by Isabella in her son's name. This was followed by the Treaty of Edinburgh, by which England acknowledged the independence of Scotland under Robert the Bruce, who was now proclaimed Scotland's king. Having had his life saved because of a Scottish emblem, Pietro was sensitive to news from that mysterious, distant land.

At the other end of the world, a crusader navy defeated Muslim pirates in the Gulf of Edremit. This was greeted with jubilation throughout all Christian lands, remarkable only because the victory had been so minor to receive such acclaim.

But that news was quickly snuffed out by far more sensational fare. Charles IV of France was dead, the fifth victim of the Curse of the Templars, as it was fast becoming known. Fourteen years before, burning upon his pyre, the last Grand Master of the Knights Templar had called out a curse upon the French king and his heirs down to the thirteenth generation.

But it seemed that the curse was now cheated. Charles IV had died without a son, marking the end of the main Capetian line. His successor was his cousin Philip of Valois, though this was not without contention. Under the Salic law, the young English king had a better claim through his mother. Bankers began pulling their money out of France as everyone wondered what this would do to the new truce, and if the curse would extend to indirect heirs as well.

Of nearer import was a letter from Bonagratia of Bergamo. He'd endured a wretched time in Italy, debating Christ's poverty with Bernardo Gui and the rest. And there had been some grisly deaths that put everyone off their food. But the end result was that Bonagratia's mentor, Michael of Cesena, had returned with them to Avignon to present the Franciscan case directly to the pope. Pietro wished him luck, but doubted his success. In the New Babylon, money spoke with the voice of God, while poverty went dumb.

Pietro spent the winter with Tharwat in a house he'd bought in Vicenza, very near Morsicato's. He followed Katerina's advice and also purchased a home in Verona not far from the via Cappello and the Piazza delle Erbe, barely a stone's throw from Cangrande's palace. Thinking ahead, he made sure his new house could be easily fortified.

But he spent no time in Verona, remaining in Vicenza to write letters, practice law, and play chess with Tharwat. Who seemed suddenly old. It was as if before Avignon he had been impervious to age, but the dam had now burst and the years flooded upon him all at once. He became slightly hunched, as if pulling into himself. Never loquacious, he was even less talkative now. Morsicato baited him mercilessly, and only occasionally would Tharwat respond in his old, tersely combative way.

Easter came early that year, on the third of April. Spring followed it two weeks later, melting the snow and clearing the roads – it had been a particularly brutal winter, slowing travelers and messengers alike. The arrival of warmth was a relief, and Pietro ordered the large windows unshuttered and thrown wide each day.

On a Friday towards the end of May, Pietro was sitting in his ground-floor study, playing chess with Tharwat, when suddenly a young man came to a skidding stop beside the open window. Without preamble, without even a greeting, he said, "O, thank heaven! I've done something foolish, Nuncle. Can you ride?"

Taken aback, Pietro was about to challenge the young fellow when his eyes opened in wonder. The curls were longer and darker than ever before, a deep chestnut with no trace of blond. Wiry thinness had become sinewy strength. The tenor voice had dropped to almost a baritone. Just turned fourteen, adolescence had made all the features of his face grow at different rates. There was even a trace of real stubble - he had to shave every day, or else this.

The eyes, however, were just the same. So too the smile. Pietro felt as if he'd been hit in the sternum. *Two years, almost two and a half. I've missed so much...*

Standing, he opened his arms. "Cesco!"

"Yes yes, well met, pat pat on the shoulder," replied Cesco, rolling his eyes in a wonderfully familiar way. "Loving embraces and congratulations on your salvation must wait. I need a horse, and some discretion. Do you have either?"

"Both, I hope," said Pietro, rising. "What's wrong?"

"I'll tell you as we ride." Cesco turned to look at the Moor and said something in a swift Arabic that made Tharwat smile and answer in kind. Cesco laughed, displaying neither pity nor horror at Tharwat's new scars. "Then be useful and tell the doctor to follow us. We may need him. Ah! Another conspirator!"

Detto came racing into view. He'd grown more than Cesco, promising to be at least as tall as his father. They'd stopped being boys. They were now young men.

"Is he there?" asked a breathless Detto. "If the palace grooms see me, my mother will know I slipped the leash—"

"He's here, Penelope to my Odd Zeus. Nuncle, please. It's urgent."

It was the look in Cesco's eyes that made Pietro stir. "Hardly the reunion I'd envisioned. Tharwat?"

"Go," said the Moor, pushing himself to his feet and shuffling off. "I'll have the doctor right behind you."

"Have the groom saddle four fresh horses," called Cesco after him. When the Moor was out of sight, Cesco bit his lip and furrowed his brow. "Your letters didn't lie. He's old."

"He's always been old."

"But now he's frail. Schiesse. I was hoping he would leap up and show he'd been fooling."

"So is this a prank?" asked Pietro.

Cesco rubbed the back of his neck ruefully. "Not at all. I blundered, and we have to head off trouble. This is a nice house, by the way. Where are the stables?"

Pietro couldn't resist any longer. Laughing, he reached through the large window and pulled the boy – young man! – into an embrace, ruffling his hair.

Cesco struggled for a moment, then laughed and hugged him back. "Missed you too, Nuncle. Now please, can we go?"

ACT IV

Children of an Idle Brain

Twenty-Eight

Hooves hammering the old Roman road, the quartet raced north upon some of the best horses in the Feltro. Ser Alaghieri naturally purchased all his horses from his old friend Montecchio, who had horse-breeding in his veins.

Bouncing in his saddle, Detto clung on for dear life. He was exhausted, having ridden all the previous day up from Rome, sleeping in snatches for just a few hours in fields before Cesco had them up and off again.

Detto wasn't supposed to have been in Rome at all. But there was talk of the Emperor giving a massive hunt, and Petruchio wouldn't have missed that for the world. So Detto had cheerfully followed his master to Rome, eager to consort with Cesco, whom he hadn't seen for months.

Naturally Cesco was constantly busy – the life of an imperial page was far beyond that of a mere squire. But they'd found time to race about the Roman ruins, pretending to be Caesar and Brutus or Antony and Augustus, or reenacting the Year of the Four Emperors, where Nero, Galba, Otho, and Vitellius had fallen in quick succession, leaving only Vespasian standing. They'd played Romulus and Remus, leaping over broken walls and trying to murder each other. Detto had balked only when Cesco suggested they try taking milk from a wolf, feeling a great relief that a year apart had not altered their friendship.

Then came the hunt, just two days past. It was one made for active men, a par force hunt rather than 'bow and stable.' The hue and cry was part of the fun, spears and bows were in hand, though the arrows were not poisoned, a practice that had fallen out of favour since Emperor John II Komnenos of Constantinople had accidentally taken one in the arm and died. Poison was an unwelcome topic at court.

A boar had been released before dawn, and the mastiffs trailed it with vigour. Ludwig rode in the front ranks, seen by all. Cangrande behaved himself, riding near the front, but not in the lead.

All was going well until Riccardo Annibaldi, one of the many Roman nobles, decided to gain favour with the Emperor by putting the upstart Scaliger in his place. "My lord della Scala," Riccardo had called out while the hounds cast for the scent. "I'm surprised to find you in such hearty spirit, like our prey. I have often thought of you as more the wily deer, elusive and swift – though you have clearly survived the breaking of your heart's bone."

It was commonly known that the deer had a thin, weak bone right in the center of its heart that kept it from dying of fright. If the bone broke, the animal fell dead of fear. Annibaldi was referencing Cangrande's actions from the Battle of Ponte Corbo seven years earlier, when he'd been wounded and fled for his life.

If Annibaldi had expected to lay the lord of Verona low with that insult, he mistook his man. Cangrande had laughed in his face. "I have never been compared to the fleet and clever deer! But perhaps I shall give up the hound and adopt it. Better by far than the Roman wolf, who gives suck to any boy that happens along!"

The overt reference was to the she-wolf that had suckled Romulus and Remus so long ago. But the subtext was hardly unclear. As men laughed all around them, Annibaldi had reddened, finding himself without retort.

Cangrande then went on to show his mettle by leaping from his horse and chasing the cornered boar with not a spear, but a sword. He'd slain the beast in a most daring style, and was roundly acclaimed for his amazing feat of bravery.

The Emperor was none too pleased to have his prey, the German boar, slain by the Italian Scaliger. And when Cangrande's comment was repeated in his ear, he took it quite personally. He had just been crowned King of the Romans. Surely the slur against manhood had been aimed at him.

"Scheisse," Cesco had groaned. He'd taken to swearing in German. "This will be trouble. Damn."

"What?" asked Detto.

"I was actually enjoying the day, so of course it was interrupted. Whenever the Fates give me a good moment, they make me pay for it tenfold."

Detto had pulled a face. "Idiot. You're the luckiest tool around."

"Maybe that explains it. Trust me, this won't go unanswered."

At first it had seemed Cesco was mistaken. The Emperor did not react. Indeed, at the feast that evening he congratulated the Scaliger for his daring and offered him the best of the boar to eat.

It wasn't until the next day at dawn that Cesco appeared beside Detto's bed. "Shh. Wake up. We have to ride."

Now, as they forded a stream, he explained to Pietro and Morsicato what he'd told Detto yesterday on the ride from Rome. "The Emperor wants to strike at Verona's pride, and I foolishly gave him the perfect tool. I've made a point not to reveal any Veronese secrets. Herkos odonton. But I slipped up. He was admiring a sword the Greyhound gave me at Christmas, and I mentioned that it came from Cangrande's forge. He asked about it, and I described the technological wonders the Scaliger employs there. I stupidly mentioned how very proud Cangrande was of his forge. I said nothing of where precisely the forge was located, but I did mention the Adige. It wouldn't have been too hard for him to send spies north. They would have seen the false forge a few miles downstream. Perhaps they would have stopped there. But I fear not."

Riding on Cesco's other side, Ser Alaghieri was rubbing his thigh. After two years in France, he was woefully unused to the saddle. "But why do you think Ludwig's—"

"I saw who he was closeted with the night before last. Not men of birth or standing, but men in need of money. One is skilled at arson. And they rode north before dawn yesterday. I'm praying we reach the forge before them. If we can warn Rienzi, they won't be able to carry out their orders."

"Won't you be in trouble?" demanded Morsicato. "Slipping away like this?"

"Oh yes," said Cesco cheerfully. "One way or another, a bridge has been burnt."

Ser Alaghieri and the doctor accepted this story without question. Cesco had admitted making a mistake, which gave the tale a ring of truth.

Detto knew better. On the ride from Rome, he'd asked another question. "The forge belongs to Rienzi, doesn't it?"

"Yes."

"Isn't his crest the flaming beaver?"

"You know, I think it is," Cesco had answered coolly.

"So this wasn't a mistake. You let it slip on purpose."

"What, you think I've forgotten our friend Death?" Cesco's grin had not changed, only become more itself. "In truth, my hope was to goad the Emperor into making a visit, and so smoke the flaming beaver out of its dam. Instead the Bavarian is going to tweak Cangrande's nose by burning it down, making the crest a reality. So I really did make a mistake."

Now they rode west, passing between Tregnano and Badia, crossing the rivers d'Illasi and Fibbio. They'd covered nearly thirty miles when they reached the via Brennero, the road running parallel to the Adige.

"Detto, where do you think we are?" Cesco had a terrible sense of direction, whereas Detto's internal map was excellent.

"Somewhere north of Sant'Ambrogio. Caprino's about six miles northwest from here, I think, across the river. I don't know where the forge is."

"If you're right, it's north of here," said Cesco. "It was covered in snow when I was here. The Moor would know. Damn."

Pietro stroked his horse's neck. "We need to slow down. The horses are exhausted. We should have changed them at Tregnano."

"And subject ourselves to countless questions?"

"If speed is of the essence, the delay would have paid for itself."

Cesco nodded curtly. "Spilt milk. We'll walk them along the water's edge. Come on." He kicked his horse into a trot down into the Adige Valley.

They reached the river, which was flowing heavily thanks to the snowmelt from the Alps, rushing past with fury and power. Cesco dismounted, and the others did the same. Together they walked their mounts north along the river's eastern edge, making aimless conversation.

Suddenly Cesco brushed at his chin, a look of distaste on his face. Morsicato said, "What's the matter?"

"Nothing a razor and some water won't fix."

The doctor puffed out his broad chest. "And what's wrong with a beard?"

"Ha! I've watched you with that thing for ten years. At meals you eat as much hair as food."

"Lets me enjoy the meal again later. It's a good sign, though, your whiskers. Means you're healthy."

"Healthy enough, anyway," said Cesco.

Pietro was squinting at Cesco's hand. "That's a new scar."

Cesco held up his right hand, showing off the shiny line of a healed wound on its back. "Goes straight through. See?" Proudly he turned his hand around to show a matching scar on his palm. He'd been stabbed through the hand.

"How did that happen?"

"I was playing knuckle-knives and I slipped. It wasn't immediately fatal, but it seems to have bisected my lifeline. Alas. Still, I'm one-third of the way to my own stigmata!" Cesco laughed, and they all resigned themselves to not knowing how he'd really gotten it.

Yet Morsicato couldn't stop staring at him. "Dear God, what do you want, old man?"

"A trip to Corsica," said Morsicato, "but I don't think that's in the stars. How are you feeling?"

"Well, since you ask, I've had this recurring stabbing pain."

"Where?"

Cesco pointed at the seat of his hose. "Here."

"Very funny. I'm your doctor, I'm allowed to at least ask after your health – it's my profession, you know."

"You profess it is. I think you're really a nosy busybody."

"Nosy busybody is repetitive."

"Over and over again."

Though amused, Pietro brought them back to the purpose. "How much farther, do you think?"

Cesco shrugged. "We came at it from the other side, last time. But if we keep to the water's edge, we should find it." He grinned at Pietro. "So how was France? Are you saved?"

"In more ways than one, as you well know." Pietro had written all his news to Cesco long before. "With Pathino dead, there's one less enemy in the world for you to fret over."

Cesco scratched at the small scar beside his eye. "I thought I felt this itch last fall. I'm delighted to hear it was caused by the death of the man who gave it me. Tell me everything. There's nothing like a well-told tale."

"And this is a tale that deserves telling," said Morsicato, who had heard it several times. Indeed, as over the next hour Ser Alaghieri related the events of his French stay, Morsicato kept jumping in to add colour Pietro had forgotten.

In describing the second confrontation with Gui, Ser Alaghieri was interrupted by Cesco. "I wish I could have been there! So bold – Nuncle, I find I am profoundly proud of you."

While Pietro laughed, Detto's head turned. "Cesco—"

Cesco ignored him, carrying on. "You certainly threw caution to the wind. Were you thinking of Plato? That to die is to gain, for eternity is only a single night!"

"Nothing so bleak as that," answered Pietro. "I was actually remembering Caesar – 'let the dice fly high'."

"I should make that my motto. But I'd be accused of both theft and pretention. Better to make my own—"

"Cesco!" hissed Detto, urgently this time.

They all stilled at once, stopping their horses to listen. It was difficult over the roar of the flowing water, but they could just hear it – men's voices calling out urgently. Then a huge rending of stone and wood. The cries became pained and frantic.

"Too late!" cried Cesco. Leaping into their saddles, they followed the sounds of confusion directly upstream.

Rounding a bend, the scene before them was straight from L'Inferno. The buildings spanning the water were ablaze. On the far side, the giant water-wheel was burning too, rising high in flames then dousing itself in the churning waters below, creating clouds of steam among the smoke. Yet in spite of the chaos, the waterwheel kept on turning.

"O Christ Almighty," muttered Cesco.

"Don't blaspheme," said Pietro.

"Nuncle, the bellows – they're still working, feeding the fire!"

"Cacat!" swore Pietro, sawing his reins. "Come on!"

They raced the half-mile upstream until they were as close as their horses would dare go. On both sides of the river men raced about trying to douse the flames.

As they dropped from their saddles, Detto said plaintively, "What do we do?"

"Let it go," said Morsicato simply. "If we send for more help, perhaps some of it can be salvaged. But from what I see, they don't have enough men to even check the fire, much less put it out. Four more pairs of hands are useless here."

"He's probably right," said Pietro. There were only a dozen men in sight, all working mightily. "We must send word to Rienzi. Tell him to send carts for these men. And not to hunt for the arsonists."

"Not hunt for them?" asked Morsicato.

Pietro turned away from the fire and lowered his voice. "If they're caught and are found to be from the Emperor, things will grow ugly. As matters stand, Cangrande will suspect this was Ludwig's doing. But with definitive proof, he must either beggar his pride and accept this crime, or break with Ludwig. Which do you think he'd do?"

Morsicato ran a palm over his sweating scalp. "Start a war."

Cesco looked to his foster father. "You're very good at this, Nuncle. So you go to Rienzi. He'll take it best from a knight."

"And you?"

"We'll stay, try to help. The doctor may be needed, and I owe them my help. This is my fault," added Cesco bitterly.

Nodding approvingly, Pietro ruffled the boy's hair as he remounted. "I'll be back. Doctor, don't let them do anything foolish."

"Who, us?" Cesco shook his head. "Don't worry, Nuncle. I've been foolish enough already."

As Pietro rode up the road back south towards Sant'Ambrogio to find another bridge across, Cesco, Detto, and Morsicato struggled forward through gusts of smoke billowing at them, towards the edge of the bridge.

Here four men were trying to make a bucket line, but they were too few to make it effective. One of them took in a lungful of smoke and had to reel away, stumbling towards Detto. He coughed and vomited on the grass beside the road. Under Morsicato's instruction, Cesco ran back to the horses and plucked a skin of water from his saddle. The man accepted the water greedily then turned a smoke-black face towards them. "Th-thanks! Now, grab a pail, get something to – carry water!"

"Why fight it?" Cesco could hardly be heard over the roar of the flames and rushing water below. "Let it burn! The Scaliger will build another!"

"The smith and his boy! Inside – trapped!"

Remembering the massive smith, victor of the wrestling at the tourney two summers past, Detto looked at the burning forge again. A gaping maw of a door was there, the wood burned away. The walls were built of brick and stone, and were mostly intact. It was the surrounding structure and the bridge itself that were burning and falling into the water.

But the smoke – if they weren't dead, they would be soon.

Morsicato was looking at Cesco. "Don't even think about it. You'd be dead inside of two minutes."

Cesco nodded. "You're right. There's no going in that door. Let me go get more supplies from the saddles."

Morsicato grunted approvingly. While he tended the coughing man, Detto chased after Cesco, skidding to a halt beside the three mounts.

Out of the doctor's view, Cesco quickly dropped his sword, tugged off his boots, and pulled off his doublet, leaving him in just his tunic and hose. Then he hefted the doctor's saddlebags, which doubtless had a bundle of medical tools. He also plucked a rope from his own saddle. "I'm going to need help," he said quietly.

Understanding they were going for a swim, Detto likewise kicked off his boots and dropped his weapon. He started to remove his dagger too, but Cesco grabbed his hand and shook his head. They might need their knives.

The wind was blowing towards them and they had to muffle their faces in their sleeves as they raced past the burning bridge. Cesco threw the saddlebags next to where Morsicato knelt, then they kept running along the river's edge. Stinging smoke made Detto blink back tears.

Then they were upwind of the smoke, a dozen yards upstream of the growing inferno. Cesco grabbed Detto's head and put his lips right up to

666

his ear. "Wade into the water and swim over to the wheel. It'll be hard."

"I'll try to not die," answered Detto, stepping into the biting cold Adige. "Ahh! What are we doing?"

"First we stop the wheel."

That made sense. The still-turning waterwheel was powering the bellows, feeding air into the heart of the blaze.

Behind them Morsicato was shouting, but they kept wading in up to their thighs, fighting to stay upright against the push of the water. The level was higher on this side of the forge, and they weren't very far along at all when Cesco dove forward, throwing his head under the water and kicking off. Detto did the same and instantly the noise lessened, becoming an indiscriminate roar.

Having spent countless hours in the waters off Ravenna, both Cesco and Detto were good swimmers. Often Ser Alaghieri would go with them – he was a particularly strong swimmer, whereas the doctor was not. No fear, then, of him diving in to drag them out.

Yet the pressure of the water was fierce. Swept along, they had to struggle to swim sideways. We should have gone in further upstream.

Breaking the surface for air, Detto found he was much closer to the bridge than he'd thought – horribly close. A few more seconds and he'd plow right into it, smashing up against the stone base.

That fear was replaced by another when a large piece of flaming wood smacked the water just before him. Detto flailed backwards with his arms and legs. "Christ!"

"Down!" Cesco's hand clamped on his head and Detto found himself thrust underneath the burning debris, swimming beneath the water, heading for the wheel.

Surfacing again, he grasped the edge of the frame that held it in place. Seconds later Cesco arrived, unslinging the sodden rope from his shoulder. He handed one end to Detto. "Tie it—!" He coughed up some water, then continued. "Tie it to something." Taking a deep breath, Cesco placed one hand on the turning wheel itself and let himself be pulled beneath the surface.

Fingers fumbling, Detto struggled with the rope. After two attempts, he wrapped it around the large wooden strut framing the wheel. Tying it off was difficult one-handed, especially as the water threatened to carry him away if he released his grip for even a moment. He was just finishing a third knot, pulling the rope with his teeth, when the rope went suddenly taut. He yanked his hand back, but it still stung as the rope snapped hard, biting his fingers against the wood.

The wet rope strained and creaked. The wheel groaned, then stopped completely. There was no telling how long the rope would hold, but as long as it did, the fire wouldn't be fed.

Pushing off the strut, Detto grabbed onto the wheel and hauled himself hand over hand along it until he found a foothold. Hefting himself out of the water and onto the wheel's frame, he felt as though he'd just shed a pair of hundred pound weights on his legs.

The smoke was not too terrible here below the fire, though the shifting wind brought it down in curtains. Detto stared around, trying to discover where Cesco had vanished to. Above him he saw the gaping mouth of the opening for the wheel, crowned with fire. Where did he go? Is he trapped under water? Should I jump back in?

A gust of wind cleared the smoke, allowing Detto to see the far side of the wheel. Cesco's end of the rope was interlaced through the shafts of the wheel leading all the way up to the top. The rope's end was obscured through the opening. Cesco had used the wheel's own motion to carry him up through the gap, weaving his body through the wheel as he did so. How he'd tied off the rope at the top without the wheel ripping it from his hands Detto could only guess.

Instead of relief, Detto was angry. He's doing it again! He's in the forge all alone! Going off without me, keeping the worst danger for himself! Anger fuelling his strength, Detto began climbing up his side of the wheel. It was slippery. His bare feet sought for footing in the cross-sections of wood. He slipped once, banging his chin against the crossbar of the wheel.

Over on the shore, the doctor was shouting at him to climb down and bring that fool Cesco with him. Detto didn't answer, his brow furled in concentration as he climbed. The wheel was wobbling, straining against the rope. If the strands parted, Detto would be plunged back into the water.

After an eternity of grasping and reaching, clutching and clawing, Detto achieved the top, wriggling through the gap between the wheel and the floor.

At once he was engulfed in smoke. Covering his mouth with his sleeve, Detto crawled along the floor, feeling his way through the wheelhouse. He spied Cesco's end of rope, caught in the gears of the bellows, fraying every second, sawed by the pressure of the river pushing against wheel.

Slithering forward, Detto could barely keep his eyes open, they were stinging so. The heat from the walls and ceiling was blistering. Even the wooden floor was warm, scalding his knees and the heels of his palms. Keeping low, he tried to call out, choking halfway through his shout of "Cesco!"

From somewhere above he heard a cough. Calling out again, this time he heard two sharp thumps from overhead – someone was beating on the floor. Crawling desperately forward, he banged his head against the bottom rungs of a ladder. Drawing in as much good air as there was, Detto climbed.

He emerged through an open trapdoor into the forge itself. Twice as big as the room below, here the smoke was less, the chimney above the hearth pulling much of it up and out. Several anvils were spaced methodically though the room, tools scattered across the floor. The walls were solid stone and brick, but the wooden floor was smoking and the ceiling was alight, dropping burning embers to start more small fires all across the room.

Rising through the smoking floorboards were shafts powered by the wheel that worked the huge leather bellows, as large as the hearth itself. The hearth was half on fire, the bricks fallen on one side and the wall beyond burning.

A man and a boy were slumped on the floor near the hearth. Standing near them, Cesco was heaving on something connected to the hearth. Detto stumbled to his side, and Cesco let go of the lever to pull his friend to the floor where the air was clearer.

"Too heavy," panted Cesco, pointing to the smith and his apprentice. "Can't get them out through the wheel. Exit's burning. We have to open the ash gate." Coughing, he indicated the base of the hearth.

From below there was a sharp crack and at once the bellows began churning, feeding air to the hearth. The rope had broken, releasing the wheel once more. Every few seconds the flames around them leapt higher, fed by the rush of air from the bellows.

Swearing, Cesco leapt to the bellows and slashed the hard leather with his knife. Detto did the same and managed to pierce it twice, but there must have been an inner seal – the fire in the hearth kept blazing with the bellows' every breath.

"Fut!" Cesco pointed a blackened finger at the tuyere, a metal pipe bolted to the bottom of the hearth that delivered air to the base of the fire. "Open the sump! I'll work on the gate!"

Obeying, Detto stepped up and heaved the valve on the tuyere. It had a sump in the bottom to catch cinders and keep them away from the air blast. The valve on the bottom allowed the sump to be emptied, then closed to block air from escaping. If he could open it, less air would reach the fire.

The hot pipe scalded Detto's hands, but he didn't let it go, and after a few seconds he had the valve turning. The air to the hearth didn't end, but it lessened.

When it had turned it as far as it would go, Detto released the hot metal and turned to help Cesco with the lever of the ash gate. Built into the hearth's floor, the ash gate allowed easy cleaning of the hearth by dumping ash and cinders into the river. The panel pivoted on a single bolt held closed by a counterweight. It was the lever of the counterweight Cesco was struggling with. Cesco had removed his tunic and bundled it around the lever as he heaved on it.

The moment Detto added his weight the lever released, the bolt slipped, and the grate at the floor of the hearth opened.

Cesco pulled a face. "I loosened it."

Laughing, Detto inhaled smoke and gagged. "Let's go," he rasped.

The firepot in the hearth blazed on, but without the full force of the bellows feeding it, there was enough room for them to jump into the river below. This was the only space beneath the forge that was clear of impediment, as the builders had made certain no offending ember could ignite the structure from below. Not that it was a concern at the moment. The arsonists had started several fires at once. It was possible the blaze would even topple the stone bridge itself.

As they pulled the unconscious forms of the massive smith and his apprentice to the edge of the hearth, an ember fell on Cesco's shoulder, scalding him. He slapped at it, then said, "The boy first." They lifted the boy and held his feet through the opening. "One, two, three." Letting go, they watched him fall into the water with a splash. They hoped the men fighting the fire saw him, or else he'd surely drown.

Next they dragged the huge blacksmith up and over, a much tighter fit. Detto remembered being impressed with the man's muscles at the wrestling match. Now those muscles made getting him through the ash gate much harder. If he got stuck, all three of them were going to die.

The licking flames in the broken firepot left him untouched, but they accidentally leaned the smith's backside against the base of the stone pot, scalding him. He twitched in response, jerking half awake and ripping himself from their hands. This sent him through the gate to fall heavily into the water below.

Detto pushed Cesco ahead of him. "Go!"

Cesco didn't argue, but leapt into space. Detto waited a moment so he wouldn't land on top of his friend, then did the same, casting himself back into the river.

I only just got dry, he thought as he fell, flapping his arms and sucking in clean air for the few moments he could. Then the breath was knocked from him as he plunged into the water feet first.

Detto kicked his legs and tried to find the surface as the river pulled him along. His main concern was finding Cesco, then the other two and dragging them to shore. If the water didn't wake them, they won't last long—

Detto's thoughts were broken by a sharp blow to the back of his head. He had a moment of lightness, a feeling of his muscles going slack.

Then darkness claimed him.

Twenty-Nine

Warmth. The skin on Detto's back prickled familiarly and he felt straw beneath him. Inhaling air, he tasted smoke, and instantly strained to sit up.

A gentle hand restrained him. "Living is dying, breathing is eating, and sleeping is a wool blanket. Welcome back, Pollux. Awake and sing."

"Cesco, what—?" Detto looked around, finding himself surrounded by the walls of a house that was not burning. The smoke he'd smelled was rising from a taper hanging from the ceiling. His hands were wrapped in cloth.

"Arise, Barak, and lead thy captivity captive," intoned Cesco. "In this case, slumber. You've been out for the better part of three hours. You had the doctor worried."

"And whose fault is that?" demanded Morsicato, appearing at Detto's bedside. Hands brushed Detto's hair back, examining his scalp. Detto flinched as a hot poker burned his head, but when he looked up he only saw the doctor restoppering a vial. "You took a hard blow."

"But, being so hard-headed, it did no damage," added Cesco.

"Two young fools," grumbled the doctor, "running into a burning building. I thought I'd need either a shovel to bury you or a broom to sweep you up."

"How are the smith and the boy?" asked Detto.

"The boy's fine," said Cesco quickly. "We fished him out right away."

"Yes, youth is resilient. Age isn't so fortunate." Morsicato pointed to a huge form lying supine on a nearby pallet. "I won't be able to tell about him until he wakes."

"Apart from a burn on his arse," Cesco explained, "there's a nasty welt on his head and a dent in his skull."

Morsicato grunted. "If he doesn't wake by morning, I may have to open it up."

"His skull?" Detto was mortified.

"Can I watch?" asked Cesco.

"No," said Morsicato firmly.

A door opened and Pietro entered. With him were Gaspardo Rienzi and his son, followed by servants with trays of meat, cheese, and bread. "We heard voices. Your patients are up?"

"Yes, and in need of food. Even if they're not hungry." Morsicato gave Cesco a sharp look.

"I'm eating, I'm eating." Cesco helped himself from the tray.

Detto sat up. "You just woke up too?"

Cesco shrugged. "I needed a nap."

Morsicato snorted as Ser Alaghieri said, "Detto, Cesco almost drowned saving you. He'd dragged the smith's boy close to shore when he saw you weren't with him and dove back in."

Cesco speared a hunk of beef with his knife. "And after drinking half the river down, I need to eat." He wolfed the meat at a single bite.

"Chew your food. Idiot." Morsicato stretched his arms, looking weary. "Detto, fool that you are, you were trapped underwater by a piece of the bridge. Cesco couldn't move it, but wouldn't leave you. You both nearly drowned. What were you two thinking?"

"That this was my fault," replied Cesco.

Ser Alaghieri came to stand over him. "I told you, no foolishness."

Cesco pointed at the smith. "I don't think he'd say we were foolish. I'm not sure, but he might even thank us for braving the fire."

"Bravery is often foolish," said Pietro, ruffling Cesco's hair. "God, you haven't changed."

"I hope that is a good thing." Cesco noticed Rienzi and his son. "Thank you, kind signor, for sheltering us in your home."

Detto looked around and realized that this was no hut, nor no palace, but a finely appointed home. Plain, but comfortable.

"You're welcome," said the ruddy-faced man through gritted teeth. He clearly did not like having them there. His son was even more vigourous in his dislike. "What's that about this being your fault?"

"Nothing less than truth, Adamo," replied Cesco, reaching for a hunk of cheese.

Adamo! Detto remembered him now from the tourney. This had to be the mysterious Death! Detto was suddenly very interested in their host and his son. Were they safe, staying in the same house with them? Did Cesco have a plan?

Without naming the Emperor, Cesco explained that the burning of the forge was a powerful man's blow against Cangrande. "You may take it as a great compliment – the Greyhound is proud enough of your forge that it is deemed a valuable target."

"Excellent," sneered Adamo. "We'll eat that compliment, shall we, while our livelihood is a smoking hulk."

Ser Alaghieri was patient. "Stones may be replaced. Lives cannot. And none were lost."

"Death spat us back," added Detto, looking directly at Adamo. The fellow showed only hostility, while Cesco grinned.

"Listen to the knight, boy," said his father warningly. "We owe these young men a debt."

Cesco waved this off. "Hardly. I owed you – I bragged too much of your forge. If you could spare a flask of wine, I'd call all debts settled."

Rienzi raised his voice. "Lia! Where's that wine? Adamo, go see where your sister has got to."

"I'm here, father." Lia came in with a tray of goblets and a stone flask. She glided into the range of the taper and Detto saw a creamy face framed by dark curls.

Two years had worked wonders for her. She had curves where there had been none before. Her eyes were long-lashed, and alight with scorn.

Far from his attentiveness at the tourney, Cesco now hardly seemed to notice her. Whereas Detto, in that awkward stage where women were suddenly 'other', felt extremely uncomfortable. Naked except for the blanket, he pulled it up to hide his chest.

Lia poured. "Will wine hurt them, doctor?"

Morsicato took the first goblet for himself. "Not any more than they seem to hurt themselves."

Detto accepted a goblet without making eye-contact. Pietro said, "The Scaliger will certainly be grateful for the safe housing of his heir."

"Better than he deserves," muttered Adamo.

Rienzi's consternation was growing with each passing second. "That's enough, Adamo." Shoving his boy out of the door, he said, "They require rest.

Doctor, please let me know of any change in Carlo's condition. Come, Lia."

The girl set down the tray beside Cesco, who poured himself wine without giving her a second glance. This seemed to please her – Detto glimpsed the ghost of a smile before she turned to depart. Her father closed the door firmly behind her.

"Not a Scaligeri enthusiast," said Cesco between bites. He held out a piece of meat to Detto, who suddenly realized how hungry he was.

"Can't imagine why." Morsicato broke some crusty bread in half and gnawed on the soft inside. "The man has a positive talent for irritating people."

"Yet Cangrande has clearly favoured him," observed Pietro. "He oversees the rents hereabouts, and has the running of the forge under his control."

Cesco jerked a greasy thumb at the man on the pallet. "The loss of Carlo might very well end that lucrative business. I hope he lives, if only so we don't get knifed in our beds."

"I don't think we're in any danger," said Morsicato. "Now eat. You too, Pietro! Then we should all get some rest."

Pietro winced as he sat. "Doctor – do you have any salves for saddle sores?"

They ate until they couldn't swallow any more, chatting softly. There was so much for Cesco and his foster father to say to each other, so much to express, though as always Cesco reached it obliquely. He joked again about the new scar, and told funny tales of the nobles in the Emperor's court. Pietro matched him with tales from Avignon. Several times they had to shush themselves for laughing, and they spent a good half hour in serious debate over Christ's poverty, with Cesco playing the Devil's advocate, arguing the papal side.

Their conversations were interrupted when the smith Carlo stirred. Morsicato waved them to silence as the smith grunted, sighed, rolled over, and began to snore.

Stroking his forked beard, the doctor heaved a sigh of his own. "He'll be fine now. Though he'll have a fierce headache in the morning. But we can all get some rest."

Propping himself up on a bolster near the unconscious smith, Morsicato was soon snoring, too. Pietro laid himself on a pile of straw on the floor and was quietly asleep in no time.

Detto couldn't sleep. Images of fire and water kept filling his head, making him shiver. He shifted this way and that, feeling his naked skin brush the blanket over him and the straw prickling him from under the thin cover beneath him.

"If you don't stop fidgeting, I'll smother you," whispered Cesco.

"Sorry," grunted Detto.

"It's a quiet house, isn't it?"

"Yes."

"No servants chatting, nothing from the yard."

"No."

"Quiet."

"Yes."

The doctor snored loudly, breaking his own rhythm, which was in counterpoint to the smith's.

"Except them, of course."

"Yes."

"Do I snore?" asked Cesco.

"Hmm?"

"I asked if I snored."

"No," said Detto.

"Good. Neither do you."

"That's good." Detto rolled once more and settled in. One moment he was listening to the drone of Morsicato's breathing and the next it was as if a candle in his head had been blown out. From painfully awake, his mind collapsed to complete, blissful unconsciousness.

Cesco had lied. Detto did snore. His breathing provided an alternate rhythm to the other two, tenor, baritone, and bass, each one's lungs determining their intervals. When all three were firmly established, and Pietro unmoving as well, Cesco rose. In the dark room he sought for his clothes – his hose had survived and his boots had been retrieved. For a shirt, he wrapped Ser Alaghieri's riding cloak about his shoulders.

Sneaking past the sleeping knight, he eased the door open and slipped into the hall, shutting it softly behind him. He was on the first floor, with a spiral staircase leading both down and up, and a lone hallway leading to another set of rooms. A warm night, no fires were lit anywhere. Nor candles. The house was dark but for the starlight creeping through slatted shutters. Those same slats brought a gust of night air flapping the edges of Cesco's borrowed cloak, brushing his skin.

He made a choice. Abandoning the hallway for the stairs, he climbed to the household suites. A large casa, it was sparely furnished. Il signor Rienzi was not a man of possessions. Cesco was appreciative. It made the house easy to navigate in darkness.

Reaching the next floor, he gazed into the shadows for a time. There were more stairs halfway down the hall, probably leading to the servants' rooms. Beyond the stairs, two doors could just be made out, facing each other. Both rooms were dark, no light creeping from beneath either door.

Cesco turned about, imagining the layout of the house. Ignoring the door across the hall, he gripped the handle to the one beside the stairs. If he chose poorly, it could easily be his life.

Slowly lowering the catch, he eased the door open. It creaked for a moment, but he was already through, easing it shut again. Waiting for his eyes to adjust, he moved towards the bed and the figure in it.

There was a snap, then another. Pulse racing, Cesco froze as a candlewick sprang to life – not from the bed, but from the window seat.

So. Not unexpected.

The girl Lia was standing beside the window, far from the bed. She dropped the flint in her fingers and picked up a very small crossbow.

Cesco held her eyes, waiting. When she didn't scream or cry for help, he took a step forward. Immediately the bolt of the bow was leveled at his chest.

Hands high, he eased himself down onto the chest at the foot of her bed. "I hope you haven't been waiting long."

Her voice was as low as his. "Longer than I expected."

"Detto had a troubled time falling asleep."

"How did you know which was mine?"

"You are your father's precious jewel. He would keep you on the top floor, and at the back of the house, far from the front yard in case of attack."

The girl said nothing.

"We've not been properly introduced. My name is Francesco della Scala, sometimes Pierfrancesco, Franz to his Highness the Emperor Ludwig, but Cesco to my friends. And you?"

The girl didn't answer.

Cesco shook his head at his own stupidity. "But of course, I was told already. Rosalia Rienzi, a triumph of alliteration. Perhaps you are named for the saint, La Santuzza, daughter of the Lord of the Roses. Or is it a festival name from old Rome? Whatever the origin, you are the Radiant Rosalia, Lia to your father, she of the Glorious Shield. But that's not your true self, is it?"

"Isn't it?"

"Of course not. Your name is Death."

Standing up languidly, he flung open her trunk. She didn't stop him as he rummaged through it.

"Ah-ha." Emerging victorious, his fingers plucked at a string and the bundle in his hands opened to reveal a hood and a man's shirt and hose. "Nothing is secret that shall not be made manifest."

The girl made no move, bore no expression save a vague hostility.

"Did you know it's a sin to pose as a man?"

"Then you're as guilty as I am."

"Figs." Cesco fiddled with the hood. "Do you find it interferes with your archery?"

"Yes yes, you've proven how clever you are. Now stop beating the dead with your small stick. What do you want?"

Dropping Death's raiments back into the trunk, he resumed his seat. "My stick being so small, I suppose I'll settle for talk with you."

"It will have to be at me. I have nothing to say to a bastard without enough self-regard to shave the hairs on his face."

Cesco touched his cheek, feeling the nascent whiskers. "Disappointment colours my soul. I apologize, I've been riding for two days in hope of averting a tragedy."

"One that I imagine you arranged, just for this interview."

"You flatter yourself. While I did let slip the existence of your father's prize, I had thought the Emperor would call and make it his own. What an honour that would have been, and what a reward – your father could thumb his nose at mine with impunity, being in imperial employ. Alas, the best laid plans, and mine."

"Fine. You erred, and attempted amends. What do you want with me?"

"I strive to pile Ossa on Olympus, and Ossa Pelion with its leafy forests, that I might scale the heavens."

A corner of her mouth twitched, and she matched him Homer for Homer. "You ought not to practice childish ways, since you are no longer that age."

"All strangers and beggars are from Zeus, and a gift, though small, is precious."

She rolled her eyes, flipping her dark hair over one shoulder. "There is a time for many words, and there is also a time for sleep." The crossbow didn't waver.

He was very aware of her neck where it met her shoulder. The pulse was visible, dancing in the candlelight. "True enough. Therefore I will state my business and be gone."

"Your business," she repeated tonelessly.

"A favour. Two, in fact. No no, relax. I am no Cianfa." When she frowned, searching, he laughed. "That was unfair – a personal reference, not a literary one. I apologize. I like that you're well-read."

"I regret I ever learned to read if it means a moment longer of your company."

"And well-spoken, if a trifle rude."

"Rude? Rude?" Standing, Lia almost shook with laughter. "You come with delusions of panache and cleverness into my room in the middle of a summer's night—"

"—and you pressed a knife against my throat on a snowy night, dressed in rags like a Tatterdemalion Prince. We are neither of us virginal in this. But to the purpose. I have two requests. Firstly, you must cease all attempts on the Scaliger's life. I know you have held your hand since Trent, and I thank you."

"I assumed you'd deduced my identity. And I was right."

Cesco took another step nearer. "So was I."

"So you're here to threaten me?" Her eyes were clear, her head held defiantly high. "Leave off attacking your father, or you'll expose me?"

He was just feet away from her now, the small crossbow still aimed at his chest. "I was actually hoping you'd expose yourself."

"Arrogant, preening peacock. You are as crude as – I can't think of anything as crude as you."

"Tongue-tied?"

"It's the sour taste you leave."

"How could you know, when you haven't tasted me?"

"I suppose if I scream you'll reveal those clothes are mine."

"I'd have to, just to save my skin."

"My father wouldn't believe you."

"But he might believe Detto. I think if my cousin saw you in the right light…"

Lia's face screwed up in fury. "You're just like him!"

"Detto? I wish. Or perhaps you mean my noble progenitor. I noticed your father has no love for my namesake."

"Nor have I."

"Saving it all for me, I hope."

"Your father deserves to die. He's a tyrant."

"Yet your father serves him faithfully. Your smith makes his swords. Your brother grows on his money. An interesting form of protest." Cesco pressed his chest against the end of the crossbow, the point at his heart. "I haven't asked my second favour yet."

Lia was barely breathing. "If you mean to have your way with me, I'll kill you first."

"I'm sure." Smiling, Cesco bent to kiss the hand on the trigger, barely brushing her wrist with his lips. Then he raised his head and looked her in the eye. "My favour is simple. May I see you again?"

Thirty

The smith Carlo woke with the morning light and didn't speak like a man out of wits. Cesco was disappointed that surgery was not required, but Morsicato promised him, "The next time a skull needs splitting, I'll call you in for practice."

Reassured that his prized smith could speak in full thoughts, Rienzi practically threw them out, so eager he was to hasten their departure. But he couldn't be forthrightly rude, so he gathered his household in the yard beside the stables to offer thanks to the brave boys. His handsome children Adamo and Lia were there to see the backs of them. Adamo glowered, especially seeing that Cesco and Detto were dressed in his best clothes. Lia simply looked bored.

Cesco and Detto accepted a gift of bread from the mother of the apprentice they'd saved, and shook hands with the fellow himself. He was called Agapeto, and was much their age, but a bastard – one without a famous sire in need of an heir. Cesco couldn't help wonder how different they were, and if he could have survived doing the same chore day after day. His mind reeled at the thought of such stagnation. But then he was already in a foul mood.

Just as he was preparing to ride, a mounted visitor entered the yard and called out his greeting. Rienzi introduced the newcomer. "Signor della Scala, Ser Alaghieri, Ser Morsicato, this is my close friend and neighbour, Abramo Tiberio."

"Call me Bramo, everyone does." Tiberio looked to be in his mid-fifties, a heavy, bearded man whose hair was as long as it was white. He was like something from another age, too wild for these civilized times. Cesco leaned out of the saddle to shake the man's hand and felt a grip of iron. Detto, too, was no weakling – he could almost hold his own in a wrestling match with his father – but Tiberio's grip was bone-crushing.

Adamo's face lit up when he saw Bramo, but Lia had disappeared inside just as he turned to greet her. There was a mote of talk as Tiberio congratulated everyone on the daring rescue of the smith. Alaghieri shook Rienzi's hand, and Morsicato gave final instructions about the invalid's care. Then they mounted and rode away from the household, neatly nestled behind waist-high walls in a bowl of the Adige valley.

"That was the most resentful gratitude I've ever seen," complained Cesco. "I wonder what the old dog did to earn such enmity."

"Maybe he tried to kill Rienzi, too," said Morsicato sourly.

Pietro's head came around so fast Cesco thought it might fall off. He gave the doctor a hard look, then turned his eyes back to the road. Oh ho. A story there. But for another time. Cesco was in no mood to draw it out.

Pietro had sent ahead to Cangrande's palace at Caprino, ordering it opened for the Scaliger's heir. They arrived to find the order carried out by none other than Tullio d'Isola, the aged Grand Butler of Cangrande's household. "Ser Alaghieri! So good to find you well. I hear there was some excitement yesterday? The forge is a tragedy, to be sure, but thank God no lives were lost."

"Thank these idiot boys as well," said Pietro, who found himself punching Cesco on the shoulder – he'd claimed to be too old to have his hair ruffled.

"Daring," admired d'Isola. "Just like their fathers. What can I do for you?"

Cesco slipped off his riding gloves. "I, for one, would like a bath and a shave."

"Excellent, my lord. Follow me."

Pietro was flummoxed. "Cesco – we must write to Cangrande, you must send your apologies to the Emperor. There's much to be done!"

"You do it, then. I feel hairy and filthy like the boar in mud, and I'm going to have a bath."

Detto went with Cesco, leaving the doctor and Pietro to hand the horses off to the waiting grooms. "I hope I wasn't so rude at fourteen."

"We all were. It's the age." Morsicato snorted. "I'm wondering when he got so fastidious! The boy I remember came home with grass-stained knees every day of his life."

"I don't know," said Pietro, just as bemused. "But then the boy we remember didn't need to shave."

"Hmph. At his age, I practically had a full beard."

"Is that where all the hair from your head went?"

"No, that's on my chest and nethers." Morsicato laughed. "Come, while you compose your letter, let's see if there's any food."

It was then that Pietro noticed a carriage having its wheel repaired in the stable yard. "I wonder who that belongs to," he said as they passed.

"Tullio, most like. Come along, I'm famished."

But as they passed the carriage, the crest on the door made Pietro lose his appetite.

It wasn't until he was half-through with the barber that Cesco learned that Detto's mother, the Lady Katerina da Nogarola, was in the palace. At the moment

Detto was eating – unlike Cesco, he had not luxuriated in a hot bath for almost an hour. Sighing, Cesco allowed the servant to finish scraping his face, then dressed and crossed the courtyard to Bailardino's suite.

Katerina look up from a book. "You're quite handsome today."

"I dressed just for you." Cesco wondered if the book was just a device, something to be caught doing. He doubted that she spent so much of her time reading – she didn't have the squint.

She was seated far from a window, but he had the impression that it was a station she had just taken up. He glanced about and, sure enough, there was an impression in the pillow on the window seat.

Her smile was perfect. So like her brother's. "I could never fool you. Even when you were small. Yes, I've been waiting."

"Waiting two years, in fact. Probably more. If patience is a virtue, you are the most virtuous of all ladies." Cesco sat in a chair neither close nor far. "I apologize for the delay. Have you seen Detto?"

"Not yet."

"Yet you sent for me, and at a moment when he was not present. I am amazed you have such time for me. Your own sons' interests must keep you busy."

"My sons are well provided for. If I take an interest in you, it is your good fortune."

"For which I thank my lucky stars every night, lady." He was speaking sharply, his dark mood of the morning unmended.

"It is of the stars I wish to speak. But first – do you trust me?"

Cesco laughed. "Oh Auntie Katerina, how can you ask? I trust in everyone. I trust the mountain lion and the shark, I trust the eagle and the monkey, I trust the scorpion and the buzzard."

"Trust them to do what?"

"Be themselves."

She was silent for a moment. "I want your confidence."

"I have every confidence in you, lady."

In spite of his goading, the lady did not succumb to frustration. "Cesco, you may not know, but it was I who took you in as a baby, when your life was in danger. You came to live with me in the palace in Vicenza."

"I've heard that. Do I owe you for that? I don't have my purse on me..."

"Please stop talking if you have nothing to say."

"I apologize, I thought you were trying to get me talking. Bringing up the palace, have you fixed that fountain in the yard?"

The lady blinked. "It works."

"There's a flaw – a crevice, just under the lip. I used to hide my toys there to keep you from taking them away. I found it again when I returned. They were still there." He grinned at her.

"So you do remember living with me."

"Bits and pieces. I think I resent you very much."

The lady smiled, revealing the only lingering evidence of her stroke. Her lopsided smile now resembled Pietro's. She said, "I accept your resentment."

"Better than indifference, I suppose."

"Anything is."

"You say my life was in danger. From whom?"

"Gregorio Pathino and the Count of San Bonifacio," said Katerina.

"Both now dead. Thank heavens. I was afraid it was someone else. A more feminine hand..."

When Katerina's eyes narrowed, the creases at their corners grew deep. "To whom have you been talking?"

She's afraid of something. That's interesting. "O, I enjoy conversing so much that I often forget who my partners are."

"I would have thought that Ser Alaghieri possessed more discretion."

"He is the soul of it," replied Cesco. "He has never revealed anything to me I didn't already know."

697

Katerina looked slightly concerned. "Cesco, I want you to know, these are lies. Whatever they say, I would never hurt you."

Nothing about him altered, but Katerina had the fleeting impression of Cesco's surprise. Mentioning a feminine threat, he had been referring to Cangrande's wife, in league with Pathino and Bonifacio. To learn that Katerina had tried to kill him was enlightening. He canted his head to one side. "If you say so, lady."

"To prove it, I have something here I wish you to see." She produced three scrolls. "I've long wanted to show these to you. You remember, I tried once before."

"When we were so rudely interrupted by the Scaliger. I remember. You called them a weapon. They must be devastating in nature. Since that day we have never been alone, you and I. I confess I am relieved it's paper you wish to share. I feared more amorous designs."

Katerina recoiled. "Don't be foul, even if it does come naturally. I am not easily shocked. Here. Take up your star-chart. Or rather, one of them."

Cesco felt a hunger open up deep within him. How many times had he begged to see his chart? How many times had he been put off? They had kept his birthday from him for years, and also the location of his birth, so that he might never make one himself – he had the skill. "Tharwat made this?"

"Yes. At my request."

Cesco fitted his thumb under the seal to break it, then paused. "Since you first brought these up, I've wondered – why do I merit three separate charts? Are they different? How is that possible?"

"Open them and you shall see."

There was something in her voice. Thumb still under the closed wax seal, he slowly lowered the rolled parchment to his side. "I'm rather tired at present. Perhaps later."

"Don't you want to read it?"

"Not particularly, no."

Donna Katerina rose to her full height. Almost as tall as her brother, she had several inches on her guest. "I insist."

His confusion vanished, his jaw set. "I decline." He held the scroll out again, hovering just above the taper flame.

Both her hands flew up. "Don't!"

The parchment began to smoke, but didn't catch fire. "I don't like playing games when I know neither the rules nor the stakes. I am no one's pawn, Auntie. Whatever your war with your brother is all about, you won't win it through me." He tossed the scroll aside, unburnt.

Katerina sank slowly into her chair. "You are a treasure of surprises."

"We spoke of my childhood. I remember very little of it before Ravenna. But I do remember that pleasing you was as important as it was impossible. So I have decided not to bother."

"You have pleased me. I applaud your restraint."

"Or you would, if you had a second paw. Do you see flattery as my weakness? I won't read it, so I'm a good boy. But as I don't want to be good, I have to read it, no?"

"Poor child. Another riddle."

"Oh, is that my Achilles' heel? Must I succumb to every puzzle? This is excellent – a catalogue of my perceived weaknesses. Yes, I enjoy games. But, as I think I mentioned, I play on my own terms. Not yours, not his. Wage your war through other pieces, Auntie. This one will scorch your remaining hand."

"Mixed metaphors and this constant harping on my hand. Would you like to see it?" She peeled the glove off her left hand and held it up, palm glistening and exposed.

"I've seen worse. Why, there was an imperial man-at-arms last winter with frostbite on his manhood. He would sooner have lost his nose. There was a sight to make the milk curdle in your bosom, if it weren't already turned to gall."

"Are you this insolent with my brother?"

"Ask him yourself."

She rotated her hand around to show him her palm. His nose curled up but he didn't turn away. "It is monstrous, is it not?"

"Young though I am, I have scars too." He held up his left hand, showing her the scarred palm. "Perhaps when I'm grown I'll be as monstrous as you."

"Aren't you interested in learning how this happened?"

"Not in the least."

"I was saving your life."

"Did you ever consider that it might not need saving?" He stepped up and before she could withdraw it took her hand in his. Bowing low, he kissed it. "When Tharwat wishes to share my stars with me, I will be interested. No one else." Turning, Cesco departed.

Outside her chamber, he wanted to break into a run. He wanted to scream. Howl. Tear his hair, gnash his teeth. Most of all he wanted to go back and beg her forgiveness.

He forced himself to walk steadily. How is that woman inside my head? I hardly know her! I barely remember her at all! Why does her voice cut me like a knife? Keeping an even gait, he descended to the kitchens to tell Detto his mother was here, and wished to see him.

Behind him, Katerina closed the door, sealing herself in the empty room. "Well. That could have gone worse."

Like so many Scaligeri country palaces, this one was built in a square that opened on a central garden. Cesco was crossing this yard when he encountered the Capitano's Grand Butler.

"My lord," said Tullio. "A message for you. A rider came with it just this half hour. He wouldn't say who it was from."

Cesco took the scrap of paper and tore away the seal. Reading it over, his right eyebrow arched a bit and the left side of his mouth curled. His mood suddenly mended, the world looking brighter and more full of possibility than it had mere moments earlier. "This rider – by any chance was he a youth about my age?"

"Yes," said Tullio. "But he had a hood over his head and I couldn't see his face."

"A bit warm for a hood, don't you think?" But Cesco was already moving off, the question clearly rhetorical. "Thank you, Tullio, my dear dear friend. If anyone asks, I'm off to hunt the hart."

He broke into a run, singing as he disappeared:

Why let the stricken Deer go weep,
The Hart ungalled play:
For some must watch, while some must sleep;
So runs the world away.

Then as the stricken deer
Withdraws himself alone,
So do I seek some secret place
Where I may make my moan.

There do my flowing eyes
Shew forth my melting hart,
So that the streams of those two wells
Right well declare my smart!

Thirty-One

Darkness had fallen. Bats were beginning to glide through the air overhead, unseen but present. Horses had been stabled, chickens cooped, and the detritus of a day's work in the Rienzi household stowed safely away.

Nestled in a secluded part of the yard, covered in leaves and bracken, Cesco watched the main house. He'd slipped away from the hunting palace, excusing himself perfectly – he'd told the doctor he was tired, told Pietro that he was avoiding Katerina, and insisted Detto deserved time alone with his mother. He'd then dressed in hunting greens and browns as ragged as the ones Lia had worn as Death, and ridden out on a horse borrowed not from the stables but a traveler, who would find a purse far richer than the horse he'd lost.

Arriving just before dusk, he'd headed straight for the perfect perch to observe the house – he'd seen it that morning. So far he'd seen the father now and again through the open windows. Rienzi seemed to like his solitude, and took interruption badly. The son was often visible as well, strutting about and offering petty orders to those who couldn't help but obey.

The girl had appeared only once, coming into the yard to draw water from the well. Cesco might have hissed to her then, but her father had called her in. The paterfamilias seems on edge. Cesco wondered what, if anything, she'd told him. Perhaps it was just Rienzi's habit to be protective of his daughter. Yet instinct told Cesco that this was uncommon, that the father was going to unusual lengths to fortify the house.

Well, there was an attack on their forge. Only natural to be on their guard, lest Cangrande's enemies strike again.

It was reckless of him to come. He knew it. In many ways he didn't know why he had. This had never happened to him before. He felt like he was walking in a fog, feeling his way along a treacherous street. All through the morning he'd replayed their confrontation in his head, critical of his every utterance. How does one woo? His examples were extreme. Cianfa Donati was an antithesis. He'd often seen Cangrande order some woman to his rooms, but he'd never witnessed the Scaliger honestly try to win a woman.

Oddly, his best example came from the Veronese Petruchio and Paduan Kate, married some dozen years now. Yes, they veiled their love-talk in banter and barbs, but their fondness seemed genuine. It was the best example he had.

He'd sought Lia out last night, not because he'd wanted to, but rather because he'd been unable not to. The scene had played out, with him playing the role of an ass, a cad, a bounder. Arrogant, preening peacock, she'd called him. Every word was a sword stroke, as if they were dueling.

Yet he wished to be stabbed. He just couldn't bring himself to drop his guard.

Then he'd done it. Said the thing that cost him more than he could have dreamed, giving voice to his desire. May I see you again?

In answer, she had laughed in his face.

He'd said something, he didn't remember what, and retreated to curl into a ball in his bed and relive that awful moment over and over. Sleep hadn't come, so he'd lit a candle and written a note that was part apology, part justification, part pontification. But he penned it in a code of his own making. If she wanted to read it, she'd have to spend the time to decypher it. Which alone meant that he mattered. Are these lovers' games? I feel both a fool and alive.

He'd relived his humiliation all morning, taking out his anger upon Donna Katerina, who surely deserved it. Then he'd seen the note, in her own hand. In his own code. She'd broken it, and written back.

He held the note tightly in his hand. It was too dark to read it, but he'd memorized it:

> Odysseus,
>
> The answer is yes. Tonight. Come in Death's weeds. My window will be open. I don't like waiting.
>
> – Penelope

Obsessively wondering what she had in mind, Cesco felt shamefully exciting stirrings, both physical and emotional, when he laid eyes on her at a distance, drawing water from the well. His hands shook, his mouth dried up, and his manhood grew stiff, forcing him to shift as a slight dampness emerged around the tip. Dear God, is this what passed between grandfather Dante and his Beatrice? Is this the way it's done?

He knew about the physical act of love, but had so far denied it to himself. Not that there hadn't been opportunities. Many a noble had tried to buy Cesco with their daughters or wives, hoping to bind the Emperor's favourite, who also happened to be the heir to a rich and strong Italian city. Some of the girls had even been beautiful. But the price was too high. A moment of pleasure, or worse, of becoming one of those smitten, besotted men who chase after a woman like a dog after their own tail, making fools of themselves.

As I am now? He put that thought aside.

Unsure how to proceed with the fairer sex, Cesco chose to embrace the example of his foster-father. He didn't need to be told that this rumour of Pietro fathering a bastard on a friend's sister was absurd. Cesco knew that if such were the case, Pietro would have married the girl straight off. Pietro simply wanted no entanglements, nothing to sully his reputation.

Whereas Cangrande's reputation was thoroughly sullied, much to men's approval. Odd how men admire a rutting dog more than a virtuous celibate.

Sex was part of the challenge Cangrande had laid down. From their first interview three years ago, the Scaliger kept hinting that Cesco should take a girl to bed. Did he wish to make Cesco despise love-making, and so lessen its power? That was possible. Perhaps even clever. Many men were undone by their lusts.

Or did Cangrande fear Cesco did not like women? Sometimes Cesco fretted over that as well. There had been times this last year when he found himself aroused in exclusively male company. But it was rarely the shape of men that drew him to attention. It was always when he watched a knight perform a brave feat, or an acrobat make a daring leap, or a singer pluck his heart from his breast like one of his lute's strings.

Talent. Intelligence. Cleverness. Daring. These were the qualities that attracted Cesco. And in Lia, they all converge.

Hidden, waiting for the household to bed down, he had a great deal of time to kill. He divided his attention between reliving the previous scene and planning the coming one. It was not his habit to script himself, but he was unable to stop.

He tried to force his mind back to Katerina and the star-chart. How he'd hungered to open that scroll! Casting it aside was perhaps the hardest thing he'd ever done. He knew – knew – the answer to many mysteries lay within. But he'd seen a matching hunger in Katerina's eyes, and she was not on his list of people to gratify.

Only one person was on that list today.

Finally it was dark enough. Lights extinguished, the house had gone to bed. Emerging, Cesco stretched his aching muscles, then clambered over the low wall and started to circle the outskirts of the yard. At the back of the house, three flights up, Lia's window was wide open, and entirely dark. Feeling weightless, Cesco imagined he could fly right up to it.

Fancy was not the same as cleverness, so he forced himself to wait an extra ten minutes, crouching beside the stable and listening to the snores of the boy within. Finished counting, Cesco briskly crossed the yard to make a few preparations, in case he needed a quick escape. Then he hoisted himself onto the lowest windowsill and set his fingers and feet to finding holds.

He slipped halfway up, his foot scraping down the wall. Catching himself, he hung by his fingers, listening. No barking dog, no whispered offers of help. Only the empty invitation of the open window above. Silently he found his feet and continued his ascent, trembling more with excitement than exertion.

Barely a minute after he'd started, he grasped the sill. He heard the rustling of bedclothes inside the room. With a rush of anticipation he pulled himself into a crouch on the window.

The room was shadowed, the only light coming from the stars outside. He let one foot down onto the floor, moving towards the bed.

"Penelope?"

The figure shifted, making the bed itself creak, groaning under a weight. Instincts flaring, Cesco pulled the hood closer, further obscuring his face. In rough German he said, "Thank God your oaf of a father isn't very bright. He'll never know about this."

Like a wraith rising from a grave, the figure in the bed stood, the coverlet flying across the room. Starlight lanced the sword in the figure's hand. "She's not here, despoiler! Arsonist! Murderer!"

It was the brother, angry angry Adamo. Ducking, Cesco kept to his Germanic guise. "It's not what it looks like, mein herr. Well, it is – but my intentions are entirely honourable." Cesco threw his back against a wall as the sword pierced the plaster just inches from his head. It stuck there.

Laughing, Cesco lashed out with his foot, taking the wind from the irate brother. But young Rienzi kept hold of his sword, which tore free from the wall and sliced along Cesco's left shoulder.

The gasping Adamo reeled across the room. Back-lit by the window behind him, he held his sword high. "We were warned – you German bastard. The Greyhound's heir sent – sent a warning that your master – had threatened my sister." While Cesco frowned in utter bemusement at that story, Adamo raised his voice. "He's here! He's here!"

This was no time to untangle Lia's lies. Dropping his good shoulder, Cesco threw himself against the door, pinning it shut just as two burly men-at-arms tried to come through it. Predictably, Adamo came at him, hacking downwards in a heavy blow. Cesco rolled away from the blow, knocking Adamo into the door and elbowing young Rienzi in the neck as he passed.

"You can't get away!" shouted Adamo as Cesco hopped up to the windowsill, then was struck dumb as Cesco leapt into space. He was struck again as the door flung wide and his father rushed in, lantern in hand.

Falling, Cesco pulled up his legs and threw out his arms. A line from Paradiso had him laughing. 'O human race, born to fly upward, wherefore at a little wind dost thou so fall?' His grandfather would be so proud...

Cesco landed in the hay cart he'd rolled beneath the window for just such an escape. The hay cushioned his landing, but he barked one elbow painfully against the cart's side.

No time for injuries! Your legs work fine! Rolling over backwards, he landed on all fours, raising little clouds of dust. Pushing off the earth, he ran for the low stone wall surrounding the yard as above him Rienzi shouted, "After him! To horse! To horse! Despoiler!"

Cesco kicked up his heels, mind racing. 'The Greyhound's heir sent a warning.' So they don't know it's me. In fact, I'm the hero - if I survive. 'Come in

Death's weeds,' she told me. Ha! Clever. And how did she know I'd pretend to be a German when I sensed danger?

Because it's what she would have done. I like this girl more and more, thought Cesco as behind him the house blazed and dogs were loosed. He vaulted the wall one-handed, coming down into a pile of bracken – the same pile he'd hidden in. His temper flared for a moment as he kicked himself free, then he was laughing again. What a stupid way to die.

Dodging behind a tree, he paused there, panting and thinking. He had to make for his horse, a mile to the south. That meant circling the house again, which would take time on foot. Especially if they had dogs after him. He touched his shoulder. It wasn't a bad cut, but the cloth was damp with his blood. Was he dripping any? Had he left any behind? If he had, a good hound would track his scent easily.

No, better to steal one of their horses and ride away in style. She wants panache? I'll give her panache. Scrambling up the tree, he waited.

Rienzi was mounting in the yard, a firebrand in his hand. "This is the Emperor's minion, an arsonist lapdog who nearly killed Carlo and Agapeto! Now he's tried to insult my daughter. I don't care if the Greyhound wants him alive, I want him dead! D'you hear me, you bastard? You're dead!!"

"We'll catch him, father," said Adamo, mounting his own horse and raising a second firebrand. "Come on!"

Rienzi's men spread out in search of Cesco's trail, thinking he was trying to escape them. Cesco waited until the bulk of the hunters had moved off in various directions, then crawled further out on the limb of the leafy tree, hoping it wouldn't sway. He waited until he was over the path out of the yard, a good fifteen feet off the ground.

Lia's brother came along behind the dog, who was snuffling the earth for traces. By the light of the torch in his hand, Adamo's eyes swept right and left, but never up. Hee hee!

The moment his prey was directly beneath him, Cesco flipped down to hang by his hands, then dropped behind Adamo in the saddle. His right elbow clubbed the young man in the ear, sending him toppling even as his left hand plucked the torch from the falling Adamo's grip. Cesco didn't bother with the reins but kicked his heels into the mare and bolted off, bearing the torch high over his head. "Horrido! Horrido!" shouted Cesco, mocking them with the Germanic hunting cry he'd heard so often these last eighteen months.

"Adamo! You fool!" cried old Rienzi as his son sputtered in the dirt. "There he goes! After him! After him! Get up, fool boy!"

There were three riders ahead on the path ahead of him, but they were facing the wrong way. Cesco thundered at them, swinging the firebrand overhead, making their horses scatter as he threaded between them. One swung a sword, but missed. Other riders whirled about and spurred in pursuit. Old Rienzi gave his son a hand up and they rode double as they chased the bobbing, flickering light of Cesco's stolen torch.

The hunted horse weaved in and out of the trees, causing the firelight to vanish for seconds at a time. At one of these their prey must have ducked, for the light sank down and stayed low. A minute later the horseman seemed to grow indecisive, slowing before making a turn, then shying away from a second turn at the last moment, losing more precious ground.

"We've got him!" called Adamo as he held on to his fat father for dear life. The riders around them spread out, denying the bastard any chance of doubling back.

The instant they came level with the running horse, they knew something was wrong. A moment later they saw why. The firebrand was stuck firmly in a loop of rein around the saddlehorn, pointing straight up to heaven. The saddle itself was empty.

Rienzi's men regrouped. It was only when they took count did they discover one of their number was missing. He'd been at the back of the pack. Retracing their route they found the man unconscious on the ground. His horse was gone.

"God *damn* it! Find him! Find the bastard!!"

Riding his third stolen mount of the day, Cesco was chuckling until he reached the place he'd left his first, the one that bore his saddle-bags with his own clothes and sword.

It wasn't there.

Dismounting, he turned about, looking in every direction. This is the place, I'm sure of it...

On the branch where he'd tethered his mount he noticed something glimmering in the moonlight. A hair-brooch, clipped around a slip of paper. Taking it down, he read:

> Try the clearing – and learn to take bet-
> ter care of your horse.

Cesco's jaw shot out as he pulled a face somewhere between a grin and a grimace. "O, I like this girl so very much, I may just have to kill her."

Careful to avoid Rienzi's men, he rode towards the clearing by the Adige where they'd first met, her knife to his throat. It took some little time to find it, and when he arrived he found that same knife buried in the ground right where Cangrande had been sleeping. Around the haft was another scrap of parchment, tied with an expensive ribbon. Dismounting, Cesco stood for a moment, scanning the forest from cover. Seeing nothing in the wood waiting for him, he took the risk and ran forward. Every moment he half-expected the girl to shoot her crossbow at him from cover.

No bolt came. Cesco plucked the knife out of the ground and tore the note free. The moon above was bright enough to read by if he squinted.

> Poor bird, how you are beguiled. How you wish fowl were fish – smoked salmon, perhaps.

Cesco tucked the note in the pouch at his belt. Returning to his horse, he retraced the path to the ruins of the bridge. Smoke still rose from the structures on either end.

He rode back and forth, resisting the urge to call out for her. At last he spied something on the grassy slope on this side of the water. Dismounting again, he slid down the rise.

It was his sword, rammed into the earth like Excalibur. Beside it was an arrow, the same kind she'd shot at Susanna. Around the shaft, just below the fletching, was wrapped another note:

> A fish on a hook makes poor sport. Swim home, little fish. Know ye not that they which run in a race run all, but one receiveth the prize?

Closing his eyes, Cesco shook his head. She can't let the game end now – she wouldn't. Tucking the note into his shirt, he pried his sword from the ground. Wiping it absently on his sleeve, he looked around. There had to be something more.

There was. A quarter mile down the riverbank, on this side of the water, was a hut, well out of sight of the road. It was humble, with part of the roof fallen. Not habitable for any long stretch of time.

Cesco eyed it with a smile. If I were ending the game, I'd want to watch and see how the fool reacts.

Leaving his stolen horse, Cesco sauntered towards the hut watchful for signs of another message or another ambush. Reaching the hut without sign of either, but on the ground he found traces of a horse. So. Mayhap the game isn't done.

He opened the hut door. The room inside was spare. A small truckle-bed, a table, a chair. Not even a firepit for cooking.

Cesco saw the note, neatly folded and standing on the edge of the bed. Unfolding it, he read it by the moonlight streaming in through a hole in the roof:

> Odysseus,
>
> I couldn't wait forever.
>
>
> Penelope

Outside Cesco heard horses and the cries of men and knew he'd been found again.

Dawn was just breaking when Cesco wearily hauled his bedraggled hide into the Scaligeri palace at Caprino. After plunging into the river and swimming for safety, he'd had to come back on foot.

Greeted by servants, he told them tales of a midnight hunt for a wily prey, omitting the fact that he was speaking of himself. Having amused them, he was starting towards his suite on the second floor when a groom said, "Your horse is well, too, young lord."

"My horse?"

"Yes, lord. The lad who you sent back with it told me it had to be ready for a ride today."

Cesco blinked, then smiled. "A good lad. Did he stay?"

"No, my lord."

"I see." Cesco started walking again, then turned abruptly. "Where are my saddle-bags?"

"In your rooms, lord."

Offering thanks, Cesco nearly ran to his rooms, his energy restored. Yes, there they were, lying across a chair. Tearing them open Cesco found one last note, written in a hand he now knew very well:

> Poor Odysseus. Blown back to where he started. Stay where you are, come no more. Are you so eager for Death's embrace? Very well. On the anniversary of the Vandalism of Rome, in the place of our second meeting, at dusk. I'll be waiting.

But who will you be, wondered Cesco, grinning to himself. Death, or Penelope?

Bundling up the note with the others, all now damp with running ink, Cesco fell into his bed. Vandalism of Rome. That was the second of June, the day the Vandals had sacked the city of Rome nine hundred years before. The place of our second meeting.

That was the Arena in Verona. The use of second also confirmed the date. Clever, clever girl. I must make ready a proper welcome...

They returned to Verona the next day, the last of May. The letter to Cangrande might have reached Rome by now, but it was too soon to expect an answer, so Detto went to stay in the Nogarola house with his mother, while Cesco had Tullio prepare the Scaliger's new palace for himself. "If I'm going to be in trouble, I may as well earn it."

Pietro himself took up residence for the first time in his Verona house, though he spent most of his time at the palace with Cesco. "Thank heaven Mastino and Fuchs are with Cangrande."

"After their disastrous invasion of Padua, he could hardly let them out of his sight this summer," laughed Cesco.

"Have you written your apology to the Emperor yet?"

"I'm still composing it. In my head."

The second of June dawned bright and clear as only an Italian morning can. Cesco awoke with the sun, full of anticipation. He'd laid out a map, and riddles, and a rooftop race to rival the one he'd run with Cangrande – he knew the city so much better now. And he also had access to the catacombs, the old Roman tunnels that ran beneath the palaces. He skipped down the stairs to his breakfast, and was positively glowing when he saw Ser Alaghieri enter, followed by three men in the robes of Franciscans. "Ah! Praise to thee, my Lord, for all thy creatures. Above all, Brother Sun, who brings us the day and lends us his light. Have some bread."

"Francesco, I'm glad to see you up and dressed. There's no time to waste. We have to ride."

Cesco frowned. "Ride? To where?"

"Rome." Ser Alaghieri gave him a lopsided smile. "I need a horse, and some discretion. Do you have either?"

"Both, I hope. And you may have them. But not me. I've some plans today, plans I've gone to great pains to—"

Ser Alaghieri cut across him. "Cesco, whatever game you have in mind, it will have to wait. This," he waved his hand to one of the cowled men, "is William of Occam. This here is Bonagratia of Bergamo. And this is Michael of Cesena, head of the Franciscan Order. They have fled Avignon, running for their lives, and need an introduction to the Emperor. You're going to give it to them."

Looking at the august assembly before him, Cesco laughed so that he wouldn't weep.

Before they departed he penned a coded note that he entrusted to Detto, on pain of torture, death, ridicule, and the loss of friendship, to deliver to anyone standing in the Arena at dusk. The note itself read:

> Poor foole. We are star-crossed, it seems.
> Against my will I am called to vandalize
> Rome myself. But I'll be back. Besides,
> Penelope should be used to waiting.

In hindsight, it was a far better revenge than anything he'd planned. He rode to Rome whistling a cheery tune.

Thirty-Two

Cesco's return to the imperial court created a sensation, as he'd brought with him three of the most famous religious thinkers in the world. He sent ahead to inform Cangrande, who in turn informed the Emperor of the whereabouts of his wayward page. An obvious story was concocted – that, hearing of the flight of his three Avignonnese friends, Ser Alaghieri had written to his foster son, and Cesco had scampered headlong and heedless to help. This convenient tale allowed both Emperor and Scaliger to gloss over the burning of the forge, which was lamented by both as a most regrettable accident. Larger issues loomed.

As the Emperor was still visiting Pisa, it was a shorter ride to intercept him. Pietro had not been back to Pisa since the death of his father's old patron, Uguccione della Faggiuola, who'd been exiled by his backstabbing protégé, Castruccio Castracani. Faggiuola had died ten years before, besieging Padua with Cangrande. Pietro and his father had both attended the funeral for the gregarious, affable, long-haired warlord.

For Pietro, Pisa was a city full of youthful memories. He'd lived here for months, studying with a youth called Lucentio who'd later gone to Padua to continue his education and ended up marrying the sister to Petruchio's wife. Life was full of odd and improbable coincidence.

The ride had been entertaining and joyful, with Cesco and Occam arguing over the moral value of physical, overt actions versus acts of will.

"A man may sin in his heart," argued Cesco, "but surely unless he commits the sin, he has done nothing wrong."

"Ah, has the young master forgotten that the Lord forbids covetousness of neighbour's property and wives?"

"Of property," corrected Cesco, a twinkling smile in his eye. "It was the blessed Sant'Agostino who edged in another commandment against what was said to be his own failing. I commend his creativity, merging the first and second commandments to make room for his own – but I wonder if he did not perhaps go too far, making a commandment to remind himself not to be lustful."

"An excellent point, and most amusingly stated, but entirely peripheral to the question at hand. The Lord prohibits both the action of stealing and the desire to steal, or covetousness. Therefore we may logically deduce that it is the desire to steal that is sinful, the acting upon it merely the consequence of human weakness. Therefore morality exists, not in deeds, but in the desire to do those deeds."

"If deeds have no morality, then what do you say to a man who desires to steal, but overcomes his base desire and refrains? Is he not to be commended? Admired? He has, after all, resisted temptation!"

"Would it not be better not to feel temptation at all?"

"Would it not be lovely to fly?" retorted Cesco. "Wishing a man's nature to be else than it is seems folly. Men are men, and feel as men, weak as God made us. If we do not act upon those feelings, do not commit the sin, are we not saved?"

"Not if you sin in your heart."

"Am I to understand that wanting to do a thing is as bad as actually doing it?"

"That is precisely correct."

"Then I thank you from the bottom of my sinful heart! Since I'm already condemned for the sins of my heart, there is no earthly reason not to make them the sins of my hand."

"That is not my point at all." Occam turned to Pietro. "I see why you like him. But couldn't you have raised him to be a trifle less perverse?"

Enjoying the debate, Pietro shrugged. "I did try."

"It's in my nature," replied Cesco with mock rue-fulness. "I cannot quell my tongue, because it is attached directly to my brain, which is a four-horse cart racing day and night across uneven ground. I enjoy it when someone rides up alongside and keeps pace with me for even the briefest times."

"A racing cart with what destination?" asked Occam.

"Won't know until we get there."

When Pietro arrived at Cangrande's borrowed Roman palace with Cesco and the fugitive ecclesiastics in tow, an exultant Scaliger kissed him on both cheeks. "You're going to be excommunicated again!"

Pietro half laughed. "I'm hoping I'm too small to notice. You're quite cheerful."

"They came to Verona! I shine with reflected glory. I do admire your talent for picking important friends. This only adds to the notion that Verona is the new Athens, the center of the world."

"The center of the world was at Delphi," said Cesco. "Where the Omphalos was located. The bellybutton of the world. I'd like to see that. Is it an innie, or an outie?"

Cangrande glanced at Cesco. "A protrusion, I think. An intrusion is always unwelcome."

"Even from Marathon, with news of victory?"

"Alas, if only you had been as fleet as he, my forge would still be standing."

Cesco slipped from his saddle to bow deeply. "It was the will of Fortune, of Providence. Had I been as swift as thought and prevented the deed, you'd have a rift with the Bavarian. Count this as a blessing. He cannot but feel the churl, filled with after-the-fact regret, as you bring him three wonderful weapons against his mortal enemy the Pope after he treated you so poorly. It gives you the moral high ground."

"That explains my confusion – the terrain is so very unfamiliar. Ser Alaghieri, won't you introduce me to your friends?"

As Cangrande honoured Michael of Cesena, charmed Bonagratia, and vigourously fenced with Occam, Pietro studied him. Older, but younger. The physical heaviness of two years ago was gone. Lean, hard, and happy, his eyes danced again. In the years following Ponte Corbo and his sister's stroke, the Scaliger had lost his purpose. Pietro recognized now that he was a sword honed only in battle. Without like steel to clash against, it rusted and tarnished. Since Cesco's advent, his sister's return, and the arrival of Ludwig, he had found all the challenge his heart desired, and was flourishing.

What happens when there are no more challenges? How far will he go to seek out stimulation, prove his supremacy?

That night at the Duomo of Pisa, before a huge assembly of Italian, German, and French dignitaries and nobles, Emperor Ludwig welcomed Michael of Cesena, Bonagratia of Bergamo, and William of Occam into his company under the delighted eyes of the Colonna brothers and the nervous shifting of the new anti-Pope. Last month Ludwig had taken his friend, a defrocked priest named Pietro Rainalducci of Corbario, and proclaimed him Pope Nicholas V. The new Pope was in his sixties, and looked massively uncomfortable. He'd come to the clergy late, after separating from his wife at the age of forty, and eighteen years under orders had not prepared him for the role he was now forced to play.

It was a remarkably Franciscan affair, as the few Dominicans who deigned to rub shoulders with the Emperor at all had all abjured the taint of welcoming three notorious heretics who refused to accept that Christ had owned property.

Ludwig spoke first. He began by thanking his young protégé, Franz der Hund, and his two fathers, Lord Cangrande della Scala and Ser Pietro Alaghieri, for escorting the trio of Franciscans to his welcoming arms. If Ludwig harboured suspicions that Cesco had meant to betray him, they were not in evidence. He then moved on to speak of the great achievements of these three refugees, and the eternal shame of those who denied their dedication to God and His divine plan.

After he was finished, all three Franciscans made speeches. Bonagratia began, receiving laughs as he cheerfully whipped the crowd into a fervor against the Avignon pope.

Occam's speech was welcome for its brevity. He knelt before the Emperor and said simply, "Tu me defendas gladio, ego te defendam calamo."

Having exceptional Latin, Pietro effortlessly translated Occam's admirably succinct statement. Defend me with the sword, I will defend you with the pen.

Last of all, Michael received Ludwig's embrace, then turned to the crowd. "Today, the prophecy of Paul to Timothy is fulfilled. 'The time will come when they will not endure sound doctrine; but after their own lusts shall they heap to themselves teachers, having itching ears; and they shall turn away their ears from the truth, and shall be turned unto fables. But watch thou in all things, do the work of an evangelist, make full proof of thy ministry.' So we have done, my fellows and I. We have abandoned the new Babylon, where the one and only head of the Holy Roman Church, Jesus Christ, is held in captivity, bound with chains of gold. High Priests and Elders, Scribes and Pharisees, behave now just as they did when they crucified the Savior. They have banished we three worshippers of Christ. But we are not without hope. The Lord's hand is not shortened. He works through His agents, proved with the elevation of the rightful head of the temporal arm of His Will on Earth, the Holy Roman Emperor before us, Ludwig IV, God bless, preserve, and keep him. Under his rule, we live in trust in the Most High that the new Babylonian Captivity will end, that the whole Church will resume its rightful seat upon the Rock of the Faith, Peter's seat upon Vatican Hill. But if this be not God's Will, yet I am sure that neither death, nor life, sword, spear, angel, devil, nor any other creature, will separate us from the love of God, and from the defending of the Christian Faith!"

It was an excellent speech, and Pietro would have been more impressed had he not seen Occam standing, eyes closed, lips barely moving. He was reciting the speech in time with Michael. Which meant that Occam, the great thinker, had written it for Michael, the great orator.

731

Looking at the assembled crowd, Pietro saw a pair of familiar faces – his boyhood friend Lucentio, looking fit and able, with his ancient father Vincentio the merchant. Pietro made a mental note to renew that old acquaintance.

But it could not happen tonight – there was too much demand for his company. Immediately following the ceremony, Pietro was embraced by Cardinal Sciarrillo Colonna. "I told you I'd see you soon! While I was sorry your master would not allow you to attend the coronation, it's allowed you a much more lustrous entrance! Well done!"

Pietro thanked him. "But it was hardly more remarkable than your own advent! I thought you entirely ensconced in Avignon."

The patrician head shook from side to side. "I can only whore myself for so long. It is not a place for mending the soul. As your friend Cardinal Gui has learned. I'm told he returned from his Italian mission a much less strident presence. I am not certain if that was due to his adventures there, or his encounter with you. But he is not as fearsome as once he was."

Good. Aloud, Pietro passed that by. "I confess, your Eminence, when I heard that the Emperor meant to appoint a pope, I was certain he'd choose you."

"What, and risk me someday slapping him in the face? Or myself? No, he wanted a man of straw, a mild, weak-willed religious simpleton."

"He seems to have chosen his man correctly, then."

"Oh, Rainalducci – or Pope Nicholas, as we must now call him, I suppose – is at heart a good man. Not a venal bone in his body, which might explain why his wife threw him out. But let's not mistake, the Emperor was not choosing a head for the Church. He was choosing a puppet, through which he can attack Avignon. Do you think I would consent to such a role?"

"Even if you would, your grace, you would find it impossible. You'd cut your strings right off."

Sciarrillo laughed heartily. "I would at that! Even if it meant collapsing in a heap. Now, where is that boy of yours? I've met him often these last weeks, and he always amuses me. He has a mouth made for slapping!"

"Or kissing," said Cesco, appearing. "I have been conversing with your lay brother, Lord Stefano. We were trying to decide how to replicate the Pisan drainage system on Roman roofs."

Arriving in Cesco's wake, Lord Stefano Colonna looked entirely at his ease. Roman to his core, even in Pisa he exuded a calm ownership of the world around him. The four of them spent a deal of time conversing, then the elderly Colonna brothers moved on to hold court over other men.

As they departed, Cesco shook his head. "When I met Stefano I began to understand the longevity of the old Roman Empire. A nobleman born. I look at Ludwig and there is no comparison. Colonna should be emperor. It's in his blood."

"And if he were killed, Sciarrillo would be Caesar in his place, slapping everyone. For every good emperor of the blood, there were five bad ones. Heredity cannot supplant ability."

"Thank heavens, then, that I have both the ability and the blood. And thanks to you, that blood is now legitimate. I am no longer a bastard."

"You will always be il veltro."

"Il veltro del Veltro, you mean," said Cesco, laughing.

Pietro smiled wanly. The time was coming when he was going to have to tell Cesco. If he didn't, Katerina would, as a weapon against her brother. Pietro was certain that was why she'd come to Caprino.

And why shouldn't he know? There's no betrayal, no disillusionment here! Unlike Cangrande, Cesco is the Greyhound! Every sign points to the chart that says he'll be the savior, not to the dark one where everything goes awry, where his talents are wasted, where his worser nature takes control.

But there was always the third chart, the one Pietro had suggested, the one with two falling stars, crossing in the middle of the heavens. So long as that one existed, taunting them, it was best not to show him any of them. Soon. Soon.

Cangrande joined them on the Duomo steps, just below the nearly finished bell tower. "A thoroughly successful evening. Reunions abound, alliances strengthened, and an end to an idyll."

"Was that Passerino you were talking with?"

"Indeed. I apologized for my laxity as his neighbour and friend, and he pledged a renewed love for me and all things Veronese. Such amiable amity! He is feeling the bite of my displeasure, though I doubt he suspects those are my teeth in his neck. His power is sadly waning. Last summer he lost his hold on Modena, and the Gonzaga clan is getting in everywhere. They have the money and their own army of mercenaries. See there? That's Guido Gonzaga in the striped cape and slashed doublet. Rakish devil, is he not? Passerino is desperately trying to ignore his presence. Alas, too late. His friends, the Este family, might be thinking they've backed the wrong horse. I expect things to come to a head soon. To save himself and retain control of Mantua, he must either embrace me forever or rebel in earnest. My new good-standing with the Emperor does not make his decision any easier."

"You sound sorry for him."

"Do I? I suppose I am sorry he turned against me. But he had his shot, and out of friendship I've let him live. But a life free of stress? That's asking too much." Cangrande looked Cesco over, head to heel. "Ludwig and I spoke of you just now."

Cesco ran his fingers through his long curling hair, sighing ruefully. "The ending idyll you mentioned. I assume that, though he has stated his gratitude in the warmest terms, the great Emperor has released me from his service?"

"He did it in the form of returning my hostage to me, an act of graciousness. He thanked me for the loan of you, and said that my dutiful service this last year has erased all doubts. This last event has set the seal on my loyalty. He has even offered to assist me in rebuilding my lost forge, of which he has heard so much." Here was a dark smile for Cesco, who mirrored it in the spirit of mockery.

"Did he perhaps mention that I had tried to prevent his arsonists from achieving their goal?"

"On the contrary, he praised you to the heavens, and said that if ever you wish to join him in Germany, you are most welcome. He took great pains to express his deep and abiding relief that your disappearance had such a happy outcome for everyone."

Cesco clucked his tongue. "Alas, I fear he doesn't trust me anymore."

"Why should he? When it came to a real choice, him or me, you chose me. I am as surprised as he."

Cesco broke a leg, sweeping into a magnificent bow. "I hope to keep surprising you for all the days to come."

Cangrande let that pass. "It does gall me that the forge goes unanswered. We cannot strike at the benevolent Emperor. But I would know the names of the men sent to do the deed?"

Cesco's expression became sly. "You needn't fear for them."

"Are they beyond our reach?"

"Not at all. But you needn't trouble yourself. I've taken care of meting out a touch of retribution."

Pietro didn't like the sound of that. Cangrande himself looked bemused. "What did you do?"

Cesco's eyes shone with innocence. "Arranged a measure of justice, is all."

A shiver ran down Pietro's spine. Had he been gone too long? Had the boy changed? Was cold-blooded murder now part of his character? "Tell me, right now, that you haven't contracted hired killers."

Cesco's smile became less placid, more active. "Of a sort. They are skilled in making men die."

"Cesco—"

"Relax, Nuncle. Had the blacksmith or his apprentice died, I would certainly have had them torched in their lodgings, burning them as living candles for their own journey to Hell. But as no one died, they are guilty only of burning down the source of Verona's swords. I deemed it only just and right to give a burn to their swords as well."

"What on Earth..?" demanded Pietro.

"In plain terms, please," said Cangrande.

"In the plainest of terms, I fear it is unseemly. But if I must..." He paused to grin wickedly. "I hired a pair of whores ripe with the pox to visit them, with the Emperor's compliments. Their swords will be burning for years to come."

Cangrande burst out laughing, drawing eyes with his magnificent smile. Then he amazed everyone, Pietro most of all, by drawing Cesco into a fierce embrace and ruffling his hair. Cesco blinked in surprise, then ducked and the two of them began slapping and wrestling affectionately on the Duomo steps.

Pietro was laughing too, but there were tears in his eyes. Pathino was dead. Cangrande and Cesco were allies, perhaps even friends. Pietro was back among the saved. Who knew – could Antony and Mari bury the hatchet? At that moment, everything was right with the world and the future seemed to hold only brightness and light. Anything was possible.

Anything.

Thirty-Three

It took nearly a month for Cesco and Cangrande to extricate themselves from the imperial court, and longer for Pietro – as the son of Dante, he was invited to stay and recite his father's works for the emperor's amusement. He did more than that, lecturing on them. Between compliments at his erudition, he was often informed that his reading was wonderful, though he lacked his foster son's flair. His only answer was, "Well I know it."

While in Pisa, Pietro made good his vow to renew his old acquaintance with Lucentio and his father Vincentio, who'd been old fifteen years ago. Calling at the large house, Pietro was instantly welcomed by the aged trader, whose wealth did not seem as vast as of yore. By some remarks he let slip, it was clear that his daughter-in-law had a taste for fine things and that Lucentio was incapable of crossing her. But Vincentio still had his fleet of trading ships, including his three prized argosies, which he promised to show to Pietro the moment they returned to port.

As there is nothing so charming as boyhood nostalgia, Lucentio was over-joyed to see Pietro. After the embraces he immediately summoned his wife Bianca. "You must meet her, Pietro. She is the treasure of my life."

She took her time in coming, but at last appeared dressed in the finest patterned gown, its sleek, elegant lines emphasizing her form, following the contours of her body. A wide neckline, fitted sleeves, and full skirts with a small train. But despite being married she wore no headdress, allowing her silky brown hair to fall past her shoulders, parted frame her face in wispy locks.

Pietro knew her sister well, but Bianca looked nothing like Petruchio's wife. Kate Bonaventura seemed to always be in motion, her beauty as much of inner life as outer flesh. Kate had curling red hair and green eyes that danced with intelligence and wit, and when she laughed the world laughed with her. Whereas Bianca's perfect smile never seemed to move, the better to show off her dimpled cheeks. Her handsome chin had a dimple too, her nose (slightly thicker than her sister's) was still straight and true, and her eyebrows were perfect dark arches. Under them, Bianca's eyes were a watery blue with a dark ring about them. They were mocking eyes, lively, but without kindness.

From the first moment Pietro could see she was a terrible flirt, as she hooked her arm in his and tried to lead him into the garden. "Ser Alaghieri! I'm tremendously pleased to meet you. I've heard such stories! Verona, Ravenna, Bologna, Avignon! Tell me, did you visit Paris?"

"Not since I was a boy," said Pietro. "I went with my father."

"Your father, he did like to travel, didn't he? Walking among the damned in Hell. O, you must stay here as our guest! You have so many stories to tell!"

Having just escaped a friend's household with a flirtatious woman in it, Pietro resolutely declined the offer. Lucentio looked relieved, and Pietro realized that his reputation as a thrower of bastards was at work here in Pisa, too. But he did visit as often as he could slip free of the imperial court, so that he and Lucentio could wax nostalgic for days past.

Meanwhile, further north, Verona was subject to a series of feasts through July to formally welcome Cangrande and Cesco back. There were hunts and games, and Cesco loudly proclaimed his determination to participate in the Palio this next year if it was the death of him. He'd missed three of them now, hadn't even seen them. Though several months off, it was a perfect statement of intent – he belonged to Verona, not the Holy Roman Empire. He went so far

as to set up races among the young men each fortnight to prepare – a horseback race the first Friday
of the month, a footrace on the third. He won the
horserace in July, but lost the footrace to Detto, who
shoved him off the Ponte Pietra in the Adige. Cesco
came up laughing to give Detto the fig.

The second horse race was won by Paride, great-
nephew to Cangrande's wife. The twin sons of Petruchio had been right in it until the end, when they'd
fallen off their horses as they struck at each other
wildly.

As they passed the finish line, Cesco glanced at
Detto. "You were holding back."

Detto lowered his voice conspiratorially. "We can't
win every event. It would be ungracious."

Cesco nodded gravely, his eyes dancing. "So I
think."

A week after Paride's triumph, Cangrande escaped the sweltering heat by taking his whole court
to Caprino. Cesco had worked it subtly, making sure
the trip was the Scaliger's idea, not his own. They
traveled on the fourteenth of August, and on the
morning of the fifteenth the massed assembly of
men rode out to chase wherever the hounds led.

As two years earlier, Cangrande rode beside his
heir. But this time the jostling was friendly, the ca-
maraderie unforced, the laughter shared. When the

buck was sighted, Cesco loosed a shaft to frighten it into Cangrande's aim.

Pietro had gained permission from Ludwig to come north for the hunt, though with strict instructions to rejoin the imperial court in Rome. Riding beside Morsicato, Pietro watched it all with a full, if stricken, heart.

Seeing his expression, the doctor said, "What's the matter?"

"Nothing!" said Pietro quickly. "Cangrande and Cesco are at last the allies they should always have been. The way things should be."

He felt Morsicato's eyes on him, but said nothing further. If he felt a pang of sadness, of loss, it was selfish, and he had to work to banish such emotions from his heart.

Just as they were loosing the hounds for a second chase, a rider came galloping up, manner urgent. "What, again?" lamented Cesco. "Shall we never finish a hunt?"

Cangrande's answer was curious. "Too soon, too soon." But he rode to meet the messenger, passing a few hurried words out of earshot of the rest. Pietro thought the rider looked familiar, in his striped cape and slashed farsetto.

Cangrande returned. "Alas, my friends, we must end our sport and ride for quite a different catch! Our new troops will be blooded, the old ones will earn their pay. But I think it should be a younger man who leads them. We'll let them draw straws for it. Come – back to the palace!"

"Is it Padua?" demanded Mastino eagerly. He'd not been allowed to stray from the Scaliger's side all summer, lest he renew his ill-advised breaking of the truce.

"No," said Cangrande shortly. "Come, I'll explain as we ride!"

For the first time, Cesco became mulish. "I haven't gotten my kill in for the day."

"Come along and I promise you shall," replied Cangrande significantly.

Cesco bowed his head. "I appreciate the offer – truly. But I think someone not of the blood would make a better choice for such game."

Cangrande stared shrewdly at his heir. "Who would you suggest?"

"Castelbarco the Younger. If you like I shall be your voice in Verona."

Cangrande nodded. "It will be as you suggest. I'll make the depositions. Stay and collect the hounds, while I–"

"–while you let slip the dogs of war," Cesco finished.

"Just so." Grinning, Cangrande sawed the reins to turn his mount, then spurred back towards the palace, the whole of the party in his wake save Pietro, Morsicato, Detto, and Cesco.

Cesco gave his friend a grim face. "Behold, the hour is at hand."

Detto gave him a ghost of a smile. "Verily, I say. In the face."

Cesco giggled. "In the face."

After long years of reading it on his own, Pietro knew his Bible better than ever. So he recognized even an oblique reference to the passage in the Gospel of Matthew. The Great Betrayal. "What's this about? Who was that man? He looked familiar…"

"A Gonzaga," said Cesco helpfully. "Guido, to be specific, brother to Ser Filippino. We saw him in Pisa, if you'll recall. A star ascendant."

Pietro remembered now. Yes, he'd seen Guido Gonzaga at the imperial court in Pisa, and again when Ludwig returned to Rome. A shifty-eyed condottiero, leader of a band of mercenaries. "The Gonzaga are Mantuan, aren't they?"

"Decidedly. You doubtless recall the slightly scorched fresco in Lord Capulletto's yard? Here the story is repeated. Cangrande is David, of course. The role of wife is a communal one, something you don't often look for in wives. Today the part of Uriah will be performed by our beloved, and soon to be lamented, Bonaccolsi. His ear must be twitching even now. Ho-ha, happiness and God be with him. As the hounds are already loosed, shall we hunt?"

"Wait a moment," said Morsicato, grasping Cesco's shoulder even as his mind raced to catch up. "He's replacing Bonaccolsi? Now?"

Cesco's eyes were on the treeline for some reason. "You seem surprised."

"I'm only surprised you're not more interested. You have a score to settle with him. He was part of the attempt to poison you."

"And his partner, the dandy Dandolo, threw Nuncle Pietro into a Venetian cell for months. Should he seek to revenge himself, or is it enough that justice is achieved? Besides, if the Capitano is bent on overthrowing his best former friend, I am the last person he should send. As I suggested, he should choose someone without ties to the family. He may send in sending Paride as an emissary of the clan, but I think Castelbarco the Younger will do nicely. That way it is Verona, not the Scaliger, turning on our ally. Preserves his honour."

Detto blew a raspberry. He'd once revered his uncle Cangrande. That had changed years ago, during the early stages of Cesco's hawking. The lines were drawn within the family, and Detto only knew two sides – for Cesco, or against him. Detto's father was a neutral, but his mother was certainly for Cesco. His brother Val would be, when he was old enough. But that was it. Cangrande, Mastino, Alberto, even young Paride – they were all Cesco's enemies. And therefore, Detto's.

Morsicato was still fretting. "I don't like it. He's taking an active hand in Bonaccolsi's downfall? They're brothers-in-law, for God's sake. His sister married Passerino's brother! I don't think he realizes how badly this is going to go down among the people."

"Perhaps he doesn't care," observed Pietro. "I must confess, he's been very patient."

The doctor shook his head violently. "I worry this means a real change. The only time he's ever tried to kill his friends was in secret. If he's doing it in the open…"

Cesco turned in his saddle. "Medicus meus, you sound as if you speak from experience! Has he ever tried to kill you?"

Rather than laugh, Morsicato said nothing, just chewing on his beard. Pietro kicked his horse into a trot, saying, "We should round up the hounds before they find the scent and can't be distracted."

It was Cesco who had the scent of something. "Tell me about it, dottore, please. When did his heavy hand aim for you?" The doctor did not respond, and Cesco threw up his hands in theatrical frustration. "Oh for the love of God, Mary, and all virgins! I'm a year away from being a man, and still you think you have to protect me! I'm fourteen, not four! I need to know! Secrets have to come to light to be any use! You're leaving me baiting the bear in a dark pit with a dull goad. I've managed to avoid the bear for three years, but if you think he's mad, I need to have a light at least, if not a spear."

Still the doctor was silent, and Cesco lifted his chin to address the bright clouds overhead. "Dear Lord, protect this good, noble, stoic, immovable, imbecilic man. I used reason, allegory, and blasphemy. I even said please. He is like Pietro's namesake, a rock."

Pietro and Morsicato exchanged a look. Pietro shrugged. "You know part of the story already. It was the same night Detto's mother burned her hand. You and he were both kidnapped."

"By my own kinsman, the late and unlamented Pathino." Cesco touched the scar by his eye. "You traced us and rescued me—"

"We got trapped in a cave. Pathino caused a landslide. They had to dig us out."

Cesco's face blossomed in amazement. "I didn't know that!"

"Detto's father took him right home – you had a broken arm," added Morsicato in an aside to Detto, who was fascinated.

"Then you, Donna Katerina, my father and I got into a carriage belonging to Cangrande's wife. But the doctor had recognized her drivers. They'd tried to kill you in your bed a few months earlier."

"How did I escape that time?"

"Hid in the rafters until I came," said Morsicato.

Cesco's eyes were round as shields. "I must remember to pick at you less in the future. Go on, go on!"

The doctor finished the tale. "I told Cangrande about the drivers and we made to chase them. Just the two of us. When we were close, Cangrande distracted me, then hit me over the head. Had Cesco been killed, I would have too. But since Pietro, Katerina, and Dante all escaped, there was no point. Too many people knew of Giovanna's treachery. We were exiled instead. The Scaliger's way of protecting his wife."

They rode on for a time, chasing the music of hounds and echo in conjunction. Then all at once Cesco began to sing:

Che pur la corona
Ne porta Verona

Per quel che si suona
Del dire e del fare!

Destrier et corsiere,
Masnate at bandiere,
Coraccie et lamiere
Vedrai remutare!

Sentirai poi li giach
Che fan guei padach -
Giach, giach, giach, gaich, gaich!
Quando gli odo andare!

———————

Indeed a crown
Verona wears,
This trumpet blown
This deed declares!

Warhorse and charger,
Fighting man, banner,
Cuirass and sword,
All a-charging!

Hear the tramp, tramp,
Foot soldiers stamp.
Tramp tramp tramp tramp tramp!
Hear how they go!

751

Pietro felt a lump in his throat. "That's the song I taught you while we were buried. As long as we sang, we were alive."

Cesco was maddeningly calm. "Clever fellow. What was it Dante used to say? 'Parenting is the art of distraction.' A philosophy to which I think Cangrande subscribes. I thought I was sent away for my protection."

"It's true," said Pietro. "One of the people he was protecting you from was his wife."

"Practical. Even in murder." Cesco shrugged, then smiled at Morsicato. "I'm very glad you are not dead, doctor."

"But you would have done the same," sniffed the doctor in disgust.

"Not at all. I don't plan to marry such a bitch. Hey ho! The hounds!"

The greyhounds and mastiffs were circling out, flushing a hare from cover. The best thing to do was to was to take the game, then round up the dogs. Pietro, Morsicato, and Detto all went after it, and argued whose bolt had been truest until it was seen that the doctor had hit home.

They were just beginning to gather up the dogs when Pietro looked around. "Where's Cesco?"

In the covert of the wood, Cesco dismounted beside the waiting Lia, who was nuzzling one of the hunting hounds that had slipped the pack. She was again dressed in her hood and rags, but the foot of height and curve of shape she'd added since last he'd seen her in them made the disguise less effective.

"I heard you were back in residence," she said.

"I meant for you to hear. I've been in Verona a month. You haven't come."

"No excuse to."

"Can you find an excuse to come Friday?"

"Why?"

"To watch me race, of course."

"I've run a race with you, and won."

"Depends on where you place the finishing line. And if we're given an equal start."

"Oh, poor little boy whining about the rules," she teased, talking to the dog. "As it happens, we're heading for Verona tomorrow morning. With your master the bastard back, we've begun rebuilding the forge, and father needs men and equipment. It's a chance for me to buy some pretty dresses, he says."

"He hasn't seen you in this? It's quite becoming. Tell me, why do you hate him so?"

Him could only mean one person. "You've seen how he treats my father. Worse than one of his hounds." Lia scrubbed the greyhound's neck, and it gave her a flickering kiss. "But with the rebuilding, he's been generous. Almost kind. Though don't let my brother hear me saying that. The family line is to hate the hand that feeds us."

"And is that your line? Do you hate all Scaligeri?"

Lia's nose crinkled under the hood, and again she addressed the hound. "I thought he was a hunter, not a fisher. But he'll catch no compliments in his net today."

Wounded, Cesco turned his head. "The hunters hunt me. What of tomorrow? Shall we keep our appointment from months past? Or shall Odysseus become the patient waiter?"

Lia continued rubbing the hound's ear. Cesco felt her nearness as if she were the moon, pulling the tides of his blood. At last she said, "Very well. Midday, the day after next."

"The Arena?"

She rolled her eyes. "What excuse could I have for going there? No – San Zeno's. I'll tell them I've gone to confession."

"Indeed! To confess your love for me. I'll be there at the very prick of noon."

She did not answer, nor did she roll her eyes. Instead she did something wonderful. She blushed! She was as excited as he.

"This hungry dog must leave you." Cesco took the greyhound by its collar. "But tomorrow he will have kisses for you aplenty."

"If he insists, remind him to chew mint leaf. And use less tongue."

"No promises, and thus no lies!" Laughing and skipping, Cesco left the wood and called haloo to his companions.

Neither he nor she spied a shadow in the glade. Only the dog had noticed the watcher. But as the hound knew him well, it had said nothing.

Returned to the palace at Caprino, they found it all up in arms as everyone packed. At last they heard the actual news from Mantua. Tensions had been rising all summer, coming to a head that morning in a confrontation between Passerino's son – named for the Scaliger, who was his god-father – and Filippino Gonzaga. Filippino had called to his brother's mercenaries for help, but facing the might of Mantua that would not be enough, so Guido had come at once to seek Verona's aid.

It was a manufactured crisis, but one that Cangrande had not expected quite yet. His cat's paws, the Gonzaga, had clearly seized the main chance when they'd seen it, and now Cangrande had to scramble to make sure Bonaccolsi fell.

Already the Scaliger had sent a party of soldiers to aid in deposing his good friend Passerino, and more would have to follow. This news caused a great deal of consternation among the Veronese. Those not in the know of Bonaccolsi's longstanding treachery were subtly informed that this was not injustice – quite the reverse.

Cesco was even more phlegmatic. "Not past time! Though Mantua is outside the Trevisian Mark, it's been within Verona's sphere for fifteen years and more. The city should pay homage. As long as Passerino lives, he detracts from the Scaliger's sense of himself. Don't chew your beard, doctor, it's disgusting."

Detto finished the last of his wine. "Who did he send to Mantua?"

"Castelbarco's son. With cousin Paride. Who else do you send to betray a cause but a Parisian? I tell you, in two days, three at the most, we'll be in Mantua installing a new podestá."

They returned to Verona the next day, passing the Rienzi party on the road. Cesco and Lia ignored each other completely – not even a stolen glance to give them away.

Arriving back in the city, news from Mantua turned faces grim. With Castelbarco the Younger holding the Mantuan soldiers at bay, the Gonzoghi had dragged Bonaccolsi and his son from their homes. Stripped of their armour and given a moment to pray, they were beheaded in the street. Word was already spreading that Passerino's last words were a plea to speak to his friend the Scaliger.

Verona's nobles shared dark looks, and not a few crossed themselves. Two touched their own necks. Cangrande expressed his sorrow by commanding a large feast. Tullio clucked his tongue as he hobbled off to oversee preparations.

But the feast never took place. Young Paride returned bearing news that the Mantuan people were gathering in the streets, demanding an explanation for the murder of their leader. Young Castelbarco was barricaded in the palace with the whole Gonzaga clan, awaiting aid from the Scaliger.

"The fools. Can't they even perform a coup without my being there?" Annoyed, Cangrande called up his nobles and gave the order to ride.

Having come to feast, Antony Capulletto paused before returning home to don his armour. "My lord, this is damn ticklish. You know I have in-laws in Mantua? Of course you do. My wife's sister married Ser Vitruvio, and they live there, where he–"

"Capulletto, I really don't have time for your–"

"My wife's in Mantua," said Antony bluntly. "Little baggage went off to visit her sister to get over the latest…"

Cangrande had the good grace to pause and clap Capulletto on the shoulder. "I'm so sorry. Both your sons – it's a crime. Your daughter is well?"

Antony's face lit up. "An angel. Completely devoted to me, of course. But, as I said, her mother's gone off to Mantua. If it's not asking too much…"

"I'll send a detachment of men to see she's safe. Do you want to lead them?"

"No no! I'd rather ride with the others. I just needed to be sure – she isn't much, but…"

"She's your wife, and she's given you your angel. It's just bad luck the boys died. Now arm, mount, and ride close to me. Let's make sure the House of Capulletto is even more famous for the next son."

Antony bowed. "Thank you, lord."

Soon the flower of Veronese nobility was gathered in the Piazza dei Signori. Yet one face was missing. Cangrande clapped his hands loudly. "Cesco! No time for your foolery!"

"He's not here, my lord," said a page.

"Well, somebody find him!"

When the mortified pages returned alone, Cangrande glowered. "You've searched the whole palace? And the grounds?" The answer was a fearful affirmative. "Damn him. Where's Detto?"

The huge voice of Bailardino roared out, cutting through the noise of the yard. "Bailardetto da Nogarola! To me!"

Detto came running from his place behind Petruchio and skidded to a halt between his uncle and father. "Where is he, boy?"

Detto looked blank. "He isn't here?" Cangrande's jaw clenched but before he could utter his cutting answer, Detto said, "I haven't seen him since the order was given, my lord. I've been busy with Lord Bonaventura's armour."

Cangrande slammed a fist into his mailed palm. "Just when we were getting along. Do you have any notion what he's up to?" Detto shook his head. "Well, it seems I must travel without my squire. Nico, may I borrow yours?"

"Of course, my lord. Hop to it, boy!"

As Paride ran to take up station behind the Scaliger, clutching the reins that should have been Cesco's, Mastino leaned in close to the Capitano. "Uncle, let me find him."

Cangrande sighed in exasperation. "I can't have my whole family disappearing just as I show my face in Mantua. How can I give order to a city when my own family is in chaos?"

Mastino was insistent. "At least let me send some-one to find where he's gone."

"As you like. The rest of you – to Mantua!"

Thirty-Four

17 August 1328

It was midmorning on a Wednesday, and the sun was as bright as a late summer sun could be. The city was all aflutter about the goings-on in Mantua, but there was no fear. Already rumour had spread that the coup was Cangrande's doing, and for citizens that had prospered in the seventeen years of his rule, that was enough. They trusted their clever, daring, open-handed lord. After all, he was the Greyhound!

It was a morning for activity. With most of the lords gone, the city had an easy air. Swimming in the Adige, games of dice or cards, boxing and wrestling – almost a holiday.

It certainly was one for Thibault Capulletto. With the lord of the house absent, the thirteen-year-old abandoned the volume of San Francesco's works he was supposed to be memorizing and instead recovered his favourite Fechtbuch from its hiding place, retrieved his wooden sword from under his straw mattress, then ran across to the door to the roof.

The rooftop on the northeast corner of the household was just one story off the ground, overlooking the walled cobblestone yard. This L-shaped roof over Capulletto's office and guest-house held a dovecote, and the gentle cooing was always a happy, soothing sound.

Emerging, Thibault saw with bitter disappointment that others had beaten him to this sunny perch. On a stool in the shade of the dovecote sat Angelica, his old nurse. At her knee, sprawled in relaxation, was her husband, the enormous and gregarious Andriolo. It wasn't often that both master and mistress were away. What a day for it, too, with a sky so clear and blue, not a cloud in sight.

Angelica's charge was there as well. Thibault's little cousin Giulietta was enjoying the sunshine in a more active way, racing around Angelica's legs, chasing a butterfly wafting on the air.

Thibault liked his cousin well enough. She was a decent companion on walks, always animated, and quite an admirer of her dashing cousin Thibault. The only time she had grown morose was when her baby brother died last year. She'd been too little to mourn the first one, but at two she had liked the little baby named for her father, and his death had smote her. Whereas Thibault had felt nothing but satisfaction that his uncle had no heir.

Quickly dodging around the dovecote, Thibault found a place in the light of the ascending sun. Sword in hand, open book before him, he set his feet to imitate the woodcut print figure in the book. Weapon poised just so, he dueled an imaginary opponent who looked not unlike his uncle. He cut and parried, turned and thrust, ducked and danced. Grunting, he blocked the phantom follow-through and cut again. This time his invisible foe was caught off-guard and Thibault delivered the killing blow. "Ha!"

Giulietta came toddling around the corner of the dovecote, forcing Thibault to check his next series of blows. "Watch it!"

"Tibby, Tibby, where's my sword?"

"You don't get a sword, Cricket. You're a girl."

"When I'm five I'll have a sword."

"You won't know how to use it."

"I will! I'm very good. See?" She was pointing at a massive bump on her brow she'd gotten the day before. Running in the cobblestone yard below, she'd taken a spill and landed plumb on her face. She'd started to cry, but Andriolo had rushed forward and scooped her up. Brushing the earth from her skirts and hoisting her onto his shoulders, he'd diverted her before the crying could set in. "Ah, my little Giulia! You're not so clever yet! When you're old enough to know better, you'll fall on your back, won't you?"

Blinking away her tears with a smile, Giulietta had giggled and shouted, "Aye!"

That answer had provoked gales of laughter from Angelica, who spent all afternoon repeating the exchange to whomever would listen. When Thibault had heard it, he'd only scowled. "You just don't understand," Angelica had said, pityingly. "One day you will!"

Thibault understood the joke. He just didn't find it funny. Of course, he wasn't thinking of his cousin on her back. He was thinking of Tessa. At each repetition of this story his mind's eye had conjured a picture of Tessa on her back beneath the hulking shape of his uncle.

It wasn't just imagination – he'd spied on them often enough to have the scene seared into his memory like a brand. He cut the air again, the wooden sword hissing, but hurting nothing.

Tessa was in Mantua now, in danger. Thibault wanted to steal a horse and ride to her rescue. But Andriolo, anticipating that, had had all the remaining horses unshod. Besides, Thibault didn't even know which way Mantua was. He'd never been anywhere, hardly even allowed out of the house.

Grunt. Stab. Thirteen – a squire's age. He was almost a man. He should be serving some nobleman, learning the art of war. The moment he turned fifteen, he knew, he'd run off and join a mercenary band, and rise to the rank of condottiero and fight for money and glory. Or even better, become a champion-for-hire, a duelist who wandered the land, living by his sword alone.

Until then, he practiced. Evading his cousin, who was spinning in circles now, Thibault came around the corner, swinging away. On her shaded stool, Angelica had her blouse open, rubbing something from a jar onto her nipples. With any other woman Thibault might have stopped to watch, but he'd seen so much of the nurse's breasts over the years they lacked all novelty.

He resumed his attack on a restored enemy, thinking this time of how to balance his feet. Halfway through he went limp with disappointment. "Riolo! Come fight with me!"

"Theobaldo, leave me be." The groom's plaintive note was comical in one so large. "It's too nice a day to play at swords."

"But –"

"Ah-ah-ah!" Angelica shook a finger at him, her bosoms swinging and jiggling. "You know better, Thibault, you little scoundrel! Wasn't he almost sent packing last time? Your fault entirely. He warned you, I warned you, God above, her ladyship warned you not to anger your uncle. But you insisted and my kind-hearted husband got no end of grief and a flurry of backhands beside. Heaven knows I don't agree with your uncle, but as long as he's the master, no one is allowed to spar with you and you know it. I can't say why, when you're so keen on it, but he must have his reasons. We're doing enough just letting you copy your books. If he ever learned you had such things he'd burn the entire library and you with it!"

Thibault hadn't heard half her speech, smarting over being called little. He was as tall as she! And the goop on her finger was shiny. "What's that you're doing?"

Shooting a sly glance at Giulietta, Angelica dropped her voice to a whisper. "Wormwood. Have to get her off the teat. Past time, really," she added with real sadness.

"Go easy with that muck," said Andriolo softly. "The girl may be going off the teat, but I'm not!"

"You beast!" Angelica swatted at him, but he ducked and slipped under her skirts to bite her bare ankle. She yelped in delight.

Giving up on the butterfly, Giulietta came tottering towards her cousin in that rocking, straight-legged run children use. "I'll fight, Tibby!"

Thibault sighed. "Fine. Come on then, Cricket." He nudged a stick with his toe, making sure to keep away from his precious fight-book.

Giulietta rushed forward and tried to raise the wooden weapon, teetering unsteadily and almost hitting herself in the face as she heaved it upright.

The nurse laid her jar aside. "Thibault, don't you dare let her." In three steps she was taking the wooden sword from Thibault's hand.

"Oi!" he cried. "I was practicing."

But the nurse was wheeling about, grinning. Her husband, grinning too, stood slowly, his hands held high. Then Angelica ran at him and chased him all around the rooftop, swatting at him with the stick, an oath with every blow, Giulietta at her heels, swinging her stick and mimicking every move and word.

Disgusted, Thibault rescued his book and settled himself into the dovecote's shade, resolutely studying the move on the next page.

Having evaded detection all night, Cesco emerged from the palace spruced and trimmed just after eleven bells. It was tempting to be purposefully late and make her wait. But she would likely leave if he were a minute past his time meeting her at San Zeno's.

Having fished for souls all his life along the banks of the Adige, Zeno was Verona's patron saint. His church lay to the northwest of the Piazza dei Signori, all massive stone. Attached was a cloister, staffed mainly by German monks. Within were glorious carvings and frescos. But it was the doorway of the church that was most famous. Carved reliefs in the shape of scenes from Genesis surrounded the bronze doors themselves. The right-hand door showed selected pieces of the Old Testament, the left-hand the New. One might have guessed, however, that the latter was the longer, because jammed into the lower parts of the Old Testament were four likenesses of San Zeno and one of San Michele.

Back in Ravenna, when Pietro had described the doors, his strongest recollection was of the image of Zeno fishing. On his first visit to the basilica, Cesco had sought for it and laughed quite inappropriately. What Pietro had failed to mention was that Zeno had been a Moor.

Nodding now to the bronze saint, Cesco entered the coolness of the church, eyes questing as they adjusted to the dimness. Several elderly women and a few wizened men were on their knees in prayer. Rosalia was not among them.

"Looking for someone, son?"

Cesco turned to find Fra Lorenzo smiling and brushing dirt from the knees of his robes.

"For God," said Cesco briskly. "But I never find Him home."

Lorenzo's face darkened. "Watch your tongue, little lordling. You blaspheme often enough in common life, but it's ten times as sinful in the house of the Lord."

"Good. I never want to do anything by halves. Why are you here? Have you switched orders?"

"A-ha, a-ha," said Lorenzo drily. "No, my Benedictine brothers are having a blight on one of their lunaria del papa flowers."

"Nothing worse. Now if you'll excuse me—"

Lorenzo stepped into his path. "Are you here to confess?"

"That would be a confession in itself."

"Perhaps if you unburden your soul you will find what you are looking for."

Cesco sighed. As Cangrande's heir he was forced several times a week to be seen publicly entering confession. Each time he invented a plethora of sins, for he was damned if he was going to entrust his real ones to the men he was destined to rule. That was a lesson he'd learned over and over, from Capitano and Emperor both: the Church was a valuable ally, but only God was infallible. His mortal agents here on Earth were no more than mere men, and no good ever came from giving other men power.

"Very well." Making a knee, Cesco crossed to the niche devoted to this particular sacrament, inventing as he went some plausible venal thoughts that would sate Lorenzo's need to cleanse, yet require no great penance.

Entering the wooden confessional, Cesco knelt. He heard the door open and close on the other side of the paneled divide and said the required words.

Fluent in Latin, it was his habit to conduct his entire recitation of sins in that tongue, usually baffling the 'learned' man on the other side of the divide.

But this time he had barely begun his account of coveting an imaginary horse when he was cut off by the person on the other side of the divider. "No. Speak of coveting something more precious."

Cloaked in darkness, Cesco allowed himself to blink. "The most precious creature in all the world. I hope you haven't been waiting long."

"Long enough." Lia's voice was a low whisper. "Penelope eternal."

"Tell me, how have you suborned the church?"

"Fra Lorenzo has a kindly heart, disposed to help those—"

"—those in love?"

"—under siege, I was going to say. Did I speak of love?"

"Very well, back to safer ground. If you know Lorenzo, perhaps you know my aunt. She is called Suor Beatrice."

"I know her well. In fact, it was she who introduced me to Fra Lorenzo." Lia sounded sly. "She's a great reader, and illuminated much of her father's work for me. And also taught me to copy in fine style."

"She did the same for me. When was this teaching?"

"This summer. I came to Verona in June for a missed appointment, so I spent a month with the sisters."

"Ah yes! Sadly I was called back to the company of the Emperor. Does that impress you?"

"I quiver with awe. Which of the three sparks sets your heart on fire?"

"All three together. Exactly what part of you is quivering awfully?"

"You always rush to the crude."

"Else I should be called prude. You do not know the company I keep. Did you seek out Suor Beatrice to question her about me?"

"About her father. I already know too much about you."

"You can know about a thing, but until you've experienced it you know nothing."

"Then I shall happily cling to my ignorance."

That had Cesco laughing. "How well do you know my foster-grandfather?"

"As well as I do his guide. Tell me, the Emperor – did you serve as his whipping boy?"

"His footstool."

"Modesty! Here I thought you suffered from a swelled head."

"Shall we discuss what on my person is swelling?"

"Please, no. This is a holy place."

"We are made in God's image. Well, I am, anyway. You're from extra bits."

"Flesh is sinful. Do you have any shame at all?"

"Having not eaten of the Tree of Knowledge, I am shameless."

"Then I shall be ashamed for us both."

"Do you need to make confession?"

"I rather hoped you'd confess yourself to me."

"What shall I confess, pray?"

"That's up to you, O Capitano in training." Though her words were taunting, her tone was breathless. He thought he heard in her the same trembling skittishness as he, a frenzy identical to the one burbling in his breast.

Or perhaps she was afraid of him. That was certainly possible. I have to know. "I confess that you are a complete mystery to me. That's a good thing, by the by. I confess that since I first deduced who you were, you've not been far from my thoughts. I confess that knowing you makes me want to be better than I am. That, to be the man that you want me to be – or that I imagine you wanted me to be–" He paused.

Beyond the screen, she shifted urgently. "Yes?"

"It's funny – I didn't realize until just this second."

"What?"

"It will mean nothing to you."

"Say."

"I was offered a glimpse into my future. I refused. I didn't realize until this moment I had done it for your sake."

"Mine?"

"I did not want our future tarnished by predictions. That which is unknown is possible. Only in knowing the limits do they exist."

"The old saw: 'Once you see your Fate, your Fate sees you.' But what has that to do with me?"

"Before you, I was sure I was destined to be brilliant and die young, leaving no trace of my passing."

"Like a poem set on fire."

"A pretty analogy. But now I've quite another future in mind."

Was it possible to hear a blush? "A fine burden to lay at my feet."

"That's not all I'll lay there. Rosalia Rienzi, I–" He halted, unsure.

"Oh dear God. Is this the part where you protest your love, having spent a full ten minutes in my company?"

"Fourteen minutes. But fine, we'll skip poetic protestations. Tell me, why did you invite me to your home that night?"

"You have a reputation for recklessness. I wanted to learn how far you'd go."

Cesco made no reply, felt stupid in spite of his high humour.

He heard her take a long breath. "I needed to know how far you'd go."

"Am I in earnest, you mean?"

"Yes."

A slow smile spread across Cesco's face. "Yes. I seek death in your lap, and burial in your arms."

She laughed in spite of herself, a full-throated sound. There was an urgent cough from outside, and she hushed to a whisper. "Fra Lorenzo is watching out for us. He worries we'll be caught."

"A blessing on him and all his endeavors."

She laughed again. "You are sure of yourself."

"Isn't that better than groaning for love?"

"Much," she said. "And one of the odder wooing scenes I've heard of."

"You must speak with the lord Detto serves. His stories make us look like turtledoves."

"That explains your technique. Fine words, a hint of blackmail, and I would fall into your arms?"

"It worked with all the other girls."

"There've been dozens, I suppose."

"Hundreds. But none tried to kill me first, so I turned them away."

"I didn't try to kill you. I just threatened to."

"Splitting hairs."

"I wanted to know how far you'd go."

"To hell and back. It runs in the family – well, the adopted one."

She wasn't joking any longer. "If I am to fall…"

"…you need to know I am willing to fall with you."

"Are you?"

His hands were shaking. It seemed his whole body was shaking. A tingly flush filled his jaw and shoulders. Trembling, Cesco braced himself. "Yes. Yes I—"

"What's that?!" screamed Lia.

All around them came a horrible grinding, like huge stone wheels set in motion. It wasn't just Cesco shaking, but the whole confessional. Thrown against the wooden wall, he barely heard Lia cry out under the seismic roar.

Struggling to his feet, he darted out of the box, flung back the curtain, and yanked her out. Lorenzo was shouting, but Cesco couldn't understand a word.

The paving stones beneath their feet were like liquid, an ocean churning in a tempest.

Pulling Lia along after him, Cesco scrambled for the door. With a furious tug the girl pulled free from his grasp and ran the opposite direction, towards the split-level altar. Cesco spun and saw a half dozen widows on their knees, screaming to God, struggling to rise. Lia reached the nearest and knelt behind her, bracing her.

Cesco was there moments later, pulling the widow up. Lorenzo and another friar arrived to lend their hands. Cesco said nothing, wit extinguished in the need for action.

At the Capulletti household, Giulietta was half laughing, half screaming, unsure how to react to all the panic around her. The moment the ground had begun shaking, Thibault had scooped her into his arms. Andriolo was shouting at his wife, "Run, woman! Run!" But she was already past him, pushing Thibault to the edge of the roof. "Jump, fool!"

He obeyed, leaping down into the open yard. For a wonderful moment as he hung in the air, everything was steady. Then he touched down and was immediately thrown to his side. He curled around his little cousin, protecting her as best he could. She was screaming full on now, right in his ear.

A moment later Andriolo fell to the cobblestones, landing on all fours then twisting to catch his wife. Her chest landed on his hip and he cried out, but then started laughing. "Thank God for your breasts!"

Wind knocked out of her, she managed only a weak smile. Then she scuttled forward and tore Giulietta from Thibault's grip, dragging her to the center of the yard and holding her close. Andriolo wrapped protective arms tightly about them both as the world shook around them.

Thibault stayed where he was, holding on to the shaking earth, realizing what he had done. He'd saved her! In a moment of terror, he'd saved her! This made up for Susanna, surely! Proved he was no coward, that he had steel in his soul, that he was meant for better things than the cloister! He was a hero. Surely, surely they would all see it now. Surely they would see!

There was a tremendous crash outside San Zeno, a great rending. Then the earth became mute, leaving behind the screams and tears and prayers of those who had lived through the ordeal.

It was only then, amid all-too-human noises, that the word earthquake came to Cesco. In the thick of it all he had known was that the natural order of the world had been undone, Fortune playing them all for fools.

Able to give commands, something like order was restored. "Out of doors!" shouted Fra Lorenzo. "There will be more!"

That got them all moving, flooding out of the basilica's famous doors. In the Piazza San Zeno, dozens of people clutched each other for support. A huge cloud of dust was still rising into the air a few blocks away, and Cesco noticed that one of the fabled towers of Verona wasn't there anymore.

For an eternity everyone stared about. Most were panting. Some were huddled up, weeping. A few prayed, sure it was doomsday at last.

Lia was helping one of the widows to a seat when Cesco knelt beside her. "Are you hurt?"

She ignored him. "How are you, mother?" The widow mumbled something and patted Lia several times on the head.

Reassured, Cesco crossed to Lorenzo, who was engaged in much the same task as Lia. "Where are the other brothers?"

"In the inner yard, I hope."

"Can I leave them to you? I have to go to the palace. The Scaliger's in Mantua with Castelbarco, Mastino – everybody. There's no one with authority."

"Go, go!"

Glancing at Lia, Cesco hesitated. "I–"

"I'll see to her. Go!"

Cesco tore off at a run, cursing Fortune, God, and poor timing.

Thirty-Five

Another building collapsed as the first aftershock rumbled underfoot. Cesco slowed to watch it crumble, sloping its head to its foundation. Beside him in the crowded street, residents watched their home fall inwards. Cesco knew any promise of aid would be cold comfort.

The instant the earth ceased its second dance, he pressed on. Reaching the Piazza dei Signori, he saw both palaces were still standing. In the middle of the square was a herd of confused and bleating sheep, the citizens and staff who laboured at the heart of Verona.

There were no steps from which to address them, always a fault with this square, in Cesco's opinion. Without breaking stride he scrambled up the ornate marble frieze that arched over the public entrance to the old palace, heedless of the risk should a third quake hit. He started talking, but few men had the wit to listen, all calling and shouting amongst themselves.

Putting his fingers to his lips he blew a piercing whistle. Heads turned, a relative silence fell.

"I'll be brief. If you are here, you know the need for order. Don't panic. The people need guidance, they must see only calm and determination. First we must send bands of men to all the fallen houses and dig for survivors. I need volunteers – quick now!"

Men stepped up, and Cesco gave them particular orders. All but two of the volunteers were palace guards, the misfits being lawyers of all things.

The effect of his brisk and concise orders was to calm the rest of the inhabitants of the piazza. As the rescue parties started off he dealt with water, livestock, and shelter for the dispossessed.

He was just finishing when another aftershock rocked the city, at least as rough as the quake itself. The marble arch beneath him was barely two feet wide. He threw himself against a carved marble crest in the wall behind him, fingers scrabbling for a hold in the carved rungs of the Scaligeri ladder. His feet slipped, but he hung stubbornly on, refusing to fall.

The moment it was over, men rushed forward to help him down, but he swung back to resume his post and continued speaking as if nothing had happened. "Anyone homeless by nightfall is to be brought here and housed at the Capitano's expense. If that's not enough, we'll put up tents and straw in the Arena – it's stood for a thousand odd years, it will be fine. Tonight we deal with the city. Tomorrow riders will be sent to every village, hamlet, hut, hovel, and shack to assess the damage. Verona will not let her sons fall prey to the whims of the earth!"

"Shouldn't someone tell the Capitano?" called a voice.

"As soon as there is news to tell. He must have felt the quake, so he'll be on his way as soon as he can. But you all know him – he values action! One more thing," he added. "Pass the word that any man found looting will be hanged on the spot. Now go, all of you, find employment. The Scaligeri have matters in hand!"

Leaping down, Cesco raced into the new palace and ordered Tullio d'Isola to open the doors and make up beds.

"My lord…" Tullio began, without finishing. His head was bleeding, and clearly his wits had been shaken along with his body.

"I'll send someone to help. Until she comes, have beds put in the Grand Salon."

"She, Master Cesco? She who?"

But Cesco was already dashing back outside to find the one person he trusted most within the city walls.

The nuns in their habits were standing in the street before their abbey, which had withstood matters well so far. The Abbess was trying to organize them when Cesco appeared. Damn, why do they all have to look alike? "Beatrice! Suor Beatrice!"

Antonia turned, and swept him into a hug. He kissed her cheek, then pushed free. "I need you at the palace, overseeing the dispossessed. Tullio's not up to the task at present."

"Where's Katerina? Giovanna?"

"Katerina's in Vicenza. She'll have her hands full there. I don't know where Giovanna is, nor do I care. I need you here, running things." He noticed Lia emerging from the crowd and smiled. "I see I am not the first to think of your help. You're well, lady?"

Rosalia curtsied. "Yes, my lord. I came to help."

Fra Lorenzo appeared. "I've delivered my charge, and I've medicines to prepare."

"Go. Auntie, I need you in the palace now. Take Rosalia with you."

Antonia hesitated, looking to the Abbess. "I cannot break the rules of the Order..."

Cesco spoke sharply. "I don't have time to debate chain of command. I know you, I trust you, you're in charge." He turned to the Abbess. "Mother, I'm calling Suor Beatrice up as a conscript. Verona needs her. There is no one more capable in a crisis."

"I quite agree. Suor Beatrice, choose a half dozen sisters to go with you and take command of the palace. Be what you are meant to be – what God has made you."

Antonia was frowning as she nodded. Then, as if a lever had been thrown, she became the woman Cesco remembered. Plucking six nuns by name, she walked briskly back to the Piazza dei Signori to take charge. As Rosalia followed, Cesco wanted to say something, but instead went off in a different direction – men were watching him, and their relationship, whatever it turned out to be, had to remain secret. For now.

Returning to the house he'd watched fall, he began digging through the debris. Eager to show their worth, the men following him joined in. Within minutes they were uniformed in grit, and Cesco sent milling women to the wells to collect water – the dust was choking.

They saved one man and recovered three dead from that building, the first of many disaster sites Cesco visited. Everywhere he went he gave commands and saw them followed. No one questioned his orders. He was Cangrande's heir, a natural leader, assuming authority as easily as a hawk took flight.

He made sure no one saw him sag with blinding fatigue, or consume the little wafers he snuck from the pouch at his belt – an indulgence he had not allowed himself in months. After that he was unaware of time until the sun was fully set. But by now his followers were able to anticipate his thoughts. Torches appeared, allowing men to continue digging. Sometimes there were miracles, such as the baby girl still in her cradle. But most often it was a lifeless form that was heaved from the rubble. Then Cesco set about comforting the family and directing them to the palace for food and rest.

He was everywhere in the night, never resting, never stopping. He assured all those who'd lost homes or businesses that if their guilds couldn't build them up again, he would. Not the city, not the Capitano – himself, out of his own purse. His grand gesture of opening the palace for all those turned out of doors was deemed the most generous act in a hundred years, nay, a thousand.

He was not so generous with looters. There were some, of course, and he forced himself to go and see to the hangings in person, so that everyone knew he was serious.

During one such hanging, Cesco thought he saw Fuchs in the crowd. What's he doing here? Before he could order Mastino's pet German to help, he'd vanished. If he was even there at all. It had been a long time since Cesco had tasted hashish.

Long after dark Cesco was walking down the busy street with thirty followers. Suddenly he halted, holding up a hand for silence. Immediately the throng stilled, straining to listen.

After a few moments they heard it too – a child's cry. Cesco raced towards the long tunnel from which the cry originated. The doors were open, and Cesco plunged in, recognizing the house at once. There was pain for him here, his greatest failure. A girl's cries, then silence. Not again.

Inside a little blonde girl with a tear-drop face was sobbing, but Cesco could see nothing damaged past broken windows and a fallen dovecote on a roof.

Realizing who the girl had to be, Cesco approached her. Kneeling he took her little hands in his and turned her to face him. "Little Giulia, are you hurt?"

The girl blinked at him and hiccupped, shy of the young man caked in dust and grit.

Cesco nipped her under the chin with his forefinger and thumb. "Don't be scared, little one. While I draw breath, nothing will hurt you. You are well?"

Giulietta cast a reproachful look at her nurse, who swooped the girl up. "Oh Lord, it's nothing, the little fool. She's scared and she wants to suckle me, but I'm weaning her – wormwood all over my dugs." She lifted a breast as if offering it. "She keeps trying, then pulling such faces – look at her now, she's angry with me."

Cesco had to laugh. "But the house is solid? Everyone's safe?"

If the nurse had not, Andriolo recognized him. "Thank you, my lord, but this house is as solid as your own. Are there many hurt?"

Just then Thibault emerged into the yard. He recognized Cesco right off. "What's he doing here?"

"Devil take my soul, if it isn't Whiskers! Hello, Puss-Puss. When are you going to come out to the tilting yard?"

Bristling, Thibault scowled. "We don't need you." Andriolo cuffed him hard on the shoulder and Thibault glared at him. "What? We don't! I saved her. More than you were able to for Susanna!"

Unflinching, Cesco finally saw recognition in the nurse's eyes. *Yes, lady. I am the one who got your daughter's throat cut. No wonder you try to forget me.*

Whereas Andriolo was forever grateful to Cesco, the vehicle of his revenge. The groom asked if there was anything they could do to help. "We could use your muscles tonight," replied Cesco. "There's much yet to do and not a moment to lose. And the homeless are overflowing the palaces. If you could find some and put them up, my – the Scaliger will absorb the cost."

Something brushed Cesco's hand. Giulietta was looking at him without a trace of shyness now, peering at his face.

He knelt again. "Yes?"

"You're all dirty."

"I know," he said ruefully. "When this is over I shall have to be beaten like an old tapestry."

Still frowning at his face, Giulietta suddenly spat in her hand and rubbed vigourously at his surprised face.

The nurse lurched forward, dragging her away. "Such manners! Naughty child! I have no idea where she learned such things!"

Cesco was laughing again, a sound both real and very tired. "I do need a bath, don't I?"

"Aye!"

"I shall make it my first order of business when this night is through." Patting the little girl on the head, Cesco beckoned to Andriolo and the other Capulletti servants to follow him out.

Just as he was entering the darkness of the tunnel he turned about. Thibault was still there. Cesco held open his hands. "Coming, Monsieur Rat-Catcher?"

By dawn the city was at peace. In some places the rubble still shifted, and a doused fire was still smoking. But the crisis was over, and the name on everyone's lips was Francesco.

The rising sun found him standing alone at the well in the volto dei Centurioni, just off the Piazza dei Signori, washing his neck and arms. He was just dunking his head in a bucket when the shivering overcame him.

He sat heavily, leaning his back against one of the well's rose-marble pillars. The smell of the well had overwhelmed him. He'd forgotten what even a light dose of hashish would do to the senses, if unprepared for it. It was too close to the day he had overindulged, and failed. It was his friend, and his enemy.

The gift of the Moor, who is my friend, yet made my star chart. Charts. My future, set down in ink. But until I read them, they are not set in stone. In bone. In the earth.

Eyes closed, he sat until the fit had passed, then continued to rest, head hung low.

Suddenly a shadow loomed over him. "Whoever you are, give me time to be mortal. In short order I shall resume super-human efforts, like standing."

"You did well. No wonder you're asleep on your feet."

"Worse. I float somewhere between that and death."

Lorenzo frowned deeply. "You've been indulging again."

Cesco groaned. "Yes, I am weak. Certainly it was better that I should not have been able to stay up all night, brimming with energy and clear-headedness. Far more important to remain pure and collapse from exhaustion! Tcha!"

Fra Lorenzo knew just what knife would wound. "You wish your Madonna Rienzi to see you like this?"

Cesco's exhaustion showed in his answer, for it was entirely honest. "If she'll be mine, I may never indulge again."

"Excellent! Here she comes."

Cesco's eyes snapped open to behold the truth of this. Rosalia looked as spent as he felt. He had checked on her several times through the night, disguising it as looking in on Suor Beatrice. Now here she was, seeking him out.

His will proving stronger than his fatigue, Cesco leapt to his feet. From the corner of his mouth he whispered. "Mum, brother, mum."

Rosalia approached them, smiling thinly. "Good day, father."

"God's blessings, daughter. You did His work yesterday."

"Well, He seemed to have His hands full."

Cesco opened his mouth, closed it, then looked to Fra Lorenzo. "Haven't you work elsewhere, brother?"

Looking between the young couple, Lorenzo heaved a smiling sigh. "I suppose I do." Upon Cesco he bestowed a final look of disapproval. "My lord, I will take your earlier comment as an oath, sworn before a man of God."

"If it pleases the Lord to aid me, I will make the oath in whatever church you need me to build."

The remark didn't quite please the friar, but he nodded, then grinned at the pair before removing himself from the scene.

Rosalia was bemused. "What exactly is he making you swear?"

"To give up oath-making. How are you, lady? I kept expecting to see you in a man's weeds, pulling rock at my side."

"If I thought for a moment that I'd have been more help that way, I'd have been by your side the livelong night. But the palace was over-run. Your aunt was amazing. I admire her greatly, I think."

"Enough to become a nun?"

"Only if there is no better offer."

"I'll see what I can do. But I'm glad you weren't with me. For every three knocked about, there was one crushed. It was quite horrible."

"I can handle horror. I spar with you, after all."

A silence fell while they simply gazed at each other. Suddenly Lia said, "That was quite a display. You're the city's new darling."

"I did it to impress you. Otherwise I would have crawled into bed and let the sheep tend themselves."

"Poor sheep."

"Don't get too swept away by my heroism. A wise man once told me, no man is just one thing."

"Are you telling me to stay away from you?"

"Caveat emptor."

"Oh, I get to bid on you?"

"If you like. But I am for sale to no one else."

She gazed at him, a desperate curiosity about her eyes. "That was quite a risk, wasn't it? I can't imagine you're used to laying yourself naked."

"No more than you are." If she expected him to make a ribald joke, he surprised her by taking her hand. "All I am, I give to you."

Rosalia said nothing. But she did not withdraw her hand.

To break the tension, Cesco forced a chuckle. "I remember once telling Ser Alaghieri he was a fool for indulging in love. I had no idea."

"You are no fool." She pressed his hand to her heart. "Or if you are, I am one too."

He wanted to leave it there, say nothing more. Yet there was one insistent impediment. "What of Cangrande?"

"I already promised."

"I don't mean that. You hate him."

"My father does. He despises the Greyhound."

"Good or ill, I doubt anyone has ever been indifferent to him, or ever could be." He smiled briefly. "Though it might be interesting to try. No, I am asking because I am made of him, and I'm afraid I'm very like him. Do you not hate me, too?"

Lia pursed her lips. "My father detests him, deems him an arrogant villain. I have done the same, for his sake. But as you said, no man is just one thing. If he created you, then that might just redeem him."

Cesco also felt her pulse beating against his fingers. Felt the softness of her skin. Felt his own heart hammering his throat. Turning his hand in hers, he laced his fingers in her, leaned his face close to hers. Both were barely breathing. For perhaps the first time in his life, Cesco had no words. Which was good. To speak was to ruin the moment.

At last he felt his legs tremble and knew it was not emotion, nor another earthquake, but fatigue. He rocked back and gave her a weak smile. "I'm falling down on my feet. I need to sleep." He looked that their entwined fingers. "But I can't seem to let go of you."

"You don't have to. Suor Beatrice sent me to find you and make you rest. There is a bed prepared. Come."

She led him back through the square and into Cangrande's new palace, where there was indeed a comfortable bed awaiting him, and where he would have the best sleep he'd ever had in his whole life, his fingers still locked in Rosalia's grip as she stayed beside his bed the rest of the morning, asleep in a chair.

Thirty-Six

Cangrande returned to Verona on the evening after the earthquake, having outstripped even the heartiest of his retine by several miles, only to find his city in good order. His people were active and cheerful, grateful for all he'd done. Which was the more remarkable, as he'd done nothing at all. But the orders given in his name by his heir had only amplified the people's love for him, and he received their gratitude gracefully.

He hadn't been able to get away without jeopardizing the fragile peace in Mantua, so he'd first sent the elder Castelbarco back with Capulletto and his recovered wife, along with a dozen knights, to restore the peace.

But it seemed the peace had not been in question. Entering the Piazza dei Signori, he surveyed the minimal damage to the two palaces, the Domus Bladorum, the Domus Nuova, and the Giurisconsulti. A façade had gone from one, and a massive crack in a marble column had left a chunk missing the size of a wild boar. Small price to pay.

Dismounting amid a swarm of attendants, Cangrande was informed that the young master was in the Domus Nuova, and the last of the dispossessed were being found more appropriate lodgings. If the Scaliger wished to rest, his own suite was, of course, untouched.

Thanking everyone for their obvious efforts on Verona's behalf, Cangrande sought out the boy.

Inside the Domus Nuova, Cesco was not sitting in the Capitano's seat, but near enough to claim it, standing on the dais. He was busy giving orders, which Cangrande noted were obeyed at once. Castelbarco offered advice, but Cesco's was the guiding hand. Dressed in a plain shirt and trousers instead of hose, the boy was the image of practicality.

The moment Cangrande appeared, Cesco said, "Oh thank God!"

The Scaliger was in sartorial splendour, finery donned for addressing the Mantuan people, finery now streaked with mud and sweat from the hard ride. Cangrande stripped off first gloves then doublet as he strode through the chamber. "Did you not enjoy your day as Capitano?"

"One day as Capitano is a day too long."

"Yet you look well rested. You must share your secret." Cangrande looked to Castelbarco. "How did he do? Are we at war? Did he sell the Arena? My lands? My household stuff?"

"He did well, as far as I can see," said Castelbarco, stretching. "I've done nothing at all, and now you're here, I'm heading for my bed."

"Sleep well, my friend. You have my thanks." Dismissing all the rest, Cangrande settled upon his backless throne.

The doors closed. They were alone. Cesco offered up a roll of paper. "A list of damages. I'm sure there's more in the outer suburbs, but this is a fair start. Crews are already at work rebuilding the most necessary. The first funeral is the day after tomorrow. We weren't sure when you'd return, and I knew you'd want to attend."

Taking the offered sheet, Cangrande scanned it. "The cheesehouse?"

"And the brothel beside it. They fell in on each other."

"There's a jest there somewhere, but I'm too exhausted to coin it. I suppose it's fortunate for everyone that you didn't ride to Mantua with the rest of us. Premonition?"

"If only. I had an appointment I did not wish to miss."

"With a girl, I hope."

It was perhaps the thousandth time the Scaliger had teased Cesco's persistent virginity. It was the first time he saw the boy squirm. Suddenly he grinned. "It was, wasn't it? You sly dog! Well past time, but better late than never."

Cesco knew what Cangrande was thinking, and let him think it. "I'm forgiven, then?"

"Oh, absolutely. On top of my manly pride in you, the city seems at ease."

"Every order was issued in your name. That comforted the people."

"My Metatron, as it were."

"Mercury to your Jupiter."

"I had a dog named Jupiter once. And Ser Alaghieri had one of his pups, a hound called Mercury. That coin at your neck was his."

Cesco fingered the coin at his neck, vaguely recalling the dog in question. He remembered it dying for him.

Shaking himself, Cesco asked about Mantua, and Cangrande looked up from the paper. "Oh, they took the change from Bonaccolsi to Gonzaga phlegmatically. They seemed utterly indifferent to the alteration. But then Bonaccolsi has not been too popular of late – high prices for food, random vandals, thefts and cut-purses – Mantua has been infested."

"I trust that will end now the Gonzaga are in charge?"

"As they were Gonzaga's thieves and cut-purses, I trust so." Cangrande grinned his allegria.

"Any word from the army?"

"I gave orders that soldiers stop all traffic east and south. The Paduans will hear about this soon, but too late to take advantage of it – not in the shape they're in." Cangrande glanced down. "I need fresh clothes."

"Stay. I'm still your squire."

"Actually, you've been supplanted. By Paride," added Cangrande.

"Oh? Well, he's a fine fellow. Still, I'll send fresh clothes. You shouldn't have to fight the crowds to get into your own house."

"I heard of my generosity. Housed at my cost?"

"I fed them venison and your best wine."

"So it's crusty bread and stale beer for me. I've had worse."

"I'll fetch the clothes." Cesco took three steps, then paused.

"What is it?" asked the Capitano. "Uncertainty is unlike you."

Half turned, Cesco said, "Did I do well?"

"A rather foolish question. If you hadn't, I'd let you know it. Or are you fishing for compliments?"

"No. I have a request."

"Oh, a reward! Very well. A new hound? A hawk?"

Cesco laughed at that. "I'm after a different kind of bird. I'd like your permission to choose my own bride."

Genuinely surprised, Cangrande groaned in mockery. "No! No, please, no! Tell me that having tasted of the fruit, you don't want to marry the tree?"

Cesco's eyes were veiled in a manner too familiar to the Scaliger – he'd seen it in his glass each morning. "I would not call her a tree, though I do admire her limbs."

"Her name?"

Cesco shook his head. "I have no right to name her until I have her consent."

Cangrande's lips curled. Anyone else might have supposed the expression was a smile. Cesco knew better. "I intended you for an alliance. I was used for one, at your age."

"And see how well that worked out."

"A hit! But nonetheless, you are a valuable piece of property, not to be wasted."

"Had you already chosen the ally?"

"I have several candidates, but nothing set in stone."

"Shall I kneel, go prostrate, beg?"

"It couldn't hurt."

"It might, actually. What will it take to gain this boon?"

Cangrande considered. "The job of Capitano has many facets. You have done Verona a great service, and proved yourself a good steward. When I am sure you're also a good leader in foreign matters, I'll consider it. Not till then. Now go – I'm reeking of sweat and need a change."

The boy gone, Cangrande considered. A girl. It even made him smile.

Antony Capulletto arrived home in a thundering hurry. Leaping from his horse before it even emerged from the arched tunnel he started calling at once. "Giulietta! Giulietta! Where are you, my girl? Daddy's home!"

A squeal emerged from inside the house. Antony dashed up a flight of steps and saw her tottling towards him, arms wide. He went down on his knees and embraced her fervently, murmuring breathless endearments into his daughter's hair. "Oh, look at that bump! A perilous knock! Are you well, sweeting? Are you well?"

Angelica was there, looking at them fondly. It was Thibault, gazing into the yard from the far balcony, who said, "Where's Tessa?"

Antony ignored the question, chuckling as he played with his little girl's grasping fingers.

Angelica repeated the question. "What, isn't the mistress with you?"

"No, she isn't," said Antony in a song-song voice as he played with Giulietta. "No she isn't. I had to leave her behind – yes I did. I had to get home to my Guilietta, my little Giulia, yes I did. She couldn't keep up, no she couldn't, not in her condition, no."

Angelica perked up at once. "Is she—?"

"Yes," said Antony, glancing up before returning his attention to Guilietta. "You're going to have another brother, yes. And this one will be strong, and you'll be able to play with him. But you'll always be my little darling, won't you? Yes you will! Yes you will!"

The nurse started chattering away excitedly, her voice mingling with Antony's teasing comments to his daughter. In the ruckus no one noticed Thibault slip out of the salon and up to his room. He closed the door and sat down on his bed, a flurry of emotions mingling into one sour expression.

Lifting a pillow, he clutched it tightly, pressing it down on his knees so hard his arms shook. Then he pressed his face into it and screamed.

Mastino entered his chamber sore and annoyed, and was more annoyed when he saw Fuchs drinking wine in complete comfort.

The German put down the cup and rose. "How was the ride, my lord?"

"Wretched. Paride yapped the whole ride back, question after question, prattling tattle. I have no use for small talk. Nor for so-called friends sitting comfortably on their asses while I ride back and forth across the Feltro in the company of fools." Exhausted, he collapsed fully clothed onto a mattress, then started. "This bed's been slept in!"

"Thank your cousin. He let homeless rabble sleep in the palace last night. Your rooms were assigned to the cheesemaker's family. I tried to stave them off, but his orders outweighed mine."

Mastino leapt to his feet, shaking with outrage. "The cheesemaker! In my rooms! In my bed!"

"To be fair, he put the homeless whores up in his own suite of rooms. Which brings us to an interesting development."

Mastino's head came up. "He's got a whore?"

Fuchs smiled. "Better. A girl. Young, innocent. Maybe a year or so older than he. The trottel appears to be in love."

"Her name?"

"I will find out."

"As soon as possible." Mastino kicked the bed frame. "And send someone to burn this. I can't sleep where some grubby peasant fucked his wife."

Bowing, Fuchs departed.

They had arranged a time and a place. Ser Alaghieri's house in Verona was empty, but for a lone house-keeper who lived in her own abode at night. Climbing over roofs and doubling back over his trail, spending time in a church, then in a fallen house, Cesco finally entered the balcony window certain he had not been followed.

There was no light within, and he wondered if she had come at all. But as he closed the shutters on the window he heard her voice from the darkness. "Just like Odysseus. Always late."

Air poured from his lungs, his fearful breath released. "I wasn't sure you would be here."

"My family believes I am with Suor Beatrice. I hope she does not betray us."

"Never," said Cesco. "The shutters are fastened. Shall I find a light?"

"I have one." The doors of a shuttered lantern opened, and the room was lit by a dim candle. Lia was seated in the master bed, dressed only in a shift, a shawl around her shoulders.

Gazing at her, Cesco put a hand to his heart. "I seem to have trouble breathing."

Lia blushed, a smile on her face. "It must be the climb."

"That must be it. Or relief. I was afraid you'd dress as the man, and I'd have to wear the gown."

She laughed at that, then pointed at her clothes, draped neatly over a chair. "There they are if you want them." She stopped herself from making the obvious next statement. You'll have to undress first.

Instead of disrobing, Cesco came and sat on the edge of the bed, near her but not too near, his back half to her. "I'm glad you came. I wasn't sure."

"I came to make you sure. And to be sure myself."

"I asked Cangrande permission to marry whom I liked."

"Did you give him my name?"

"Time enough to upset our parents. And I did not want him bothering you."

"So what did you tell him?"

"That I was ensorcelled. Bewitched. Ensnared in an older woman's charms."

She hit him on the arm. "Older woman! I'll be sixteen in November."

"Tell me the date, I'll have Tharwat make you a chart."

"Who?"

"My friend, the Moor."

"The one who struck me with the knife?"

"To be fair, he did not then know that you would turn out to be my Beatrice. He's good with charts, but cannot actually see the future."

"So, what did he say?"

"Cangrande? If I do one more great deed for Verona, he'll allow it. I'm already planning."

"I'm sure you are." She brushed the hair from his eyes. "You look much better than you did this morning."

"I slept. For perhaps the first time in my life, I had a restful sleep. Thanks to you."

"Did you come here to sleep again?" Her question was fraught with meaning.

"I came to see you. I want nothing more. To sleep beside you would be enough."

"You want nothing more?" she teased, though her teasing had an edge to it.

Cesco's heart was hammering, flooding his veins and filling his ears with a pounding sound. "We don't have to," he said, trying desperately to be noble.

Lia was sitting very still. "Of course we don't."

"You could get pregnant."

"Yes, I could. Does that worry you?"

"Yes." Smiling at her, Cesco stroked her cheek. "I'm afraid that if you are pregnant when we marry, everyone will think it was because of the baby, not for love."

She melted, leaning her cheek against his back. "A romantic. I would never have dreamed." Reaching around him, she put her hand on his. He grasped her fingers, and she squeezed them. Her voice was hurt, almost fearful. "Don't you want to?"

"Yes." His voice was strangled, and he had to clear it. "I do. Desperately, in fact. It's just that I think—"

"That's the answer, then."

"What?"

Turning him towards her, Lia took Cesco's face in her hands. "Don't think."

She kissed him, chin high, lips barely brushing. He closed his eyes, not kissing back, just breathing her in, terrified of ruining the moment.

Slowly he moved his lips, pressing them back, and their kiss moved from tender and tentative to passionate.

When they banged their noses, they both laughed, and the laughter was like a tonic. Perfection was impossible, and laughing was sharing their fear, confirmed they were together, not alone.

She took off his tunic, pulling it over his head. When Cesco slipped his hand inside the neck of her shift, he half expected her to turn, or slap him away. But Lia allowed him to touch her breast, stroke it, run his fingertip around her stiff nipple. Then, to prove he was not only interested in the forbidden, he slid his hand to her back, pulling her close into renewed kisses. Here his hand was strong and confident, stroking her back up and down, feeling the curve, his hand with each stroke exploring lower, his excitement building as he reached the curve at the base of her spine, and lower to her bottom.

By now he was in danger of tearing the shift at the neck, and she pushed him away. He withdrew instantly, tremulous. But she was not offended. Rising to her knees, she gave him a blinking smile and, pulling the shift over her head, dropped it beside the bed.

He stared at her naked body, feeling the fear, the trust, the hope, the desire, everything that was in her. She was naked before him, and he wanted nothing more than to earn that honour. He kissed her, and laid her back on the bed.

Cesco's clothes were more troublesome. Lia tried to manage the points of his hose, but they were complicated and he had to help. Suddenly he was free, kicking away the last clinging wool.

Overcome with shyness, he pressed against her to hide the awkward thing between his legs. They rolled back and forth, legs twining, hands seeking, mouths exploring necks and shoulders and ears and breasts. The wetness on her belly from him was matched by the moisture against his thigh, pressed hard between her legs.

And so, with wordless consent, Cesco rolled on top of her. Their foreheads pressed together, breathing heavily, Lia opened herself to him.

Intellectual knowledge was not the same as experience. Seeing a joust in a book did not make one a master with a lance, whatever natural skill one had. Cesco pressed against her and pushed, and pushed, but nothing felt the way he expected or imagined it should.

At last she reached her hands down between them, took hold of him, and guided him into her.

As they pressed and arched, both kept wondering, Is this right? Not the morality, but the act itself. Were they doing it right? Was this how? Then Cesco felt a moment where his body went still, an irresistible urge to hold himself perfectly motionless. His breath caught, and he pressed deeply inside her once more before relaxing, kissing the space between her breasts.

Withdrawing and falling off to one side, in the dim light he saw blood on him, and on her thighs. "Are you all right?" he panted. She nodded, then smiled and kissed him reassuringly before stealing the light and going to another room for a few minutes.

It was an agonizing wait for him, and he remained perfectly still, like a frightened bird about to take flight. When she returned she was still smiling, and she moved to the bed, cleaning him with a damp cloth, then pressing herself against him once more. He relaxed into her embrace.

They talked, making light conversation. She joked about another earthquake, making him chuckle at the absurdity of the idea. He examined the puckered scar on her arm where she had been stabbed, and laughed at the story she'd invented to cover it. She talked of watching him almost die in the Arena, how she had wanted nothing more, and how much that shamed her.

This brought the talk back to love, and marriage, and forever. They kissed and clung, and as they did their bodies responded again, and the kissing and clinging became more urgent.

The second time was not as good. They both felt the need to prove themselves, to be more adult, more confidant, more sure. The result was almost angry, pushing and thrusting against each other. When it was done they recoiled, bruised of body and feeling. There was no talk of love, only awkward bits of conversation.

Thinking to be solicitous, Cesco padded downstairs and produced some cheese and a bottle of wine. Over that midnight meal they talked again of love, of marriage, of dreams. Dreams of the future, of hope. Dreams of what they wanted life to be. Dreams that they could now share.

The third time was slow, exploratory, the lightest of brushes and kisses, as if their joy was sea foam that could vanish at too hard a breathing. This time she was the one who wanted the world to stop, arching her back while the sensation pervaded her, stopping her breath and tensing every muscle. In that moment Cesco felt like a man, and when he finished he was crying, a smile upon his face as he buried it in her breasts, clinging to her as if his very life depended upon it. She stroked his hair, and kissed his forehead, and laughed at him, and he could laugh too. They were no longer unsure of themselves. The act would take time to figure out. But Lia and Cesco were certain.

Nothing would ever change that.

Nothing could.

ACT V

Sins of the Father

Thirty-Seven

Three days after the quake, Antonia took a much-needed respite from her ministrations to the dispossessed. The moment Cangrande arrived at the palace she'd returned to the abbey and thrown herself into similar efforts there, looking after homeless children and women who had no other refuge.

On the fourth day, the Abbess came to her and said, "Rest. You're one of the few useful girls here, and I can't have you collapsing when we need you."

Antonia disobeyed, of course, simply resuming her work where the Abbess couldn't see her. For the first time in two years, she felt like herself again. Having become a victim, it had become her identity. Worse, since she had decided to endure the attacks in exchange for Cesco's solace, she'd felt herself a willing victim. At least the boy had no idea what she had endured for his sake. Of course, Cesco that he did not know made her resentful, which was intellectually unjust but emotionally quite real.

Told repeatedly as a child how capable, how forceful, how certain she was, that had been her identity, even when she herself did not feel capable, forceful, or certain. Perhaps, she'd always thought, if I pretend to have those attributes, they will be there. So determined to live up to the ideal of her father, she had been relentless and fearless in his interests. Then he had died, and her sense of self became wrapped up in being an efficient novitiate, on serving God – and on raising Cesco.

Which had lasted right up to the moment she had accepted personal disaster and perhaps even the ruin of her relationship with the Lord for the sake of a posturing, preening, brilliant boy.

In the two years since the attacks, she built a personality based upon her weakness. Her weakness to endure had driven Cesco away. Her weakness of body had allowed the attacks to occur. Her weakness of mind that she couldn't move past them. Weakness became her new definition of self, and each time she repeated the word weak, it became more true. All her accomplishments belonged to someone else, another person who had lived in her body and then vanished like a dream.

Then all at once Cesco had appeared, in crisis as always, and needed her. Not the weak her, but the strong, capable, confident her that he remembered. The woman he trusted above all others.

As if a lever had been thrown or a veil lifted, she found herself doing what was expected of her. There was no time for fear or doubt. These people needed help and, helping them, she had discovered she was still strong and capable.

Confidence would take longer to return. But she had turned a corner. Perhaps, as Pietro had taken to saying of Cangrande, no one was just one thing. Perhaps it was possible to be capable and afraid. Perhaps it was a question of facing the fear.

Having rediscovered a purpose beyond copying Bibles and praying, she was loath to let it go. So even when ordered to bed she'd taken only the briefest of naps, returning a few hours later to the aid of the city her father had loved, his second home.

Catching her, the Abbess scolded Suor Beatrice. "You will have nothing left for yourself, daughter."

"I want nothing for myself," replied Suor Beatrice simply.

The Abbess was a knowing woman, and she was enormously proud of the girl she had started to think of as an actual daughter, in spirit if not the flesh. She saw much of herself in the girl, and had endured at least at much in the world of men. Watching Antonia emerge from her fearful shell was watching a butterfly break its cocoon – beautiful, but fragile. If the girl wasn't careful, she would work herself to such a state that she would collapse. Work and prayer was the order of their Order, but rest did not go amiss.

Yet if Suor Beatrice would not sleep, she could be made to relax in another way. "Daughter, I have had a request from one of the great ladies of the city that you come visit her. Donna Montecchio asked for you by name."

With a pang of guilt, Antonia realized it had been several weeks since she'd seen Gianozza. She'd run into Antony, almost literally, two days after the earthquake and learned that his family was well. But she had no idea how the Montecchio household had fared. "Is anyone hurt?"

"She didn't say. She only asked if you could call. I release you from work here for the rest of the day."

"But…"

"You've done enough. Go see your friend."

Feeling a twinge of her old annoyance, Antonia traced the Adige, grumbling to herself. Why was she not being allowed to be useful? Had she been wrong? Was her help somehow lacking?

No, a voice said.

Then why send me away? she demanded. Why force me to go on a social call? What good does it do? What is she trying to tell me?

She wrestled with those questions without answer until she came to Montecchio's massive home just south of the Duomo. Ushered in, she waited in the sitting room and listened to Romeo and his cousin

Benvolio playing outside. At least the boys weren't hurt.

Romeo, it seemed, owned quite a wonderful imagination, leading his cousin on fantastic quests about the yard. Their relationship reminded her of Cesco and Detto, a lively leader and a stolid follower. Except that Romeo's exploits were limited to breaking a vase or getting his hose grubby. How old must he be now, seven? Eight? A nice boy. A trifle too worried about being liked, but with his mother and father, that was to be expected.

Shifting in her seat and smoothing out the folds of her habit, Antonia tried to banish her tension. She actually didn't much enjoy visiting Gianozza, but felt obligated. The poor girl had so few friends. Montecchio was well-loved by everyone (except, of course, Capulletto), but his wife was not nearly as popular. Much admired for her beauty, she bore the brunt of the blame for the rift between the two friends. Had she married Antony and cuckolded him, then he would have been the laughingstock. But since he was allowed to escape the engagement with his honour, she was deemed a disobedient daughter, a headstrong girl, willful and unladylike. For some reason none of the blame attached to Mariotto, who was at least half as culpable as his bride.

817

But that wasn't why the society ladies shied away from this house. Gianozza had a habit of behaving in a disturbingly dramatic manner. Everything was a crisis, everything was dire.

These days most of her anxiety focused on Romeo – his health, his appearance, his education, his wild ways (which were not particularly wild by Cesco's standards). Yet none of it seemed genuine. Antonia suspected that she did not enjoy being in a room if she were not the focus of the attention. It was something Antonia had noticed more and more. Confronting her only fed the fire.

Still and all, Gianozza had been a good friend, and there had been times these last two years when her dramatic prattle had yielded to talk of poetry, allowing Antonia some feminine company outside the cloister. For that reason alone, she was grateful. And they had been young together. That often counted a great deal more than it should.

Gianozza came sweeping into the room. "Antonia! How are you?"

Smiling and enduring an embrace, she said, "I'm well, and the abbey was untouched, thank God. But Gianozza, you must call me Suor Beatrice now, remember?"

"Oh, of course! I keep forgetting! Forgive me!"

"Nothing to forgive," said Antonia, settling in again to sit. "How are you and yours? Is anyone hurt?"

"Oh, well, let me tell you!" Gianozza threw herself onto a cushioned chair and launched into a complete recounting of the events starting an hour before the quake and concluding that very morning. Briefly, Romeo and Benvolio had been playing along the river tossing stones when the ground had erupted and a wave had leapt up and knocked both boys backwards. Startled, they'd run to the house declaring that there was a catapult attacking the river. The incredible story they'd created about ancient foundations being rocked, shaking the whole city until it was about to fall in on itself and open a path to the Underworld was so charming that Gianozza had been reluctant to tell them what had really happened. Apparently the boys took it in stride, though Romeo seemed a little crestfallen. But they embraced the new explanation and went to help the grooms get the stables clear and keep the horses calm.

Antonia tried not to bristle. There was no emergency, nothing useful to be done here. Just Gianozza's need for attention.

Gianozza continued talking almost without pause. "The next day Mari came racing back, Benvenito with him. You should have seen them, it was so darling, their concern. Of course we might have died, so they were right to fret, but just looking at him I was reminded how much I love him and how we were meant to be together. I mean, even if we never have another child, this is the life I was meant to lead. Mariotto and Romeo – or my two Romeos." Mariotto's baptismal name was Romeo.

Gianozza prattled away for several minutes, and Antonia found her mind wandering. Where was the girl with the love of poetry and reading? Where was the strength of character that let her say no to her family and marry the man she chose instead? Did she ever exist, or was it all a shadow of vanity? And what was she teaching her son? From what Antonia had seen, Romeo shared his mother's penchant for the dramatic. Maybe if he spent more time with his father... But Mariotto had grown up without a mother, so he made sure his son spent a good deal of time near his mother's apron-strings.

Gianozza snapped Antonia out of her reverie by saying, "You'll interested in this. I've had a letter from home."

"Oh?" Home was always Padua. Gianozza was related to the highest of Paduan nobility, the Carrarese.

"From my cousin Taddea – you know, Il Grande's daughter? That's her. Well, she's become a decent letter-writer, and there's really nothing else to do in Padua at the moment, all boarded up in her house. From what she says no one of noble birth dares step out into the street for fear of being kidnapped and ransomed. Of course, it's not the commoners doing the kidnapping, it's the other nobles – especially Ubertino. Taddea says that it's hard to tell which is worse, cousin Ubertino in the city wreaking havoc or his little brother Niccolo and the exiles destroying the countryside. Marsilio doesn't know what to do, so he does nothing. My family is crazy," she concluded.

"All families are, I think," observed Antonia.

Gianozza barely heard her. "It's about power and responsibility. They want the one without the other. For all they fight against the Greyhound, they could learn a lot from him. Taddea says that Marsilio more often references him than her late father. Certainly he wants to lead men the same way. The time he spent as a prisoner here taught him a lot about how a leader behaves. But Taddea says that without Heinrich of Carinthia's men, he has to use the whole Paduan army guarding the city from both without and within, just to let city life continue."

"At least they did not attack after the quake," observed Antonia. It had been a real fear.

Gianozza laughed. "They couldn't if they'd wanted to! Their soldiers were tied up helping our cousin Rolando Rossi retake Parma. Which leaves Padua even more defenseless. Things are so bad that Taddea wants to leave the city, but she daren't, not with the exiles snapping up everything in the countryside."

"But she's part of Niccolo's own family," protested Antonia. "Surely he wouldn't hurt her."

"If it's Niccolo who captures her. There are a lot of exiles who hate all Carrarese, and being Marsilio's close cousin is almost a death-sentence. Poor Marsilio, he's really stuck. I know you're not fond of him for your brother's sake, what with the duel and all, but I still can't help loving him for helping me marry my one true love–" And she was off again.

Antonia sat with an attentive expression, but her mind was racing. An old feeling was returning. Not just usefulness, but cleverness – no, clear-sightedness.

An hour later, as she walked back to the abbey, Suor Beatrice thought hard, piecing bits of rumour together, trying not to let fear or weakness cloud her judgment. Because she'd had an idea.

Her old self was not one to shy away from difficult decisions, yet this bold idea daunted her. She had to ask the Abbess about it.

Lia had convinced her father to let her spend the rest of the summer in Verona to help the sisters of Santa Maria in Organo care for the victims of the earthquake. Staying in her father's house, with her father's servants looking over her, she was careful not to meet her lover often. Part of their caution was fear of discovery, but also a dread of ruining what was between them.

Yet they couldn't stop writing. It was coded, of course, with them teasing each other by changing the code just a little each time, forcing the other to spend maddening minutes – sometimes hours! – working it out.

Two days after their first night together, Lia wrote:

> Francesco,
>
> O goodness, what is that smothering my mind? Doubts? Fears? Faults? The latter is what I believe it may be. Why can I not just accept that I have found someone wonderful, perfect, all I could have ever dreamed?
>
> Perhaps I find it impossible to truly be-lieve that anything can be perfect. I think I'm on a scavenger hunt for our

faults. Not our flaws – we are clearly flawed, you and I. But a fault in us. I need to find something wrong – which is in itself wrong, I know. Then again, can what comes from inside be wrong? How can something involving me, at this age, be perfect? Everlasting? Does it have to be everlasting? Is anything?

I think it has to be. I do not understand frivolous relationships, the crushes girls my age have on boys for a month. Maybe I'm not thinking enough to know for certain if you're right or wrong. I don't want you to be wrong. So I drown my thoughts with thoughts of you. Circles!

You really are part of my life now. Mine. Everything I think about, I think of it with you in mind. I thought of our house, our carriage. I can see us everywhere. I miss your hand in mine, it is phantom fingers I grasp now. I slept with your hat under my pillow and dreamt of you so vividly that I was surprised when I woke and you weren't there.

When I cancel out existence, leave only my heart to explain, one fact comes clear: I love you. (I have a horrid belief that you're not allowed to say that and mean it).

Reach out and take my hand

Now listen to the silence here

Keep your eyes closed

Don't see me

Just love me

With your arms. Anywhere.

Drenched in clichés,
Rosalia

Cesco's reply was, for him, remarkably simple:

Love,

Don't think.

Love

In the meanwhile, Cesco racked his brains for some way to do another great deed for Verona and thus win the right to choose his bride. But for some reason he couldn't concentrate, could hardly walk without bumping into things, so full were his thoughts with her. Detto laughed at him without knowing why, and Cesco could not help himself smiling too.

The Abbess was adamant that Cangrande should be told about Suor Beatrice's idea. "It is an excellent notion. But it requires swift action. You must suggest it to him at once."

Here was the sticking point – Antonia couldn't bring herself to be alone with the Scaliger. The end of the attacks had not ended her speculation as to the identity of her attacker. She ran over every possible man in her mind, but always her thoughts came back to Cangrande. Having no way of knowing that Cesco had eliminated the Scaliger as a suspect – unaware Cesco even knew of her plight – Antonia focused on the phrase 'No quarter'. From whom was Cesco seeking quarter? From Cangrande. Over the last two years she'd seen the Scaliger in public. Even the sound of his voice made her want to flee, to hide. Her brother had always said he was a demon. Was Pietro more right than he knew?

With such dark thoughts swirling about him, she couldn't bring herself to offer him a solution to his longest running war. Yet her idea wouldn't just benefit the Scaliger. It was good for Verona, and someday Verona would belong to Cesco.

Yet she couldn't face Cangrande alone! "Mother, couldn't you bring it to him?"

"I could," said the Abbess. "But he may not listen to me. I have been too long outside such affairs. He may deem me a silly woman, a mother hen with no sense of how the world works. You, on the other hand, are the daughter of Dante, sister to one of his most valued knights, and just ran his whole palace in the midst of the crisis. He cannot dismiss you."

Antonia had begun to shake her head halfway through the list of praises. "Even if I could, I would never present it with enough confidence to persuade him."

Knowing exactly what Suor Beatrice's fear was, Abbess Verdiana hoped to make her face it. But the girl's reluctance could not be allowed to extinguish so good an idea. "Why not pass it to your brother, then? Let him take credit for the notion. The Scaliger will receive it even better from a man." She sniffed to show what she thought of that.

"Pietro's back in Rome, with the Emperor and the exiled clergy," protested Antonia. "This must be done quickly."

The Abbess pressed her lips together thoughtfully. "That leaves one option. The boy. Cangrande's heir has already shown remarkable faith in you – faith that is entirely justified, by the by. He trusts you, respects you, and values you. And in the war between father and son, such an idea as this must surely give him a victory."

Antonia nodded, slowly at first, then more enthusiastically. "Very well. I'll tell him at once."

The Abbess smiled. "Let us invite him to dine. I'd like to meet him properly."

War was in the air. Everyone felt it. In Verona there was talk of invading Padua. Meanwhile, sensing Verona's weakness in the aftermath of the earthquake, Treviso sent raiding parties into Veronese territories. Cangrande had to deal with that, so he took an armed party of his favourite nobles and soldiers to scare the Trevisians off.

Out of pique (or perhaps, Cesco had to admit, a sense of fairness) the Capitano had kept Paride on as his squire. As he'd shown such an affinity for the people, Cesco had been demoted to secretary, which kept him at the palace, greeting visitors and answering letters.

In public he lamented this mind-numbing work, but secretly Cesco delighted in the posting. Lia's latest note was an invitation for another midnight meeting.

That morning, bathed and refreshed, he announced himself ready to greet all comers. It was a slow day for work, and after dealing with a few disputes that didn't need the Capitano's attention, he delved into letters. There were never many, but the ones the city received were long and often densely scrawled. Cesco had no trouble, however, decyphering the squiggles into words, and he was done and bored when the invitation arrived to take his midday meal at the abbey.

Arriving, he was allowed to embrace Suor Beatrice as a family member would. "Auntie!"

"Hello, dear." He was as tall as she was now, and still growing. And though his grip was gentleness itself she could feel the strength in his arms. "You look well. But tired."

"I can say the same about you. Hard work suits you. It can't be good to be crabbed up over parchment all day long – look at grandfather! He was so hunched and squinty at the end... 'Antonia!'" he cried in imitation of the old poet. "'You haven't translated that Ovid right – it's *I once thought to be,* not *I once wished to be.* Gad, Devil take it!' "

The impression was so good that Antonia laughed outright, her eyes welling. So focused on his genius, she had forgotten her father's quirks. "Francesco della Scala, allow me to properly introduce Abbess Verdiana. Mother, this is—"

"—Cesco," he finished for her. "Plain Cesco. I feel as though an apology is in order, though for what I cannot recall."

"Perhaps for running roughshod over my authority by conscripting Suor Beatrice to your purpose."

Cesco's eyes were twinkling. "That's right! You were very rude. But for the sake of my beloved auntie, I forgive you without an apology. What's to eat?"

Antonia sucked in her breath, but the Abbess' eyes twinkled. "I had forgotten what a young Scaliger is like. You treat your inborn cleverness, a gift from the Lord, as a bludgeon, hitting targets indiscriminately. It is beneath you. But likewise, I forgive you. Please, enter and enjoy our humble fare."

Cesco's spirits seemed remarkably imperturbable, as if he were spiritually armoured against all assaults. So he laughed happily and offered the Abbess his arm, which she accepted.

It was an interesting meal. After talk of the earthquake and the feeding of the poor, they discussed the general needs of the abbey. Cesco seemed genuinely interested in the running of the choir. Of course he knew a great deal about copying. "I grew up ink-stained," he confided to the Abbess, leaning close. "Sometimes I fear it blackened my soul."

"Then you're using too much alum to bind it," retorted Antonia, so tartly that they all laughed – she had been egged into it.

Cesco looked around. "This is a marvelous old building. I adore the columns. Are they original?"

Abbess Verdiana nodded. "As is the crypt. Alas, much was destroyed in the last earthquake, two hundred years ago. The same one that felled most of the Arena's outer wall. Thank heavens when they rebuilt they constructed it to withstand such another as we just had."

"How old is this convent?"

"Five hundred eighty-three. In 745 two sisters – birth sisters – instituted a monastery for women in their home. Their names were Autconda and Natalia, and they left their house to the order they founded."

"Generous of them. I'm glad it endures. I'm always astonished there are Benedictine houses anywhere, what with Franciscans and Dominicans stealing all the glory. You and San Zeno, the last of by-gone days."

Again Abbess Verdiana nodded. "We may not be in fashion, but our simple life and strong work ethic sees us through. Are you never still?"

Through their talk Cesco's leg had bounced to a rhythm all its own, as if music was playing only he could hear. "Time enough to be still when I'm dead." He studied her face. "Saint Verdiana. An odd choice. Presuming you chose it yourself."

The Abbess bowed her head. "I'm surprised you've heard of her at all. She is hardly famous."

"Nor was she a Benedictine. I thought she was Dominican."

"They have claimed her, as did the Franciscans – she was visited by the blessed Saint Francis, they say. But I have a personal connection to the sainted lady. She was my kin on my mother's side."

"Oh? And reclusiveness doesn't run in the family? You don't feel the pull to wall yourself into a cell for thirty years?"

"Thirty-four. Alas, I fear I am not as holy as my namesake. Nor do I enjoy confined spaces."

"Practical. So tell me, what brings about this invitation? Does the convent need a new wall? Fresh tapestries? A new fresco? It is a time of building, I'm afraid, and the masons are required for more urgent work. But I will happily add your name to any list of buildings needing work."

"On the contrary. We – and by we I mean Suor Beatrice – invited you here to offer aid, not ask what you can do for us."

Cesco looked to Antonia. "I'm on the edge of my seat."

Pursing her lips, Antonia began. "I was talking with Donna Montecchio yesterday. Among the topics was the news from Padua. I'm sure you've heard much the same, and I know the Scaliger is considering invading. But as I thought about it, I had a different idea." She explained, outlining it all. At the end she said, "Am I right? Is it possible?"

Cesco sat back on his chair. "It's not *im*possible. Just highly unlikely. And why involve good Nuncle Pietro at all?"

"Pietro has to be a part of it. It removes the threat of…"

Cesco frowned. "Threat of what?"

Antonia paused to frame her reply, but the Abbess solved her dilemma. "Ser Alaghieri was a part of the Dente uprising three years ago. If that were known—"

"—Carrara would put yet another price on his head." Cesco clucked his tongue. "For such a nice man, so many people want him dead. Or perhaps that's the reason. No, wait – it can't be, because the same number want me dead as well." Though he rambled, he was eyeing the Abbess shrewdly. "We seem to be remarkably free with the family secrets here. This sainted claustrophobe knows a whole level of intrigue that has missed me entirely."

"We have no secrets in this house," said the Abbess.

Cesco looked back and forth between the two women, and it seemed on the tip of his tongue to ask something. But instead he nodded. "So, you think Padua will fall. Perhaps the may. Yet they could survive a tumble. They have before, you know. This war has lasted twenty years, more or less. Both sides have had near-fatal turns. If Carinthia decides to send some troops, they're saved. Or Treviso – though Treviso has been very shy of Padua lately. I think the Trevisians are of your mind and would rather keep their soldiers alive for their own defense. But to oppose Verona's expansion, Venice might step in. Even Florence. Or the exiles might turn on us. It's all happened before. The only reason they haven't unraveled up to now are the Carrarese – they're a strong family, however corrupt. Not unlike my own," he added, flashing a grin. "Ser Alaghieri hates Marsilio with a passion. Will he even agree?"

"If he doesn't," said Antonia, "he's not the man we both know. So – what do you think?"

Cesco sat limply in his chair, eyes in the middle distance. Abruptly he leapt up out of his seat and began pacing, fingers drumming the air at his sides. The Abbess and Suor Beatrice watched as he paused, turned, paced again, then checked himself again.

Finally he slapped his hands together. Grinning, he crossed to kiss Antonia on the cheek. "Suor Beatrice, you have no idea how grateful I am. This will work."

"But how can we include Pietro when he's in Rome?"

"Nothing easier. We play a trick."

Thirty-Eight

Tonight's midnight meeting was clearly to be a game. The moment Cesco arrived at the appointed station, he was chased by a man whose chickens had gone missing. Running, he heard a taunting laugh ahead of him, and caught sight of her against the moon, once more in man's attire. Clearly she'd spent the last week learning the city.

But no one knew Verona better than Cesco, save perhaps Cangrande. He led his pursuers down a wrong turn and managed to cut her off, so that they thought she was he, forcing Rosalia to hide.

When Cesco found her, she was hip-deep in water at the bottom of a well. "Are you coming up, Narcissa," he asked lightly, "or should I join you in your bath?"

"Let me come up," she said. "I've already fallen, and it would be dangerous for you to descend any further." Refusing his offer of aid, she climbed out on her own. Teeth chattering as the chill air touched her hosed legs, she said, "Turn around."

He made a show of not complying as she took off her leggings. Her man's shirt was long enough to keep her from too much immodesty, but sight her bare calves made it difficult to think.

"And what are you looking at?" she teased.

"A pair of alabaster candlesticks. How do you walk on such thin little twigs?"

"How do you keep your balance with that massively swollen head?"

"Simple," he said, drawing near to her. "I think of you." He kissed her neck. "And the blood drains right away from my ego."

"Idiot..." Her skin prickled as his kisses continued. He murmured something into her skin and she laughed. "What was that?"

"I was remarking on your scent. How do you manage to smell nice after falling down a well?"

"I bathe regularly – something I cannot recommend highly enough."

Laughing, he buried his face in her skin again. What he did next made her grateful for the dark night that hid her blushes. She quickly stepped away. "Where did you–?"

He flopped down on the ground. "I read a lot. And I've been hiring Verona's better whores for instruction."

"It's money well-spent. Next time I'll pay their fee." She sat down beside him.

"Thank God. That way I won't have to go to the Capitano and account for my dwindling fortune."

"I'm curious – you always refer to him by his title. Why?"

"He has forbidden more familiar forms of address," said Cesco. "Says I haven't earned it."

"Do you like him at all?"

"I admire him a great deal," said Cesco, stretching out in the darkness. "But because you dislike him, I would I could choose a different set of parents."

"And who would they be?"

He paused in real thought. "Ser Alaghieri would be my father," he answered at last. "My first choice for mother would be his sister, but since that is both horrible and disgusting outside of old Egypt's royalty, I think my mother would be a woman I met once several years ago."

"Who was she?"

"My real mother, actually. Or so I'm told. I'll never know for certain."

"I never knew my mother, either," said Lia.

"Half-orphans, both." He stroked her hair. "We'll just have to make sure that we both know our children." She shied away. "What did I say now?"

She hugged her knees. "You are foolishly romantic, you know."

"It's a wonderful kind of foolery."

"Yes it is. My hero. You've saved me."

"From what?"

"You remember Tiberio? Our neighbour who arrived the morning after the disaster?"

"Which disaster was that?"

She laughed at that. "Disaster does seem to follow us – the bridge, the forge, an earthquake. But you know what one I mean."

"Tiberio. Came into your yard just as we were leaving after our first night together."

"Is that how you count them? My father wants me to marry him."

That brought Cesco up short. "Tiberio?"

"Imagine how I feel. Old Bramo the wild-man. He once tore a wolf's leg off with his bare hands, they say."

"And then used it to beat the wolf to death. I'm stunned you didn't swoon into his arms on first sight. But you might have got lost in that thicket of hair. Shall I grow a beard like his?"

"I dare you to try." She rolled over onto him, pinning his arms beneath her hands. "Kiss me, fool."

He did, then recoiled. "Dear God!"

"What's that?"

He gestured at her clothes. "I could be kissing a boy!"

"What do you want me to do about it?"

"Take them off, of course."

"I wasn't born just for your pleasure."

"I see," said Cesco, gazing up at her. "Taste this apple, said Eve, keeping it just out of reach."

"At least Eve was her own woman," said Lia. "So am I."

"Nay, you lie, in faith. You are mine as I am yours."

"If I am yours, then why do you want me?"

"Don't fish for compliments."

Her eyes twinkled. "What if I like compliments?"

"Ask for them," said Cesco, "and they're yours."

"Compliment me."

"Beautiful Lia, if you cut me, my flesh would smoke, not bleed. My heart is on fire—"

"A good start."

"You're brilliant. Beautiful. Venus and Diana in one. I look into your eyes and feel I've known you all my life."

"A body would never know you were raised by a poet."

"Fine. Then follow me." He threw her off him and dashed away.

They went swimming in the Adige, dipping in and out of the starlit water, well away from bridges and homes and prying eyes. They splashed, blew bubbles, and tried to surprise each other by bursting up from underneath. When they were thoroughly chilled they crawled up onto the bank and lay separated by a few feet, gasping. They still had bits and pieces of clothing on.

"It's impossible," she said. "Isn't it? As if we were meant to be."

"We are," he said simply.

Lia hitched herself up on one elbow. "You believe that?"

"No. I mean, yes, but that wasn't what I was saying. I'm saying that we aren't meant to be, some distant day in the future. We are, now. We just are." He laughed, leaning in to kiss her. "Though I never expected to be in the snares of an older woman."

She pushed his face away with the flat of her palm. "Silence is a virtue. I can see you're going to be difficult to manage. Medio tutissimus ibis, but you'll never be happy there."

"This may be heresy," said Cesco, nuzzling her neck, "but to hell with Ovid. Safety and happiness have very little in common. You'd best put a hashashin on retainer, just to be sure of me. I can arrange an introduction..." His voice trailed off, his gaze on the water. Then, with a sudden nod of his head, he rolled over, pulled something out of one dry boot on the bank, and threw it into the river where it made barely a splash.

"What was that about?" she asked.

Cesco was wiping something sticky from his hands. "Keeping a priestly promise."

At that moment Cangrande was arriving at his sister's palace in Vicenza. After a brief skirmish with the Trevisians at Castelfranco, he'd left the bulk of his forces idling down the westward road. Those with him straggled in and, well aware he'd be out again at dawn, collapsed in their beds. The sole exception was Bailardino, who sat up with his brother-in-law and discussed various plans, from the forge and local taxes to a possible invasion of Padua and a siege on Treviso.

Katerina da Nogarola entered unannounced, with only her cane to support her. Both men stood, and Bail crossed to buss his wife dutifully on her cheek. Accepting it, she turned to face her brother. "If you finally have a moment for me."

"Only a moment." Cangrande sat and began massaging his aching calves.

Katerina glanced at her husband. There was a pause, then Bail scowled. "I'll be in our rooms – if you have a moment for me." They could hear him stomping off down the corridor.

Cangrande arched his eyebrows. "I sense all is not domestic bliss."

"He'll be fine," said Katerina dismissively. "I want to know what you've told Cesco."

"About what?"

"About his destiny."

Cangrande stiffened visibly, a sign of his fatigue – he never showed her a genuine reaction if he could help it. "What makes you think I said something?"

Katerina sat down. "I offered to show him the charts."

Cangrande waited, knowing there was more.

Katerina said, "He refused."

He arched a brow. "He has sense after all. Surprising."

"He also intimated that I had once tried to kill him."

Cangrande grinned. "How these stories do get around."

"You didn't tell him anything?"

"Naught at all. Recounting your perfidies to my heir is not high on my list. Perhaps it was your pet, Pietro. So, did you force the knowledge of his destiny upon him?"

"He knows the charts exist and that I have them in my possession. Someday soon he will come for them. He cannot resist for long."

"Who can ever resist you, sister my sweet?"

"Only you," said Katerina.

"And Cesco, it seems! Ha! He's found what he needs without you, darling sister. The perfect shield to your arrows. Do you wonder what would sate his thirst for knowledge? What could it be? Hmm."

Katerina sighed at her brother. "Francesco, you are at your worst when you try to be mysterious. Clearly you're dying to tell me something. Do so or leave. I have no patience with you in one of your moods."

"Oh, let me play a little!" protested Cangrande. "A hint, a simple hint."

Katerina placed her hands over her ears and closed her eyes. "I'm not listening."

Crossing and leaning his lips just behind her ear, his voice was almost a purr. "What is the secret name of Rome?"

Katerina's eyes snapped open. Slowly her hands came down. Her face was stricken. "Dear lord — no."

"But yes!"

"He's in love?"

"Desperately!" The Scaliger threw his hands into the air. "Yes, brace yourself sister! Our little protégé has fallen backwards into some teenage romance. Moreover, he's asked if he may choose his own bride. I'm considering saying yes."

"But – no, Francesco, you can't! It's not – not what's in the chart–"

Cangrande's brilliant smile lost none of its luster. "I know."

"Three loves – there are three loves, but not his wife! He can't marry for love!"

"I know. Believe me, I know. But you know my feelings. Even at this late date, I'll do what I can to prove your precious charts wrong. If it means making my damned heir damnably happy, I suppose I can suffer it. How can you object? His happiness is all you've ever claimed to want."

Katerina could not help herself. She rose to the bait. "I want him to live his destiny."

"Who better to choose that destiny than the lad himself? Yes, you've quite made up my mind. Thank you. I'll let him know at once – he has my permission to wed this girl. Be she trollop or heiress, she shall be his wife."

Seeing her brother make to leave, Katerina stood. "And what of the oracle? What if this is the love she meant? The one that begins within a year of your death."

Cangrande lingered for a moment, then shrugged. "People fall in and out of love every day – I know I do. Yet I remain. I cannot live in fear. A man cannot control his stars, but he can control his actions. Mine shall not shame me. And before I die, I will be all I am meant to be, and more." His smile became less fixed, more wry. "The joy of it is, I'm beginning to like him. I could even pity him. And if a normal life is what he wishes, then I shall do my best to give it him. Good night, sweet sister." He departed, whistling as he went.

Mastino had not been allowed to go to Vicenza – too near his disastrous alliance with Niccolo da Carrara. That joint venture had gone from a bonfire to a pile of ashes, and as a result he wasn't allowed to even go near a war. No, he had to remain in the old palace, inert, not even allowed to do public business – that was left for the bastard heir, who wasn't even a bastard anymore, according to the church.

I threw my dice, and lost. Now I must wait for another opportunity.

A light rap on the door announced Fuchs. Mastino grunted. "About time. You'd best have something."

"Not something," replied Fuchs in his heavily Germanic Italian. "Everything."

"You got her name?"

"Her name, and much, much more."

As Fuchs related what he'd learned about the girl, a look of delight spread over Mastino's face. "Christ."

"It opens up a world of possibilities, does it not?"

"It does," said Mastino. "I want to be the one to break the news to the happy couple. The timing has to be just right. So I want your word – no spoiling it."

Fuchs promised, sure he would be allowed to watch the scene to come.

The young lovers retired to Ser Alaghieri's house to warm themselves and make love in a proper bed. Before dawn they began to dress, though their progress regressed a couple times. But finally, as he laced the cuffs to his sleeves, Cesco said, "I have to go away."

No sigh, no protestation. "To where?"

"To the end of war, and the beginning of our peace."

"Your riddles are getting worse."

"The Capitano promised that if I do one more great deed for Verona, I can marry where I choose."

Lia smiled. "So you're going to do what, conquer Jerusalem?"

"If you asked me to. But there's another, riper target closer at hand. I'll tell you all about it when I return."

Grabbing the front of his doublet roughly, she pulled him close. "See that you do. Come back."

Laughing, Cesco kissed her. "There's no danger to this whatsoever. In fact, there's a Damoclean sword cut down, and a happy measure of revenge. In a week, we'll be free to wed."

She leaned her forehead against his. "I cannot wait."

Keeping his forehead against hers, Cesco removed the thong with the old Roman coin from around his neck, transferring it to hers. "There. A fair trade. All I have ever been, for all I will ever be."

Thirty-Nine

Pisa

25 August 1328

Leaping from his horse, Pietro Alaghieri tied it to a hitch and began to walk swiftly towards the center of town, a bundle under his arm. He was a worried man. The coded note had arrived by an expensive messenger who had ridden through the night, changing horses twice. The message was in his sister's hand, in their private code. Yet the message was abrupt, even for her:

> Pietro,
>
> Be standing in the center of Knight's Square in Pisa at noon on the 25th of this month. It is a matter of the utmost importance. Do not come armed. Wear your judge's robes.
>
> *Antonia*

Cryptic. Ominous. The part about not coming armed was especially disturbing. Judge's robes? Was he needed here on some legal matter? What the devil was going on? He'd barely had time to offer his apologies to Ludwig's steward, though he doubted he would be missed. Occam was the new darling of the imperial court, and why not? The man was an outright genius, and while not perhaps an admirer of the Emperor, he detested the Pope in Avignon. The amount of logical abuse heaped upon the holy gnome's head had everyone in Rome clutching their sides for laughing.

In private, Occam had lamented his state to Pietro. "This has been a needless humiliation of a man who, I say myself, is as cautious and moderate as the household dog. I am no rabid radical by nature. But as even a good dog will turn on its master if beaten enough, so they insist upon turning me into the thing they accused me of being – an enemy to Pope John. Very well. I come late to the cause, but I will be its most devout crusader. For the danger I fight against is nothing less than papal heresy!"

Shaken from these thoughts by the familiar clamour of hammers and anvils, Pietro reached Knight's Square and paused, looking about. This place had hardly changed since he was a young teen. Also known as la Piazza delle Sette Vie for the seven streets that intersected here, this had once been the forum of the *Portus Pisanus*, the Roman harbour that had been Pisa's origin. Knight's Square was now the city center, much as the Piazza dei Signori was in Verona, with offices and law courts. Not far from here, in days gone by, Pietro had studied with Lucentio.

In celebration of the city's independence, several buildings had been joined to create a palace for both the people and the Anziani. Uguccione da Faggiuola, his father's former patron, had lived in that building there, until he'd been driven out. And just as Santa Maria Antica adjoined the Scaligeri palace, there was the church of San Sebastiano alle Fabbriche Maggiori, named for the blacksmiths just around the corner.

It was always crowded at midday, and Pietro had to step in the lee of an angled façade to don his judge's robe. As this was not a formal occasion, he did not wear the crimson robe, but the summer colour of a deep green, lined with taffeta. Then he pulled on his *collobium*, a knee-length tabard. Though he could have hidden a sword under his bulky robes, he had obeyed Antonia – mostly. There was a knife on his belt, and another in his boot.

Taking a breath, he plunged into the bustle of the square, eyes darting for Antonia, when he heard a laconic greeting. "Ah, the prodigal uncle."

Pietro whirled about in shock. "Cesco! Good God, you startled me. What the devil are you doing here?"

"Invoking God and Satan in a single breath. You're certainly prepared for any eventuality."

"What's going on?" demanded Pietro. "What's happened? Is Antonia—?"

"Everyone is well, Nuncle. But they will be better after this day's business. Now brace yourself for a shock and try not to do anything rash. We are not alone."

The ludicrousness of Cesco's warning against rashness was driven from Pietro's mind as he followed the lad's outstretched hand and saw a face from his past.

He was older now, older than his years, with white starting from his temple, as the dueling strains of his office and his family drained the life from him. Pietro had seen this face on the other end of a sword on four separate occasions, most recently in the Dente uprising three years earlier. It was still a remarkably handsome face, a touch darker than most inhabitants of the Feltro, more like a Genoese. But Marsilio da Carrara was the essence of Padua and its fabled pride, *patavinitas.*

Disbelieving his eyes, Pietro's hand groped for the sword that wasn't there. Cesco said, "Tut! I'm very glad you are obedient, Nuncle. Swords are not needed here, trust me."

Pietro noted the sword on Carrara's hip. "He's armed."

"Alas, he is less obedient than you. Being of an uncharitable mind, he also showed up an hour before his time."

It had been far longer since Carrara had lain eyes on Pietro, and it had taken him until now to recognize the face of his old foe. His left hand dropped to hold his sword, his right ready to draw. "I rode sixty miles for *him*?"

Pietro braced himself, ready to fight the moment Carrara's steel cleared the leather. "Cesco, what is this?"

"A trick," replied Cesco. "Both of you lured here under false pretenses – well, are there any other kind? But it's for your own good."

"How did you break my family's code?" Carrara demanded.

"You've been using the same one for five years at least," replied Cesco easily. "A few of us Veronese do bear brains, you know."

"Noted." Thus far Carrara's eyes had been on Pietro. They moved to study the young man with the thick hair and large eyes. "Cesco. Francesco. The bastard of Verona."

"Ah, how remiss of me! Marsilio de Carrara, I am indeed Francesco della Scala, scourge of scoundrels, the legitimized illegitimate, and heir to the Greyhound who holds you in such high esteem that he plans even now to invade your city." Cesco bowed deeply. "And allow me to reintroduce you to Ser Pietro Alaghieri, son of Dante, Knight of the Mastiff, and Special Consul to the Scaliger. You two are already acquainted, are you not?"

Carrara ignored that. "Cangrande's invading? Is that why you've lured me here?"

"He won't. What we do here today will make it unnecessary."

Carrara's gaze turned once more to Pietro. "So it's revenge, is it?"

Pietro opened his hands slightly, showing his lack of arms. "I had nothing to do with this."

Cesco clapped Pietro on the shoulder. "Don't be so modest! Marsilio – may I call you Marsilio? The whole thing was his idea, and a good one it was, too. You'll be thanking him by the end of the day."

"Thanking him!" Carrara almost spat.

"How better to show goodwill on both sides than patching up an old feud? Now, can the pair of you stop posturing like cocks on a fence long enough to stop all these good men from staring? There is business to discuss."

Slowly Carrara lowered his right hand, hooking its thumb onto his belt to keep it near his sword's grip.

As he straightened, so did Pietro. "Cesco, what are you up to?"

"It was your idea!" repeated Cesco in a chiding tone. "But if modesty prevents you from explaining it, allow me." Standing in the middle of the crowded square, he launched into a long speech. Slowly – slowly – the two enemies altered their focus from each other to him. By the time he reached his conclusion, both were staring pensively into space.

"I think that covers everything. Isn't that right?" Cesco turned to Pietro, eyebrows raised.

When Pietro said nothing, Carrara prompted him. "Well?"

"Well, what?" Pietro was distracted, thinking hard.

"Is what he says true? Was this your idea? Or is this just another trick, like the ones the Pup so adores?"

Pietro the knight wasn't about to lie. But Pietro the lawyer saw the advantages of a careful omission. "I think it's a good idea."

Carrara was clearly thinking hard as well. "And what guarantees do I have?"

Cesco watched a circling fly. "How fortunate that we have a lawyer here who also happens to be a judge of Verona. Why don't you let him draft an agreement?"

"He'll cheat me. He always cheats. Cheated in Vicenza, in the Arena." Carrara looked at Pietro. "You were with Dente, weren't you?"

Fuming at the accusation of cheating, Pietro took a breath. *A knight does not tell lies.* "Yes, I was. How did you know?"

"You were the judge he got to condemn me, and you bore me a grudge. Makes sense you were there. Just like in Vicenza, in disguise. You never fight as yourself."

"I did in the Arena."

"Yes, and got the Scaliger to save you. You would never lay a finger on me in a fair fight."

Wondering if he was about to fight another duel, Pietro pointed at Carrara's thigh. "I probably gave you a scar."

Carrara's initial scowl turned into a smile as cold as his stare. "Then we're a matched set. At least I gave better than I got."

Cesco saw matters getting away from his delicate plot. "Well, now that you're to be allies, you'll never have a cause to strike each other. Ser Alaghieri will draw up the contract, and you can have every lawyer in the world pore over it. All that this requires is your word. So shake hands and let's go inside before we melt."

Marsilio glanced at Cesco. "You speak for the Scaliger?"

"I speak for Verona."

"But Cangrande knows you are here?"

"Yes."

Pietro knew Cesco well enough to know a lie when he heard one. But he was beginning to see what his proposal would mean – for Verona, for Padua, for all of Italy. It was brilliant. *If* they could pull it off.

Carrara stood in the center of Knight's Square, looking as fine and regal as any noble of the blood. Pietro and Cesco waited. This all depended on Carrara's sense and ambition overcoming his pride.

But his pride needed a sop. "Very well. Tell your master I agree. But first, I want Ser Alaghieri here to admit the truth. That I won our duel."

Childish, petulant, arrogant, prideful. Carrara was still all these things. It was true that the duel had ended with Marsilio holding a blade to Pietro's throat. But only because he had acted dishonourably. For all his talk of cheating, he had himself played false by attacking Pietro's bad leg, against all the rules of chivalry.

Then Pietro thought about the cause of the duel. Carrara had driven a wedge between Montecchio and Capulletto. Carrara's cousin had been engaged to marry Antony, but Carrara had aided Mari to marry the girl in secret. Pietro had challenged him to the duel to make him pay. In that he had failed, and Mari and Antony were as far from being friends as ever.

"Yes, Marsilio. I admit it. You won."

The next few minutes were taken up with where to go while they thrashed out the finer points of the contract. They finally settled on the house of Vincentio. Lucentio was Pietro's friend, but had married into a Paduan family, making his father's house neutral ground.

Welcomed and closeted in private, that fine old establishment became the site of the most extraordinary negotiation in Veronese history. They stayed up through the night, arguing and spelling out every fine point, wrangling over every possible objection, with Cesco prodding both adult men when they became intransigent over some small point.

It was nearly dawn when Pietro finished drawing up two identical documents. "Of course you realize this has no weight until the Scaliger signs it."

"I understood it the last five times you said it." Marsilio snorted out a laugh. "You really *are* a lawyer, aren't you?"

As Pietro bristled, Cesco sighed ostentatiously. Despite the truce, these two would never approach amity.

"Four day's time?" asked Carrara.

Pietro was reluctant, but there was nothing for it – Carrara had insisted. "Yes. Tuesday the Thirtieth. The Doge's palace."

Taking his copy, Carrara departed at once for the long ride back to Padua, whereas Pietro and Cesco accepted Lucentio's invitation to sleep in one of the guest suites. Their journey could wait for the afternoon.

Bedding down in their shared room, Cesco fell back on his pillow. "I'm sorry, Nuncle. You were meant to arrive before him, so I could explain it all."

Pietro nodded as he closed his eyes. "It was a good plan."

"It means you have to brave Dandolo again. That was deliberate on Carrara's part. He must have heard of your imprisonment."

"Of course it was deliberate," answered Pietro with a snort. "But I'll be safe. I'm no longer an excommunicant, and Bonaccolsi is dead. I'm no threat to Dandolo anymore, therefore he has no reason to arrest me." He sounded far more sure than he was.

"I should have made him choose the Emperor as host instead. Rome would serve."

"For a Guelph? No. Venice is neutral, at least officially. It's all worked out. Well done."

"It was your sister's idea, actually."

"Antonia?" Smiling, Pietro was too tired to sit up. "Well done, little sister. Was she trying to remove the Paduan sword of Damocles from my head?"

"Yes. Though I was afraid your confession in the square would spoil the milk of concord. Must you be so honest?"

"Cesco, if there's one lesson I've learned as I've gotten older, it's this – secrets are more trouble than they're worth. The strain of keeping a secret is far harder than dealing with the consequences of the truth. I know in statecraft there are things that must be kept close to the vest. But in my life, I want no more secrets."

"The truth will set you free?" Cesco was only part mocking.

"Knowing is always better than not knowing. And, as I found in Avignon, God rewards the truth."

"He's the only one, then," murmured Cesco as he drifted into slumber.

Vicenza

"The Jew."

It was said so softly that, seated across the chessboard, Morsicato barely heard it. "What did you say?"

"MAB. We can trace her through the Jew." The Moor said it plainly, yet the words were so nonsensical that the doctor began to fear that delirium had set in.

It had been exciting to ride and be a part of the great meeting, Occam and the Emperor. But Morsicato's practice was just reviving, and he had one patient in his care for whom he was very concerned.

Yet when he'd come back from Rome in mid-July, he'd found the Moor suddenly mobile. As Esta told him the day he arrived, "He comes by every morning and takes me for a walk. Not far, and not quickly. But further every day. It's helped me regain my strength, too. And he's so quiet, but a good listener."

Morsicato chuckled at that. If Tharwat had been the chattiest person on Earth, he would barely have gotten a word in edgewise. Cesco himself barely managed. Esta was a gladiator of the gab.

Still, news of these walks was as pleasing as it was surprising. Until now, the Moor had shown no interest in recovery. He'd sat there, playing chess and drinking water mixed with poppy-syrup, uninterested in Paduan troubles or dealings with emperors and popes, barely interested in eating or sleeping. It was as if he had been reduced to a mind, and that mind cared for nothing but the stimulation right before it.

Something had changed that, and Morsicato was fairly sure what it had been. Cesco. The very sight of the boy, in that briefest of moments, had awakened the Moor's will. That day, he had been unable to ride. He still was, but now he could walk two miles on his healing ankles without missing a step. And in the afternoons he was raising a stick, a thin, whippy stick, and retraining his body in the ways of the sword. A good sign – though, missing an eye, he would never be what he had been.

This morning there had even been a visitor – a Spanish princeling, no less. Told where to find Tharwat al-Dhaamin, he called in great style, dressed to the hilt in silks, taffeta, and ruffles. His name was Pedro of Aragon, and though he owned a natural arrogance, it seemed tempered by an equally natural generosity. He insisted no one stand on ceremony in his presence, and he seated himself just at the Moor's knee. "My father told me, if I was ever in need of a prophecy, to call upon the Arūs, the great Theodoro of Cadiz. Indeed, I recall you visiting with your master the great Ignazzio when I was but a boy of ten."

From his chair, Tharwat bowed his head. "I am surprised you remember."

"Could I forget? You frightened me then, and your master was killed that very night, almost on our doorstep. A most vicious murder. Was the culprit ever brought to justice?"

Tharwat had nodded. "Yes."

"I am glad to hear it," said the tousle-haired prince. Despite his affected clothing, there was something centered about the twenty-three-year-old Don Pedro. "But, to the reason for my visit. I am about to visit a place called Bellamonte. I mean to woo an heiress. But, in order to do so, I must undertake an oath. It seems there is some kind of test. Should I fail that test, I must vow never again to woo a woman for my wife. Before I throw my die, I wish a little assurance. So I ask you, who can see into the future – shall I wed? Shall I have heirs?"

"Stars do not always reveal such things. Not in such precise terms. And I am not as skilled as others in the use of the pendulum." Tharwat had then smiled, but with his lips closed to hide his missing teeth. "Still, for the care your father gave dead Ignazio, I shall try."

Don Pedro had left looking happier. Whatever befell in Bellamonte, he had an errand to run in Pisa, but that when these tasks were over he would call again for a longer conversation.

Now Morsicato was afraid that either his recent exertions or else the plying of his arts had broken the Moor's mind. "What are you talking about?"

"Cesco's mother. Pietro and I have been searching for her. Three years. But there's a path we did not explore. The money."

"What money? What Jew?"

"There is a Jew in Venice. He is related to Manuel. Unpleasant, but honest. Had a lovely wife, though now a widower. He has handled Cangrande's secret accounts for years. Gave money to Ignazzio, to me, to Pietro. Why not to Donna Maria as well?"

It was the most Tharwat had spoken since he'd returned from Avignon. and he had dropped a hornet's nest in Morsicato's lap. "Cesco's mother?" asked the doctor incredulously. "You've met her?"

"Once. Ser Alaghieri, twice. I traced her, but she was kidnapped, tortured, and probably killed. We have been looking."

"Why?" asked Morsicato baldly. "Cesco's been legitimized now, there's nothing for his mother to swear to."

"They wish it to be secret. Any secret could harm the boy. If I can help him, I will." Tharwat rose. "I must go to Venice."

As nothing Morsicato could say would dissuade him (and the doctor said a great deal), there was nothing for it but to join Tharwat on another trip to Venice.

So the wheel began to turn.

Forty

Verona
27 August 1328

"I'm going to kill him," said Cangrande evenly. "It's as simple as that. I'm going to kill him."

The Anziani had sent to complain that their business hadn't been conducted since the day before yesterday. This morning the Scaliger had returned to his city, along with his entire retinue, to find his heir missing yet again.

Summoning a meeting of the city council at the Domus Nuova, Cangrande spent the first dozen minutes calmly but thoroughly berating his absent heir. "First he disappears when I need a squire. Now he's abandoned his post here at the palace. He wasn't here at all yesterday?"

"No, lord," answered Tullio d'Isola stoically.

Cangrande nodded. "I'm going to kill him. I have to, if only to avert total anarchy. What, does he think he's so special he doesn't have to obey my orders?"

"I'm sure there's a good reason, my lord." Paride owned a deep voice for one so young (he was just Detto's age), but it still broke from time to time. It did so now, and he flushed, but pressed on. "He's always looking out for your best interests."

"Commendably loyal of you, Paride," said Cangrande. "But my interests are best served by following my orders."

"Maybe he's got a woman somewhere," said Alblivious innocently. Mastino shot a covert glance at Fuchs, whose lips curled at the edges.

"We've all got women somewhere!" cried the Scaliger. "Wives, mistresses, whores, we've all got them – sorry, father," he said to Bishop Guelco who was present at court.

"No no. I have them too – well, not the wife," added the bishop. The crowd of nobles laughed.

"It's not funny, dammit!" Cangrande slammed his hands together. "He's off gallivanting around the countryside while the city is still rebuilding and we're on the brink of war! It's inexcusable!"

The doors flew open. "So I won't excuse it!"

Heads turned to witness Cesco's entrance. It was a marvelous reversal of Cesco's first day in this building, when he'd been on the podium and Cangrande had appeared suddenly, resurrected from the dead. This time it was Cangrande seated and Cesco calmly striding up the aisle, peeling off his gloves and tracking dirt from a hard ride.

Before anyone could say anything, another figure entered, causing a clamour of delight. "Ser Alaghieri!" Pietro's friends rushed over to greet him, Montecchio and Capulletto elbowing each other out of the way.

Sparing Pietro a narrow glance, Cangrande eyed his heir. Hat in hand, Cesco stopped before the dais and gazed placidly back. When the furor had subsided, Cangrande said, "Well?"

"We agreed, no excuses."

"An explanation, then."

"Perhaps we should close the doors?" Cangrande nodded and the doors were closed. At once the nobles resumed their stools and benches. The Scaliger's heir was clearly brimming with news. "Ser Alaghieri and I have just come from Pisa."

"Another holiday with the Emperor?"

"No, actually. I just felt like going for a ride."

"I see," said Cangrande. "A week ago you asked a favour of me. I was on the verge of granting it. But if you can't be bothered with even a decent excuse..."

Cesco was coy. "Well, something interesting did happen while we were there."

Cangrande rolled his eyes. "It is a poor showman who mistakes tediousness for tension. I promise you, we are all agog. So out with it. What happened in Pisa?"

"We won the war with Padua," said Cesco.

The crowd of nobles stirred. Cangrande suddenly wished he'd treated this as a family affair, locking the nobles out. Too late now. "And how did we manage that?"

Cesco stepped aside and waved at Pietro. "It was all Ser Alaghieri's doing. He'd heard tell, as we all have, of the deteriorating situation in Padua. But, unlike the rest of us, he determined to do something about it. He arranged a meeting, at great personal risk I might add, with Marsilio de Carrara."

Echoing murmurs as the nobles eyed Pietro with admiration. Pietro turned red as Cesco swept on. "Yes, Ser Alaghieri set aside his personal animosity in favour of Verona's greater good. Face to face, standing together in the house of Lord Bonaventura's in-laws, Pietro laid out all the options available to Carrara in the plainest terms. Carinthia has failed him, Treviso has abandoned him, and the Venetians won't send him any more money. Padua has to fall. The question is, to whom? Shall it fall to his cousin Niccolo and his measly band of exiles? Or shall it fall to Cangrande, the famous Greyhound of Verona? Wouldn't he prefer handing control of the city to a foreigner than to a blood relation who'd rebelled against him? And wouldn't it be better if, rather than shed any more blood in a pointless siege, he and the

Scaliger could reach an amicable settlement? Especially if that meant he remained in power in Padua as the Greyhound's representative?"

Stunned faces on all sides. Cesco nodded, his own eyes wide. "Yes, I know! Ser Alaghieri took all this upon himself, proposing it to his sworn enemy! And Carrara has accepted! The war is over without a blow being struck! Padua belongs to Verona, thanks to Pietro Alaghieri, Knight of the Mastiff! For all that he was born a Florentine, he is a true Veronese patriot!"

A swell of spontaneous applause greeted an embarrassed Pietro, and he found himself clapped on the shoulder and shaken by the hand.

Cangrande smiled sweetly. "And you just happened to be there?"

"Pure coincidence," said Cesco winningly.

"Then you'd best step aside, boy, and let the men deal in this – since you had no hand in it. Ser Alaghieri, what were the terms of this negotiation?"

"I have them here." Withdrawing a long sheet of parchment from a flat leather case, Pietro handed it to the Scaliger. "Carrara is aware that nothing is official without your personal approval."

Grunting, Cangrande seated himself and starting to read, sipping the wine that was never far from his hand. The crowd looked on in breathless anticipation. Were the terms good enough? Would he accept?

Slowly – very slowly – Cangrande began to smile.

"Your pardon, lord," said Bernardo Ervari, rising to his feet. "But since you seem to be considering them, would you mind sharing the terms with the council?"

"Not at all," said Cangrande jovially. "Our beloved Ser Alaghieri has anticipated my every hope. I am to become Lord of Padua, but will graciously leave the Paduans to be ruled by their own laws. There will be no retributions for acts committed during the course of the war, though Marsilio has reserved the right to deal with the exiles." Everyone present knew that all but the wealthiest would die. Carrara's cousin Niccolo certainly would. No Veronese would shed a tear for him. "Marsilio benefits personally from this surrender, taking over the rights to the lands of all the banished. Ah, I see Ser Alaghieri has added a codicil exempting Nico da Lozzo from any punishment, and a return of his Paduan lands. Well done," said Cangrande, even as Nico strode over to shake Pietro by the hand.

The next provision made Cangrande smile's even broader. "Mastino!" The nineteen-year-old stepped warily forward. "It seems congratulations are in order. You're to be married."

Mastino blanched. "To whom?"

"To Taddea de Carrara, daughter of the late Il Grande and Marsilio's cousin." Ignoring Mastino's reaction to the news of his betrothal to a notorious feather-brain, the Scaliger glanced at his heir. "It's a shame we couldn't bind those ties even closer, isn't it?"

"It is," agreed Cesco. "But I was–"

"Expecting?" Cangrande supplied.

"Hoping," corrected Cesco. "I was *hoping* to be already spoken for."

Cangrande wafted the parchment through the air. "We shall see." He returned to reading, a pensive expression across his face. "The matter is to be decided in Venice, three days from now. Why so soon?"

"Best strike while the iron is hot, before word of the agreement slips out." No one wondered why, if Alaghieri was the true architect of this agreement, it was the heir who was answering.

Cangrande sat and considered while the assembly watched him, hoping. At last he said, "I see one problem."

"What's that, my lord?"

Cangrande gestured at his nephew. "Mastino. He led his own troops along with Niccolo's exiles. Marsilio may ignore that, but not the people. Mastino della Scala led Veronese soldiers against Padua, in defiance of the truce. A marriage isn't enough. What do we do about Mastino?"

Cesco smiled sweetly in Mastino's direction. "I don't suppose we could execute him?" he asked lightly, then hurried on. "No, probably not. Don't want to leave his bride bereft. How about disowning him?"

Stepping forward, Mastino's hand dropped to the knife at his belt. Cangrande snapped his fingers repeatedly. "Down, my mastiff, down! The pup is just teasing. He knows what is acceptable and what isn't. He's just waiting to tell us his real idea."

"Which is what?" scowled Mastino.

Cesco shrugged. "It's easy, really. It wasn't Mastino in the armour."

"What?!" demanded Mastino.

Cesco put a hand to his heart, feigning shock. "A scandal, is it not? Last summer someone stole your helmet and impersonated you. This kind of thing has happened before, you know – I hear uncle Pietro there once wore the armour of the Count of San Bonifacio. This time the trick was done to sow discord between our fair cities and break our fragile truce. Probably some agent of the Emperor, looking to make our beloved Capitano lose face in this region."

"No one will believe that!" said Mastino.

"Certainly not," agreed Cesco. "But it's enough for a wink and a nod. Especially if we throw someone else to the dogs."

"So to speak," said Cangrande.

"So to speak," agreed Cesco.

"Whom did you have in mind?" But Cangrande was quick. His eyes had already found the man in question.

"Why, il signor Fuchs, of course. Who has access to both Mastino's men and gear? Why, il signor Fuchs, of course. Who would Mastino's men follow even unto death? Why, il signor Fuchs, of course. Who is German, not Italian, and therefore more likely to be in the thrall of a German emperor? Why, il signor Fuchs, of course. As he's not a native Veronese, exiling him won't cost you a florin here at home. We'll have to come up with a good story – probably he was bribed by the Emperor's men, and Mastino, finding the money and some incriminating papers among his effects, turned him in at once. I think that will be enough for the Paduans. If not, we can always have him dragged to Padua in chains. Nothing like a public execution for a boost in popularity, even if everyone knows the charges are trumped up."

Throughout the whole speech Cesco had not turned, and nothing in his voice conveyed either satisfaction or contempt. Rather he spoke dispassionately, as if Fuchs' exile and ruin was a matter of no moment.

Listening in growing horror, Fuchs felt the eyes of every man turn upon him, and was suddenly aware how few friends he had made here over the last four years. "You cannot—!"

"Don't tell me what I can do," said Cangrande coldly. "To end this war in Verona's favour, I would do all that he describes and a great deal more." Cangrande rose, pulling himself up to his full height. "An edict will be published at the end of the day tomorrow declaring Niklas Fuchs guilty of treason for usurping Mastino's authority and breaking the truce with Padua. That gives you twenty-four hours to disappear. If ever you are found in Veronese lands, you will be killed on sight."

Just that fast, Fuchs became an outlaw and public enemy. Stunned though he was, Fuchs wasn't about to go without a fight. He turned to Mastino. "My lord?"

Mastino had the good grace to look Fuchs in the eyes, yet he remained perfectly still. Scowling, Fuchs turned back to Cangrande. "What if the troops say it was not me?"

Before Cangrande could answer, Mastino crossed to lay a hand on Fuch's shoulder. The German experienced a moment of hope before he heard the Mastiff say, "My friend, attempt that and I'll have to kill you myself."

No one had ever said Mastino was slow. He had grasped the situation, and the escape being offered him. Still, his eagerness to abandon a friend would not soon be forgotten by the watching crowd.

"Besides," said Cesco brightly as he turned to face Fuchs at last, "who would come forward just to put his own neck on the chopping block? And Niccolo's exiles won't be allowed to testify who it was under the helmet – they'll be fled or dead. No, all in all, I think you will find every hand against you. Nothing personal, Niklas," he added. "You've just reached your deadline."

Fuchs eyes met Cesco's for the first time. There was true hatred present in both sets, blue and green.

"Best start running now," said Mariotto Montecchio, a grimly satisfied smile on his face.

He was not alone in smiling. "Mention this to anyone," added Antony Capulletto, "and you'll find no bolt-hole safe."

The sight of those two implacable enemies united drove home the hopelessness of his situation. Fuchs stood a second longer, a bewildered look on his face. Then, with a dark glare for the Scaliger's heir, he stalked from the hall, leaving the doors wide behind him.

Cangrande ordered the doors shut once more, then slowly looked each man present in the face. "My lord Capulletto is quite correct. What we learned here today must, by its very nature, remain a secret for some weeks more. The Paduans will revolt if they discover their leader has been negotiating with us, and drag the war on for a dozen more years out of pique. I, for one, am tired of this war. I think you are too. Therefore I ask each of you to hold this information closer than you hold your wives, your lovers, even your dogs."

Chuckles, but every head was nodding.

"Good then. Tullio, please start packing my finest weeds. I'm off to Venice at dawn tomorrow. In the meanwhile, I say we celebrate this turn of events by giving a welcome feast to our trusted friend Ser Pietro, whom I declare a full Consul of Verona and promote to member of the Anziani! No less than he deserves! To the Great Hall! Mastino, lead the way!"

Pietro accepted the congratulations of the Veronese nobility with mixed feelings – it had been Antonia's idea and Cesco's execution. He had only negotiated the details. But he had to play the part they'd written him. He was embraced by Mari and Antony, by Nico and Petruchio. Bailardino actually had tears in his eyes, sallow-faced Ervari was jumping up and down, and Castelbarco was sitting as if struck by a stunning hammer.

Pietro suddenly realized what this really meant to them all. Twenty years of war, over. Success. Victory. Slowly his smile grew to match theirs.

The mass of men went to a happier meal than any they could recall. Before Cesco could join them, however, Cangrande grabbed him by the collar. "Where are you going?"

"To the Great Hall?" said Cesco innocently.

"To the stables," corrected the Scaliger. "What has this celebration to do with you? By your own confession you were shirking your duties. Your first chore is to rake out my private stables and rub down every horse in it. But I'll save a hunk of meat for you."

Cesco was utterly unperturbed. "Keep the meat. How does this deed stack up?"

Cangrande stared into the middle distance, a wry half-grin playing at the corners of his mouth. "It stacks up very nicely indeed. When the ink is dry on this agreement, you have my permission to marry where you choose."

Bowing low, Cesco skipped off to the stables with a heart full of joy.

Watching him go, Cangrande's famous smile turned inwards. For his sister was correct. Based on the star-charts, if the boy wed for love, he was not the Greyhound.

Which meant there was yet room for another to snatch that title. And with the conquering of Padua, Cangrande was one step closer to fulfilling his own destiny of ruling all the Feltro.

His heart almost as full as his heir's, Cangrande went off to join the feast.

Fuchs heard the reveling while he packed. Another man might have wept for rage and shook from frustration, but his eyes were clear, his hands steady as he closed the last loop on his saddlebags. His jousting gear he would have to send for. Mastino would do him the courtesy of sending it.

He said as much when, after the meeting, he slipped out of the feast for a brief, final chat. "This is not banishment forever. In a year, perhaps sooner, when Padua is firmly in Cangrande's power, I'll arrange for your recall."

"You will try." Fuchs was not hopeful. He'd long since taken the measure of Cangrande's steel, and of Mastino's friendship, and knew which was stronger.

"I'll try," agreed Mastino. "That little shit. Thinks he's so clever! Well, at least you've given me the tool I need to end his little love affair."

Fuchs paused in his packing to look Mastino in the eye. "He has to be alive for you to use it."

Mastino came off the wall he was leaning against. "No! No, Fuchs. We can hurt him, break him, make him wish he'd never been born. But you cannot kill him."

"I can kill anyone I choose," answered Fuchs carefully.

Hearing the threat, Mastino grew equally cold. "Not if you wish to return to Verona. There is a curse upon us, my grandfather's curse. Any of us who sheds the blood of a relative is damned. That extends not just to shedding the blood ourselves, but people doing it for us."

Fuchs returned to stuffing his spare tunics in his saddlebags. "I won't be doing it for you."

"No matter, I'll take no chances." Grabbing Fuchs by the arm, Mastino turned him so they were face to face. "I want your word, Fuchs – you'll not kill him."

"Or what?"

"Or no money, no armour, nothing. You leave Verona with the clothes on your back. Try making a name for yourself in the lists without armour. But if you obey me, I'll open an account in – Bruges? Madrid? Wherever they like tourneys. You can spend the next year or two becoming famous, at my expense."

"I want revenge!" snarled Fuchs.

Mastino's grip tightened. "And you'll have it. But he has to live to feel it. Your word, Fuchs."

Reluctantly, Fuchs nodded. "My word."

"And the girl. Leave it to me to find the very moment for it, the perfect spy of the time. But let me tell him. Promise me."

Fuchs nodded a second time, even more reluctantly.

"Or the other matter We agreed, he must never know that, above all."

A third nod. That one, at least, was easy. Neither one wanted to share that secret.

Mastino stared hard, as if his gaze could discern the strength of Fuchs' word. Then with a nod he clapped his friend on the shoulder and departed, without even an apology.

Full of rage, Fuchs put on his best riding cloak, hefted his saddle-bags, and went down to the stables of the old palace. In his ears rang the joys and clamours of the Veronese nobles celebrating the end of the war. That he was the sacrifice required mattered not a whit to them.

These fauler unecht nobles, thought Fuchs, who had counted on Mastino to ennoble him. Think the rest of us are dirt. I will show them.

This thought was still in his mind when he heard a cheerful voice from inside the stable. "Ah! Just in time. I've saddled your horse for you."

It was the heir, preening in his victory. Fuchs stopped in his tracks, tempted beyond words to draw his sword and flay the skin from this little bastard.

Cesco read his thoughts. Stepping away from Fuchs' horse, he rubbed his own belly, drawing attention to the sword hilt just inches from his fingers. "Please, do. I'm not as small as once I was, and I was trained by the best – including you. I'm quite eager to try my hand at a real duel."

"Another time, giftzwerg, another place." Bushing past, Fuchs began checking the cinches of his saddle. It would be just like the bastard to fray a cord so it would snap while he was on the road.

Cesco leaned casually against a stone pillar, crossing his legs at the ankle. "O, I am patient beyond words. But I'm glad for this meeting. You see, I so wanted you to know why. After all, I could have disgraced anyone. Why heap odium upon you?"

Fuchs shrugged. "You need no motive for your little schemes."

"Perhaps not. But once in Ravenna, long ago, I interrupted a rather ugly seduction. Ever since that night, I have had a real distaste for rapists."

Fuchs straightened, a smile playing on the edge of his lips as he shifted his saddlebags into place. "You knew."

"Suspected. The look on your face when I mentioned deadlines confirmed it. That night I could only guess by size and speed. But you never take your shirt off in public, at least when I'm around. Is it because I scarred you? I hope the spikes hurt."

"Not half so much as my spike hurt her."

Cesco's body jolted off the pillar, and an eager Fuchs readied himself to draw.

After a moment that vibrated with violence, the bastard stepped back, out of the enclosure of the stables. "Not here, and not now. But soon. Go where you like. There is no place you are safe from me. You hurt the closest thing I have to a mother. In return, I will destroy you inch by inch."

Fuchs turned back to his horse, that same smile playing about his mouth. "You have no idea how badly I've hurt you. You and your mother, both. But you will. Just you wait. You've ruined me. But I'll ruin you, too."

Cesco seemed utterly unconcerned. "Then we have that in common. We are the destroyers of hopes, wreckers of dreams. But I am here and you are not. Write the vision, and make it plain upon tables, that he may run that readeth it." Stepping aside,

Cesco made a sweep with his arm. "In other words, friend Fuchs – run. Run for your life."

Forty-One

With Ser Alaghieri in Verona, the lovers could not use his house to meet – or at least, not the inside. They sat upon his roof instead, gazing at the stars as they held hands.

After a time, Cesco turned to her. "You do want to marry me, don't you?"

Lia gasped, choked, and laughed all at once. Cesco grinned. "I'll take that as a yes."

She struck him with the back of her hand. "Was that supposed to be a proposal?"

Cesco shrugged. "I only wanted to be sure. I asked Cangrande, but I don't remember actually asking you. It seemed an established fact."

"Better late than never, I suppose. If marriage is, in fact, a necessary evil, must we follow ritual pro forma? Shall we read the banns this night? You could shout them from the rooftops."

"I could ask your father first. What do you think he'd say?"

"I think we'd best act first, tell after."

"A widow instead of a fallen woman. Wisely, wisely."

She grabbed a handful of soot from the chimney behind her and smeared it across his face. "Now who's fallen?"

Begrimed, Cesco leaned in for a kiss. "Purge me with hyssop, and I shall be clean, O God."

"Wash me, and I shall be whiter than snow," she said, returning the act in kind.

"Create in me a clean heart…"

"He that hath clean hands, and a pure heart, who has not lifted up his soul unto vanity, nor sworn deceitfully…" They were both giggling as their faces grew sootier.

"*What God hath cleansed,*" he said, falling over and placing his head in her lap, "*that call not thou common.*"

"O! Common, am I?" She cut off Cesco's protest with a raised hand. "In silence man can most readily preserve his integrity."

"Eckhart! Nice. Silence gives the proper grace to women."

"Sophocles? Or Socrates?"

"The former."

"I'm wishing this wine were the latter's," said Lia. She kissed his eyelids. "Let there be a sacred silence."

"Do you, my Muse's priestess, sing for girls and boys songs not heard before?"

Lia stroked his hair. "I haven't heard this song before."

"Nor I."

"It is late. I'll be missed. Though we could do this all night."

"Yes, we could. Do you speak Arabic?"

"No. Will you teach me?"

He reached up to run one knuckle softly along her cheek. "Tomorrow."

"And tomorrow?"

"And tomorrow. Inshallah." She looked curiously down at him. "God willing."

"God willing," she said, smiling.

Amazingly, the coming meeting between Cangrande della Scala and Marsilio de Carrara remained a secret. Cangrande made as if he were visiting Vicenza, taking a large retinue. Tellingly, he left Nico da Lozzo, a Paduan, in charge of Verona – the exile turncloak would be persona non grata at this particular meeting.

They set out upon Monday morning. It was the twenty-ninth day of August, and the air was thick and hot. Riding at the front with the Scaliger were the men he had chosen to travel to Venice. Bailardino and Castelbarco were the elders, representing the interests of Vicenza and Verona. Petruchio was married to a Paduan, so he was needed. And Montecchio's wife was cousin to Carrara, so he would be allowed to come, whereas Capulletto would definitely not. He'd supplied arms to Padua in secret, which was embarrassing to Cangrande, and he hated Carrara with a passion, which was moreso.

Antony was not pleased to be left when Mariotto was to attend, but there was nothing he could say. He'd remain with the troops on the road to Treviso, watching for incursions.

Mastino had to come, as he was to marry Carrara's cousin. Castelbarco asked his son to come along, grooming him to take the family place in Verona's affairs, and Petruchio had invited both his boys. Paride was there, acting as the Capitano's squire. And Cesco and Detto were allowed to ride along, Detto to squire Petruchio and Cesco because he'd earned it.

As the supposed architect of the peace, Pietro would have a place of honour in the assembly. But he spent the first leg of the journey riding beside Cesco. "You'll be knighted for this. Even if I get the credit, you'll get a knighthood."

Cesco rode easily, his whole body languidly happy. "I was hoping for something even better." But as to what he had in mind, he remained mum.

They stopped in Vicenza to change horses, and Pietro and Cesco called upon the house of Morsicato, expecting to find the doctor and the Moor deeply engaged in chess. But they found only Esta.

"Where have they gone?" asked Pietro in concern. The last time he'd seen Tharwat, the Moor had been hardly able to walk.

"Gone? To Venice. Very secret they were about it, too. You men and your little conspiracies. As if keeping secrets from a wife is ever clever."

Pietro and Cesco exchanged puzzled stares. "Venice? How did they know?"

Cesco shrugged, laughing. "We knew he was good with the charts, but I had no idea he could predict the future so accurately!"

Entering Venice's Yellow Crescent, Morsicato felt decidedly uneasy. The eyes here were furtive, unfriendly. He'd always ignored the rumours of well-poisoning, Satanic rituals, flesh-eating, and the burning of live children. In fact, he'd learned a good deal of medicine from his Hebrew colleagues. But Jewish doctors were not allowed to treat Christian patients, one of many steps to keep them insular, separate from society. Jews were not allowed to marry Christians, to sell staple foods or any clothing to Christians, to hold land or mortgage. And, most recently, on top of their yellow badges they were now ordered to wear hats with a point to represent a devil's horn.

Yet, in an ironic twist, they were needed. Desperately so. It was heretical for any Christian to levy interest on a loan. But since Jews were damned already, they were allowed to lend at high rates – so long as the state received two-thirds of the interest levied. Indeed, usury was the only profitable enterprise a Jew was allowed. Ironic, as ancient Judaic law declared usury an abomination, which was why Christ had thrown the money-lenders from the Temple. Modern Christian law forced Jews to handle money and be the bankers of the world, making them religiously unclean in the process.

No wonder, then, that the gazes upon them were unwelcoming. Morsicato could not tell if it was for just for himself, or also for his companion. For all that Moors were unwelcome in Venice, the doctor would have thought these people, also anathema, would at least tolerate him. But they seemed more suspicious of the astrologer's presence than of Morsicato's.

Perhaps it was the Moor's appearance – the old burn scars on his neck, the new scars on his hands, the eyepatch, the slack area in his cheek where teeth had been removed. Tharwat was clearly a man who had been tortured throughout his life. It was possible that the residents viewed such a man as dangerous, inviting trouble down upon their heads.

Tharwat knew the way, so the doctor followed, matching his pace. It was slower than of old, but even, If the Moor was in pain, he did not show it. Eventually they came to a tall, thin building with a heavy oak door. "This is the house."

Morsicato stepped up and knocked. A moment later the door was swung wide and they were faced with a repulsively ugly young servant who did not wear the yellow star or the horned cap. A Christian servant?

If the fellow thought the duo of a bald doctor with a forked beard and a one-eyed Moor was odd, he gave no sign. "Yes, masters?"

"We're here to see Shalakh," answered Tharwat, his rasping voice low but clear.

The servant grinned. "The devil you say."

"We really do," said Morsicato.

"I'm sure. I mean to say, you seek the devil my master? I wonder you don't hear him, ser. There he is, conversing with two good Christians, the merchant and his friend."

Following the servant's crooked finger, Morsicato saw a short man, slim and forbidding in his fine gabardine robes. He wore a trim mouth-beard, and beneath it was a wry smile, at once grave and mocking.

The Moor nodded. "That is he."

The two men Shalakh was talking to were fair enough, pure Italian. One was thin and sad-faced, no hat upon his head, his rich clothes in disorder as if he could not be bothered with his appearance. His companion was a hair shorter but much more dapper, and was holding his own hat in his hand. Both eyed the Jew with suspicion.

Thanking the ugly servant, Morsicato and Tharwat drew near the conversation, halting just short of the three men. There they waited, standing in the square at the end of the Crescent, lingering unobtrusively until the interview was over so they might catch Shalakh alone. Their business was not for outside ears.

This was evidently not true of the Venetians' business. From where they stood, Morsicato could not help over-hearing the exchange. As the Jew's servant had indicated, Shalakh was talking quite loudly.

"…Signore, for years you've railed to the whole Rialto about my profession, called me a – what was it? Oh yes, an 'unbelieving heathen dog'. You have actually spat in my face for being skilled at the only profession I am allowed. Passing you in the street, I've felt the back of your foot. Now I ask you, have you ever heard me complain?"

"Not much," replied the Venetian merchant sarcastically.

"Exactly so! I've borne it all with quiet patience – well, we are accustomed to unjust suffering. And now you need my help? 'Jew, we need money,' you say. What should I say to you in return? Should I be the man you think I am and reply, does a dog have money? Or should I lie under your boot and beg you to take my hard-earned ducati, pretending that we're friends? What would you think of me then?"

"Say whatever you like." The shorter man turned to his companion. "Antonio, there's no need for this."

"Wait, Bassanio." The merchant called Antonio pushed his friend aside. "Jew, you are right. We are not friends. But isn't it better to lend money to an enemy? That way, if you aren't repaid you won't hesitate to take whatever vengeance that subtle mind of yours can come up with."

Shalakh's hands flung to his chest. "You wound me! You positively do! Here I am, charity itself, offering you my hand. Your friend there needs money? He shall have it! And, what's more, I'll lend it without a drop of interest. What do you say to that?"

Antonio blinked, clearly surprised. "I say – that is very kind of you. Almost…"

"Almost Christian?" Shalakh's eyes narrowed in mockery. Then his brow furrowed. "This will hurt my business."

"How is that possible?" asked Antonio. "I would think having my business should enhance your reputation."

Folding his hands, Shalakh worried his lower lip. "You don't know my people. If my brother lenders hear I let such a sum go without surety, I will be considered a risk." His clouded brow cleared and he let loose a throaty laugh. "I have it! To show them that I have not lost my wits or my pride, let's have a bond. You swear to repay me within three months – plenty of time to make good the debt. But we'll have a contract that says if you fail to pay me, I can have a pound of your flesh!" He chortled. "You see? My brethren will deem me a marvel, thinking I have you in my power. And your friends will see that I won't lend you money for interest, the same way you lend to your friends. Neither of us loses face. A good joke, no?"

The Venetian merchant was smiling at the ridiculous nature of the bond. Morsicato wasn't a lawyer, but he misliked the terms of the bond.

The merchant's friend Bassanio seemed to be thinking along the same lines. "Antonio, don't do it. I'll get the money another way."

Antonio gave him a strange look. "I thought I was your last chance."

Bassanio dropped his head. "You are. My ship sails tonight. But I'd rather not have the money than see you take such a risk."

Shalakh threw up his hands to the open sky. "O Abraham! How suspicious these gentiles are! But then I suppose they have reason. Their Savior was betrayed by a Jew, after all. At least he had silver in return. Signor Bassanio, if this bond is broken, tell me – what do I gain from it? What on Earth would I do with a pound of Antonio's flesh – if I could get even that! You should eat more, Master Antonio, you're looking almost Hebrew in your thinness. But again, what would I do with it? It's not good currency, and if you're right about me and I think all Christians are swine, then I certainly can't eat it!" He laughed again with such good nature that Antonio actually laughed with him, if not deeply then at least honestly.

Shalakh smiled at the one called Bassanio. "I'm a practical man. Your friend knows this. I'm buying his friendship. Being his enemy is hard on my business." He glanced again at Antonio. "That is, my friend, if you feel safe. If not, why then, adieu – that's French for to God, you to yours, me to mine."

The Venetian Antonio grasped the Jew by the arm. "Shalakh, wait! Bassanio, don't worry! I have ships out all over the world, and in two months I'll have the money to pay this fellow back three times over." Releasing Shalakh's arm, the merchant offered his own hand. "I will take this bond."

Shalakh took the Venetian merchant's hand, shook it once, and released it. "Very good! As I told you, I don't have three thousand ducati on hand at present, but I'll send right now to my neighbour Tubal and borrow it. Once I have the silver on hand, I'll send you a note and meet you – at your convenience – at the notary so we can have this matter settled."

"Then Godspeed, gentle Jew. Yours and mine." They parted, with the one called Bassanio looking worried and his friend shrugging unconcernedly.

Shalakh turned and swept right past Morsicato, muttering something about Christians as he passed. Tharwat cleared his throat, causing the money-lender to look up sharply. "The Arūs. An unexpected honour." He managed to make the honour sound unwelcome and offensive. "Time has been unkind to you, I see. Are you here for yourself, or your master?"

"Myself. We have important business." With a wave of his hand he indicated Morsicato. Shalakh inclined his head, and Morsicato did the same. "May we walk home with you?"

Shalakh shrugged in disdainful resignation. "Well." Together they moved towards Shalakh's house.

Morsicato attempted light conversation. "We heard your offer to that merchant. Very generous."

The doctor half expected the usurer to excoriate him for eavesdropping. But Shalakh seemed in an affable mood. "It was, wasn't it? Still, truth be told, I can't afford Antonio as an enemy at the moment. There's another rumour of debt-cancellation, which has all my brethren running scared like sheep at the scent of a wolf. And Antonio undercuts my business by lending money interest-free to his friends and other good Venetians. Perhaps now the Christians will see me in a more favourable light and make use of my services."

They reached his door. The house itself was very fine, well-made if lacking in outward adornment. Jewish craftsmen were skilled, and its austerity added a certain elegance.

"Do you mind entering a Hebrew domicile?" With their consent, he led them up a set of stairs and into a room with only two entrances and no windows. This room served as Shalakh's office, as far as visitors were allowed. Waving them into chairs, he remained standing behind his desk. "This man is..?"

The doctor chose to introduce himself. "Ser Giuseppe Morsicato, personal physician to the Nogarola family."

Shalakh gave Morsicato a quick up-and-down glance, clicked his tongue, and returned his gaze to the Moor. "You are still in the employ of the Scaliger?"

"Among others. I was sorry to hear of the passing of your wife," said Tharwat. "Leah was a lovely woman, and kind."

Shalakh frowned defensively, but saw nothing pointed or malicious in Tharwat's face. "Thank you." Unconsciously he touched a beautiful turquoise ring on his finger. He suddenly looked down at it, scowled, and pulled it off. Placing the ring in a drawer of his desk, he became brisk. "What is your business? Do you require money? As you heard, I have very little ready cash at hand, but I can supply a modest need."

Tharwat shook his head. "We come for information."

"That will take longer. Please excuse me a moment." Shalakh lifted a wax tablet and carved a few odd-looking sigils into it. "I must send a message, then I will hear your request. Launce! Launcelot! Where is that fool?"

Instead of the servant's voice, they heard a young woman call from upstairs, "He's out back, father, beating the rugs!"

Shalakh scowled. "Then you come here, girl!"

There was a tremendous sigh, audible through the floorboards, followed by footsteps, and suddenly a teenaged girl was framed in the doorway. She was ravishingly lovely. There was an exotic air to her, something old, earthy, primal. Her modest clothes couldn't hide the swing to her hips. "Yes, father?"

"My daughter Jessica," said Shalakh carelessly to his guests as he crossed and held the wax tablet out to her. "Girl, tell that idiot to go over to Tubal's, give him this, and say I'll explain later."

She took the tablet of wax and departed without a glance in the guests' direction. There was a furtiveness about her, as if she were guilty of something. Living in Shalakh's house, there must have been a great many rules.

Closing the door behind her, Shalakh returned to his desk. There was a little scroll with numbers on it, marking the current exchange rate for various currencies. Few regions of the world had sufficiently reliable access to silver or gold to mint coins. The Venetian ducato was an exception, and was accepted all over the civilized world as one of the few stable currencies.

Behind Shalakh's desk, a massive metal box served as a chair. Since money was officially considered a creation of Satan, a money-lender's strongbox could hardly be imagined without a Devil engraved on the lid. But Shalakh's was not so adorned. It was plain, and covered with a comfortable looking cushion, well-used. Shalakh settled himself onto it. "Well?"

He'd addressed Tharwat, so the Moor did the talking. "We need to trace someone Verona supplies with money."

The Jew's left eye twitched. "Does his Highness the Scaliger know of your query?"

Tharwat produced a parchment bearing Cangrande's seal. Morsicato chose not to ask where he had gotten a copy.

Shalakh pushed his nose up to the parchment, reading and staring at the seal suspiciously. Morsicato tried to look unconcerned. Finally the Jew grunted and handed the paper back. "Very good. Who, precisely, are you looking for? The paper doesn't say."

"A lady of about forty years, known to us as Donna Maria."

Shalakh straightened, taking him to his full height, which was not in itself impressive. Yet for all his short stature, he was a remarkably forceful presence. Morsicato could imagine him standing toe-to-toe with even Cangrande and holding his own.

Shalakh gazed at his guests. "Why?"

"We want to find her."

"You have wasted your time, and mine. I cannot help you. Good day." Rising, Shalakh started to cross to the door again.

Morsicato leapt up and grasped the Jew's arm as he passed. "Wait. You clearly know who we're talking about."

Shalakh turned with such a look of anger that the doctor almost let go. "I will not have hands laid on me in my own house. I may have no recourse at law if you accost me, but I do have friends in many cities-"

Morsicato withdrew his hand, but did not step away. "I won't accost you if you answer me. You know her."

A sneer. "Yes."

"What is her name?"

Shalakh looked at him pityingly. "Donna Maria."

"Her family name."

"We never used one. Please leave."

"Shalakh." Tharwat's rasping voice was soft, but there was steel beneath the purr. "We must know."

The money-lender stood for a time, then crossed behind his desk and resumed his seat. Morsicato mirrored his action, and Tharwat nodded. "If there was no name, how was the draft to be honoured?"

"There was a seal to be shown," said Shalakh. "With it she could have whatever funds she required. Or send me a note with the proper words and the seal in a certain place and I would send a draft wherever she directed."

"So where is she?" asked Morsicato.

Shalakh smiled serenely. "I have no idea. Please leave."

Tharwat placed a hand on the doctor's arm, pulling him back into his seat. "Where did you send the last draft of money?"

"I sent one for one hundred twenty ducati to a banker in London."

"London?" echoed Morsicato.

"When was this?" asked Tharwat.

"Three years ago. In fact, almost exactly three years. I received the order at the beginning of your August, in the year of your lord 1325."

The same month she disappeared, thought Morsicato, who had pressed Tharwat for all that was known of Cesco's mysterious mother.

Tharwat posed another question. "Do you do much business in London?"

"No. My tribe has very little to do with the English these days. Ever since their king Edward I, may the Lord spit in his eye, ran all Hebrews out forty years ago, we've had to use agents. There is no profit to be had."

"Please give us the banker's name. It will be a place to start."

Shalakh said the name and both men committed it to memory. They would not trust writing it down.

"It won't do you any good," added Shalakh.

"And why is that?"

"I sent that draft three years ago," said Shalakh in triumph. "It was never honoured. The money sits here, gathering interest in my capable hands. She never collected it."

Tharwat was grim. "I never thought she did."

Forty-Two

It was another half hour before they departed the house of Shalakh. Morsicato left carrying a bundle of papers. It had taken some real convincing for the Jew to part with it, because therein lay every record of money passed from Cangrande to Donna Maria over a period of fifteen years – since Cesco's conception, it seemed. The money would be no use in tracing her, of course. Wherever her kidnappers had taken her, she was unable to collect the sum awaiting her in London. But it was Tharwat's hope that these papers held some clue to her history. Even just her surname would help.

While their host had vanished into his back room to find these records, Morsicato had seen the daughter, Jessica, slip down the stairs and press a sealed fold of paper into the servant Launcelot's hand just before he went out. Seeing Morsicato's eye upon her through the open door, she pressed her finger to her lips, eyes imploring. He mimicked her, smiling under his beard. A love affair. Hopefully not with the servant. More like he was the conveyor of love – a curious Cupid if ever there was one.

Now, as they were leaving the Yellow Crescent, Morsicato saw the Jew's servant conversing with the merchant's friend from an hour earlier, Bassanio. With Launcelot was a doddering old man who bore his features, whose back was bent both with age and a massive hump.

The medical part of Morsicato's brain wondered if the younger man's ugliness came about because of the father's deformity? Or was it due to becoming a father at so advanced an age? Does a man's seed age with him? There's a paper in that... Meanwhile the romantic in him wondered, Was the girl's note for Bassanio? Or is he another in a chain of Cupids?

Tharwat's gait was slowing now, exhaustion from the journey setting in. They paused by the edge of the bridge that he might recover, and Morsicato could not help hearing the odd pair, father and son, falling over themselves to ingratiate themselves with the handsome young noble. Finally Bassanio waved them to silence. "Enough. Your master already made your wish known, Launcelot. If you wish it, I will take both of you into service. But be warned – though I have hopes, I am not yet a rich man."

Launcelot bowed. "You are rich in that you serve God, master."

Bassanio laughed. "If that's enough, then go to my house and put on my livery. Then take leave of your old master and collect your things. I set sail for Bel-lamonte tonight. But first I dine tonight with your former master and Signor Antonio."

"A merry supper that will be," said Launcelot wryly. "Please say you are serving pork? His rant would provide the evening's entertainment."

"Lamb. But don't fret, there will be entertainment. Antonio's hired revelers and actors for a show, and doubtless the masquers will be in the streets. God knows Gratiano and Lorenzo like the smallest excuse to don false faces!"

"Signor Lorenzo?" said Launcelot knowingly. "Master, will you tell your friend that I have a letter for him?"

"Tell him yourself, you'll see him at my house. Now go, or we'll all miss our boats."

Bassanio was greeted by another friend, moving away from Morsicato and Tharwat. So, not Bassanio. But if Morsicato judged matters correctly, tonight while Shalakh dined with the Christians, a Christian was going to steal his most valuable treasure – a treasure most willing to be stolen. Good for them, thought the doctor, dimly remembering what youth-ful love was like.

Cangrande's band of Veronese nobles arrived in Venice in the late afternoon. "Did you send anyone ahead?" asked Pietro.

"Only to arrange lodging, not to inform anyone. I don't want Ambassador Dandolo to know we're coming until we're at the Doge's doorstep. A peace treaty between Verona and Padua is not good for Venice. The Doge may be too old to care, but Dandolo has his eye on that office, and if he attains it, his first concern will be making certain Verona doesn't dominate mainland trade. We already control all the alpine passes to Germany and France. If we hold all of the Feltro, we could carve away their European trade, just as Genoa is trying to do with the East. The Venetians live in their ships, but that doesn't mean they can ignore land."

Cesco was riding on Cangrande's other side. "I think Ser Alaghieri was fretting on a more personal level. The last time he was in Venice, he spent his time locked in darkness with rats nipping his toes."

"Thanks for reminding me," said Pietro, concealing a shiver. "But I'm actually more concerned for you – both of you. Dandolo's only reason to harass me would be pique, and he's far too reasonable a man to act that way. But if everything you say is true – and it is, I heard Dandolo himself say so – he has every reason to be afraid of you. And coming here with

Cesco, Mastino, and Paride means he can imprison all of Verona's potential leaders in one fell swoop."

"You don't consider Alblivious leader material?" asked Cesco, and they all laughed. Alberto della Scala had been left behind.

"Ah, but I have a secret weapon," said Cangrande in answer to Pietro's question. "The Emperor owes me a favour for delivering Occam. And our boy here is known to stand high in Ludwig's favour. Venice cannot risk the wrath of the Holy Roman Empire. Besides, brokering this peace will be a feather in Venice's cap. When the details are made public, they can reap the praise for being trusted arbiters, neutral ground for two enemies to settle their differences."

"Even if they didn't want those differences settled."

"Even then. Venice is the model for opportunism. We could all learn something from the unwalled fortress of the Serenissima."

Arriving, they retired to a palace rented under a false name. It was in the busy San Polo district, near the Naranzeria, the square where oranges were housed and sold. Their arrival was masked by the bustle of market life all around them. Cangrande, Bailardino, and Castelbarco all bathed and dressed in their best finery in preparation to call at the Doge's palace. Pietro, it was decided, should stay indoors until it was certain he would not be arrested again. "As an escaped prisoner, in the company of the two young men who helped you escape, it might be considered impolitic to bring you tonight."

"They might be afraid we'll poison them all again," said Cesco.

"They'd be right to," said Mastino sotto voce.

Mariotto chose to stay with Pietro. Petruchio had promised his twin sons a night on the town, and Mastino's interest was piqued when Petruchio mentioned a gambling establishment. They all left together.

As the formal party reached the door, they encountered Cesco and Detto, dressed in plain clothes. "We thought we might take the air."

Cangrande grimaced. "For God's sake, keep out of trouble. And take Paride with you. He's a good lad, but in need of friends."

Detto pulled a face, but Cesco said, "Of course! We shall teach him to swim, and he can befriend the fishes."

They all knew why Cangrande had added young Paride to the boys' excursion. With him in tow, the daring duo would restrain their excesses – at least, that was the hope. So it was that the three cousins, Cesco, Detto, and Paride, set forth into the sweltering August evening, just as the sun was setting.

"What's that smell?" demanded Paride, wrinkling his nose.

"The effluvium of humanity," replied Cesco, pointing to the water just feet away from them. "Before we explore, shall we first indulge in the local fruit?"

With their faces buried in fresh oranges, they walked up to the Rialto bridge. "Here it is, the rivoaltus. The bridge is a new one, just sixty years old. The heart of the city."

"The Doge's palace is here?" asked Paride, confused.

"No," scoffed Detto.

"But he said this was the heart of the—"

"A city's heart is not its government, but its market. This is where things are traded and sold. This is where the money is. Fitting, also, that the abattoir is also here."

"You've been here before," said Paride.

"Twice," agreed Cesco. "Once to effect Ser Alaghieri's release from captivity, and once the year before that. A holiday," he added, sharing a knowing look with Detto.

"I'm still amazed we survived," said Detto, grinning at the memory. "Both the trip and the punishment afterwards."

"Tell me." Paride sounded almost wistful. "I never have any adventures…"

As Detto told the story, with Cesco providing wry commentary, they strolled along the edge of the Canal Grande, the water lapping just inches away, occasionally licking over the edge of the paved walkway to dampen their shoes.

"...so when the guards caught him, he was hanging upside-down by his knees, trying to get a better look."

Paride was laughing. "At an old Roman bust?"

Cesco grinned. "I have an affinity for troubled souls, and he certainly was one."

They passed men in masques with skins of wine and musical instruments. "It's not Carnevale, is it?" asked Paride, who had heard of the festival all his life.

"Not unless we've turned the calendar back. There must be some feast or other – Venetians are always looking for reasons to hide their faces."

"Are they so hideous?" asked Detto.

"Or so beautiful," countered Cesco. "They may be protecting us from enslavement. Incubi and succubi rather than demons and gorgons."

Detto pulled a face. "I'm not sure which I'd fear more."

Tossing the rind of his second orange into the water, Paride rubbed his hands together. "So – what are we going to do?"

"Do?" asked Detto innocently.

"Whatever do you mean?" asked Cesco.

"I mean you two are always getting into mischief and I want my share! When you planned to go out tonight, what were you going to do?"

Exchanging a look, Detto shrugged, and Cesco said, "We were going to find the doctor and the Moor and see what they're up to."

"Why?"

"They wouldn't come to Venice for no reason. Firstly, it's dangerous – when last they came, Tharwat and Morsicato both deceived the Doge and poisoned his household, with our help. Our birth may excuse us, but I doubt the Venetians look kindly on them. As I recall, Tharwat had to fight his way out, and even if he did not kill his opponents – something we cannot rule out – they certainly owe him a bad turn."

"And the Moor is still recovering from being tortured in France," added Detto darkly. "It must be something important for him to come here."

Paride's excitement was palpable. "Then let's find them!"

"If you insist!" said Cesco, laughing.

As the night grew darker and torches were lit, the trio passed more and more men wearing the masques of varnished leather. As they entered a shadowy arched tunnel beside the water, Detto had an idea. "We should buy some faces! Blend in."

Cesco clapped his hands. "Come upon them in secret. Pretend we're robbers."

"Maybe we can make the doctor shave his beard again!"

"That would be a shame. He's so proud of it."

"I also want to explore the Arsenale," said Detto. "The last time we were here, I didn't get to—"

He was cut off by a wet smacking sound. Cesco whirled in time to see Detto's sinking head leaving a bloody smear on the bricks of the tunnel wall. Paride cried out as a booted heel caught him in the chest and set him flying into the water.

A man in a hooded black cloak leapt over Detto's limp body and wrapped his gloved fingers around Cesco's throat.

Cesco fought, scrabbling desperately at the hands choking off his air. He reached for the knife at his belt, but his attacker swept his feet out from under him and they fell together, driving the breath from Cesco's lungs, the man's knees pinning Cesco's wrists to the ground.

Lights swirled and danced before his eyes. Through his last sliver of consciousness, Cesco saw a grotesque face under the cloak's hood. It was a masque, a masque of a demon laughing and snarling.

A demon Cesco knew.

Forty-Three

Having paid their respects to the Doge and fixed a time for the next day's meeting, Cangrande, Bail, and Castelbarco returned to the rented palace near the Naranzeria. They were just sitting down to a late meal, regaling Pietro with the Doge's surprised welcome, when Paride burst into the chamber. Dripping and frightened, he described the attack in a very few words. "I don't know how many there were. When I got out of the water, I found Detto and got him into a house."

Bail was out of his seat. "He's alive?"

Thirteen years old, Paride was surprisingly steady. "He was when I left. They're looking after him now."

Bail was already moving towards the door, everyone behind him. Reaching Paride, Cangrande demanded, "And Cesco?"

"Gone."

This was clearly no prank, no game on the part of the boys, but deadly serious. As they ran through the streets after Paride, Pietro said, "Dandolo?"

Cangrande was able to run and talk easily. "How would he even have known?" There was a fortifying wineskin in his hand, and he took a pull from it. "This is either Carrara, or someone inside our council. And to target Cesco…"

"Fuchs," said Pietro at once.

"Fuchs," agreed Cangrande. He turned to young Castelbarco. "Find Mastino. Make sure he has no hand in this. If he's with Petruchio, say nothing of this. Just send me word – is Mastino with Bonaventura, or no."

Wheeling about, young Castelbarco ran off while his father puffed to keep pace with the rest. All around them on the street were masques, and men carrying bundles, or leaping into the multi-coloured gondolas and punting from side to side of the Grand Canal. A man could disappear tonight and never be found.

Paride led them first to the house that held Detto. Shouldering past the owners, Bail knelt beside the low table his eldest son had been laid upon. "Detto? Detto?"

The boy's face was bloodied, and his breathing was awkward, probably due to his nose being broken. There was swelling around both eyes and a huge bump the size of a goose-egg upon his forehead. But he would live.

Pietro snapped his fingers. "Morsicato's in town. With Tharwat."

Bail's voice was the crack of a whip. "Send for him."

Paride said that it was the doctor they had been off to seek, but that he didn't know where Morsicato might be staying.

"We'll hire servants to find them," said Cangrande. "Now show me where it happened."

Leaving Bailardino with Detto, they stepped outside and turned down a shadowed archway along the water's edge. Cangrande plucked a torch from its sconce and waved it around. There was the smear of Detto's blood on the wall, and another where he had fallen. But there was no other trace of blood.

"Not stabbed, then." Pietro didn't feel any relief.

"Taken," agreed Cangrande. "But where? Paride, how long were you in the water?"

Though shaken, the young man's voice was firm and certain. "A minute, two at most. But I came out over there—" he pointed off a ways towards a pole sticking out of the water "—and had to run over that walkway to get back."

"Three minutes, then. In the crowd. Cesco would have been unconscious, or else he'd have screamed bloody murder."

Pietro was reliving the night a six month-old Cesco had been snatched by a scarecrow and carried through a crowd, then pitched to a leopard.

The scarecrow was dead now, but this night's events seemed so much worse...

All around them were men in false faces of varnished leather as the impromptu revels kicked off a summer's eve in Venice. Pietro saw several men in a gondola heading off towards the Yellow Crescent, their masques bold and their bodies alternately exuberant and furtive – they were drunk.

"The water!" he said suddenly. "I always forget – it's the real way to travel in Venice. Say Fuchs had a gondola ready. He tosses Cesco in, covers him, and punts off."

"But to where?" asked Cangrande.

Neither man had any idea.

His throat was sore. That was the first thing Cesco noticed when he awoke. He swallowed several times, licking his lips and coughing to clear it. But it still hurt. He tried to reach up to rub it—

He heard a rattle of the chain as his hands jerked to a stop, at the end of their tether. His wrists were shackled, bolted to the floor.

With a rush of fear and excitement he was instantly awake. Rolling from his back onto his knees, he tried to look around him, but it was dark, impossibly dark. He tried to look at his hands...

There was something wrong with his eyes! They hurt, and with every attempt to blink he felt a tug, a pull, a resistance, like someone plucking out his eyelashes. Squeezing his eyes shut, he tried again, real panic gripping him now. My eyes! What's wrong with my eyes?

Bending down towards the floor, he put his face close to his hands and delicately ran his fingertips over his eyelids. Above and below the lashes he felt thin thread, almost as fine as fishing line, in a criss-cross pattern. There were small knots at both edges.

His eyelids had been sewn shut.

A deep chuckle from across the room made him freeze. "Just like they do when transporting a bird. You appreciate the irony? You are a disobedient falcon, kept in flack."

Fuchs. Slowly Cesco straightened, feeling terror like he'd never known.

A harsh voice, a voice that could have been Cangrande's or Katerina's or Dante's, an adult voice, hard and uncompromising, began issuing instructions inside his head. No eyes? They're not gone forever. Until you get them back, use your other senses!

The smell of tar. Water. Damp wood. The slight swaying. On a ship. Through his eyelids he could tell there was only a dim light, a candle or a covered lantern. He pulled on his chain. It rattled back and

918

forth, and his fingers found the large metal loop set into the planked floor through which the chain was threaded. The loop was large enough for him to put his hand through. Some kind of securer for cargo. A freight vessel.

Speaking, he tried to force casualness into his tremoring voice. "Where are we going?"

Somewhere to his left, Fuchs snorted. "You aren't wondering why you're not dead?"

"If you like. Why am I not dead?"

"I gave my word. Your family and their stupid superstitions." Boards shifted as Fuchs came closer. "But I only promised not to kill you. There was nothing about not hurting you."

The next minute was about endurance as Fuchs punched, kicked, slapped, and beat Cesco. There was only a foot and a half of chain between Cesco's hands, and with it looped through the solid bolt on the floor, there was little he could do to avoid the blows except curl into a ball. "Bastard! Du arschfickender hurensohn!" The only part of him that Fuchs did not hit was the face – doubtless he didn't want to break the stitches holding his victim's eyes closed.

Breathing hard, Fuchs finally backed away with a satisfied grunt. "A long time have you had that coming. A long time."

Sickened by blows to his stomach and a kick to his groin, Cesco whimpered something.

"What?"

Cesco swallowed blood and said again, "Only a German could be so rude to his verbs."

"Always so clever. I wonder if your new owners will find you so amusing."

"Owners," repeated Cesco.

The scuff of Fuchs' boot, the scrape of something being dragged closer, a creak of wood as Fuchs sat down. "Forgive me, your earlier question I did not answer. You asked where we are going. I am going back to land, and then on to Bonn to endure my year of exile. You, bastard, are going in the opposite direction."

Cesco's breath was returning. There was no pain so long as he didn't move. "How far? China?"

"Anatolia. Mohammedans pay a good price for young men in Bursa's slave markets. Especially pretty young men. You leave in just a few minutes, before anyone can mount a search. Do you have any questions before you go?"

Cesco didn't, really. All he could think of was Rosalia, waiting in vain for him to return and marry her. He had to get free. And to do that, he had to learn more. Which meant he had to keep Fuchs talking. "Does Mastino know?"

"No. He has his own revenge planned. If you ever return to Verona – it is possible, you are clever – he'll be waiting." Fuchs leaned closer. "I was hoping you would wake up sooner. I so wanted to give you the same I gave your dear auntie. She liked it, I think. She wriggled under me and kept silent, when one shout would have betrayed me. So she must have enjoyed our midnight liaisons, don't you think?"

With his eyes sewn shut, Cesco couldn't help his mind's eye conjuring the image Fuchs was painting. Hot tears pooled beneath his sewn lids, leaking out at the corners. With a bellow of rage he yanked at the chain and reached towards Fuchs' voice, straining against his bonds.

Laughing, Fuchs slapped his fingers away. "The closest thing to a mother, you called her. Does that make me almost your father? As close to a father as you'll ever know. Or should we call her sister now? Yes, Suor Beatrice was quite the treat, and all mine. Verhurtes drecksgür." Fuchs leaned even closer, whispering right in Cesco's bruised and bloodied ear. "But she was nowhere near as giving as your real mother. That bitch died screaming at the end of my knife."

Morsicato was unearthed at an inn not far away, the Moor with him. They were ferried over at once. As the doctor stepped off the gondola he looked at the assembled faces in surprise. "Pietro? They told me Cangrande was in the city. What's the boy done now?"

Pietro didn't have the heart to smile. "He's been kidnapped. We think by Fuchs. Detto's hurt."

Morsicato became brisk. "Where?"

"In there." Morsicato entered the house, leaving Pietro to offer a hand to Tharwat.

The Moor surprised Pietro by clambering out on his own, though with less grace than of old. "Fuchs?"

"We think so." Pietro quickly explained the treaty with Padua, and the sacrifice of Mastino's German friend. "If Mastino's involved, he shows no sign. He's gambling with the three Bonaventura men, and enjoying himself." Pietro frowned. "Do I remember right – one of the charts had a crisis right about now."

"Yes," said the Moor. "The third chart. The crossed stars. His life is altered from this moment onward. Not for the better."

The night Cesco had been born there were reports of shooting stars. One story had the star falling favourably. One, disastrously. It had been Pietro who had seen the possibility of a third chart, a chart with two stars crossing in the sky. That chart was the most tempestuous. He might still become the legendary Greyhound, but his life would be ruled by Mercury, with violence, heart-break, and death wherever he went.

Which was why Pietro was desperate to have that chart not be the true one. "But if we save him...this could just be a bad night, not a life-changing moment, yes? It might not be that event at all?"

Tharwat was grim. "If this is the moment. If we save him. Only time will tell."

Pietro grasped Tharwat's arm. "We can't let it happen. We can't."

From behind him came Cangrande's voice threw Pietro's long-ago words back at him. "A man may control his actions, but not his stars. Now come."

"Where?"

"If we are to save him, we must act swiftly. All ships must remain in this harbour until we can search them, and there is only one man who can give that order. We are off to see the Doge. Come. Paride, you too! You there – we need your boat!"

Pietro looked at Tharwat, who stood erect and said, "I will not slow you." They stepped together back into multi-coloured vessel bobbing at the bottom of the steps.

Climbing in behind the Scaliger, Paride said for the hundredth time, "I'm sorry."

"Stop." From Cangrande, the word was a command. "You did well. Driver, the Doge's palace. Move!"

Cesco lay entirely still, hardly daring to breathe. Moving hurt. Some ribs were probably broken, and his legs and arms were bruised and swollen. His wrists chafed against the shackles. And he wanted to reach up and tear the stitches from his eyelids like he'd wanted nothing else in his life.

Or so he had thought until this moment. Suddenly all he could think of was killing, of slaughter, of spilling so much blood that the sea beneath the boards would turn red. "My mother."

"Your loving mother," gloated Fuchs softly. "Die möpse, so soft, so white and round. And her voice! Even screaming she had that lilt in her voice. Scots, she said. She said a lot before the end. Blutige sau. Cursed me, I think. I didn't understand most of it. She had gone someplace, in her mind. Her death was a mercy."

Groaning, Cesco curled low as if in pain, hiding his hands as he strained to pull one free of the cuff. But there was no give. The Venus mound below his thumb was too wide to slip through. "Why?"

"Why? Because it was a secret. Because it was something hidden, and what is hidden is powerful. Not that her secrets will help you. Nothing she said was to your good. Though she spoke well of you. Said you were very like your father – I'm sure she meant it as a compliment. She called for you, too, at the end. Praying for salvation. But it was some other name she called you by, a strange one. Not Mercury…"

"Mercutio." Cesco's whispered voice was as heavy as his heart. He'd hoped Fuchs was lying, or that he'd found the wrong woman. But his mother had given him that name during their meeting three years earlier. Our only meeting in this world.

"That was it! Mercutio! What an odd name. Mercutio. The little Mercury. Do you wish you had wings on your feet now, Mercutio?"

Giving up on the shackles, Cesco raised his head. "Does Mastino know?"

"Why?"

Cesco answered in a voice devoid of emotion. "I'm deciding who has to die."

Fuchs laughed loudly. "O, if you only knew the things kept from you, bodies would be piled all the way back to Verona! But no, Mastino didn't know. Kidnap, yes. Murder, no. How he raged when I told him she was dead! He wanted answers, but fears the curse. He even abhorred where I hid the body as being too obvious! Fool. He fears much - you most of all. His nemesis. He will thank me when you are gone. He will take his rightful place, he will rule Verona, be all that Cangrande is and more, and I will be his champion."

"Not while I'm alive."

"I know it," agreed Fuchs. "Better to kill you now. But I have sworn. If you die by my hand or my order, Mastino will think he is cursed. Belief is powerful. Curses have power if a man believes in them. Your mother cursed me, your aunt Antonia as well, most like. Yet I am well! Because I do not believe. But because Mastino believes, I must not kill you. Yet," he added, almost playfully, "should you die whipped by some heathen hand in a far off place, he will not feel the sting of the curse. You will just be gone."

Cesco's teeth were grinding. "I will live longer than you."

Fuchs knelt close again, his foul breath filling Cesco's nose. "You want a chance, yes? A chance to be free, to escape? Then have it."

A handle was pressed into his hand. The handle to a knife. Cesco felt it quickly, fingers exploring. It was only three inches long, dull and rusted. Fuchs chortled. "No point and almost no edge. Like you. But if a hawk was desperate enough, he could claw away the threads on his eye - rough work, the eye might not survive. Or the bird could scratch through enough flesh to be free of the shackles – he might not lose the whole claw. If it was a man, it could use it to stab its neck and end it all. You prize your wits so highly, use them to sharpen this blade." Fuchs leaned even closer, pressing his lips to Cesco's ear. "While you're making your choice, I think I will stop on my way to across the Alps to call at the Rienzi house, so she can curse me too. I will taste all your women."

With a howl from his soul Cesco lunged, sweeping the dull blade back and forth as far as the chain would reach. "If you touch her, Fuchs, if you touch her, I swear, you will die harder than any man ever has!"

Fuchs had retreated just out of danger, his delight a hearty rumble. "I do love empty threats. Do your worst. Curse me too. But know that it is you who are cursed. Don't you feel it? Mothers, sisters, wives – any woman who loves you is a fool. For they are doomed from the moment you—"

He stopped as they both heard running footfalls above them. A hatch opened. "Master, master! The Doge's men – they are searching all ships!"

"Already?" snapped Fuchs angrily. "Damn!"

Cangrande's gondola had gone barely a quarter mile before they heard voices raised in angry cries. "What's happening? Can you tell?"

"No." Pietro squinted through the darkness at a cluster of torch-bearing gondolas. "Something's amiss over there."

"Driver, that way!"

There was nothing to do but strain their ears and eyes for some clue. "They seem to be looking for someone."

"A woman," said Cangrande. "That's a woman's name."

As they drew closer the livery of the men in the boats became clear. "Those are the Doge's men, lord," said the gondola driver.

They were hailed and ordered to come closer. "Do it," ordered Cangrande. As they pulled near, a man with long moustaches and an official air said, "Are there any women on board?"

"None," said Cangrande. "What is happening?"

The man scowled. "A fool's errand. The daughter of some old Jew has run off on him, with all his gold."

"Shalakh's daughter," murmured Tharwat, a wistful half-smile on his face. "Thank you, girl."

The Venetian official carried on. "Serves him right, I say. But the Doge knows this Jew, half the Christians in the city owe him money, so we're searching

928

all the ships and boats and skiffs to discover where she's gone."

He was about to order his driver to push on when Cangrande leapt across into his boat and began giving urgent explanations, followed by orders.

The hatch had closed again, and there was more clatter above deck, panic. They were going to be caught.

Cesco was thinking fast. In a moment more Fuchs would realize he had no chance to carry out his scheme. His only way out would be to murder the only witness, lose the body overboard, and act all innocence when the searchers came aboard. If he blended with the crew and escaped detection, he might survive.

But only if Cesco was dead.

Shackled, without sight, there was no chance to evade death. All Fuchs had to do was draw his sword and bring it down on Cesco's head. It was attack, or die.

First order of business, then, was freeing himself from his bonds. This was going to hurt.

Rising as high as his chain would allow, Cesco put all his weight behind his knee as he drove it down upon his hand, forcing himself not to flinch or hold back. There was a sickening crunch as the bones in his hand broke, and despite bracing himself he grunted in pain, but the noise from above decks drowned out both sounds. Kneeling, he pulled hard on his left shackle, forcing the broken hand painfully through the wrist cuff, shuddering with the agony of it. But the broken bones moved, made way, and in moments his hand slipped free.

There was movement in the room. Fuchs might have glanced over, seen him. There was only time for one try He yanked hard with his right wrist, and the chain passed through the ring on the floor, the empty cuff rattling as it cleared the loop. Cesco kept his arm flying, swinging the chain as a weapon at where it had sounded like Fuchs was standing. The chain connected, and Cesco heard a grunt and a curse.

He didn't swing it again, but ran straight for the sound, the blunt knife in his good hand, and leapt. Fuchs' right arm was across his body, trying to free his sword. Unable to grip with his left hand, Cesco pressed himself close and struck with his elbow while his feet sought out knee or heel. Hooking one, he pulled back. Fuchs fell, Cesco on top of him.

Fuchs was strong, and expert. In the old training days, he had bested Cesco at most duels. But Cesco was no longer a boy of eleven. He was fourteen, and had spent a year of that struggling and wrestling with a man three times his age, a master of the art of war. He'd fought with every weapon and every disadvantage possible. Often he'd been made to fight in darkness, perfect training for this life-or-death struggle.

They grappled, using knees and elbows and heads. Feeling teeth biting into his shoulder, Cesco recoiled and kneed Fuchs in the head. Cesco brought that same knee down to pin his enemy's right arm to the floor, pressing his other knee on Fuchs' sternum. He raised his short weapon, aiming to plunge it into the soft spot under Fuchs' chin, or his neck, or his eye.

Anticipating this, the German jouster grasped with his free left hand just as Cesco's hand plunged. He missed the incoming wrist, but caught the chain. Fuchs yanked hard towards his legs, and Cesco's straining hand stopped short of finding flesh.

Cesco redoubled his effort, pressing hard. Both grunted and snarled, but Fuchs was a grown man. Slowly, slowly, Cesco's hand was pulled backwards, away from Fuchs' face.

The German gave a triumphant snarl. In a moment he would have Cesco's arm pinned to the floor and he could roll away and beat the boy to death with his own chain, or stab him with the short knife...

Cesco twisted, taking his arm in the direction Fuchs was pulling, down towards the German's legs.

Chain momentarily slack, he plunged the dull knife into the soft meat of Fuchs' inner thigh, where Morsicato had told him the blood was carried through the body on its way up to the heart. The femoral artery.

Fuchs cried out in surprise. He tried to rise, but Cesco kicked out, his heel finding Fuchs' jaw. The young man then scissored his legs around his enemy's torso, pinning him back onto the ground.

Feeling wet warmth on his thigh, Fuchs yanked up on the chain. But Cesco's hand was still gripped tight around the hilt of the knife, and the yanking only dragged the dull blade upwards through the German's flesh. Fuchs grunted, twisted, tried to dislodge the youth who was clamped tightly to him like a leech, draining him of precious blood.

"Do you believe now, Signore?" demanded Cesco through gritted teeth as he twisted the blade viciously. "Do you believe in curses now?"

The fight was fading from Fuchs. His head was light. His arms had no strength. He felt not so much pain as a sleepy sadness. But he forced himself to utter one last defiance. "Geh zum Teufel."

Cesco twisted the blade one more time. "You first."

Fuchs died. Cesco felt the blood stop pumping, coming in weaker and weaker spurts until it was just a trickle across his fingers.

As Fuchs' life ended, so Cesco's senses seemed to return. He was again aware of the tramping of feet overhead. Hardly any time had passed, and his situation had not changed – if he was found here, the captain and crew would be hanged. So they would be coming to make sure Fuchs had removed the incriminating evidence.

By feel alone he made his way to the wooden stairway and climbed until he was just below the hatch. He found the latch and listened, hoping for a shout or a loud noise to distract those above so he might slip out unseen.

Instead the hatch was suddenly hauled wide as the captain came to check on his passengers. Seeing the wrong one dead in a welter of blood, he cried out.

Cesco propelled himself upwards, right arm swinging the chain in wild molinelli over his head. Blind, he had no way to know which way to run, so he turned right towards where the ship's starboard rail should be. He ran into it, hard, just as a hand grasped his hair. Twisting his head away, he flung himself backwards, overboard, into the water.

Plunging, he kicked and flailed, pushing himself hard away from the ship. He hadn't taken a good breath and was forced to surface, gasping. Instantly he heard shouts. Gulping down air, he dove and kicked again, hoping he was putting distance between himself and the slave ship.

Swimming was almost impossible. Sightless, one hand broken, the other weighted down with a chain, he struggled in the water, surfacing from time to time to more shouting.

The final time he surfaced he heard cries from close by, men calling, "There he is!" and "Quick, before he sinks!" and "Get him aboard!" Cesco couldn't tell if these were friends, foes, or entirely Indifferent to him. All he knew was that if he remained in the water, he would surely drown. Swimming awkwardly for the shouting, he banged his head against the side of a gondola.

Hands hauled him out of the water. He immediately recoiled when they tried to cover him in cloth, fearful they would muffle him. "Don't touch me! Don't touch me!"

"Boy, you're safe—"

"Don't touch me!" Cesco kept screaming it, over and over, hysteria crashing over him in waves. He swung the chain and threw himself back and back into the front of the gondola where no one ever stood. "Nobody touch me! Don't touch me!"

Slowly, slowly, he recognized voices. Alaghieri. The Arūs. Paride. All calling, soothing, comforting. They seemed like from another world.

It was Cangrande's voice that broke through his panicked veil. "Cesco. Cesco, you're safe. You're safe. It's over. You're free."

"Free?" asked Cesco blindly, his unbroken hand outstretched.

"You're safe," said Cangrande again.

Cesco's lip quavered. "Father?"

He was instantly swept into an embrace. The first ever. And as Cangrande held him, the Scaliger said the only words Cesco had ever wanted to hear.

"You're safe. You're safe. I'm so proud of you."

Forty-Four

"You knew she was dead?"

Cesco was lying very still under a damp cloth. The bones of his left hand had been straightened and set in sticking plaster. After snipping the knots at the edges of his eyes, Morsicato had covered the stitches with olive oil to loosen the threads. Rather than pull them out and risk damaging the lids, they were letting the strands work themselves free.

It meant he had to lie still. But he could still ask questions, and when he was alone with Pietro and Tharwat, he'd told them of his mother's death. Only to find out they already knew.

"We weren't certain," insisted Pietro. "There was some blood. But no sign of..."

"There was no body," said the Moor bluntly. "And no grave. We could not know she was dead."

"But you suspected she was."

"Yes," admitted Pietro.

"You could have warned me." Cesco's accusing tone was entirely justified.

"We should have."

"But you didn't. Because you think there are things I shouldn't know. Like my star-chart."

The three of them sat in silence for a long time. Predictably, it was Pietro who finally answered. "We aren't trying to conceal things from you. We're trying—"

"—to protect me? Excellent job so far."

"You're alive," rasped Tharwat.

"Thanks to my hawking, not your protection. I hated him for it, but he made me strong, gave me skills. I survived because I could rely on myself. That's the lesson. I need to be independent. Autonomous. So tell me this – is there anything else you've been hiding?"

Cesco could almost hear Pietro and Tharwat exchange a look. "Your mother left a message," said Pietro slowly.

Cesco swallowed. "For me?"

"We think so. It was in code."

"A puzzle," added Tharwat. "She knew you already."

"And I never knew her at all." Though that was not their fault, it was difficult not to blame them. "What kind of puzzle?"

They explained it, laying it out for his mind's eye. He sat wondering at it, getting no further than they had. But he would. For he was sure this was a message just for him.

Tharwat was in the process of explaining that he and the doctor had come to Venice in order to trace her when there was a knock. Cesco heard a door creak open and Paride say, "Pardon, Ser Alaghieri, but they're leaving."

"Very well." Cesco could hear the reluctance as Pietro rose to his feet. The meeting with Carrara had to go forward, and Pietro had to be there. Cesco would miss the seal being set upon his handiwork. But after all, it hadn't been his idea. It had been Antonia's.

Antonia. It was tempting to wound Pietro by revealing her secret. See? I keep things from you too! But that secret was not his to tell. He'd avenged her honour, if such things mattered. And knowing that he, too, was keeping secrets to protect his family calmed him, dampening his anger at those who loved him.

As Pietro exited, Cangrande came to the door – Cesco knew him by his step. "Boy. We are going."

"Pay my respects to Carrara," replied Cesco with as much cheer as he could muster.

"I shall. If this goes well, he will owe you a great debt." There was a pause. "As will I."

"How great?" asked Cesco.

"Pick a date," said Cangrande, the smile evident in his voice.

After they had gone, the doctor checked on him. The strands were halfway free, curling of their own volition. "I can tease them out now, if you like."

"Please." Cesco braced himself, gripping his good fist and gritting his teeth. The sensation was bizarre and awful, as the tugging pulled his lids away from his eyeballs. But it did not hurt, and in moments one eye was free.

"Keep it shut a little while longer," advised Morsicato as he started his tweezers tugging on the other eye.

"For a man with such stubby fingers, you are remarkably gentle."

"And for a boy who has such a loathing of cats, you have as many lives as one."

"Only nine? I've used more than that already." The last strand came free and Cesco could not wait any longer – he blinked, winked, squinched his eyes, then opened them.

The world was blurry, but no moreso than when one awakened from after a long sleep. He cuffed his eyes and sighed. "I can see." He was not so proud to hide his tears of relief.

Morsicato returned downstairs to check on Detto, who had awakened with a splitting headache. When he was gone, Tharwat said, "If you wish to con your charts, I will show them to you."

Cesco looked at the Moor, pleased to be looking at anything at all. "Why?"

"Because you have the right."

"Why more than one?" demanded Cesco, and Tharwat explained the anomalies of the shooting stars, without explaining the results. "And why is Donna Katerina so eager for me to see them?"

"Because two of them predict a great destiny, and she wishes to solidify her place in that. She wishes her life to have meaning."

Cesco considered that for a long time. "Why does Cangrande hate her?"

"Because his chart was not as grand as she led him to believe."

Again Cesco sat, quietly thinking. "He feels trapped by the prediction."

"Yes."

"So would I. Wouldn't I?"

"There is more confusion in your charts, because of the stars. But I think so."

"When you see Fate," murmured Cesco softly, "Fate sees you, too." He thought of the future. Of Rosalia. Quite unexpectedly, he smiled. "No. Thank you, no. Let Fortuna turn her wheel unobserved. I am happy to let life unfold as it will."

The astrologer nodded his head. "Good."

The return from the Doge's palace was as full of triumph as any Roman parade. Hearing the victors entering below, Cesco, Tharwat, and Morsicato met the Triumph's leaders at the top steps of their borrowed palace.

After congratulating him on the return of his eyes, Cangrande at once launched into the tale of the day. "O, what a time! What a day! The pity is it will need to remain secret! But such long faces in the Doge's palace, and such happy tidings for all good men!" He wrapped an arm about Pietro's shoulders. "This one! How well you did. Whatever bait Carrara laid, you ignored it, doggedly keeping your lawyer's robe over your knight's sword."

"I take it things went well?" asked Cesco wryly.

"Well? There was never such a day. Pity the Doge could not do more than greet us. But he has his hands full all with this other business of last night. It seems Manuel's cousin, the money-lender with the odd name, had a terrible loss last night, and he's busily lodging suits against all sorts of people this morning. He has – or at least, had – enough money and clout to garner the Doge's attention."

"His daughter has run away," explained Pietro, who remembered Jessica well, and yet was somehow surprised. "With a Christian."

"And with all her father's gold and gems," added Petruchio with a smile. He liked willful women. "They called at her house in masques, and lifted her down from a window into a gondola, together with the contents of his treasure box and desk."

"An excellent dowry." Cangrande was just as amused. "But I fear for any good Christian soul that owes him money at present. Despite the ruckus he raised last night, she has escaped, and he is not now in a forgiving kind of mood. He is alternately incoherent with rage and quite pitiful. When I spoke to him he barely knew who I was. Kept muttering, 'O my daughter! O my ducati!' "

Cesco had never met this Shalakh, and though his miraculous salvation had come thanks to the search for the Jew's missing daughter, he wasn't interested in her escape or the money-lender's suffering. There were more important matters to hand. "But the meeting with Padua – that went well?"

"Perfectly! Marsilio was allowed to make some gibes, which I suffered nobly. Then Ser Alaghieri read the bond, we quarreled over a few minor points, which I graciously conceded to leave his pride intact. We agreed to burn the contracts in time – if this is to work, there can be no evidence that Carrara is colluding with Padua's fearsome enemy, the Scaliger. Then handshakes, oaths, signatures, seals,

942

kisses, and done! We were finished by dinner time, and there was nothing left but the wine!" Of which Cangrande had clearly had the lion's share. Even for a man who was never far from spirits, he was unusually flushed.

"Who acted as witness?" asked Cesco.

Grinning, Cangrande turned to Pietro, who said, "Dandolo."

"Oh? He didn't take exception to Ser Alaghieri's prominent place?"

"On the contrary," laughed Cangrande, "he graciously acknowledged Ser Alaghieri's presence, praised him for the peace accord, and offered hearty congratulations upon Pietro's return to the saved. He then called forth the warrant for his arrest and tore it up before our eyes – as well as one for someone called Theodoro of Cadiz, along with his unnamed, beardless assistant." Morsicato grunted in half-amusement.

"I'll still be watching for soldiers when we leave the city," said Pietro. But he was smiling. Of all the places that had wanted him dead, only Florence remained. That, he could live with.

There were others downstairs, filing in. Petruchio's son Hortensio had no head for drink, and his brother was having to half-carry him in. Both were singing. Montecchio was grinning broadly, foreseeing a great new market for horses open up under his cousin-in-law, Carrara.

Then in came the man Cesco had been waiting to see. "Congratulations, cousin! I suppose we must transfer the title of Arūs from the Moor to you, for you are to be Padua's bridegroom!"

Pausing at the door, Mastino glanced up to the top of the stairs. Here was a look of death if ever one had been given. Medusa could not have been more frightening. Nor more frightened, seeing herself reflected. For Cesco was certain his gaze carried as much death in it as his cousin's.

Yet Mastino came forward and offered a heartfelt apology, voicing his joy at Cesco's clever deliverance. "I swear, cousin, I had no idea what Fuchs had planned."

"I believe you," said Cesco, because he did.

"And they tell me he kidnapped your mother, killed her. I knew nothing about that, either. I swear it."

"I believe you," said Cesco, because he didn't. He even elaborated. "In fact, the late Fuchs didn't seem to think highly of you. He called you weak. Said you didn't have it in you to kill a member of the family, even one so removed as my mother. So he did it himself."

Mastino shook his head. "If I'd known…"

"I know." Cesco felt Cangrande and Pietro watching him. "We are not friends, but we are cousins. There is only so far we can go."

Mastino nodded vigourously. "And we both want what's best for Verona."

"Yes. Yes we do. So I say again, congratulations on your impending wedding."

Mastino grinned at him. "Thank you. I hope she's as pretty as Montecchio's wife. A shame Carrara doesn't have another girl cousin for you. We could have made it a double wedding, a grand affair!"

Cesco smiled at him. "What an excellent notion. Perhaps we should look about for a wife for me." He glanced at Cangrande, who grinned in return, lowering his head in a single nod.

They set out for Verona the next day, Cangrande and Cesco riding at the head of the party, engaged in light-hearted persiflage. Twice snubbed by Cesco, Pietro fell back to ride with Tharwat and Morsicato, clearly feeling the sting of Cesco's displeasure. It was the Moor who said softly, "You realize what is happening. He is rejecting us, his surrogate fathers, because at last he has his real one. They are forging the bond I feared would never be formed. They are becoming united in purpose and spirit. So while this may be hurtful to you and me for a time, this is nevertheless excellent for the world. With these two united, can you imagine what Verona can achieve?"

Pietro recalled the end of the prophecy of the Greyhound. "A new age of man." He shook his head. "Good for them. Certainly Cesco has been good for Cangrande. He seems more—"

"Human," said Morsicato.

"Yes." Pietro watched the leading pair as they broke into an impromptu race. Cesco's hair was even darkening, giving way to a deeper chestnut. In a few years he would look just as Cangrande had as a young lord. "I suppose that's life. Children grow up and don't need you anymore."

"Not life," said Tharwat. "Fatherhood. And never fear – he will always belong partly to you."

Pietro smiled wryly. "I hope that doesn't hold him back."

Morsicato was frowning. "Did I hear him right yesterday? Does he want to get married? Why on Earth would he want to do a fool thing like that?"

The other two, bachelors, laughed at the married man.

Back among Verona's lords, those few days of waiting had been almost unendurable. It felt as if a hushed haze had fallen over the Piazza dei Signori. Everyone went breathlessly about their business – trials were held, complaints were heard, deals were made. Those with an interest in trade started quietly feeling out suppliers in Abano and Campo San Piero, two cities close to Padua.

Cangrande returned in the middle of the night of the 1st of September. The morning of the 2nd, the Anziani assembled in the Domus Nuova without being called. The doors closed, Cangrande strode to the dais and told them what they longed to hear.

"Tomorrow Marsilio de Carrara will lay the groundwork by having himself declared sole ruler of Padua, giving him exclusive power to treat with us. Two days after that he'll let slip in conversation that Mastino and Taddea are betrothed and, because of that, I've ordered all hostility to cease. I've already dispatched a massive personal gift of fruit and wine to the citizens of Padua to honour the union. I left Mastino to wait in Vicenza and, if all goes well, the very next day he will travel to Padua with a detachment of lances. What happens next depends on the mood of the Paduan people. If they welcome Mastino, Carrara will inform the Paduan Anziani that he's handing the city over to me. Provided there is no uprising, I will enter Padua on the Tenth. Nine days from now, the war will be over."

They did not cheer this time. The secret was too precious, too fragile. They hardly breathed, lest it go awry. Adding to this, Cangrande reminded everyone that secrecy was still paramount. "Herkos odonton. A hundred things could still go awry. Let's not tempt fate." He stepped off the dais and headed for the exit, to arrange against those hundred things and a hundred more.

Pausing beside Cesco, he murmured sotto voce, "Make sure your mystery bride is ready to enter polite society by the Fourteenth. That's when the banns will be read. Mastino's idea was excellent. Two birds, one stone. Damned if I'm paying for two weddings."

Bowing deeply, Cesco said nothing. He didn't have to. He was practically glowing.

The moment the doors opened, everyone filed out. Detto caught Cesco by the arm. "Married? Truly?" Cesco nodded and Detto groaned. "I didn't think you were serious! Who is she?"

Cesco couldn't resist himself. "Death."

"Death?" Detto's reaction was all Cesco could have wished. Confusion. Memory. More confusion – Death had been their name for the boy, the boy who they'd traced to a girl changing clothes, the Rienzi flag, Rienzi had a son and a daughter, a girl named—

"Rosalia?"

"Shh. It's a secret." But Cesco was unable to hide his delight.

Bewildered, Detto kept shaking his head. "Truly? Truly? Married. To her."

"Truly. Married. To her."

"Well, I guess – congratulations." Detto stuck out his hand, and Cesco grasped it. "Though I hate to lose my best friend so young."

"You're not losing a friend. You're gaining a sister. We are brothers!" Releasing the handclasp, Cesco punched Detto in the shoulder. "Besides, now that you know, I need your help."

"With what?"

"Who else but my brother would I ask to be my best man?"

The following week carried a tide of good news for the conspirators. On the Third of September Marsilio de Carrara was declared Capitano di Padua. Two days later rumours started flying of a secret betrothal between the Scaligeri and the Carrarese. The following morning Cangrande's public gifts began to arrive – baskets of grapes and cherries, barrels of wine, all for the union of Mastino della Scala and Taddea de Carrara. For an over-taxed, frightened populace, the gifts were a wonder, and they all began to hope.

Next came the risky part, as details of Carrara's deal with Verona were let slip. At first Paduans gathered in an angry mob to protest being chattel. But Carrara, never afraid of personal danger, walked out among them and addressed the crowd, telling them that the average Paduan would feel greater security than they had in recent years, and prosperity would follow. "The only men in danger are those who have abused you, terrified you, stolen from you, these past two years."

Mollified, the crowd quickly changed sides, cheering for Carrara and for the foreign ruler they had demonized for two decades.

Hearing he was now beloved in Padua, Cangrande laughed and laughed.

Meanwhile, another conspiracy was gathering speed. Meeting Lia on a rooftop late on the night of his return, Cesco told her all that had happened. She kissed the fingers of his broken hand, sticking like sausages from the splints and plaster wrapping Morsicato had concocted.

"I wish I could see your eyes," she said, for it was an overcast night, clouds covering the stars.

"They look the same, or so everyone tells me. The lids are just a little tender now. The doctor says there will be some scarring, but it shouldn't be bad. With my eyes open, I'll look the same. Though I had a dream the other night that I could see through them even when closed. Like a peeper through the chink in a wall."

"He's dead?" demanded Lia, too upset to be amused.

"Dead as if Death herself had kissed him." Cesco's fingers brushed the coin about her neck. "He called me Mercutio, after my mother. He meant to taunt me. He forgot that the caduceus is the symbol of Death's messenger, carried by him who will guide the dead to Hell. So I lived up to my name and led him there myself."

She did not like his joking. Taking his face between her hands she said, "Shut up. You almost died. I would have been alone. Forever. So promise me. 'I. Will. Not. Die.' "

For the first time ever Cesco was grateful for Fuchs. He'd shown Cesco that Rosalia truly cared. Kissing her, he whispered, "I will not die until you give permission. I promise."

She looked straight at him in the darkness, and he imagined he could see the intensity of her fierce green eyes. Finally she nodded, satisfied. "Good."

They decided not to meet again until he was in Padua and sent for her. "Detto has agreed to play the best man and kidnap my bride for me. It would help if you didn't try to elude him."

Lia's eyes twinkled in the starlight. "No promises. He may not ride fast enough."

They laid their plans. On the night of the Twelfth, Lia and Detto would ride for Padua, arriving by the morning of the Fourteenth, when Mastino would be formally betrothed to Taddea de Carrara.

"You want to steal a little of his thunder."

"As much as I can," agreed Cesco. "We'll announce the wedding, and let Cangrande and your father wrangle over the details. Then at the end of the month we'll get married. Plenty of time to change your mind."

"And leave your caduceus hanging out to carry off other women? Better I suffer for all womankind."

"Noble of you."

"Isn't it?"

Cesco stopped smiling, looked away. "There's something I have to ask you to do. I need you to deliver a message. I should do it myself, but—"

"But?"

"I'm afraid to."

Concerned, Lia put an arm about him. "It must be serious."

"As serious as can be. I need you not to question or even try to figure it out. It has nothing to do with anything. Just tell Suor Beatrice that he is dead. That's all you need to tell her."

"That Fuchs is dead?"

"Don't say Fuchs. Just say, 'He is dead. Cesco says he is dead.' She'll understand."

On the Sixth of September, Mastino entered Padua to tumultuous cheers. The Paduan Anziani's reception to Carrara's pact with Cangrande was less warm, but at last they conceded he'd hammered out better terms than anyone else could have. So the general announcement went forth – henceforth, their great city would by ruled by the Greyhound.

News of the Fall of Padua (for so it was called by both friend and foe) reverberated like a thunderclap in a canyon. The leaders of Pisa and Bologna sat up and took notice. The Florentine Signoria, completely and faithfully tied to the Guelph cause, took the time to write the Scaliger a note in admiration of his skill at both war and diplomacy. They expressed a hope that his election (the word they used) would impose peace upon warring factions and bring well-being and stability to Padua's citizens. Comparing him to King David, they paraphrased Psalm 119:165, saying 'great peace will have those who love your law and nothing can make them stumble.' The letter closed with another Psalm: 'In our days may justice flourish and may peace abound.'

In Rome, the anti-pope was equally lavish in his praise, and Ludwig himself sent a hearty congratulations, along with a wry remark of how there were now more soldiers free to fight any imperial battles on the horizon.

In Cangrande's own lands, citizens rejoiced. Festivals raged from Mantua to Vicenza, and in Verona the members of the Guilds clad themselves in silk and linen dyed all the colours of the rainbow and paraded themselves through the streets, dancing and singing.

Only one corner of the Feltro was devoid of festivity. Treviso, still staunchly Guelph, looked upon the Fall of Padua as the knell of doom. There was now nothing to distract the Scaliger from the last hold-out city in his domain. They set about rebuilding their barricades and harvesting every scrap of food they could pick, pluck, shuck, or unearth to place in the granaries within their walls. They sharpened their swords, practiced their drills, and waited for the spring, and war.

The day that Cangrande and Cesco rode out for Vicenza to prepare for their entrance to Padua, Rosalia did as her love had asked. Finding a moment alone at the convent, she relayed the message just as Cesco had told her. "Suor Beatrice? I have a message from Cesco. I am to tell you, he is dead."

At first Antonia did not understand. She'd already heard the whole tale from Pietro, and again from Gianozza, who of course was full of gossip. But when she'd called at the palace for Cesco, Suor Beatrice was informed that he was out.

Now he was sending her cryptic messages. "Who is dead? Fuchs? I heard."

Rosalia shook her head in frustration. "I must not be saying it the right way. He told me to tell you, 'He is dead.' I asked if he meant Fuchs, and he said to say only that—"

"He is dead." Understanding swept over Antonia, wave after crashing wave. Knees buckling, her eyes filled with tears even as she began to laugh, a pit opening in her stomach, a lightness across her shoulders.

Then the darkness returned. He knew? He knew, and never said..? O, Cesco!

Rosalia did not know what she was watching, and had promised not to guess. But it was impossible not to see something near the truth. Kneeling, she wrapped her arms about Suor Beatrice and held the older woman while tears of humiliation, relief, guilt, anger, remorse, and joy poured out all at once. Holding her tight, Lia knew that Cesco had brought about some kind of justice.

Forty-Five

On the tenth of September, 1328, Cangrande della Scala, Capitano di Verona, Imperial Vicar of the Trevisian Mark, made his triumphal entry into Padua. His victory was all the sweeter for the fact that he was genuinely welcomed by the people. They cheered him hoarse, strewed his path with flowers, and waved banners bearing the ladder and the hound.

He was preceded by all the nobility of Verona. Castelbarco and his son. Bailardino Nogarola and his brother Antonio, with Detto and Valentino between them. Antony Capulletto with his uncle (though without his nephew). Petruchio Bonaventura with both his sons, waving to the city that remembered him – and his wife! – all too well. Giuseppe Morsicato. Tharwat al-Dhaamin, who received his share of amazed pointing and gasps. Mariotto Montecchio and his brother-in-law, Benvenito Lenoti. Ziliberto dell'Angelo. Bernardo Ervari. Massimiliano da Villafranca. Dozens of others. Everyone had come, glittering in their finest armour, horses barded and bedecked in caparisons, pages riding with banners overhead.

Pietro Alaghieri rode beside his brother Jacopo, re-called from his studies for this glorious day. Both waved wildly, their faces bursting with joy. Above them flew the new family crest Pietro had designed while in Avignon. The old symbol for the Alaghieri family had been per pale or and sable a fess argent. But now the crest was a single wing, seen from the side, as if in flight. It was both more recognizable and far more apt – the family name in Latin, Alagerius, was a pun on Virgil's aliger, meaning 'wing-bearing'. Though not overfond of his big brother, Poco had heartily approved the change. Cesco had laughed himself sick for some reason.

Next came the immediate family. Alberto della Scala. Paride della Scala. They were followed by the bridegroom, Mastino della Scala, who had been feted once already. Then the mysterious heir, Francesco della Scala, who waved with one hand while the other was hidden beneath a rich crimson half-cape.

At last came the Capitano di Verona himself, as magnificent as he had ever been. Tall and broad-shouldered, he was a naturally imposing figure even without fancy dress. But today Cangrande wore armour of sliver and gold, polished so brightly that the crowds were blinded at every turn. The armour had been etched with acid, creating geometric swirls in the metal. Over his shoulders hung the scarlet cape of a Roman general, and the banner behind him carried not only his family ladder and his personal greyhound, but also the twin-headed eagle of the Holy Roman Empire.

Under one arm he carried his famous helmet, the Houndshelm. The people of Padua knew that inhuman visage well, having seen it a dozen times in battles just beyond the city walls. The massive snarling hound's head that rose from the top of the helmet, silver wings reaching to either side, was symbolically subdued, held down by its master, who in his right hand carried an olive branch, the universal symbol of peace.

The horse beneath him was massive, its pure white hair draped in red cloth, its tail and mane dyed a bright red. White and red – the colours of Padua.

The people cheered and cheered, weeping and throwing flowers into his path. In that moment he was Caesar after crushing the Gauls, Charlemagne returning to Aachen, King Arthur after the battle of Badon Hill. But he was even better, because this was a bloodless victory, and it was the enemy rejoicing his entry to their city. He was their savior, their hero, the blessing they had been praying for.

So secure was Cangrande in this victory that he was willing to share it. Beside him rode Marsilio da Carrara, just as fine, and with his own crest of the four carriage wheels being carried behind him. Next came the combined clergy of the two cities and Vicenza besides, all bearing crosses and chanting litanies and Te Deums. Behind them surged a crowd of Veronese peasants and merchants come to witness their lord's victory and celebrate with their old enemies, now their brothers.

The parade was heading for the Bishop of Padua's palace, where Cangrande was to stay, when suddenly their way was blocked by a group of boys bearing a ladder stolen from some shop. "Long live Cangrande! Long live Cangrande!" They cheered even louder when the Scaliger reached into his heavy leather bag and scattered gold coins at their feet. A red-headed man in his twenties shoved past the boys, knocking them down in order to scoop up the gold. Grown men laughed as the boys pummeled him and pelted him with dung. But he scampered away with a handful of gold, grinning.

As they waited for the boys to disperse, Cangrande leaned towards Carrara, his famous allegria as bright as it had ever been. "This may be the best day of my life. I will look back at this as the pinnacle of my achievements, and whatever comes next will pale in comparison. Thank you."

"This is your day, lord." Carrara's smile was nearly as broad. For so many years he had worked to hate the Scaliger, only to find that he admired no one else. The Scaliger understood power and its uses. That being true, Marsilio de Carrara was determined to sit at the master's knee and learn. He was only thirty-four years old, and his race was far from run.

The Paduans began a new chant. Beaming, Cangrande canted his head to listen. Carrara saw the great man's face change, grow rigid, his smile becoming fixed. What's wrong? He listened to what his countrymen were saying.

"Grazie a Dio per il Veltro! Il Veltro ci ha salvati!"

Thank God for the Greyhound! The Greyhound has saved us!

The Scaliger actually stopped to correct the crowd. "My name is Cangrande! I am a mere man! I am no myth!"

Loving him all the more for his modesty, the cries of Greyhound continued. Hearing it, Pietro watched Cangrande. The Scaliger hid it well, but if one knew to look for it, one could see the rage, the hurt, the disappointment. This day is ruined for him. Soiled. Stained. Spoiled. He worked so hard for this, tried to achieve it on his own, only to have victory handed to him by Cesco. That's the most galling part – this Triumph belongs to Cesco. Cangrande knows it, and it's killing him.

Watching fearfully for the reaction, Pietro saw a startling change come over Cangrande. The Scaliger looked to where Cesco was riding right before him and slowly the rage vanished, the hurt became pride, and all at once something Pietro had never seen in Cangrande came to the fore. There was only one word for that look. It was fatherly.

Tharwat was right. This is as it should be. They have mended the old wounds. They will be united, and the world will be the better for it. In that moment, surrounded by cheering crowds and full hearts, anything seemed possible.

Even when they reached their destination and dismounted, waving to the jubilant throngs, the crowd went on cheering for the Greyhound. Only Pietro, Tharwat, and Morsicato appreciated the irony.

For, all unknowing, the people of Padua were cheering the right man. Cesco had brought peace to Padua, and now they cheered him by his rightful title – the Greyhound.

Just after dusk on the Twelfth, Detto met Rosalia beside Verona's Ponte Pietra. She was once more dressed in man's garb, and they would be just two young men riding along the road.

"Hello," he said.

Her smile was disarming, wry, and mocking all at once. "Hello."

Detto felt awkward – he was thirteen, not yet a man, she was sixteen, and a woman. But his best friend, cousin, and blood-brother wanted to marry her, and was trusting Detto to bring her safely. He'd ridden all day, and the night ahead promised to be harder. "Well, if you're ready, we'd best get going."

Lia looked him over. "You must be tired. Would you like to sleep a few hours? They won't miss me until morning."

Detto shook his head. "I'm a heavy sleeper. Once out, I'm out. I'll be fine on the road."

Her smile changed. "It's good to know yourself. But then I knew he'd chosen his only friend wisely. I hope his choice of brides is as unerring."

"So do I." It slipped out before he could catch it.

She only laughed. "Traditionally the best man was the strongest and best armed, present to back up the groom as he kidnapped the bride. This time, though, the groom is absent and it is the best man who is guilty of kidnapping – or, technically, theft. After all, an unwed girl is very much her father's property."

Detto found it in him to bow. "I'm sure you belong only to yourself."

"Pretty to think so. But I belong entirely to him."

Detto nodded, knowing just whom she meant. "As do I."

Lia came close and kissed his cheek. "Then we are united."

He blushed, then said suddenly, "Who taught you to shoot a bow?"

She looked at him, startled. Then they grinned at each other and the tension vanished as they both dissolved into laughter.

Next she was climbing Into the saddle of the fresh horse he'd brought for her. "I left a sealed note to be taken to my father. It explains everything. I'm committed now." She noted that Detto had strapped a sword onto Lia's saddle, a mirror to his own. "Smart. Was that his idea, or yours?"

"Mine," said Detto proudly. He stepped into his stirrup and heaved his frame up onto the horse. Large for his age, he might pass for sixteen. He wondered if Lia knew any other girls…

They rode through the night until they reached the area around Vicenza, then slept for a few hours in one of his uncle's castles. At midday they set out again. The journey was easy. They were never molested or even questioned as they passed over bridges and down the road along the Bacchiglione River. She talked most of the way, telling him stories and asking for little details of Cesco's life. She learned that her love hated cats, which she found adorable and determined to tease him over. She heard more about the awful night with Fuchs, and before that the details of the tourney, which she had seen but not understood.

Detto found himself talking more and more, about himself, about Cesco, about their friendship, how much it meant to him. Things he had shared with no one else. By the end of the journey he felt nearly as comfortable with Lia as he did with Cesco.

"So you approve?" she quizzed.

She was so similar to Cesco that Detto, long familiar with his friend's tones and undertones, was able to pierce the wryness to hear the plea beneath.

"Yes," Detto assured her. "I cannot imagine him happy with anyone but you."

In answer, Lia sniffled a little and shot him a relieved smile. The fact that she wanted his approval made Detto like her all the more.

They arrived at Padua by the second hour of the morning, quickly making their way to a suite of rooms Cesco had set aside for her. These rooms were in a casa owned by Petruchio's father-in-law, il Signor Minola, whom Cesco had charmed upon first meeting.

Cesco was there, trying to be easy in his mind, alternately playing chess against himself and reading from a copy of Plutarch's Lives. The moment they came in, Cesco was up and striding forward, arms wide. "Thank God. I was terrified something had happened."

"I'm sorry," said Rosalia, winking at Detto as she hugged Cesco. "My spirit was iron, but my flesh was paper. I needed sleep."

"No, I did," said Detto. He had not yet seen them together – not in this way, at least. Somehow they fit. Two wheels in the same windmill, meshing together to grind the wheat. He let Cesco shake his hand, then withdrew, leaving the two lovers alone. He didn't know why – he was losing a friend after all – but he was happy.

Once Detto was gone and the door was locked, Cesco looked her over. "Promise me this is the last time you will dress like a man."

Lia cocked her hip and head at the same time. "How about this – only one of us will dress as a man at any time."

Pulling her close, he unbuckled her belt and began working the points of her hose. "Better still, we could just swear off clothes forever."

"But then how will we know which is the woman, and which the man?"

"We'll know."

They fell together, giggling and sighing, into the bed, and did not sleep until the dawn.

Pietro rose at the bells to the first prayer, dressing in his finest doublet and hose. Mastino's official betrothal was to take place that evening at the Church of San Giacomo by the city's north gate, the closest holy site to Verona, symbolizing their fresh amity.

After praying and being blessed, he went across to the Bishop's palace where Cangrande had taken to holding court. He was curiously excited. By now everyone around Cangrande knew that Cesco had some girl he wanted to marry, that he'd kept her a secret, and that Detto had slipped away to bring her to Padua. It was charming, and there was speculation aplenty – she was a whore, she was cross-eyed, she was a Moorish princess, she was a witch. Petruchio was even taking bets.

Pietro suspected she was just lowly born, or else so high-born as to be out of reach. Whatever the reason for the secrecy, Pietro could hardly wait to learn what kind of bride his ward had chosen.

I ought to think of marrying. My trouble is that I've not met anyone I feel pulled towards. Maybe my father's love poetry ruined me. Look at Antonia – a nun. Poco's a whoremaster, loving every woman for a half-hour at a time. And I'm waiting for – what? True love? My own Beatrice? I should just ask Cangrande to arrange a marriage for me and be done.

The morning dragged on with no sign of Cesco as Cangrande went about the day's business. The Scaliger ordered a special dispensation for the traditional Paduan faires honouring Santa Giustina and San Prosdocimo in October and November, and offered a guarantee against reprisals of those from other cities or families, that the markets could thrive. He dispensed justice and made a formal donation to the city treasury in order to facilitate street cleaning and to begin infrastructure programs – new wells, new towers, new bridges. Padua under Cangrande would be a prosperous place. To that end he appointed Bernardo Ervari as Padua's new podestá – a functionary with no personal ambition who never rubbed anyone the wrong way, yet had enough steel not to be trampled under Carrara's hooves.

When Detto finally dragged himself into the borrowed palace, scrubbing the sleep from his eyes, Cangrande pulled a wry face. "Ah! You've returned. Bail, we seem to have raised squires who go gallivanting off whenever they damn well please."

Bail ruffled his son's hair. "I blame your influence. You never did like order."

968

"I like order fine, when I'm the one giving the orders."

Everyone laughed, including Pietro. He was feeling that old sensation, the one he'd had when he was young and Cangrande seemed an invincible genius. All the old hurts and mistrusts were fading, leaving only the great man he should have been all along. He was even drinking less wine.

Cangrande scratched out a few words on a piece of parchment beside him. "I take it you've brought my heir's mysterious bride. I have to pen the announcement for this evening. Do you think he would object now, at this very late date, if you were to give us a hint as to her identity?"

From his expression it was clear Detto was considering. Everyone waited, Petruchio the most anxious, ready to make book.

Finally Detto shrugged. "I don't see why not. Her name is Rosalia Rienzi."

No gasps, no exclamations, just curious murmurs – some people knew the Rienzi name, others did not. Petruchio looked so disappointed that several men laughed. It took Pietro several seconds to recall the house near the forge, and longer still to remember the girl. Straight dark hair, green eyes, well shaped. That was the girl Cesco had chosen? Pietro was bemused. Surprising. I didn't really notice her. But I suppose I'll get to know her when she and Cesco...

"Rienzi?"

The dead tone of the question that made Pietro turn. There was a look on Cangrande's face, such a look as Pietro had seen only once before. Anguish, horror, absolute dread.

But beneath it all this time there was no triumph. Only sadness, and a grim resignation.

"Where is he now?"

Cesco and Lia were awake again, pressing their bodies against each other, when there was a rattle at the door. Busy with each other, they ignored it.

A key turned in the lock, and the door flew open. Rosalia pulled the blanket up to hide her chest, but did not cry out. Cesco saw the figure in the doorway and hissed.

Mastino stood there, expectant triumph etched across his face. Seeing the couple in bed together, his grin grew wider. "Ah, true love. How magnificent. I'd heard it existed. I'm so happy to see it bloom." Walking into the room, he closed the door behind him, making sure of the latch. "And happier still that you have not waited to consummate your relationship. I so wanted you to know every pleasure of each other's company. You deserve it."

Naked, Cesco rolled half out of bed, reaching for his sword.

Mastino held up his hands. "I come unarmed! Or at least, with no implements of steel or wood. My only weapon is the truth. They say it will set you free. We'll see if that's so."

Drawing dangerously nearer, he sat at the edge of the bed. "Rosalia, we have not been introduced. I am Mastino della Scala, your betrothed's cousin. I hope my intrusion isn't too upsetting. I feel like we're family already. And I owe our friend here a debt which I hope to pay, at least in part, right now."

Still half in the bed, half out, one leg on the floor, Cesco snarled, "What do you want?"

"I realize, cos, I have been remiss. I haven't congratulated you on no longer being a bastard. Can I tell you, I was a little dismayed when Ser Alaghieri had you legitimized, but now I am overjoyed. You are Cangrande's son, for all the world to see. It's in writing, with the seal of the pope. No more jokes of il veltro del Veltro." His voice became honeyed acid. "It makes this all the sweeter. I told you years ago, you're cursed. The best part is I didn't have to raise a finger. Fortune has done my work for me."

Looking murder with his eyes, Cesco repeated, "What do you want?"

Mastino smiled. "Such a temper! I'm just here to tell you a story. Think of it as a gift, a wedding present from beyond the grave. Fuchs was a fool to try what he did. I understand the impulse, of course. I'd like nothing better then to see you dead."

"The feeling, I assure you, is mutual."

Lia nodded. "I'm learning the feeling myself"

"Of course you are. Peas in a pod, you two. But back to Fuchs. For all his faults, he is – was – remarkably loyal. He promised not to kill you, and he didn't. He also promised to keep a secret. I was desperately afraid that, during your final confrontation, temptation would overwhelm him. But it seems he stayed stolid and steadfast. So sad. If he'd just left you alone, he could have come home in short order. I guess revenge was too appealing."

Seething, Cesco only half heard the words coming out of Mastino's mouth. "Say what you have to say and get out."

Mastino plucked idly at the blanket beside him at the foot of the bed. "Oh, is that any way to treat me, cos? I merely came to greet my family's newest member. Rosalia Rienzi. A beautiful name. What do the poets call that, Cesco? When the first letters are all the same? No? No matter, where was I? Oh yes.

Rienzi. Fuchs was out riding near the Rienzi place and he just happened to pass the time with one of the maids. Her name was Giacinta. Do you know her, Lia? Of course you do. Well, Fuchs was a handsome man, quite dashing, before you murdered him. And when he chose, he could be very charming. As he charmed this Giacinta, our little hyacinth told him a story. Would you like to hear it?"

Cesco and Lia were both wary, silent.

Eager now, Mastino was breathing hard as he spoke. "Once upon a time a great lord, the greatest in the land, took a fancy to a fine lady. He was young and proud and he never let anything stand in his way, not even the protests of her husband. And she was willing – of course she was, who wouldn't be?"

"No," said Lia softly.

"Of course the silly bitch got pregnant. But she was in love, and wouldn't get rid of it. She'd already had one child by her husband, a boy, so she would force him to acknowledge this one, too. And after she had it, she would continue her affair with the great man."

"No," said Cesco, even softer.

"But the child killed her, leaving the cuckolded husband to raise the baby as his own. He even loved it, the maid said, after his fashion. But he hated the lord, despite having to go on serving him. Hated him with everything in him." Smiling, Mastino's eyes fixed on Cesco. "Hearing Lia's name just now made me remember that story. I wonder why."

Lia was curled in a ball upon the bed, the blanket pulled up to her chin. Cesco was frozen. "No."

"Yes," hissed Mastino, drinking his enemy's suffering like ambrosia. "A bastard for a bastard. Fitting, don't you think?"

Instinctively, Cesco turned and reached out for her. But she recoiled from his touch with such a look of horror as he had never seen. Looking into her deep green eyes, he saw himself reflected there, and understood why he felt as if he'd known those eyes all his life…

Of the collection of charts that Tharwat al-Dhaamin had made, one at least could be discarded.

FIN

Afterword

Historical Apologies and Addendums

First off – I know, and I'm sorry. It hurt to write it. But I've named this series *Star-Cross'd* for a reason. Trust me, this is far from over.

The war between Verona and Padua ended with neither bang nor whimper, but with bells – wedding bells. In time these two cities would be enemies again, but for the rest of Cangrande's lifetime all was peaceful between the two powers. Indeed, Marsilio da Carrara is said to have emulated the Scaliger in every way, idolizing his former enemy the way he'd never done with his famous uncle.

At this moment in time, Cesco's fictional existence coincides neatly with the history of one of Cangrande's bastard sons called Franceschino (a name I was loath to saddle him with). Fiction will branch off again soon, but since little is known about Franceschino after 1330, I am happy to provide a vehicle for his life, conflating the historical person with the Shakespearean character. It won't be the last time our lad infuses fiction with history.

Speaking of fiction, Pietro's time in Avignon is purely that, though his friendship with Petrarch is not. Despite Pietro likely penning his first commentary on his father's epic years later, Petrarch was certainly familiar with said commentaries, so it seemed apt to merge these elements. As I have come across no records of Pietro's whereabouts during this time (I'm sure they're out there, lurking, waiting to refute me), I've once again made him serve my story as much as his own. The sojourn in Avignon opened up our stage a little, and will play a vital role a couple books from now...

While I am confessing: this is not actually Book Three. We're still in Book Two.

In designing the series, the events that took place in VOICE OF THE FALCONER were only the first part of my intended second novel. FORTUNE'S FOOL is the middle part, and the next book is the final part. This was all one novel until I realized I had too much story to tell comfortably. So it got cut up, retooling each part to have its own arc.

I tell you this so that when the next one comes out you can read all three the way I imagined them. The Master Of Verona stands alone, but the events of these three books were designed to flow in and out of each other in one fell swoop. Cangrande, Katerina, Pathino, and Dandolo play a long game. So do I.

◆ ◇ ◆

These major sources are worth citing again: A.M. Allen's A HISTORY Of Verona; PADUA UNDER THE CARRARA by Benjamin J. Kohl; Emanuele Carli's DANTE E GLI ALLIGHIERI A VERONA; GLI SCALIGERI, edited by Arnaldo Mondadori; DANTE: THE POET, THE POLITICAL THINKER, THE MAN by Barbara Reynolds; Frances Stonor Saunders' THE DEVIL'S BROKER. The translation of the Rustico di Filippo poem comes from an anthology by Marc A. Cirigliano.

Adding to these previous sources, we have AVIGNON IN FLOWER by Marzieh Gail, a marvelous combination of the history of the Avignon popes and the life of Petrarch; THE POPE'S PALACE AT AVIGNON by Dr. Gabriel Colombe; and THE PALACE OF THE POPES AT AVIGNON, by Sylvain Gagniere, a guidebook of sorts. And there's Babylon On The Rhone, a collection of letters about Avignon by Dante, Petrarch, and Catherine of Siena.

Then there's the COMENTUM SUPER POEMA COMEDIE DANTIS, by Pietro Alighieri. A 720-page Latin tome, it contains Pietro's explanations of his father's intent, and shows Pietro to be, in the words of my translator, an amazingly erudite and well-educated man, in his time or any other. I wish I'd

977

had a copy years ago, but I'm delighted to own it now (more on said translator later).

For this novel I found myself sharing characters and subject matter with Umberto Eco's masterpiece, THE NAME OF THE ROSE. I've tried not to contradict anything Eco created, and I've even taken the liberty of referencing the fictional meeting that is the setting for his story. If I can create a world where Dante, Shakespeare, Petrarch, and Eco intersect, I will deem my career well spent.

Speaking of Petrarch, there are conflicting dates for the death of his father, so I have used the year most often cited. As for Petrarch's sister, Lucia is partly (mostly) invention. There is a mention of a marriage contract between two families, the bride being Pietro Petracco's unnamed daughter. There is also speculation that the reason Petrarch never mentions his sister is due to a great shame she brought the family. In AVIGNON IN FLOWER, the author hints at the girl having an affair with an ecclesiastic, which would certainly have added to Petrarch's disgust for 'the new Babylon.' Complete conjecture, but it makes for an excellent story.

Readers should also note that Mercutio mentions Petrarch in his litany of lovers as he teases Romeo (R&J, Act II, scene iv): "Now is he for the numbers Petrarch flowed in: Laura to his lady was but a kitchen-wench; marry, she had a better love to berhyme her..." So many pieces of this story seem fortuitous, and few moreso than that.

Once again, we have someone referencing Francesca di Rimini as a role model for love, despite her being in Hell. To me this is like hearing Send In The Clowns or Every Breath You Take at wedding receptions. Those are not romantic songs. One is depressing, the other creepy and stalkery. Somehow people associate them with love. Brrr. Sends chills up my spine.

Funny story. When I finished the first draft of this novel, I immediately sent a copy to my friend Mike Nussbaum. Described by David Mamet as 'an irascible motherfucker,' Mike wins the prize for Most Remarkable Life, having been entrusted by Eisenhower to send the official communication ending WWII in Europe, returning to the states to be an exterminator, then retiring from that to become a successful stage and screen actor (you saw him in Men In Black among other films, and he was in the original Glengarry Glen Ross).

Mike had read a draft of THE MASTER Of Verona backstage during a show we did together at the

Chicago Shakespeare Theatre (he repaid me wonderfully by turning me on to Patrick O'Brian's novels). When I sent Mike the sequel, he'd just been cast as both Friar Lawrence and Shylock at CST, so he found this book amusingly relevant. He raved about it to Barbara Gaines, CST's artistic director, who was at the helm of Merchant. She called me in, more to talk about the book than audition, but somehow I ended up playing a minor role in the show.

That production changed the ending of this book a great deal. Discovering the play from the inside for the first time, it began supplanting the climax I'd already written. So I must thank Mike, Barbara, and the rest of the cast and crew for illuminating Merchant for me and sending me back to the damn drawing board.

By the same token, purists will object – Merchant mentions Mexico, placing the action in the 16th century at the earliest. Thus I am flatly contradicting Shakespeare, something I've done only inadvertently before (Petruchio's line about a 'demi-cannon' I genuinely forgot). I can only bow my head in shame. Or give my detractors the fig. Which I do. Cheerily.

Teenage sex. Human nature being what it is, I'm sure it was just as prevalent then as it is today, if not moreso. Children experiment, push boundaries, imitate adult behavior. Add hormones to that combustible mix and it becomes positively explosive. And in a world where girls were married as soon as they menstruated and boys became men at fifteen, teenage sex was condoned even earlier than it is today.

In my first book I prudently (or prudishly) shied away from writing sex scenes, with one off-camera episode between Mariotto and Gianozza, two years after they got married. As a reader, I'm only interested in scenes that move the plot forward, and that applies to sex scenes as well. In the second novel, there was the childhood encounter of Thibault and Tessa, told in hindsight.

In this novel, however, sex is essential to the plot. I have so much strife planned for Cesco in the years to come, I thought he deserved one moment of perfect happiness. And I took inspiration from a certain famous speech of his...

But all this left me writing about a fourteen-year-old boy having his first sexual encounters. Fortunately I have Shakespeare to guide me. Whenever teenagers have sex (most notably Romeo and Juliet themselves), bad things happen. Even if they're married. I simply applied that rule here. I gave these two the first time everyone wishes they had, and things still go south. Poor Cesco – he just can't win for winning.

Some notes about names. Two of my early readers pointed out my casual slipping back and forth between languages for names, and they're entirely right. I've used a form of Francis for both Petrarch and Verona's Bishop, though both men were Italian and would certainly have been called Francesco. With Petrarch the answer is easy – he has embraced all things French, so he becomes François. Maybe Bishop Francis went to England once. Who knows? It's a mystery.

Why change their names at all? Because I already have far too many Francescos running around. Cangrande, Cesco, and the Venetian Dandolo are all called Francesco. Adding two more would only compound the confusion. And trust me, the confusion is real – in an early draft, I believed that Cardinal Bertrand de Poyet was a different person than Bertrando del Poggetto, not one and the same man. Just as in Shakespeare's day, names were fluid. Francesco della Scala becomes Cesco becomes Franz der Hund. I so often cause confusion, here I'm just trying to avoid it.

A few quick hits:

- The business with the Pot of Fire is interesting to me, and also necessary. Romeo mentions a 'gun' in R&J, and despite the Mexico business above, I'm trying very hard to allow each Shakespearean reference to have grounding in the world I'm crafting. And while the date and unfortunate explosion are the children of my brain, the first recorded uses of gunpowder in Europe were in just these kinds of demonstrations in France.

- The insults Tessa uses for Gianozza I choose not to translate because again I am too prudish. Tessa is quite the foul-minded thirteen-year-old.

- William Montagu was a very real personage, an important player in the rise of England's Edward III. His appearance in this novel, though brief, is not happenstance. And yes, the medieval mêlée was the original Capture the Flag game.

- Back in Italy, the business with the bridge at the imperial coronation is perfectly true, though the Visconti were most likely responsible for its downfall, not our two boys.

- Speaking of the Visconti, the more eagle-eyed of the Shakespeareans may have noticed me slipping in the future Duke of Milan and his daughter Sylvia. Valentino has to have someone to fall in love with. After all, he is a gentleman of Verona...

- The date of the earthquake comes not from history but from Shakespeare. The Nurse mentions it in her first scene, while telling one of her bawdy tales. She also mentions that during the earthquake her lord and lady were in Mantua. Given my fictional timing of Juliet's birth and the historical downfall of Passerino Bonaccolsi, the confluence was far too perfect to ignore. In writing as in life, it is often better to be lucky than good.

- The slap. Yes, I am aware that most consider Colonna's slap of the pope to be metaphorical, not literal. But he was a bold man, and placed in his position, I don't see him resisting the impulse. I think the slap-as-metaphor is a sop to those appalled by such an action. And besides, it makes for a better story.

- Both in the opening poem and the Prologue I've referenced a Wallace Stevens quote some 600 years before its time. But the sentiment is an old one, and I could think of no better phrasing than Stevens, who remains one of the finest American poets in our canon. That particular poem has long resonated with me.

- I've added three new crests for this novel, and changed one. The burning badger and the shooting star crests are pure invention. The other new one, a bear holding a bunch of cherries, is the Petrarca family crest. And I've removed the frills from the Scaligeri crest, leaving the ladder in its simplicity.

- Yes, I've once again hidden two anagrams in the text. I'm astonished that people have found them, but found them they have.

Lastly, a true apology. It's odd that, as the author, I should have qualms about my own story-structure. One would think I have complete control over the tale I tell – and I suppose I do. Still, I confess I loathe jumps in time. I did it in MoV and I do it to an even greater degree here, but it drives me nuts. Yet, because I've decided to portray real events, I am constrained by their sequence.

On the other hand, it provides me the possibility of going back in years to come and fleshing out my tale with shorter books, a la Bernard Cornwell. I've already written short stories about Cesco's time with Dante, as well as a few that touch on events from Shakespeare and history that didn't fit into the greater narrative. I'm absolutely certain I'll tell tales of the combined exploits of Cangrande and Cesco as they occur to me – those months of hawking are rife with possibilities. And though I did not include them in this novel, I have very concrete plans for the year Cesco spent with Emperor Ludwig in Milan and Rome.

Mercutio – The Lost Years, volumes I-XXXIII. Look for them about the time my kids are picking colleges.

Once again, huge thanks to both author Judith Testa and my Veronese friend Marina Bonomi for fixing my ongoing series of Italian (and English) infelicities. They, along with the amazing Constance Cedras and Mary Matthews, also caught many blatant errors in this text, pointing them out with precise kindness. All mistakes, therefore, are entirely mine. They did try to warn me.

As before, I am indebted to Professor Martin Walsh at the University of Michigan, this time for his research into the Emperor Ludwig. While it was easy to discover the major events about the Bavarian, learning about the man and his habits was far more difficult. I couldn't have managed without Martin, who delved into the German texts for me and came up with gold.

Then there's John Lobur, Associate Professor of Latin at the University of Mississippi. A high school friend, John's been astonishingly generous with his time and talent, translating whole passages of Pietro's commentary for me at a moment's notice. I'd scan pages and send them, then he'd read aloud the translation over the phone while I madly transcribed his words. It was fun, educational, and extraordinarily useful. John's been a resource for every novel I've written, all because he stuck with our middle school Latin class when I dropped it after a year. I envy his dedication and his knowledge, and treasure his friendship.

Huge thanks to author MJ Rose for all she's done for these books, and for me. Go read her novels, now.

Thanks again to Tara Sullivan, godmother to my kids and to these books. Thanks to Stephanie Heller for a lot of hard and generous insight, as well as being an avid reader.

Great swathes of this book were written in an apartment rented by my parents as a Chicago nest for them to visit their grandchildren without intruding. Just down the hall from our place, it became my bolt-hole, a refuge from the Mickey Mouse Clubhouse, Little Einsteins, Cars, and whatever else the kids were momentarily obsessed with. Mom, Dad, thanks for that. And again the maps were drawn by my mother, Jill Blixt, from whom my creativity is derived.

Dash & Evie – at the present moment, I can't imagine loving you more. Yet tomorrow I know I will. I can't wait to see the people you'll become.

Janice Lee - my choice is made. I will have no other.

The next book is entitled THE PRINCE'S DOOM.

Ave,
DB

Dear reader,

We hope you enjoyed reading *Fortune's Fool*. Please take a moment to leave a review, even if it's a short one. Your opinion is important to us.

Discover more books by David Blixt at https://www.nextchapter.pub/authors/david-blixt-historical-fiction-author

Want to know when one of our books is free or discounted? Join the newsletter at http://eepurl.com/bqqB3H

Best regards,
David Blixt and the Next Chapter Team

The story continues in:
The Prince's Doom by David Blixt

To read the first chapter for free, please head to:
https://www.nextchapter.pub/books/the-princes-doom

About the Author

Consistently described as 'intricate,' 'taut,' and 'breathtaking', David Blixt's written work combines a love of theatre with a deep respect for the quirks and passions of history. His novels span the early Roman Empire (the COLOSSUS series, his play EVE OF IDES) to early Renaissance Italy (the STAR-CROSS'D series) up through the Elizabethan era with HER MAJESTY'S WILL. His latest novel, WHAT GIRLS ARE GOOD FOR: A NOVEL OF NELLIE BLY follows the early career of pioneering undercover journalist Nellie Bly as, fueled by outrage and compassion in equal measure, she breaks into the newspaper business and sets about her journey to the madhouse on Blackwell's Island.

As an actor, David has made a career out of Shakespeare, with especial attention to *Romeo & Juliet*, in which he has played every major male role save Benvolio. Other favorite roles include Macbeth, Iachimo in *Cymbeline*, Benedick in *Much Ado About Nothing*, Mark Antony in *Julius Caesar*, Petruchio in *The Taming of the Shrew*, Leontes in *The Winter's Tale*, Kent in *King Lear*, and Orsino in *Twelfth Night*. David is the resident fight director for two Shakespeare companies, and for 8 years has taught stage combat at the Chicago High School For The Arts.

David continues to write, act, and travel. He has ridden camels around the pyramids at Giza, been thrown out of the Vatican Museum and been blessed by Pope John-Paul II, scaled the Roman ramp at Masada, crashed a hot-air balloon, leapt from cliffs on small Greek islands, dined with Counts and criminals, climbed to the top of Mount Sinai, and sat in the Prince's chair in Verona's palace. But David is happiest at his desk, weaving tales of brilliant people in dire and dramatic straits.

Living in Chicago with his wife and two children, David describes himself as "actor, author, father, husband. In reverse order."

http://www.davidblixt.com/

Fortune's Fool
ISBN: 978-4-86751-120-6 (Large Print)

Published by
Next Chapter
1-60-20 Minami-Otsuka
170-0005 Toshima-Ku, Tokyo
+818035793528
20th July 2021

Lightning Source UK Ltd.
Milton Keynes UK
UKHW010946060821
388423UK00003B/483